Educational Research and Inquiry

Also available from Continuum

Questionnaire, Design, Interviewing and Attitude Measurement, A. N. Oppenheim

Research Question, Richard Andrews

Developing a Questionnaire, 2nd Edition, Bill Gillham

Educational Research and Inquiry

Qualitative and Quantitative Approaches

Edited by

Dimitra Hartas

continuum

Continuum International Publishing Group

The Tower Building	80 Maiden Lane
11 York Road	Suite 704
London	New York
SE1 7NX	NY 10038

www.continuumbooks.com

© Dimitra Hartas and Contributors 2010

British Library Cataloguing-in-Publication Data
A catalogue record for this book is available from the British Library.

ISBN: 9781441178718 (paperback)
   9781441183798 (hardcover)

Library of Congress Cataloging-in-Publication Data
Educational research and inquiry: qualitative and quantitative approaches.[edited by] Dimitra Hartas.
     p.   cm.
   ISBN 978-1-4411-8379-8 – ISBN 978-1-4411-7871-8
  1. Education–Research–Methodology. 2. Qualitative research. 3. Quantitative research. I. Hartas, Dimitra, 1966– II. Title.
   LB1028.E3133 2009
   370.7′2–dc22

200934278

Typeset by BookEns Limited, Royston, Herts
Printed and bound in Great Britain by CPI Antony Rowe, Chippenham, Wiltshire.

Contents

Authors' Biographies

Pia Christensen is Professor of Anthropology and Childhood Studies at the University of Warwick. Her extensive ethnographic research with children and young people has been conducted in families, schools and in local communities in Denmark and the UK, and currently includes research into children's urban childhoods where she combines ethnography with new technologies to understand children's mobility. Her theoretical interests focus on how agency is constituted in children's everyday lives, how concepts of life course can be used in and developed through the study of children, ethical questions in research with children and children and sustainability. She has published widely on children's understanding of, and agency in, health, learning, risk engagement, food, time and space. Her latest books include *Children in the City: home, neighbourhood and community*, co-edited with M. O'Brien (RoutledgeFalmer, 2003) and *Research with Children: Perspectives and Practices*, co-edited with A. James (Routledge, 2nd edn, 2008).

Will Gibson is a senior lecturer in the Warwick Institute of Education. Drawing on perspectives from interactional sociology, Will's research concerns the examination of diverse empirical areas of social practice, including healthcare, online discourse and musical performance. One of his current research projects involves examining the practical work of optometrists in assessing eyesight. Will has written a number of articles and a book that explore issues in qualitative research methodology.

Denis Gleeson is Professor of Education at the University of Warwick and teaches alongside a number of colleagues in this volume on WIE's Graduate Foundation and Advanced Research Methods Training Programmes. He has received numerous grants from ESRC and other bodies for his work in the sociology of education, employment and society with particular reference to learning cultures, professionalism, management and governance in post-compulsory education. He is currently chair of *The Sociological Review* and an associate editor of *Gender, Work and Organisation*.

Dimitra Hartas is an associate professor in special educational needs at the Warwick Institute of Education, and a BPS chartered psychologist. Her research interests include language and social/emotional difficulties in children, children's rights and disability, young people's participation and voice, and interprofessional collaboration within the SEN and disability context. She has been involved in a number of government-funded research studies in collaboration with colleagues from the Centre for Educational Development, Appraisal and Research (CEDAR) at the University of Warwick and other universities. Her recent publications include *The Right to Childhoods: Critical Perspectives on Rights, Difference and Knowledge in a Transient World* (Continuum, 2008).

Andrew J. Hobson is an associate professor in the Teacher and Leadership Research Centre at the University of Nottingham, where he teaches on MA and EdD programmes and supervises doctoral research candidates. He has previously been employed as a teacher and head of social science in secondary and further education, as a senior research officer at the National Foundation for Educational Research, and as lecturer in educational research at the University of Leeds. His main research interests relate to mentoring and other aspects of the experiences of beginning teachers. He directed the longitudinal (2003–9) 'Becoming a Teacher' research project in England, funded by the Department for Children, Schools and Families (DCSF), the General Teaching Council for England (GTC) and the Training and Development Agency for Schools (TDA). His recent publications include *Navigating Initial Teacher Training* (Routledge, 2009), with A. Malderez and L. Tracey.

Kristiina Kumpulainen is Professor in Pedagogy at the University of Warwick. She received her PhD in Education from the University of Exeter in 1994, which focused on collaborative interaction, writing, and learning processes with computers. More recently, her research work has concentrated on methodological questions in the analysis of social interaction, discourse and learning, collaborative interaction and social knowledge construction, multimedia-enriched education and learning, as well as on the use of digital video technology in educational practice and professional learning. Professor Kumpulainen has a strong record in pursuing internationally recognized research in the areas of learning sciences and education with a specific focus on (a) sociocultural approaches to teaching and learning; (b) dialogue, social knowledge construction and learning; (c) design, use, and evaluation of learning technologies in education; and (d) new models of professional teacher education and learning. Her research projects have been funded by the Academy Finland, the Cultural Foundation of Finland, The Ministry of Education in Finland and The European Union.

Geoff Lindsay is director of the Centre for Educational Development, Appraisal and Research at the University of Warwick where he is also Professor of Special Educational Needs and Educational Psychology and chair of the Humanities and Social Sciences Research Ethics Committee. He is also convenor of the European Federation of Psychologists' Associations' Standing Committee on Ethics and was a member of the British Psychological Society's (BPS) Professional Conduct Board and past chair of the BPS Investigatory Committee. He is a past president of the BPS. He has researched ethical dilemmas of professionals and written and presented papers and workshops on developing ethical practice in a number of different countries. He is joint author with C. Koene, H. Ovreide and F. Lang of *Ethics for European Psychologists* (Hogrefe, 2008).

Andrew Loxley is currently the director of research in the School of Education at the Trinity College (TCD) in Dublin, and the founding member of the school's Cultures, Academic Values in Education (CAVE) research group. A sociologist by trade and PhD graduate from the University of Bath, he has been involved in a number of small- and large-scale research projects both in Ireland and in the UK over the past 15 years and writes on the issue of social inclusion, as well higher education policy and practice and research methodology. He has been in TCD since 2002 and before that was a lecturer in the School of Education at the University of Leeds.

Alan Pritchard is an associate professor in the Warwick Institute of Education, University of Warwick. He has taught in schools, worked as an educational adviser and was the deputy head of a large middle school before joining the staff at Warwick in 1992. He has undertaken research and published widely in the academic press, and spoken at academic conferences around the world. He was invited as a visiting scholar to Central Queensland University in Australia during 2003. He has published eight books, including titles concerned with learning, the use of computer technologies in schools and the efficient use of the internet for educational purposes. His most recent book, *Studying and Learning at University* (Sage, 2008), is comprehensive guide to the ways, means, whys and wherefores of academic study.

Jon Prosser teaches international education management in the School of Education and Visual Methods and is also a member of the Leeds Social Science Institute at Leeds University. He is involved in three ESRC projects: 'Building Capacity in Visual Methods', which is part of the Researcher Development Initiative; 'Realities', based at the University of Manchester and part of the ESRC National Centre for Research Methods; and a study of visual ethics with the National Centre for Research Methods, University of Southampton.

Wendy Robinson is a professor of education at the Graduate School of Education at the University of Exeter. Her main research interests have developed out of her early work in the history of education. She is keen to explore ways of bringing new historical perspectives on the theory and practice of education to bear on current educational policy, especially in relation to end users of educational research, such as local authorities, schools, teachers and students. A secondment to the National Academy of Gifted and Talented Youth (NAGTY) as deputy director of research provided a focus for her research interests in the broader field of pedagogy, teacher effectiveness and pupil achievement, initially concentrated in a programme of research in gifted and talented education. She is currently working on a meta-analysis of teacher continued professional development, using historical, documentary and oral history methods.

Steve Strand joined the University of Warwick in April 2005 as Reader in Education. He is deputy director of research, course director for the MA in Educational Research Methods and the MA in Educational Studies, and teaches both foundation and advanced quantitative research methods. Previously (1998–2005), he was senior assessment consultant at Nfer Nelson, the UK's leading educational test and assessment publisher. Prior to that he was head of research and evaluation at Wandsworth Local Education Authority (1990–8) and head of assessment and evaluation at Croydon local education authority (1988–90), and in these roles was responsible for pioneering work on 'value added' analyses of school performance. He holds a first class BA Hons and PhD in psychology. Steve has worked extensively with government departments, local authorities and individual schools on the analysis of pupil attainment, school effectiveness and differential pupil progress.

Andrew Townsend is Assistant Professor in Educational Enquiry in the Institute of Education at the University of Warwick. This post is principally concerned with supporting action research conducted by education professionals studying for masters-level programmes. Before taking up his current post he worked as a consultant, researching, supporting and evaluating professional development and action research projects. This interest in change and development through action research was cultivated during a ten-year teaching career. Recent work has included researching and publishing on the process and outcomes of collaborative and networked enquiry, and supporting student voice and practitioner research projects. He has also used action research in externally funded research, establishing groups of practitioners as partners in research.

David Wray taught in a variety of schools for ten years and is currently Professor of Literacy Education at the University of Warwick. He has published 50 books and over 140 chapters and articles on aspects of literacy and language teaching and is best known for his work on developing teaching strategies to help pupils access the curriculum through literacy. This has resulted in such innovations as the Extending Interactions with Texts (EXIT) model to guide the teaching of reading to learn, and writing frames to help with the writing of factual text types. His work was made an integral part of the UK National Literacy Strategy in 1997.

Michael Wyness is Associate Professor in Childhood Studies at the Institute of Education the University of Warwick. Previously he has taught at the Universities of Northampton, Stirling and Edinburgh. His research interests are in the sociologies of childhood and education. In particular, he has worked in the fields of home-school relations, social policy relating to children and childhood and theories of childhood. His current book is *Childhood and Society: An Introduction to the Sociology of Childhood* (Palgrave, 2006). His previous books were *Contesting Childhood* (2000) and *Schooling Welfare and Parental Responsibility* (1995) both for RoutledgeFalmer. He has also written widely in a number of refereed journals and is currently working on projects in relation to primary-secondary transitions and social trust in schools. He is currently on the editorial board of *Children and Society*.

Preface

This volume emerged from numerous discussions with colleagues from the Warwick Institute of Education and other UK institutions about research skills training at a higher-degree level, and the dilemmas of balancing a sound grounding in research methods, i.e., qualitative, quantitative and mixed, with a wider understanding of the theoretical, methodological and ethical issues that underpin all phases of educational research. To avoid a narrow focus on research methods, this book was structured in a way that new researchers may find it easier to:

- engage with the contested nature of educational research and the current issues and debates with regard to its purpose and meaningfulness;
- become aware of the philosophical, ethical and pragmatic nature of qualitative, quantitative and mixed-method research;
- set the parameters of a research topic in terms of formulating research questions, reviewing existing research and considering the ethical issues that surround the conduct of research and the challenges of researching children and young people;
- become familiar with qualitative and quantitative strategies of inquiry and the procedures for data collection and analyses; and
- write and present research findings in ways that engage the end users of research.

The thought processes during research are not linear but iterative in that every new step we make helps us refine and calibrate the previous ones. Having said this, we accept that research methods can alter the research questions directly or indirectly and vice versa, but stress the importance of establishing an inquiry and starting from the research topic and research questions. We acknowledge that it is not possible, nor is it desirable, to categorize research into singular paradigms and research practices, stressing the need for engaging with diverse methodologies, theories and perspectives, and delineating their emerging influences with regard to research in education.

In this volume, we engage with strategies of inquiry and their interpretive frameworks, and draw links between techniques for making sense of data and their underpinning theoretical and methodological assumptions. We hope that new researchers will be supported to carry out research not only at the ends of the qualitative-quantitative continuum but also in the spaces between. Increasingly, there is an expectation that research in education and the knowledge generated from it within communities of practice can act as a platform for social action to stimulate social changes at a local and national level. This may be realized by embracing research as a cooperative action, and developing the epistemological and methodological tools that transform research into a dialogue and a site for critique.

Dimitra Hartas, University of Warwick

Acknowledgements

In this journey through the complex territory of research in education with its array of diverse, and often confusing genres that range from experiments and surveys to discourse analyses, visual semiotics and action research, I would like to express my thanks to colleagues from the Warwick Institute of Education and the Universities of Exeter, Leeds and Nottingham, as well as from the London Institute of Education and the Trinity College in Dublin. This volume would not exist without them. They brought a variety of perspectives to construct a rich tapestry of research in education.

We are grateful to the UK Data Archive, a service provider for the Economic and Social Data Service (ESDS) at the University of Essex, and colleagues from the Centre for Longitudinal Studies, who have graciously given us access to use subsets of data from two national datasets, namely the Millennium Cohort Study (third survey), and the Young People Social Attitudes, to illustrate quantitative data analyses presented in this volume and offer students access to real-life data to practise newly-learnt statistical skills.

This volume is dedicated to all present and future postgraduate students in education who, through the challenges of undertaking research in the ever-changing field of education, will develop a critical consciousness to accept uncertainty and negotiate their identities as teachers, researchers and policy-makers. We hope that, through discussions on the nature and the practical considerations of inquiry in education, they will be encouraged to engage in reflexive practices in diverse educational contexts and communities.

Introduction
Dimitra Hartas

This book is about research in education. Educational inquiry, due to its inherent diversity, requires a new thinking of the epistemological frameworks and methodological tools to examine mainstream academic knowledge and assumptions about teaching and learning, as well as the positionality of researchers, teachers and their communities. Educational research is polyphonic and shares many characteristics with pluralistic research in terms of recognizing multiple social accounts and educational contexts, and transforming power relationships (Grant *et al.* 2004). It has the potential to challenge 'established canons, paradigms, theories, explanations and research methods' (Banks and Banks 1993: 8) with the view of creating knowledge to sustain social action against inequality and power structures and their impact on learning.

In much social and educational research, a disproportionate emphasis has been placed on the value of methods. Although a thorough understanding of research methodologies and their underlying epistemological premises is crucial, in this book we took an iterative and dialectical approach by acknowledging the non-linear nature of research and placing an equal weight on all its phases. Across chapters, methods and ways of making sense of data are discussed in the context of inquiry, encouraging students and new researchers to bridge qualitative and quantitative methods, reflect on research ethics and engage with the broader theoretical and methodological issues.

In this volume, we present diverse epistemologies, and stress the need to bring together explanatory models with exploratory and reflexive practices towards the generation of knowledge that is dialogic, value-centered and action-orientated, and relevant to people's social and historical circumstances. We share the view that developing sound and innovative methodologies, which are much needed in educational research, cannot be decontextualized, requiring a clear theoretical and epistemological framework to account for consensus as well as dissent, both central to research.

We believe it is pedagogically appropriate to present quantitative and qualitative methods and analyses as being complementary, linked to the research conceptualization and design. Quantitative, qualitative and mixed-method approaches are contextualized by drawing links between the research questions, the choice of methodology and the theoretical and epistemological frameworks that underpin it. Training in research methodology should not occur in a vacuum because it is less likely to lead to better research (Boote and Beile 2005). We hope that the readers will appreciate the diversity in research in education and balance the emphasis on methods with an understanding of the field and the theoretical and methodological assumptions that underpin inquiry.

Educational researchers work at the crossroads of many disciplines, and thus mono-disciplinary perspectives and singular research identities are not conducive to tackling complex problems in education. The contributors to this book all share a commitment to improving the teaching and learning of research in education in a manner that supports its polyphonic character and rich landscape across paradigmatic transitions. Implicit in their contributions is a range of views about epistemology, methodology and the values that underpin educational research and its communities.

The Phases of Research

The structure of this volume reflects the phases that researchers typically go through when conducting research. Although there is heterogeneity in the ways we conduct research, especially qualitative research (e.g. ethnography, case study, conversation analysis, document analyses, interview studies), it is useful to have a framework to guide us through the research cycles. The book is divided into five parts. These are: Educational Research and Inquiry: Foundations; Conceptualizing and Planning Research in Education; Methodology and Research Designs in Education – Strategies of Inquiry; Making Sense of Research in Education – Analysing our Data; and Presentation of Educational Research.

Parts I and II deal with the pre-empirical phases of research. Here the reader is presented with issues to be considered in formulating research questions. These are: (a) philosophical (e.g. ontological, epistemological); (b) practical/technical (e.g. sources of data, data collection and recording, resource availability – time, money, materials); (c) personal (e.g. the researcher's prior experiences, political standpoint; motivations – political, emotional, professional, social class, race, gender, sexual orientation); and (d) ethical (e.g. codes of professional practice, self-regulation, dissemination of results). Parts III and IV deal with the empirical phases of research, which involve decisions about the research design and techniques for data collection and analysis. Finally, Part V deals with writing and presenting research in education.

Part I contains four chapters which focus on the theoretical and epistemological foundations of research in education.

Chapter 1 engages with the shifting landscape of educational research. Internationally, since the 1990s, passionate debates about the validity, applicability and trustworthiness of educational research have been articulated by governments, researchers and policy-makers. The tensions in educational research have been articulated in terms of its increasing politicization and the resurfacing of paradigmatic divisions. In this climate, the nature of inquiry, the values and positionality of the researchers and the researched, and the polarization of qualitative and quantitative research require new arguments. A way forward may be to go beyond paradigmatic divisions and support the creation of communities of practice where inquiry in education is relevant to the lives of researchers and the researched.

Chapter 2 presents the diverse epistemologies that underpin educational inquiry. It discusses empiricism, positivism, postpositivism and critical realism as worldviews that relate to quantitative research, and critical theory, postmodernism and social constructivism as the most common paradigms in qualitative research. The ultimate aim is to engage with paradigms that bridge qualitative and quantitative research approaches. The positivist and postpositivist worldviews approach knowledge as objective and capable of encapsulating absolute truth and certainty. From a poststructuralist/postmodern point of view, knowledge is not given but continually contested and revisable. Citical theory and social constructivism view knowledge as socially constructed, with transformative and emancipatory potential. This type of knowledge is relational and in contrast to that traditionally developed within the positivist paradigm, characterized by hierarchical relationships and generalizable abstract ideas. Chapter 2 concludes with a discussion on bridging diverse worldviews to promote mixed-method research in education.

Chapter 3 introduces qualitative analysis as a method of inquiry in education and discusses the interwoven nature of theory and analysis. Gibson offers an overview of qualitative research designs and presents a framework of data collection methods deemed appropriate within the context of qualitative methodologies. He questions the use of the singular 'method' in qualitative research, arguing that there are as many 'approaches' as there are qualitative researchers. To him, each empirical research experience and theoretical context lead to something distinctive in the 'approach' being taken. Indeed, the ways that people reflect on these experiences and contexts in writing about social and educational research are exactly the things that can make research methods stimulating.

Chapter 4 focuses on pre-empirical considerations, namely, population and sampling as well as reliability and validity, which influence the conceptualization of quantitative research designs. Clarifying these issues is important to create a solid foundation for quantitative research as an inquiry, regardless of its type (experimental or nonexperimental) and the routes (group comparisons or relationships between variables) we take to address the research questions. Clearly, a thorough consideration of the sampling, validity and reliability can set the stage for a rigorous research design which brings together the research questions and the methodology in a cohesive whole. The chapter concludes with a discussion about reliability and validity as criteria to judge the meaningfulness of quantitative research, and offers a vignette to illustrate the points made.

Part II has three chapters that aim to introduce new researchers to the initial thoughts and processes when conducting research in education. It deals with issues such as conceptualizing a research design, formulating the research questions and planning about participants, reviewing the available literature to define the parameters of a study and considering the ethics of research in education.

Chapter 5 discusses the processes involved in conceptualizing a research design and formulating research questions. The notion of 'fitness for purpose' between the methodologies and the research questions driving the study is discussed and examples are used to illuminate the interaction between research questions and research design, stressing their dialectical nature. Gleeson warns of the danger in seeing theory as being separate from the research design and the policy implications of education research. Such separation is triggered partly by the pragmatics of getting the research methods right and partly by scepticism about a 'grand theory' and its relationship with practice in education. The notion of 'fitness for purpose' between research questions and the way they shape the research design and classroom practice are key elements in a study, stressing the dialectical nature of the relationship between research questions and research design as a first step in *doing* research.

Chapter 6 focuses on doing a literature review in terms of locating and accessing sources; applying evaluative criteria towards a critical review of research studies and other materials; analysing and synthesizing the information; and writing up. The purpose of doing a literature review is highlighted, and its theoretical and methodological benefits are discussed along the lines of becoming aware of others' work, extending ideas and calibrating research question(s) and identifying existing research gaps to enable us to develop original research ideas. Finally, issues regarding reviewing studies in cross-cultural contexts (e.g. international research) and plagiarism are discussed.

Chapter 7 discusses the ethical issues in educational research. Lindsay considers research to be an intrusive process; we enter into the lives of participants to varying degrees. It is therefore necessary to undertake research within an ethical and legal framework. This chapter raises awareness of the major codes of ethics (e.g. those of the British Educational Research Association) and discusses the basis for ethical guidance and the need for ethical codes. It also raises issues of ethics with regard to a research design, recruitment of participants, informed consent and data storage to mention but a few, and the ways in which research might be conducted to comply with their implications. Ethical issues concerned with researching children, working with schools, parents and teachers are also discussed.

Part III contains ten chapters that present a wide range of strategies of inquiry across qualitative, quantitative and mixed-method research, elaborating on research designs and their relevant methodologies. Although certain methodological approaches are more qualitative than quantitative in their orientation, we hope that we have challenged the artificial divides between qualitative and quantitative research by stressing that they can (and should) work in a complementary fashion.

Chapter 8 discusses action research as a participative inquiry that has transformative potential for developing a personal and a collective voice, and for community engagement. Townsend approaches reflexivity and an understanding of the self as important dimensions in developing and evaluating educational practices through research. He offers alternative views and models of action research for new researchers to follow and, against which, to critique their own practice. The intention is not to restrict or limit the possible pathways that action researchers could follow, but rather these models are intended to show how the principles of action research could be realized in practice.

Chapter 9 discusses the challenges of ethnographic encounters with young people. Starting with the question 'What is a child?', Christensen engages with recent sociological and anthropological research with children. She highlights the challenges to research when changing the perspective from learning *about* children's lives to learning *from* children, stressing the need to develop dialogical practices in research and engage with children's 'cultures of communication'. Finally, the implications of promoting child agency are highlighted through a problem case scenario (i.e. talking about children's health), juxtaposing the role of the researcher and the researched with the complexity of children's lives.

Chapter 10 examines a comparative case study approach as a prominent qualitative research method in education. The comparison of case studies is implicit in research that offers an in-depth analysis from small samples. The chapter explicitly draws out the methodological significance of case studies in terms of their potential to illuminate key cultural and institutional differences when examining organizational structures, and offers a comparative analysis of data from different research sites. Wyness draws on a recently completed project on young people's negotiation of democratic structures and participation in educational and civic settings to illustrate the use of comparative case studies in education.

Chapter 11 discusses the nature of researching classroom interaction and talk. The social and contextual nature of human learning has received a great deal of emphasis in recent research on teaching and learning, with more attention now being paid to the practices leading to the social construction of knowledge in learning situations. Because of this developing research agenda, new methodological questions concerning the analysis of classroom interaction and learning have arisen. How, for example, can researchers unpick and describe qualitative differences within and between interactions in a variety of learning settings? Wray and Kumpulainen review and critique approaches to studying and analysing classroom interaction, and especially the discourse that characterizes it. The chapter is centred on an account of a programme of research into classroom interaction and social learning, and uses the methodological decisions made during that programme as a set of pegs on which to hang discussion of methodological issues in this field.

Chapter 12 examines the possibilities and potential of documentary research. Drawing largely from historical methods, the contribution of documentary research has often been overlooked in educational studies. This elision is unfortunate and often leads to deeply decontextualized and ahistorical perspectives in current educational research. In this chapter, Robinson demonstrates how documentary research is used in stand-alone projects and in the context of multimethod projects. The chapter deals with the practicalities of undertaking documentary research, including issues of access to documents, the selection of documents and the critical analysis and interpretation of documentary material. A set of documents is used to illustrate the main processes involved, from the generation of research questions to the final dissemination of the findings.

Chapter 13 deals with the application of a visual methodology in the exploration of the visual culture of schools. The use of a visual methodology is fairly new and raises important ontological and methodological questions with regard to the object of research (e.g. what counts as image), the type of visual methods that are useful and the ways of interpreting visual data through the application of visual semiotics and other strategies of inquiry. Prosser and Loxley have explored innovative ways of using and interpreting image as an important element of visual research in education. The chapter concludes with a discussion on the ethical issues that visual researchers are likely to encounter.

Chapter 14 deals with interviewing as an educational research method. Hobson and Townsend present a cluster of the most frequently used methods of generating data in educational (and social) research, namely research interviews. They describe interviewing as a 'cluster' of methods because the existence and use of a wide variety of different kinds of interview means that in some respects it is simplistic to speak of 'the interview' as a single method. The authors offer definitions and typologies of interviewing, and discuss the advantages and limitations of several types of interview (e.g. structured and less structured interviews). Finally, they present group interviews and focus group discussions as core methodologies in conducting research in education.

Chapter 15 examines two main types of quantitative research design, namely, experimental and quasi-experimental, including design experiments. Distinctions between these designs are drawn and examples from educational research studies for each design are provided. Key elements of these designs, such as the notion of control (e.g. experimental and control groups, blind and double-blind experiment), randomization, a-priori hypotheses, pre- and post-measures, intervention/treatment, placebo, causality and objectivity are discussed. Finally, the chapter concludes with a discussion on the advantages and limitations of each design type.

Chapter 16 discusses the theoretical and practical considerations for non-experimental research (i.e., survey research, which is the most commonly used method in education). Survey research designs are flexible and tend to incorporate questionnaires for data collection. The advantages and disadvantages of survey research are discussed, and the theoretical and methodological considerations involved in questionnaire construction, including web-based surveys, are presented. Finally, some practical advice is offered on how to construct questionnaires to avoid common pitfalls.

Chapter 17 is concerned with the evaluation of educational policy and practice through research. Increasingly, the need for evidence on accountability and resource management in education requires the use of evaluation research. Different models of evaluation are presented, emphasizing participatory evaluation and the dilemmas that emerge from it, especially when exploring possibilities for social change. The use of mixed methods in evaluation is discussed, and two studies (PGCE Plus and the Capital Modernization initiative) are offered to illustrate the processes involved in evaluating programmes and policy initiatives in education.

Part IV comprises seven chapters that present a range of analytical tools for qualitative and quantitative data analysis. This part deals mainly with quantitative data analysis because types of qualitative data analysis were discussed within the context of qualitative research methodologies in Part III. The chapters on quantitative data analysis offer a basis to engage in explorations of data (e.g. describe and summarize data and make inferences about the population from which the sample is drawn). These chapters do not assume any prior knowledge of statistics. Their aim is to help the reader to develop an understanding of quantitative data analysis by discussing how we decide upon a statistical technique and, most crucially, why. These discussions involve considerations of the nature of data and the assumptions that underpin statistical techniques, as well as the limitations that these techniques bring with them.

Chapter 18 offers an overview of the processes involved in qualitative data analysis. It mainly focuses on transcription, and its different types and applications. Gibson applies the principles of treating data analysis as an iterative feature of the research process rather than a separate 'stage', and of building the design of one's research around the generation of relevant data. He briefly introduces the use of computer software (i.e. CAQDAS) that facilitates the analysis of qualitative data. Finally, he discusses the theoretical and methodological framework of a thematic analysis and its relevance to qualitative analysis in education.

Chapter 19 introduces new researchers to the key concepts and assumptions as they relate to quantitative research design and analysis. Part of deciding upon a quantitative research design and its associated statistical techniques is to consider issues related to the identification of variables, hypothesis-testing, probability and statistical power. The technical requirements that underpin statistical analyses should be considered carefully. However, what is crucial is to ensure that the quantitative analyses we employ are consistent with the research aims and questions, and that the decisions about sampling and hypothesis-testing link directly to the research design.

Chapter 20 deals with the practicalities of preparing, coding and inputting data in SPSS (Statistical Package for the Social Sciences) 15/16. This is to help new researchers in getting started with data entry into the Data Editor of SPSS, creating and labelling variables, and saving and retrieving files. Two important functions, 'recode' and 'select' are presented to be used for the purpose of preparing quantitative data before employing statistical techniques.

Chapter 21 goes through the first steps in exploring quantitative data to gain an overall view (e.g. frequency of responses to screen the data and correct any errors found with the data before we start the analyses). Descriptive statistics are discussed as a way of gaining an overview of the data through the calculation of the central tendency measures (i.e. mean, mode and median) and dispersion (i.e. variance and standard deviation). The distinction between descriptive and inferential statistics is discussed, and three types of analysis are introduced, namely univariate, bivariate and multivariate. The distinction between parametric and nonparametric data is discussed, highlighting its implications for choosing statistical techniques. The chapter concludes by presenting a cross-tabulation and contingency analysis, explaining the use of the chi-square test.

Chapter 22 presents statistical techniques that are used to explore differences between groups of people. Traditionally, within experimental and quasi-experimental designs, comparisons between experimental and control groups have been important to make causal inferences about the effects of the treatment/intervention received by the experimental group. Thus, the focus of this chapter is on comparing groups and, more specifically, comparing two or more means of the scores obtained across groups. To this end, two statistical analyses are presented and illustrated here: independent t-test and n-way analysis of variance (one-way and two-way ANOVA). With a two-way ANOVA (independent factorial analysis), we examine two independent variables simultaneously, and compare several means to determine the main and, most importantly, the interaction effects of the independent variables on the dependent variable.

Chapter 23 starts by describing simple associations between two outcomes, both in the forms of simple two-way tables and as scatterplots showing the relationship between two continuous variables. It builds from graphical presentation through to statistical concepts of correlation and partial correlation, and on to complex statistical models such as multiple regression and logistic regression. Throughout the presentation of the statistical techniques, an emphasis is given on *why* researchers would want to employ these techniques, by linking them to clear research questions (e.g. *Which factors are the best predictors of getting a degree? Do boys and girls differ in their educational attainment?*). To this end, the chapter employs datasets using real longitudinal data, drawn from the British Birth Cohort Studies and other sources.

Chapter 24 presents an exploratory factor analysis, elaborating on its aims and the phases involved in it, namely initial screening of variables/items, factor extraction and factor rotation. It discusses the methodological and statistical issues involved in factor generation and rotation, offering an example to illustrate the use of a principal component analysis for calculating the common variance (communality) and the loading (coefficients) of each variable to factors. Finally, the chapter concludes with considerations about whether the generated factors approximate the original variables, and the extent to which they ensure a good fit.

Part V contains one chapter offering advice on and practical examples of ways of presenting and writing research in education.

Chapter 25 covers the presentation and writing of research, focusing on issues of style, format, audience, purpose, plagiarism and referencing. Since good research can be spoiled by its presentation, it is valuable to include guidance for those who are perhaps new to the field. Presenting findings and analysis effectively, whether by written report, journal article, conference paper or by means of the spoken word, is a crucially important part of the process of undertaking research. Finally, considerations of both the nature of the research (e.g. quantitative or qualitative), and the nature of the audience (e.g. academics, practitioners, lay people), are essential and discussed here with clarity.

On Reading and Using this Volume

This volume was written with the requirements of postgraduate students and new researchers in mind, presenting a broad range of theoretical and methodological knowledge. Most chapters were written as an introduction to research in education but some require more background knowledge than others. Although the methodological approaches presented in this book are by no means exhaustive, the range of chapters can offer guidance to students in education of what is available and what is possible in educational research. The chapters are organized in a way that reflects the phases of undertaking a piece of research. It is useful to read the description of the chapters offered in the introduction, before you embark on reading the entire chapter in order to gain an overall idea of the range of material covered.

Here are some tips on how to use this book.

- At first, it may be useful to browse through the book to see what is available in terms of identifying the landscape of theoretical and methodological approaches regarding educational research.
- The five parts of the book follow the steps that we typically take in conceptualizing and conducting research. For example, Chapters 1, 2, 3, 4 and 5 guide you in exploring research questions and the epistemological and ontological traditions that underlie the theoretical and methodological bases of educational research.
- It is helpful to consider the theory-method-practice relationship that underpins research designs and to explore how research questions fit within certain epistemological frameworks.

With regard to the last point, an attempt has been made in almost all the chapters to reflect on the theory-method-practice relationship, engaging with the difficult task of translating theoretical perspectives into methodological frameworks while, at the same time, identifying their practical implications. To guide this metamorphosis, while reading the chapters in this book, we set the following questions:

- What are the key arguments in each chapter?
- What are the theoretical assumptions that underpin the questions asked?
- What are the assumptions that underpin the methodological approaches taken?
- What are the key terms?
- What kind of questions is a given method of inquiry designed to address? What kind of questions does it not address?
- What data do we need to address these questions?
- What kind of analysis is deemed to be appropriate for the data collected?
- What are the theoretical assumptions that guide decisions about research design, data collection and analyses?
- How does a methodological approach contribute to researching issues in education?
- How do we account for the social and political influences on research in education?

Pedagogic features

Several pedagogic features are offered in this volume to present text in ways that are more likely to facilitate access to, at times, complex material. These are as follows.

- *Boxes* are used to exemplify or summarize an idea or a series of steps towards a specific goal. They also list important points and offer brief overviews of the main points covered in a chapter.
- *Checklists* aim at highlighting the steps that we take towards a specific task. They function as a guide or set of 'road signs' for the procedures that we plan to undertake as educational researchers.
- *Summaries* at the end of each chapter are offered to bring together the key issues covered in the chapter. The aim is to reinforce the important points in the chapter that you need to make a note of before you move to another chapter.
- *Glossary*: a glossary with full definitions of key terms is offered at the end of the book.
- *Web companion:* a range of materials that educational researchers may find helpful to use the book effectively. These are:
  - revision questions for each chapter to give the opportunity to reflect on the key issues covered
  - web links and additional resources to support new researchers in extending their study of research methods, offering opportunities for interactive learning
  - exercises for most chapters where learners can use real-life datasets (i.e. LSYPE, Millennium Cohort Study, YPSA) to carry out statistical analyses and also qualitative analyses
  - checklists and frameworks to guide researchers through the conceptualization and conduct of research, delineating the phases/cycles of research and the sort of considerations we need to make to complete a research project
- *Frequently-asked questions* can be found at http://education.hartas.continuumbooks.com to clarify common (or not so common) misconceptions and draw attention to important issues.
- *Key terms* lists can be found at http://education.hartas.continuumbooks.com, with their definitions included in the glossary.
- *Further reading:* a list is offered at http://education.hartas.continuumbooks.com with further reading material and a brief annotation for those who want to extend their knowledge on particular topics.

References

Banks, J. A. and Banks, C. (1993) *Multicultural Education: Issues and Perspectives,* 2nd edn. Boston, MA: Allyn & Bacon.

Boote, D. N. and Beile, P. (2005) 'Scholars before researchers: on the centrality of the dissertation literature review in research preparation', *Educational Researcher,* 34(6): 3–15.

Grant, C., Elsbree, A. and Fondrie, S. (2004) 'A decade of research on the changing terrain of multicultural education research', in J. A. Banks and C. A. Banks (eds) *Handbook of Research on Multicultural Education,* 2nd edn. San Francisco: Jossey Bass.

Part I
Educational Research and Inquiry: Foundations

Educational Research and Inquiry: Key Issues and Debates

1

Dimitra Hartas

Introduction

This chapter discusses educational research as inquiry and brings together key issues and debates on its purpose, governance and increasing politicization. The studies reviewed here point to a diversity that collectively maps onto what is known as 'educational research'. Although diversity strengthens research in education, it may exacerbate inherent problems with the increasing politicization of research and perpetuation of paradigmatic division. Understanding the rich landscape of educational research is not straightforward. Nor are the responses to the intense criticisms directed towards educational research and the rise of a new orthodoxy of science.

By the end of this chapter, you should be able to:

- reflect on the nature of educational research as inquiry
- outline the current criticisms of educational research
- understand the increasing politicization of educational research
- critically engage with the paradigmatic divisions and dichotomies between qualitative and quantitative research
- understand the importance of creating communities of practice to govern research in education

What is Educational Research?

Education is a diverse and ever-evolving field with a multidisciplinary orientation to scholarship. Increasingly, the investigation of educational phenomena is characterized by a perennial criticism of the usefulness and relevance of educational research to policy and classroom practice, and the battles over the rigour and trustworthiness of the ways we conduct research. The complexity of doing research in education increases as more and more people need to learn more things and commit to learning for longer than ever before. We seem to be at a crossroads of redefining education and the scholarship produced within it. In both the developing and developed world, formal education faces great challenges in supporting young people to tackle complex problems and contribute actively to their communities. These challenges have encouraged innovative thinking about education and educational inquiry and stimulated debates on the instrumentality of knowledge and the view of learning as a means to an end. Within this context, research and scholarship in education have become a moving target.

As societies become globalized and diverse, education appears to play a prominent role in preparing individuals as citizens to engage with their communities and offer solutions to complex problems of environment, citizenship, poverty, social justice and the rise of polarized societies. The diversity inherent in education highlights the tensions between educational practices as they operate at a local level and educational policies at a global level. Moreover, lifelong learning and the digital revolution have transformed the spatial and temporal parameters of schooling, and ultimately the scope of education and the nature of knowledge. In a knowledge-based society, where the pursuit of knowledge is not restricted to a specific locality (e.g. the classroom), medium (e.g. teacher/computer-mediated instruction) or time (e.g. school years/lifelong learning) the role of communities of practice is crucial to set the parameters of inquiry in education and govern the politics and ethics of knowledge-making.

Research studies in education have often borrowed theoretical and methodological frameworks from other disciplines (e.g. psychology, sociology, anthropology). This is crucial because education relies on multiple perspectives to develop multidimensional policy and practice. However, there is a growing criticism that we, as educational researchers, tend to situate inquiry outside the field of education, within other related disciplines (Ball and Forzani 2007). This view raises the need to focus on the 'instructional dynamics' of the ways in which instructional activities mediate learning and the interaction among students, teachers and classrooms as contexts and instructional tool and materials. This type of research is needed to clarify not only what is happening (e.g. class size affects academic performance) but also *how* and *why* is happening. The argument for the centrality of educational research is pertinent especially in a climate where the capacity to demonstrate whether, how and under what circumstances instructional programmes and learning initiatives work and offer evidence on their effectiveness is paramount.

Educational research is transdisciplinary and strives to capture the complexity of educating and learning, and elucidate the link between current pedagogy and tomorrow's citizens. However, educational researchers tend to focus too much on the past and the present of knowledge, engaging in a limited reflection on what a future knowledge society would look like, and whether the need for expert knowledge is likely to bring scepticism and controversy, at best, and suspicion at worst, especially if the knowledge produced is not localized and transferable. To tackle complex questions such as 'What motivates learners to learn?', 'Is a reading programme effective and why?', 'What makes a school truly inclusive?' and 'Does parental school involvement support children's learning?', the diverse tapestry of education as a human science should be preserved.

Educational Research as Inquiry

The process of constructing knowledge through research is guided by frameworks that enable researchers and communities of practice to ask questions about ontology (what it is, what is there to be known, what the object of research is); epistemology (questions about the nature of knowledge, such as what does it mean to know?); paradigm (a set of ideas, assumptions and beliefs that guide action, a worldview); methodology (the specific ways of examining, the 'how' of gaining knowledge); and theory (the construction of knowledge through developing and validating interpretive frameworks) (see Box 1.1).

Box 1.1 Educational research as an inquiry

Notions of ontology, epistemology, paradigms, methodology and theory can be summarized as:
What is there to be known (ontology)?
What strategy shall I follow to collect and analyse my data (method)?
From whom and how (methodology)?
Within what framework (epistemology, paradigms, methodology)?
How is theory developed – cycles of theory verification and theory generation?

(Punch 2006: 63, paraphrased)

Ontology

Ontology, as a branch of philosophy, is the science of what is, of the kinds and structures of the objects, properties and relations in every area of reality (Smith 2003). In simple terms, ontology seeks the classification and explanation of entities, in that 'what it is' and 'what there is to be known' are articulated in a descriptive as well as explanatory manner. Each scientific field has its own preferred ontology, defined by the field's assumptions, worldviews and the canonical formulations of its theories. Philosophical ontologists have engaged with the world, as studied by the sciences, and also with domains of practical activity such as education, applying the tools of philosophical ontology to solve problems by providing a full description. There are often clues of what something is in its full description, which stresses the importance of describing what the phenomenon is before developing any explanatory frameworks (Miles and Huberman 1994).

Epistemology

Epistemology is the philosophy of knowledge, a system of thought that articulates specific beliefs about the nature of knowledge, what it means to know, what is knowable and the methods of knowing. Epistemology is articulated through questions such as:

- What is knowledge?
- Are there different kinds of knowledge?
- Are there good and valid procedures for constructing and understanding knowledge?
- How can we know if we are wrong?
- How sure we are about knowledge?

To understand what knowledge is and how it is developed through research, Oancea (Oancea 2005: 174–5) offered four continua on which attributes of knowledge are placed:

- *Cumulativeness:* knowledge that is cumulative in terms of adding to an existing body of knowledge in linear or more complex ways vs. *non-cumulativeness* in which new knowledge presents a rapture, a shift from previous knowledge.
- *Convergence:* with different communities of research working together vs. *divergence.*
- *Rationality:* knowledge growth is governed by rules or criteria (probabilistic, semantic, linguistic, mathematical) vs. *non-rationality.*
- *Teleology:* research is goal-oriented and its fitness of purpose is the criterion to judge its outcome, vs. *non-teleology* where research's side-effects and byproducts are equally as important as its main or intended outcomes.

To construct knowledge and reflect on its nature we use a lens, a worldview, which provides us with theories, models, exemplars, values and methods shared by a community of scholars. This worldview is called a *paradigm*, and is deeply 'embedded in the socialization of adherents and practitioners' (Patton 1990: 37).

Paradigms and paradigmatic transitions

Thomas Kuhn, in *The Structure of Scientific Revolutions* (1962), introduced the construct of *paradigm* to make sense of the conceptual changes in physical sciences. To describe a paradigm, Kuhn invoked Piaget's conceptualization of cognitive schemata – that is, cognitive structures that facilitate our understanding of the world. However, it is important to note that cognitive schemata are psychological structures whereas paradigms reflect a worldview that is constructed and shared by a community of practice (Donmoyer 2006).

Patton also defined paradigm as a 'world view, a general perspective, a way of breaking down the complexity of the real world'. In this context 'paradigms tell [researchers] what is important, legitimate, and reasonable'. Paradigms are also normative, 'telling the practitioner what to do without the necessity of long existential or epistemological consideration' (1990: 37). Put simply, paradigms offer researchers an agreed-upon conceptual framework within which to operate. A paradigm can function as a 'double-edged sword' in that, on the one hand, it provides a conceptual framework, to reduce the complexity of social reality and, on the other hand, it may limit the scope of an inquiry. Nevertheless, it is important to note that paradigms offer frameworks for inquiry, not a substitute for knowledge.

Over the years, the notion of paradigm has entered the popular culture, and 'paradigm talk' has become very popular among researchers, administrators and the public at large. Since the 1980s, educational researchers have seen a paradigm proliferation with 'paradigm shifts' taking place to replace one way of thinking about the nature of knowledge with another (Donmoyer 2006). In 1985, Guba and Lincoln referred to two paradigms, namely positivist/naturalist and constructivist. By 1994, new paradigms, including neo-Marxism, feminism, materialism and critical theory (poststructuralism and postmodernism) had become present in the educational community (Guba and Lincoln 1994).

When a community of practice goes through reform, a revolutionary transition from an old paradigm to a new one often resolves the crisis. The new paradigm employs a different conceptual framework, and sets new problems as well as rules (exemplars) for their solutions. Kuhn observed that, when a paradigmatic transition takes place, 'the profession will have changed its view of the field, its methods, and its goals' (1970: 85). For Kuhn, the change of paradigm is not rule-governed. Nor does it amount to a slow transition from one paradigm to the other; it is rather an abrupt change in which the new paradigm completely replaces the old one. Paradigmatic shifts are capable of shaping the scope and aims of research and our understandings about the nature of knowledge, stimulating shifts in epistemology, methodology and theory.

Once we have set up the theoretical framework to underpin our inquiry, we need to study the methods or strategies by which we examine the phenomenon under investigation. The process of how we 'come to know' refers to the *methodology*.

Methodology

Methodology focuses on the specific *ways*, the *strategies* or *methods* we use to understand social reality. In educational research, a disproportionate emphasis has been placed on the value and the objective power of methods. Janesick coined the term 'methodolatry, a combination of method and idolatry' to describe our preoccupation with focusing on methods so much as to marginalize the scope of an inquiry and the story we want to tell (1994: 215). Placing too much emphasis on methods rather than on research as an inquiry is likely to reduce research *to* a method. Thomas and James (2006) argue that the imposition of methods is likely to break the narrative, the accounts of the participants, by 'sanitizing' them through grounded theory analyses.

These views about the role of methods are important as new researchers try to reconcile the nature of an inquiry and the methods that are employed to collect and make sense of data. There is always a danger that research is reduced to a mere collection of activities that fit into a singular method. Moreover, relying on a single method does not constitute science because it is unlikely to unravel the complexities that the study of educational phenomena entails. The development of science requires contest and debates, willingness to accept uncertainty and embrace multiplicity and plurality by encouraging the use of multiple methods, as in design experiments, action research or ethnography.

The American Educational Research Association (AERA) actively encourages 'the robust methodological pluralism of educational inquiry' and warns against a 'blanket' approach to research by stressing that the 'methodological adequacy of a piece of work' should be understood and judged in relation to the 'methodological requirements of its type [...] the significance of the results in the context of the problems internal to its own tradition, and not the requirements and aspirations of types to which it does not belong' (2002: 103–5). To this end, a fit between the method and the purpose and circumstances of research is crucial. There are many legitimate research frameworks and paradigms, and no single method is good or bad or scientific or unscientific. As a general rule, we should start from the questions we seek to answer, and then develop the methodological frameworks to inform our choice of methods. In this way, we start from the inquiry and not from the method.

Establishing the parameters of an inquiry can be facilitated through a review of the literature in the chosen field of study (see Chapter 6), and from personal and professional experience and insight. Once the first steps towards formulating research questions have been taken, the methodological approaches can be considered. This does not mean that the research questions will remain unchanged. As we think about methods and their underlying epistemological frameworks, the research questions are refined further. The process of moving from an inquiry to the methods is not linear; it is rather iterative: the research topic/questions set the basis for thinking about methods, and the methodological approaches refine the research questions. This dynamic symbiosis between the research questions and the methodological approaches offers a unified theoretical and epistemological framework to explain how people's meaning and social reality take shape and change over time.

Developing a worldview and studying the methods to conduct research is guided by theory. Within inquiry, theory is a thinking tool and a provisional end product (Mouzelis 1995).

Theory

Theory in educational research entails multiple meanings, fluid explanations, interpretive frameworks, epistemological positions and personal reflections (Thomas 1997) that should be guided by the data collected but not limited to it (Layder 1993). Thomas and James consider theory to be 'about conjecture [...] and creativity' that goes beyond everyday patterning, syllogisms and ways of trying to understand the world (2006: 773), and beyond what Schatzman calls 'common interpretive acts' (1991: 304). Social scientists are thought to operate within two kinds of theory, namely theory for the purpose of mapping out a problem area (Nadel 1957: 1) and theory 'as a set of statements that tells us something about the social world that can be proved or disproved by empirical investigation' (Thomas and James 2006: 774). Another way of describing the two types of theory is *theory generation* and *theory verification* (Punch 2006). Theories for mapping an educational phenomenon involve understanding and interpretation (theory generation), whereas theory as a process of confirming a priori hypotheses involves explanation through inference-making and prediction (theory verification).

Theory generation and theory verification rely on two broad methods of logic, namely inductive and deductive reasoning. Typically, in quantitative research, we engage with theory verification through deductive reasoning which works from the more general to the more specific (top-down approach) as follows:

- theory
- hypothesis formulation (a priori hypothesis)
- observation
- theory verification (or not)

Deductive reasoning is often referred to as a hypothetico-deductive approach to inquiry in that it relies on the formulation of hypotheses based on previous theory and research findings and the collection of data to confirm/reject them. Deductive reasoning builds upon previous theories that have been systematically confirmed or rejected, rather than theories as they emerge from data. One criticism of deductive reasoning is encapsulated in the phrase 'putting the cart before the horse' in that theory is a priori and not generated through engagement with the participants' narratives and views of the world. For quantitative researchers, the view that theory emerges from the data is critiqued along the lines of 'everything goes', arguing that lack of an a priori theory means lack of a framework to guide inquiry.

The value of prediction, an important element of deductive reasoning, has been criticized when it comes to explaining the social and natural world. As Thomas and James argue, referring to Ptolemy's prediction of the movement of the planets based on an earth-centric view, 'predictive accuracy does not make for explanatory veracity' (2006: 777). In other words, prediction may seem plausible even when it is based on false assumptions. Within deductive reasoning, we arrive at theory through a systematic and extensive data collection, where explanations are tested for the purpose of verification or falsification, and generalizations are based on the explanations that have been verified.

On the other hand, studies with a qualitative methodology are more likely to engage with inductive reasoning, with theory emerging from the data. Inductive reasoning works from specific observations to broader generalizations and theories, progressing through:

- observation
- identifying emerging patterns
- forming tentative hypotheses (data-driven hypotheses)
- generating theories based on the themes/ideas as they emerge from the data

Inductive reasoning is also referred to as empirico-inductive or data-driven reasoning, and underpins grounded theory (see Chapter 3). Inductive reasoning has received criticism along the lines of an 'everydayness of inductive reasoning', questioning the notion of generating theory and how it differs from explanations or predictions. For Thomas and James, theory offers a 'canonical apparatus which allows us to make inferences based on inductive processes' (2006: 771).

Theory verification and theory generation operate from distinct conceptual bases; they are situated within different epistemological, methodological and paradigmatic traditions. Theory generation has been linked to qualitative research, whereas theory verification is assumed to take place within quantitative research. However, theory verification and generation are not dichotomous processes. Research studies can go through cycles of theory verification and theory generation, regardless of their epistemological and methodological orientation. For example, theory generation may be a priority when studying a new topic, in order to establish the ontology of a phenomenon (what it is), before moving into theory verification.

Wolcott (1994) coined the phrases 'theory first' and 'theory after' to describe theory verification and theory generation, respectively. Perhaps, 'theory all round' may be a more appropriate phrase to highlight the processes whereby theory informs but also extends research to create new knowledge through cycles of interpretation and explanation in an iterative manner. The distinction between a priori hypotheses that characterize deductive reasoning and hermeneutic interpretations as incurring at the end of an inquiry is problematic because 'meaning exists at the beginning of any research as well as at the end, as the choice of the theme to be investigated, the awakening of the desire to investigate, as the gaining of the new problematic' (Gadamer 1975: 251).

Both inductive and deductive types of inquiry have received extensive criticism along the lines of restricting the fluidity of imagination and creativity (Thomas and James 2006). Through deductive reasoning, the notion of discovery of knowledge is stressed as being the purpose of research. Although the notion of discovery makes sense in the context of natural science – for example, the discovery of the DNA sequence – within education the notion of invention or construction is more appropriate. Discovery presupposes that something already exists, although it is hidden, in the form we discover it. Invention or construct, on the other hand, is a product of our mental, psychological and social experiences. Thomas and James talk about all these things which make us human and inform our mental and psychological lives: personal histories, emotions, hopes for the future, artefacts and a sense of purpose. This fabric of our humanity is present when we approach research and removing it is neither feasible nor desirable. It is meaningless to argue that the methods of an inquiry do not rely on previous knowledge and experiences, and to consider inquiry to be a sort of 'epiphany *ex nihilo*', that is untouched by our histories.

What makes us human guides us to make meaning during research in that our identity, moral values and the judgements we make are not separate from the research process itself, and shape the voices of the researchers and the researched in significant ways. Increasingly, more and more emphasis is placed on issues of diversity, identity and morality within educational inquiry, moving towards a humanistic model to account for power relationships and counteract the increasing politicization of educational research.

Researcher Identity, Positionality and Values

Epistemology, methodology and the choice of paradigms are all influenced by the values and beliefs, as well as the identities, of the researchers and the researched (Greenbank 2003). Researchers are 'embodied agents whose identity shapes their work', suggesting that research ideas emerge from our biographies and relate to our emotions and identities, challenging a value-free objectivity in educational research (Hammersley 2005: 148). Similarly, Iano (1986), in her critique on research in special needs education, detests the notion of neutrality and value-free research, considering it to be problematic in the context of disability and education rights. She argues that removing systems of belief and norms from educational research is faulty in that beliefs and values constitute the basis of education.

Educators' judgements reflect moral responsibility, which cannot be reconciled with the notion of a value-free and reductionistic science. At the same time, an over-reliance of important decisions on morality and social values alone may be problematic. Educational research has been criticized for being impartial, with the interpretations and conclusions reached being influenced by the researcher's political bias and values (e.g. Tooley and Darby 1998). There is a fine line between value-laden and partisan research, and researchers often operate in the spaces where research is value relevant. The strife for neutrality is not feasible, nor is desirable, because values should determine the object of research as well as the epistemological and methodological approaches, arguing for research to be value-conscious (Abraham 1996), trustworthy (Lather 1986) and error-free (Romm 1997). The establishment of partnerships between the researcher and the researched, an unbiased sampling process, triangulation of data and the adoption of a grounded approach to data analysis are likely to moderate a researcher's values to avoid bias (Greenbank 2003).

Partnerships raise important issues regarding the ethics and politics of voice and representation that are particularly relevant for qualitative research in education. Researchers strive to ensure accuracy in the representations of fieldwork experiences and participants' accounts, transparency in the way they present evidence and openness about their positionality and biases. However, there are challenges with regard to whose voices, beliefs and moral values are represented in these accounts, and who makes decisions about what constitutes evidence and how it emerges from researchers' constructions of the participants' constructions about social reality (Geertz 1983: 9). In addition to these concerns, some researchers may not be consciously aware of compromising moral values to achieve certain social and personal aspirations, stressing the need for a reflexive approach to include subjective information and multiple voices as part of the data (Williams 2000).

Criticisms of Educational Research

In the last decade, criticisms regarding the validity, usefulness and relevance of educational research have become prominent. Many articles have appeared in the *Educational Researcher* (e.g. Cobb *et al.* 2002; Shavelson *et al.* 2003; Freeman *et al.* 2007) stimulating debates on what counts as evidence and the value of research in education. The growing 'crisis' in educational research has become international. This crisis has been articulated along moral purpose, legitimation of the community of educational researchers, the position of research within wider social, economic and political contexts, and its capability for growth (e.g. Goodson 1999; Lomax 1999; Edwards 2002; Oancea 2005).

In the UK, the criticisms regarding educational research were articulated by government representatives in the main, such as the Department for Education and Skills (DfES), the Office for Standards in Education (Ofsted), the National Foundation for Educational Research (NFER) and the Teacher Training Agency (TTA) (e.g. Tooley and Darby 1988; Hargreaves 1996; Hillage *et al.*

1998; Woodhead 1998). Hargreaves' TTA annual lecture in 1996 acted as a catalyst in the growing body of criticism of educational research. He raised concerns with regard to the capacity of educational research to be cumulative and relevant to classroom practice. In his 2000 ESRC lecture, David Blunkett (Secretary of State for Education and Employment, 1997–2001) also raised concerns about the applicability of educational research, urging it to move away from being 'ivory tower' and contribute to policy and practice.

The criticism offered about educational research can be summarized (Oancea 2005: 166) in terms of:

- *The commissioning of the research:* the ways in which educational research was funded, raising concerns about transparency, political and ideological bias and being supply-driven.
- *The abilities, practices and attitudes of the actors involved:* the researchers were guilty of insufficient methodological training, and of not taking into consideration the research users.
- *The organization of the research:* the whole process of publishing research, from peer reviewing and monitoring, to lack of partnership and user involvement and limited dissemination.
- *Methodology:* non-reliable and inconclusive, lack of rigour, using qualitative methods without any triangulation, sampling bias, ideological bias in interpreting the results, superficial literature, flaws in empirical research.
- *Research outcomes:* use of jargon and over-theoretical language, non-cumulative research findings, irrelevant to practical problems in the field, difficult to transfer in the school context and poor cost-effectiveness.

In the USA, educational research has been described as 'broken', and in the words of Michael Castle, 'Congress must work to make it more useful [...] Research needs to be conducted on a more scientific basis. Educators and policy makers need objective, reliable research' (National Research Council 2002: 28). The US National Research Council redefined scientific educational research along the lines of 'causal analysis by means of experiment as the only way to improve educational research' (Erickson and Gutierrez 2002: 22). This view constructs science as a linear accumulation of knowledge derived from causal explanations between factors through experimental research, for example, randomized trial designs. In the *No Child is Left Behind* legislation of (US Department of Education 2001), research is described as involving:

> the application of rigorous, systematic and objective procedures to obtain reliable and valid knowledge relevant to education activities and programs; and [...] employs systematic, empirical methods that draw on observation or experiment; involves rigorous data analyses that are adequate to test the stated hypotheses and justify the general conclusions drawn; relies on measurements or observational methods that provide reliable and valid data [...] is evaluated using experimental or quasi-experimental designs in which individuals, entities, programs or activities are assigned to different conditions and with appropriate controls to evaluate the effects of the condition of interest, with a preference for random assignment experiments, or other designs to the extent such designs contain within-condition or across condition controls [...]

This definition privileges the use of quantitative research, which is perceived as being objective and valid, and carried out via experimental designs. Experimental research in education has an important role to play. However, within the evidence-based movement, quantitative research methodologies are approached in a fundamentalist manner, allowing for dichotomies between qualitative and quantitative research to resurface, offering a distorted view of science (e.g. Berliner 2002).

Nearly two decades ago, Toulmin challenged what seems to be today a drive to establish authoritative principles through evidence-based practice, contesting the search for a 'permanent, unique set of authoritative principles for human knowledge' which 'proves to be just a dream, which has its appeal in moments of intellectual crisis, but fades away when matters are viewed under a calmer and clearer light' (Toulmin 1990: 174). Other theorists in education agree that the current climate of intellectual crisis is heightened by the misuse of science and a sense of hypocrisy when it comes to policy decisions based on research findings (e.g. Berliner 2002; Whitty 2006).

Furthermore, concerns have been raised about efforts to 'legislate scientific practice and mandate research design' which 'threaten to harden the boundaries of what counts as science', moving towards hard-science models of research (Freeman *et al.* 2007: 25). The distinction between 'hard' and 'soft' science is misleading because it stipulates that research within hard sciences is more rigorous compared to that within soft sciences, encouraging a 'culture of science' that accepts certainty. Erickson and Gutierrez argue that 'the accumulation of knowledge in actual science is not at all continuous – it moves by fits and starts. Real science is not about certainty but about uncertainty' (2002: 22). A prescriptive approach to research – i.e. research as a tool for scientific prediction – contradicts the very nature of educational research as inquiry, and is likely to reduce its creativity and resourcefulness (Hammersley 2005).

The 'new orthodoxy' of educational research favours quantitative research approaches (Hodkinson 2004) by arguing for an authoritative framework of knowledge that is value free and ahistorical, and thus less relevant to the needs of a civic society. This view of research is likely to pose obstacles to the rise of a scholarship with emancipatory potential (e.g. research on difference and human rights of marginalized groups). As Archer (1995: 2) argues

> we would betray ourselves, as well as our readers, by offering any form of social scientism, the 'laws' which are held to be unaffected by the uses and abuses we make of our freedoms, for this renders moral responsibility meaningless and political action worthless and self-reflection pointless. Equally, we delude one another by the pretense that society is simply what we choose to make it and make of it.

'Scientism' refers to the application of natural science frameworks to understand social phenomena. Within the positivist tradition, quantitative research has been criticized for using methodologies and assumptions from the natural sciences and applying them to the human sciences. In its broader sense, 'scientism' refers to the reduction of science to a method, regardless of whether the method is quantitative or qualitative. Scientism is not located within a specific paradigm and does not privilege a certain epistemology over another. Rather, it emanates from bad research practices, which can take place across methodological paradigms.

The discourse that frames the criticism of educational research is managerial, focusing on standards for good practice, development of criteria to judge research and value for money (Tooley and Darby 1998), relevance for practice and user involvement (Hargreaves 1996) and evidence-based policy and practice, quality assurance and fitness for purpose (Hillage *et al.* 1998).

Notions of quality control/assurance, transmission, outputs, policy development, as well as the process of 'legitimizing the criticism itself' have stimulated passionate debates about a wide range of topics, including school effectiveness, evidence-based policy and practice, literacy research and class size research (Oancea 2005: 167).

The focus on policy-relevant and policy-driven research as being the only valid form of research poses challenges for educational researchers (Freeman *et al.* 2007). In an era of paradigmatic transitions, the need for reform in education has been expressed with much intensity and extreme positions have often been taken. Whether the criticism of research is as an 'impetus for change' or a 'regulation mechanism', as an 'ideological device' or an 'expression of skepticism', or a disenchantment discourse', the criticism itself also changes and adapts to new realities (Oancea 2005: 178).

To research education in an era of globalization and transition requires methodologies that are responsive to change and uncertainty. The criticisms and challenges that educational research faces may prove to be a healthy and productive phase that highlights the need for adaptability to increasingly complex social and educational phenomena, and may lead to a rethinking of the nature of knowledge. Understanding and responding to the criticism in educational research is likely to advance research, as long as we are clear about the foundations of the criticism itself. Whether research is to deliver answers about 'what works' or offer the means of creating a public space where critique and dialogue are supported to 'produce localised and transferable knowledge' should be at the centre of the debate (Oancea 2005: 158).

The relationship between educational research, policy and practice is not a straightforward one. The process whereby research critically informs decisions to improve educational action cannot be confined to an engineered application of research or an evidence-based 'social engineering approach' to educational improvement (Erickson and Gutierrez 2002). Government and policy-makers expect educational research to provide immediately applicable solutions to complex problems. Educational research based on a narrowly defined notion of evidence of what works is problematic, especially in a field that changes rapidly, with teaching and learning being influenced by multiple factors. 'What works today' may not work tomorrow. The most important questions to ask are 'why it works', 'in what contexts' and, most importantly, 'what it is' (Whitty 2006). As Edwards (2002) has argued, the purpose of educational research should be defined in terms of conceptual change and effectiveness of practice, and also its capacity to raise 'difficult questions'.

The current landscape of educational research is characterized by a lack of 'common purpose' (Bredo 2006: 28). To untangle the multiplicity of purposes of quantitative research requires a strong epistemological position by a community of inquirers. Most crucially, political and institutional changes need to take place to ensure that educational research, quantitative research in particular, is not sidetracked by a political rhetoric, and does not contribute to partisan political views. Rather, educational research is a public inquiry responsive to the needs of individuals and communities, especially in diverse societies.

The Politicization of Educational Research

Furlong, among others, argues that educational research is increasingly used by politicians and governments to support the rise of the 'new managerialism' by providing answers 'that can guide national policy, allowing the government to take legitimate control over ever more specific areas of educational practice including pedagogy' (2004: 353). Inglis (2004) comments that the role of government has been reduced to regulate and manage rather than govern, resulting in an audit-based and managerialist culture. The emphasis on evidence-based practice has become 'the tool for over-regulation that supports political discourses of accountability and performance' (Lather 2004: 763) and uses research as a control system. Wright (2006) observes that 'evidence-based everything' has shifted our thinking about the relationship between academic research and real world policy and practice. In this climate, research is not about scientific rigour, but about becoming a tool 'to support government policies and strengthen management control' (Lather 2004: 763). Politicized research does not account for different epistemologies and paradigms and their contribution to knowledge. Nor does it accept that different research traditions can truly contribute to knowledge.

Some in the educational research community experience conflict because corporations and the government have shown an increasing interest in positivist approaches to science and educational inquiry to maximize efficiency and strengthen authority by using research to promote policy. Often, quantitative research in education has been misused for political purposes, being reduced to a method applied towards meeting policy agendas, and a tool to justify social engineering (e.g. Berliner 2002; Bredo 2006). On the one hand, quantitative research methods are perceived as being scientifically rigorous and, on the other hand, findings from quantitative studies that do not conform to certain political and ideological agendas are neglected. The influence of political decision-making on educational research is illustrated in class size research and the withdrawal of funds for initiatives targeting class size by the US Department of Education (e.g. Camilli *et al.* 2003).

Reflecting on the increasing politicization of research, Wright argues that the era of the 'paradigm wars' did not end in the 1980s, but has re-emerged in the present, stressing that the assumption that those wars were ended 'was a collective overly optimistic (mis)reading of a simmering situation that is now threatening to boil over once again into open hostilities' (2006: 797). The current danger in research in education, however, has not arisen from paradigmatic divisions but from the misuse and misinterpretation of science, and the acceptance of an ideology-driven research that dovetails with political concerns and agendas. The politicization of research, triggered by over-regulation and federal mandates, may be a paradigmatic transition or a complete rapture that aims to redefine the purpose of educational research and practice to support governmental policies. What constitutes political action as worthless is not the epistemic basis of quantitative research per se, but its politicization and the interests of funding bodies in research findings, and these are entirely non-epistemic issues.

At this point, it is important to differentiate between epistemological diversity (and the battles that characterize it) and the use of research for political purposes to provide a 'quick fix' to complex social and educational problems. During the era of the paradigm wars, exploring dualisms in epistemology and methodology was crucial in developing research strategies that were responsive to diversity. Disagreement between different communities of research and practice is important, as long as it is genuine and has a clear pedagogic basis (Furlong 2004). The current criticisms about educational research, however, are more about 'a hidden managerialist agenda that has little to do with research findings and their implication for practice' (Davies 2003: 100). This view is also supported by Lather who argues against an 'extremely interventionist regulatory climate policed by statutory bodies' that has created the need to use research as 'a neo-liberal weapon of crisis management' (2004: 762). Essentially, what is understood by Wright as the 'hegemony of positivism' is the hegemony of a managerialist culture and political ideologies.

Flyvbjerg also expresses concerns about the politicization of research by referring to the synergies between postpositivist science and the broader audit society, arguing that both are based on a technical rationality (Flyvbjerg and Sampson 2001). He frames the debate along the lines of an alliance between positivism and neo-liberal ideologies, stressing that research that relies on fundamentally different epistemological stances cannot be reconciled easily. This view, however, may further polarize educational research by suggesting that certain types of research – i.e. quantitative research – are flawed by virtue of being traditionally located within the positivist paradigm. It is erroneous to think that, for example, emancipatory research with capacity for social action cannot be accomplished by analysing and interpreting the quantitative properties of social/educational phenomena. Explanation and interpretation are not competing entities and can coexist across qualitative and quantitative research to compact polarization (see Chapter 2 for a discussion on bridging paradigms).

Polarization of Qualitative and Quantitative Research

The debates on the polarization of qualitative and quantitative research that dominated the second half of the twentieth century are far from over. They have been reinvigorated with a recent emphasis on evidence-based research, which differentiates between hard and soft sciences (Berliner 2002). Berliner argues that education is 'the hardest-to-do science', in that educators and other social scientists encounter shifting realities, 'local conditions that limit generalisation and theory building', the 'ubiquity of interactions' and the 'decade by findings' interaction (2002: 18–20). Educational scientists deal with contexts and human variation, as well as unpredictability and continually changing political, ideological and cultural landscapes and networks of social interaction. Delineating all the factors that, at any given time, interact and influence an event, as well as determining the magnitude and direction of its influence are not always straightforward tasks. On top of these factors, there is an 'expiration date' or 'short half-life of findings' of educational research, considering that social and educational phenomena change and adapt as we study them and form new social entities (Berliner 2002: 20).

The dichotomy between qualitative and quantitative research is artificial in that we need to combine both approaches to ask questions about 'what works' but also to establish 'what it is' (Erickson and Gutierrez 2002). Establishing 'what it is' can be achieved through qualitative research which accounts for the social context and the dynamic interactions between the persons involved and the adjustments they make as a response to changes. Investigating the effects of an educational intervention should not solely rely on drawing causal inferences from the outcomes, but also document every aspect of the intervention and the adjustments required in its context.

Some theorists have placed inquiry in education and the knowledge it generates on a continuum. Punch argues that prespecified research questions, tightly structured design and prestructured data can coexist with general guiding questions, loosely structured design and data that is not prestructured (2006: 23). For Ercikan and Roth, on the one end of the continuum 'knowledge [...] is characterized by contingency, particularity, being affected by the context, and concretization', whereas, on the other end, 'knowledge [...] is characterized by standardization, universality, distance, and abstraction' (2006: 20). Educational inquiry involves elements that are simultaneously particular and universal, concrete and abstract, or specific and general, suggesting that dualisms in constructing knowledge are meaningless because educational phenomena and our knowledge about them entail both qualitative and quantitative dimensions.

Education, as a public policy field, responds to diversity by embracing diverse paradigmatic positions and constructing diverse bodies of knowledge through multiple perspectives and research methodologies. One-dimensional thinking and fragmentation in educational research is likely to bring unidimensional policy decision-making (Donmoyer 2006). If the purpose of research is to understand complex social and educational phenomena, then multiplicity and polyphony in the modes of inquiry are required to respond to the different needs of individuals and groups in society.

Beyond paradigmatic divisions: creating communities of practice

Research is not constructed in isolation; it defines and is defined by a community of practitioners with their own norms and codes of conduct, showing mutual engagement, joint enterprise and a shared repertoire of actions, discourses, tools and perspectives (Edwards 2002; Hodkinson 2004). Educational research flourishes in a community of practice where strong links are developed between researchers and practitioners (teachers, policy-makers, administrators), with practitioners' research playing a paramount role. Knowledge is influenced by the community/discipline within which it is located. Such community should value debate, resolution and diversity in perspectives and epistemological lenses, rather than standardization of ideas and research approaches (Taylor 1995).

Furlong argues for the need to 'defend a rich and diverse range of approaches to research, promoting debates about quality within different sub-communities and encouraging open discussion across epistemological and methodological boundaries' (2004: 343). If we are to embrace a community of practice, it is worth asking whether paradigmatic tensions are fruitful in building collaborative workings among researchers from fundamentally different paradigmatic positions. The increasing politicization of educational research is likely to destroy communities of practice by dividing them into those where good research is evidenced and the 'other', where poor research is produced. Lack of community and a shared code of practices are likely to leave a vacuum to be exploited by political groups.

Educational inquiry can benefit from a dialogue with diverse communities of practice and across paradigmatic divisions that do not involve acceptance or opposition but understanding of different views. Traditionally, educational research is situated within heterogeneous communities of practice, in terms of interdisciplinary and cross-disciplinary areas of study, with researchers viewing 'the enterprise through divergent epistemological lenses, employing various methods, and even holding competing objectives' (Feuer *et al.* 2002: 9). In addition to being heterogeneous, communities of educational researchers tend to be organized around personal networks, institutional alliances and members' political orientation, rather than around methodological approaches (Hammersley 2005). The diversity built in the communities of research makes the need for governing educational research even more pressing.

Governing Educational Research

Increasingly, educational researchers accept the need to develop systems of governance; the question is not, as Hammersley argues, 'control or not control', but 'what kinds of control, exercised how and by whom and (above all) to what end' (2005: 144). Although the judgement about methods should be left to researchers, the general rules need to be laid down to set the boundaries of educational inquiry, ensuring a fair representation of competing approaches. This requires an open dialogue with diverse communities of practice to defend both deviations from within as well as pressures from outside governmental agencies that may use educational research for political purposes. In education, as is probably the case in other disciplines, there is a fine balance between over-regulation and under-regulation of research practices. Over-regulation is likely to stifle creativity and limit the nature of research by imposing rigid, recipe-like frameworks. On the other hand, under-regulation is likely to result in fragmentation, conflicting approaches to research design and, possibly, intellectual disengagement.

Governance in educational research has been understood along the lines of developing and applying standards of evidence. Norms and standards are not necessarily against good and innovative research practice, as long as they emerge from within communities of practice defined by their theoretical and paradigmatic traditions. Although it is important to develop systematic and scientific ways to conduct research, researchers should resist political mandates whose sole aim is to control the type of research that is getting funded, inhibiting the development of alternative methodologies (Freeman *et al.* 2007). Paradigmatic traditions and their methodological requirements are not static, requiring innovative research designs to capture fluidity, as well as constant adaptation of standards.

The promotion of a scientific culture is not confined to specific approaches or methods to generate evidence and increase knowledge. It requires nurturing and reinforcement by developing 'norms and practices, and an ethos of honesty, openness and continuous reflection' (Feuer *et al.* 2002: 4). The development of a scientific culture should be a joint endeavour with the responsibility falling on both the individuals and educational institutions. Whitty (2006: 172) stresses the need for encouraging an active community of educational researchers to support debates about the quality, purpose, content and methodologies of educational research; promoting cooperation and discussion with policy-makers and practitioners; defending and developing an independent research culture committed to open inquiry and the improvement of education; and enhancing the professional services it provides for its members.

Education is not a static entity and nor is educational inquiry. Educational research is heterogeneous and diverse and capable of tackling the complexity and uncertainty of the real world and the changing nature of knowledge. And this is what makes it exciting. The complexity of educational research becomes evident when we research phenomena that we cannot comprehend, when we 'consider something possible although we cannot understand the conditions of possibility' (Luhmann and Schorr 2000: 158). New epistemologies and methodologies are required to approach research as interaction and cooperation that is capable of creating 'spaces of possibilities' for teachers and learners (Davis and Sumara 2006). As researchers in education, we have an 'epistemic responsibility' but also a responsibility towards learners and educators.

Summary

In this chapter, we highlighted the shifting landscape of educational research. Internationally, since the 1990s, passionate debates about the validity, applicability and trustworthiness of educational research have been articulated by government offices, researchers and policy-makers. Over the years, several terms have been coined to capture current trends in educational research, conceptualizing research as evidence-based practice, a response to the rise of an accountability and audit culture where evidence is needed to justify policy. The tensions in educational research have been articulated along the lines of the new paradigm wars that emerge from the increasing politicization of research. In this climate, issues such as the nature of inquiry, the values and positionality of the researchers and the researched and the polarization of qualitative and quantitative research require new arguments. Perhaps a way forward is to go beyond paradigmatic divisions and support the creation of communities of practice where inquiry in education is relevant to the lives of researchers and the researched.

References

Abraham, J. (1996) 'Positivism, prejudice and progress in the sociology of education: who's afraid of values?', *British Journal of Sociology of Education*, 17(1): 81–6.

AERA (American Educational Research Association) (2002) *Ethical Standards of the American Educational Research Association: Cases and Commentary*. Washington, DC: AERA.

Archer, B. (1995) The nature of research, co-design, *Interdisciplinary Journal of Design*, 6–13.

Ball, S., Loewenberg, D. and Forzani, F. (2007) 'What makes education research 'educational'?, *Educational Researcher*, 36(9): 529–40.

Berliner, D. C. (2002) Comment: educational research: the hardest science of all, *Educational Researcher*, 31(8): 18–20.

Bredo, E. (2006) 'Philosophies of educational research', in J. L. Green, G. Camilli and P. B. Elmore (eds.) *Handbook of Complementary Methods in Education Research*. Mahwah, NJ: AERA/Lawrence Erlbaum.

Camilli, G., Vargas, S. and Yurecko, M. (2003). Teaching children to read: the fragile link between science and federal education policy, *Education Policy Analysis Archives*, 11(15), http://epaa.asu.edu/epaa/v11n15/, accessed 5 November 2009.

Cobb, P., Confrey, J., diSessa, A., Lehrer, R. and Shauble, L. (2002) 'Design experiments in educational research', *Educational Researcher*, 32(1): 9–13.

Davies, B. (2003) 'Death to critique and dissent? The policies and practices of new managerialism and of "evidence-based practice"', *Gender and Education*, 1 (1): 91–103.

Davis, B., and Sumara, D. (2006) *Complexity and Education. Inquiries into Learning, Teaching and Research*. Mahwah, NJ: Lawrence Erlbaum.

Donmoyer, R. (2006) 'Take my paradigm, please! The legacy of Kuhn's construct in educational research', *The International Journal of Qualitative Studies in Education*, 19(1): 11–34.

Edwards, A. (2002) 'Responsible research: ways of being a researcher', *British Educational Research Journal*, 28(2): 157–68.

Ercikan, K., and Roth, W. M. (2006) 'What good is polarizing research into qualitative and quantitative?, *Educational Researcher*, 35(5): 14–23.

Erickson, F., and Gutierrez, K. (2002) 'Comment: culture, rigor, and science in educational research', *Educational Researcher*, 31(8): 21–4.

Feuer, M., Towne, L. and Shavelson, R. (2002) 'Scientific culture and educational research', *Educational Researcher*, 31(8): 4–14.

Flyvbjerg, B. and Sampson, S. (2001) Making Social Science Matter: Why Social Inquiry Fails and How it Can Succeed Again. Cambridge: Cambridge University Press.

Freeman, M., deMarrais, K., Preissle, J., Roulston, K. and Pierre, E. (2007) 'Standards of evidence in qualitative research: an incitement to discourse', *Educational Researcher*, 36(1): 25–32.

Furlong, J. (2004) 'BERA at 30: have we come of age?, *British Educational Research Journal*, 30(3): 343–58.

Gadamer, H. G. (1975) *Truth and Method*. New York: Seabury.

Gage, N. L. (1989) 'The paradigm wars and their aftermath: A "historical" sketch of research on teaching since 1989', *Educational Researcher*, 18(7): 4–10.

Geertz, C. (1983) *Local Knowledge: Further Essays in Interpretive Anthropology*. New York: Basic Books.

Glaser, B. and Strauss, A. (1999) *The Discovery of Grounded Theory: Strategies for Qualitative Research*. New York: Aldine & Gruyter.

Goodson, I. (1999) 'The educational researcher as a public intellectual', *British Educational Research* Journal, 25(3): 277–97.

Greenbank (2003) 'The role of values in educational research: the case for reflexivity', *British Educational Research Journal*, 29(6): 791–801.

Guba, E. G., and Lincoln, Y. S. (1994) *Competing Paradigms in Qualitative Research*. Newbury Park, CA: Sage.

Hammersley, M. (2005) 'Countering the new orthodoxy in educational research: a response to Phil Hodkinson', *British Educational Research Journal*, 31(2): 139–55.

Hargreaves, D. H. (1996) 'Teaching as a research-based profession: possibilities and prospects', *The Teacher Training Agency Annual Lecture*. London: TTA.

Hillage, J., Pearson, R., Anderson, A. and Tamkin, P. (1998) *Excellence in Research on Schools*. London: DfEE.

Hodkinson, P. (2004) 'Research as a form of work: expertise, community and methodological objectivity', *British Educational Research Journal,* 30(1): 9–26.

Howe, K. (1988) 'Against the quantitative-qualitative incompatibility thesis, or dogmas die hard', *Educational Researcher,* 17(8): 10–16.

Iano, R. (1986) 'The study and development of teaching: with implications for the advancement of special education', *Remedial and Special Education (RASE):* 7(5): 50–61.

Inglis, F. (2004) *Culture.* Cambridge: Polity Press.

Janesick, V. J. (1994) 'The dance of qualitative research design: metaphor, methodolatry, and meaning', in N. K. Denzin and Y. S. Lincoln (eds) *Handbook of Qualitative Research.* Thousand Oaks, CA: Sage.

Kuhn, T. S. (1962) *The Structure of Scientific Revolutions.* Chicago: Chicago University Press.

Kuhn, T. S. (1970) *The Structure of Scientific Revolutions,* 2nd edn. Chicago: Chicago University Press.

Lather, P. (1986) 'Research as praxis', *Harvard Educational Review,* 56(3): 257–77.

Lather, P. (2004) 'Scientific research in education: a critical perspective', *British Educational Research Journal,* 30(6): 759–72.

Layder, D. (1993) 'Grounded theory and field research', in *New Strategies in Social Research: An Introduction and Guide.* Cambridge: Polity Press.

Lincoln, Y. S. (2002) 'On the nature of qualitative evidence', paper presented at the annual meeting of the Association for the Study of Higher Education, Sacramento, CA, November.

Lincoln, Y. S. and Guba, E. G. (1985) *Naturalistic Inquiry.* Beverly Hills, CA: Sage.

Lomax, P. (1999) 'Working together for educative community through research', *British Educational Research Journal,* 25(1): 5–21.

Luhmann, N. and Schorr, K-E. (2000) 'Problems of reflection in the system of education', *European Studies in Education,* 13.

Miles, E. G. and Huberman, A. M. (1994) *Qualitative Data Analysis: An Expanded Sourcebook.* London: Sage.

Mouzelis, N. (1995) *Sociological Theory: What Went Wrong?* London: Routledge

Nadel, S. F. (1957) *The Theory of Social Structure.* Glencoe, IL: Free Press.

Naroll, R. (1962) *Data quality control – A new research technique: Prolegomena to a Cross-Cultural Study of Culture Stress.* New York: Free Press.

National Research Council (2002) 'Scientific research in education', in R. J. Shavelson and L. Towne (eds) *Committee on Scientific Principles for Education Research.* Washington, DC: National Academy Press.

Oancea, A. (2005) 'Criticisms of educational research: key topics and levels of analysis', *British Educational Research Journal,* 31(2): 157–83.

Pallas, A. M. (2003) 'Preparing education doctoral students for epistemological diversity', *Educational Researcher,* 30(5): 6–11.

Patton, M. Q. (1990) *Qualitative Evaluation and Research Methods,* 2nd edn. Newbury Park, CA: Sage.

Punch, K. (2006) *Introduction to Social Research. Quantitative and Qualitative Approaches.* London: Sage.

Romm, N. (1997) 'Becoming more accountable: a comment on Hammersley and Gomm', *Sociological Research Online,* 2(3).

Schatzman, L. (1991) 'Dimensional analysis: notes on an alternative approach to the grounding of theory in qualitative research', in A. L. Strauss and D. R. Maines (eds) *Social Organization and Social Process.* Aldine: Transaction.

Shavelson, R., Phillips, D., Towne, L. and Feuer, M. (2003) 'On the science of education design studies', *Educational Researcher,* 32(1): 25–8.

Smith, B. (2003) 'Ontology', in L. Floridi (ed.) *Blackwell Guide to the Philosophy of Computing and Information*. Oxford: Blackwell.

Smith, J. and Heshusius, L. (1986) 'Closing down the conversation: the end of the quantitative-qualitative debate among educational inquirers', *Educational Researcher*, 15(1): 4–12.

Smith, J. K., and Hodkinson, P. (2005) 'Relativism, criteria, and politics', in N. K. Denzin and Y. S. Lincoln (eds) *The Handbook of Qualitative Research*, 3rd edn. Thousand Oaks, CA: Sage.

Taylor, C. (1995) *Philosophical Arguments*. Cambridge, MA: Harvard University Press.

Thomas, G. (1997) 'What's the use of theory?' *Harvard Educational Review*, 67(1): 75–104.

Thomas, G. and James, D. (2006) 'Re-inventing grounded theory: some questions about theory, ground and discovery', *British Educational Research Journal*, 32(6): 767–95.

Tooley, J. and Darby, D. (1998) *Education Research: An Ofsted Critique*. London: Ofsted.

Toulmin, S. (1990) *Cosmopolis: The Hidden Agenda of Modernity*. New York: The Free Press.

US Department of Education (2001) *No Child is Left Behind of 2001*, Public Law 107–10. Washington, DC: US Department of Education.

Whitty, G. (2006) 'Education(al) research and education policy making: is conflict inevitable?', *British Educational Research Journal*, 32(2): 159–76.

Williams, M. (2000) 'Models of character education: perspectives and developmental issues', *Journal of Humanistic Counseling, Education & Development*, 39(1): 32–41.

Wilson, B. J. (1994) 'A challenge to communication empiricists: let's be more forthcoming about what we do', *Western Journal of Communication*, 58(1): 25–31.

Wolcott, H. (1994) *Transforming Qualitative Data: Descriptions, Analysis and Interpretation*. London: Sage.

Woodhead, C. (1998) Introduction, in J. Tooley and D. Darby, *Educational Research: A Critique*. London: Ofsted.

Wright, H. (2006) 'Qualitative researchers on paradigm proliferation in educational research: a question-and-answer session as multi-voiced text', *International Journal of Qualitative Studies in Education*, 19(1): 77–95.

The Epistemological Context of Quantitative and Qualitative Research | 2

Dimitra Hartas

Chapter Outline

Introduction

Research in education is situated within diverse epistemological traditions (e.g. positivism, critical theory, pragmatism, postmodernism), creating a rich intellectual and methodological landscape. At times, however, diverse epistemologies offer a fragmented vision of the ways in which knowledge is generated through research. Our understanding of social reality becomes blurred, and questions about what counts as knowledge have no easy answers. Pallas (2003: 6) articulated the confusion that emerges from a kaleidoscope of epistemologies and their contribution to understanding the nature of truth as follows:

> Experienced researchers and novices alike find it hard to keep up with the cacophony of diverse epistemologies. Behind the welter of names – positivism, naturalism, post-positivism, relativism, feminist standpoint epistemology, foundationalism, postmodernism, each with an array of sub-species – lie important questions: Is there a single, absolute truth about educational phenomena, or are there multiple truths? (Or is the concept of truth itself so problematic as to be of no value in understanding the world?) Can we count on our senses, or on reason, to distinguish that which is true about the world from that which is false? Are there methods that can lead us close to understanding, or are there inherent indeterminacies in all methods? Is knowledge of the world discovered or constructed? Can knowledge of the world be evaluated independent of the social and historical contexts in which it exists, or is it always contingent upon, or relative to, particular circumstances?

This chapter offers a glimpse of different epistemologies and paradigms, or worldviews, that have influenced quantitative and qualitative research in education and social sciences. In so doing, we hope to shed light on the processes of meaning-making during research and the paradigmatic transitions from knowledge as absolute and abstract to knowledge as a human endeavour, constructed via research that is communal and polyphonic with a capacity for social transformation.

By the end of this chapter, you should be able to:

- discuss the major paradigms (e.g. empiricism, positivism, critical realism) that underpin quantitative research in education
- understand the worldviews (e.g. critical theory, postmodernism, social constructivism) that relate to qualitative research in education
- critically engage with paradigmatic transitions and epistemologies that bridge qualitative and quantitative approaches to research

The Paradigms in Quantitative Research

Quantitative research was originally situated within the philosophical tradition of empiricism and logical positivism, with the latter being influenced by Enlightenment thinking. In the 1950s, the main principles of logical positivism were challenged by postpositivists, resulting in paradigmatic transitions to critical realism and pragmatism.

Empiricism

The main premise of empiricism is that experience (*empeiria*) is the only source of information about the world that offers justification for substantive claims about the nature of knowledge. Empiricism, in its initial form, originated in the post-Hippocratic school of medicine, under the leadership of Philinos of Cos and Serapion of Alexandria, and claimed that all medical knowledge arises out of one's own observations, the observations of others and analogical reasoning (Psillos 1999).

Empiricism took its modern form with John Locke (1632–1704), who argued that all knowledge comes from experience (Locke [1894] 1974). In his view, the sensory organs transmit basic information from the external world to the human brain, which then analyses, combines and abstracts these 'elementary ideas' to form complex concepts and gain general knowledge about the external world. A question that arises from this assertion is that if all knowledge comes from experience, people with different experiences would construct different bodies of knowledge, making the process of reaching consensus very difficult. Locke's response to this was that the 'primary qualities' of things such as shape, size and movement can be easily observed and agreed upon, whereas the 'secondary qualities' such as taste or colour are more subjective and may stimulate different interpretations (Locke [1894] 1974: 17). Although people have different experiences, they are likely to agree upon the primary qualities of things (e.g. the shape or size of objects) that are observed directly. A variety in interpretation is likely to emerge with the secondary qualities whose properties are subjective in nature. Locke proposed a type of 'foundationalist epistemology', in that the directly observable primary qualities of things set the foundation of knowledge (Bredo 2006: 7).

Empiricism accepts that knowledge is gained through observation, stressing the need to differentiate between what is actually observed and what is observable, and by whom. A theory-free observational language was thought to create a neutral ground on which competing theories could be compared and confirmed. To empiricists, a value-free language captures 'the given' in an experience, which acts as a foundation of all knowledge. Questions as to whether things can exist unperceived and whether there can be causal knowledge derived from observable events have not been tackled within the empiricist paradigm.

Leibniz, as cited in Psillos (1999), claimed that we are all empiricists in 'three-quarters of our actions', but the fourth quarter is based on other (non-empirical) modes of knowing. Empiricism is far from being a tight doctrine. Although a consensus has been reached among empiricists that knowledge cannot be achieved by relying on experience alone, they have disagreed over its exact limits and the role of observation in understanding social reality.

Box 2.1 What is empiricism?

Empiricism claims that experience, and a value-free language that describes it, is the foundation of all knowledge. To empiricists, causal knowledge is derived from observation, although they stress the need to differentiate between what is actually observed and what is observable, and by whom.

Classical positivism

Auguste Comte (1798–1857) is regarded as the founder of classical positivism, the epistemological position that knowledge can be derived from directly observed phenomena, as opposed to unobserved entities or metaphysical views. Comte argued that knowledge develops at three stages, namely the 'theological' or 'fictitious' stage, the 'metaphysical' or 'abstract' stage and the 'scientific' or 'positive' stage (Bredo 2006: 7). His view was that science should rely on what is positively observed, without making any inferences about social phenomena based on unobserved entities or internal states of mind.

Comte argued that social phenomena must be studied in the same scientific manner as the world of nature. Natural science has succeeded in establishing the lawfulness of natural phenomena, and thus the same epistemic basis can be extended to the study of social phenomena (Comte [1896] 1974). According to him, society is subject to basic laws just as the natural world is, although he did acknowledge that society presents added complexities. He coined 'social physics' to describe the new discipline to understand social reality based on laws and principles of natural sciences.

Logical positivism

Logical positivism was the product of the Vienna Circle (1920s and 1930s), which was comprised of mathematicians and philosophers who articulated the nature and principles of knowledge that became the 'gold standard' for the physical sciences. Logical positivism has its roots in empiricism, and goes back to Aristotle, Bacon and Kant. The word 'logical' in the name refers to a belief that logic is important for philosophy and the social sciences, whereas the term 'positivism' denotes a form of empiricism. Logical positivism was a philosophical move to disentangle the natural sciences from religious and metaphysical beliefs, stressing the importance of logic (the notion of logic distinguished *logical* from *classical* positivism). As a paradigm, logical positivism separated *logos* (reason) from *mythos* (myth or metaphysical beliefs), advocating a type of science that is based strictly on the mathematical notion of proof. Logical positivists have been criticized for having a limited view of logic, situated in the context of mathematics.

The logical positivists conceptualized objective knowledge to exist independently from an observer and to abide by universal laws. Through an exploration of causal relationships, knowledge can be predicted, measured and quantified. The logical positivists differentiated between two types of knowledge, namely, logical/mathematical and natural/scientific knowledge. The logical/mathematical knowledge relied on the formation of propositions derived from definitions, whereas the natural/scientific knowledge relied on synthetic statements of relationships that cannot be known just by going back to the definitions. To illustrate this, Bredo (2006: 8) refers to a proposition taken from the natural sciences: 'the pressure of a closed container will increase at a certain rate with an increase in the temperature'. He argues that this proposition cannot be ascertained by relying on the definitions of 'pressure' and 'temperature'; it requires more synthetic statements that go beyond the definitions per se.

An important premise of logical positivism is that social phenomena can be measured and thus understood through value-free observation, in a manner similar to the methods adopted by the natural sciences. The 'verifiability theory of meaning' asserts that a proposition can be verified or falsified based on evidence derived from directly observed entities (Carnap [1935] 1966: 209). To Carnap, statements that can be verified via experience are 'meaningful', whereas those that cannot are 'without sense'. Objectivity, static reality, reason, causality and replicability are the main principles that underlie positivism (see Box 2.2). The logical positivists argued that these principles should guide experimentation, comparison and observation.

Box 2.2 The principles of logical positivism

- Experimentation, comparison, and observation are the only ways to understand a phenomenon, discern natural laws and make generalizations.
- Reality is independent of human experience and knowledge exists independent of the observer (objectivity).
- Research is value-free.
- The construction of knowledge is based on a deductive analysis of causal relations.

Logical positivism has been an influential paradigm in psychology and education for almost half a century, manifested in psychometrics (a branch of psychology) and social learning theories such as behaviourism (see Box 2.3). Its orthodoxy has been challenged by many theorists in the social sciences, arguing that positivism has offered a mechanistic view of human development and learning, and has reduced the complexity of human experience.

Box 2.3 Examples of logical positivist thinking

Within psychology, psychometrics focuses on assessing intelligence to make educational recommendations based on evidence derived from quantitative research. Burt in the UK, Binet in France and Terman in the USA focused on the development of intelligence tests to be used as tools to separate pupils according to their ability. Psychometrics has attracted a great deal of criticism from psychologists and educators alike, who argue against a concept of intelligence as a fixed entity that can be 'positively' observed and quantified.

Another example of positivist thinking in psychology and education is Skinner's theory of behaviourism. Behaviourism was influenced by logical positivism, advocating directly observed and measured behaviours as the basis for gaining knowledge about human action. Skinner disregarded internal states such as thoughts or feelings as being valid sources of knowledge, and advocated the use of highly controlled experiments and neutral language to avoid ambiguity and limit interpretation that goes beyond observed entities. Behaviourism and its positivist framework have been criticized as being reductionistic in terms of simplifying human nature into observable behaviours/responses within highly controlled conditions.

Criticism of positivism

Since the 1950s, the logical positivist tradition has been challenged by theorists and researchers in the social sciences and humanities. Sellars (1956) challenged the 'myth of the given' and rejected the dogma of empiricism and positivism that knowledge can be objective, gained through a value-free approach to science. Moreover, Peirce (1958) argued that positivism is self-contradictory in that there are no direct observations that can verify the truth of the positivism itself. Positivism has received a wide range of criticism, attacking not only its epistemological and ontological basis but also claims that it has been responsible for many social problems. Its critics have contested the mechanical view of science that logical positivism is thought to promote, where interpretation, values, ethics and expression of uncertainty and ambiguity have no place (see Box 2.4).

In *Cosmopolis*, Toulmin (1990) traced the evolution in western thought from the Renaissance humanists to the Vienna Circle of logical positivists. In his view, logical positivism, as a philosophical position, devalued the 'oral, the particular, the local, the timely and the practical [...] for formally "rational" theory-grounded, abstract, universal and timeless concepts. Soon enough the flight from the particular, concrete, transitory and practical aspects of human experience became a feature of cultural life in general' (pp. 75–6). Moreover, he argued that it removed the 'reasonable uncertainties and hesitations of 16th century skeptics in favour of a new, mathematical kind of rational certainties and proof'.

The idea that knowledge is objective and value-free has been defeated on both theoretical and empirical grounds (e.g. Paul *et al.* 2007). On the objectivity of knowledge, Kuhn (1970) argued that all observation is theory-laden, stressing that there cannot possibly be a theory-neutral observation framework. Each theory (or paradigm) determines the meaning of all terms that occur in it and there is no such a thing as a neutral language to assess different theories (or paradigms).

Box 2.4 Criticisms of logical positivism

- Separation between facts and theory (data being independent of the theories under investigation).
- Separation between facts and values (science, and the language used, are value-free).
- Claims can only be falsified, not verified (Popper 1959).
- Individualistic conception of science rather than a community of inquirers, or Kuhn's view of science as a social enterprise (Bredo 2006: 10–11).

Postpositivism

Like the logical positivists, the postpositivists accept that reality is independent of our thinking about it, and that observation and measurement are at the core of a scientific endeavour. However, they refute the belief that observation sets the epistemic foundation of all knowledge, in that observation is laden with theory, beliefs and values that can be accepted by all sides of a theoretical divide. The postpositivists recognize that observation can contain error, stressing the need to be critical about making statements about social reality with certainty (see Box 2.5).

Box 2.5: From positivism to postpositivism

- Objective observation → observation that is theory laden.
- Absolute truth → observation being fallible and theory revisable.
- Objectivity as an individual endeavour → objectivity as a collective enterprise.
- Language as being neutral → language being imbued with meaning, language as discourse.
- Reality as experienced → reality as shaped by language/discourse.

The view that observation can contain error makes it fallible and theory revisable, acknowledging the importance of multiple measures and observations, and stressing the need for triangulation through multiple sources of data. Moreover, the postpositivists accept that researchers are inherently biased by their cultural and social/political positioning and experience, and argue for objectivity that relies on 'the rational pursuit of inquiry' (Hammersley 2005: 149), accepting that, although researchers have their own preconceived notions of truth, they should subject their views to a rational scrutiny by their peers. Objectivity is not an individual but a social endeavour that can be achieved collectively, in a community of theorists and researchers who scrutinize each other's work. Within a community of practice, postpositivists argue, a natural selection theory of knowledge occurs, leading to the 'survival of the fittest' theory.

Karl Popper (1959) refuted that scientific laws can be verified. He argued that, because a phenomenon has been observed to take place in the past does not mean that it will continue to do so in the future. This view questions the notion of prediction, generalization and induction when examining social reality, stressing that scientific facts can never be verified, only falsified. According to this view, what makes 'a claim scientific is not the fact that it has been verified, but rather the fact that it is at least potentially falsifiable by empirical observations and has been subject to stringent attempts at such disproof' (Bredo 2006: 10).

Popper's view bears important implications when testing hypotheses; he urges researchers to look for disconfirming evidence rather than focusing on confirming their hypothesis. This may be achieved by testing the null hypothesis rather than the alternative hypothesis, and confirming the alternative hypothesis only when the null hypothesis has been rejected (see Chapter 19 on hypothesis testing). In the current climate of politicization of educational research, there is a dangerous allure for researchers to use data to confirm their own views, especially if they dovetail with certain political agendas. Thus, it is important to stress that a proposition (hypothesis) remains falsifiable by future events, and when a claim is verified it is done temporarily, until future evidence discredits it. This approach to knowledge is less dogmatic, compared to that offered by the logical positivists (Bredo 2006).

Criticism of postpositivism

The positivists define 'real' in terms of experience, whereas the postpositivists define reality in terms of language/discourse (Patomaki and Wight 2000). For the postpositivists, the components of reality are 'sociolinguistically constructed' (George 1994: 156). Some have expressed more radical views about reality, claiming that 'nothing exists outside of discourse' (Campbell 1998: 24). The critical realists have critiqued this view, commenting that if reality is a mere sociolinguistic construction, then an entity exists if we say it exists and does not exist when it is not an object of discourse. Assuming the goal of science is to investigate if things are as described, we have no way of knowing if a sociolinguistically constructed world is the 'real' world (see Box 2.6).

Bhaskar (1989) observes that, for both the positivists and postpositivists, social reality has an anthropocentric basis by being tied to human perception and language/discourse. In other words, an entity exists if it is experienced directly or is an object of discourse. However, Patomaki and Wight argue that 'to be' means more than 'to be experienced' or 'to be spoken', stressing that social reality cannot be confined within experience and discourse (2000: 217). Bhaskar (1989) observes that, within positivism and postpositivism, epistemology (what is to be known) and ontology (what it is) are tangled: what is known (epistemological question) *is* what can be experienced (what it is, which is an ontological question).

Box 2.6 Criticisms of postpositivism

- Reality is sociolinguistically constructed ('nothing exists outside discourse').
- Epistemology (what is to be known) and ontology (what it is) are tangled (epistemic fallacy).
- Social reality is not composed of experiences and discourses only.

Critical realism

Although critical realism is located within the postpositivist tradition, it differs from empirical realism (positivist) and linguistic realism (postpositivist) in two regards. First, the critical realists argue that the world is composed of not only events, experiences and discourses but also underlying structures and power relationships, which exist regardless of experience and discourse. Secondly, reality consists of many levels (underlying structures vs. surface or direct experience) that are understood as functioning not necessarily in harmony with each other, but out of phase (Patomaki and Wight 2000). The existence of underlying structures and tensions can stimulate capabilities and possibilities, although they may not always be realized. With this in mind, science is a process of illuminating these structures and processes and the ways in which they shape events (see Box 2.7).

Box 2.7 What is critical realism?

- Critical realism accepts that social reality consists of multiple levels (e.g. underlying structures and direct experiences).
- It argues against the view that social reality is experience (positivists) or a sociolinguistic construction (postpositivists).
- It defends the role of science in illuminating complex structures and systems, and accepts that an investigation can be fallible, stressing the importance of revision.
- It attempts to 'reclaim reality' rather than 'merely accept reality, reject reality or retreat from it' (Patomaki and Wight 2000: 235).

The critical realists challenge causal explanatory models, favouring models for explanatory narratives. They also question the meaningfulness of interpretations that involve the delineation of cause and effect relationships among the factors examined in a study. According to Nash (2005: 2101), 'realism rejects the account of causation as constant conjunction, opposes the law-like interpretations of variables, regards models as representations of reality and argues that explanations should, wherever possible, be given in terms of generative mechanisms'.

Although the critical realists have expressed criticisms against a natural science framework to understand social reality, they accept that a scientific understanding of the world is desirable as long as it 'affords only a particular angle or slant of reality, picked out precisely for its explanatory scope and power' (Bhaskar 1993: 15). Critical realism is, as Kemp and Holmwood (2003: 165) argue, the 'main defender of the idea that social inquiry can be scientific' if we accept science 'not as a supreme or overriding value, but only one among others to be balanced (in a balance that cannot be wholly judged by science) in ergonic, emancipatory and eudaimonistic activity'.

Realists argue against universally occurring regularities or sequences of cause and effect, stressing that events are often determined by multiple influences (Kemp and Holmwood 2003). However, the view that universal regularities may not exist does not mean that a scientific approach to understanding social events and relationships is flawed and should be abandoned. Rather than focusing on identifying universal regularities, the purpose of a scientific inquiry should be the identification of structures, defined as 'entities that have the causal powers to influence events' (Kemp and Holmwood 2003: 166). The existence of such a structure does not necessarily bring a particular outcome, in that many structures may operate at any given time, applying multiple influences without actually explaining the event itself.

The critical realism is critical because researchers accept that their investigations are fallible, and stress the importance of a critical examination of values and facts. For critical realists, knowledge is gained through neither induction nor deduction but by a process of explanation of a phenomenon at deeper levels. As we gain knowledge, we constantly revise previous knowledge and understandings. Patomaki and Wight (2000: 224) summarize critical realism as:

- an ontological realism (there is a reality, which is differentiated, structured and layered, and independent of mind)
- an epistemological relativism (all beliefs are socially produced and hence potentially fallible)
- a judgemental rationalism (despite epistemological relativism, it is still possible, in principle, to provide justifiable grounds for preferring one theory over another)

Pragmatism

Pragmatism, as a philosophical movement in America, was originally articulated by Peirce and James, and was later taken up and transformed by Dewey at the University of Chicago (Stuhr 2000). The pragmatists attributed a practical, utilitarian function to knowledge, conceived as an instrument that guides action and facilitates adaptation to reality. For pragmatists, knowledge is theory- and value-laden and capable of shaping human values. The contemporary philosophy of science has shown that a separation between theory and data, facts and values does not correspond to the real world. Knowledge and ideas are seen as artefacts or activities that function as a platform for action and organization of human behaviour.

Like the critical realists, the pragmatists hold that truth is not absolute but relative to the time, place and purpose of an inquiry, and verifiable as discoveries are made. With this in mind, an inquiry does not offer guaranteed knowledge based on past experience but rather a sufficient knowledge to make predictions regarding present action. The truth is to be found in the process of verification, stressing that a research approach should be determined by the research question (fitness of purpose) alone, and that research findings are tentatively confirmed until new findings emerge that either confirm or reject them (see Table 2.1).

The proponents of scientific realism and pragmatism have attempted to disengage quantitative research from its positivist tradition by accepting the value of causal relationships in addition to interpretivist approaches to meaning-making. They argue that quantification is necessary to science and the 'assumptions of positivism are not inherent to quantification itself'; it is possible to identify 'systematic patterns that will allow the possibility of empirical controls for the purposes of scientific inquiry' (Nash 2005: 186–7).

As Oslen and Morgan (2005: 257) argue, it is not 'how analytical statistics do what they do' but 'how can we interpret what we do with analytical statistics'. For example, in the hands of positivists, multilevel analyses of relationships between nested variables are seen as an accurate

Table 2.1 Moving from empiricism and positivism to critical realism and pragmatism

| Epistemological continuum in quantitative research | | | | | |
Empiricism →	Classical positivism→	Logical positivism→	Postpositivism→	Critical realism	Pragmatism
Objective observation (value-free science)	Objective observation (value-free science)	Objective observation (value-free, theory-free science)	Theory- and value-laden observation	Theory- and value-laden observation (subjectivity)	Theory- and value-laden observation (subjectivity)[1]
Absolute truth	Absolute truth that relies on positively observed entities	Absolute truth	Observation being fallible and theory revisable	Truth is verifiable and changeable	Truth is verifiable and changeable
Atomistic view of research	Atomistic view of research	Atomistic view of research	Research as a collective endeavour	Research as a collective endeavour	Research as a collective endeavour
Neutral language (theory-free observation language)	Neutral language	Language of logic	Language as a discourse	Language for interpretation and narrative	Language for interpretation and narrative
Knowledge gained via experience (no a priori knowledge)	Knowledge gained via direct observations	Knowledge gained via deduction of causal relations	Knowledge as sociolinguistically constructed	Knowledge relates to time, place and inquiry (critical analysis of vales/facts)	Knowledge as guiding action
Reality as experienced/ observed (independent of observer)	Reality as experienced/ observed (independent of observer)	Reality as experienced/ observed (independent of observer)	Reality as shaped by language/ discourse	Reality consists of multiple layers	Reality consists of multiple layers
Science is based on experience	Science to explore causal relationships	Science to explore causal relationships	Science as a process of verification	Science as a way to illuminate structures and processes	Science as one of the approaches to understand social reality

[1] Ercikan and Roth (2006) challenge the assumption that 'objectivity' and 'subjectivity' are properties of quantitative and qualitative research, respectively, conceived as two poles of the research continuum. They argue that this assumption reinforces dualism in our thinking about the nature of research.

representation of these relationships, whereas realists may derive explanations about the structure of relationships among factors. Through a statistical analysis we cannot achieve absolute representations of reality; however, power, capacities and generative mechanisms can be traced through correlational analyses and other non-parametric analyses of data (2005).

The Paradigms in Qualitative Research

The paradigms in quantitative research, be they empiricist or postpositivist, have offered some valuable worldviews to understand educational phenomena. They are, however, vulnerable to assumptions that social reality can be examined in similar ways as phenomena in the natural sciences. The social world is of a different kind, and social reality has a historical and political basis, shaped by people's action and construction of meaning, and their experiences of power structures and agency (see Table 2.2). With such a view of social reality, understanding truth as an abstracted and objective entity through our senses is no longer desirable. Some challenge the concept of truth as being problematic and irrelevant in understanding social reality (Pallas 2003), emphasizing the need for educational inquiry that brings together both deductive and interpretive models.

Table 2-2: Worldviews in qualitative research

Social Constructivism	Critical Theory	Structuralism	Poststructuralism	Postmodernism
Knowledge is socially constructed – a human product	Knowledge is socially distributed and its goal is human emancipation	Knowledge is foundational and is derived from understanding the function of linguistic, cultural structures	Knowledge is intertwined with social and political structures – there is no objective viewpoint	Knowledge is contested and polyphonic – no single authority is privileged – grand narratives are challenged
Reality is understood through human activity - it cannot be discovered because it does not exist prior to being constructed	Reality is examined via approaching participants as agents and producers of their own culture and histories	Reality is understood by exploring linguistic and social structures	Reality cannot be understood objectively by stepping outside of discourse – language is not neutral	Reality is not abstract and ordered, based on reason and universal truths. It encapsulates the local and the particular
Associated with work of social learning theorists such as Vygotsky and Bruner (learning as relational), as well as with research on communities of practices and social interactions	Examples of emancipatory research are found in research on multi-cultural education and disability (eg, marginalisation, rights, voice), focusing on agents' own knowledge and self-understanding	Examples of structuralism are found in the work of Piaget (a structure of cognitive development common to all children) and Noam Chomsky (a structure common to all languages)	Associated with Foucault, whose work focuses on delineating the history of claims about truth via 'discursive practices'	Associated with work on challenging scientific knowledge and notions of certainty, predictability and law-like cause-and-effect relationships
Research that draws upon this worldview relies on rich descriptions of context and approaches experience as mediated by society, culture and history.	Research is relevant to people's historical and political contexts, and contributes to their life.	Research is to explore these structures in that, it is difficult to operate outside them – make them the object of research	Research challenges social and political structures that legitimise knowledge and social reproduction	Research that raises questions about social justice and focuses on local contexts

Social constructivism

Social constructivism emphasizes the culture and the social context that surround people's lives and help us to understand society and construct knowledge based on this understanding (Derry 1999). The social constructivists believe that reality is understood through human activity, and it cannot be discovered because it does not exist prior to its social construction. To social constructivists, knowledge is a human product that is socially and culturally constructed (Gredler 1997; Ernest 1998). Individuals create their own subjective meanings of their experiences through interactions with each other and their surrounding environment. Harding and Hintikka (1983: x) argue that 'knowledge should be grounded on human experience' and bounded by people's social interactions, and the language used during these interactions. They welcome diversity and multiplicity in these meanings and challenge mechanistic views of social reality. The constructivists argue that by becoming actively involved in meaning-making we assume responsibility, whereas the acceptance of an 'objective true', based on universal laws, removes responsibility from individuals. These shifts in knowledge creation require its users, be they teachers or pupils, to be 'more socially accountable and reflexive', with the role of the teacher/educator and pupils being negotiated in the context of communities of practice (Gibbons *et al.* 1994).

Social constructivism is closely associated with the work of many educational and child development theorists such as Vygotsky and Bruner. In education, much research has explicitly or implicitly drawn upon constructivist ideas and practices, approaching learning as being relational, a product of 'engagement, imagination and alignment' of individuals with the world (Wenger 2000: 231). For example, research by Lave and Wenger (1991) examined the relations among practitioners, their practice and the social organization and political economy of communities of practice. In such communities, learning occurs through engagement with the structures and discourse of the community (e.g. how its members talk, act, model certain behaviours, patterns of collaboration and attitudes towards outsiders and conduct their lives).

Educational research that draws upon constructivism strives to empower participants' perspectives and ideas, and obtain rich descriptions of the contexts that surround their lives. Individuals' experiences are often mediated by historical, cultural and social circumstances, requiring strategies of inquiry (e.g. unstructured interviews, case studies, narratives, action research) that offer an in-depth exploration of their experiences. The findings from such research rely on interpretation of multiple perspectives as they are constructed and voiced in the context of social interactions. In teaching and learning, social constructivist approaches underpin reciprocal teaching, peer collaboration, cognitive apprenticeships, problem-based instruction and other methods that involve learning with others (Shunk 2000).

Pring (2004: 50–1) summarizes aspects of constructivism as follows:

- Each person lives in a world of ideas, and it is through these ideas that the world (physical and social) is constructed. There is no way to step outside this world of ideas to check whether or not they accurately represent a world existing independently of the ideas themselves.
- Communication with other people, therefore, lies in a 'negotiation' of their respective world of ideas. A consensus is reached.

- Such notions as 'truth' need therefore to be eliminated, because given the above there can be no correspondence between our conceptions of reality and that reality itself.
- Furthermore, the distinction between 'objective' and 'subjective' needs to be redefined since there can be nothing objective in the sense of that which exists independently of the world of ideas – which has been constructed.
- Development of our thinking lies in the constant negotiation of meanings between people who only partly share each other's ideas. Therefore there are as many realities as there are conceptions of it – multiple realities.

Critical theory

Critical theory originates in the European Marxist tradition known as the Frankfurt School. A 'critical' theory is different from a 'traditional' theory to the extent that it seeks human emancipation, 'to liberate human beings from the circumstances that enslave them' (Horkheimer 1982: 244). A critical theory provides the descriptive and philosophical framework for social inquiry aimed at emancipation in all its forms. Broadly, many philosophical approaches are clustered under critical theory, including feminism, race theory and postcolonialism. The critical theorists argue that, to examine social reality, we need to understand structure and agency, regularity and normativity, stressing that research should have a moral rather an instrumental role, and is expected to challenge human oppression and achieve emancipation.

The critical theory worldview, as conceived within the Frankfurt School, is based upon three principles: it must be explanatory, practical and normative. That is, it must explain the factors that work against emancipation in society, identify the actors to change it and provide both clear norms for criticism and achievable practical goals for social transformation. To examine social reality from a critical theory perspective is to approach participants as agents and 'producers of their own historical form of life' (Horkeimer 1993: 21). This view challenges the technocratic models of social scientists as detached observers and favours contextualized social relationships and a socially distributed practical knowledge. The critical theorists argue for the importance of first- and second-person understanding in an attempt to move away from a technocratic view of social inquiry whose sole purpose is to offer solutions to practical problems. In this regard, a critical theory and its approach to social inquiry have much in common with pragmatism (Bohman 1999a, 1999b). Both strive to generate knowledge that is relevant to people's historical and political contexts, and capable of making an important contribution to their lives.

The critical theorists challenge a single unifying theory of science and accept diversity by employing many theories that capture different historical and political situations. They argue that social inquiry should start with agents' own pretheoretical knowledge and self-understandings to ensure pluralism in the perspectives offered. Within a pluralistic inquiry, criticism is verified by the participants, and the verification should be part of the process of the inquiry itself. Habermas (1988: 3) accepts that various theories and methods have 'a relative legitimacy', and they should be critiqued in relation to each other and brought into a peaceful coexistence. With this in mind, a critical theory brings together diverse theoretical and methodological perspectives and assumptions to explain their relative merits and limitations. Habermas (1987: 375) also accepts that critical theory is not a 'competitor'; rather, 'starting from its concept of the rise of modern societies, it attempts to explain the specific limitations and relative rights of those approaches'.

Moreover, Habermas critiqued what he perceived as an instrumental rationality, the view that social issues and problems can be resolved instrumentally, through research that emphasizes efficiency, accountability and shared norms and assumptions. This is evident in educational reforms whose goals are efficiency and educational effectiveness. At present, a discourse of targets, effectiveness and efficiency, rather than purpose or values, dominates the educational systems of many western countries. In a context where education is defined by measurable outputs, consumer responsiveness, efficiency, public inspection and profitability, research is less likely to account for the historical and political context of education. From a critical theory worldview, pluralism and reflexivity, achieved by evaluating multiple perspectives and people's experiences, are crucial elements for a social inquiry with emancipatory potential.

Emancipatory research

Emancipatory research is seen as operating within a critical theory paradigm. Its main goal is human emancipation, and it draws mainly upon the philosophical positions developed by Marcuse, Habermas and Freire. A key argument of emancipatory research is that mainstream research has produced theoretical understandings that are not always relevant to or empowering of individuals who are marginalized. Emancipatory research often has a political agenda and focuses on issues of social justice.

An example of emancipatory research is multicultural education research, which has generated knowledge that challenges structural inequalities and institutionalized discrimination (Banks 2006). Research and the generation of knowledge about a situation have the potential for change and transformation of the people involved. An emancipatory inquiry has the following characteristics (Banks 2006: 776):

- seeks to describe cultures and experiences from the perspectives of the group being studied
- seeks to describe the experiences, values and perspectives of marginalized groups in accurate, valid and sensitive ways
- constructs concepts, theories, paradigms, explanations and narratives that challenge established and institutionalized knowledge
- develops counternarratives to mainstream accounts and narratives
- views scientific knowledge as having both subjective and objective components that are interactive
- seeks to reveal the ways in which research is influenced by the lives, cultures and positionality of researchers
- assumes that scientific knowledge should enhance justice and equality within society

Transformative research asks questions about the lives of people who have been marginalized or discriminated against (Banks 2006). As with multicultural education, researching difference by approaching individuals from diverse racial, ethnic, linguistic, ability/disability and social perspectives can be emancipatory because it encourages people to express their views about issues that concern their lives, especially those experiencing disadvantage, by trying to see the world through their eyes (Ragin 1994). Emancipatory research has the potential to demystify the structures that surround people who have experienced marginalization and powerlessness, and raise social awareness by articulating/representing their situation in new light to tackle questions about legitimacy of knowledge, power structures and the influence of social and political contexts on people's experiences, agency and participation rights.

Structuralism and poststructuralism

In the 1960s, in France, the structuralists drew upon the ideas of Marx, Freud and Saussure, and argued that humans are not simply constrained by structures – linguistic, cultural or socio-economic. Rather, we play an active role in producing these structures and thus it is almost impossible to operate outside them. The notion that cultural or linguistic tools can constitute objects of research is at the centre of a structuralist worldview. In a structural analysis, these tools are defined by the rules that are set for an activity of which the behaviour under investigation is a part. For example, if we want to explore pupil participation in class, the structural analysis will involve not only the behaviour (i.e. pupil participation) but also the rule-governed elements that surround it. These elements may be conversational exchanges, the physical arrangement of the classroom, or teacher verbal and nonverbal cues that are influenced by the classroom rules. A study by Mehan (1979) found that interactions in a classroom are structured along a pattern of teacher asking questions – pupils offering answers – teachers evaluating the answers. A structuralist would argue that this structure of teacher-pupil interaction is not externally imposed but produced by both teachers and pupils to organize behaviour in a hierarchical manner (Bredo 2006: 17).

The work of Jean Piaget, with his theory on cognitive schemata as the basis of human cognitive functioning, draws upon the principles of structuralism. Also, Noam Chomsky's language acquisition device relies on the assumption that there are structures common to all languages. A common criticism of structuralism is that it offers a foundationalist worldview, in that it examines structures in text, discourse or cognitive/linguistic functioning in order to establish certain foundations of knowledge.

The poststructuralists challenged a foundationalist worldview, arguing that the structures themselves should become the object of investigation. Foucault, a representative of the poststructuralist worldview, accepted that language and society are shaped by rule-governed systems, but disagreed with the structuralists on two counts. First, he did not think that there were definite underlying structures that could explain the human condition and, secondly, he thought that it was impossible to step outside of discourse and survey social reality objectively (Foucault 1980).

Foucault focused on the 'discursive practices' or 'serious speech acts' that are thought to shape knowledge, delineating the history of truth claims. He viewed knowledge as being intertwined with socioeconomic and political structures, stressing that there is no objective viewpoint but a multi-perspectival way of examining social structures and discourses. To him, there is no ultimate truth to be uncovered and any explanations offered should be situated within the context within which individuals operate and form relationships. Interpretation and not absolute truths is the cornerstone of poststructuralist knowledge (Foucault 1980).

To the poststructuralists, language is not a neutral, transparent tool used to transmit information about absolute truths and the 'world out there'. Language is central as 'both carrier and creator of a culture's epistemological codes' (Punch 2005: 140). Lyotard referred to Wittgenstein's 'language games' to articulate the processes and structures that shape discourse and, ultimately, explain and legitimize knowledge. Wittgenstein viewed language as an integral component of the social, political and cultural context within which it is used, even being defined by its use. Similar views are expressed by Jacques Derrida, who argued that language or 'texts' are not a natural reflection of social reality, stressing the importance of uncovering the multiple meanings of such texts. Influenced by Heidegger and Nietzsche, Derrida accepted that all text has ambiguity and, because of this, the possibility of a final and complete interpretation is impossible. Poststructuralism shares a similar conceptual platform with postmodernism in that both worldviews are not foundationalist and do not accept a singular authority towards knowledge construction.

Postmodernism

A theme of the late twentieth century was that there are no certainties, and thus there are no special means to construct knowledge about the human world. Lather (1991: xx) observes that 'we seem somewhere in the midst of a shift away from a view of knowledge as disinterested and towards a conceptualisation of knowledge as constructed, contested, incessantly perspectival and polyphonic'. Parker (1997: 122) also acknowledges this shift and 'the capacity to articulate doubt', which is 'the mark of the attitude of seriousness; of an ability to recognize the true depth and gravity of a situation [. . .] This idea of open-mindedness – the exhortation constantly to question, criticize and change –issues in a culture of radical doubt'.

Within a postmodern worldview, no single authority is privileged and the grand narratives are challenged along the lines of 'whose true?' and 'under what circumstances?', an idea or a perspective is considered to be true (Lyotard 1984). Postmodernism has risen as a 'response to the loss of faith in the traditional religious and political orthodoxies' (Lather 1991: 159). This loss of faith has become evident through the collapse of communism (a grand political narrative), the increasing questioning of religions (e.g. Christianity) and the liberal foundations of western civilisation. Among postmodernists, grand narratives are oppressive, operating to the exclusion of others and prescribing ethical and political views in society that regulate decision-making and codes of conduct.

The nature of knowledge has been framed by discourses that draw on distinctive traditions of philosophical, educational, psychological and political thought, and by frameworks that translate knowledge into practice. In the era of Enlightenment (e.g. Kant's *Critique of Judgement*), knowledge was understood as a 'mental aptitude' that was characterized by originality, with some people having a greater capacity than others to gain knowledge. The notion of knowledge as a universal property was critiqued by Bourdieu (1984), who, among others, contested the universality of knowledge and argued for the importance of a context (*habitus*) in shaping knowledge and aesthetics. Bourdieu's critique offers a democratic view of knowledge by stressing its emancipatory role in mitigating against inequality, hierarchies and prejudices.

The Enlightenment project, whose main premise was that, through reason and science, people will achieve knowledge, and, eventually, become liberated, has also been under scrutiny. In *The Dialectic of Enlightenment*, Horkheimer and Adorno (1972) argued that reason has not liberated individuals. Rather than being liberating and progressive, a conceptual and organizational framework based on reason has become dominating and instrumental, creating a 'totally administered society'. Moss (1999: 142–52) offers a critique of the Enlightenment project and its assumption about knowledge as being foundationalist and universal, relying on dualistic categories of thought:

> The Enlightenment project is inscribed with certain values and assumptions: the possibility of an ordered world, certain, controllable and predictable, built on foundations of universal, knowable and decontextualised criteria and laws; knowledge as an objective mirror of the real world, unaffected by values and politics; the separation of reason and emotion, one of many dualisms; linear progress to a universal civilisation without cultural differences; the superiority of the West, whose institutions and values provide the basis for this universal civilisation; and one true, reason-dictated solution for every problem.

From a postmodern worldview, the nature of knowledge is fundamentally different from the scientific knowledge that arose within positivist traditions. Scientific knowledge is thought to reflect a social reality that is based on cause-and-effect relationships, which do not always account for the complexity and fundamental uncertainty involved in understanding a social reality. Scientific knowledge, what Lyotard called the 'grand meta-narrative of science', has been dominant over the last century and, in recent years, has received intense criticism. Apple (1991: vii) argues that:

> the programme of making everything knowable through the supposedly impersonal norms and procedures of 'science' has been radically questioned. The hope of constructing a 'grand narrative', either intellectual or political, that will give us the ultimate truth and will lead us to freedom has been shattered in many ways.

Apple's criticism of scientific knowledge centres on the realization that science has not always benefited people, especially those who experience disadvantage and have been excluded from institutional arrangements based on scientific advances. This raises ethical questions about the validity and usefulness of scientific knowledge, in terms of who has access and who benefits from it.

Bridging Diverse Worldviews

Often, quantitative and qualitative research methodologies have been used in a manner that has allowed for dichotomies between qualitative and quantitative research to resurface. Although much emphasis on paradigmatic divisions can make research appear fragmented and repetitive, being aware of different worldviews is crucial to ensure that research does not become a mere collection of activities. Increasingly, researchers in education argue for a worldview that does not approach educational issues and learning in an instrumental manner. Rather, we need a research epistemology that explores possibilities by giving voice to people who are directly affected by social and educational situations, and to encourage researchers to develop a capacity for reflection on both means and ends in education. Such a worldview is likely to bring together causal and interpretive models to examine the dynamics of complex systems where research practices are intensive and fine-grained to ensure that complexity is mapped sufficiently.

Acknowledging change and complexity in education can challenge current thinking about teaching and learning. In this regard, educational research carries high expectations to develop a new learning science (Jolles *et al.* 2005). Increasingly, the kinds of problems that educators must confront are very complex and cannot be solved without understanding how social, economic, cultural, political and individual factors interact to create the kind of conditions seen in schools and communities. This awareness has stimulated the integration of different worldviews to support mixed-research methodologies for educators to engage with inquiry.

More and more, in educational research, an eclectic approach to diverse worldviews is taken, combining both qualitative and quantitative strategies of inquiry (e.g. mixed-method designs). In so doing, we challenge dichotomies and perceived incompatibilities that may arise from combining different paradigms and philosophical positions, taking the view that 'social reality is both causal and contextual, and social knowledge is both propositional and constructed [...] multiple methods are not only welcomed but required' (Greene and Caracelli 2003: 99). This view suggests that the conceptualization and execution of research should not be restricted by the empiricism-interpretivism debate, in that quantitative analyses of an experimental intervention are as important as detailed and contextual descriptions of the intervention itself. For example, the research on the impact of class size on academic achievement may involve an experimental design (relevant to a postpositivist), combined with case studies and ethnographic observations to capture pupils' and teachers' classroom experiences and voices (relevant to social constructivism/critical theory). Finally, the implications of class size research findings may be emancipatory in that issues of social justice and access to good quality education come to the fore, and the resulting policy may transform young people's lives.

Within the context of mixed-method research, integrated worldviews may offer the intellectual platform for educational research as a cooperative action to emerge, and address the ways in which knowledge in education translates into policy and practice at a local level. Educational research that is pluralistic and action-oriented draws upon principles of social justice, equality and empathy for young people and their communities, which become part of the research process and propel social transformation.

Summary

In this chapter, we engaged with diverse epistemological positions to present different worldviews of educational inquiry. The positivist and postpositivist worldviews approach knowledge as objective and capable of encapsulating absolute truth and certainty. From a poststructuralist/postmodernist point of view, knowledge is not given but continually contested and revisable. This view of knowledge brings risks, and requires individuals to have the conviction to explore possibilities that may bring more uncertainty. In this context, research inquiry relies on multiple perspectives and discourses rather than normative views of knowing.

Critical theory and social constructivism approach knowledge as being socially constructed, with transformative and emancipatory potential. This type of knowledge is relational and in contrast to that traditionally developed within the positivist paradigm, is characterized by hierarchical relationships and generalizable, abstract ideas. Knowledge as a relational entity signifies the move of educational inquiry towards the construction of an 'embedded knowledge' shaped by human experience. Finally, the bridging of diverse worldviews is likely to promote mixed-method research in education that combines methods to create a complementary form of educational inquiry.

References

Apple, M. W. (1991) 'The politics of curriculum and teaching, National Association of Secondary School Principals (NASSP)', *Bulletin*, 75(532): 39–50.

Banks, J. (2006) 'Improving race relations in schools: from theory and research to practice', *Journal of Social Issues*, 62(3): 607–14.

Bhaskar, R. (1989) *Reclaiming Reality: A Critical Introduction to Contemporary Philosophy*. London: Verso.

Bhaskar, R. (1993) *Dialectic: The Pulse of Freedom*. London: Verso.

Bohman, J. (1999a) 'Democracy as inquiry, inquiry as democratic: pragmatism, social science, and the cognitive division of labor', *American Journal of Political Science*, 43: 590–607.

Bohman, J. (1999b) 'Theories, practices, and pluralism: a pragmatic interpretation of critical social science', *Philosophy of the Social Sciences*, 29: 459–80.

Bourdieu, P. (1984) *Homo Academicus*, trans. Peter Collier. Cambridge: Polity.

Bredo, E. (2006) 'Philosophies of educational research', in J. L. Green, G. Camilli and P. B. Elmore (eds) *Handbook of Complementary Methods in Education Research*. Mahwah, NJ: AERA/Lawrence Erlbaum.

Campbell, D. (1998) *National Deconstruction: Violence, Identity and Justice in Bosnia*. London: University of Minnesota Press.

Carnap, R. ([1935] 1966) *The Rejection of Metaphysics. 20th-Century Philosophy: The Analytic Tradition*. New York: The Free Press.

Comte, A. ([1896] 1974) *Positive Philosophy*. London: Ball.

Derry, S. J. (1999) 'A fish called peer learning: searching for common themes', in A. M. O'Donnell and A. King (eds) *Cognitive Perspectives on Peer Learning*. Mahwah, NJ: Lawrence Erlbaum.

Ercikan, K. and Roth, W. (2006). What good is polarizing research into qualitative and quantitative? *Educational Researcher,* 35(5): 14–23.

Ernest, P. (1998) *Social Constructivism as a Philosophy of Mathematics*. Albany, NY: Suny Press.

Foucault, M. (1980) 'Truth and power', in C. Gordon (ed.) *Power/Knowledge: Selected Interviews and Other Writings, 1972–1977*. London: Harvester Wheatsheaf.

George, J. (1994) Discourses of Global Politics: A Critical Re-introduction to International Relations. Boulder, CO: Lynne Rienner.

Gibbons, M., Limoges, C., Nowotny, H., Schwartzman, S., Scott, P. and Trow, M. (1994) *The New Production of Knowledge: The Dynamics of Science and Research in Contemporary Society*. Stockholm: Sage.

Gredler, M. E. (1997) *Learning and Instruction: Theory into Practice*, 3rd edn. Upper Saddle River, NJ: Prentice Hall.

Greene, J. C., and Caracelli, V. J. (2003) 'Making paradigmatic sense of mixed method practice', in A. Tashakkori, and C. Teddlie (eds) *Handbook of Mixed Methods in Social and Behavioural Research*. Thousand Oaks, CA: Sage.

Habermas, J. (1987) *The Theory of Communicative Action*, vols 1 and 2. Boston, MA: Beacon Press.

Habermas, J. (1988) *The Logic of the Social Sciences*. Cambridge, MA: MIT Press.

Hammersley, M. (2005) 'Countering the new orthodoxy in educational research: a response to Phil Hodkinson', *British Educational Research Journal*, 31(2): 139–55.

Harding, S. and Hintikka, M. (1983) *Discovering Reality*. Dordrecht: D. Reidel.

Horkheimer, M. (1993) Between Philosophy and Social Science. Cambridge, Mass: MIT Press.

Horkheimer, M. (1982) *Critical Theory*. New York: Seabury Press.

Horkheimer, M. and Adorno, T. W. (1972) *The Dialectic of Enlightenment*. New York: Seabury.

Jolles, J., de Groot, R., van Benthem, J., Dekkers, H., de Glopper, C., Uijlings, H. and Wolff-Albers, A. (2005) *Leer het Brein Kennen* [*Understanding the Brain*]. Den Haag: NWO.

Kemp, S. and Holmwood, J. (2003) 'Realism, regularity and social explanation', *Journal for the Theory of Social Behaviour*, 33(2): 165–87.

Kuhn, T. S. (1970) *The Structure of Scientific Revolutions*, 2nd edn. Chicago: Chicago University Press.

Lather, P. (1991) *Getting Smart: Feminist Research and Pedagogy with/in the Postmodern*. London: Routledge.

Lave, J. and Wegner, E. (1991) *Situated Learning: Legitimate Peripheral Participation*. Cambridge: Cambridge University Press.

Locke, J. ([1894] 1974) *An Essay Concerning Human Understanding*, vol. 1. Oxford: Clarendon.

Lyotard, J-F. (1984) *The Postmodern Condition: A Report on Knowledge*. Minneapolis, MN: University of Minnesota Press.

Mehan, H. (1979) *Learning Lessons: Social Organization in the Classroom*. Cambridge, MA: Harvard University Press.

Moss, P. (1999) 'Early childhood institutions as a democratic and emancipatory project', in L. Abbott and H. Moylett (eds) *Early Childhood Transformed*. London: Routledge.

Nash, R. (2005) 'Explanation and quantification in educational research: the arguments of critical and scientific realism', *British Educational Research Journal*, 31(2): 185–204.

Olsen, W., and Morgan, J. (2005) 'A critical epistemology of analytical statistics: addressing the skeptical realist', *Journal for the Theory of Social Behaviour*, 35(3): 255–84.

Pallas, A.M. (2003) 'Preparing education doctoral students for epistemological diversity', *Educational Researcher*, 30(5): 6–11.

Parker, S. (1997) *Reflective Teaching in the Postmodern World*. Buckingham: Open University Press.

Patomaki, H., and Wight, C. (2000) 'After positivism? The promises of critical realism', *International Studies Quarterly*, 44: 213–37.

Paul, J. L., Fowler, K. and Cranston-Gingras, A. (2007) 'Perspectives shaping and challenging research approaches in special education', in D. J. Gallagher (ed.) *The Sage Handbook of Special Education*. London: Sage.

Peirce, C. S. (1958) *Values in a Universe of Chance. Selected Writings of S. Peirce*. Garden City, NY: Doubleday.

Popper, K. R. (1959) *The Logic of Scientific Discovery*. London: Hutchinson.

Pring, R. (2004) *Philosophy of Educational Research*. London: Continuum.

Psillos, S. (1999) *Scientific Realism: How Science Tracks Truth*. London: Routledge.

Punch, K. (2005) *Introduction to Social Research: Qualitative and Quantitative Approaches*. London: Sage.

Ragin, C. (1994) *Constructing Social Research: The Unity and Diversity of Method*. Newbury Park, CA: Pine Forge Press.

Sellars, W. (1956) 'Empiricism and the philosophy of mind', in H. Feigl and M. Scriven (eds) *Minnesota Studies in the Philosophy of Science, Volume I: The Foundations of Science and the Concepts of Psychology and Psychoanalysis*. Minneapolis, MN: University of Minnesota Press.

Shunk, D. H. (2000) *Learning Theories: An Educational Perspective*, 3rd edn. Upper Saddle River, NJ: Prentice Hall.

Stuhr, J. J. (ed.) (2000) *Pragmatism and Classical American Philosophy: Essential Readings and Interpretive Essays*, 2nd edn. New York: Oxford University Press.

Toulmin, S. (1990) *Cosmopolis, The Hidden Agenda of Modernity*. New York: The Free Press.

Wenger, E. (2000) 'Communities of practice and social learning systems', *Organization*, 7(2): 225–46.

3

Qualitative Research as a Method of Inquiry in Education

Will Gibson

Chapter Outline

Introduction

The high volume of research texts that deal with qualitative research inquiry, from very varied disciplinary perspectives and in relation to all kinds of empirical domains, shows that the use of the singular 'a method' in the title of this chapter could be seen as somewhat problematic. In some senses, there are as many 'approaches' as there are qualitative researchers, as each empirical research experience and theoretical context lead to something distinctive in the 'approach' being taken. The ways that researchers address these experiences and contexts in writing about social and educational research are exactly the things that can make research methods output stimulating.

Precisely because qualitative research is characterized by a large variety of distinctive approaches to dealing with data, it can be very difficult for researchers to know how to orientate themselves to this range. In this chapter, I suggest that instead of approaching this problem with the question 'Which of these approaches should I use?', we may more productively concentrate in detail on their own empirical context of work, the particular research issues we are bringing into it, and the types of data we require in order to deal with our research topics. This helps to create integrated and aligned research projects, and a stable basis for considering *if* any of the existing methodologies or approaches that are encountered are relevant or not. It is crucial to emphasize that using a formalized methodology is not a *requirement* of data analysis (even if it is a well-established convention). What is necessary, however, is that the data are effectively put to work to deal with the research issues.

By the end of this chapter, you should be able to:

- understand the interplay between theory and analysis, research design and analysis and data collection and analysis
- reflect on your own research context and problematic, and approach the range of qualitative approaches with the question 'How does this approach relate to what I am doing?'
- understand the distinction between 'a priori' and 'empirical' theory
- think about data collection as a 'lived analysis', to accurately characterize the active role of the researcher in deciding 'what is to count as relevant'

Approaches to Analysis in Qualitative Research

Wolcott (1994) has listed over 50 different approaches to dealing with data. These approaches are often discipline-specific or directed towards very particular ends. In their famous outline of grounded theory, Barney Glaser and Anselm Strauss (1967) articulated a clear methodology for developing theory from data. This approach has little in common with, say, Harvey Sacks' suggested methods (1995) for analysing talk in social interaction (actually, Sacks' approach is not best thought of as a research method, but as a very distinctive approach to conducting sociological inquiry – see Sharrock and Anderson 1986). Similarly, the 'cross case analysis' outlined by Matthew Miles and Michael Huberman (1994) is radically different to, for example, Joan Leach's (2000) description of rhetorical analysis and to Norman Fairclough's critical discourse analysis (1995). These approaches are characterized by very different analytic aims, (e.g. producing a theory about a dataset, as in grounded theory; understanding the methods of conversational organization, as in conversation analysis; or understanding the processes of argumentation, as in rhetorical analysis).

These distinct aims involve different ideas about 'what is to count as data' and different methods and concepts for dealing with that data. While some researchers may be able to identify easily their work with an established and definable strategy/approach such as the above, not all researchers can, and this can lead to difficulties. New researchers often approach qualitative research by thinking that they need to 'pick' one of these approaches to use in their study. While this can certainly work sometimes, it is pretty difficult to know where to start or how to go about making the selection. Instead of thinking about qualitative analysis in this way, I suggest that a better starting point is to work through the particular research context very closely, and to think about the specific conceptual issues being dealt with.

Non-linear analysis

Data analysis involves working through a conceptual problem in relation to a set of data. This data will have been *designed* and *produced* through the research process specifically so that the research problem can be dealt with. When people get to the stage of having some data to work with, they will already have established some key analytic problems to think about in relation to that data. One way to put this is to say that 'a good deal of analytic work will have been undertaken before researchers get to working with their data'.

Analysis of data does not typically occur in a linear way. A useful way to think about this point is to reflect on the hypothetico-deductive model of research, which characterizes the process as a sequential movement through distinct stages. In this model, the research process begins by formulating a question that is then positioned in relation to literature, and used to design a study that will generate some data for analysis. In this view, data analysis occurs at a particular point in the research process (i.e. after a problem has been formulated, a study has been designed and data have been collected). However, research practices are much less rigid than this model implies, particularly in qualitative research. For example, research questions – or topics, interests, issues or concerns – are often iteratively developed through research, and frequently change as the researcher gains more knowledge and insight into a given area. The analysis of data may actually lead researchers to alter their question slightly, or to become focused on something quite different to their original interests. Similarly, the gathering of data occurs in tandem with analysis, as the interrogation of data leads researchers to ask new questions about their research setting, to think about their existing concerns in new ways and, as a consequence, to collect new data in order to answer those questions. Analysis, as with every aspect of qualitative social/educational research (such as formulating questions, interrogating literature, designing research, gathering data and writing) is a research *practice* rather than a research *stage*. Although there may be a point in research where a researcher is doing more of one kind of thing than another, there are no fixed boundaries between these practices as researchers very often shuttle between them and use them to inform each other.

In this chapter I wish to work through the implications of these more fluid pictures of research by, firstly, thinking about the role of theory in relation so data analysis and, secondly, working through the design and conduct of research. In these ways I hope to provide a pragmatic orientation to approaching qualitative research in ways that involve foregrounding analysis.

Theory and analysis

Theory is one of the key concerns researchers have when approaching the analysis of data. It is common for researchers to want or expect a theory or theoretical orientation to help them in their data work, and this is often precisely one of the interests that people have when they are exploring 'off-the-shelf' analytic approaches. Any theoretical resource, however, will need to be worked through in relation to the specific context of its use before it can be put to use. As a means of helping researchers think about and orientate to the broad range of analytic approaches, and as a mechanism for working through the generation of conceptual ideas, I would like to draw a distinction between two approaches to theory development in qualitative research: *a priori* theorizing and *empirical* theorizing. In a priori theorizing, theory and theoretical conceptions are specified prior to data work. In empirical theorizing, analytic concepts and frameworks are developed through the analysis of data.

These two approaches to theory are not necessarily (and probably not *usually*) mutually exclusive, as most theoretical outputs are formulated and situated in relation to other work *and* as a result of engagement with the data. These do not necessarily represent *alternatives*, but simply *differences* to which researchers very often orientate their work. So, instead of asking the questions 'Is this approach a priori or empirical?' or 'Am I doing a priori or empirical analysis?' it may be more productive to think 'What aspects of this/my work may be thought of as "a priori" and which aspects as "empirical"'. I will come back to this point shortly.

A priori theorizing

Some approaches to qualitative analysis contain well-formulated conceptions of the types of issues they are interested in and the sorts of data required to deal with them. These approaches, which I refer to as 'a priori' approaches, are characterized by the following:

- well-defined theoretical aims
- specified concepts for analysis
- reflection on, and specifications of, the processes of pursuing analysis using those concepts

The usual character of an a priori approach is a pre-existing body of concepts and ideas that are put to work in the course of doing analysis. Many approaches to analysis have this character, such as critical discourse analysis, rhetorical analysis, semiotic analysis and critical narrative analysis, to name but a few. To work within these approaches/paradigms is to orientate to their body of work and assumptions. Of course, 'orientate to' does not mean 'agree with' or even 'stick within the confines of', but it does mean that there is existing theoretical and conceptual work that is used to organize analysis from the outset of a research project. This is very distinct to the next approach to analysis that I will describe.

Empirical theorizing

Grounded theory involves the production of theory through the examination of data. In their early articulation of this approach, Glaser and Strauss (1967) argued that the aim of creating theory that both fits one's data and is appropriate to the setting being explored is a more productive approach than the a priori production of theories and concepts that may or may not be relevant to a given setting. They outlined a methodology for producing theory through research, and for developing contextually relevant concepts and theoretical formulations.

A significant aspect of the approach to theory outlined in their first book involved creating a clear separation between the analytic resources brought to a research setting and those derived from it. Glaser and Strauss suggested that researchers should attempt to minimize the extent to which they use resources such as preformulated theory or common-sense assumptions as a means of making sense of the setting. To give an illustration, researchers should be careful not to base their research on theoretical notions derived from existing research literature. It would be a mistake, for example, to enter a setting with a clearly defined notion of 'dependence' or 'power' or 'exploitation' and to use these to explain the relationship between two sets of actors, as this would be to prespecify a theoretical relationship without empirical interrogation. In grounded theory, any theoretical concept must be derived from an examination of the data produced through the research.

Since this initial formulation, Glaser and Strauss diverged somewhat in their characterization of approaches to the production of grounded theory, with slightly different emphases on the relation between external and empirically generated analysis. Strauss's collaborations with Juliet Corbin produced a more 'flexible' approach to the use of 'external' theory, arguing that it may play some useful role in analysis. Such differences, and the methodological debates they provoked (see Charmaz, 2000) are not my concern here, but it is important to emphasize that the debates and differences have emerged precisely around the issue of the relationship between an empirically derived and an externally imposed theory.

The aim of generating theoretical concepts through research is regarded in the original grounded theory approach (Glaser and Strauss 1967) as quite different to the use of prespecified analytic frameworks. However, while these processes *might* in some cases be distinct, they are not often entirely separated, and most social and educational research involves some combination of both approaches. Indeed, the polemical debates within grounded theory and its primary contributors illustrate the difficulties of keeping these two aspects entirely separate. Theory in qualitative research is usually both a matter of using the resources that one has at hand (such as literature, analytic concepts and distinctions, common-sense assumptions, research design) as a means of directing the interrogation of data *and* of producing new analytic categories and distinctions through the interrogation of data.

I provide this distinction between 'a priori' and 'empirical' theory to help researchers think about the range of approaches that they will invariably come into contact with in their reading about qualitative data analysis and about qualitative research more generally. I do not wish to suggest that researchers need to *choose* one of these approaches. Indeed, as I noted in the introduction, for those researchers who do not readily identify themselves with a particular tradition of research, such as those discussed above, it is probably more helpful to reflect on one's own research setting and work. One way to do this is to use an 'a priori and 'empirical' distinction to reflect on one's own context of work. The question 'What aspects of my work may be thought of as "a priori" and which as "empirical"?' I posed earlier may be of some use. Through it, researchers may begin to think about the theoretical commitments that their work entails (a priori theory), and about the ways that data might be used to develop it (empirical theory). This does not require any particular theorized methodology for data work, but merely involves a close attention to one's own concerns and their relation to the work of other scholars.

Research Design and Qualitative Analysis

Research design involves working out a specific way of following through a research question or set of questions in relation to a set of data. There is a distinction to be made between specific research designs (such as experimental designs, survey designs, case studies or ethnography) and the process of designing research. The former refers to enshrined sets of practices that specify particular modes and strategies for organizing and carrying out research. In some cases, such as in ethnography and survey research, these strategies are tightly related to particular epistemological preferences and assumptions (see Chapters 9 and 16 in this volume). The process of designing research, however, need not entail the orientation to any of these particular modes of research, and may simply involve specifying the research questions and topics that are to be explored; the sample of people under study; the particular modes of data collection that are to be used; and so on. In what follows, I provide a brief introduction to some of these processes in the context of qualitative research and illustrate their relevance for the analysis of data.

Formulating research questions

Usually, the research process begins by trying to outline the area of interest to be investigated. As mentioned in the introduction to this chapter, research is not a neatly linear process and it is quite usual for research interests to alter as research progresses. However, formulating research questions can nonetheless be a useful way to begin a research project, even if they will likely be subject to modification. One neat way to start the process of thinking about research interests is to produce a 'concept map' that outlines the key conceptual foci to be used and worked through in the research. Box 3.1 provides an example of a concept map used in the context of a study of training visually impaired computer users.

Once some key terms and concepts have been provisionally established, researchers can work through these in the production of particular research questions (see Chapter 5 on the process of formulating research questions). These questions provide further specifications of how the concepts are to be taken forward within the research. Box 3.1 shows some examples of research questions that could be developed from the concept map. Not all qualitative research involves the pursuit of specified questions in this way, and researchers often follow loose and exploratory concerns or interests that are formulated in quite general terms. In such instances, the formulation of questions in the above ways can still be useful for thinking through the direction of those concerns. Further, research questions are certainly not static. On the contrary, as qualitative research is an iterative practice, it should be expected that the assumptions that inform the production of questions are themselves under investigation and may well turn out to require modification.

Box 3.1 A concept map in a study of visual impairment and computer use

Concepts and issues
Visual impairment – forms of impairment/levels of impairment/life stages/congenital vs. developmental

Computer use – recreation/gaming/web searching/social networking/information-gathering/writing/music production

Training – improving skills/assessing skills/developing career prospects/making products and practices accessible

Research questions
What are the distinctive issues faced in training congenital and developmentally visually impaired computer users to search the web?
How can we assess the accessibility of social networking software for visually impaired teenagers?
How valuable are online networks of collaborative support for advanced cataract suffers?

Research design

A research design is a strategy for addressing a specified research question or concern. To put the matter like this is to imply that there is a divide between question formulation and design construction. However, these two 'processes' are usually developed in tandem: after all, there would be little point in developing a very elegant but utterly impractical research question.

It is perhaps more useful, then, to conceptualize research designs as approaches to thinking through research topics. The benefits of this view are that data remain a central concern throughout the research, and the research process is organized as a means to an analytic end (namely, exploring the research question). One way to pursue a design is to think through all the possible forms of data that could be produced by the various research methods available to the researcher. While, in principle, researchers can use any research method to answer any question, in most instances they do not have a completely free choice about the methods they use, the preferences of the personnel involved in the research, the limitations of time and money or the professional expertise available within the research team. All these factors will delimit a range of possible methods that are practically available.

A particularly productive way to begin the design process is to reflect on the various types of data that each available method may produce, and to think about how that data may be used to address the research problem. For example, researchers can reflect on the types of information that they might glean from interviews or observational work or on the differences in data that may be generated by focus groups as opposed to interviews. In my example of assessing the accessibility of social networking software for partially sighted users, a researcher could observe the users' interaction with a social networking site and note the problems that they have in using, for example, a screen reader as a means of navigating the online environment. This data would give rich insights into the actual practices that the users engage in (literally, how they use the screen reader to work through the information), but may require specialist knowledge to interpret the actions that a researcher may not necessarily posses.

Alternatively, researchers could interview the users about their experiences. The data produced through this approach would lose much of the detail provided by observations as the talk would only loosely reference 'what went on'. However, it may give detailed understandings of the users' motives, strategies, contextual problems and so on that are hard to gain through observation alone. The relevance of one form of data over another will depend largely on the nature of the questions being asked. By thinking through the relation between data type and research question in these ways, researchers can help to create a constructive alignment between their data and research questions/interests.

Sampling

The construction of a sample for a research project is a fundamental part of working through a research problem and its crystalization as a defined research strategy. In qualitative research, the concern of specifying one's sampling procedures is a matter of working out which people from the available population(s) have the most theoretical relevance to the given research project. To return to the example of the partially sighted computer users, researchers may be interested in particular forms of visual impairment (such as congenital visual disorders) or they might want to develop a sample that has representation from users with a variety of conditions. Similarly, the interest may be in a particular age group, a type of assistive technology, or with a particular community of people. Samples are specified in order to enable the central interests of the research to be explored in relation to relevant data. As with so much in qualitative research, samples are very often iteratively developed, as the collection and interrogation of data may reveal interesting features that lead the researcher to develop new interests and new samples to explore those interests. The process of data collection itself is evolutionary and the creation and management of a relevant sample must occur in orientation to the analytic purpose of the project.

Data collection and qualitative analysis

The dominant modes of data collection in qualitative research are interview and observations. They are not the only methods of course – researchers may also examine documents or artefacts, or invite research participants to produce textual or other resources for the researcher to work with. In the main though, researchers tend to rely mostly on either some form of interview and/or observation work. In this section, I briefly discuss each of these in turn, and outline how analysis is a central referent in the formulation and enactment of data collection strategies.

Interviews

Through interviews (including focus groups, face-to-face questionnaires, telephone and computer-mediated interviews) researchers create a discourse that is used to investigate their research questions (see Chapter 14 for a detailed discussion of interviews). The aim in the creation of such discourse is that it is centrally focused on the research questions being explored. The formulation of the specific questions/topics to be examined in the interviews is a central aspect of the design of interviews. (I discuss this in more detail below in relation to structured, semistructured and unstructured approaches.) Further, the *mode* in which the interview is to be conducted (e.g. face to face; telephone; computer-mediated discourse, etc.) is also an important concern. Researchers need to use a medium of data collection that will produce data that are relevant to their analysis. For example, if a researcher intends to conduct a form of discourse analysis, then it may be more appropriate to use verbal interviews rather than text-based ones (although the relevance of this depends on the exact nature of the question being asked and the form of discourse analysis being used).

Researchers need also to be careful that the description they provide to the participants does not create problems for their analysis. The information provided will be used by the participants to construct what they see as 'relevant talk'. With this in mind, the information provided by the researcher to frame the interview needs to be carefully selected to make sure that the participants can 'design' their talk in appropriate ways. The choice of the setting for the interview can also have a bearing on the nature of the data produced. Some settings may be more conducive to the production of talk than others, and some modes of communication may be more familiar to certain groups of people than others.

In *structured interviews* researchers precisely formulate the wording and order of the questions that are to be asked within the interviews prior to entering the setting. The research questions and topic(s) are the key referent in structuring the interview questions. All interviewees are asked the same questions in the same way to facilitate the comparative analysis of the data that are produced through the interviews. The subsequent analysis of data is structured around the questions and relevant analytic issues.

In *semistructured interviews*, the central analytic interests of the project are used to create topical themes that are to be addressed within the interviews. In this type of approach, the questions may well be improvised in the research setting, with the researcher(s) asking the questions at points that are appropriate to the discussion and with wording that is sensitive to the unfolding discourse. Interviewers often probe their research participants for more information on issues that seem particularly analytically relevant. Semistructured interviews involve a researcher working through their analytic interests in real time, creating distinctive and unique discourse events that are topically similar to each other in the issues that are addressed.

In *unstructured interviews*, researchers engage with their research participants with very little (if any) predefinition of the topics that need to be covered. There are two dominant contexts in which researchers use unstructured approaches: (a) when they are at an early stage of formulating their research interests and are interested in using these interviews as a means of constructing a focused research approach, or (b), when they are interested in exploring a very open research question such as 'What does this set of people know about x?'.

These interview types should not be thought of as firm divisions, rather as analytic commitments and foci. Researchers may begin their project using unstructured interviews, and move on to using semi- or even structured interviews. These 'types' do not relate to formalized and separate methodologies, but to analytic concerns. In Chapter 14 of this volume, a critical discussion is offered of the advantages and disadvantages of different types of interview, raising issues of validity, reliability and the impact of a human element when interacting with research participants.

Observation

Structured observations, like structured interviews, entail the creation of detailed outlines of one's analytic concerns and their relevance for the research settings prior to undertaking the observations. Researchers use *observation schedules* to describe these interests, and to help them to systematically record particular kinds of information about things that occur in the setting. In this respect, observation schedules are resources that analytically focus the researcher on particular events in the setting. In contrast, *unstructured* observations typically involve an attempt to see how some observational setting works before creating an analytic focus. Often, unstructured observations are used as a precursor to the conduct of more focused observations. While they may not be predesigned, the production of unstructured observations is nonetheless analytic, as it entails the researcher making judgements, on the spur of the moment, based on the relevance of the unfolding events to their project.

In unstructured observations researchers use fieldnotes, video or audio recordings, or a combination of these to record their data. Where fieldnotes are used, the researcher constructs a narrative of the events being investigated, and does so, as I have said, with reference to their existing and emerging interests. Fieldnotes usually record both *contextual information* (such as time of event, participants, location, and so on) and *detailed* information (such as what actually happened in a given setting). Detailed information refers to the main events in a given observation and may include central structural features, problems, unintelligible events, confirmations of previous observations and so on. While it is a slightly artificial distinction, it is common for researches to keep 'description' and 'analysis' separate in their fieldnotes – i.e. the things that happened and their interpretations of these things.

As all of these examples of data collection illustrate, the production of data through the *enactment* of research methods is always analytic – i.e. it is directed towards the generation of data that fit and help the researcher to work through a particular research interest. Further, data are *actively considered* throughout the research process; all but the most structured forms of interview involve working out in situ 'what is to count as relevant data', and data collection is probably best thought of as 'analysis in action'. In all cases, analysis is at the heart of the collection (or rather, the *generation*) of data.

Summary

I began this chapter by pointing to the difficulty that many researchers in education face when thinking about qualitative analysis, including but not limited to the wide range of available approaches or frameworks to analysis, and the problem of knowing how to orientate towards these approaches. I suggested that rather than approach this range with the question 'Which of these approaches should I use?', it is usually more useful to simply clarify one's own research interests and problematic.

I outlined a distinction between a priori and empirical theory, and suggested that this may be useful for both making sense of the broad variety of approaches to qualitative data analysis, and for thinking through one's own theoretical commitments. I discussed the ways in which research design and practice can be thought about in relation to data analysis – i.e. as means of generating analytically relevant data. My aim has been to encourage an approach to qualitative research that treats data work as a continuation of the existing research concerns and interests.

The wide variety of distinctive approaches to qualitative data analysis is not best thought of as a selection from which a researcher needs to choose. It is better to reflect carefully on one's own research context and problematic, and approach this range with the question 'How does this approach relate to what I am doing?'

Data work involves continuing to think through analytic problems that have been used throughout the research to design some data in order to deal with a particular problem. Researchers nearly always come to data collection and analysis with some clear ideas about what they want to achieve. However, data work very often involves thinking through the research problem and design, and may well have some impact on both of those aspects.

The distinction between 'a priori' and 'empirical' theory can be very useful for both making sense of the wide variety of approaches to qualitative data analysis, and for thinking through one's own conceptual framework. Designing data collection methods is a matter of working through analytic interests in order to produce data that are relevant to the research interests. In less structured forms of research, data collection is best thought of as a 'lived analysis', as this most accurately characterizes the active role of the researcher in deciding 'what is to count as relevant'.

References

Charmaz, K. (2000) 'Grounded theory: objectivist and constructivist methods', in N. Denzin (ed.) *The Handbook of Qualitative Research*. London: Sage.

Fairclough, N. (1995) *Critical Discourse Analysis: the Critical Study of Language*. London: Longman.

Glaser, B., and Strauss, A. (1967) *The Discovery of Grounded Theory: Strategies for Qualitative Research*. New York: Aldine.

Leach, J. (2000) 'Rhetorical analysis', in M. Bauer and G. Gaskell (eds) *Qualitative Researching with Text, Image and Sound: A Practical Handbook*. London: Sage.

Marshall, C., and Rossman, G. B. (2006) *Designing Qualitative Research*. London: Sage.

Miles, M. B., and Huberman, A. M. (1994) *Qualitative Data Analysis: An Expanded Sourcebook*. London: Sage.

Sacks, H. (1995) *Lectures in Conversation*, vols 1 and 2. London: Blackwell.

Sharrock, W. W., and Anderson, B. (1986) *The Ethnomethodologists*. London: Tavistock.

Wolcott, H. (1994) *Transforming Qualitative Data: Descriptions, Analysis and Interpretation*. London: Sage.

Quantitative Research as a Method of Inquiry in Education

4

Dimitra Hartas

Chapter Outline

Introduction

Traditionally, quantitative research in education has been within experimental designs that aimed at replicating scientific methods – for example, observation and experiment – used in the natural sciences. As discussed in Chapter 2, the epistemological roots of quantitative research are in the empiricism and positivism, with an emphasis on control and manipulation of variables in order to establish cause-and-effect relationships via hypothesis-testing. In quantitative research, we develop a research design, formulate research questions and test specific hypotheses based on previous theories and research findings to verify (or not) theory and generalize the findings to contexts beyond the study. In the 1960s, the scope of quantitative research began to widen to include research designs (e.g. quasi-experimental designs and surveys) which enabled educational research in naturalistic settings. The move to explore methodological approaches outside the framework of experiments was stimulated by the limitations that experimental research poses in exploring educational phenomena within artificial, lab-like settings, which are less relevant to the places where teaching and learning take place (a detailed discussion on experiments is presented in Chapter 15).

By the end of this chapter, you should be able to:

- understand different sampling methods and consider their strengths and limitations
- appreciate the implications of sampling techniques with regard to the validity and generalizability of a study
- understand concepts such as validity and reliability as important criteria to judge the quality of quantitative research

What is Quantitative Research?

Quantitative research is typically defined along the notion that data are presented in a numerical form that is suitable for mathematical analyses (Aliaga and Gunderson 2002). Other definitions of quantitative research focus on the assumptions that underpin the positivist tradition within which educational research was originally located, in terms of being hypothesis-driven, applying deductive logic, discovering causal relationships and achieving objectivity (see Box 4.1).

There are two main routes in conducting quantitative research, namely group comparison and exploration of relationships among variables. A group comparison route involves comparisons between different groups or within the same group at different points in time. This route originates in experimental and quasi-experimental research where the effects of a treatment on an outcome are tested by exploring the differences between the experimental and comparison groups. The relationship between variables route examines degrees of association between variables, or how much variance in a variable is accounted for by another (common variance). This route is typically taken in survey research (nonexperimental research), which aims at exploring relationships among variables in naturally occurring educational situations. These two routes rely on different theoretical and methodological assumptions and involve different statistical approaches (see Chapters 21, 22 and 23).

In this volume, the epistemology, research design and data analyses in quantitative research are discussed and illustrated with examples in a number of chapters (i.e. experimental and quasi-experimental designs, survey research, key concepts and assumptions in quantitative research, exploring quantitative data, between-group differences, correlation and regression and factor analysis). At the foundation stage of quantitative research, along with knowledge of the content domain and the formulation of research questions, it is important to think about the research participants and the strategies whereby we form a sample from a population. We also need to consider the reliability and validity of a study to ensure that the methodological approaches we take are trustworthy and meaningful. Sampling, reliability and validity are crucial aspects of a quantitative research design, and should be addressed right from the start.

Box 4.1 Doing quantitative research

- The rationale for the research design is explained by establishing the fitness of purpose between the research questions (hypotheses) and the methods employed.
- The aims of research are guided by a coherent conceptual framework that delineates the epistemological and paradigmatic traditions (e.g. postpositivism) within which quantitative research is located, as well as the context of current research, whose parameters are established though a literature review.
- Quantitative research has multiple purposes. A truth-seeking purpose, a developmental purpose, an intervention/change in practice purpose and a public policy change purpose (Donmoyer 2006).
- The strategies employed for data collection and data analyses should be justified thoroughly.
- The data are actively interrogated and cross-examined (triangulated).
- The claims are supported by the research findings, and are located in the wider research context.
- The implications with regard to theory, policy and practice are delineated.

Population and Sample

Among the first things we identify in a research study are the people or units of analysis that we plan to study. A *population* is a group of individuals or organizations that share the same characteristic that is of interest to our study – for example, Year 3 mathematics teachers. What defines a population is not its size (it may be small or large) but the presence of a specific characteristic. In the context of quantitative research, one way of thinking about population is by asking the question, 'Who do I want to generalize the findings *to?*' In other words, a population is the group to which we want to generalize the findings obtained for the sample. In every study, there is a theoretical and a pragmatic or target population. A theoretical population displays the characteristics/attributes we want to study. However, due to resource limitations, it is not always feasible to access all those who share the characteristics of interest. Hence, we carry out research work with the pragmatic population, to which access is feasible considering the scope and parameters of a research study.

Once the population is defined, a *sample* is selected. A sample is a section or a subgroup of the population we intend to study. How the sample is selected is very important for the validity of a study. To generalize research findings from the sample to the population, the sample has to be representative of the population from which it was drawn. Sample representativeness means that the individuals or the units of analysis display the characteristics and attributes that are typical of the population. To achieve this, we should form the research sample via a systematic or probabilistic sampling, to distinguish it from an unsystematic or nonprobabilistic sampling.

Probabilistic sampling

A probabilistic sampling involves a random selection to ensure that all participants or units of an analysis have an equal opportunity to be chosen from the target population. Random selection is the process of randomly drawing a sample of persons or units from a population to ensure that the sample is representative of the population. There are four types of probabilistic (random) sampling, namely, simple random sampling, systematic random sampling, stratified random sampling and cluster random sampling (Cresswell 2005: 146).

In *simple random sampling* the participants or units of analysis are selected randomly from a population with the intent that the sample is representative of this population. The idea behind random sampling is that any bias in the population is distributed equally in the sample. Simple random sampling can be accomplished easily. For example, we put the names or numbers in a hat and pull out as many as we need to comprise a sample. However, this technique is not efficient, especially with a small target population.

Systematic random sampling is very similar to the simple random sampling. The main distinction is that, with systematic random sampling, we apply a rule (e.g., select every nth participant or unit from the population randomly). Suppose that the target population is N = 100 and that we want to draw a sample of n = 10. To form a systematic random sample, we need to calculate the so-called *interval size* by dividing the total population size with the sample size. In this example, the interval size is 100/10 = 10, thus we select every tenth person or unit from the population until we select ten units to form the sample. It is important that the units of the population are ordered randomly *before* we start the selection process. A systematic random sample is more precise than a simple random sample.

Stratified random sampling is another type of random sampling where we divide the population (e.g. primary-school pupils) into subgroups (e.g. Year 4 pupils, Year 6 pupils) and then apply a simple random sampling with each subgroup to form the sample. For example, the target population is all pupils in a primary school, and we want to create a random sample to ensure that pupils from all years will be included in it. In so doing, we divide the population into subgroups (Year 1 to Year 6) and, through random sampling, select a number of pupils from each year. This process ensures that pupils from all years are represented in the sample.

A stratified random sample can be proportionate or disproportionate. To form a proportionate random sample we use the same sampling fraction with all subgroups, whereas with a disproportionate sample we use a different sampling fraction. In the primary school example, a proportionate sample involves the same percentage of pupils from each year, whereas a disproportionate sample involves a higher or lower percentage of pupils from certain years. The idea behind stratified sampling is to ensure that certain groups/categories are represented in the sample. This sampling method has social justice implications especially with regard to the inclusion of groups such as homeless people or individuals from certain minority ethnic groups who have not had a fair representation in research.

Finally, randomized designs can be individual or 'cluster random'. An individual randomized design involves a random assignment of individuals to groups, whereas a cluster design refers to assigning clusters (classroom, schools) to groups. In *cluster random sampling*, we divide the target population into clusters, typically along geographic or socioeconomic boundaries, and apply a simple random sampling within each cluster. Cluster random sampling allows us to select individuals from a large geographic area in an efficient and economic manner.

In a real-life research, we tend to use multiple methods of sampling in order to maximize efficiency and effectiveness, through a process called *multistage sampling*. With a multistage approach we are in a better position to obtain a rich sample in a systematic way (Trochim 2006). For example, suppose that we want to collect data from pupils with Special Educational Needs (SEN) in England. This is a time- and resource-demanding process, which can benefit greatly from employing different sampling methods. Because the population is geographically diverse, we may start with a cluster random sampling to select a number of clusters – i.e. local authorities (LAs) from a geographic area. Within each LA, it is not feasible to collect data from every single pupil with SEN. To overcome this problem, we may employ a stratified sample to ensure that, for example, minority ethnic pupils with SEN in each LA are represented (in a proportionate or disproportionate manner). (In this example, we assume that ethnicity is a factor relevant to the scope of the research.) Finally, within each strata, we may employ a simple random selection of pupils with SEN. As this example illustrates, we can have three or four stages of sampling, depending on the scope and practicalities of a study, and the resources available to carry it out.

A randomization can take place at the level of sample selection and group assignment. Random selection and random assignment 'serve different purposes' (Cresswell,2005: 284). A random selection aims at forming samples that are representative of the population from which they are drawn to maximize generalizability and thus external validity. A random assignment involves randomly assigning persons or units of analysis to different groups (e.g. experimental and control groups) in a study. A random assignment purports to distribute bias equally among the groups by equating them, to increase control over the effects of extraneous factors and, ultimately, maximize the internal validity of a study. Specifically, a random assignment ensures that unsystematic variation due to extraneous factors (e.g. differences in ability or the amount of sleep the participants had the night before taking a test) are not systematic but randomly distributed across groups.

Both a random selection and assignment are important; however, a random selection may not be always feasible due to practical reasons (e.g. small sample sizes). In some studies, random assignment is given priority over random selection in that establishing a good internal validity is often more desirable than maximizing the external validity. As discussed in Chapter 15, a random assignment is crucial in experimental designs to ensure that bias is distributed equally and thus control is maximized over extraneous factors. In some types of research, such as a computer-mediated research (e.g. web-based surveys), a researcher has limited control over the participants' characteristics and attributes, making the notion of sample representativeness debateable.

Nonprobabilistic sampling

In educational research, for practical reasons, we cannot always select groups and/or assign persons to groups randomly. Sometimes we select participants who display a characteristic of interest, and who are available and accessible. In these cases, we employ *nonprobabilistic* sampling techniques. The samples obtained may or may not be representative of the population; we have no way of knowing. Thus, we cannot make generalizations about the population based on what we know about the sample. Also, without a random allocation, we cannot tell whether the groups are equivalent. Two nonprobabilistic sampling techniques, namely convenience sampling and purposive sampling, are often employed in educational research.

Convenience sampling is an easy way to select participants based on who is available and who would like to volunteer. Although this is a convenient way to select a sample, we need to be aware of selectivity bias in that the characteristics or attributes of individuals may not be distributed equally. For example, individuals who function as volunteers are likely to present characteristics such as motivation, interest or extreme views about certain issues, which may set them apart from the target population, introducing bias in the results.

Purposive sampling is a sampling technique with a purpose. For example, we may want to sample children between 5 and 7 years from a particular school with which we have negotiated access. Several types of purposive sampling (e.g. snowball sampling, expert sampling, quota sampling) can be employed depending on the purpose of the study.

With *snowball sampling* we start selecting a few individuals who meet the criteria for inclusion in our study, and we ask them to identify others who are likely to meet the same criteria. The advantages of this type of sampling are that we are likely to form a good sample size because the participants identified through this process tend to be more motivated to complete questionnaires or attend interviews than are complete strangers. This sampling technique may suit research studies with an original or under-researched focus, such as studies that explore a new territory where it is not easy to identify and recruit participants. As with convenience sampling, a snowball sample is less likely to be representative of the target population.

With *expert sampling* we select a group of individuals who are known to be experts in a specific domain. This is a useful technique if a study seeks to investigate the views of individuals who are experts in a particular area (e.g. key personnel in a school or LA).

With *quota sampling* we select individuals or units of analysis according to a specific quota. It is important to decide and justify the characteristic upon which we base the quota (Trochim 2006). In many cases, a quota sample is proportional in that it accounts for the number of cases but also the representation of the characteristics in these cases. Suppose we want to compile a sample that represents the main ethnic minorities (i.e. white, Indian-Bangladeshi and Afro-Caribbean, mixed heritage) in a country. If we know that the population of a country where we conduct the research is comprised of 75 per cent white, 15 per cent Indian-Bangladeshi, 5 per cent Afro-Caribbean and 5 per cent mixed heritage, then these percentages set the criteria for compiling the quota sample.

The sampling techniques discussed in this chapter have a quantitative research orientation. For a discussion on participant recruitment and the issues associated with conducting research with children within the context of qualitative research see Chapters 7 and 9.

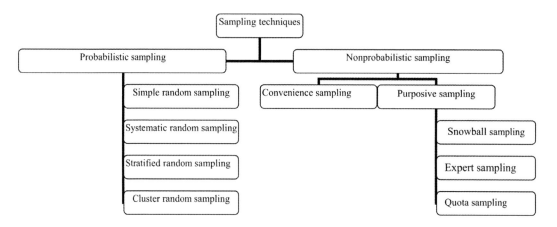

Figure 4.1 Sampling techniques

The sample size

The size of a sample depends on the nature and the purpose of an inquiry and it should be determined from the outset of a study. Qualitative studies tend to involve a small number of participants to collect in-depth and contextualized information about social phenomena. In contrast, quantitative research studies aim to select as many participants as possible, in that the larger the sample the more confident we can be that it is similar to the population from which it is drawn. In other words, with large sample sizes, the sampling error is minimized (the difference between the sample estimate and the true population score).

When deciding upon the sample size, we should consider the statistical objectives set by data analysis procedures and the affordability of the sample. The choice of statistical techniques depends, among other factors, on the sample size. Cresswell (2005: 150) estimated the following sample sizes for different types of research:

- in an experimental study, which involves group comparisons, approximately 15 participants per group (or cell)
- in a correlational study, which explores the relationship between variables, 30 participants
- for survey research, 350 participants approximately

When selecting participants, we need to strike a balance between affordability and meeting the statistical objectives set by data analysis procedures: this means selecting a sample that is large enough to meet the statistical objectives but not too large as to waste resources and time. Most crucially, we should be realistic about the number of participants we can access and the nature of the information we can obtain from them.

An important consideration of a quantitative research design is to ensure that the methodological approaches taken to address the research questions are consistent, trustworthy and meaningful, and that the procedures implemented for data analysis and interpretation are systematic, stable and coherent. To this end, the reliability and validity of a study are important criteria to judge its quality.

Reliability and Validity in Quantitative Research

Reliability

Reliability refers to the consistency and stability of a measurement, and is concerned with whether the results of a study are replicable (repeatable). Replicability can be achieved by offering adequate details on the definitions of constructs/variables and the procedures employed to collect and analyse data. The consistency of a measurement is examined in terms of consistency over time (stability), equivalence and internal consistency (see Figure 4.2).

Consistency over time (repeated measurement)

Consistency over time refers to the degree to which a measurement is the same each time it is obtained under the same conditions with the same participants. In short, consistency refers to the

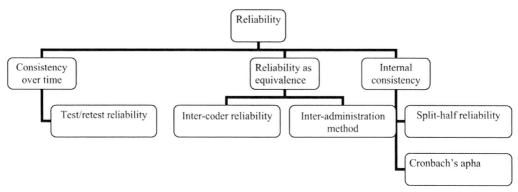

Figure 4.2 Reliability

repeatability of a measurement. A measure is considered reliable if a person obtains the same scores on the same test given twice. It is important to note that reliability is not measured but estimated through test/retest and split-half procedures.

Test/retest reliability involves the process of using two very similar (or equivalent) tests on the same participants at two different points in time. We compute the correlation coefficient (r) between the two separate measurements, expecting to see stability in the trait measured between Test 1 and Test 2. A correlation coefficient above 0.6 indicates good reliability. An important consideration with test/retest is to determine the time elapsed between Test 1 and Test 2. By allowing a brief time, respondents may remember how they responded the fist time ('carryover effect'), resulting in overestimating reliability. By allowing a longer time between the first and second test, we may observe differences in the responses due to developmental changes, maturation or 'learning effect' in the respondents. One or two weeks is often recommended as an optimal interval of time between tests (Muijs 2004).

Reliability as equivalence

Reliability as equivalence is established by estimating the degree of agreement between two sets of measures obtained via two administration methods of the same instrument/test (administration method reliability). Also, it can be established by having two independent raters coding the same event (inter-coder reliability, see Box 4.2).

To illustrate *administration method reliability* we refer to a study by Sperle*et al.* (1997) that examined the equivalence reliability of two administration methods for the Functional Independence Measure for Children (FIM). The two administration methods were direct observation of child performance and parental interview. Thirty children between the ages of 19 months and 71 months with identified developmental disabilities were included in the study. The direct observation and interview methods were administered in a random order to each subject within a three-week period. The direct observation was completed in an educational setting, and the FIM information was obtained by either in-person or telephone interviews with parents. The correlation coefficient (ICC) for total FIM ratings was 0.93, indicating consistency between the two administration methods.

With *inter-coder reliability* we estimate the extent to which two or more individual raters agree on a coding scheme devised to code themes as they emerge through a thematic analysis. In other words, inter-coder reliability addresses the consistency of the implementation of a coding system. In practice, inter-coder reliability is estimated by asking two raters to code 25 per cent of the transcripts produced during interview or focus group discussions (same transcripts). The percentage of their agreement is estimated; anything above 65 per cent is considered to indicate a good inter-coder agreement.

Box 4.2 Example of inter-coder reliability

Two or more researchers are observing the Literacy Hour in a primary classroom. The researchers have a coding scheme to rate pupil participation during the Literacy Hour, defined along the number of oral contributions they make, instances of on-task behaviour, frequency of note-taking etc. In this case, an inter-rater reliability assesses the consistency of the coding system devised to code pupil participation. If one researcher codes a pupil's behaviour as participatory, while another researcher does not code the exact same behaviour as participatory, obviously the inter-rater reliability is compromised. An inter-rater reliability shows the extent to which two or more individuals can be consistent when observing or rating the same event. Ultimately, it shows how well the coding scheme is constructed in terms of the thematic coherence of its components.

Reliability as consistency over time is a straightforward concept when we measure concrete entities (e.g. weight), because several consecutive measurements using the same weight scale and the same person are expected to produce the same score (and if not, the lack of consistency is easily detectable). Consistency over time becomes more difficult to ascertain when measuring latent variables (i.e. constructs such as intelligence, attitudes, self-esteem) that cannot be observed and measured directly. In this case, reliability refers to the consistency of measures taken for these variables. A clear operational definition of a latent variable is thus crucial to enable us to delineate its dimensions with clarity. For example, self-esteem can be operationalized in terms of academic and social self-esteem. Depending on the purpose of a study, social self-esteem may consist of several dimensions such as being perceived by others as popular, having many friends, spending time with friends etc. For latent variables that do not measure an attribute directly, their components should be consistent with each other (internal consistency).

Internal consistency

Internal consistency refers to the conceptual coherence across all items that constitute a characteristic (in a questionnaire, items that measure the same construct are clustered together). For constructs, such as intelligence, we define their components thematically. For example, we may define intelligence along Gardner's (1999) concept of multiple intelligences (e.g. musical, mathematical, creative etc.), depending on the research questions and the scope of the study. Having delineated the components, we develop questions that, thematically, mirror or map onto these dimensions of intelligence. After collecting the responses, it is important to run a correlation (see Chapter 23) to determine if a questionnaire reliably measures the concept of intelligence. There are two ways to calculate reliability as internal consistency, namely, split-half reliability and Cronbach's alpha.

Split-half reliability offers a measure of the reliability of a test based on the correlation between scores on two arbitrarily formed halves of the test. The assumption is that if the items in both tests measure the same concept, they will be strongly related, with a correlation coefficient (r) over 0.7. To compute the correlation values among the items we use a statistical technique called *Cronbach's alpha*. In short, Cronbach's alpha splits all the items in a questionnaire every possible way and computes the correlation values for them all. In the end, a computer output generates one number for Cronbach's alpha – and like a correlation coefficient, the closer the number is to 1, the higher the reliability estimate is. Cronbach's alpha offers a less conservative estimate of reliability than does the test/retest procedure.

The reliability of a test or a questionnaire is maximized by taking care to develop items that conceptually relate to the construct of the study (internal consistency). This can be helped by phrasing the questions/statements in a clear and unambiguous way (see Chapter 16 on how to construct the items of a survey), and by having defined the terms in the research questions with precision. Most crucially, we need to have a good knowledge of the field, mainly achieved via a thorough literature review.

Validity

The validity of a study is an important criterion regarding the meaningfulness of the results and the overall value of research. The concept of validity is concerned with the question as to whether we measure what we set out to measure, and this question goes to the heart of an inquiry. In many ways, establishing the validity is more important than achieving reliability, in that the results of a study may be reliable but not valid, making the entire research exercise worthless. The process of establishing validity is dialectic and ongoing rather than a fixed feature of an instrument/test. Smith (2003: 472) argues that 'validation as a process is never complete, always subject to new information and insights, and always referring to a social world – of moving back and forth among purpose, data, theories, inferences and audiences'.

There are four types of validity commonly examined in social and educational research. These are: internal validity, construct validity (i.e. content, convergent and discriminate validity and criterion validity), external validity and ecological validity (see Figure 4.3).

Internal validity

Internal validity is concerned with whether there is a connection or a causal relationship between the variables – i.e., independent and dependent variables. This type of validity is relevant to experimental and quasi-experimental designs where causal relationships are examined by controlling for variables other than the independent variables that may contribute to the variation in the outcome. Through control, mainly achieved via randomization, the threats to internal validity are minimized. In experimental designs, the internal validity is more important

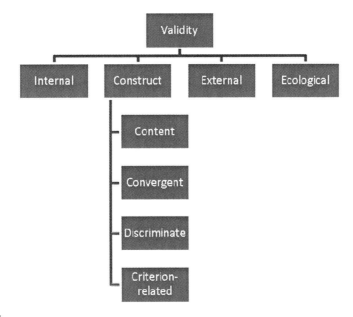

Figure 4.3 Validity

than the external validity. For example, the study by Finn and Achilles (1990) examined the relationship between class size and academic achievement. If the study achieves a good internal validity (by controlling for extraneous factors), then it can be inferred, with a degree of confidence, that variation in academic achievement is explained by class size (small class sizes increase academic performance).

Construct validity

Construct validity is concerned with whether the measures of the dimensions of a construct actually reflect the construct itself, or, in other words, whether the operationalization (definition) of a construct is consistent with its measurable components. Construct validity refers to the conceptual coherence between a construct, such as social self-esteem, and the dimensions used to operationalize it (e.g. popularity, friendship, peer acceptance). Construct validity is important for latent variables (those that cannot be observed directly) because to measure them we need to identify the components that comprise them. Well-defined constructs consist of components that are theoretically related. However, if the conceptual components do not map onto the construct, measuring them would not be the same as measuring the construct itself (it would be a case of measuring not the construct in the study but a different conceptual entity altogether). The operationalization of key terms in the research questions plays an important role in achieving construct validity.

Construct validity refers to content, convergent, discriminate and criterion-related types of validity. Content validity addresses whether the operationalization of a construct actually reflects the content domain, relevant to the construct. To achieve content validity, we need to have a thorough understanding of the content domain, which is achieved by reviewing the relevant literature. For example, suppose that the construct is intelligence; before any attempt to operationalize it, we need to acquire a thorough understanding of the literature on intelligence and its underlying components. A good knowledge of different theoretical models of intelligence (e.g. Sternberg's triarchic theory of intelligence or Gardner's theory of multiple intelligences) is important to identify the dimensions of intelligence to be studied. In so doing, we offer a theoretical justification as to why we operationalized intelligence the way we did. The least we can achieve in terms of construct validity is face validity, to ascertain whether 'on its face' a definition appears to be a good translation of the construct. This is probably the weakest type of construct validity.

Convergent validity is the actual general agreement among ratings, gathered independently of one another, on variables that are theoretically related (e.g. the degree of agreement on independent measures of components of intelligence, such as analytical thinking or verbal skills, assuming that these define intelligence). *Discriminate validity* refers to a lack of a relationship among measures which are taken on variables that are not theoretically related (e.g. sociometric measures on popularity and interpersonal skills measures on friendship).[1]

Criterion validity, also called *instrumental validity*, relates to the accuracy of a measure or procedure by comparing it with another measure or procedure which has been demonstrated to be valid. For example, when developing a new test (e.g. a sociometric test), we want to ascertain whether it relates to other tests for peer popularity, If it does relate to other tests on social skills, it means that it has the potential to predict certain outcomes regarding social skills development. There are two subtypes of criterion validity: predictive validity and concurrent validity.

Predictive validity refers to whether a new test or instrument (e.g. a sociometric test) predicts outcomes which are thought to be theoretically related. For example, when implementing a social skills training programme to support children with social/emotional difficulties, the measures taken from a sociometric test with a good predictive validity help us to predict whether certain children are suitable candidates for the programme (children who are expected/predicted to benefit more from the programme).

Concurrent validity refers to the extent to which measures taken from a test measuring a specific behaviour relate to measures taken from other tests that are thought to measure similar behaviours. For example, measures taken from a sociometric test are expected, at least in theory, to relate to measures taken from a peer popularity checklist. If not, then we need to consider the content domains that these tests cover and delineate their conceptual similarities. Both predictive and concurrent validity are important when developing a new instrument, such as a behaviour checklist or sociometric questionnaire.

External validity

External validity refers to our ability to generalize the results beyond the context of a specific study. In the study on the impact of class size on academic achievement, a question of external validity is the extent to which the results can be generalized to other classrooms beyond those originally involved in the study. For some research studies, especially experiments, achieving external validity is not always very important. In fact, external validity is often compromised to ensure that the internal validity is attained. In addition to internal validity, external validity is useful in survey research. The relative importance of internal and external validity is determined by the purpose of the research, the desirability of objectivity, the necessity of generalization and the relevance of findings to the intervention. As already discussed, both internal and external validity are very much influenced by sampling techniques (e.g. random assignment and random selection).

Ecological validity

Ecological validity is concerned with the extent to which the findings from a study reflect people's attitudes and their everyday experiences. A criticism regarding experimental research is that the findings do not always relate to natural educational settings. Bryman (2004: 29) comments that research findings with little relevance to people's lives are 'artefacts of the social scientist's arsenal of data collection and analytic tools'. The terms *external* and *ecological* validity are often used interchangeably. Conceptually, they are very similar because both refer to the generalizability of research findings. However, the ecological validity is concerned with not only whether the results can be generalized but also their relevance to people's lives. For example, the results from a questionnaire may have a good internal and external validity but limited ecological validity if the people who completed it felt that the content of the questions did not reflect their life experiences. Furthermore, a questionnaire may be seen by some participants as an exercise that is removed from their typical interactions and conversations. The notion of relevance is central to ecological validity, especially with regard to the transference of research findings in naturalistic contexts.

Generalizability

Traditionally, generalizability has been viewed as a property of a quantitative research.[2] Within the positivist tradition, generalizability is understood in terms of assertions that research findings are 'truly universal, unrestricted to time and space [...] always and everywhere the case, provided only that the appropriate conditions are justified' (Kaplan 1964: 91). This understanding of generalizability is problematic and bears little relevance to educational research whose goal is to understand behaviour and relationships as they operate in local contexts. Generalization should take into account the particulars of a context in that generalizations are representative of the context and the specific attributes of the participants.

Threats to validity

There are many threats to validity, with some being integral to the research design, the purpose and context of a study and our knowledge of the field to enable us 'deconstruct' key terms and ideas in ways that map onto the content domain to be directly measured. The research vignette in Box 4.3 illustrates key issues with regard to the reliability and validity of a study and their implications for rigour in a quantitative research design.

Box 4.3 A research vignette

Suppose that we would like to examine ways of supporting the social self-esteem of children with dyslexia. There is research to suggest that children with dyslexia are more likely to show a low self-esteem during their interactions with peers. For the purpose of this research we want to test the effectiveness of social coaching as a technique for supporting the development of social problem-solving skills, perspective-taking (showing empathy) and communication skills in children with dyslexia. The research plan is to engage a group of ten Year 5 and Year 6 children with dyslexia (volunteers) in a number of social coaching sessions for three weeks, and then test possible improvements (impact of social coaching) in their social self-esteem and peer interactions.

Initially, we give the group of children a questionnaire to get some baseline measures on their social self-esteem by asking them questions about their peer interactions, how confident they are during peer interactions, whether they show helping behaviours towards others, what they say to resolve conflict and help another person in distress etc. During the coaching sessions that take place at the end of the school day, we engage the children in role-playing by giving them two hypothetical situations. The first is about a child who feels embarrassed about his poor reading aloud. The second is about a child who feels sad because he was not invited to a birthday party. During these sessions, we model appropriate behaviour and conversational skills in terms of things to say to make the distressed children feel better.

At the end of the coaching sessions, we give the group a post-questionnaire with questions about friendship (e.g. how many friends they have, how often they see them, how confident they are to find a friend and the things they would like to do with friends), to check whether there has been any improvement in their peer interactions. We also choose a subgroup of the most talkative children and carry out an interview to talk about how they feel during peer interactions and whether they feel confident to talk about their learning difficulties with their peers.

To consider the issues regarding reliability and validity that emerge from the vignette in Box 4.3, we need to start from the research questions and the research design. This study set out to investigate the impact of coaching sessions on the social self-esteem of children with dyslexia. The construct of social self-esteem cannot be directly measured, and thus we need to define it and identify its underlying components. A key procedure is to operationalize social self-esteem in terms of measurable components. This has implications for both the internal and construct validity of the study in that not having a clear idea of what we are measuring will have a negative impact on the rigour of the research design and the methodological approaches we plan to take.

The next step is to ensure the consistency between the aspects of social self-esteem that we set to investigate and the aspects of social coaching on which we focus. In the vignette, social coaching focused on modelling behaviours such as social problem-solving skills, perspective-taking (showing empathy) and communication skills. This raises the question of how these social coaching aspects map onto our definition of social self-esteem. Not having defined social self-esteem, we are not in a position to know whether social coaching, as it is presented here, is relevant to social self-esteem.

There is also a lack of clarity in how the pre- and post- measures (a) relate to each other and (b) relate to social self-esteem. The pre-questionnaire (baseline measures) focuses on confidence during peer interactions, helping behaviours towards others, and capacity to resolve conflict and help another person in distress. The post-questionnaire shifts the focus to friendships. Although there are links between friendships and confidence during peer interactions and capacity to resolve conflict, from pre- to post- measures we do not measure the same entity, and we do not know whether what we measure relates to social self-esteem. To complicate things further, the treatment (i.e., social coaching) appears to focus on academic self-esteem (a child feels embarrassed about his poor reading aloud), and exclusion from peer interactions (child who has not been invited to a birthday party). So, again, how do these aspects relate to the outcome (social self-esteem)?

The confusion with defining what we measure and whether the pre- and post- measures reflect the outcome compromises the construct validity of the study. Also, the internal validity is compromised, given that the design of this study does not control for confounding factors. As discussed, internal validity is concerned with whether there is a connection between the variables, (i.e. social coaching and social self-esteem). To delineate the relationship it is crucial to ensure that there are no confounding factors to influence it. In this study, little care was given to control for confounding variables, mainly due to lack of a control group and random assignment of children to groups. Without a control group we cannot be certain that changes in children's social self-esteem would not have happened anyway regardless of social coaching (see Maturation, below). A lack of random assignment means that bias (e.g. opportunities for peer interactions) is not evenly distributed across groups. Also, the way children were selected for the study (volunteers) and for the interviews (talkative children) introduces a response bias. As already mentioned, volunteers are likely to possess characteristics that set them apart from others. Likewise, children who are more talkative than the rest also introduce a bias, especially given that conversational skills play an important role in social self-esteem. Finally, in terms of external validity, the group of children is a convenient sample (nonprobabilistic). Thus, external validity is also compromised.

Considering the administration method reliability, with regard to the post- measures, we are less likely to get a consistency because the areas explored during the interviews and the post-questionnaire are not conceptually similar. The interview focuses on feelings during peer interactions whereas the post- questionnaire focuses on friendship. Although these areas are interrelated, they are conceptually distinct. Moreover, an inter-rated reliability check would have been useful to establish the extent to which two independent raters agree on the themes emerging from the interviews. If the coding scheme does not relate to the key issues as stated by the research questions or the issues have not been defined accurately, this will compromise inter-rater reliability.

The concerns discussed here emanate from a poorly-designed and executed study. However, even a well-designed study presents threats to validity. Common threats to internal validity include:

- *History:* this refers to events and situations that have already occurred in a setting and are beyond the control of the research study (background, contextual factors, relationships among participants).
- *Instrumentation/testing:* this results from procedures not being followed consistently during testing. Also, the validity of a study can be compromised when participants become sensitized to being tested (e.g. studies in which pre- testing and post- testing occurs within a small time interval).

- *Attrition*: this threat refers to changes in the participants, who may leave the study voluntarily or due to circumstances beyond their control (e.g. moving into a different school or out of the geographical area). Attrition is more likely to occur in longitudinal studies that span long time periods.
- *Maturation*: this emanates from natural changes the participants may experience over the course of a study. In experimental designs, where there is a control group, the effects of maturation can be 'controlled' in that participants in both experimental and control groups are equally likely to experience natural changes. However, in studies without a control group, it is debatable as to whether the changes attributed to intervention would not have happened anyway due to maturation.
- *Selection*: the sample selection procedures play an important role in ensuring that the findings of a study are reliable and valid. Probabilistic samples that utilize randomization, (i.e. random allocation of persons to groups) ensure (to a degree) that the groups are equivalent, with factors likely to affect the outcome being distributed equally across the groups.
- *Hawthorne effect*: this refers to changes in the participants' attitudes and behaviour (e.g. becoming more cautious or socially aware), triggered by taking a part in a research study. As with maturation, the use of a control group can mitigate against this threat to validity.

A common threat to external validity is *selection*, where research findings cannot be generalized to different ethnic and socioeconomic groups unless this was considered during the selection process by forming a sample that is representative of a population and which also involves proportions of ethnic and SES groups. This potential threat to generalization may be alleviated through random selection, a stratified random selection in particular, where a strata from different ethnic and social groups is taken to form the sample.

Box 4.4 Checklist: reliability and validity

- Do two very similar tests on the same participants produce very similar results (consistency over time: test/ retest reliability)?
- Do two independent coders agree on a coding scheme (consistency over time: inter-coder reliability)?
- Are the items in a questionnaire of high quality (e.g. unambiguous questions – internal consistency)?
- Do the questions/items clustered together actually reflect the characteristic I want to examine (internal consistency)?
- What is the goal of my study (in terms of objectivity, generalizability)?
- Have I controlled for extraneous factors (via random selection and random assignment)?
- Do I have a control group (internal validity)?
- Have my sampling techniques (e.g. random selection) produced a representative sample (external validity)?
- Have I defined the main construct(s) of my study along dimensions that can be directly measured (construct validity)?
- Have I delineated the content domain (construct validity)?
- Can a test differentiate between concepts that are related and those that are not (convergent/discriminate validity)?
- Do the dimensions of a construct map onto the content domain (content validity)?
- Does a test on reading predict future outcomes with regard to reading development (criterion-related validity – predictive validity)?
- Do the measures taken from my test relate to measures taken from other tests that measure similar areas (criterion-related validity – concurrent validity)?

Summary

In this chapter we discussed pre-empirical considerations, namely, population and sampling issues as well as reliability and validity, which influence the development of a quantitative research design. Clarifying these issues is crucial for a solid foundation for quantitative research as an inquiry, regardless of the type of quantitative research (experimental or nonexperimental) and the routes (group comparisons or relationships between variables) we take to address the research questions. Clearly, a thorough consideration of the sampling, validity and reliability sets the stage for a rigorous research design which brings together the research questions and the methodology in a cohesive whole.

Notes

1   The concepts of popularity and friendship, although both relating to social skills, are conceptually distinct in that popularity refers to a wider notion of peer acceptance, whereas friendship involves interpersonal skills (e.g. communication, capacity for empathy, disclosure).
2   Qualitative research is also concerned with generalizing knowledge across contexts (Ercikan and Roth 2006).

References

Aliaga, M. and Gunderson, B. (2002) *Interactive Statistics*, 2nd edn. Upper Saddle River, NJ: Prentice Hall.

Bryman, A. (2004) *Social Research Methods*, 2nd edn. Oxford: Oxford University Press.

Cresswell, J. W. (2005) *Research Methods in Education*, 6th edn. London: Routledge.

Donmoyer, R. (2006) Take my paradigm ... please! The legacy of Kuhn's construct in educational research, *International Journal of Qualitative Studies in Education*, 19(1): 11–34.

Ercikan, K. and Roth, W.M. (2006) 'What good is polarizing research into qualitative and quantitative?', *Educational Researcher*, 35(5): 14–23.

Finn, J. and Achilles, C. (1990) 'Answers and questions about class size: a statewide experiment', *American Educational Research Journal*, 27(3): 557–77.

Gardner, H. (1999) *Intelligence Reframed: Multiple Intelligences for the 21st Century*. New York: Basic Books.

Johnson, B. and Christensen, L. (2004) *Educational Research: Quantitative, Qualitative, and Mixed Approaches*, 2nd edn. Boston, MA: Pearson Education.

Kaplan, A. (1964) *The Conduct of Inquiry: Methodology for Behavioral Science*. San Francisco: Chandler Publishing.

Muijs, D. (2004) *Doing Quantitative Research in Education with SPSS*. London: Sage.

Smith, B. (2003) 'Ontology', in L. Floridi (ed.) *Blackwell Guide to the Philosophy of Computing and Information*. Oxford: Blackwell.

Sperle. P. A., Ottenbacher, K. J., Braun, S. L., Lane, S. J. and Nochajski, S. (1997) 'Equivalence reliability of the functional independence measure for children (WeeFIM) administration methods', *American Journal of Occupational Therapy*, 51(1): 35–41.

Trochim, W. M. (2006) 'Nonprobability sampling', www.socialresearchmethods.net/kb/sampnon.php, accessed 23 October 2009.

Part II
Conceptualizing and Planning Research in Education

Research Questions and Research Design 5

Denis Gleeson

Chapter Outline

Introduction

This chapter sets the scene for conceptualizing and planning research in education. It focuses on issues relating to the formulation of research questions, and their role in constructing a conceptual framework (or over-arching theory) that influences the research design. It addresses the ways in which research questions and problems influence research planning, the deployment of research methods and the outcomes of educational research. There is a danger in seeing theory as separate from research design that affects the quality and impact of education research. This is partly influenced by the pragmatics of getting the research methods right and partly by scepticism about 'grand theory' and its relationship with practice in education. The notion of 'fitness for purpose' between research questions and the way they shape research design and practice is a key element of this chapter. It provides insight into the dialectical nature of the relationship between research questions and research design as a first step in *doing* research.

By the end of this chapter, you should be able to:

- identify the research questions you are trying to answer
- understand how the questions you ask influence the conceptual and methodological approach you adopt
- understand the iterative connection between theory and method in research design
- recognize that the outcomes of your research, in terms of findings, data analysis and conclusions, are strongly influenced by the formative thought processes that run through your research work

The Changing Context of Educational Research

In recent years, there has been a widespread debate about the purpose and quality of educational research. Much of the debate has focused on the failure of research to inform and help improve practice in education and education policy. This has led to further criticism of the scope and nature of educational research (whether it is too broad or too narrow), its connections with the social sciences (is it too inward-looking, uncritical and policy dominated), whether it constitutes a discipline or a field of inquiry and whether it is rigorous enough. Running parallel with such scrutiny are deeper questions concerning the purpose of educational research: whether it is *on*, *with* or *for* education policy and practice and what is its critical function in relation to cognate disciplines of the social sciences?

These and other issues capture something of the complexity of educational research among its key stakeholders – parents, learners, professionals, government, employers, practitioners, academics, community and other bodies – all of whom have different expectations of achieving improvement in education. Whatever position individual researchers may take on this issue, it is as well to recognize the contested nature of education research, as this has a bearing on the contexts in which education research takes place and the research questions we pose. Far from viewing this as a problem to be overcome, it is an opportunity for educational research to be innovative in and around contradictions between policy and practice through which new insights and solutions may flourish. This suggests that education research does not operate in a vacuum and is value-laden. Though this has major implications for doing educational research, it is also not a problem to be overcome but rather one that informs the context in which reflexive research is conducted. What is meant by reflexive research is how well the researcher 'tells the story' of the processes that went into the research, including the conclusions and outcomes. Telling this story starts at the beginning rather than at the end of the research process and involves the following questions:

- Why am I doing research (the existential and pragmatic question)?
- What is the problem I want to address and why?
- How is my research to be constructed?
- What approach will give my research credibility and authority?
- What is it worth saying, to whom and for what purpose?
- What are the social, cultural and contextual factors that produce research?
- To what extent will the research empower those involved?

In this chapter, I approach these questions through a range of preparatory *thought processes*, which impact on the way you approach the design of your own research. However, before getting started, it is worth noting Gorard and Taylor's (2004: 16) warning against seeing methods as the main starting point of research:

> Students have been heard to exclaim before deciding on a topic and research questions that they intend to use 'qualitative' methods of data collection or analysis, or that they are committed to the idea of a questionnaire [. . .] Don't fit your proposed study to your favourite approach (a case of the cart pulling the horse), and then try to disguise this as philosophical, rather than a methodological decision. This is why all researchers need some knowledge of all methods.

To think first about research methods as a way of addressing the topic and second about developing a perspective or questioning approach is a temptation for the beginning researcher and an easy trap to fall into. Beginning researchers should aim 'to attain the eyes of the artist, for it is art that teaches the sensitivity of being attentive to significances that normally remain uncelebrated' (Ruddock 1991: 106).

Doing Educational Research: First Thoughts

Central to the journey of doing research is the process of designing a study that is clear in its purposes and with the methods necessary to investigate them. The study will need to begin by stating with clarity the topics and issues which require investigation. Why is the research needed? What are the concerns facing policy-makers and practitioners, learners and parents? And, what are the gaps in our knowledge? Reading the background literature in the appropriate fields of study will enable you, as a researcher, to develop the conceptual and analytical frameworks needed to give the study shape and focus. So too will your social and professional experience of the field involved. Together, the originating concerns and the conceptual frameworks enable the formulation of research questions and hypotheses that are the prerequisite for a study with clarity and focus.

Though the process is not clear-cut and there are no formulaic procedures, and despite the tendency to confuse research design with *method* and '*what works*', there is an art, craft and science element to the serendipity principles involved. As we shall observe the research questions drive the process of research design and investigation to provide the evidence to test hypotheses and the methods which are appropriate to the investigation.

A precursor to doing educational research requires us to understand what constitutes the complexity of its nature and purpose as a:

- field of enquiry drawing on different disciplines, theories and traditions in and beyond the social sciences
- multidisciplinary field which combines quantitative, qualitative, documentary and related perspectives
- field that focuses on pedagogy, policy and practice
- contested and value-oriented terrain;
- multifaceted discipline that serves different audiences
- differentiated domain ('from birth to grave')
- process and outcome, which are related
- domain that is socially, culturally and historically located

The principles involved in investigating research problems, formulating research questions and constructing a research design are many and diverse. The process involves more than just method and constitutes, as Ruddock (1991) argues, an art as much as a science. Denzin and Lincoln (2000) take the analogy further by suggesting that the multiple thought processes involved can be viewed as a 'trade' in which research design becomes a form of *bricolage* and the researcher *bricoleur* (2000: 3):

> A bricoleur is a 'jack of all trades' or a kind of do it yourself person. The bricoleur produces a bricolage, that is, a pieced together close knit set of practices that provide solutions to a problem in a concrete fashion. The solution (bricolage) which is the result of the bricoleur's method is an (emergent) construction.

What problem, whose problem?

What constitutes a research problem should not be confused with 'social problems' or providing answers to 'problems' posed by politicians, policy-makers, government, big business, pressure groups or those in power. Whose problem one might ask? This is not to deny that social and economic problems exist or that research should not address real-world issues. Rather, it is to understand that the 'making and taking of problems' is not a disinterested process at any level of research, big or small. How the researcher addresses what constitutes his or her research problem, and the thought processes involved, strongly influence the autonomy and integrity of what is said. Without transparent agreement-making between sponsors (e.g. school, government agency, religious body) and researchers, the kind of autonomy and independence expected of critical social science research may become compromised. However, as Silverman (2001: 7) ironically notes, 'by beginning from a clearly defined social science perspective, we can later address such social problems with considerable force and persuasiveness'.

The initial thought processes involved in identifying a research problem and designing a research plan are many and diverse. They involve a combination of the following:

- asking questions, hunch-making and posing hypotheses
- exploring the significance and rationale of a proposed study: 'for whom and why?'
- theorizing the study in its historical and contemporary context
- examining how the study builds on existing knowledge in the field, including literature reviews and other sources
- testing ideas about the use of appropriate research methods for data collection and analysis
- considering ethical dimensions including participant involvement in the research, use and outcomes of the research
- reflecting on the research role and how it is perceived by the researcher as a creative process: as an art, craft or science

What constitutes a researchable problem is influenced by a complex dialectical process linking the researcher's identity, position and experience with their understanding of themselves, their work and relationship with society. This relationship is both an individual and social one involving the researcher in different roles as a student, practitioner, parent and member of a community, that structure forms of social interaction that predispose the researcher to an interest in what is happening in society. As an extension of this process the *sociological imagination* that drives the research process is sensitive to historical, political, cultural and contextual issues that surface in relation to rights, principles of social justice and the needs of people in society.

According to Mills (1959: 14–17), what constitutes a researchable problem is steeped in understanding the relationship between 'personal troubles and public issues'. For Mills the *sociological imagination* constitutes a form of practical reasoning that influences the way social problems are conceptualized or theoretically understood. Personal or private troubles relate to the individual's biography, experience and actions whereas public issues transcend the local context that form part of the larger structure of social, historical and economic life:

consider unemployment, when in a city of 100,000 only one man is unemployed that is his personal trouble, and for its relief we properly look to the character of the man, his skills and his immediate opportunities. But when in a nation of 50 million employees, 15 million men are unemployed that is an issue, and we may not hope to find its solution within the range of opportunities open to any one individual. The very structure of opportunities has collapsed. Both the correct statement of the problem and the range of possible solutions require us to consider the economic and political institutions of society, and not merely the personal situation and character of a scatter of individuals.

(Mills 1959: 15)

The contemporary relevance of this example contributes to the thought processes of research design mentioned earlier. The first concerns how the researcher defines and understands the particular and general aspects of the *problem* to which the research questions relate. The second draws attention to the neglected ways in which the researcher's identity and experience are culturally bound up in the biographical, historical and social structures that interconnect the 'researcher with the researched'. All too often the failure of educational research is that it weighs too heavily on one side or the other of the so-called 'structure' or 'agency' divide. It focuses either too much, for example, on the 'micro politics' of the school and classroom or the 'macro politics' of policy formation without a reference to what Bourdieu (1999) calls a relational analysis of the two.

According to McCulloch (2004) both the public and private spheres engage in what Habermas refers to as 'mutual infiltration' and 'reciprocal permeation' (see Habermas 1992: 145–51). This again returns us to the question of who research is *for* – 'in, with or for society' – and what is the relationship between the *particular* (context) and the *general* (bigger picture) in doing educational research. Ranson (2008: 3) provides a narrative example of how he addressed this in his own research:

In my study of governing bodies, I sought to clarify three layers of reality that I wished to research. In the study the research defined the object of civil society to be a social reality as important as the more observable characteristics of school governing bodies.

1. The *school governing body* itself: its composition, practices, structures and cultural codes. The tasks of such research drew upon the language and purposes of education administration; what were the powers, roles and responsibilities of governing bodies, and what contribution did they make to the task of improving school performance;
2. The *local community*: its social capital and relationship to the school as a public institution. The task of research at this level drew upon the languages and purposes of public management: the extent of authority, trust and legitimacy of a public service;
3. *Civil society*: the role of volunteer citizens and their relationship to professional knowledge. Research here draws on the language of political science of the relationship of public services to democratic participation.

The nature of the relationship between the specific object of a study, for example the context of the school curriculum, pedagogy or governance, and how it is situated in wider social relations of education, economy and society is contested and will be followed up in the sections that follow.

Starting Points

A starting point in the process of formulating research questions and the research design is to identify the object of the study and the issues that define the focus of the research. While it is relatively easy to pick from a wide range of topics that may interest us, it is more difficult to identify one that is researchable even within our own sphere of professional experience. Though prospective researchers usually have a good idea about a topic, for example in relation to the busyness (*habitus*) of their classroom or workplace, they are not often aware of and receptive to its problematics. A precondition of practitioner-based research is for the professional to become temporarily a stranger in their own institution or workplace, to allow themselves the distance required to reflect and see things from different perspectives (Ruddock 1991).

Identifying a suitable topic for research initially appears to be a straightforward matter. However, beginning researchers often have a tendency to define their topic too broadly and seek to find causal explanations for major issues such as crime, unemployment, racism, truancy or underachievement or 'how the mind works'. While laudable, such explanations are beyond the scope of the lone researcher, argues Silverman (2001: 5): 'As I tell my students your aim should be to say "a lot about a little (problem)". This means avoiding the temptation to say "a lot about a lot"'. The significance of Silverman's comments alerts us to certain pragmatic and theoretical issues that guide the research planning process. These include being selective about the topic in hand, understanding what is manageable in terms of time and resources and identifying/sharpening the focus of the research. This involves a questioning that addresses why this topic is significant and to whom (see Box 5.1). Such initial questioning shapes further thought processes about what constitutes the nature of the *problem* to which the research is addressed.

Box 5.1 Why formulate research questions?

- Set the scope and parameters of your study.
- Offer a framework for the literature review.
- Guide epistemological questions about the nature of knowledge.
- Assist in the construction of a research design.
- Guide decisions about research methods.
- Structure the analysis of data and the writing up.

The process of formulating research questions commences with identifying the topic and issues that constitute the object of a study. This involves defining and identifying the research problems to which the research questions are addressed. Though there is no set formula, the following provide insight into some of the thought processes involved in formulating research questions and constructing the research design in particular, and justifying the significance of research in general.

- Define the research topic and problem under consideration. How it is situated and understood in the available research literature and policy-practice debates?
- Offer a rationale for its significance and importance as a researchable area.
- Distinguish between research purpose, aims, objectives, topics, questions and hypotheses.
- Assess the ways in which a problem can be researched using different methodologies derived from the research questions and hypotheses.
- Consider the logistics of testing different theories and methods and justify your choice.
- Develop initial ideas for designing and piloting a micro study.
- Assess the contribution of the study to and for the advancement of knowledge, policy and practice.

The phases of getting the research started

Formulating research questions is a process that is iterative and dialectical in nature. It involves many theoretical and practical considerations (see Box 5.2). To make this task manageable, I break down the process into three phases; each phase involves a series of exercises that will, hopefully, assist you in starting your research on sound ground.

Box 5.2 Things to consider when formulating research questions

- State the questions with clarity (define the key terms).
- Be realistic with regard to whether the research questions can be researched, considering the timeframe of your study and the resources available.
- Situate them in the context of existing research to allow you to make connections between theory and research.
- Justify their importance in terms of theory, policy and practice.
- Ensure the overall coherence of the research questions (how well they sit together) to help you articulate the core argument of your study.
- Balance the questions on a narrow-broad continuum.

Phase 1: how to set the parameters of your research topic and formulate research questions

- Draft several short statements outlining your initial ideas for a research project and discuss them with your supervisor or colleagues.
- On the basis of their responses, write a one-paragraph introduction to your study.
- Add another two paragraphs setting out some of the key research questions relating to the topic and focus of study identified in the first paragraph.
- Locate one or two texts and journals to which your study connects. Compare and contrast the way in which different researchers discuss their research approach.
- Write up your initial thoughts and conclusions and return to your supervisor, fellow students and colleagues to discuss them.

When you have completed this exercise and evaluated the responses, make some further brief notes guided by the following supplementary questions. These will feed into the next phases discussed in the chapter.

- What is known and what are the gaps in our knowledge about the issue or topic you want to research?
- What ideas (theories, hunches, hypotheses) can be drawn upon to explain or interpret the issue?
- What kind of framework or set of ideas and questions will enable you to further explain the issue you have chosen to study?
- What is the policy-practice relevance of the research?
- Why is the research needed: for whom and why?

When addressing these questions bear in mind the perennial critiques of educational research – either too broad or too narrow and being largely atheoretical.

Phase 2: initial plan for a study

Following up Phase 1, you are asked to advise a colleague who has been requested to undertake a study in their own school. The study involves obtaining the views of school staff on the effectiveness of personalised learning (or a topic of your choice) recently introduced in the school. Its introduction has raised controversy among staff concerning the relationship between formal and nonformal learning, how it is assessed, additional workload and lack of preparation time and staff training. Discuss how the researcher should design an initial plan for a study, by considering the following questions:

- What is the nature of the research brief and why is it significant to the school?
- What is the nature of the problem which the study addresses?
- What obstacles do you envisage in undertaking the research and how will these be overcome?
- How will the main aims and objectives be communicated to participants and how will they be involved in the study?
- How will the study build on existing knowledge and contribute to outcomes envisaged in the research brief?
- What theories and hypotheses will be tested during the course of the study?

Phase 3: articulating the scope of a study

Following up on the two previous phases, write out the thought processes involved in articulating the scope, focus, research questions and research design of your project. Do this by filling in the blanks to these lead questions.

> The study addresses the following topic (*name the working title and topic*). It explores a number of research questions (*state three of them*) that address a particular issue or problem (*state problem or issue*) that forms the focus or basis of the study (*state the focus and rationale*). The focus of the study is identified in a range of literature sources and research studies (*state two or three examples*). The study draws on a number of theoretical approaches (*briefly identify and explain*) that inform or guide the main methods of data collection and analysis (*provide examples and rationale*). Some of the ethical issues and any problems I envisage in undertaking the research (*state briefly*) including envisaged outcomes of the research (*provide example*).
>
> (Adapted from Cresswell 2003: 127)

Once you have completed these three phases, you should be in a position to flesh out a more detailed research plan that you can discuss with a mentor, tutor or colleagues. Remember that

---

Box 5.3 An overview of getting started

1   Background (the justification and need for the research)

- Why is the research needed: what issues are emerging from practice or gaps in policy, knowledge and research literature, that suggest the need for the research?
- What is the policy-practice relevance of the study?
- What are the purposes and *aims* of the study?

2   Frameworks of analysis (review of knowledge and conceptual development)

- Develop an analytical framework which clarifies the object(s) of the study as well as the ideas and concepts which are judged to be most relevant to interpret and explain the particular problem or issue that has been chosen for study.
- What is known and what are the gaps in knowledge and experience of the issue?
- What ideas and theories or concepts are currently drawn upon to interpret and explain the issue?

3   Research design (constructing the focus and design of an investigation)

- What are the principal *research questions*?
- What *design* will best address these questions?
- What kind of *knowledge* (e.g. qualitative/quantitative/documentary/visual) is needed (epistemology)?
- What kind of *investigation* will develop the knowledge/evidence to answer the questions?
- What *methods* are necessary to gather the appropriate information (e.g. documents, questionnaires, interviews, observation, diaries, visual)?
- What is the *timetable* and resource(s) for the research?

---

there is no set order to how you set out your research design so long as it interconnects different aspects of the points and issues raised so far in the chapter.

Theorizing Research: Theory as a Practical Activity

The nature of the relationship between theory and research is interconnected with the dimensions of questioning and problem-posing discussed so far. It is part and parcel of explaining the nature and significance of a field of study that offers a perspective or a way of looking at a research issue or problem. While theory is often seen as irrelevant to practice, the approach I take here is one of viewing theory as a form of practice, with the two being inseparable.

The term 'theory' is best understood as an over-arching term that often holds different interpretations among qualitative and quantitative researchers. However, adherence to a particular 'grand theory' (e.g. constructionist, cognitive, Marxist, postmodern, structural functionalist) may appear daunting to the beginning researcher. It often distracts attention away from identifying a researchable topic in the same way that reaching for the nearest methods manual can. Thomas (1997) in his paper 'What's the use of theory?', outlines four uses of theory: as thinking and reflection; as tighter or looser hypotheses or hunches; as explanations for adding to knowledge in different fields; and as formally expressed statements of science. This view regarding the uses of theory is compatible with understanding theory as a lens through which the researcher plays with ideas, hunches and hypotheses or ways of looking that are precursors of research design. Theory as a practical activity is also akin to a kaleidoscope through which many different shapes and colours can be simultaneously observed at the same time (Silverman 2000). With this in mind, theory as a practical activity is articulated as a

- form of understanding and an explanation of complex and often invisible variables and processes (e.g. 'the hidden curriculum')
- kaleidoscope that takes into account different shapes and colours (e.g. meaning and understanding)
- lens through which social issues are understood (e.g. racism, feminism, class)
- set of concepts that define and explain often diverse or contradictory phenomena;
- proposition about the relationship between things, a relational concept;
- way of making sense of the world and a way of testing research, data and theory

As a concluding remark, I would like to stress the danger in seeing theory as separate from the thought processes of a research design and how a research problem is constructed within and through the reflexive experiences of the researcher. Contrary to popular conception, asking questions, problem-posing and theory construction are all part of a practical way of thinking that, in Denscombe's view, provides 'propositions about the relationship between things' (1988: 240).

Summary

In this chapter, I discussed issues regarding the identification of research topics, formulation of research questions and their influence in constructing a research design. One of my aims has been to offer a balanced view on the importance of theory in doing research, stressing the practical contribution of theory to the thought processes involved in research, especially at the 'getting started' phases. Moreover, I offered initial theoretical views and practical examples to illuminate the thought processes involved in developing the research topic and research questions of a study, capturing the tension between theory and early decisions about choosing research methods.

Acknowledgement

The author gratefully acknowledges the input and contribution of Warwick colleagues involved in the Graduate Foundations and Advanced Research Methods Programme, in particular Dimitra Hartas, Steve Strand and Stewart Ranson, with whom he works in close collaboration.

References

Bourdieu, P. (1999) *The Logic of Practice*. Cambridge: Polity Press
Cresswell, J. W. (2003) *Research Design: Qualitative, Quantitative and Mixed Methods Approach*. London: Sage.
Denscombe, M. (1998) *The Good Research Guide*. Buckingham: Open University Press.
Denzin, N. and Lincoln, Y. (2000) *Handbook of Qualitative Research*. London: Sage.

Gorard, S. and Taylor, C. (2004) *Combining Methods in Educational and Social Research*. Maidenhead: Open University Press.

Habermas, J. (1992) *The Structural Transformation of the Public Sphere*. London: Policy.

McCulloch, G. (2004) *Documentary Research in Education, History and the Social Sciences*. London: Routledge.

Mills, C. W. (1959) *The Sociological Imagination*. Harmondsworth: Pelican.

Ranson, S. (2008) 'Researching schools governance: a case example, unpublished graduate research training programme, University of Warwick.

Ruddock, J. (1991) *Innovation and Change: Developing Involvement and Understanding in Education*. Buckingham: Open University Press.

Silverman, D. (2001) *Interpreting Qualitative Data*. London: Sage

Thomas, G. (1997) 'What's the use of theory?' *Harvard Educational Review*, 67(1): 75–104.

6 Doing a Literature Review

Dimitra Hartas

Chapter Outline

Introduction

A literature review is an integral part of a research process. It involves a review of relevant research studies and other documents (e.g. policy or historical documents), and offers a critical analysis and synthesis of previous research work. A good literature review brings together diverse perspectives, enhances the quality of an inquiry and has the potential to extend scholarship. Through a literature review, we gain numerous theoretical and methodological benefits in terms of becoming aware of others' work and identifying existing research gaps, which in turn enable us to develop, extend and calibrate original research ideas. Furthermore, a critical review can stimulate and generate new perspectives and contribute to the advancement of knowledge through a continuity in scholarship. Shulman (1999) describes the process of generating new knowledge based on prior scholarship and research as 'generativity'.

In educational research, there is a growing concern about placing too much emphasis on the methodology (see 'methodolatry' in Chapter 1) at the expense of developing a thorough understanding of the field and generating new perspectives and theory. Boote and Beile (2005: 12) observed a 'broader culture of education research that artificially distinguishes between literature review, on the one hand, and methods and analytic techniques, on the other'. The separation between theory and methodology has implications for educational research, in which, due to its multidisciplinary nature and diversity in perspectives, shared knowledge is hardly established. Moreover, critics of educational research have pointed out that for research to be useful and relevant, it has to be cumulative and 'build on and learn from prior research and scholarship on the topic' (Boote and Beile, 2005: 5). These criticisms may be explained by the compartmentalization of theory and methods, and superficiality in our approach to understanding educational theories. Conducting a rigorous and systematic review may counteract these criticisms by inculcating the norms and practices of an academic culture, with its emphasis on the analytic, the intellectual, the universal and the theoretical (Labaree 2003).

Although the current volume is devoted to research methods, in this chapter the purpose and function of literature reviews are defended, and the process of doing a review is discussed along the lines of locating and accessing sources, analysing and synthesizing information and generating new perspectives.

By the end of this chapter, you should be able to:

- understand the multiple purposes and function of a literature review;
- describe the stages of a review – i.e. getting started – accessing materials and resources, organizing notes – and the main phase which involves the writing up (introduction, main body, conclusion)
- consider and apply the steps involved in engaging critically with the reviewed studies

Why do a Literature Review?

A critical review of a literature is likely to stimulate a 'progressive problem shift' that yields new perspectives regarding the research topic, with more explanatory and predictive powers than those offered by existing perspectives (Strike and Posne 1983: 356–7). Commenting on the importance of a literature review, Lather (1999) stressed that a synthetic review should serve a critical role in gatekeeping and policing, and lead to a new productive work, rather than merely mirroring the research in a field.

Currently research training in education has placed little emphasis on the literature review, which is often perceived as a mere summary of findings from previous studies. It is not uncommon for doctoral students in education to conduct the literature review *after* they have decided on the research questions and methodological approaches for their research. The increasing emphasis on research methodology leaves little space for supporting students to develop systematic approaches towards a literature review. In educational research, with its 'messy and complex nature', doing a thorough literature review is particularly important to understanding educational ideas through a synthesis and an analysis of research designs and findings from existing research (Boote and Beile 2005: 3).

Before embarking on a research project, we have to prepare the ground, and a big part of this preparation is to review prior research in the field of specialization. A literature review is supposed to set both the theoretical and methodological foundations of research by:

- clarifying the issues under consideration
- developing new perspectives that have a better exploratory and predictive power, and a capacity to shift previous ones (generative capacity of research)
- setting the principles that characterize good theoretical work, namely, consistency, elegance, parsimony and fruitfulness (Strike and Posner 1983)

With regard to these principles, 'consistency' refers to the conceptual thread that runs through the research questions/aims, literature review, methodology and results in a study. 'Parsimony' refers to using language in a succinct manner, avoiding repetition. 'Elegance' is reflected in the way language is used to clarify concepts and produce an output that flows logically, offering clear and well-reasoned arguments. Finally, a literature review has to be 'fruitful' in producing conclusions that shed light on key issues in the field of study, and in identifying the strengths and limitations of previous research.

A literature review fulfills multiple purposes. Some of these are to:

- identify limitations in previous studies and existing gasps in knowledge, and set the boundaries/scope of the investigation by delineating what has been learned and accomplished in a particular field and what gaps still exist
- offer a theoretical framework for a research study by setting the context of the study, delineating and justifying the research topic and forming research questions (marking the area of investigation)
- assist in narrowing down the research topic and refining the research question(s), justifying the significance of the research topic in terms of theory, policy and practice
- assist in making and justifying decisions about the choice of research methodologies
- situate research within the wider evidence-based context to analyse and synthesize our findings in ways that provide new perspectives (generative capacity)
- set the framework within which new findings are placed and discussed, as well as the implications of a study
- provide a sense of continuity in scholarship by drawing links between the old and new knowledge; identifying areas that require further research; and extending knowledge by delineating emerging research issues and trends
- help us to develop an international perspective by bringing together studies that are conducted within diverse social and political/policy contexts

Reflecting on these purposes, it is apparent that a review of the literature takes place at different phases during the course of research. At the initial stages, a review of current research studies helps us locate the field and identify the main studies and theoretical and methodological frameworks. The next stage of a review is concerned with methodological issues, focusing on qualitative, quantitative and mixed methodologies, to gain an understanding about the range of methodologies used by other educational researchers. With quantitative research, a review of existing studies justifies a priori views that may underpin the formulation of hypotheses through deductive reasoning. For qualitative studies, a review can assist in developing a framework for thematic analyses of the qualitative data, illustrating the process of generating knowledge through induction.

Research methods do not operate in a vacuum and a systematic literature review can set the framework for a good methodology (Mullins and Kiley 2002). A review enables us to:

- elucidate/refine research questions
- construct and justify the research design by referring to designs employed in previous research
- develop the instruments for data collection (the development of items for a survey or an interview schedule).

Towards the end of a study, a review of the literature can assist us in locating the findings within the wider research context, and drawing implications by delineating the continuity in scholarship.

Box 6.1 The purposes of a literature review

- Distinguish between what has been done and what needs to be done.
- Identify the strengths and the innovative aspects of previous research, and the patterns and trends that contribute to a collective understanding.
- Identify the topics/areas that are important for understanding educational research.
- Gain a new perspective and generate new knowledge (e.g. theoretical models, conceptual frameworks).
- Establish the context within which the research study is located.
- Rationalize and justify the significance of the research topic.
- Familiarize yourself with the terminology relevant to educational research.
- Understand diverse theoretical and methodological approaches taken by previous research.
- Place your findings in the wider research context (Hart 1999).

Why do a Review of International Literature?

Educational research has become internationalized, and this trend is reflected in the increasing number of cross-cultural studies in education, and the large number of novice and established researchers who conduct research in international contexts. Although international studies contribute to our understanding of cross-cultural educational research, issues such as translating, synthesizing and, most importantly, interpreting international research findings require further consideration. The absence of a shared cultural experience makes interpretation of research challenging. Reviewing international research studies requires us to be aware of the variability of the cultural interpretations and the culture-specific approaches to meaning construction.

To engage with research in international contexts, we need to develop the tools, the translation methods and insight necessary for accessing and interpreting knowledge in non-western contexts, and capture the many layers of meaning. A review of international literature is likely to support the analysis and interpretation of data collected in non-western contexts by familiarizing ourselves with the cultural conceptions, codes of reference and assumptions, to enable a critical stance towards cross-cultural evidence and scholarship at an international level.

Barna (1998) summarized the challenges encountered during conducting and reviewing cross-cultural research. These include:

- assumptions of similarities
- language differences that go beyond language competency and mere translation – the pragmatics of language and social/cultural knowledge
- nonverbal misinterpretations;
- preconceptions and stereotypes
- lack of shared cultural assumptions

These issues should be considered when we review international research or conduct research within international contexts because they are likely to influence both theoretical and methodological aspects of the research.

The Phases of a Literature Review

There are two phases to conducting a literature review, namely, the 'getting started' phase, which involves database searches and the organization of materials and notes, and the 'main phase', which is the writing.

The 'getting started' phase

Although how we start a review depends on our prior knowledge of the field and prior experience of a research-related, academic writing, a good starting point is to look at some examples of literature review, systematic EPPI reviews in particular (see http://eppi.ioe.ac.uk). This offers a good introduction to the nature and requirements of doing a review of research studies and other documents. After this initial exposure, we may take the following steps:

1   Think about the key concepts/themes that reflect or map onto your research topic. This will establish the relevance of the research studies you plan to review to your research topic.

2   Define the terms used in your research questions as they emerge from the research topic. This allows you to develop a list with key words for the initial search.

3   Use the key terms to access resources/databases: you can do the searching by subject or author. Locate key resources and indexes for a subject area. Also, use catalogue key word search by typing the topic and literature review – for example, if the topic is language development then type 'child language development and literature review'.

4   Determine the scope of the literature review in terms how extensive the search will be (coverage). A good strategy is to start with key concepts/themes that are of direct interest to our research and then expand to include other relevant topics. This strategy has the advantage of keeping the search focused in terms of narrowing down the topic and calibrating the research questions.

5   Locate the first key articles to establish the initial bibliographical framework before expanding to include other relevant studies.

6   Review up-to-date studies, preferably those published in referred journals (primary sources/original research). You may also include secondary sources such as books or internet sites (with caution!) or older landmark studies that have made an important contribution to education and social sciences.

7   Take a multidisciplinary approach by reading studies located within other disciplines. The nature of topics in education and child development require us to read research from other related fields such as psychology, sociology and the political sciences.

8   Take care to record the references systematically and accurately as you search. This saves you valuable time and reduces the possibility of plagiarism arising from misquoting or not referencing material properly, especially text that is taken verbatim from source (software programmes such as Endnote can assist with this task).

9   Organize your work and maximize efficiency by keeping detailed written notes as you read the material. After you have reviewed a good number of studies and made notes, organize the notes by forming thematic clusters that group the notes according to the main themes/topics of your review. It is important to delineate the criteria that you use to structure your work with clarity.

10   Last but not least, good time management is crucial in terms of helping you to stay in control and carry out work that is thoroughly and comprehensively done.

Sources

To do a systematic search of sources and materials, it is important to compile a systematic database by searching journals, specialist websites and 'citation tracking' (i.e. checking the reference lists in relevant reports) (see Endnote: 'A Selection of Databases in Education-related Fields'). The type and extent of searches depends on the nature of the research in the area of interest. It is advisable to combine different methods of searching, including

- electronic database searching
- hand-searching of key journals
- searching specialist websites
- general search engines on the internet such as 'Google' and 'Google Scholar'
- personal contacts, authors and experts in the field (http://eppi.ioe.ac.uk)

Tips for doing searches

During searches, you may consider the following tips:

- a well-defined research question and well-justified inclusion/exclusion criteria are necessary to enable you carry out successful searches
- identification of the disciplines involved in a research topic may assist in deciding on the types of databases (e.g. ERIC –an educational research database; Psychlit – a psychological database; or sociological databases)
- a combination of key words and thesaurus terms is useful when setting the conceptual parameters of a construct
- a balance between sensitivity (i.e. finding all articles in a topic area) and specificity (i.e. finding only relevant articles) is crucial to retain depth and breadth
- words such as AND, OR and NOT should be used carefully (e.g. for a wide search use OR, to reduce/specify the search use AND, to make it very specific use NOT)

The main phase

This phase involves the writing of the review, stressing the importance of applying evaluative criteria to engage critically with the material (see 'Evaluative criteria of a Literature Review' later in this chapter). Typically, a literature review is structured along the following lines.

1 Introduction: it is useful to start a review with an introduction where you present the main topics and offer a justification regarding their importance. The purpose of the introduction is to introduce the main topic of the review, justify its importance and signpost the content by stating the key ideas/themes upon which the review is based. In other words, an introduction sets the scene and offers a 'roadmap' for the reader.
2 Main body: this should be organized around relevant themes/topics. Within each theme, you should present all the relevant ideas and ensure coherence in the development of arguments (see Figure 6.1). It is crucial to avoid a merely descriptive account. A critical engagement with the materials involve the capacity to
    - compare/contrast different views
    - synthesize diverse pieces of information
    - identify points of contest or clashing worldviews, consensus or lack of it on a topic, and reconcile conflicting accounts

- capture the major debates in the field
- make your own interpretations and back them up with research findings
- engage in a critical appraisal of the materials throughout.

3 Conclusion: this offers a summary of the key points in a review by drawing together the most important themes. The final sentences should reflect the insights gained from the review (the key findings/themes that emerge from the reviewed studies). If the review is merely a descriptive account then it would be difficult to deduce the key issues that define a research topic. The following questions may assist in structuring the conclusion:

- What are the gaps in knowledge (develop questions for further research)?
- What are the strengths and the innovative aspects/dimensions of previous research studies?
- What are the theoretical and methodological limitations of the studies reviewed?
- What are the implications of current research findings in terms of theory, policy and practice?
- How does the review inform your research in terms of refining the research questions, assisting you with decisions about methodology, sharpening the focus of your research and justifying the importance of your research?

4 Reference list: present the references by following a convention (e.g. American Psychological Association (APA) or Harvard style).

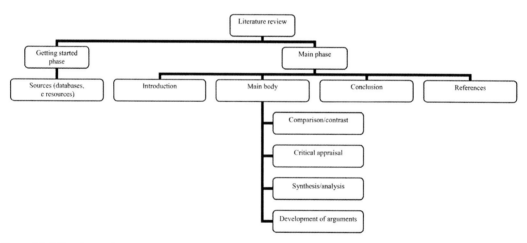

Figure 6.1 A literature review

Box 6.2 Tips on writing (e.g. constructing sentences/paragraphs and using headings)

- Organize a literature review along sections and subsections that are presented in a logical order to enable you to cluster ideas and themes together.
- The use of headings is important to assist you with a logical presentation of diverse and often complex material. Each section should focus on one theme or set of interrelated ideas to allow you discuss it in depth, rather than raising too many issues at once and treating them in a superficial manner.
- Each paragraph should contain a single idea/theme that is discussed by comparing/contrasting different views and approaches.
- Avoid having too many short paragraphs consisting of two or three sentences to ensure that the writing does not appear fragmented.

Box 6.3 Tips on the language use

- Avoid vague language by keeping the expression simple (e.g. short sentences) and clear.
- Avoid the use of jargon because it obscures meaning.
- Use language in ways that allow you to show analytical thinking and criticality (taking a critical and evaluative stance towards a perspective or an idea).

Box 6.4 A 'good' and a 'poor' literature review

A 'good' literature review:
- Takes an analytical approach towards evidence by 'unpicking' ideas/views.
- Is a synthesis of diverse pieces of information.
- Involves a critical analysis of the material to assess the meaningfulness and relevance of information.
- Offers a critical appraisal of the key issues.
- Is concise and clear.
- Captures the main debates in the field.
- Generates new knowledge and insights.
- Has a balanced breadth and depth.

A 'poor' literature review:
- Offers merely descriptive accounts of the main issues.
- Engages in a limited critical analysis and offers unsubstantiated personal views.
- Raises too many issues and treats them superficially ('glossing over' the key issues).
- Lacks clarity, direction and purpose.
- Does not make a clear and cohesive case by developing logical arguments.
- Presents themes/ideas in an arbitrary manner.
- Includes dated and irrelevant material.
- Makes inappropriate generalizations that cannot be supported with the evidence offered.
- Includes many secondary sources, and sources from the internet that are not peer reviewed.
- Includes a great deal of text taken verbatim without paraphrasing or interpreting it.
- Does not signpost clearly when paraphrasing or using text verbatim.
- Includes confusing referencing.
- Engages in limited interpretation of findings.

How to Write a Critical Literature Review

A factor that determines the success of a review is our capacity to go beyond simply summarizing studies and engage critically with the ideas presented. A good 'literature review should not be understood as merely an exhaustive summary of prior research'; it is rather 'a form of scholarship requiring a broad range of skills and knowledge' (Boote and Beileok 2005: 5). A critical engagement with previous research sustains the continuity of scholarship by building on others' work. Analysis and synthesis of previous research are prerequisites for scholarship in terms of identifying an interesting and timely topic for research and deciding upon 'fit for purpose' methodologies. LeCompte *et al.* comment that lack of an 'integrative and critical grounding in previous investigation' is likely to weaken a subsequent piece of research (2003: 124).

A critical review shows that we have approached existing research with insight and the capacity to

- compare/contrast and juxtapose findings and different theoretical and methodological approaches
- appraise critically by applying evaluative standards and criteria with reference to your own study
- analyse and synthesize findings in ways that permit new perspectives by drawing links between the research questions and aims, methodology and findings
- develop well-reasoned arguments

To make the process manageable, a critical literature review can be broken down into the steps shown in Table 6.1.

Table 6.1 The four steps towards a critical review of the literature

Compare and contrast	*Critical appraisal*	*Analysis and synthesis*	*Development of arguments*
Conceptual similarities and differences found in the: • research topics and aims of the studies selected for the review • theoretical frameworks (epistemology, paradigm) and rationale offered • research design, methodological approaches and sampling • data analyses procedures • research findings and implications.	Along the dimensions of: • coverage • suitability • quality/authority • relevance • currency/implications • up-to-date-ness • appropriateness of methodology	Offers the platform to: • identify research gaps • place the topic within the broader scholarly literature • articulate emerging issues • gain new perspectives or acknowledge a shift in the original perspective	To make a case by: • indicating a direction and a sense of purpose • clustering interrelated ideas • presenting ideas in a logical manner • using evidence to support the presented ideas • building a case that can be followed step by step

Note: although the four steps are depicted as occurring in a linear fashion, the process of a critical review is iterative and dialectical.

Step 1: compare/contrast

A comparison/contrast between ideas involves the identification of conceptual similarities and differences across a number of papers on the same or related research topics. This is a particularly useful technique when comparing different theoretical models to delineate their dimensions and offer a rationale as to why we adopt them to structure our review. Comparisons across studies may be organized along the conceptual similarities and differences found in the:

- research topics and aims of the studies selected for the review
- theoretical frameworks (epistemology, paradigm) and rationale
- research design, methodological approaches and sampling
- data analysis procedures
- research findings and implications

A comparison helps us to bring together important aspects from all the reviewed studies. Once you have identified and summarized the similarities and differences across research studies, you are ready to move to the next phase of writing, which is analytical/synthetic and evaluative. Literature reviews that stop at summarizing information across studies lack a critical analysis dimension. Analytical and evaluative writing is an integral component of a critical engagement with the summarized materials.

Step 2: a critical appraisal

A critical appraisal of research studies can be facilitated through the application of evaluative criteria. The evaluative criteria presented here, namely coverage, suitability, quality/authority, relevance, currency and up-to-date-ness, have been adapted from Bruce's typology (2001). In addition, Boote and Beileok (2005) stress the need for an appraisal of the methodology of the studies selected for a review.

Coverage, as an evaluative criterion, refers to how well a review covers the studies in the field of specialization, and offers a justification of the studies that are included and those that are excluded from the review. The coverage criterion enables a sharper and well-justified focus of the review in particular and the research study in general. A good review is thorough in terms of covering the field of a study. However, this does not mean that we should review every single study written in the area of specialization. Rather, it means that we are aware of the wider research in a field and have applied criteria to justify the inclusion/exclusion of studies.

Coverage also relates to the originality of the topic: the more original the topic the fewer the studies available for a review. In other words, the breadth of reviewing depends on the extent to which the topic of interest is researched. For under-researched topics, initial searches yield a small number of studies, requiring a widening of the search. When very little is written on a topic, Bruce (2001) suggests that analogous studies in similar fields should be sought. With a plethora of research on a topic, the focus should be on a specific aspect. In this case, you need to justify carefully why you focused on this aspect by identifying the key issues and their relevance to your research questions. Finally, when you explore a new area and have not decided the research topic, it is advisable to read widely before you set the parameters of a study.

The decision about the extent to which you need to be selective or comprehensive depends on the purpose and rationale of your study. It is important to balance the depth and breadth of the reviewed studies, and justify your decision about coverage because it is inherent in the justification of the research topic. Moreover, it is important to evaluate the validity of sources, especially internet-based sources, in terms of the extent to which they are authoritative and peer reviewed.

Moreover, the reviewed studies should be examined through the prism of suitability, quality/authority, relevance, currency and up-to-date-ness. Suitability refers to how well the reviewed studies suit the topic and aims of your research. The quality of the research studies is an important issue, in the light of an increasing criticism of educational research (see Chapter 1). Assuring the quality of the sources can be particularly challenging considering that an overwhelming amount of reviews and studies are posted on the internet, requiring you to distinguish studies that are peer reviewed and valid from those which are not.

Relevance is linked to how well the research questions have been formulated, and how clear the aims and the objectives of the research are. The process of formulating questions relies on a good review of existing studies, stressing the interdependence and the dialectical relationship between reading and synthesizing existing research and developing further research topics and questions.

Currency refers to the significance of the studies reviewed in terms of how influential they are in shaping theory, policy and practice. The notion of significance is debatable and difficult to judge in that some studies are more theory- than policy- or practice-orientated. However, being able to draw links between research findings and an educational policy and practice is important in that one of the criticisms of educational research is that it does not always translate into classroom practice.

The up-to-date-ness criterion refers to how recent a study is. This is particularly important for educational research where issues and debates in the field tend to gain momentum at a certain point.

Finally, a methodological appraisal involves the identification and appraisal of the main methodologies and research techniques used in the studies reviewed, mainly focusing on their advantages and limitations. It also addresses how well the literature review provides the theoretical framework to assist in the choice of methods. For example, new perspectives generated from the literature review may stimulate a paradigm shift, or introduce a new epistemology to frame the research design. Through a methodological appraisal, you will develop an appreciation of the ways in which researchers' methodological choices have affected the research findings by considering the strengths and weaknesses of the research methods. This may stimulate new methodologies and provide a justification about their appropriateness. As Boote and Beileok argue, 'researchers cannot appropriate sophisticated research methods if their understanding of the phenomena they are investigating is rudimentary and unsystematic' (2005: 10).

Step 3: an analysis and synthesis

Analytical writing involves 'teasing out' or 'deconstructing' ideas, asking questions about meaning, and interrogating its context and the factors that shape the process of meaning-making. Synthesizing findings from diverse sources, as Lather (1999) and Strike and Posner (1983) suggest, is likely to stimulate new perspectives by critically integrating and extending ideas, and capturing current debates and the contested nature of the issues under investigation. A synthesis of the findings from the reviewed studies may also offer a new explanatory framework by identifying gaps in your current knowledge and theorizing on the polyphony of the perspectives offered.

A good analysis and synthesis of a selected literature on a topic offer the platform to:

- distinguish what has been done in the field from what needs to be done
- place the topic or problem in the broader scholarly literature (e.g. the historical and policy context of the field)
- acquire subject-specific terminology
- articulate important issues relevant to the topic and the emerging variables
- gain a new perspective on the literature or acknowledge a shift in the perspective (Hart 1999)

The last point, gaining a new perspective, involves a conceptual shift, where different understandings about the topic of interest are synthesized to create new concepts. This process of extending existing concepts by formulating new ones is an important outcome of an analysis and synthesis of diverse research studies. Moreover, a good synthesis supports the interpretation of the findings of a review, and goes beyond the review itself. As such, the conclusions from a review are based on an accurate interpretation of diverse information as well as other types of knowledge, such as tacit practice knowledge and user experiences.

Step 4: the development of arguments

In a review, the development of well-reasoned arguments can be achieved by:

- showing a direction and a sense of purpose via the presentation of ideas in a logical manner where the reader can follow, step-by-step, the process of making a case and offering specific viewpoints
- presenting interrelated ideas/themes in ways that are supported by evidence from the reviewed studies
- presenting ideas/themes in a logical sequence with clarity and parsimony

The checklist in Box 6.5 brings together a number of questions that you need to ask as you do a literature review to ensure that you apply the evaluative criteria discussed in this chapter.

Box 6.5 Checklist: evaluative criteria towards a critical review of the literature

- What are the scope and relevance of the reviewed studies (coverage, relevance, currency)?
- Could the key topics have been approached more effectively from a different epistemological stance (e.g. interpretivist rather than postpositivist) (suitability, relevance, quality/authority)?
- What is the theoretical framework (e.g. developmental psychology, a sociological or feminist approach) that underpins the reviewed studies (coverage, suitability, relevance, quality/authority)?
- What are the methodological considerations (e.g. sampling, choice of research design, participants, statistical techniques used, modes of inquiry) of the reviewed studies (methodological appraisal, suitability, relevance, quality/authority)?
- What are the components of the author's argument? How is it constructed (relevance, quality/authority, purpose/direction)?
- What are the implications of the research findings (relevance, currency, significance)?
- Do the reviewed studies deal with timely issues in education (up-to-date-ness, relevance)?

Summary

This chapter has three aims: first, it stresses the important contribution of a literature review to offering a robust theoretical framework to a research study and to the continuity in scholarship. Secondly, it offers practical advice on the phases and the structure of a literature review, from getting started to organizing materials and notes and engaging with the writing. Thirdly, it focuses on how to engage in a critical analysis and appraisal of the material. A critical engagement with the reviewed studies can be quite challenging, and so we break down this process into four manageable steps that involve a comparison and contrasting of the materials; the application of evaluative criteria to facilitate a critical appraisal; an analysis and synthesis of ideas to form new perspectives; and, finally, the development of well-reasoned arguments.

Box 6.6 Checklist: doing a literature review

- Have I identified my research topic and the initial research questions?
- Have I defined the key terms?
- Have I produced a list with key words or phrases to use in search engines?
- Can I access databases and indexes to locate the studies I need?
- What is the scope of the literature review for my study? How broad or narrow should the search be?
- Have I found enough materials to make a start?
- Are they relevant and up-to-date?
- Have I organized the materials/sources properly?
- Have I produced an introduction that sets the scene, justifies the review and offers a 'roadmap' of what the review involves?
- Have I compared and contrasted different studies?
- Have I engaged critically with the selected studies?
- Have I produced a coherent synthesis of theoretical frameworks and findings by stating arguments and offering evidence to substantiate them?
- Do the conceptual clusters reflect the research questions of my study?
- What are the conclusions drawn? Do they fit with the introduction and the main body of the review?
- What new perspectives on the topic of interest have emerged?
- What limitations exist in the reviewed studies?
- In what ways has the review has been useful in setting the parameters for my study?
- Is the review written with the intended audience in mind?
- What is the overall fit between the literature review and my research? (Does my study intend to fill the emerging gaps?)

References

Barna, L. (1998) 'Stumbling blocks in intercultural communication', in M. J. Bennett (ed.) *Basic Concepts in Intercultural Communication: Selected Readings.* Yarmouth, ME: Intercultural Press.

Boote, D. N., and Beileok, P. (2005) 'Scholars before researchers: on the centrality of the dissertation literature review in research preparation', *Educational Researcher*, 34(6): 3–15.

Bruce, C. S. (2001) 'Interpreting the scope of their literature reviews: significant differences in research students' concerns', *New Library World*, 102(4): 158–66.

Hart, C. (1999) *Doing a Literature Review: Releasing the Social Science Research Imagination.* London: Sage.

Labaree, D. F. (2003) 'The peculiar problems of preparing educational researchers', *Educational Researcher*, 32(1): 13–22.

Lather, P. (1999) 'To be of use: the work of reviewing', *Review of Educational Research*, 69(1): 2–7.

LeCompte, M. D., Klingner, J. K., Campbell, S. A. and Menk, D. W. (2003) 'Editors' introduction', *Review of Educational Research*, 73(2): 123–4.

Mullins, G. and Kiley, M. (2002) '"It's a PhD, not a Nobel Prize": how experienced examiners assess research theses', *Studies in Higher Education*, 27(4): 369–86.

Shulman, L. S. (1999) 'Professing educational scholarship', in E. C. Lagemann and L. S. Shulman (eds) *Issues in Education Research: Problems and Possibilities*. San Francisco: Jossey-Bass.

Strike, K. and Posner, G. (1983) 'Types of synthesis and their criteria', in S. A. Ward and L. J. Reed (eds) *Knowledge Structure and Use: Implications for Synthesis and Interpretation*. Philadelphia, PA: Temple University Press.

Ethical Considerations and Legal Issues in Educational Research

Geoff Lindsay

Introduction

In this chapter, I shall explore the ethical issues that arise when conducting educational research. The general orientation of the chapter is to eschew an approach that is instrumental – how do I get past this barrier that is standing in the way of my getting on with my research? Rather, the premise is that ethical consideration is an important element in research practice in parallel with technical questions of design, validity and reliability of results, and interpretation. Fundamentally, the argument is that careful thinking about research ethics will *enhance* research.

By the end of this chapter, you should be able to:

- discuss the ethical principles that underpin research in education
- trace the evolution in the development of regulatory systems and ethics codes in education and related disciplines
- understand the nature and basis of ethical guidance
- appreciate that consideration of ethics permeates all phases of research

Why Have Ethical Guidance?

This chapter will argue that an ethical code may be a helpful source of guidance but the more important starting point is that the researcher reflects upon ethical issues by starting from ethical principles. However, it is also worth considering why ethical codes have been developed and whether researchers need an ethical code such as that developed by the British Educational Research Association (BERA) (2004).

Arguments in favour of ethical codes take several forms. A code provides explicit guidance which is intended to have practical utility. Furthermore, an ethical code sets out what is considered acceptable or even 'good'. Hence, the code is a manifestation of the moral position of those who develop and confirm the code, typically an organization. The immediate beneficiaries of an ethical code are those to whom it applies – educational researchers in our case – by guiding research practice. The effect of such codes is also, and ultimately, to regulate practice for the benefit of others. This includes both those directly affected (e.g. research participants) and a wider audience, which may include society in general. For example, there may be a positive impact on those not in the original study.

It is also worth noting that an ethical code may be beneficial to the group to which it applies, such as educational researchers. Professions are characterized by particular skills and knowledge derived from organized training and experience. In addition, adherence to an ethical code, or its equivalent, is a characteristic of professions. For a group of practitioners in a developing field to have an ethical code may be seen as a marker, an indication, that they have 'arrived' as a profession. Consequently, although the arguments in favour of an ethical code are primarily outward-looking (protection of the public) there are benefits to the professionals also. This is particularly pertinent to a new professional group although the development of different professions has taken a variety of paths in this respect. There is a long tradition of an ethical code in medicine that can be traced to the Hippocratic Oath, but other professions have been more tardy. In psychology, for example, the American Psychological Association (APA) had been in existence for about half a century before it started to develop its first formal ethical code. The teaching profession in England did not have a comparable code until the setting up of the General Teaching Council for England (GTCE) in 2000 and its approval of a code of conduct and practice in 2004 (see www.gtce.org.uk/publications/pub_reg, accessed 27 July 2008).

The development of the APA code is instructive as it is well documented and illustrates the tensions that can arise. The APA code arose after the Second World War at a time when a large number of psychologists had become engaged in practice rather than academic teaching and research, partly as a result of the war effort but also due to the demand for psychologists in industry and mental health provision. Educational psychology was a slower discipline to develop as a separate entity, although in England Cyril Burt was appointed the first (and at that time only) educational psychologist to the London County Council in 1913. In the USA, Hobbs (1948: 80) argued that psychologists had a growing sense of unity and professional esteem and felt the need for setting the agreed foundations of professional practice: 'to ensure public welfare to promote sound relationships with allied professions, to reduce intra-group misunderstandings, to promote professional standing of the group as a whole'.

Hobbs argued that an unwritten code was no longer tenable. But note the range of reasons provided, and as discussed above. Hall (1952) however, in an article entitled 'Crooks, codes and cant' took a different line, arguing that not only was there no need for an ethical code, its existence could have a negative effect as 'the crooked operator reads the code to see how much he can get away with' (p. 430), Nevertheless, the APA did develop its code, the first edition of which came into operation in 1953. It is also of note that the APA code has subsequently been through several revisions until its present form (see www.apa.org/ethics, accessed 27 July 2008).

Do We Need Ethical Codes?

The brief summary of the development of the APA code indicates that there are different views on the need for an ethical code. However, there is evidence both from professional practice and research that supports the need for and benefit of standardized guidance on ethical practice. One source is the existence of unethical practice. Where a regulatory system has been set up for a profession then it is possible to collect evidence of alleged misdemeanors. Various regulatory bodies publish reports of alleged unethical behaviour and the investigations and adjudications that follow. In England, the General Medical Council (GMC), General Teaching Council (GTC), British Psychological Society (BPS) and the Health Professions Council (HPC), for example, all provide such information. These reports indicate that there is unethical practice, including that arising from research and scholarship, although it is important to note that it is on a very small scale (Lindsay *et al.* 2008b).

Another source of evidence is research into ethical decision-making and the ways in which professionals deal with ethical dilemmas. For example, studies in the USA (e.g. Pope and Vetter 1991) and UK (Lindsay and Colley 1995; Lindsay and Clarkson 1999) have demonstrated that psychologists and psychotherapists encounter ethical dilemmas in their practice, including research. These findings have been supported by studies in other countries. The results suggest that dilemmas can arise even if a professional knows of the relevant ethical guidance; however, having that guidance assists the decision-making process (Lindsay 2008).

The case for educational researchers needing an ethical code is based partly on the points made so far. However, there is now a further reason which concerns the increased presence of regulatory systems for research practice. This is relatively new in many areas of educational research. Unlike medical practitioners and psychologists, for example, educational researchers are not regulated by a system of specific qualifications. Before practising law or dentistry, for example, it is necessary to be recognized as having successfully gained a qualification approved by a regulatory body. In educational research, by contrast, there is no comparable requirement. Although a doctorate may be regarded as an appropriate indicator of research competence, it is not a requirement. Furthermore, there have been initiatives actively to promote the conduct of research by those without even a masters-level qualification, for example the support for research undertaken by teachers.

The BERA (2004) has published ethical guidelines which are available to assist education researchers (see www.bera.ac.uk/publications/guides.php, accessed, 27 July 2008). The original 1992 guidelines were approved only after a good deal of debate and criticism (guidelines were first proposed in 1974). It is interesting to note that the original content was addressed not only to the practice of researchers but also to that of organizations such as funding bodies, and reflected concerns about the political context in which educational researchers practised. For example, there might be concerns that government sponsored and funded research leads to contractual control over the design, publication and even the process of research (Simon 1995). This is an unusual approach to ethical guidance and the 2004 version has a more traditional focus on the researcher, but the sociopolitical context in which professionals practise is pertinent. In the next section, I shall start to consider the basis for ethical guidance, beginning with ethical principles but taking into account the broader context.

The Basis of Ethical Guidance

There have been three main approaches to the development of ethical codes. The first entails an empirical investigation of the ethical challenges faced by the professionals concerned. This has the benefit of being rooted in practice and so helps to ensure any guidance is ecologically valid. The original APA code used this approach. The second approach is to identify key issues that are thought (typically by an expert committee set up to develop the guidance) to present ethical challenges. Drawing upon their own experience and any other source of guidance the committee may identify issues such as confidentiality, working with children, working for government funding bodies etc. The third approach is to identify the key ethical principles that apply and to work from these to determine more specific manifestations of the principles in action. A good example of this approach is the European Federation of Psychologists Association's (EFPA) *Meta-code of Ethics* (see Lindsay *et al.* 2008b).

Principle ethics

This approach attempts to identify *universal principles*. Universality is important if the guidance is to be appropriate for all those to whom it is addressed. In practice, universality typically concerns a particular country, or a smaller political unit, although there are currently attempts to devise a 'Universal Declaration of Ethics' that will be applicable to psychologists worldwide.

Five principles that may be identified are:

- non-maleficence
- fidelity
- beneficence
- justice
- autonomy

These principles form a sound basis for ethical codes for various professions although they are not uncontentious. The principle of *non-maleficence* requires the educational researcher to avoid harm. While this may generally be an admirable principle, is it always appropriate? In some medical research a degree of harm may be inevitable, for example researching a new surgical procedure. In education, an investigation of a disciplinary procedure may lead to pupils suffering discomfort or more unpleasant effects. Hence, in considering this principle it is necessary to take into consideration the balance of good versus harm. This first principle, therefore, raises the issues of relativity and identifies that interpreting how to be guided by a principle will not be like following a cookbook.

The principle of *fidelity* stresses the need for accuracy, for example of measures and their interpretation. Poor measurement leading to inaccurate data (even if unintended) and the reporting of inaccurate data (whether intentional or not) is addressed by this principle. There are, however, studies which deliberately report false data or interpretations as part of their design, for example those using deception as a process.

The principle of *beneficence* may be interpreted as a requirement not only to avoid harm but actively to do good. This is often a challenge for educational research. Studies of interventions (e.g. for literacy) may produce more improvement in the experimental condition but many studies are investigative, illuminative and/or exploratory. Here there may be no clear benefit to participants, at least in the short run, perhaps never. Hopefully there will be benefit to others, pupils who are subsequently given the new literacy programme, for example.

The principle of *justice* may also be difficult to build into consideration of educational research. For some, this is not a problem and their research may be driven or at least guided by a strong desire to promote justice. This raises the distinction between the research itself and the wider agenda of which it may be part, although some researchers might argue that this separation is artificial.

Finally the principle of *autonomy* suggests the importance of a particular view of the person, to accord and promote autonomy. This has a degree of culture specificity, particularly in western culture, and may be contrasted with, say, collegiality where the group (e.g. a village or the country) is seen as more important than the individual. In educational research there may be studies where autonomy is a clearly stated aim, where the method can be developed to optimize the participant's degree of autonomy within the project, for example to engage the participant in having some control over the study as a whole or in part. In many, if not most, studies it is also possible to carry out the research in a manner that optimizes a respect for the autonomy of the participant. Indeed, the shift in language from 'subject' to 'participant' partly reflects this.

These five principles, therefore, provide a useful basis but are not without difficulties in interpretation and implementation.

Virtue ethics

One distinction made in ethical codes concerns whether the code is intended to identify the *bottom line*, the minimum standard of practice that is acceptable, or whether it is intended to be *aspirational*, encouraging the professional to seek the highest level of practice. Implicit in the latter is that professionals may seek but not achieve these higher levels whereas in the former case the professional is expected at least to meet the 'minimum' standards.

Prudence concerns the care with which the research is conducted. For example, an educational researcher may need to show prudence in selecting the sample and also in how to carry out the study. When working with young children, for example, the question of child protection is a very important consideration to address.

Integrity concerns the honesty and fairness of the research enterprise. As an example of aspirational ethics, the requirement here may be for a researcher to ensure not only that data and interpretations are accurate but also that the fullest amount of interpretation is provided. The interpretation of results may include a number of alternative explanations, not only a discussion of whether the research hypothesis is supported.

Respectfulness may also be demonstrated at different levels. The aspiration is to offer the highest level of respect, not just that which is acceptable. For example, the researcher would need to consider optimizing comfort (rather than avoiding discomfort) or optimizing the participant's active engagement (rather than providing minimum necessary information).

There are other principles that may be used as organizers of ethical guidance, such as equity (or equitability) which implies even-handedness; openness, implying the fullest disclosure of information; and benevolence (or goodwill) – see Francis (1999). It is apparent that there is a degree of overlap between the major constructs presented here as examples of both principle and virtue ethics and within each grouping. What is important, however, is the recognition that an approach based on virtue ethics is aspirational and intended to be motivational, to support the practitioner in seeking, and achieving, the highest levels of ethical practice.

Another distinction that may be made is between the different philosophical bases of ethical codes, relating to their derivation from moral philosophy. A *teleological* philosophy stresses a utilitarian approach where the greatest good for the greatest number is a key concept. Compare this with a *deontological* basis where there are absolutes and certain outcomes are therefore intrinsically right. Each has its strengths and limitations. Absolutes can be very useful but only if their absoluteness is uncontentious. In practice, certainty in educational research, absolutism is not easy to promote. For example, is there an absolute, uncontentious, approach to involving participants in research? On the other hand, a utilitarian approach may lead to vagueness or be based on assertions rather than evidence. For example, can an analysis of the greatest good for the greatest number be carried out if results are uncertain?

Cost vs benefits

Implicit in the discussions so far is the notion of *relativism*: ethical judgments for educational researchers will often not be susceptible to simple, formulaic decisions for action but, rather, will require the weighing up of different factors. Ethical decisions require consideration of both the costs of an action and of the benefits from that (or alternative) action. The researcher must attempt to eliminate costs and benefits and then determine the ratio, not in a precise mathematical sense, but conceptually.

Both benefits and costs may be explored with reference to a number of different players:

- research participant(s)
- the institution (e.g. a school)
- society as a whole
- the researcher

Benefits may be tangible: the participant may gain from an intervention, from a payment for time allocated, for example; the researcher may gain by attaining a research degree; a school might benefit from either the results of the study or the process of being part of the study, or both.

Society's gain, by contrast, is almost certainly long term in educational research. Costs also may be tangible – for example, loss of time, opportunity costs for an alternative action such as a different intervention. Benefits and costs may also be less tangible. A school may benefit from the research having taken place even if there was no effect that was specifically due to the research itself. The interest and presence of a researcher may have knock-on effects, a version of the well-established 'Hawthorne effect'.

Ethics and values

The last factor to be considered in relation to the nature of ethics is the question of values. Personal and societal values are shaped by a number of influences. The most powerful are probably the religious and political contexts of a particular society. There will be an interaction between these factors and both the personal and the societal. For example, a country where a religion exerts a strong influence may well be characterized by a powerful religious impact on its laws and societal structures as well as individuals' personal belief systems. These will then interact.

Values are also influenced by non-religious ways of thinking – for example, humanism – and by political and economic belief systems – for example, capitalism, socialism or the 'third way'. An important question is whether, and to what degree, ethical codes are or should be influenced by value systems (Lindsay 1995). If you return to the discussion of ethical principles above you might like to reflect on the degree to which those different principles relate to your personal values.

Values may change, however. Rokeach and Ball-Rokeach (1989) carried out a study of changes in values among American adults over a ten-year period. Equality (brotherhood, equality for all) went down the hierarchy from fourth to twelfth whereas 'a comfortable life' went higher, from thirteenth to eighth. This raises the question of the stability of ethics and hence of ethical codes. The APA code, as mentioned above, has been through a number of different versions with substantial changes; the BERA code also changed substantially between its two versions. Some changes reflected structural and organizational variations rather than different core ethical guidance. The EFPA *Meta-code* for psychologists hardly altered between its 1995 and 2005 revisions (Lindsay *et al.* 2008b). On the other hand, some elements of codes do change, sometimes substantially. With respect to research ethics there may be relatively few changes for education, but medical research is raising new ethical dilemmas each year as science develops, for example, the use of cloning and stem cell research.

Ethical Issues in Research

In this section, I shall focus on more specific issues concerning educational research. First, however, it is important to make the general point that all research is, by its very nature, intrusive to some degree. The exception to this statement may to some extent be observational research, particularly in public places (e.g. a playground) with non-identified participants and also the use of anonymous datasets (secondary data). However, even in these examples a degree of intrusiveness may be postulated. Even though an individual is not identified or named, the results of either study will relate to specific groups and the publication of those results may be sensitive and have an impact on participants. Take, for example, a study of pupil development that presents the results differentiated by ethnicity. This issue was pertinent to one of our studies which analysed the total pupil dataset in England (about 6.5 million pupils) to explore the relationship between special educational needs and ethnicity (Lindsay *et al.* 2006; Strand and Lindsay 2009). No individual was identified: the study presented comparisons by minority ethnic group. However, there is a contentious historical legacy from research in this area necessitating that we recognized the research, and especially the results, as sensitive sociopolitically and not simply as objective, value-free science.

Intrusiveness increases as a result of the activity with which a participant engages and also by their degree of exposure. A group reading test leading to anonymous data may take a relatively short time and lead to very limited exposure; interviews with adolescents on their gender identity are inherently more intrusive. In considering intrusiveness there are several relevant factors. First is the vulnerability of the participant, a function of their age and developmental status. This is partly an issue of cognitive competence but there may also be emotional factors (see informed consent, below). Second is the type and degree of potential negative consequence. Typically in educational research we do not undertake studies designed deliberately to have negative impacts but it is also important to consider unintentional negative consequences that may occur. This process should include reflections on the possible medium- to long-term effects. A person may be genuinely willing to provide information on a sensitive personal topic but may regret this five years later when their personal circumstances have changed. Anonymity is key here, but may not be assured – in many studies anonymity cannot be guaranteed.

It is the responsibility of the researcher to take appropriate care to minimize the degree of intrusiveness to that which is necessary for the study and to minimize the risk of negative consequences (see also supervision, below).

Design

Research design is not only a technical matter of identifying the appropriate method to study the research questions specified. Inferior design will most probably result in inferior research. As a consequence, findings may be difficult if not impossible to analyse appropriately and interpretation of findings is compromised. Invalid, unreliable and misleading results are possible outcomes of such research. At best this may represent a waste of resources (participants' time, funder's financial support) but if the poor design is not appreciated the researcher may publish inappropriate results.

Recruitment of sample

We have no right to access research participants: all must be done by their consent except for naturalistic observation in a public place or anonymous datasets of secondary data where this is not practical. Identification and recruitment of participants will often require the permission of one or more 'gatekeepers' in addition to the informed consent of the participants, for example, the head teacher and local authority (LA). Where different professionals are involved there may be other agencies.

It is necessary to disentangle issues of access from those of consent and, in the latter case, levels of consent. For example, in a recent study for the Department for Children, Schools and Families (DCSF) and Department of Health (DH) investigating provision for children and young people with speech, language and communication needs (SLCN), we needed DCSF and DH to approach the LAs and primary care trusts (PCTs) respectively to confirm their willingness to be case studies in our project (Lindsay *et al.* 2008a). It was also necessary to gain health service approval to approach the trusts, a process (ROCR-Lite) that required information on the time needed and type of data to be collected. Next came the process of LAs and PCTs identifying individual senior managers for interview. They in turn provided informed consent for their own involvement and the LA manager provided access to head teachers for interview. Head teachers then gave informed consent and also access to heads of specialist resources for pupils with SLCN in relevant schools; heads of these resources gave informed consent to be interviewed.

This example shows the different, but sometimes intertwined, processes of access and consent. Also, it is always necessary to provide appropriate information for each organization or individual concerned. Each element of these processes requires careful, ethically justified information. Furthermore, the determination of the sample itself requires ethical as well as technical consideration so that the sample can be justified in terms of intrusiveness and also the avoidance of bias. A sample is biased relative to the research design. Inducements, for example, may bias selection whether financial or intimations that a participant will gain another benefit such as an improvement from an intervention.

Informed consent

Informed consent is at the heart of ethical research practice. It incorporates issues of clarity of purpose, trust, honesty and integrity. The first question to ask is how will informed consent be obtained? The inclusion of 'informed' in this term is crucial. Consent may be presumed, enforced, hijacked and given on behalf of another or given in ignorance. To ensure consent is informed it is necessary to consider several issues.

First, the competence of the potential participant to give informed consent must be assessed. As educationists, we often undertake research with children. Age is a key marker but it is not sufficient. Cognitive competence to give informed consent is a function of the child's developmental status and the law recognizes that it is this rather than chronological age that is the key guiding factor. But emotional factors may play a part. For example, a teacher may be perfectly competent to consent to engagement as a research participant from a cognitive point of view but the topic may raise important emotional reactions (e.g. a bereavement) such that it may not be reasonable to assume informed consent.

Second, being informed requires clear, comprehensive and accurate information. For adults, an information sheet can be very useful and is recommended. Even if a participant prefers an oral explanation, having to produce such a sheet helps to focus the researcher's thinking. It is important not to swamp the participant with unnecessary detail – 'comprehensive' need not mean 'overwhelming'. The concept of 'need to know' is useful in assessing the information to present.

Young children will normally require an oral explanation expressed in a manner that communicates effectively. The key information to be provided will typically include a description of the aims of the study, why the participant has been selected, what they will be asked to do, and what will happen to the findings, including issues of confidentiality and anonymity. Where English is an additional language for a participant, a communication in the most appropriate language (and medium) must be considered.

The second question is how the informed consent will be recorded. There is an increasing tendency to adopt a 'safety first' approach and require a written confirmation that the participant has read and understood the information and consent. This active and explicit recording of consent certainly assists defensive practice, but is it necessarily appropriate? In several studies recently I have asked interviewees whether they would prefer to sign such a form or have me record their consent. All the professionals to whom I have offered this choice have chosen a note of an oral consent. However, there may be times when such an informal approach is unwise. An important factor to assist a decision is the degree of risk to the participant and the sensitivity of the topic. Higher levels on either scale suggest the necessity for a written record. Furthermore, written consent is advised when carrying out a research study as a student (e.g. for a doctorate). Records of consent should be stored safely (see data storage, below).

Where the participant cannot be assumed to be capable of informed consent then another must provide this. This may result from the level of maturity of the participant or the complexity of the action for which consent is sought. A third factor once more is the degree of risk of harm, of any kind. Parental consent will often be essential although in some cases an appropriate professional may act *in loco parentis*. It is not necessary in England from a legal perspective always to gain parental consent on behalf of a young person under 16 years of age if they are competent to make the necessary decision, but usually this will be the preferred option. Not only does it avoid the question of having to be able to show that the young people are competent, it also respects the parental role and responsibility.

Even where a competent adult provides informed consent on behalf of a child, it is still necessary from an ethical point of view (see respect principle, below) to gain the child's *assent*. This term is used to indicate that it has a lower level of force and that consent may not be inferred. Nevertheless, this ensures that the researcher actively engages with the participant to explain as fully as possible the nature of what is expected of the child and secures their agreement to participate.

In all cases the participant should be informed that they are free to withdraw at any time, without penalty. If there is a possibility of any adverse consequences these should be discussed and any contrary indications for the participant's involvement should be identified (e.g. possible effects of a VDU presentation on a participant with epilepsy).

Furthermore, it is the researcher's responsibility to ensure that consent is *freely given*. In some schools, for example, and in some cultures, consent is assumed to be within the gift of the head teacher and the staff must comply. When researching in such a setting the researcher should consider the cultural factors that should be respected and balance these as appropriate against the ethical standards appropriate in the UK.

Box 7.1 Issues regarding informed consent

- Provide a comprehensive and accurate informed consent.
- Consider the language used (especially with regard to children and persons from minority linguistic backgrounds).
- Decide about ways of recording informed consent (oral vs. written).
- Decide on storage of informed consent.
- Consider parental consent for children.
- Ensure children's input (child assent).

Privacy, anonymity and confidentiality

The discussion of intrusiveness focused attention on the impact of research on a participant's privacy: in short, privacy is compromised. It is incumbent upon the researcher, therefore, to ensure that the degree to which this occurs is as limited as possible. This will require negotiation as part of the process of gaining informed consent.

Anonymity may be assured in some studies, for example, the completion of a questionnaire which has no identifier and data are not presented at an individual level. This is less easy, possibly even impossible, in an interview study, especially where the number of interviewees is small and their identification cannot easily be hidden. For example, one of my doctoral students is undertaking research that involves interviews with very senior officials in specific countries. In such cases, there may be only one person who could be in that role. In other cases anonymity may be easier to preserve, but still cannot be guaranteed. For example, in our recent study of 18 LAs in the Parenting Early Intervention Pathfinder we interviewed a large number of parenting group facilitators, parents and also lead officers in each LA (Lindsay *et al.* 2008). Each interviewee was coded by an LA code plus a code for the type of interviewee. Both were allocated randomly. This sets a high likelihood of anonymity being preserved but it is not infallible as the interview itself, when parts are quoted, may lead some readers to have a reasonable idea of a person's identity.

Although anonymity cannot be assured, it is the researcher's responsibility to limit the likelihood of identification. Occasionally this may bring a conflict if a participant actively wants *not* to be anonymous. In such cases it is necessary to consider the impact of disclosure on others (if any) in the study and also the potential for that participant to regret making this decision at a later stage, when the situation cannot be retrieved. If in doubt, it is better to take the conservative approach and anonymize.

The information provided by a research participant should be treated as confidential unless the study requires otherwise and this is agreed with the participants. The coding of interviews, as described above, allows important and relevant information to be used for the purpose of research while maintaining the anonymity of the participant. Ensuring confidentiality also pertains to the recording and storing of information. For example, it is good practice never to put an interviewee's name or other identifying information on fieldnotes or transcripts. Codes should always be kept separate from the data to which they apply.

In most educational research, maintaining confidentiality is relatively straightforward. However, in some studies serious ethical dilemmas may arise. For example, a researcher may be given information that implies the participant is at risk. Child protection protocols may require a researcher immediately to report certain information. One corollary is that a researcher should never give a blanket assurance of confidentiality, a position that could be untenable. It is worth noting that this is an area where practice has changed over the recent past, even among professionals involved in therapy rather than research, and this goes some way to explain why the most common ethical dilemmas for psychologists, in many countries, are concerned with confidentiality (Lindsay and Colley 1995). Some research may have as its aim the identification of poor (or worse) practice, or at least aim to critique practice. This is more complex and may raise serious ethical dilemmas regarding the conflict between maintaining confidentiality and the responsibility to report. For example, a study of Office for Standards in Education (Ofsted) inspections may produce findings critical of that organization, but its identity cannot be hidden. A study of a 'failing' school could seek to anonymize the school – or not. The presumption in the latter case should be not to identify the school.

Box 7.2 Ethical issues in educational research

- Participants' chronological age.
- Participants' cognitive competence.
- Participants' social/emotional factors.
- Privacy.
- Anonymity.
- Confidentiality.
- Authorship of research output.

Data-handling and analysis

Data derived from educational research may take a variety of forms, including anonymized datasets in a computer file and interview schedules with verbatim transcriptions. Test data may also be produced. Whatever the nature of the data it is necessary to ensure its accuracy, fairness and security.

Accuracy requires careful recording at the point of acquisition and at any subsequent point of transfer, for example from one computer file to another. Accurate interpretation is not possible unless the raw data are accurate. Data should also provide a fair reflection of the phenomenon under investigation. This is dependent upon the original design and decisions about methods, including measures: the adage GIGO (garbage in, garbage out) is still applicable and applies to all kinds of information, not only numerical data processed by a computer. Incomplete test forms, questionnaires and interview schedules, for example, all pose threats to the study and from an ethical point of view it is necessary to consider appropriate treatment that provides a fair representation of the results.

A similar issue is raised by the identification of 'outliers'. It is not uncommon in statistical analysis to explore the data to check if outliers are present. As this may distort the dataset, action may be deemed justified and necessary. The same process could be applied to qualitative data, although here researchers may be more interested in keeping *in* the outliers as they provide an interesting, alternative perspective that, by definition, differs from the information and/or opinion provided by the main body of the sample.

In either case, the task for the researcher is to judge the *fair* way to represent the data, balancing the need to represent the main body of the sample as opposed to outliers. It is necessary also to be careful to avoid, especially in qualitative studies, the tendency to be seduced by the very interesting but atypical quotation. Such quotations should be clearly labelled as atypical and not over-represented in the findings.

Data storage

It is the norm in the social sciences to keep data for ten years after a study. This allows other researchers as well as the original research to examine the data, possibly to challenge or to extend analyses. Also, a number of datasets including those from the national longitudinal studies such as the British Cohort 1970 study (BCS70) make data available for other researchers.

Storage of data and consent forms requires secure facilities, whether in password protected computer files or locked and secure cabinets and rooms. Access to the data must also be restricted to those with permission. Furthermore, care is necessary to maintain an agreement regarding confidentially made with the participant. Particular issues arise with student research where data must be stored at the student's home rather than a university office. The same principles apply. Furthermore, data should not be destroyed until after the examination process and award of the degree, at a minimum.

Reporting

Ethical reporting of findings is grounded in the original design and the stages of the study leading up to this point. In addition, reporting itself must be fair, honest and accurate with interpretations that are reasonable given the data and their limitations. The most obvious form of ethical violation is the deliberate falsification of data and possibly the most famous alleged instance in an education-related field is that of Sir Cyril Burt, who undertook research on the heritability of intelligence using twin studies (e.g. Mackintosh 1995). The scale of falsification of data is unknown and the allegations against Burt have not been proven despite at least three books and other published analyses, although Mackintosh comes down on the side of 'guilty'. However, such behaviour is clearly unethical. What is less easy to judge are practices that fall short of this and may not be seen as unethical by the researcher. These include the omission of data, overemphasis of unrepresentative data to imply they are representative of a larger group and the omission of data, and discussions thereof, when those data are not supportive of the position or hypothesis of the researcher.

Interference by outside bodies may also challenge the ethical status of a research study. As mentioned earlier, Simons (1995) was concerned that this was occurring and that government intervention was influencing research. It may also be alleged that research reports and papers are not true and fair reflections of the findings as the funder (e.g. a government agency) has interfered, unethically. An example of this criticism may be found in a critique by Torrance (2003) of a study by Ann Lewis and myself of baseline assessment (Lindsay and Lewis 2003). Torrance suggests that 'It seemed to be taken for granted that as government policy was to introduce baseline assessment, the authors' (implicit) evaluation task was to assist in implementation rather than conduct a disinterested inquiry' (Torrance 2003: 169). In fact, we would argue that Torrance's interpretation does not do justice to the paper which includes a critique of government policy. However, for present purposes the point is whether it is possible to undertake government sponsored research and present findings that are critical of government policy. If not, then there would be concerns about the research from an ethical standpoint. My own experience of undertaking research funded by government agencies in the education and health domains is that no pressure has ever been applied to change findings, conclusions or recommendations other than to clarify or sharpen focus.

Authorship

The final issue to be considered is that of authorship. Authorship should reflect the input into the research and the writing of publications that arise. Research for a degree must be presented as a thesis or dissertation in the name of the student. Publications arising from research groups or teams should reflect the contributions of those team members. This has been an unclear area and sometimes a rather laissez-faire attitude has prevailed. This can work to the disadvantage of one or more parties. The APA guidance on attribution of authorship (www.apa.org) is particularly useful in this respect as it is based on principles of amount and type of contribution rather than seniority. Also important is to recognize that a senior researcher adopting a laissez-fair attitude may assist researchers whose work is promoted but disadvantage others where that team's senior colleague adopts a more systematic approach.

Determination of authorship of publications other than the thesis that arise from research by a student requires clear protocols and both discussion and agreement at an early stage. One approach is to discuss with any new research students the aims that their research will lead to publication(s) beyond the thesis and that whenever possible the supervisor would support the writing of such publications. The student would typically be first author with the supervisor second author in the case of doctoral research. At undergraduate or masters' level the supervisor is likely to have had a more fundamental role in directing the study, from conceptualization to completion, and may properly be the senior author. Discussion is required but the guiding principle is, again, the relative contribution of each person.

Ethical Approval and Ethical Decision-making

The previous section focused on the specific issues that are relevant to planning and carrying out a research project. These are the issues likely to be addressed by the ethical approval system in a higher education institution (HEI), although the system will vary from one HEI to another. Typically a researcher will need to complete a research ethics approval form which will then be scrutinized by a committee or member of staff. Education students on taught courses and those taking research degrees will also be subject to the ethical approval system. Whereas the system for staff is likely to be conducted at university or faculty level, that for student research may well be carried out within the department. It is clearly important to identify the exact system in your institution.

The guidance provided here should form a sound foundation for thinking through the ethical issues arising when planning and carrying out educational research, but no guidance can be comprehensive. Ethical decision-making cannot be done simply by following a 'cookbook' approach. Although specific issues (e.g. informed consent) can be identified there will be subtle variations or ethical dilemmas that arise in practice. Several have been alluded to so far.

To address this, a further approach based on ethical principles is advocated. This is set out at length in Lindsay *et al.* (2008b) and further examples are given in the context of educational psychology in Lindsay *et al.* (2008a). This method requires the researcher to identify the ethical principles that apply in any particular case, recognizing that there may be more than one. Lindsay *et al.* (2008b) use the EFPA *Meta-code* (www.efpa.eu) to explore these four principles for psychologists' practice but the basic approach is applicable to education researchers. These four principles have been amended from the EFPA *Meta-code* to be relevant to educational researchers:

- *The principle of respect for a person's rights and dignity.* Educational researchers accord appropriate respect to and promote the development of the fundamental rights, dignity and worth of all people. They respect the rights of individuals to privacy, confidentiality, self-determination and autonomy, consistent with the researcher's other professional obligations and with the law.
- *The principle of competence.* Educational researchers strive to ensure and maintain high standards of competence in their work. They recognize the boundaries of their particular competencies and the limitations of their expertise. They provide only those services and use only those techniques for which they are qualified by education, training or experience.
- *The principle of responsibility.* Educational researchers are aware of the professional and scientific responsibilities to the participants in their research, to the community, and to the society in which they work and live. Educational researchers avoid doing harm and are responsible for their own actions, and assure themselves, as far as possible, that their services are not misused.
- *The principle of integrity.* Educational researchers seek to promote integrity in educational research. In these activities educational researchers are honest, fair and respectful to others. They attempt to clarify for relevant parties the roles they are performing and to function appropriately in accordance with those roles.

Box 7.3 The four ethical principles for educational research

- The principle of respect for a person's rights and dignity.
- The principle of competence.
- The principle of responsibility.
- The principle of integrity.

Supervision and peer support

Those who are undertaking educational research as part of a higher degree will have a research supervisor. In this case supervision provides an opportunity to receive guidance and support on ethical as well as technical issues concerned with the research. This does not absolve the student of responsibility for their actions but the supervision will provide an experienced researcher who is able to help the student to consider the ethical issues as they arise. A system of supervision is also appropriate for junior researchers. Furthermore, experienced researchers will also benefit from discussing ethical issues with a peer, just as research design or appropriate methods of analysis might be discussed.

The main focus on ethical guidelines will come in the early stages when the project is being planned and set up, but others could occur during fieldwork or at the stage of writing a thesis, research report or journal article. In all cases the importance of discussing the ethical challenges and dilemmas with colleagues, using ethical principles and written codes of ethics as guides, cannot be over-stressed. The BERA code (2004) is a good starting point, but the other codes and guidance mentioned in this chapter are also useful sources. These provide the structures to aid your reflections and discussions with a supervisor or peer as appropriate.

Summary

The approach of this chapter has been to combine direct guidance with working from basic ethical principles. The section Ethical Issues in Research, supported by ethical codes and guidance such as the BERA revised *Ethical Guidelines for Educational Research*, the EFPA *Meta-code* and the APA code, provide a structured approach to specific ethical issues that educational researchers will typically need to address. However, not all ethical questions are easily answered by these guidelines. Sometimes ethical dilemmas arise where different guidance appears to be in conflict. Furthermore, new research methods or topics may raise issues where it is not clear how these codes and guidelines apply. For example, research using the internet including blogs raises new variants of ethical questions concerning confidentiality of data, responsibility to research participants and respect of those actively engaged in the research and those who may be affected indirectly. In these circumstances, returning to ethical principles will help the researcher to think through the issues. A supervisor and/or colleague also provide an important resource.

Finally, and especially for researchers who are developing research skills, I would urge you to recognize the importance of research ethics along with research design. Research ethics has received a bad press recently when institutions have set up cumbersome, unhelpful and time-consuming systems of ethical approval that have antagonized researchers, delayed and disrupted research and have not added value. Indeed, some appear not to have been fit for purpose and by their bureaucratization and protracted nature have even, it could be argued, been unethical themselves. This is changing. At Warwick, for example, ethical approval for education student research projects is typically turned round in a couple of days. The Humanities and Social Science Research Ethics Committee, which considers staff proposals, has set up a system designed to be rigorous but also speedy, responsive and efficient.

It is the institution's responsibility to devise a system that is appropriately rigorous but also fit for purpose. The ESRC guidelines (see www.esrcsocietytoday.ac.uk/ESRCInfoCentre/opportunities/research_ethics_framework/index.aspx?ComponentId=11292&SourcePageId=19165, accessed 27 July 2008) provide extensive advice but are also based on the principle of taking into account degree of risk as a key factor when considering how ethical issues are addressed and how the HEI considers proposals. All ESRC funded research must comply with these guidelines but the guidance is useful and applicable to all education research studies.

The responsibility of the researcher is to build in ethical considerations throughout the whole of the research process, from conceptualization to reporting; to use each research project to develop their ethical awareness and to use their growing experience to reach the levels of ethical practice to which we should all aspire.

References

British Educational Research Association (BERA) (2004) *Ethical Guidelines for Educational Research*, www.bera.ac.uk.

British Psychological Society (2006) *Code of Conduct. Ethical Principles and Guidelines*, www.bps.org.uk.

Francis, R. D. (1999) *Ethics for Psychologists: A Handbook*. Leicester: BPS Books.

General Teaching Council for England (GTCE) (2007) *Code of Conduct and Practice for Registered Teachers*. Birmingham: GTCE.

Hall, C. S. (1952) 'Crooks, codes and cant', *American Psychologist*, 7: 430–1.

Hobbs, N. (1948) 'The development of a code of ethical standards for psychology', *American Psychologist*, 3: 80–4.

Lindsay, G. (1995) 'Values, ethics and psychology', *The Psychologist: Bulletin of the British Psychological Society*, 8: 448–51.

Lindsay, G. (2008) Ethics and value systems, in B. Kelly, L. Wolfson and J. Boyle (eds) *Frameworks for Practice in Educational Psychology*. London: Jessica Kingsley.

Lindsay, G. and Clarkson, P. (1999) 'Ethical dilemmas of psychotherapists', *The Psychologist*, 12: 182–5.

Lindsay, G. and Colley, A. (1995) 'Ethical dilemmas of members of the Society', *The Psychologist*, 8: 214–17.

Lindsay, G. and Lewis, A. (2003) 'An evaluation of the use of accredited baseline assessment schemes in England', *British Educational Research Journal*, 29: 149–67.

Lindsay, G., Pather, S. and Strand, S. (2006) *Special Educational Needs and Ethnicity: Issues of Over- and Under-representation, RR 757*. Nottingham: DfES.

Lindsay, G., Desforges, Dockrell, J., Law, J., Peacey, N. and Beecham, J. (2008a) *Effective and Efficient Use of Resources in Services for Children and Young People with Speech, Language and Communication Needs*. DCSF-RW053 London: Department for Children, Schools and Families.

Lindsay, G., Koene, C., Øvreeide, H. and Lang, F. (2008b) *Ethics for European Psychologists*. Gottingen: Hogrefe.

Lindsay, G., Davis, H., Strand, S., Band, S., Cullen, M. A., Cullen, S., Hasluck, C., Evans, R. and Stewart-Brown, S. (2008) *Parenting Early Intervention Pathfinder Evaluation*. DCSF-RW054 London: Department for Children, Schools and Families.

Mackintosh, N. J. (1995) *Cyril Burt: Fraud or Framed?* Oxford: University Press.

Pope, K. S. and Vetter, V. A. (1991) 'Ethical dilemmas encountered by members of the American Psychological Association: A national survey', *American Psychologist*, 47: 397–411.

Rokeach, M. and Ball-Rokeach, S. J. (1989) 'Stability and change in American value priorities, 1968–1981', *American Psychologist*, 4: 775–84.

Simons, H. (1995) 'The politics and ethics of educational research in England: Contemporary issues', *British Educational Research Journal*, 21: 435–49.

Strand, S. and Lindsay, G. (2009) 'Ethnic disproportionality in special education: evidence from an English population study', *Journal of Special Education*, 43: 174–90.

Torrance, H. (2003) 'When is an 'evaluation' not an evaluation? When it's sponsored by the QCA? A response to Lindsay and Lewis', *British Educational Research Journal*, 29: 169–73.

Part III
Methodology and Research Designs in Education – Strategies of Inquiry

Action Research 8
Andrew Townsend

Introduction

The term 'action research' is used to describe a wide range of different approaches and yet the contention of this chapter is that these all share some common principles. These principles, it is suggested, can be traced back to some of the attributed origins of action research, and can serve as a critical lens through which action researchers can interrogate their practice. This is underpinned in the following section by an exploration of the origins of action research.

By the end of this chapter you should be able to:

- appreciate the history, nature and application of action research
- consider alternative views and models of the action research process which you can follow and against which you can critique your own practice.

The Nature and Origins of Action Research

Action research is intended to combine *research*, as an exercise in producing knowledge, and *actions* which can contribute to, or be derived from, such knowledge. Kurt Lewin is often credited as the pioneer of this approach (although there are other possible sources outlined below). He suggested that research concerned with practice needed to be based around actions:

> The research needed for social practice can best be characterized as research for social management or social engineering. It is a type of action-research, a comparative research on the conditions and effects of various forms of social action, and research leading to social action.
>
> (Lewin 1946: 35)

Lewin went further in suggesting that such an approach required a series of cycles based around planning, acting, observing and reflecting (Lewin 1948). This emphasizes the central features of action research – namely that it is concerned with practices in social situations, that it is cyclical and that, as the name suggests, it is a fusion of research and action (see Box 8.1 for a more detailed exploration of these features). Despite these apparently simplistic central features, an examination of what is currently termed action research would appear to cover a bewilderingly disparate set of approaches. One of the aspirations of this chapter is to illustrate that, in this diversity, there is a common set of principles that underpin this work.

Box 8.1 The central features of action research

Action research is:

- Concerned with practices in social situations. Action research was developed as an alternative to social research that constructed theory without influencing or changing the settings of that research. Action research is concerned more with practice than with theory. This is not to deny any role to theory as Lewin stated that there is 'nothing more practical as a good theory' (1951: 169), but the emphasis of action research is on changes to practice, not on the construction of theory.

- Cyclical. The cyclical nature of action research has been identified by a large number of authors. The main basis of this is a process of developing a plan of action, implementing those actions, observing the effects and then reflecting on the outcomes.

- A fusion of research and action. Action research is, by definition, concerned with both action *and* research. The changes in practice which are advocated through action research are achieved by both conducting research, and hence enhancing understanding, and changing practices. As outlined later in the chapter, however, research and action need not remain separate and can be fused – i.e. new actions can constitute research and research can be considered actions!

Action research is normally described as being a qualitative form of research, which is convincing inasmuch as action researchers are concerned with the 'quality' of practice and of the social settings for those practices. As Elliot (1991: 69) puts it: 'Action research might be defined as the study of a social situation with a view to improving the quality of action within it'.

Using the word 'quality' in any text relating to the public services, with their concern with concepts such as best practice, continuous improvement, tables of institutional performance etc. is a risky thing to do. And yet 'quality' in the sense used in action research is more normally concerned with the qualities perceived by the action researcher themselves and how they relate to their aspirations:

> Action research is a form of collective self-reflective enquiry undertaken by participants in social situations in order to improve the rationality and justice of their own social or educational practices, as well as their understanding of these practices and the situation in which these practices are carried out.
>
> (Kemmis and McTaggart 1988: 5)

However, despite this qualitative emphasis, action researchers tend to see meaning and interpret evidence where it has most relevance for them, and in doing so they often make use of data which would be more commonly associated with quantitative approaches (such as numerically coded questionnaires or student performance data). Bearing this in mind, it might be better to perceive action research as an over-arching approach, or methodology (Somekh 2006), which has predominantly qualitative aspirations in that it is concerned with actively changing the quality of a particular situation. But, while concerned with quality, this is an approach in which the evidence that inform such changes is drawn from a wide variety of sources and collected via a range of approaches which relate to the aspirations, understandings and convictions of the action researcher themselves, of which some may well be numerical in nature.

Although itself a contested viewpoint, seeing action research as an over-arching methodology does more accurately capture the diversity of approaches in this form of research, and reflects a common view that, rather than prescribing one particular approach or 'method', action research is more based around a series of central principles or common characteristics.

The features that were described in the opening to this section are just such common characteristics, namely that action research is based around changing practices in social situations, that it is a cyclical, or iterative, process and that it intentionally merges research and action. Other recurring themes in action research are detailed below and are related to some of the attributed origins of action research. These are derived from a range of sources and are intended to raise a number of challenges for the action researcher to consider, including:

1. What are the participatory elements of action research? This includes asking who should be participating in this process and how such participation can be achieved. If it is to be authentic participation this should be more than simple consultation.
2. What practices are of concern and how do they relate to the aspirations of the action researcher, and to other members of the community?
3. In what ways is action research reflexive and, in particular, to what extent does it incorporate an element of self-study and critique?

These main features of action research also influence the types of projects or questions which are more suitable for this approach. Action research is applied where people want to change something both as a result of and through their research. This can be seen in a number of action research reports, including those that use action research to enhance inclusive practices (Angelides *et al.* 2008), to enhance the democratic practices of schools by encouraging students to act as action researchers (Cox and Robinson-Pant 2008), or who wish to develop competence with particular pedagogical approaches, for example, phonics (Edwards 2008). With the degree of variety hinted at by just these three examples (all drawn from the same journal) it would appear that action research can cover a broad field, and yet all these approaches have a common feature: they are all concerned with actions. Rather than simply studying actions, they all aspire to achieve change. They are all concerned, in some way, with the participation of individuals in this process of change, and they all are based around the action researchers' production and use of practice-related knowledge. However, there are different emphases placed on the conduct of action research which, in some respects, are associated in the differing fields in which it is applied. These are explored in the following sections.

Community Engagement and Participative Inquiry

As suggested, the origins of action research are often attributed to Kurt Lewin (see e.g. Adleman 1993; Hopkins, 1993: 45). Lewin's work came in a variety of forms, although the common theme in each was an approach to change based on the perceptions and aspirations of the individuals who would be most affected by such change. These emphasized group decision-making and were applied in business settings and projects concerned with resolving issues of inequality and in particular in working with marginalized or minority communities (Lewin 1946; Adleman 1993). This is sometimes termed 'community action research' and has been characterized by Stringer (1999: 9) as being 'the application of the tools of anthropology and other disciplines to the practical resolution of social problems'. Community action research has the following qualities (Stringer 1999: 10):

- it is democratic, enabling the participation of all people
- it is equitable, acknowledging people's true worth
- it is liberating, providing freedom from oppressive, debilitating conditions
- it is life-enhancing, enabling the expression of people's full human potential

Thus one of the founding principles of action research was the participation of community members in a process of change which, it was aspired, would lead to a more just society. his creates a direct link with participatory research, indeed in the eyes of some, the two are inseparable:

> As we search for practical knowledge and liberating ways of knowing, working with people in their everyday lives, we can also see that action research is participative research, and all participative research must be action research [...] Action research is only possible *with*, *for* and *by* persons and communities, ideally involving all stakeholders both in the questioning and sensemaking that informs the research, *and* in the action which is its focus.
>
> (Reason and Bradbury 2001: 2)

Interestingly, however, this model of participation is often based around the action researcher as a facilitator of a wider group, establishing relationships with a particular community and then supporting them through a process of change. The weakness of such an approach is in the reliance on a partnership which has the potential to simply produce an alternative form of control, reliant on the powerful position of the researcher (Chambers 1983), thus failing to achieve genuine participation. Nevertheless this does establish one aspect of action research, namely that it is concerned with challenging social inequality and achieving societal change through active participation. This argument has also been made by other authors who call for a 'critical' approach to action research in which 'The practitioner group takes joint responsibility for the development of practice, understandings and situations, and sees these as socially-constructed in the interactive processes of educational life' (Carr and Kemmis 1986: 203).

This is critical in the sense that it relates to the emancipatory ideals of critical theory. In the view of Carr and Kemmis, the limitations in the success of practice must, necessarily, be associated with limitations in the theoretical views which underpin such practice. Thus action research has the potential to be emancipatory in that it frees people, through collective action, from the restrictions of the assumptions that are made of them and of their social context. This is distinct from some of the participatory approaches described above, in that it is reliant more on developing a community of action researchers who develop their understandings and implementation of practice through collective dialogue, and not through the inquiry process led by an external agent, although there is likely to be some form of external facilitation in each model.

Developing Practices through Reflective Inquiry

Lewin's aspirations were to implement a form of research which was orientated towards action and concerned with practice. This emphasis on developing practices has also been embraced by others, such as Stephen Corey (1953: 70) who stated: 'We are convinced that the disposition to study, as objectively as possible, the consequences of our own teaching is more likely to change and improve our practices than is reading about what someone else has discovered of his teaching.

In the UK, Lawrence Stenhouse led the development of other, education-specific, programmes of developing practices through practitioner research, stating that 'It is teachers who, in the end, will change the world of school by understanding it' (Rudduck 1995: 3). Stenhouse (1975: 144) proposed a model of the extended professional which had principles of questioning and inquiry at its heart, proposing that such extended professionals would show the following characteristics:

- the commitment to systematic questioning of one's own teaching as a basis for development
- the commitment and the skills to study one's own teaching
- the concern to question and to test theory in practice by the use of those skills

In this model of action research practitioners are supported in systematically studying their own practice, enhancing their understanding of the context of their own work and developing practices accordingly. This is more than simply an 'add on' to practice, indeed there is one sense in which characteristics shown by the practitioner-researcher are synonymous with the qualities of an effective practitioner. Whilst this is practice-focused, the aspiration to achieve change can be consistent with the social justice emphasis of the critical/emancipatory view. Indeed, the practice of teachers is often concerned with notions of equality and of the influence that their work can have on the lives, and hence life chances, of their pupils. Under these circumstances a focus on enhancing practice can be considered, by definition, to be concerned with addressing social inequality and injustice, as it is concerned with enhancing the life chances of students.

This is not to claim that the social justice agenda of advocates of critical/emancipatory action researchers is entirely practice-free. In referring to practice they provide a view of the outcomes of action research, and the productivity of work, which emphasizes the commitments which underpin actions and which is more consistent with social justice and socially responsible action:

> Action researchers can examine their own educational practices to discover the ways in which they are distorted away from these values; they can also examine the situations and institutions in which they practice to see how they are constituted so as to prevent a more rational communication, more just and democratic decision making, and productive work which provides those involved with real access to an interesting and satisfying life.
>
> (Carr and Kemmis 1986: 193–4)

Central to all of this are the action researchers themselves. In particular, emphasis is made of the part that action can play in helping individuals understand themselves, of how they relate to their context and how their actions can be developed to better achieve the aims that they have for their work. This is at the heart of the final issue to be emphasized here: reflexivity and the study of the self.

Reflexivity and understanding of the self

The term 'reflexivity' tends to be used in three main ways (see e.g. Abercrombie *et al.* 2000: 291–2). The first of these refers to theories, theoretical positions or related disciplines which routinely challenge the fundamentals of the positions that they promote. Advocates of participatory research, for example, regard it as being a reflexive discipline because it continually challenges the reality of the equal contributions of participants that it endorses (Heron and Reason 1997).

A second use of reflexivity is one associated with ethnomethodologists, who refer to the meaning that people make of the world in which they live (Pfohl 1985). This meaning is neither constructed by individuals in isolation from each other, nor is it solely acquired from society, but involves a process in which perceptions and experiences are interpreted through individual beliefs and preconceptions, in part influenced by the society of which they are a part.

While both of these have relevance for action research, it is the third form of reflexivity which is of most importance here. In a personal sense, reflexivity also refers to the ways in which people examine their own beliefs, perceptions and practices, and implement change as a result (Bourdieu 1992). Action research can be seen as a reflexive discipline as it involves the action researcher in a process of developing and understanding themselves and how they relate to their context, and taking action accordingly.

This relates to the work of Jacob Moreno, a contemporary of Lewin, who has also been attributed as one of the founders of action research (Moreno 1953; Gunz 1996; Boog 2003). If Lewin's legacy was one of change led by communities through processes of external facilitation, then Moreno's was more concerned with the personal focus of psychotherapy, instigating practices such as psychodrama and sociodrama. These are seen as methods for allowing individuals to reflect upon their context, identify limiting factors from their social setting and then freeing themselves from those limitations. This is reflexive in the sense that it is concerned with examining the individual's relationships with society, and then implementing appropriate change.

A particular form of action research which emphasizes the self-exploration of a reflexive approach is 'living education theory' which is grounded in the 'I' of the researcher (McNiff and Whitehead 2006: 41). In adopting this approach, action researchers 'use a form of thinking that sees things in relation with one another. The aim of the researcher is to hold themselves accountable for their learning and their influence in the learning of others (McNiff and Whitehead 2006: 42).

And so such an approach advocates a process of self-study, which takes into account not only the personal beliefs, preconceptions and aspirations of the action researcher, but also how they interact with and affect their immediate context (in the case of teachers their school communities). This is not intended purely as a process of developing self-understanding, but in keeping with the aspirations of action research, the core beliefs revealed by this process are intended to result in related change.

The purpose of the reflexive aspects of action research is to understand, but also challenge, the perceptions and understanding of the individual, and reveal how they relate to the context in question. By adopting such a reflexive approach, questions are posed such as:

- How do my actions relate to my beliefs?
- How have I changed from this process?
- How reasonable are my preconceptions?
- How do my perceptions relate to the context of this practice?

The challenge is to address these questions through the process of action research and not simply as a limited conceptual exercise. In other words, the action researcher should consider how to adopt reflexive practices.

Process Models of Action Research

This section describes some models which are intended to represent the action research process. The process is intended to be cyclical in that the stages of plan → act → observe → reflect ultimately lead back to planning and was described by Lewin (1948: 205) as follows:

> The first step then is to examine the idea carefully in the light of the means available. Frequently more fact-finding about the situation is required. If this first period of planning is successful, two items emerge: namely, 'an overall plan' of how to reach the objective and secondly, a decision in regard to the first step of action. Usually this planning has also somewhat modified the original idea.

This emphasizes a second, cyclical aspect of action research, that the understandings developed through phases of a project are compared against the original aims and, based upon this reflection, these aims are revised. And so the conduct of one phase leads to a developed understanding of the initial problem and an appropriate design of the following phase.

Based around this description of the process of action research, a number of authors have developed graphical representations of cycles, two of which are shown here. The first, shown in Figure 8.1, was designed by Kemmis and McTaggart (1982). While showing those repeating phases the flow diagram is intended to indicate a progression from one cycle to the next.

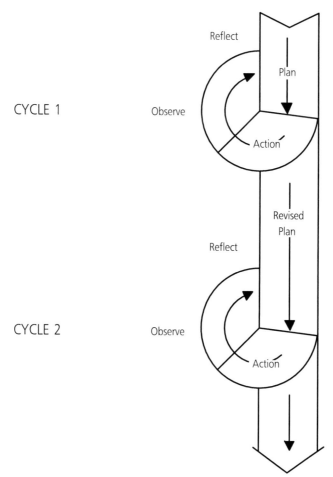

Figure 8.1 Kemmis and McTaggart's action research cycle (1982)

The second, shown in Figure 8.2, was produced by Elliott (1991) and provides a more detailed step-by-step plan. In particular it emphasizes:

- that the general idea might shift (by explicitly revisiting the original purpose of this work)
- an expanded role for reconnaissance from simply fact-finding to a more analytical and recurring theme which could also provide evaluative evidence
- that monitoring the progress of the implementation of an action step should precede monitoring the effects of the associated actions

Both of these expansions of the initial Lewinian cycle emphasize the relationship between the collection of evidence and the implementation of actions – i.e. the fusion of action and research. In some respects this calls into question the nature of data, or evidence, derived from research, and how this data relate to action. By way of an illustration, an example of integrated research and action is provided in Box 8.2.

Models, such as those shown above, are by definition speculative and are likely to be applied differently in different contexts. In addition, the initial concept of one cycle leading directly to

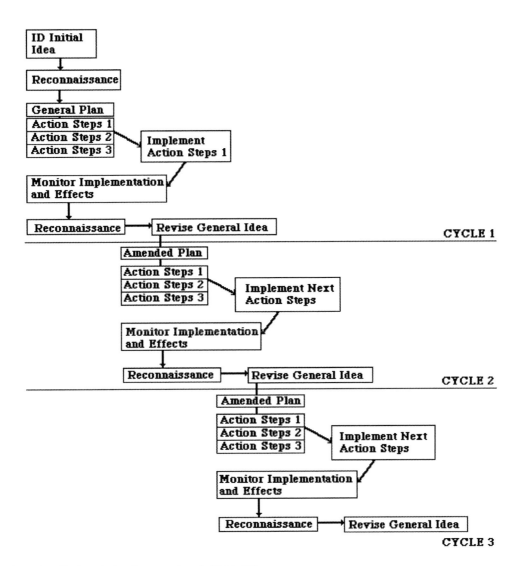

Figure 8.2 Elliott's revised action research cycle (1991: 91)

the next would suggest that the cycle is flexible, depending on what is learned at each step. All steps of the plan of action, for example, need not be implemented if the early steps elicit understanding or perceptions which make the later stages of the plan redundant. Each of the cycles shown above is accompanied by a much more lengthy explanation of the process which could not be covered here. But to provide a little more illustration of this, an extended model is outlined in Box 8.3.

Box 8.2 The nature of data in action research

This experience of one action researcher is intended to question the nature and purpose of data in action research. The action researcher in question worked in a medium-sized primary school (4–11-year-old students). This was a rather challenging school to work in and contact with parents and families was a major issue. The action researcher was concerned, as were many others in the school, with poor pupil literacy, but also with the lack of contact between the school and the parents of pupils.

Her action research was thus concerned with those two aims, to implement strategies to improve pupil literacy and to engage more fully with parents in this process. One of the first steps was to conduct a questionnaire survey of parental perceptions of children's literacy education. In particular this was intended to explore the nature of the support provided to pupils at home, but was also meant to provide a route through which parents could be informed of the project and, as a result, might choose to participate in it more actively.

This questionnaire included two questions about the nature of parental support for reading. The first asked whether parents read with their children, the second, later in the questionnaire, how long they spent engaging in such reading activities. It is perhaps unsurprising, bearing in mind status- and power-ridden relations between schools and parent bodies, that many of the answers to these questions were contradictory. One response would indicate that reading was a regular occurrence, the other that parents simply couldn't find time for such support. This could be attributed to the tendency for research participants to give socially acceptable responses, but is also a recognition of the desire to respond positively to their child's school.

However, although the contradiction in responses did challenge the extent to which the action researcher felt she could rely on the outcomes of this work, the questionnaire served another purpose. By inviting parents to take part in the work (participation was voluntary and responses anonymized), parents were also informed of the opportunity to become involved in other developments and how to register their interest. Indeed, following the application of the questionnaire, many parents did just that, and so, while some of the data derived from the questionnaire seemed to have limited benefit, the resulting enhanced engagement of parents as partners in this process was of considerable benefit in furthering mutual understanding and the subsequent development of reading practices.

This illustration is not intended to suggest that any form of research is flawless, indeed all research has its limitations and it is worth questioning the extent of the participative aspects in this example. Rather, it illustrates that the nature of data, and their collection, can serve more purposes than simply informing understanding. Changes in action and practices can also result from data collection; indeed, the aspiration of action research is that action and research are interrelated, rather than one being derived purely from the other.

An adherence to the above cycles might not necessarily incorporate some of the principles outlined above. It is possible, for example, to imagine an action research process being conducted by an individual which very closely matched one of these cycles, but which was an entirely individual affair and which, as a result, did not match the participatory principle of action research.

Box 8.3 An extended model of an action research process

Stage	Key activities
1 Refining a focus	This initial phase involves a period of reflection, dialogue (especially if action research is being conducted as part of a collective) and consultation to identify a potential focus for change.
2 Conducting reconnaissance	A phase during which the focus is refined and developed and potential actions identified. The intention of this phase is to further clarify, and possibly refine, the focus articulated in Stage 1. It also helps to understand what is already happening in relation to this focus, both within and beyond the immediate focus for action.
3 Reflecting on progress	This aspect is intended to build on the reconnaissance to consolidate what has been learned. This is not just a stage of itemizing the outcomes of reconnaissance, but rather should be an interrogation of the initial focus and identify how what has been learned from reconnaissance relates to those initial aspirations. This might include deciding that the initial focus was in some way inappropriate.
4 Planning for action	Having established the outcomes of reconnaissance, the next stage is to identify appropriate actions. Although intended to be actions which address the overall focus, this could include a second reconnaissance phase, which may be appropriate if the focus is refined, or developed, or is now judged to be inappropriate. However, the aspirations of this stage fit into three main themes: 1 What actions should now be taken? 2 How can the outcomes of these actions be observed? 3 How should the action steps proceed, including asking who else should be involved and in what ways?
5 Implementing and observing action	This is the stage at which actions are introduced. Note that this is not the first thing that happens in the action research process but that it arises from a process of reflection and reconnaissance. While the emphasis in this stage is concerned with the implementation of an action plan, two forms of observation are also carried out: observing the progress of implementation and the immediate effect of actions. Please also note that in this extended model the observing and action stages that are separate in the above cycles are combined.
6 Reflecting and evaluating change	The final stage is an opportunity to pause, take stock and ask: what has changed? In one respect this can involve a formal phase of evaluation, but is also likely to involve a period of reflection on the original purposes of the action research, and to ask, not only whether they have been addressed, but whether they and the initial perceptions have changed. The intention is that this will then lead back to Step 1 and the clarification of a revised focus.

The extended cycle described in Box 8.3 comes with two caveats. The first is that, although shown as a series of consecutive steps, each stage could overlap – for example, not all actions need to be pre-planned prior to the implementation of the first steps of the action plan. Similarly, reconnaissance does not necessarily cease with the first action step and the information gleaned from further reconnaissance, or from the outcomes of action steps, can influence subsequent steps. The second caveat is that the stages do not all need to be followed through regardless of what has been learned. It may be perfectly appropriate, for example, to conduct a second phase of reconnaissance, if the first does not sufficiently inform the focus, or if it completely changes the perceptions of the action researcher, such that the focus shifts significantly. In these circumstances it would be inappropriate to persist with developing an action plan based on the original premise, and it may be more appropriate to refocus.

Criticisms have been made of representing action research as a cycle. The suggestion is that such representations limit the development of practices as they impose a series of steps, which is perceived as being contradictory to the initial empowering aims of the practitioner research movement (Hopkins 1993). McTaggart (1996: 248) also emphasizes that, rather than being a prescribed process, action research involves a commitment to a core set of ideals or principles: 'Action research is not a method or a procedure for research but a series of commitments to observe and problematise through practice, a series of principles for conducting social enquiry'.

Indeed the very history of action research as a prescribed process is questioned, the argument being that, in describing this approach, Lewin intended purely to emphasize the difference between interpretive, action-orientated research and more traditional, positivistic approaches. The extended model shown in Box 8.3 could also be subjected to criticisms but perhaps the best way to view such models is as 'ideal' steps along a process of change.

Summary

This chapter is intended to provide an introduction to the nature, origins and facets of action research. While some authors have identified what they perceive as a division in action research communities between the practice-focused approaches of the northern hemisphere and the empowering, critical approaches of the southern hemisphere (Brown and Tandon 1983), it seems reasonable to consider that both approaches have elements of the three main themes identified here, albeit with a slightly different emphasis.

The stages identified above, and the principles upon which they are founded, are intended to represent an alternative approach to the generation of knowledge and the implementation of change that is more situated in the interests and perspectives of the individuals most affected by such change. It is, as a result, a challenge to the perceived powerful position of academics, whose research is intended to influence practitioners, but to which some practitioners find it very hard to relate. This argument, however, seems a little over-simplistic and it is perhaps better to consider the participatory principles of action research as relating to all stakeholders – i.e. action research can provide the opportunity for the development of practices through collaboration amongst all members of the educational community.

Furthermore, attempts to implement action research are often best achieved with the active support, and participation, of individuals with differing perspectives on the same issue. This would seem to suggest that collaboration between different groups of stakeholders would represent a strength to the whole.

References

Abercrombie, N., Hill, S. and Turner, B.S. (2000) *Dictionary of Sociology*, 4th edn. London: Penguin Reference.

Adleman, C. (1993) 'Kurt Lewin and the origins of action research', *Educational Action Research*, 1(1): 7–24.

Angelides, P., Georgiou, R. and Kyriakou, K. (2008) 'The implementation of a collaborative action research programme for developing inclusive practices: social learning in small internal networks', *Educational Action Research*, 16(4): 557–68.

Boog, B. W. M. (2003) 'The emancipatory character of action research, its history and the present state of the art', *Journal of Community and Applied Social Psychology*, 13(6): 426–38.

Bourdieu, P. (1992) *Invitation to a Reflexive Sociology*. Chicago: University of Chicago Press.

Brown, D., and Tandon, R. (1983) 'Ideology and political economy in inquiry: action research and participatory research', *Journal of Applied and Behavioural Science*, 19: 277–94.

Carr, W. and Kemmis, S. (1986) *Becoming Critical: Education, Knowledge and Action Research*. London: RoutledgeFarmer.

Chambers, R. (1983) *Rural Development: Putting the Last First*. London: Longman.

Corey, S. (1953) *Action Research To Improve School Practices*. New York: Teachers College Press.

Cox, S. and Robinson-Pant, A. (2008) 'Power, participation and decision making in the primary classroom: children as action researchers', *Educational Action Research*, 16(4): 457–68.

Edwards, K. (2008) 'Examining the impact of phonics intervention on secondary students' reading improvement', *Educational Action Research*, 16(4): 545–55.

Elliott, J. (1991) *Action Research for Educational Change*. Bukingham: Open University Press.

Grundy, S. (1987) *Curriculum: Product or Praxis*. London: The Falmer Press.

Gunz, J. (1996) 'Jacob L. Moreno and the origins of action research', *Educational Action Research*, 4(1): 145–8.

Heron, J. and Reason, P. (1997) 'A participatory inquiry paradigm', *Qualitative Inquiry*, 3(3): 274–94.

Hopkins, D. (1993) *A Teacher's Guide to Classroom Research*. Buckingham: Open University Press.

Kemmis, S. and McTaggart, R. (1982) *The Action Research Planner*. Geelong, Victoria: Deakin University Press.

Kemmis, S., and McTaggart, R. (1988) *The Action Research Planner*, 2nd edn. Geelong, Victoria: Deakin University Press.

Lewin, K. (1946) 'Action research and minority problems', *Journal of Social Issues*, 2(4): 34–46.

Lewin, K. (1948) *Resolving Social Conflicts*. New York: Harper.

Lewin, K. (1951) *Field Theory in Social Science: Selected Theoretical Papers*. New York: Harper & Row.

McNiff, J. and Whitehead, J. (2006) *All You Need to Know About Action Research*. London: Sage.

McTaggart, R. (1996) 'Issues for participatory action researchers', in O. Zuber-Skerritt (ed.) *New Directions in Action Research*. London: Falmer Press.

Moreno, J. (1953) *Who Shall Survive?* New York: Beacon House.

Pfohl, S. J. (1985) *Images of Deviance and Social Control: A Sociological History*. New York: McGraw-Hill.

Reason, P. and Bradbury, H. (2001) 'Introduction: inquiry and participation in search of a world worthy of human aspiration', in P. Reason, and H. Bradbury (eds) *Handbook of Action Research: Participative Inquiry and Practice*. London: Sage.

Rudduck, J. (1995) 'Introduction', in J. Rudduck (ed.) *An Education that Empowers: A Collection of Lectures in Memory of Lawrence Stenhouse.* Clevedon: Multilingual Matters.

Somekh, B. (2006) *Action Research: A Methodology for Change and Development.* Buckingham: Open University Press.

Stenhouse, L. (1975) *An Introduction to Curriculum Research and Development.* London: Heinemann.

Stringer, E. T. (1999) *Action Research.* London: Sage.

Winter, R. (1989) *Learning From Experience.* London: Falmer Press.

Ethnographic Encounters with Children

Pia Christensen

9

Introduction

This chapter discusses some of the important questions that arise in contemporary research with children and explores the challenges to researchers, who, rather than setting out to learn *about* children's lives, wish to learn *from* children themselves (Ferguson 2000). Underlying this approach is the importance of researchers listening to children, hearing what they say and fully understanding their meanings (Roberts 2000/2008). From this perspective, it is key that researchers develop dialogical practices in which children wish to take part and, instead of dedicating themselves to developing particular 'child friendly' methods, engage with children's own 'cultures of communication' (Christensen 1999a, 1999b; Christensen and James 2008). The active participation of children in research will inevitably question some taken-for-granted assumptions implied in much conventional thinking about children. In this chapter, I illustrate my discussion of these themes with ethnographic case examples, including ones from ethnographic studies that I have carried out during two decades. Ethnography provides in-depth and detailed insight into questions of children's lived experiences and practices, including into connections and interactions with their material, social and cultural worlds. Ethnography is intensive and its longitudinal character reveals, focuses and crystallizes many methodological questions and issues that researchers conducting other less intensive work with children encounter (Christensen and Prout, 2002).

By the end of this chapter, you should be able to:

- engage with the challenges of reconciling learning *about* children's lives, with learning *from* children themselves

- question preconceptions about issues of competence in childhood and reflect on the questions 'What is a child?' and 'What is an adult?'
- determine whether children's views are at the centre of research investigations
- interrogate the essentialism that researching children has often entailed

The Challenge of Researching Children

I have often been asked by students and researchers new to the field of childhood research how they can design their study so it is 'child-friendly' and 'fun' for the children taking part. Other common questions have included, 'How old do children need to be before taking part in research?' and 'Which methods are best suited for working with children?'. The thinking behind these questions can be seen as a puzzling over 'what a child is' and working with an idea of research design as a matter of deciding which 'toolbox' is needed to be well prepared for research with children. In a sense, these issues do appear to be central to 'unlocking the mystery' of conducting research with children. The researcher, like the magician in the marketplace, urgently feels the need to entice, entertain and intrigue their audience. They do this by bringing their box of tools and tricks. No audience – no performance! No fun – no children! No research?

However, research is in a sense a more straightforward matter. In order to do research with children it is necessary for the researcher to explore, clarify and critically question their own assumptions about what a child is (Van der Geest 1996), including any preconceptions the researcher has about the children who will take part in their specific study. Sometimes the expectation is that conducting research with children means engaging with people who are less capable than adults of taking part in research, or less likely to do so. Researchers may assume that children at different ages lack the necessary cognitive competencies to take part in research, including motivation and comprehension (see discussion of the development of psychological research in Woodhead and Faulkner 2000/2008). Researchers taking such approaches are assumed to take upon them a paternalistic approach as children may lack basic knowledge and insight for understanding the research. It is also often assumed that children will only engage in research if they have 'fun'.

In my experience, however, children in all age groups most of all like to be taken seriously and communicated with in ways that help them to feel that they are being treated as *partners* in research. It is important, therefore, to demonstrate through one's research practice that children's views are indeed at the centre of the investigation. Research with people of all ages has taught me that to be taken seriously and to be listened to are probably the most 'enticing' and fundamental aspects of research for the participants. One of the important rewards for taking part in research for children (as well as adults) is the researcher's genuine and sincere engagement in *attentive listening and looking* (see Christensen 1993). In this way the researcher enacts (and performs) real interest in understanding children's experiences and their aim to accurately represent children's points of view and the reality of their lives to others. It is such communicative qualities that are keys to engaging children (as well as adults) in research. Children are also often keen to know that sharing their experiences will contribute to creating change and to helping other children. Also, it should be recognized that taking part in research is hard work and time-consuming. It takes time away from children's leisure and work time (Nieuwenhuys 1993). Therefore, sometimes researchers may best appreciate children's contribution to research by payment or gifts for their time and efforts.

Research is challenging for both researcher and informants. For example, when conducting research some years ago in a hospital setting, many conversations and arrangements with nurses and doctors were carried out while chasing up and down corridors or in busy offices and rushed consultations. My brief encounters with the staff were accomplished between tasks and the encounters were often characterized by distractions and interruptions. At other times the research was a tiresome task, involving, for example, sitting with patients waiting to see a doctor, when nothing seemed to be happening. Indeed, any piece of research entails a good measure of patience and perseverance by all those involved. In essence this research setting is no different from observing children in their everyday lives at school, at home or at work when they are playing or roaming about the street, neighbourhood and playground, the brief conversations and snapshot encounters with children during break-times, or an interview that needs to be drawn to a conclusion because the child participant has lost concentration and interest. Ethnographic research can be seen as composed of encounters that require the researcher to meet the persons (participants) where they are and during what they are doing.

Research with children is not best understood as a set of issues based in a taken-for-granted (age-based) adult/child distinction (Christensen and James 2008). I wish to emphasize the necessity of researchers to question the essentialism with which the study of children conventionally has been suffused (James and Prout 1997). Furthermore, research with children does not mean that any particular methods or set of ethical standards, different from those used with other categories of research subject, are required. The questions that the researcher of children faces during the research process are not unique to working with children (Christensen and James 2008). All research raises questions about suitability. To work with any prior notion that research with children is different to research with adults is an 'error' because it evades other more important questions in research with children. It gives primacy to age and omits other aspects of children's identities such as gender, ethnicity, social, economic, cultural and political identity that are crucial when thinking and developing research practices. The choice and development of suitable methods enables the researcher to investigate and answer their research questions. However, research methodology needs also to be meaningful to the people participating in the research, which needs to be informed by their questions and concerns and take into account their particular social, historical, cultural and material contexts. Researchers therefore should not aim to be 'child friendly', but ensure that their research is 'participant friendly' (Fraser 2004).

Ethnography as a Multi-method Approach

Ethnography is a distinct type of research where the knowledge that is produced depends on fieldwork. The researcher takes part in close social interaction with informants in their milieu, over an extensive period of time. For the purpose of this discussion, I look at ethnography as a multimethod approach in so far as fieldwork frequently involves a combination of different methods (see Figure 9.1). At the core of ethnographic fieldwork are three elements. The first is *participant observation.* This is the key method that distinguishes ethnography from other qualitative studies. The second element is the *ethnographic interview.* The third is the *researcher.* I often argue that 'the researcher' is the most important tool in any qualitative or ethnographic research. The quantitative researcher needs to put much effort and care into developing, for example, a suitable and effective questionnaire, as this may be their most important tool for producing reliable data. It is the questionnaire that works in the field as a mediator between the researcher and his or her respondents to produce data. On the other hand, it is the ethnographer's qualitative researcher's conduct in the field, their skills (including interpersonal ones) and their craft that is crucial for the production of the data.

Looking at Figure 9.1 it is important to note that it does not assume that 'the more methods, the better the research'. On the contrary, the employment of multiple or mixed methods is primarily to help the researcher to investigate their research question from various angles and perspectives. A second purpose is that a combination of methods will facilitate dialogue and active participation by children because it gives them different opportunities to take part. This, in my experience, is best achieved through the researcher developing, engaging with and facilitating various forms of communication. For children to engage with research necessitates the researcher developing a practice that is in line with and reflects children's experiences, interests, values and everyday routines. It involves adopting communicative structures that children use to express and represent their views in the different contexts of their everyday lives. Taking research and children seriously does not prevent the children (or the researcher) from actually having fun (indeed

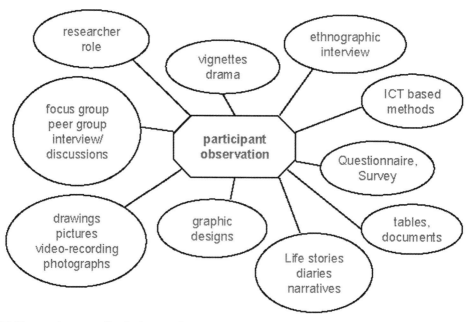

Figure 9.1 Ethnography as a multimethod approach

'shared humour' and the exchange of a smile is unique in connecting and facilitating human relations globally), but it does require researchers to engage in dialogues that connect with children on their own terms, allowing them to share both happy and sad experiences, difficult emotions and the positive and negative aspects of their interaction with the researcher.

Traditional anthropological fieldwork methods include ethnographic interviews and participant observation, supplemented with participatory techniques. Figure 9.1 shows some of the methods that have been used in research with children including visuals, writing tasks, drama, graphical designs, video and photos and peer group discussions. As is now widely recognized in research with children, studies need not to confine themselves to producing verbal accounts requiring speech, language and conversational skills. Rather, it is important to encourage children to use a diversity of means to express themselves in the communication between researcher and themselves (see also Clarke and Moss,2001). However, it is important that the way of communicating with children corresponds to their own cultures of communication.

Conducting research with children

It is important to form research relationships that children would want to maintain throughout the research process (Christensen 2004). The basis for developing research relationships is established in the very first encounters with the children, when the researcher presents and explains the aims of their study. I often introduce my research by saying, 'I am interested in how children experience their everyday life. It's important for me to get a better understanding of what it means to children themselves. What you think and what you do!' In this way, I wish to convey to the children the emphasis I put on *their own* perspectives. During the research, my aim is to perform and demonstrate my interest genuinely and in ways that are convincing to the children. For instance, when conducting formal interviews such as a peer group (or focus group) interview, I work with an underlying notion of facilitating a continuing dialogue, which children feel they have control over and which allows them independence in our conversations. Although I often introduce my general aim and purpose to the children, they are encouraged to take our conversation in a direction that allows them to introduce their own themes and also to conclude an interview on their own terms (see Box 9.1).

Box 9.1 Research as dialogue

The notion of research as a dialogical practice signifies a general move within the human and social sciences away from seeing the researcher as 'collecting' and 'gathering' data to recognizing both the researcher and the informant as active in the 'production' of data. The research process is a joint venture allowing for equity between researcher and informant. This does not omit questions of power and control in the research process but it recognizes the importance of establishing more fluid notions that actively work to establish informants as participants and partners in shaping the research.

In my first study I was interested in children's own perspectives on health and illness. This research involved interviews with 6 to 7-year-old children at school. Our conversations were relatively short and set around a specific topic. For example, small groups of children were asked to make a drawing of 'the last time you were ill' and were then interviewed individually. Each child decided when their drawing was finished and the interview would stop when the child wanted it to, although sometimes I eventually suggested that we finish because I felt they were beginning to feel 'fed up' or tired.

However, it was only in subsequent interactions with the same children, when they knew and trusted me, that I learned that our first encounters had been conditioned by the children's initial discomforts. Then I had been a 'stranger' and an 'adult', but also, as they now confided, they thought the subject of our conversations (i.e., everyday health) was sometimes 'peculiar', 'rubbish' or simply 'boring'. The problem this presented me with was how to understand children's puzzled, though not altogether disengaged, responses to my interest in their experiences of health and the everyday management of an illness. On reflection, it became obvious to me that children's openness and engagement had been restricted by their shyness and occasional mild disapproval of the subjects we talked about, both in the spontaneous group discussions sparked off among the children while making the drawings and in the conversations I had with them individually afterwards.

While I was able to carry out the interviews because of the children's cooperative and accepting manner, I began to reflect seriously on what needed to be taken into account when researching children's perspectives. It became evident that the children's accepting and cooperative response to me seemed to mirror the inherent power relation between researcher and researched. In child research this may be reinforced by more general cultural notions of power and control in generational relations between children and adults (Alderson 1995; Mayall 2000/2008; Alanen and Mayall 2003). This can especially be the case when research is carried out at school or in the classroom where children are expected to give precedence to the adult/teacher setting the agenda for many activities. The conclusion to be drawn is that one-off interviews with children, whether these are qualitative or quantitative, or use task-oriented tools or not, may appear on the surface to be quite possible to carry out in school. However, for researchers who wish to learn about children's own perspectives such arrangements are unlikely to provide a context within which children feel they can respond in accordance with their own views. This is because children will have been left little scope for engaging in a critical manner with the research questions and the research practice, even despite the fact that they may have given informed consent.

In the course of this fieldwork I developed my ability to *listen and look attentively* with children, both during our conversations and their conversations with each other. That I choose to make this point may seem crude and somehow naive. However, it was crucial to the way my relationships with the children were developed and shaped throughout the study. Working with groups of children is an engrossing experience. Its almost constant business leads one to at times feel one is in the middle of a fusillade of noise, tempo and activities. Through this, I became aware of the importance of *looking and listening* when the children asked me to. I developed a determination not to let myself be interrupted by something or somebody else until a child had completed what he or she wanted me to see or hear. I supposed that, from the children's point of view, this confirmed that I was genuinely interested and wished to learn and understand about their lives.

Research with Children as a Dialogical Practice

As I have illustrated above, my development of a dialogical research practice was prompted and shaped by the children. Their initial discomforts in engaging with the research were closely connected to the ambiguity of my role. I seemed to be an adult conducting myself like other adults they knew at school. I was therefore an 'outsider' to their social relationships with each other. At the same time, I seemed to want to engage with their lives in a way different from most adults (Fine 1987; Mandell, 1991). The children's reactions can be seen as calls for me 'to take sides'. Their mockery of my questions about 'health' showed me very directly that from their perspective I was not part of their groups. A 'choice' was therefore made clear to me. I could decide to engage with the children in my research from the position of an adult, such as the teacher, calling on the status and authority given to teachers. Alternatively, I could develop a form of communication and interaction which resonated with the children's own practices and, therefore, could be seen as acceptable by the children.

The lessons to be drawn are manifold. Most importantly, this first encounter is a reminder that research questions are very rarely posed at the request of the participants in our research. In this particular study on children's health practices and experiences the questions were posed by me and central to my interests and concern, not theirs. This, at the time new-found understanding, led me to ensure that my questions were understandable for children; that the way I designed my research engaged with their interests and concerns; and that our interactions took on a reciprocal form. I also realized, with a humility and gratitude that still remains, the many ways in which the children engaged with me: taking great effort to include me in their everyday lives, explaining their activities and relationships and even, as some children did, developing a sense of what I wanted to know. During the final stage of my fieldwork, some children were able to guess my questions and often began to answer them before I addressed them explicitly.

The theoretical implication underlines my earlier point about ethnography as a dialogical enterprise (Tedlock 1979; Baktin 1986; Tedlock and Mannheim 1995). One of the main features of my approach was to attend to what I have termed the 'cultures of communication' encountered in the field (see Box 9.2). This approach is an important step away from the idea of researchers developing and using particular methods for particular groups of people. Rather, it emphasizes the importance of seeing fieldwork (with children and adults alike) as a practical engagement with local cultural practices of communication. Thus, by observing children's language use, their conceptual meanings and their actions, the researcher is able to piece together a picture of the social interactions and the connections between people. Through getting to know the different codes of conduct and communication, and contexts and timing, the researcher learns from the children how to behave and interact with and among them. At the same time, the researcher will be able to engage with the differences constituted in the field between and among children and adults. This includes an appreciation of how different contexts – for example, the school, the home and the street – constitute a set of positions from which children and adults 'speak'.

Box 9.2 Cultures of communication

This notion relates to research as a dialogical practice. It refers to developing a practice that is in line with children's experiences, interests, values and everyday routines. It involves the researcher in engaging with the communicative structures that children use to express and represent their views in the different contexts of their everyday lives. It entails observing children's language use and understanding the meanings of children's words, notions and actions. The researcher will need to engage with codes of conduct as they already exist in the settings they work in order to understand children's social interactions and relationships. In this sense the researcher learns from the children (and other informants) how to conduct themselves, interact and communicate in ways that benefit their research. Understanding 'cultures of communication' can be gained through participant observation, conversations and reading the work of other scholars in the field.

In my example, engagement with the children and understanding their culture of communication also enabled me to better understand how I became integrated into their everyday lives. I suggest that my readiness to join in with and my respect for the communicative forms of children established reciprocity between us and thus created a route for them to enter into a dialogue with me about particular questions, interests and ways of communicating. It thus established a dialogue through which it became possible to create a better understanding of the social interactions and relations in which children are involved (Christensen and James 2000/ 2008). Much in the same vein, recent research has demonstrated how this can be successfully done with very young children by developing an imaginative array of methods for listening to them (Clarke and Moss 2001). Clarke and Moss stress that research needs to be carried out with sensitivity and respect, concluding that: 'It is not only a question of seeing the world from children's perspectives but of acknowledging their rights to express their point of view or to remain silent. We are keen that a participatory approach to listening is respectful of children's views and also of their silences' (2001).

Working out research questions: talking about health

It is worth reflecting on the kind of data that are likely to be produced through research that is more or less solely directed by the researcher's interests rather than the priorities and agendas of the respondents. This calls for a sincere consideration of whether the subject of the research makes sense to them and how it may be made to reflect their experiences and perceptions (Mauthner 1997). As described earlier, the youngest children responded to my interest in their illnesses with puzzlement, as if illness belonged to the category of rather mundane and uninteresting events in everyday life. Among the older children, I sometimes experienced straightforward resentment towards talking about illness. It seemed that they saw illness as an unsuitable subject for conversation.

To begin to understand the broader framework of children's thinking, children's accounts must be related to how they conceptualize, develop and apply understandings of their social and cultural world. For example, it was not only necessary to investigate the topic of health from a variety of different angles and over a period of time, but it was also important to consider whether or not children knew about a particular experience, how they named it and whether it was significant for them. Through our conversations and my observations I familiarized myself with their culture of communication and would make use of children's own vocabulary and formulations. This again led me into detailed questioning and reflection on children's sometimes enigmatic replies (see e.g. Christensen 1993, 1999b). This persistence was rewarded, however, by a deeper understanding of children's views and I would argue that it is through such research practices that the researcher is able to produce a 'thick description' that prevents research making unwarranted analytical jumps (see also Geertz, 1973: 6–10).

It is important to explore ideas about the exchanges between the participants in research and the set of ethical values, such as confidentiality and trust, that underscore the work we do (see Chapter 7 for a detailed discussion on research ethics). Working together with children in research requires attention to the trust and loyalty that accompany it. In my attempt to unravel particular parts of my fieldwork, I have shown how my research engagement with the children provoked new lines of thinking and research practice.

What is a Child? The Role of the Researcher

The third important tool in research, woven through my discussion so far, is the distinctive role of the fieldworker in the way research relationships are developed through the research process. In my introduction to this chapter, I argued that one of the first questions that a researcher needs to address is 'What is a child?' Researchers have long discussed the importance of attending to how they conduct themselves. Some researchers contrast the researcher's relationship to the children with that of other key adults such as teachers (Baraldi 2002). Two distinctive roles have been distinguished: the role of an 'other adult' (Fine and Sandstrom 1988; Pollard and Filer 1996; Mayall 2000/2008); and the 'least adult role'. The latter has been advocated by child researchers who have attempted to modify their adult identity and status, such as Mandell (1991) and, from a feminist perspective, Thorne (1993). For Mandell, this role involved her in rejecting exercising adult authority over children and engaging as a participant in their activities, most notably spending hours with the children in their sandpit games to the puzzlement of adult staff in the nursery. This strategy must be commended for its wholehearted effort to enter into and participate in children's social relations but is open to the criticism that it seems simply to wish away the complexity of the differences and similarities between children and adults as they are currently constituted. From this perspective the issue of power is one of social position with a preconception of children as the least powerful in the institutional settings of their everyday lives. Lærke (1998: 30), who advocates the role of the researcher as aiming to be as a 'child', describes her role in the field in this way: 'I aimed to be as "child-ish" as possible. I dressed like the children, ate with the children, stood nicely in line with the children and so forth. I did not speak with the staff on a daily basis and therefore I knew only what a pupil at school would know, which was not much with regard to the overall planning of the school day'. It is clear from this account that Lærke, as an ethnographer of children, wishes to break from her status as an 'adult' when working in the field. However, she does that through a reifying notion about what it means to be a child – by making the assumption that children are passive, separated from adults and generally ignorant of institutional life. In a piece of my own research with children aged 8–12 I asked them to comment on the role of the child researcher. As an example for discussion, I presented them (in anonymized form) with Lærke's account, above. The children felt offended, because it seemed to them that the researcher belittled children and they did not respect the adult effort to be 'childish'. For children being 'childish' is not in any way a preferable or acceptable child identity.

In contrast, the next example shows how the ethnographer sees children's relationships as informed by knowledge and news-sharing. This is the account of an anthropologist studying the lives of working children in India:

> I found nevertheless support from the children whom I met while they were at work. They did not think it awkward that I should show some interest in what they did. The thought that I was interviewing them to write down what they said excited them. Some became spontaneously my informants, reporting to me all the news that used to go from mouth to mouth. A few even sought in me their patroness, asking me for small loans with which to start a business or for loans to buy the necessities for going to school.
>
> (Nieuwenhuys 1993: 46)

While the above examples show how important it is for researchers not to make stereotypical assumptions about what a child is, in this section I will also introduce another related issue – the importance of the question 'What is an adult?', not only to the researcher but also to the children and others that take part in the study. However, the definition and meaning of 'adult' as a social and cultural category remains relatively unexplored and unproblematized in researchers' accounts. 'Adult' acts as an umbrella term that does not specify the institutional practice or status concerned – for example, 'teacher', 'parent' or 'pedagogue'. Research with children requires researchers to be accepted by both children and adults – an issue that has received some attention in the research literature and one to which several sorts of solution have been attempted. The most focus has been on the relationship between an adult ethnographer and children. Fine notes that differences between adults and children such as size and place in the hierarchy of organizations make it almost impossible for an adult ethnographer to 'pass' as a child (1987: 222). It thus seems difficult to become a 'native insider' to their social and cultural lives, the role that Geertz (1983) maintains is central to doing ethnography. Fine and Sandstrom (1988) suggest that the ethnographer of childhood has to find a way of straddling the divide between adults' and children's worlds and they suggest adopting roles such as that of 'adult friend' to the children. This maintains adult identity but softens it so as to allow a partial access to the children's experiences and perspectives.

However, in contrast, children often greet researchers who enter their lives as 'a stranger', with the frank question, 'Who are you?'. By making this enquiry children encapsulate one of the key processes of research: the working through of wider notions of 'who we are to each other'. This is an important antecedent to how we relate to each other, a process that both researchers and children engage in (see also Corsaro and Molinari 2000/2008). In my view the researcher's engagement with the detail of social interaction and the implications of social representations forms part of the process of children's genuine participation. As I will go on to demonstrate, researchers' responses to the question 'Who are you?' encapsulate the centrality of engaging with the lives of children and with the questions that are important to them.

Thus far, I have described how I fundamentally changed my approach to the children after their refusal to engage with my research. At its outset the study raised particular issues of methodology when studying children's everyday lives from their own perspective. Researchers have positioned themselves in relation to a taken-for-granted, general notion of what an adult is, assuming that this notion is somehow commonly shared across social and cultural settings. I suggest, however, that researchers need a more careful working out of the different 'versions' or representations of 'what an adult is' in everyday interactions in the particular settings of research. The apparent complexity of my role in the field was illustrated to me by a mother of one of the 10-year-old boys. We met on the football pitch outside the school on one of the last days of the fieldwork. While watching the game she said goodbye to me and then added: 'The children will miss you! But I'll tell you something – they didn't always know what to make of you. I mean, you haven't been an adult in a usual sense. They knew you weren't a teacher and that you weren't a mother, but I think sometimes they forgot that you weren't ten like themselves.'

In my research I did not aim at assuming the status of a 'child', which, from the point of view of children (or other adults), might have been perceived as patronizing and insincere. Thus in my research I have been aware of the ongoing balancing act between being recognized as an 'adult' and at the same time avoiding the preconceived ideas, practices and connotations associated with 'adulthood' or specific adult roles such as a teacher, member of staff or a parent. This status as an 'other adult' was inevitably negotiated and renegotiated with both children and adults during the entire process of the study. At one level of interactions with children, I followed the 'rules' set for adults at school – for example, regarding my own active (or not) participation in children's play or games. At another level, my participation, in general play or in a particular game, relied on following the children's rules and practices – for example, when joining in or leaving a game. I refused to adopt traditional adult roles in the institutional settings such as setting the rules of a game, telling children off, solving conflicts among the children or protecting and looking after them.

In this sense I developed an approach, later given support by Mayall (1998), that adults doing childhood research should present and perform themselves as an 'other' adult, one who is seriously interested in understanding how the social world looks from the children's perspective but without making a dubious attempt to *be* a child. Through this the researcher emerges first and foremost as a social person and secondly as a professional with a distinctive and genuine purpose.

I will conclude this section with a quotation from Pollard and Filer's ethnographic study into pupils' experiences in the late 1990s. This description of the role of the field researcher working with children bears a resemblance to my own experience as an ethnographer in the field working with children, and in this way help to summarize the points made above.

I was certainly viewed as being somewhat 'strange'. Here was an adult who was often at school, but who did not behave like a teacher, a parent, dinner supervisor or classroom assistant. He wandered around the classroom and the playground, watching activities, chatting with children, occasionally asking questions and recording their replies in his notebook. When asked what he was doing, he would explain that he was 'writing a story about what children think about school'. The children, with no other experience, accepted their pet researcher and joked about him. 'Was I a spy?', 'Was I Superman?' [...] As in my previous research with pupils, I found that children loved to be listened to and have their views taken seriously. This, of course, was simple for me because, unlike their teachers and parents, I had no responsibility for the children and no position to protect. Whilst I was never required to 'tell them off', I could indulge the children simply by being interested in them.

(Pollard and Filer 1996)

Summary

I have suggested that the participation of children in research emphasizes the dialogical qualities and the potential of, in this case, ethnography to reveal the working out of research relations over time. The dialogical approach is fruitful and necessary if children are to be actively involved in research. It requires that the ethnographer 'retrains' their attention so that they do not dominate a conversation, as adults often do. It requires a shift towards engaging with children's own cultures of communication, including the context and timing of communication, which are often key to this process. The researcher may be tempted to try and pass as a child but my experience is that children are well aware that this is a ploy. Children are very sensitive to adult-child differences precisely because they encounter them throughout their everyday lives. It is, however, possible to be a different sort of adult, one who, while not pretending to be a child, seeks throughout to respect children's views and wishes. Such a role inevitably involves a delicate balance between acting as a 'responsible adult' and maintaining the special position built up over a period of time. In everyday routines, this is not too difficult to accomplish but it can be testing in some circumstances. Research with children that builds on their active participation and wishes to engage with the complexity of their relationships will need to investigate key cultural ideas about what it means to be 'an adult', including the categories used to describe generational categories and life-course stages. The fragility of any piece of research is that, basically, it needs people who want to take part. In my experience, this is revealed through different notions of trust posed by the children, aimed at testing the reliability and genuine engagement of the 'adult' researcher in the research process.

References

Alanen, L. and Mayall, B. (eds) (2003) *Conceptualizing Child-Adult Relations*. London: RoutledgeFalmer.

Alderson, P. (1995) *Listening to Children: Children, Ethics and Social Research*. Barkingside: Barnado's.

Baktin, J. J. (1986) *Speech Genres and other Late Essays*. Austin, TX: University of Texas Press.

Baraldi, C. (2002) 'Planning childhood: children's social participation in the town of adults', in P. Christensen and M. O'Brien (eds) *Children in the City: Home, Neighbourhood and Community*. London: RoutledgeFalmer.

Christensen, P. (1993) 'The social construction of help among Danish children: the intentional act and the actual content', *Sociology of Health and Illness: A Journal of Medical Sociology*, 15(4): 488–502.

Christensen, P. (1998) 'Difference and similarity: how children are constituted in illness and its treatment', in I. Hutchby and J. Moran-Ellis (eds) *Children and Social Competence: Arenas of Action*. London: Falmer Press.

Christensen, P. (1999a) *Towards an anthropology of childhood sickness: an ethnographic study of Danish school children*, PhD thesis, University of Hull.

Christensen, P. (1999b) '"It hurts": children's cultural learning about health and illness', *Etnofoor*, 12(1): 39–53.

Christensen, P. and James, A. (2000) 2nd edn. *Research with Children: Perspectives and Practices*. London: Routledge.

Christensen, P. and James, A. (2000/2008) 'Researching children and childhood: cultures of communication', in P. Christensen and A. James (eds), *Research with Children: Perspectives and Practices*, 2nd edn. London: Falmer Press.

Christensen, P. and Prout, A. (2002) 'Working with ethical symmetry in social research with children', *Childhood: A Global Journal of Child Research*, 9(4): 474–97.

Clarke, A., and Moss, P. (2001) *Listening to Young Children: The Mosaic Approach*. London: National Children's Bureau.

Corsaro, W. A. (1997) *The Sociology of Childhood*. Thousand Oaks, CA: Pine Forge Press.

Corsaro, W. A. and Molinari, L. (2000) 'Entering and observing in children's worlds: a reflection on a longitudinal ethnography of early education in Italy', in P Christensen and A. James (eds) *Research with Children: Perspectives and Practices* 2nd edn. London: Routledge.

Ferguson, A.A. (2000) Bad Boys: Public Schools in the Making of Black Masculinity. Ann Arbor, MI: University of Michigan Press.

Fine, G. A. (1987) *With the Boys*. Chicago: Chicago University Press.

Fine, G. A. and Sandstrom, K. L. (1988) *Knowing Children: Participant Observation with Minors*. Newbury Park, CA: Sage.

Fraser, S. (2004) 'Situating empirical research', in S. Fraser, V.Lewis, S. Ding, M. Kellett and C. Robinson (eds) *Doing Research with Children and Young People*. London: Sage.

Geertz, C. (1973) *The Interpretation of Cultures*. London: Fontana.

Geertz, C. (1983) *Local Knowledge: Further Essays in Interpretive Anthropology*. New York: Basic Books.

Hallett, C. and Prout, A. (eds.) (2003) *Hearing the Voice of the Child: Social Policy for a New Century*. London: RoutledgeFalmer.

Lærke, A. (1998) 'Om at vente og ikke vide. Tid og disciplin i en engelsk primary school' (About waiting and not knowing. Time and discipline in an English primary school', *Tidsskriftet Antropologi (Journal of Anthropology)*, 38: 29–39.

Mandell, N. (1991) 'The least adult role in studying children', in F. Waksler (ed.) *Studying the Social Worlds of Children*. London: Falmer Press.

Mauthner, M. (1997) 'Methodological aspects of collecting data from children: lessons from three research projects', *Children and Society*, 11(1): 16–28.

Mayall, B. (1998) 'Researching Children', paper presented at the Centre for the Social Study of Childhood, University of Hull, May.

Mayall, B. (2000/2008) 'Conversations with children: working with generational issues', in P. Christensen, and A. James (eds) *Research with Children: Perspectives and Practices* 2nd edn. London: Routledge.

Morrow, V. and Richards, M. (1996) 'The ethics of social research with children: an overview', *Children and Society,* 10(2): 90–105.

Nieuwenhuys, O. (1993) Children's Lifeworlds: Gender, Welfare and Labour in the Developing World. London: Routledge.

Pollard, A. and Filer, A. (1996) *The Social World of Children's Learning*. London: Cassell.

Roberts, H. (2000/2008) 'Listening to Children: and Hearing them' in P. Christensen and A. James (eds) *Research with Children: Perspectives and Practices*. London: Routledge, 260–275.

Tedlock, D. (1979) 'The analogical tradition and the emergence of a dialogical anthropology', *Journal of Anthropological Research*, 35: 387–400.

Tedlock, D. and Mannheim, B. (eds) (1995) *The Dialogical Emergence of Culture*, Chicago: University of Illinois Press.

Thorne, B. (1993) *Gender Play: Girls and Boys in School*. Newark, NJ: Rutgers.

Van der Geest, S. (1996) 'Grasping the child's point of view? An anthropological reflection', in P. Bush *et al.* (eds) *Children, Medicines and Culture*. New York: Haworth Press.

Children's and Young People's Participation within Educational and Civic Settings: A Comparative Case Study Approach to Research

10

Michael Wyness

Introduction

In this chapter, I examine two related approaches within social and educational research, case study and the comparative analyses of cases. A multi-case approach allows the researcher to move beyond the single case of an instance in the pursuit of continuities and differences between equivalent cases. To illustrate this approach, I present a piece of research carried out by the author between 2001 and 2003 on the nature of children's and young people's participation within educational and civic realms. The cases discussed in this chapter are of different participatory fora within these realms, namely, school and youth councils respectively.

Given that the theoretical emphasis for this research was the child as a reflexive and knowledgeable actor within a range of social settings, the comparative case study approach will be located towards the qualitative end of the methodological spectrum.

An important methodological emphasis was to generate an understanding of the meaning and significance of children's participation from the vantage points of relevant key informants. The research sought to examine the understandings and perceptions of young people's councils among the various groups involved, including the young people, teachers and local government-based professionals. These 'subjective worlds' are crystallized through specific cases of children's participation. The comparative dimension teases out the institutional and sociogeographic differences between the cases.

First, I explore the methodology of the comparative case study approach by referring to its theoretical and epistemological assumptions. Next I link the discussion of methodology more explicitly to the research on children as political participants. I will argue that grounding the research within a framework that emphasizes the subjective realms of children as social agents directs us towards a more interpretive approach to the case study. I then discuss methods commonly used in constructing case studies, making reference to children's participation research. Finally, I focus on the comparative dimensions of the children's participation project and explore the social, political and institutional differences between cases.

By the end of this chapter, you should be able to:

- locate the comparative case study approach within an appropriate epistemological and theoretical framework
- recognize the case study approach as a means of capturing the situated, complex and multifaceted nature of social and educational settings
- identify the ways in which a comparative dimension explores similarities and differences between equivalent cases

Comparative Case Studies: Epistemological and Theoretical Origins

A key theoretical and epistemological assumption of the case study approach is the research subject as a reflexive social agent situated within a multilayered social setting. At a number of levels, the case study has an affinity with the ethnographic approach. However, the emphasis on the reflexive subject does not foreclose the possibility of a quantitative approach, especially if we view the process of completing a questionnaire as a reflexive practice. Moreover, it is possible to use the questionnaire in generating broad patterns of attitudes and practices across large geographical areas (in relation to pupils' attitudes to school councils, see Taylor and Johnson 2002).

However, using the children's participation project as an example, the survey approach would probably have told us much less about the institutional, cultural and local political basis to their participation. It would also have given us insufficient depth of insight into the ways in which children's participation was understood by the young people and adults involved in these structures. The important thing for the case study is to locate the attitudes and practices within a more grounded context as a way of providing a deeper understanding of origins, causes and motives. The emphasis in a case study is on far fewer instances and more depth of focus.

While there is, strictly speaking, no necessary relationship between case studies and methodology, the depth of analysis demanded and the illustrative purpose of case studies make them more amenable to the generation of qualitative data. The research discussed in this chapter adopted a case study approach within an interpretive methodological frame. Adelman *et al.* (1976: 141) argue that 'case study research always involves "the study of an instance in action"'. A particular situation, organization or group is intensively researched in order to capture its dynamic, complex and multifaceted nature. The case study approach emphasizes the internal coherence of the case: a depth study of one instance for its own sake. Stake (2004) refers to this as an 'intrinsic' form of case study. There is little or no attempt to generalize from the case to a class or category of broader phenomena. Generalizations are made about rather than from the case (Adelman *et al.* 1976).

The comparative approach, on the other hand, is closer to Stake's other two types, namely, the 'instrumental' and 'multi-case' types, where the emphasis is on using the case study as a means of illustrating a broader phenomenon – in my case, the political participation of children and young people (see Box 10.1). In selecting distinctive cases of participation within educational and civic realms, it became difficult to think in terms of a single case. As I have argued elsewhere, there were limited links between the school and civic councils within one research site in terms of membership or communication structures (Wyness 2005). While the research sites contained two distinct cases of children's participation, the sociogeographic location of the sites nevertheless had an important contextual purpose.

The form of case study adopted was determined by the research focus. A single case might have been appropriate where the focus was, for example, a single school and the emphasis on pupil participation within this school through the school council. The data then might have been generated from a wider range of members within the school. Thus, a sample of pupil 'constituents' as well as councillors would have told us something about the reception of the council across the school population and the meaning of participation within the school from those who had little direct interest or involvement in the council. However, the research adopted a comparative case study approach: the focus was on comparing a number of participatory structures in a number of research sites and exploring participation from the perspectives of those directly involved in the councils. The comparative case study approach inevitably involves a trade-off between the depth of analysis of the single 'intrinsic' case and the multi-case approach, but with respect to the former there are fewer claims made to any sort of ethnographic authenticity.

There are some 'family' resemblances between the case study and ethnographic approaches. The interpretive emphasis of both generates different demands in terms of generalizability as compared with statistically grounded research. The latter is about testing a theory or hypothesis against hard evidence – truth claims based on scientific evidence (see Chapter 4 for a discussion of quantitative research, including generalizability). In the case study approach, generalizing is still a valid concern, based around reasonableness and plausibility of the case or cases under review. Adelman *et al.* (1976: 143) discuss the relationship between the case study and the reader in terms of 'the shock of recognition', in that the analysis makes connections with the reader's tacit understanding of the case and its context.

> **Box 10.1 The features of a comparative case study**
>
> Locates attitudes and practices within a more grounded context.
> Approaches informants as being reflexive and capable of exercising agency.
> Examines social phenomena within multilayered contexts.
> Balances the depth of a single 'intrinsic' case and the richness of a multi-case approach.

Children's Participation and the Case Study Approach

So far, I have set out the theoretical, epistemological and methodological bases to the case study approach. I want to focus now on how these assumptions formed the basis of the research on children's and young people's participation. The theoretical and epistemological basis of the case study approach to children's participation derives from a shifting social scientific orthodoxy on the social status of children. First, children are now starting to be recognized as social actors and agents. Thus, rather than being defined as dependants with limited involvement in their social worlds, as *actors* children are constituent members of the social world: 'beings' rather than 'becomings' (Qvortrup 1994), having a more well-defined ontological status as social participants and citizens. Within a number of social contexts, this 'action' becomes *agency*. Children within the family and the community can have an influence; their voices are more likely to be heard and acknowledged, their views are more likely to be taken seriously. The research discussed in this chapter was firmly located within the new social studies of childhood (James and Prout 1997; Christensen and James 2000; Wyness 2006), with the focus being the roles children play as political representatives of their peers within educational and civic contexts. Case studies of school or pupil and civic councils allowed us to explore the institutional, cultural and local political basis to their participation.

Secondly, until relatively recently, children's views did not count as legitimate knowledge of the world. Particularly within the political domain, children's assumed intellectual and moral incompetence meant that they could not account for themselves in the world, and were unlikely to be able to make judgements on political matters (Sears and Valentino 1997). Responsible adult agents have tended to act as research proxies, mediating children's worlds in terms of accounting for their lives and experiences within the research process (Christensen and James 2000). Challenges to this social scientific orthodoxy regarding children and childhood have resulted in some accommodation of children's subjective worlds with children playing a more 'collaborative' approach within the research process.

School and civic youth councils were selected as case studies of children's political participation for a number of reasons. First, as discussed earlier, the civic realm has become a political space within which young people are now expected to participate (Matthews 2003). Yet, given that it is conventionally viewed as an adult space, one of the focal points of the research was the ways in which children negotiate this unfamiliar territory. Secondly, the educational dimension was selected in order to both expand the possible range of children's political participation, and provide a potential frame of comparison for the analysis of the youth councils. Unlike the civic realm, children are the majority population in school, yet paradoxically there is little or no space for children's political involvement (Wyness 2003). The history of school councils in the UK is of marginal teacher-oriented fora for pupils with agendas that according to Baginsky and Hannam cover little outside the 'charmed circle of lockers, dinners and uniforms' (1999: iii). Against the impetus from the introduction of citizenship education in England and Wales (QCA 1998) and the ascendance of a pupil voice agenda, the research set out to capture the ways in which schools might take a more inclusive approach to democratic practices involving pupils.[1]

Thirdly, the education and civic realms do not exhaust the possibilities for children's participation. Neither does the choice of pupil or school and youth councils within both these realms.[2] Pupil and youth councils were selected because they were children's fora, which were relatively well established within their respective realms. The prominence of children's participation within police frameworks sharpened the focus on these institutions, creating an agenda for change and improvement, which would potentially have significant consequences for these institutions (Hill *et al.* 2004). The research was thus trying to generate a picture of these more conventional and formal structures for children within a period of considerable change.

Comparative Case Studies: Methods for Data Collection

The comparative case study allows us to explore the complexity of social reality, particularly within a contemporary educational context that promotes diversity and fragmentation (Chitty 2004). Cohen and Manion (1997: 123) refer to this complexity in terms of the 'embeddedness of social truths'. An important feature of the case study is the possibility of revealing the depth of this embeddedness through a multimethod approach. I now want to discuss the methods that can be adopted in a case study by referring to the children's participation research.

There were three main research methods deployed. First, there were semistructured interviews with key participants, namely the young councillors, key local authority personnel and relevant teaching staff. The interviews sought to explore concepts and ideas relating to children's participation from the perspectives of those closely involved with the participatory structures. The interviews took two forms depending on the availability of time: group and individual interviews. The former took place predominantly with the young councillors and the latter with adult personnel. The interviews were conducted in schools and local authority settings. There was no hard and fast rule with regard to participants' age or generation-related nature of the interviews although there were a few instances where the youngsters preferred to be interviewed together. There were also a few instances where local council personnel were interviewed in pairs and there were several cases were youngsters were interviewed on their own. However, young councillors tended to be interviewed in groups because there were simply too many to be interviewed individually. Additionally, pupil councillors from the same class or year group were often interviewed together as they were usually released from classroom activities at the same time.

A second method was non-participant observation. We negotiated with the relevant personnel to attend civic council meetings in youth clubs and civic chambers, and pupil council meetings in the research schools. The aims here were to document the formal occasions when participants worked through council agendas and to get a sense of the dynamics between the various participants. The observations also allowed us to explore formal and informal processes of agenda-setting. Systematic fieldnotes were taken and predetermined features of the meetings were observed as a means of giving the observations some structure.

A third method was documentary analysis. While the data collected from the observation and interviews gave us insights into the structure, functions and understandings of the participatory fora, the review of various documents and papers relating to them gave us a third, formalized and officially recorded version of children's participation. In some cases, the official documentary data could be directly compared with our own record of events, such as formal minutes of meetings that circulated within the research settings. Other documents were publicly available accounts of these for a – among other things, mission statements, school and local authority policy material and newspaper cuttings from publicized events. Finally, national policy has focused attention on children's participation over the past few years and policy documents and statements were drawn to contextualize the other sources of data.

The issue of triangulation is a key one within case study research. The depth of a study relates to the number of perspectives in any social situation and the ability to utilize a range of methods in eliciting consistencies and conflicts of interests within the case (Adelman *et al.* 1976). I referred earlier to the importance of the location of the interview. In the small town site, there was a considerable overlap between membership of the school and town council (see Table 10.1). In

Table 10.1 Research sites (Wyness 2005)

Civic sites	Coronation	Jubilee		Marleybone		
Schools	Coronation	West End	East End	Copper Street	Golden-gate	Silver-side girls
Social geography	Small town, rural setting, white, mixed social class	Midlands city centre, working class, ethnically diverse	Midlands city centre, working class, ethnically diverse	Small town, white, mixed social class	Medium-sized town, white, affluent residential area	Medium-sized town, white, residential area
Number of pupils	1100	955	567	1200	1300	750
Council structure	Class, key stage* and whole-school councils	**Upper, lower and sixth form councils	Single school council	Single school council	Upper and lower councils	Year councils
Levels of representation	Elections at class and key stage levels	Elections at class level	Elections at class level	Elections at class level	Elections at class level	Elections at class level

*The National Curriculum in England and Wales created two key stages within each secondary school. Key Stage 3 consists of students aged between 11 and 14 (Years 7–9); Key Stage 4 consists of students aged between 14 and 16 (Years 10 and 11).
**Upper = Key Stage 4, Years 10 and 11 (ages 14–16). Lower = Key Stage 3, Years 7, 8 and 9 (ages 11–14).

some cases, councillors were interviewed twice, first in their roles as young town councillors in the town council chambers and later as school councillors in the school. The focus of the interviews in each context was different, but there were clearly areas where their representative roles in both settings overlapped. School councillors were more relaxed when they were interviewed out of school in their roles as civic councillors, and as discussed earlier, were in a stronger position to take a critical stance towards the idea of participation. There was clearly potential for a discrepancy of views, and in fact this happened on a few occasions. For example, school councillors' accounts of the effectiveness of their councils and relations between themselves and the teachers were inconsistent when comparing this data from interviews with the same councillors in school and civic settings. This does raise issues of reliability with the same respondent in some respects giving inconsistent accounts, particularly of their roles within school.

To some extent, the other methods allowed us to triangulate these views and verify them against other sources. The observational data from the school council meetings gave us limited opportunities to explore pupil-teacher relations and compare the accounts given by the pupils/youth councillors. Similarly, the documentary data on school councils can be set against these accounts. While verification may be rather limited here, the differing accounts of pupil/teacher relations and the perceived effectiveness of school councils may be useful data when comparing power relations in school and civic settings. The contextualizing of the interviews and any inconsistencies, and the range of different data, which in some respects is the 'stuff' of case studies, give us a complex but real-world view of young people's participatory structures.

Comparative Dimensions

The focus on a case study approach places considerable demands on the researcher to contextualize (Stake 2004). The participatory fora had to be situated at a number of levels, namely, social, institutional and political. An emphasis on vantage points and perspectives of those being researched further situated the research in terms of particular interest groups. Where there are a number of comparative dimensions to the analysis this contextualizing becomes a complex and multilayered process (see Box 10.2). In case study research, there were three forms of comparison: first, the focus on school councils and civic councils was to identify a limited range of categories of participation, but importantly, to explore the political and social contexts that underpinned differences in the organizational structure between the two forms. In some respects, this meant researching the educational and local political domains as distinctive contexts within which the councils were located. An analysis of the policy contexts of both domains revealed distinctive historical and political trajectories (Wyness 2005). While the research interest in children's participation brought the two domains together, one important reason for looking at the two types of council was that in the educational case, children are a majority population, with their educational and social well-being constituting a paramount concern. In the other local authority case, there appeared to be an absence of interest in things relating to children. Local authorities are commonly seen to be populated by adults; they are not recognized as places or spaces for children (Wyness 2005).

A second comparison took place across the three research sites. In relation to the civic councils there was one case per site; in the case of the school councils there were a number of cases within two of the three sites; in the civic councils, the comparison was straightforward in that the data were telling me something about the way that civic councils operate in different sociogeographical areas. Importantly, a comparison was made of how the research subjects within each site understood their roles and the purposes of their civic council. In the school council, the comparison of the research sites was complicated by the differences between the schools in two of the three sites. In both of these cases, comparisons between school councils took place within as well as between research sites.

Third, the three research sites formed the basis of a sociogeographical comparison. The different size of locations, combined with the cultural and socioeconomic make-up of the population, was chosen to capture any possible diversity in terms of the structure, practice and experience of participation. Clearly, there was a possibility that a comparison between the small-town monocultural site Coronation and the multicultural urban Jubilee city location would generate significant differences from the data (see Table 10.1). Equally, any perceived continuities across the two sites would be worthy of comment. The institutional discontinuities found within the sites between the civic and school councils were potentially overlaid and complicated by characteristics that distinguished the three research sites as possible cases in their own right.

Box 10.2 Comparison dimensions of a case study

- Between institutional and organizational forms of children's participation, namely, pupil and civic councils.
- Within each of the three research sites, particularly where there was more than one pupil council.
- Between the three research sites in terms of size and social geography.

While some councils were more intensively researched than others, the three civic councils and the six school councils could be treated as separate case studies of children's participation. What we have here is a particularly complex example of the comparative case study approach involving comparisons of these instances at a number of levels. The different levels of comparison allow for more depth of analysis and a contextual and real-world understanding of the research area (Adelman *et al.* 1976: 142). If we refer back to the third level of comparison between the three sites and take the cases of civic councils, we are in a position to identify points of convergence and clear differences between a small town, a medium-sized town and a city civic council. Our emphasis on social and geographical differences may be strengthened if we are able to identify continuities between the civic and school councils within each research site. Thus, despite the institutional differences between school and civic councillors, there may be important similarities in the way that the councillors understand and experience their roles in both educational and civic settings that neutralize these differences.

For example, in a comparison between the largest and smallest sites, councillors in the former were more 'cosmopolitan' in their outlook than those in the latter. Specifically, Jubilee Youth

Council was committed to representing the interests of diverse groups of young people from across the city. They were drawn from a much larger pool of youngsters from a larger and wider range of schools across the city (see Table 10.1). There was considerable diversity of social, cultural and educational backgrounds, and members were part of a complex network of urban youth groups. This diversity was reflected in the social and cultural composition of the two Jubilee schools in the study, which were ethnically mixed. Coronation councillors, on the other hand, all went to the sole secondary school. The town was small, political and community networks were close and much more transparent and personalized. As the school had a more direct 'feeder' relationship to the civic council, networking was limited to the schools within the local authority rather than through other civic youth groups. They also had more direct if limited involvement in the adult council than the youth councillors at Jubilee.[3]

The scale of participation in both sites was very different as were the kinds of social networks developed by the youngsters. The third form of comparison in terms of social geography focuses our attention on local characteristics that help us to make sense of the data generated at the second level of comparison. However, if we refer to the first-level comparison between civic and secondary schools, we generate a more nuanced account of young councillors' understandings of the notion of participation. The city councillors' accounts of their commitments to representing diverse groups of young people brought them into conflict with what they saw as the narrow and elitist character of school councils based largely on their own school experiences. While the social geography of Jubilee council might generate a more 'cosmopolitan' conception of citizenship than either of the other two civic councils, this cosmopolitanism was paradoxically in part a response to the perceived shortcomings of the schools that the city youth councillors currently attended (Osler and Starkey 2005). Many Jubilee youth councillors had experience of representing their peers in school councils. They were a powerful vocal minority who felt that the school council did little to strengthen the voices of a culturally, socially and educationally diverse range of pupils. Their attempts to make their youth council more representative of the city's young people brought them into conflict with the political processes associated with school councils.

Some elements of this critique could be found within one of the city schools.[4] But in the main the school councillors and adult advisers interviewed in the two city schools supported the role of the school council in providing a voice for young people in school. The point to be made here is that the institutional comparison within one research site revealed a degree of conflict in purposes between the civic and educational realm that potentially compromised any social and cultural affiliations between the youngsters within these realms.

Summary

In treating the case as an instance of an educational phenomenon, the expectation is that the analysis of actors' involvement within the case needs to accommodate a number of perspectives both from within the case and in relation to the way that the researcher sees the case. This chapter illustrated a case study approach by presenting a project which was informed by the view that the researched subjects are reflexive members of a community. In the case of children, as civic participants, this was a relatively new research innovation. The focus was on children's participation as councillors and representatives of their peers and the case study allowed us to explore the meaning of their participation from a number of vantage points. I also wanted to explore a number of cases of children's participation, in effect, locate their participation in distinctive institutional fora, and within different social and geographical sites. The comparative dimension to the research offered us the opportunity to explore a particular social phenomenon, which has national and global importance within distinctive localized settings. By adopting a multi-case approach, I was able to go beyond the particularities of a single case study. We are thus in a stronger position to make links between children's participatory structures in schools and civic arenas in distinctive sociogeographical settings and national and international trends, which highlight the importance of children's right to participate (Franklin 2002).

Box 10.3 Summary of key points

- The case study approach focuses on a number of aspects within a single case from multiple perspectives and vantage points.
- The comparative case study approach is not exclusively 'qualitative' in terms of methodology. Nevertheless, the focus on 'depth' analysis of how social and educational phenomena are constituted through social engagement is more amenable to an interpretive approach.
- A comparative case study allows the researcher to move beyond the single case and make links between localized settings and broader societal trends.

Notes

1   A foremost academic journal within the field of education, *Educational Review*, devoted a whole edition to the theme 'pupil voice'. See volume 58, edition 2 (2006).
2   For examples of children's participation in other realms, see Hill *et al.* (2004) and the children's participation blog, http://childrensparticipation.blogspot.com. In relation to other participatory initiatives in school and the civic realms see Wyness (2000) and Cambridgeshire Children's Fund (2007).
3   Although this had also to do with political choices made by Jubilee youth councillors. See Wyness (2005).
4   It is possible that this criticism was muted due to the location of the interviews within the schools. Schools are hierarchical structures and the culture in schools can make dissent and criticism more difficult.

References

Adelman, C., Jenkins, D. and Kemmis, S. (1976) 'Re-thinking case study: notes from a second Cambridge conference', *Cambridge Journal of Education*, 6(3): 139–50.

Baginsky, M. and Hannam, D. (1999) *School Councils: The Views of students And Teachers*, London: NSPCC.

Cambridgeshire Children's Fund (2007) *Cambridgeshire Children's Fund*, www.cambridgeshire.gov.uk/social/children/fund.

Chitty, C. (2004) *Education Policy in Britain*. Basingstoke: Palgrave.

Cohen L. and Manion, L. (1997) *Research Methods in Education*, 4th edn. London: Routledge.

Christensen, P. and James, A. (2000) 'Researching children and childhood: cultures of communication', in P. Christensen and A. James (eds) *Research with Children: Perspectives and Practices*. London: RoutledgeFalmer.

Franklin, B. (2002) (ed.) *The New Handbook of Children's Rights*. London: Routledge.

Hill, M., Davis, J., Prout, A. and Tisdall, K. (2004) 'Moving the participation agenda forward', *Children and Society*, 18(2): 77–96.

James, A. and Prout, A. (eds) (1997) *Constructing and Reconstructing Childhood*, 2nd edn. London: Falmer.

Matthews, H. (2003) 'Children and regeneration: setting an agenda for community participation and regeneration', *Children and Society*, 17(4): 264–76.

Osler, A. and Starkey, H. (2005) *Changing Citizenship: Democracy and Inclusion in Education*, Maidenhead: Open University Press.

QCA (Qualifications and Curriculum Authority) (1998) *Education for Citizenship and the Teaching of Democracy in Schools*. London: HMSO.

Qvortrup, J. (1994) 'Childhood matters: an introduction', in J. Qvortrup *et al.* (eds) *Childhood Matters: Social Theory, Practice and Politics*. Aldershot: Avebury.

Sears, D. and Valentino, N. (1997) 'Politics matters: political events as catalysts for pre-adolescent socialization', *American Political Science Review*, 91(1): 45–65.

Stake, R. (2004) 'Qualitative case studies', in N. Denzin and Y. Lincoln (eds) *Handbook of Qualitative Research*, 2nd edn. London: Sage.

Taylor, M. and Johnson, R. (2002) *School Councils: Their Role in Citizenship and Personal and Social Education*. Berkshire: NFER.

Wyness, M. (2000) *Contesting Childhood*. London: Falmer Press.

Wyness, M. (2003) 'Children's space and interests: constructing an agenda for student voice', *Children's Geographies*, 1(2): 223–39.

Wyness, M. (2005) 'Regulating participation: the possibilities and limits of children's and young people's councils', *The Journal of Social Sciences*, 9: 7–18.

Wyness, M. (2006) *Childhood and Society: An Introduction to the Sociology of Childhood*. Basingstoke: Palgrave.

11 Researching Classroom Interaction and Talk

David Wray and Kristiina Kumpulainen

Chapter Outline

Introduction

The social and contextual nature of human learning has received great emphasis in research on learning and instruction (Anderson *et al.* 1997; Greeno 1997). Attention has been paid to the practices, processes and conditions leading to the social construction of knowledge in different learning situations (Palincsar 1986; Lemke 1990; Fisher 1993; Tuyay *et al.* 1995). The focus of analysis has been extended from external factors influencing learning processes and achievements to the student's participation in and evolving interpretations of the learning activity (Perret-Clermont *et al.* 1991; Grossen 1994). In the midst of these changes in emphasis, new methodological questions concerning the analysis of classroom interaction and learning have arisen. Questions to which researchers have been trying to find answers are, for example:

- What qualitative differences can be found within and between interactive activities across a variety of learning contexts?
- What typically happens during classroom interaction?
- How can practitioners and researchers develop and strengthen their understandings about optimal learning within inherently social settings (e.g. classrooms)?

This chapter will review and critique some approaches to studying and analysing classroom interaction, and especially the discourse which characterizes this. It is based on an account of a programme of research into classroom interaction and social learning, and uses the methodological decisions made during that programme as a set of pegs on which to hang a discussion of methodological issues in this field.

By the end of this chapter, you should be able to:

- understand the complexity of investigating socially shared learning practices
- consider some methodological issues emerging from researching classroom interaction and talk
- understand the need to move from an analysis of classroom talk to a more holistic analysis of classroom interaction
- understand the use of analytical maps that involve functional, cognitive processing and social processing analyses of classroom interaction and talk

The Framework of Analysis

The analysis framework described here emerged as a result of a number of studies of primary-aged learners' interactions while working in peer groups on various educational tasks in Finland, Greece and the UK (Fourlas and Wray 1990; Kumpulainen and Wray 2002). The main goal of these studies was to investigate the nature of students' social activity, particularly verbal interaction, in different small group-work learning situations. The initial development of the method concentrated on the functions of students' verbal interaction as a basis for investigation of students' roles as communicators and learners in teacher-centred and peer-group centred classrooms (Fourlas and Wray 1990). This functional analysis method was later piloted, modified and applied by Kumpulainen (1994, 1996) in a study that investigated students' social interaction during the process of collaborative writing with a word processor. Due to its fine-grained categorizations, the functional analysis method was felt to give a structured overview of the nature and quality of students' verbal interaction in this learning context.

Despite the potential of the analysis method, in more recent studies of peer group learning this functional analysis of verbal interaction was found to be inadequate as a means of unravelling the complexities of socially shared learning processes. Firstly, there seemed to be a need to develop a descriptive system of analysis, which took a more holistic and multidimensional perspective on interaction. Consequently, the analysis of verbal interaction alone seemed not to be sufficient for this. Secondly, it seemed important that more attention be paid to the moment-by-moment nature of interaction in order to highlight the situated processes of meaning-making and knowledge construction within peer groups. Thirdly, it seemed important to take the individual and the group as units of analysis in order to investigate the types and forms of participation within peer groups.

In the analysis method subsequently developed, the dynamics of peer group interaction were approached from three analytic dimensions.

1 The first dimension of the analysis, termed *functional analysis*, focused on the character and purpose of student utterances in peer group interaction. It characterized the communicative strategies used by participants in social interaction.

2 The second dimension, *cognitive processing*, examined the ways in which students approached and processed learning tasks in their social interaction. It aimed at highlighting students' working strategies and situated positions towards learning, knowledge and themselves as problem-solvers.

3 The third dimension of the analysis, *social processing*, focused on the nature of the social relationships

that were developed during students' social activity. This included examining the types and forms of student participation in social interaction.

Before discussing the theoretical and methodological background of these methods and highlighting the analytical framework with some empirical examples, we will first review some of the other analysis methods used to study peer interaction that have contributed to the present analytical approach.

Investigating Collaborative Interaction in Peer Groups

Peer group interaction has been studied quite extensively in different contexts in and out of school. The research objectives and methodological solutions have been diverse, being linked with the research goals and theoretical perspectives adopted by the researchers.

One large group of studies focusing on peer interaction from the educational perspective is located in the systematic tradition, often referred to as process-product studies of peer interaction (e.g. King 1989; Tudge 1992; Light *et al.* 1994; Joiner *et al.* 1995; Teasley 1995; Webb *et al.* 1995). In these studies, peer interaction is analysed with coding schemes, which categorize interaction into predefined categories. Variables such as student achievement and performance are statistically linked to the frequency of categories as identified in the data. Usually, the development of the actual interaction process or meaning-making in interaction is not the prime interest, but the focus is rather on some specific features of the interaction and their relationship to student learning or achievement. Consequently, the process of interaction over a period of time is not highlighted by such studies. The situated nature of interaction, as represented by the contextual features impinging upon it, also often receives only cursory inspection. One advantage of process-product studies is that they enable the analysis of large amounts of data and use publicly verifiable criteria to make their categorizations.

Probably the best known of such category systems is the Flanders Interaction Analysis (Flanders 1970). This system has been used extensively in classroom observation studies (Wragg 1999; Newman 2004). It has two main uses. Firstly, it was intended to provide evidence of the differences in teaching patterns that distinguish one teaching style from another and, secondly, it has been used to try to explain differences in learning outcomes associated with different styles of teaching.

The Flanders Interaction Analysis Categories (FIAC) consist of ten categories of communication, seven used when the teacher is talking and two when a pupil is talking (and one when there is silence or confusion). An observer using the system makes timed observations, usually every three seconds, and categorizes the behaviour which he or she observes at each point into one of ten categories. These categories are shown below in Table 11.1. A very useful website explaining and exemplifying the Flanders system can be found at Nova South Eastern University Centre for Teaching and Learning (www.nova.edu/hpdtesting/ctl/fia.html).

Other research traditions have produced quite different approaches to the analysis of peer

Table 11.1 Flanders Interaction Analysis Categories (FIAC)

Teacher talk	Indirect influence	1	Accepts feelings: accepts and clarifies the feelings of the students in a non-threatening manner. Feelings may be positive or negative. Predicting and recalling feelings are included.
		2	Praises or encourages: praises or encourages student action or behaviour. Jokes that release tension, not at the expense of another individual, nodding head or saying 'uh huh?' or 'go on' are included.
		3	Accepts or uses ideas of student: clarifying, building or developing ideas or suggestions by a student. As teacher brings more of his/her own ideas into play, shift to category five.
		4	Asks questions: asking a question about content or procedure with the intent that a student may answer.
	Direct influence	5	Lectures: giving facts or opinions about content or procedures; expressing own ideas; asking rhetorical questions.
		6	Gives directions: commands, or orders with which a student is expected to comply.
		7	Criticizes or justifies authority: statements, intended to change student behaviour from non-acceptable to acceptable pattern, bawling someone out; stating why the teacher is doing what he/she is doing, extreme self-reference.
Student talk		8	Student talk – responses: talk by students in response to teacher. Teacher initiates the contact or solicits student statement.
		9	Student talk – initiation: talk by students which they initiate. If 'calling on' student is only to indicate who may talk next, observer must decide whether student wanted to talk. If he/she did, use this category.
		10	Silence or confusion: pauses, short periods of silence and periods of confusion in which communication cannot be understood by the observer.

group talk and learning. Barnes and Todd (1977, 1995), for example, developed an analytic system for studying peer group talk which was 'grounded' in the data, as opposed to being derived from a pre-existing network of categories. Consequently, their system did try to take account of the context in which peer talk was occurring. In their analysis Barnes and Todd were interested in the actual processes of interaction and the ways students developed and constructed knowledge without direct teacher presence. In analysing the dialogue among the groups of students, they considered types of talk and their impact on the construction of meaning during group interactions. This demanded an analysis of both the *social* and *cognitive* functions of conversation. They developed a system describing speech acts, which was based on two levels.

Level one consisted of:

- discourse moves (such as initiating, eliciting, extending and responding)
- logical processes (such as proposing a cause, advancing evidence, negating, suggesting a method, evaluating)

Level two comprised:

- social skills (such as competition and conflict, supportive behaviour)
- cognitive strategies (such as setting up hypotheses, constructing new questions)
- reflexivity (such as monitoring one's own speech, evaluating one's own and others' performance)

They identified 'exploratory' speech characteristics such as hesitation and changes of direction, tentativeness in voice intonation, assertions and questions made as hypotheses rather than direct assertions, invitations to modify or surmise, and self-monitoring and reflexivity. They went on to propose conditions for *collaborative* work among groups in classrooms, based on this empirical evidence. Further analysis (Barnes and Todd 1995) provided descriptive examples of the four categories of collaborative moves: initiating, eliciting, extending and qualifying.

Despite some limitations in the analytical system and the tools used for data collection (tape recorders only, thus losing any information from non-verbal elements of communication), Barnes and Todd's work made an important contribution to the analysis of peer talk since it integrated ideas from discourse and conversational analysis with research on learning and instruction. Several studies have used the Barnes and Todd framework to inquire into classroom interaction (e.g. Edwards 2005).

Many other methods of analysis of peer group interaction, either with distinct categories or more interpretative 'modes' have been developed in the past 20 years and to review all of them here would be impossible. One important analytic approach which needs to be discussed, however, since it has contributed greatly to our understanding of children's talk during small-group learning is that developed by Fisher (1993), Mercer (1994, 1996, 2000), and Mercer and Littleton (2007). What is interesting in this approach is that it tries to investigate how children use talk to think together and thus uses a group as a unit of analysis, not individual children. By taking a sociocultural approach to children's talk, it tries to show that particular ways of talking permit certain social modes of thinking. The analytic framework was derived from analyses of children's talk during collaborative peer group learning and includes three distinct modes of talk which characterize different ways of thinking together. These are:

- *disputational mode*, characterized by disagreement and individualized decision-making
- *cumulative mode*, consisting of positive but uncritical decision-making
- *exploratory mode*, which is seen as the most effective mode of speaking in fostering critical thinking and cognitive development (Mercer 1996) and is characterized by constructive and critical engagements, including argumentation and hypothesis-testing

Theoretically, this analytical framework makes an important contribution to our increasing understanding of the different modes of talk and social thinking in peer group situations. One of the limitations of the method, though, can be found in the fact that the unit of analysis is the group – the method does not take into account individual students' participation in the 'social modes of thinking'. Consequently, the method does not highlight how the different types of social thinking are actually constructed within peer groups. Moreover, by concentrating mainly on students' talk, the analysis may not always give a complete picture of the nature of knowledge construction in peer groups. Instead, a more dynamic approach to peer interaction is necessary, which focuses on the whole interactive context and its development, including non-verbal communication and the use of different tools, before we can unravel the processes and conditions for learning in peer group activity.

Towards a New Analytic Method

In the remainder of this chapter we will outline and discuss a descriptive system of analysis for investigating the situated dynamics of peer group interaction. Of particular importance are the mechanisms through which the social and cognitive features of peer group activity operate. The theoretical grounding of the analysis framework was informed by sociocultural and sociocognitive perspectives on interaction and learning (Wertsch 1985, 1991; Resnick *et al.* 1991; Cole 1996), whereas the methodological solutions were greatly influenced by the work of Barnes and Todd (1977, 1995) and Mercer (1994, 1996) as well as by interactional ethnographers (Green and Wallat 1981; Green and Mayer 1991; Tuyay *et al.* 1995).

In this method, learning is seen to take place as a result of individuals' active participation in the social practices of their environments. Learning is viewed as an interactional process that requires an understanding of language and other semiotic tools, as both personal and social resources (Halliday and Hasan 1989; Wells and Chang-Wells 1992; Cole 1996). Peer interaction is treated as a dynamic process in which language and other semiotic tools are used as instruments of communication and learning. Interaction is seen as a complex social phenomenon composed of nonverbal and social properties in addition to its verbal characteristics. Peer discourse itself is not treated as representing a person's inner cognitive world, nor even as descriptive of an outer reality, but rather as a tool-in-action shaped by participants' culturally-based definitions of the situation (Edwards and Potter 1992; Edwards 1993).

The application of the method involves a microanalysis of evolving peer interactions by focusing on three analytic dimensions, namely the functions of verbal interaction, cognitive processing and social processing. Whereas the functional analysis concentrates on students' verbal language, the analyses of students' cognitive and social processing focus on interactive dynamics as they occur across the participants. Consequently, a group is taken as a unit of analysis. The three dimensions are treated separately for analytic purposes, although it is recognized that they are closely linked together in a complex way. In actuality the dimensions cannot be separated since each element gives meaning to all the others and simultaneously obtains meaning from them.

Dimension 1: functional analysis of verbal interaction

The functional analysis of students' verbal interaction focuses on the purposes for which verbal language is used in a given context. It investigates and highlights the communicative strategies applied by individual students while taking part in interaction (Halliday and Hasan 1989). Analysis of this nature often concentrates on the illocutionary force of an utterance, that is, on its functional meaning (Austin 1962; Edwards and Westgate 1994). The functions for which students use their oral language are closely linked to the topic of discussion as well as to the individuals' expectations and evolving interpretations of the situation shaped by the sociocultural context of the activity. The functions of language used in the course of interaction serve both intra- and interpersonal purposes. On the one hand, the purposes and intentions carried by means of verbal language serve an ideational (i.e. cognitive) function. On the other hand, they serve an interpersonal function relating to the personal and social relationships between the interactors (Halliday and Hasan 1989).

The identification of language functions in peer interaction takes place on the basis of implication – that is, what a speaker can imply, suggest or mean may be different to what the speaker literally says. Consequently, the functions are not identified on the basis of specific linguistic forms. Rather, they are identified in context in terms of their retrospective and prospective effects on the actual discourse both in terms of content and form. An understanding of the functions for which students use their verbal language in interaction is greatly assisted by data gathered from direct observation, video-recording and student interviews. The functions of peer interaction are the minimum units analysed in the system. They are identified on an utterance basis and defined in terms of source, purpose and situated conversational meaning. An utterance is viewed as a meaningful unit of speech, that is, a message unit. The boundary between each utterance is linguistically marked by contextual cues. Given that an utterance may serve multiple functions, more than one function can be recorded for each utterance.

Examples of language functions identified in peer group interaction across learning situations are the *informative, expositional, reasoning, evaluative, interrogative, responsive, organizational, judgemental* (agrees/disagrees), *argumentational, compositional, revision, dictation, reading aloud, repetition, experiential* and *affective* functions.

Some of these functions describe the nature of interaction more from the activity point of view (e.g. dictation, reading aloud), whereas others take a more interpretative/cognitive (e.g. informative, reasoning, evaluative) or social perspective (e.g. affective, responsive, judgemental) on the analysis of verbal interaction. However, none of the functions should be seen as reflecting only one of these dimensions. Conversely, each function in the framework is regarded as reflecting the social-cognitive-discursive actions of the participants as they verbally interact in their social activity. The language functions used in the course of joint problem-solving often differ across situations and contexts, thus these functions presented in the analytic framework should not be understood as fixed, predefined categories. Instead, the functions must be situationally defined for each interaction situation on a post-hoc basis.

An example of the use of this system to analyse peer interaction is given below (for more information see Kumpulainen and Wray 2002: 61). As can be seen in Example 1, more than one function can occur within the same language utterance.

Example 1: functional analysis of verbal interaction

Context: two girls, Elise and Madeleine, are making an imaginative story for a school magazine. They are writing collaboratively with the computer.

	Oral interaction	Language functions
Elise:	Let's write that one day the boys decided to go to the grave.	(OR, CRE, IM)
Madeleine:	Yeah. And that they took a torch and some food with them.	(J, CRE, IM)

Both of the children were involved in creating writing and hence using their talk in the *compositional function*. In addition, since this was not a true story they seemed to be imagining the situation and hence using the *imaginative function*. Elise was also using her oral language for the *organizational function* when suggesting 'Let's write'. Madeleine, on the other hand, when agreeing to Elise's suggestion was using the *judgemental function*. In summary, Elise used her speech for the organizational (OR), compositional (CRE) and imaginative functions (IM). Madeleine, on the other hand, used her speech for the judgemental (J), compositional (CRE) and imaginative functions (IM).

In addition to the qualitative analysis permitted by this system, it can also be used to produce quantitative data. An example of this is the study originally carried out by Fourlas and Wray (1990) and reported in Kumpulainen and Wray (2002: 43–56). The aims of this study were to investigate the influence of two styles of classroom organization, teacher-centred (a teacher directing the discussion of a whole class of students) and peer-group-centred (students organized into several peer groups to discuss materials and problems) on the ways in which students used their oral language in classroom interaction. The study was carried out in three Greek primary schools, using children aged from 7 to 9 years. The research sample was eight lessons, four organized on a teacher-centred basis and four organized on a peer group basis. The data were collected and processed by means of observation, tape recordings and written transcripts. After careful examination of the data, the functional analysis system was used to investigate the nature of children's oral language in these two classroom organizational systems. Table 11.2 shows the frequency of occurrence of each language function in the talk of students in both types of lesson.

Functions such as the intentional, the responsive, the reproductional, the interrogative and the experiential were observed to occur in higher frequencies in the teacher-centred lessons. All the

Table 11.2 Frequency (%) of occurrence of language functions in the talk of students in teacher-centred and peer group-centred lessons

Language function	Teacher-centred lessons (%)	Peer group-centred lessons (%)
Intentional	25.1	1.5
Responsive	28.6	2.3
Reproductional	7.6	2.8
Interrogative	7.6	3.6
Experiential	3.0	1.5
Informative	10.5	19.3
Judgemental	9.4	18.2
Hypothetical	1.1	3.1
Argumentational	2.4	7.0
Affective	1.3	4.5
Organizational	2.5	16.2
Compositional	0.6	6.1
Heuristic	0.3	4.2
Imaginative	0.2	4.0
Expositional	0.0	1.1
External thinking	0.0	4.5

other functions were found in higher frequencies in the lessons that were peer-group-centred. Of further interest was the fact that children in the peer group lessons used oral language over the entire range of functions in respectable proportions. In contrast, in the teacher-centred lessons, children did not use the external thinking or expositional functions at all, and they used the imaginative, heuristic and compositional functions quite rarely. These findings suggest that the language experiences of students in these two classroom organizational systems were quite different, in quality and in quantity.

Dimension 2: analysis of cognitive processing

The analysis of cognitive processing examines the ways in which students approach and process learning tasks in their social activity. It aims at highlighting students' working strategies and situated positions towards knowledge, learning and themselves as problem-solvers. In the method, cognitive processes are seen as dynamic and contextual in nature, being socially constructed in students' evolving interactions in the sociocultural context of activity.

In the analytical framework we distinguished three broad modes to characterize the nature of students' cognitive processing in peer group activity:

- *Procedural processing* refers to the routine execution of tasks without thorough planning or thinking. Ideas are not developed, rather they are cumulated or disputed without constructive judgements or criticism. The students' activity is often product-oriented and concentrates on procedural handling of information.
- *Interpretative or exploratory processing*, on the other hand, refers to a situation during which thinking is made visible through language or other tools and the whole activity is focused on strategies, planning and hypothesis testing. The students' activity reflects their deep engagement and interest in the problem-solving task.
- *Off-task activity* refers to a situation during which the students' activity does not focus on the task (e.g. playing around, discussing break-time activities, 'absent minded' activity).

It is important to recognize that these three broad analytical modes are used as heuristic devices rather than distinct categories into which students' cognitive processing can be easily coded. The modes are reflected in different ways in different contexts and situations and, hence, require situational definitions.

Dimension 3: analysis of social processing

The analysis of social processing aims at characterizing the social relationships and types of participation in peer groups. The different modes in which social processing is often constructed in peer group interaction are *collaborative, tutoring, argumentative, individualistic, dominative, conflict* and *confusion* modes. The latter characterizes interaction during which there is an obvious misunderstanding or lack of shared understanding between the children. The conflict mode reflects disagreement, usually at a social level. The dominative mode reflects the distribution of power and status in the peer group. The individualistic and dominative modes are contrasts to collaborative interaction. The individualistic mode implies that students are not developing their

Example 2: cognitive processing analysis

Context: two students, Alex and Maria, were asked to construct three-dimensional objects pictorially represented, by the use of two-dimensional shapes.

	Oral interaction	Cognitive processing
Alex:	Bottom ... how come?	Speculating
Maria:	No ... but that's the bottom ... that's that sort of a triangle and the lid is that sort of a triangle ... they are connected ... it shows there how they are connected.	Explaining
Alex:	No ... look ... this is ...	
Maria:	Yeah ... it's connected.	
Alex:	Wait.	
Maria:	That could be created by side triangles in a way.	Speculating
Alex:	Triangle comes here ... triangle comes here ... triangle comes here and here comes a rectangle.	Explaining
Maria:	Yeah ... exactly and here to the roof as well.	
Alex:	Could it go here?	Speculating
Maria:	This one ... this one yeah ... wait a minute ... yeah this is the rectangle.	Testing

ideas together but rather working individually in the group. The dominative reflects an imbalance in students' social status and power. The argumentative and tutoring modes of interaction characterize the nature of collaboration between the participants. In this sense they can be regarded as sub-modes of collaborative activity. The argumentative mode implies constructive interaction in which students negotiate their differing understandings in a rational way by giving judgements and justifications. This often leads to a shared understanding of the situation. The tutoring mode shows students helping and explaining for the purpose of assisting another to understand the matter at hand. In addition, collaboration includes interaction in which participants attempt to achieve a mutual understanding of the situation, ideas are jointly negotiated, and discourse is coherent. In collaborative interaction participants often create bi-directional zones of proximal development assisting one another (Forman 1989).

It must be noted that, apart from the functional analysis of peer group interaction, the unit of analysis for the different modes of cognitive and social processing is not defined by distinct rules, such as an utterance basis. Instead the units of analysis for the modes of cognitive and social processing are based on their development in peer interaction on a moment-by-moment basis. In other respects the three dimensions on which the analytical framework concentrates all emerge from the data as a result of the researchers' and, when possible, also the interactors' interpretations of the situation.

Example 3: social processing analysis

Context: two students, Jon and Tim, were asked to construct three-dimensional objects pictorially represented, by the use of two-dimensional shapes.

	Oral interaction	Social processing
Jon:	Where is the large triangle?	Slight domination from Jon
Tim:	Oh, yeah . . .	
Jon:	Take those away.	
Tim:	Hahah . . . what are you looking for?	Tim tries to initiate collaboration
Jon:	A kind of a triangle to the centre . . . these tasks are a bit too difficult . . .	
Tim:	How about this one then?	
Jon:	It might be . . . perhaps two of these there . . .	
Tim:	Basically no.	
Jon:	Show me . . . hmm . . . let's turn to the next exercise . . . let's solve that one since it is easier . . . it is what one sees . . . hey, could it be these . . .	Slight domination from Jon
Tim:	Do you mean these small ones?	Tim tries to initiate collaboration
Jon:	These.	
Tim:	What about these big ones, I think they look big . . . like this.	
Jon:	I think . . . (indistinct)	
Tim:	I don't know . . .	Signs of conflict starting to appear

The full categories of the analysis method are summarized in Table 11.3.

Table 11.3 Analytical framework of peer group interaction

Dimension	Analytical categorization		Description
COGNITIVE PROCESSING	Exploratory/interpretative	EXPO	Critical and exploratory activity which includes planning, hypothesis-testing, evaluation, and experimenting.
	Procedural/routine	PROC	Procedural on-task activity which focuses on handling, organizing and executing the task without reflective analysis.
	Off-task	OFF	Activity not related to the task.
SOCIAL PROCESSING	Collaborative	COLL	Joint activity characterized by equal participation and meaning-making.
	Tutoring	TUTO	Student helping and assisting another student.
	Argumentative	ARGU	Students are faced with cognitive/social conflicts which are resolved and justified in a rational way.
	Individualistic	INDI	Student(s) working on individual tasks with no sharing or joint meaning-making.
	Domination	DOMI	Student dominating the work, unequal participation.
	Conflict	FLCI	Social or academic conflicts which are often left unresolved.
	Confusion	FUSI	Lack of shared understanding, student(s) do not understand the task or each other, often includes silent episodes.

Dimension	Analytical categorization		Description
DISCOURSE FUNCTIONS	Informative	I	Providing information.
	Reasoning	RE	Reasoning in language.
	Evaluative	EV	Evaluating work or action.
	Interrogative	Q	Asking questions.
	Responsive	A	Answering questions.
	Organizational	OR	Organizing or/and controlling behaviour.
	Judgemental		
	● Agrees	Ja	Expressing agreement or
	● Disagrees	Jd	disagreement.
	Argumentational	AR	Justifying information, opinions or actions.
	Compositional	CR	Creating text.
	Revision	RV	Revising text.
	Dictation	DI	Dictating.
	Reading aloud	RE	Reading text.
	Repetition	RP	Repeating spoken language.
	Experiential	E	Expressing personal experiences.
	Affectional	AF	Expressing feelings.

Analytical Maps

In our analysis, the dynamics of peer group interaction are illustrated with the help of analytical maps, which have been created for each peer group under investigation. The product of the analysis is a series of situation-specific analytical maps that describe the sequential evolution of peer group interactions as they are constructed by students interacting with and acting upon each other's messages. In addition to highlighting the dynamics of peer interaction, these maps show the element of time in the students' activity as well as some contextual information necessary for the interpretation of the social activity in question. Although a structural map is always a simplification, it gives a coherent and temporal picture of a complex situation, making comparisons across educational contexts,peer groups and students possible. Moreover, the structural maps help one return easily to the original data to check the validity of interpretation. In addition, when presenting extracts from the data, one is able to investigate the co-text, that is, the data context to which the extract belongs.

Table 11.4 Interactive dynamics between Jon and Gary

SESSION: 1.1.2 Mathematics
STUDENTS: Tim and Jon
WORKING TIME: 11.05 – 11.30

TIME	PARTICIPATION		TRANSCRIBED PEER INTERACTION	LANGUAGE FUNCTIONS	COGNITIVE PROCESSING	SOCIAL PROCESSING	CONTEXTUAL NOTES
11.16	147	JON	Where is the large triangle?	Asking for information Q(I)	Looking for a face	Slight domination from Jon's side correct faces to	Students are trying to find
	148	TIM	Oh, yeah ...	Affectional utterance (AF)	Gary is holding the construction students have		construct the geometrical object

TIME	PARTICIPATION		TRANSCRIBED PEER INTERACTION	LANGUAGE FUNCTIONS	COGNITIVE PROCESSING	SOCIAL PROCESSING	CONTEXTUAL NOTES
	149	JON	Take those away	Organizing (OR)	already made		
	150	TIM	Hahah … what are you looking for?	Affectional utterance (AF) and asking for information Q(I)		Tim initiates collaboration	
	151	JON	A kind of a triangle to the centre … these tasks are a bit too difficult.	Answering A(I) and evaluating the task (EV)	Explaining		
	152	TIM	How about this one then?	Reasoning in a question form Q(RS)	Speculating		
	153	JON	It might be … perhaps two of these there …	Reasoning (RS)			
	154	TIM	Basically no	Reasoning (RS)	Organizing working, speculating	Slight domination from Jon's side	
11.17	155	JON	Show me … hmm … let's turn to the next exercise … let's solve that one since it is easier … it is what one sees … hey, could it be these …	Organizing (OR), evaluating (EV), and reasoning (RS)			
	156	TIM	Do you mean these small ones?	Reasoning in a question form Q(RS)		Tim initiates collaboration	
	157	JON	these	answering A(RS)			
	158	TIM	What about these big ones, I think they look big … like this	Reasoning (RS)	Speculating		
	159	JON	I think … (indistinct)	–			
	160	TIM	I don't know …	Informing (I)		Signs of 'a free rider effect' starting to appear	
	161	JON	That's a bit too thick that one there … that's there … rather small …	Reasoning (RS)	Comparing cards		
	162	TIM	That's not it … heheheh …	Reasoning (RS)			
	163	JON	It's all the same really	Reasoning (RS)			
	164	TIM	Let's try both	Organizing (OR)			
	165	JON	Let's take … this is there below, isn't it? …Bigger one … hold it	Organizing (OR), reasoning (RS), and organizing (OR)	Organizing working		
	166	TIM	No, I don't want to	Disagrees (Jd)		Social conflict	

Summary

In this chapter we have explored some of the methodological issues involved in a study of classroom interaction. Our focus here has been particularly upon interactions between learners as they engage with the material of learning. A number of key methodological points have been aired, and the analysis system we have devised has been presented as one way (among many possible such ways) of responding to some of the difficulties inherent in trying to understand what are inevitably very complex processes. It should be stressed, however, that although the past 30 years has seen substantial growth in approaches to and study of classroom interactions in a range of contexts, we are still inevitably in the infancy of our understanding of what goes on inside the 'black box' of classrooms or learning situations.

References

Anderson, J. R., Reder, L. M. and Simon, H. A. (1997) 'Situative versus cognitive perspectives: form versus substance', *Educational Researcher*, 26(1): 18–21.

Austin, J. L. (1962) *How to Do Things with Words*. Oxford: Clarendon Press.

Barnes, D. and Todd, F. (1977) *Communication and Learning in Small Groups*. London: Routledge & Kegan Paul.

Barnes, D. and Todd, F. (1995) *Communication and Learning Revisited, Making Meaning through Talk*. Portsmouth, NH: Boynton/Cook Publishers, Heinemann.

Centre for Teaching and Learning (2007) *Flanders Interaction Analysis*. Fort Lauderdale, FL: Nova Southeastern University.

Cole, M. (1996) *Culture in Mind*. Cambridge, MA: Harvard University Press.

Edwards, D. (1993) 'Concepts, memory, and the organization of pedagogic discourse: a case study', *Educational Research,* 19, 205–25.

Edwards, D. and Potter, J. (1992) *Discursive Psychology*. Newbury Park, CA: Sage.

Edwards, D. and Westgate, D. (1994) *Investigating Classroom Talk*, 2nd edn. London: Falmer Press.

Edwards, J. (2005) 'Exploratory talk in peer groups: exploring the zone of proximal development', in *Fourth Congress of the European Society for Research in Mathematics Education, Sant Feliu de Guíxols, Spain*. Spain: ESRME http://cerme4.crm.es/Papers%20definitius/8/JulieAnnEdwards.pdf, accessed 19 June 2008.

Fisher, E. (1993) 'Distinctive features of pupil-pupil classroom talk and their relationship to learning: how discursive exploration might be encouraged', *Language and Education*, 7: 239–57.

Flanders, N. (1970) *Analyzing Teacher Behavior*. Reading, MA: Addison-Wesley.

Forman, E. (1989) 'The role of peer interaction in the social construction of mathematical knowledge', *International Journal of Educational Research*, 13: 55–70.

Fourlas, G. and Wray, D. (1990) 'Children's oral language: aA comparison of two classroom organisational systems', in D. Wray (ed.) *Emerging Partnerships, Current Research in Language and Literacy*. Clevedon, OH: Multilingual Matters.

Green, J. and Mayer, L. (1991) 'The embeddedness of reading in classroom life: reading as a situated process', in C. Baker and A. Luke (eds) *Toward a Critical Sociology of Reading Pedagogy*. Amsterdam: Benjamins Publishing Company.

Green, J. and Wallat, C. (1981) 'Mapping instructional conversations – a sociolinguistic ethnography', in J.

Green and C. Wallat (eds) *Ethnography and Language in Educational Settings*. Norwood, NJ: Ablex Publishing Corporation.

Greeno, J. G. (1997) 'On claims that answer the wrong questions', *Educational Researcher*, 26: 5–17.

Grossen, M. (1994) 'Theoretical and methodological consequences of a change in the unit of analysis for the study of peer interactions in a problem solving situation', *European Journal of Psychology of Education*, 11: 159–73.

Halliday, M. A. K. and Hasan, R. (1989) *Language, Context, and Text*. London: Oxford University Press.

Joiner, R., Messer, D., Light, P. and Littleton, K. (1995) 'Investigating the relationship between communicative style and productive interaction, paper presented at the sixth European Conference for Research on Learning and Instruction, Nijmegen, the Netherlands.

King, A. (1989) 'Verbal interaction and problem-solving within computer assisted cooperative learning groups', *Educational Computing Research*, 5(1): 1–15.

Kumpulainen, K. (1994) 'The nature of children's oral language interactions during collaborative writing experience at the computer', unpublished doctoral dissertation, Exeter, University of Exeter.

Kumpulainen, K. (1996) 'The nature of peer interaction in the social context created by the use of word processors', *Learning and Instruction*, 6: 243–61.

Kumpulainen, K. and Wray, D. (2002) *Classroom Interaction and Social Learning*. London: RoutledgeFalmer.

Lemke, J. L. (1990) *Talking Science: Language, Learning and Values*. Norwood, NJ: Ablex.

Light, P., Littleton, K., Messer, D. and Joiner, R. (1994) 'Social and communicative processes in computer-based problem solving', *European Journal of Psychology of Education*, 14(1): 93–109.

Mercer, N. (1994) 'The quality of talk in children's joint activity at the computer', *Journal of Computer Assisted Learning*, 10: 24–32.

Mercer, N. (1996) 'The quality of talk in children's collaborative activity in the classroom', *Learning and Instruction*, 6: 359–77.

Mercer, N. and Littleton, K. (2007) *Dialogue and the Development of Children's Thinking: A Sociocultural Approach*. London: Routledge.

Newman, M. (2004) *Problem Based Learning: An Exploration of the Method and Evaluation of its Effectiveness in a Continuing Nursing Education Programme*. London: School of Lifelong Learning & Education, Middlesex University.

Palincsar, A. S. (1986) 'The role of dialogue in providing scaffolded instruction', *Educational Psychologist*, 21: 73–98.

Perret-Clermont, A-N., Perret, J-F. and Bell, N. (1991) 'The social construction of meaning and cognitive activity in elementary school children', in L. B. Resnick, J. M. Levine and S. D.Teasley (eds) *Perspectives on Socially Shared Cognition*. Washington, DC: American Psychological Association.

Resnick, L. B., Levine, J. M. and Teasley, S. D. (eds) (1991) *Perspectives on Socially Shared Cognition*. Washington, DC: American Psychological Association.

Teasley, S. (1995) 'The role of talk in children's peer collaborations', *Developmental Psychology*, 31: 207–20.

Tudge, J. (1992) 'Processes and consequences of peer collaboration: a Vygotskian analysis', *Child Development*, 63: 1364–79.

Tuyay, S., Jennings, L. and Dixon, C. (1995) 'Classroom discourse and opportunities to learn: an ethnographic study of knowledge construction in a bilingual third grade classroom', in R. Durán (ed.) *Discourse Processes (Literacy among Latinos: Focus on School Contexts)*, 19: 75–110.

Webb, N. M., Troper, J. and Fall, J. R. (1995) 'Constructive activity and learning in collaborative small groups', *Journal of Educational Psychology*, 87, 406–23.

Wells, G. and Chang-Wells, G. L. (1992) Constructing Knowledge Together: Classrooms as Centers of Inquiry and Literacy. Portsmouth, NH: Heinemann.

Wertsch, J. (1985) *Vygotsky and the Social Formation of Mind.* Cambridge, MA: Harvard University Press.

Wertsch, J. (1991) *Voices of the Mind: A Sociocultural Approach to Mediated Action.* Cambridge, MA: Harvard University Press.

Wragg, E. C. (1999) *An introduction to Classroom Observation.* London: Routledge.

12 Documentary Research

Wendy Robinson

Introduction

The contribution and potential of documentary research have often been overlooked in education and social sciences. It is also often missing from the research methods literature (Scott 1990: 1; McCulloch 2004: 11). This elision is unfortunate and often leads to deeply uncontextualized and ahistorical perspectives in current research. This chapter demonstrates how documentary research can be used in stand-alone projects and, also, as one approach in multimethod projects. The chapter will deal with the practicalities of undertaking documentary research, including issues of access to documents, the selection of documents and the critical analysis and interpretation of documentary material. The chapter is in four parts. First, documentary research is defined and its contribution to educational and social science research discussed. Secondly, the identification and classification of different types of documents is examined. Thirdly, a framework for making sense of documentary data is considered. Finally, a case study of a piece of documentary research is uncovered to illustrate the main processes involved.

By the end of this chapter, you should be able to:

- understand what documentary research is and how it can contribute to educational and social science research
- familiarize yourself with the practicalities of undertaking documentary research, including selecting, accessing and collecting a range of different primary and secondary documents
- explain how documents are classified and categorized
- reflect on ways in which meaning can be drawn from documents

Documentary Research: Definition and Role

Documentary research is derived largely from historical methods, which are essentially concerned with the problems of selection and evaluation of evidence. It involves the use of written texts and documents as source materials. These are wide ranging and could include, for example, official government publications, reports, legal documents, newspapers, books, institutional records, personal diaries and letters. John Scott, a leading methodologist in documentary research, defines a document as 'an artefact which has as its central feature an inscribed text' (Scott 1990: 5). In the past, such documents would have been produced as hard copies, whether in manuscript or published form. However, new technology now extends the possibilities to include a host of electronic and virtual documents, which in turn raise important questions about the direction and parameters of this type of research.

Historically, documentary research was at the heart of educational and social research but its popularity waned as other research methods, particularly in qualitative fieldwork, were developed. McCulloch (2004) argues that historians comfortably use documents all the time, but that in the last 20 years documentary research has fallen out of favour with social science and educational researchers who prefer the tools of interview, questionnaire and observation, which offer a more enticing direct engagement with the subjects of study. Documents have been relegated to a very peripheral role, often being used only to provide background material. There has also been a mistrust of the methodology used in documentary research, particularly around bias, representation and interpretation. McCulloch argues convincingly for a revival of documentary studies on the grounds that documents can provide crucial links between the past and the present and particular insights into aspects of change and continuity in educational ideas and practices.

Documentary research does have a role in educational and social sciences research. Precisely because of the wealth and diversity of documentary sources, documentary research offers multiple perspectives on a problem or topic. It can be used as the sole approach to a research problem, to provide reference or background material or as a more substantive resource in a multimethod triangulated approach, particularly when used alongside interview evidence (see Box 12.1). Silverman (1995: 46), in his work on qualitative research, reminds us of the importance of documents to social science and of:

> the pervasive significance of documentary records, written and otherwise, in contemporary social settings. What follows logically from such an observation is that qualitative field research must pay careful attention to the collection and analysis of documentary reality. Such inquiry is not confined just to the inspection of documents themselves. It must also incorporate a clear understanding of how documents are produced, circulated, read, stored and used for a wide variety of purposes.

Box 12.1 The role of documentary research

- It offers multiple perspectives on a problem or topic.
- It provides a point of reference or background material.
- It functions as a substantive resource in a multimethod triangulated research approach.

Selecting, Identifying and Accessing Documentary Sources

Historiographical and methodological literature on the use of documents points to the need for a classification and categorization of different types of documents. This enables the researcher to make judgements about the relative merits of different documents. It also indicates differential levels of quality, reliability, authenticity and built-in bias that will inevitably characterize the type of data that can be gleaned from different sources. It also helps with the selection and gathering of data from as wide a range of documents as possible to generate confidence in analysis and interpretation. Ease of access to documents, whether they exist in the public or private domain, is also contingent on the particular category of document being used.

Primary versus secondary documents

Drawn from historical methodology, the main classification of documents is to distinguish between primary and secondary sources. Primary sources are broadly defined as sources created within the period studied, with secondary sources, usually in the form of books and articles, produced later. This suggests a hierarchy of documents – with those closest in time and in relationship with the topic under review being more desirable than those more removed. This division is contentious between historians and is not always straightforward. There are blurred boundaries in some cases, relating largely to the focus of the research question. For example, in my own study of initial teacher education in the early twentieth century, I used teaching method books as primary sources, and did not include any secondary sources, because my research question was concerned with the training of teachers in dominant pedagogical practices (Robinson 2004).

Classification of sources

Within the primary and secondary distinction lies a more complex hierarchy and classification of documents. Again, further classification of documents is problematic because some documents just do not fit neatly into a given category and there are always going to be blurred boundaries. The location and accessibility of documents is also related to their classification, with unpublished and harder to reach documents perhaps carrying greater weight than more widely accessible public documents. A popular convention is to distinguish between published (printed) and unpublished (manuscript) sources. Within this hierarchy, manuscript or handwritten documents, of which there is usually only one copy held in archives or a private collection, come first, followed by published pamphlets, periodicals, government reports and reports of parliamentary debates which can be easily located in libraries.

Another convention emphasizes the authorship of the source, drawing a distinction between those produced by governments (official) and those produced by corporations, associations or private individuals (semi-official and private). Some sort of distinction along the continuum between public and private is a useful way of categorizing documents. This type of distinction would embrace an approach to the whole documentary record, ranging from the most official or public of government records to the most private personal diary or letter (see Box 12.2). Rather than rank documents within a descending hierarchy of weightiness, it is probably more helpful to think about accessing a broad spectrum of documents which encapsulates a wide range of perspectives, rather than relying too heavily on one particular group. This of course has to be framed within the obvious limitations of the documentary record, which, by its very nature, is only ever going to be partial.

Box 12.2 Classification of documents

- Sources (primary vs. secondary).
- Location and accessibility (unpublished vs. public documents).
- Form (printed vs. manuscript/handwritten).
- Authorship of source (governmental/official vs. corporations/individual/semi-official/private documents).

Selection, access and location

Searching and selecting documents demands the same rigour and consistency as any other type of social/educational research. Clearly, selecting and accessing sources is influenced by the amount of time available and the size and scope of the project. Access to sources is not necessarily straightforward for a number or reasons. Published sources are relatively easy to gain access to through publicly available bibliographies and catalogues in copyright libraries. Accessing semi-official and personal documents, which are not in the public domain, is much more difficult. The conservation of unpublished records is haphazard, though in Britain there is an extensive network of local archives and record offices, which are an important resource for the documentary researcher. The availability of documents cannot be taken for granted and the documentary record is frustratingly fragile. Documents are often destroyed for political purposes or by accident. In Britain, there is a 30-year closed period on certain political documents which clearly has an implication for the study of contemporary history. Andrews neatly encapsulates the frustrations for the documentary researcher around problems of access and the survival of the documentary record:

> the material which is so central to the research suddenly changes in character or runs out; the newspaper for a particular (crucial week) has been destroyed; the discovery in the record office catalogue of some immensely exciting document leads only to the information that it disappeared mysteriously five years ago, or is damaged beyond restoration. Material which might enable a wealth of insight can be tantalisingly elusive.
>
> (Andrews 1985: 156, quoted in McCulloch 2004: 43)

Making Sense of Documents

Identifying, selecting and accessing documents is only the start of the process of documentary research. The main challenge is to read, interpret and find meaning in the documentary record. This not only demands a face-value reading of the document to elicit factual information from what is actually written, but also requires a much more difficult and tenuous engagement with hidden and obscured meaning – a critical reading between the lines. McCulloch (2004: 1) neatly captures this two-stage process: 'To understand documents is to read between the lines of our material world. We need to comprehend the words themselves to follow the plot, the basic storyline. But we need to get between the lines, to analyse their meaning and their deeper purpose, to develop a study that is based on documents' (McCulloch 2004: 1).

Seeking meaning from witting and unwitting information lies at the heart of documentary research, and this is both its biggest strength and its biggest weakness. Documentary records, however 'official' they might seem, cannot be treated as firm evidence of what they report. They need to be properly understood as social and historical constructs and in context – their place in organizational settings, the cultural values attached to them and their distinctive types and forms. In analysing and interpreting documentary data, the same crucial rule, which applies to all other forms of qualitative data analysis, should be followed – that is, to be *systematic and critical*. There are some basic established rules associated with interpreting and analysing documents and these demand that they be subjected to a rigorous external and internal criticism through key questions about authenticity, reliability, credibility and meaning.

Authenticity

First the authenticity of the document should be tested, and the author, place and date of writing and audience verified. Scott asks whether the evidence is 'genuine and of unquestionable origin' and suggests that this is absolutely essential if the researcher is to make any proper judgement about the quality of the data (1990: 7). Where copies or reproductions and edited versions of documents are produced from the original, questions of authenticity are particularly relevant.

Reliability

The reliability of the document should also be tested. This relates to difficult questions of detecting and understanding bias and appraising the truth of accounts, as well as practical considerations of the availability of relevant source material and the representativeness of documents which have survived and are able to be included in a study. Documents will never be bias free but it is important for the researcher to be able to detect and understand bias as a way of understanding the bigger picture. Documents are also susceptible to differential survival rates, which can lead to a dominance of some types of documents, notably official or 'top-down' documents, at the expense of more personal documents and documents produced from the perspectives of marginal, oppressed or subordinate groups. For many reasons documents are destroyed, lost or damaged, thus skewing the overall documentary record. Researchers need to be aware of these problems with reliability and take into account such limitations when drawing any conclusions. Problems with reliability also strengthen the case for not depending on one single source but drawing on as wide a range of documents as possible, both as a form of triangulation but also to ensure that alternative, contradictory and conflicting perspectives can be found. What John Tosh (1991: 66) advises for historical research has a useful bearing more widely on documentary research:

> It will be clear, then, that historical research is not a matter of identifying the authoritative source and then exploiting it for all it is worth, for the majority of sources are in some way inaccurate, incomplete or tainted by prejudice and self-interest. The procedure is rather to amass as many pieces of evidence as possible from a wide range of sources - preferably from all the sources which have a bearing on the problem in hand. In this way the inaccuracies and distortions of particular sources are more likely to be revealed, and the inferences drawn by the historian can be corroborated. Each type of source possesses certain strengths and weaknesses; considered together, and compared on against the other, there is at least a chance that they will reveal the true facts - or something very close to them.

Meaning

In probing the question of meaning, Scott (1990) asks whether 'the evidence is clear and comprehendible'. If specialized or technical language is used, then the evidence needs to be deciphered for the meaning to be understood. The document also needs to be read with its context in mind. Various approaches have been used by researchers to analyse documents for meaning, including hermeneutics, linguistic analysis, discourse analysis, semiotic analysis, quantitative content analysis and more grounded theory approaches (see Chapter 18 for a discussion on qualitative research analysis including grounded theory).

A Case Study in Using Documents: Sarah Jane Bannister (1858–1942)

This case study is based on a biographical study of Sarah Jane Bannister, who was a female educationist in the late nineteenth and early twentieth century in Britain. I first came across the character of Sarah Jane Bannister when I was researching the late nineteenth-century pupil-teacher system in England and Wales. Her name appeared in a wide range of historical documents that I accessed for this extensive study. The only female principal of one of 12 London School Board pupil-teacher centres in the late nineteenth century, she went on to become principal of Moorfields Teacher Training College under the London County Council. In 1898, she was represented on a departmental committee inquiry into the pupil-teacher system and her own evidence on the experience of instructing female pupil teachers, as well as her broader views on the future development of teacher training, was deemed very significant. I became very interested in the development of her professional career in education and, as I started to map this out, I began to develop a number of research questions which prompted me to undertake a focused piece of biographical research. I wanted to track her contribution to the educational world in which she operated, and understand her views on the education of girls and women and teacher education. At the same time, I wanted to find out about her personal life and consider how, at a time in history when women struggled to be accepted in the public workplace, she managed marriage and motherhood and broke down barriers to gender equality. I wanted to probe the relationship between her public/professional life and her as a person. This research depended entirely on documentary evidence and both the process and product of this work serve as a useful case study on the strengths and weaknesses of documentary research – including its possibilities and frustrating limitations.

In seeking to construct a professional and personal history of Sarah Jane Bannister, I drew upon a wide range of documents – the majority of which would be classified as official, in the form of legal documents and public government papers, and semi-official, in the form of a range educational writings, newspapers and unpublished local archive material relating to the London School Board, the London County Council and Hendon Borough Council. These included: official registration documents, such as birth, marriage and death certificates; her will; reports of her work and some of her own writing in the professional press and in the local Hendon press including the *Times Education Supplement*, *The Woman Teachers World*, *The School Master* and the *Hendon Guardian and Times*; her evidence to and role as a member of an official government committee on the pupil-teacher system; minutes and notices of the London Pupil Teacher Association; contemporary educational writings; unpublished local archive material relating to the London School Board and London County Council; and miscellaneous letters and papers from the Hendon Borough Council. Accessing these documents and amassing such a bank of documentary evidence led me to the websites, catalogues and search rooms of numerous public and local archives and copyright libraries including the British Library, the Public Record Office, Kew, the Family Records Centre, the London Metropolitan Archive, the Barnet Local Studies Centre and Hendon Library. The process of accessing, selecting and finding meaning in relevant documents was not neat or linear. Rather, it required taking leads from some documents to seek out other documents and engage in an iterative interrogation of the material. Different documents were used to triangulate and corroborate some reasonably solid facts and also to help develop the less tangible but intriguing detail about her personal and public values, attitudes and relationships. The process can be likened to piecing together a jigsaw puzzle, without a guiding picture or confidence that all the pieces are available.

The most frustrating aspect of the research was the dearth of any highly personal documents, such as personal letters or diaries, other than formal birth, marriage and death certificates and her will. While these legal documents did afford some tantalizing insights into Sarah Jane Bannister the person, the very type of unwitting, 'reading in between the lines' evidence that forms such an important part of the documentary record, these were limited and made it very difficult to answer those aspects of the research questions which were about the relationship between Sarah's personal and professional life. When undertaking documentary research it is often necessary to work with loose research questions at the initial stages and to modify and refine these as the data are gathered. My general starting research questions were concerned with investigating patterns of professional life encountered by late nineteenth-century female teacher-educators. I was also interested in broader questions about social class and gender, which transcended Sarah's own highly personal experiences into the much bigger educational picture of the time.

To illustrate how documentary research is developed, four types of documents that were used in the Sarah Jane Bannister study are examined. These include examples from civil registration documents; a will; a local newspaper; and an official government publication. In reality these were not accessed chronologically. My initial engagement with the official government publication prompted further research on Sarah and enabled me to trace other types of document.

Civil registration documents

In England and Wales, civil registration of births, marriages and deaths has been mandatory since 1837. These official legal registration documents can be traced and copies made at the General Record Office. Standard certificates contain specific biographical factual information, and are a useful resource when building a picture of a person's background, life span, social origins and family background. This required some patient detective work, leafing through numerous ledgers and cross-referencing information already gathered on estimated birth, marriage and death dates of Sarah Jane Bannister to make sure that I was accessing the right documents for the right person.

Certified copy of an entry of birth

The birth certificate reveals crucial information about the date and place of birth: Sarah Jane Stourton, 5 August 1858 at Norton St Philip, Somerset. In addition, it names Sarah's mother as Harriet Stourton, formerly Moon, and her father as John Stourton. An entry for the occupation of father, as 'journeyman mason' gives some indication of the social and economic background of the family at the time as artisan working class.

Certified copy of an entry of marriage

The marriage certificate, as well as confirming the marriage between Sarah Jane Stourton and Henry Bannister, reveals some important clues about Sarah's age and where she was living at the time of her marriage, and also the occupational status of her husband, her father and her father-in-law. Aged 23 she married Henry Bannister, a widowed schoolmaster, 15 years her senior. Henry's own father, John Mugford Bannister, was also a schoolmaster, suggesting not only that Sarah might have married into an established teaching dynasty but also that her marriage was an affirmation of her own rising social status to upper-working or lower-middle-class professional respectability. The marriage was solemnized at the parish church of Tottenhnam and Sarah's father, John Stourton, is listed as a builder, suggesting some upward social mobility from the previously recorded occupation as 'journeyman mason'.

Certified copy of an entry of death certificate

The death certificate brings the official registration documentation full circle and records Sarah's death on 16 March 1942 at the age of 83. It records her place of death at home, 1 Hill Close,

Hampstead Way, Golders Green Hendon – a very long way from her place of birth in Somerset, and the cause of death as a carcinoma of the skull and spine. It also reveals that she was, by the time of her death, widowed and that Henry had predeceased her. Most interestingly, it reveals that Sarah and Henry had a daughter, 'R. W. Bannister', who was present at the death of her mother. The daughter was unmarried.

Though formal and factual and providing important basic biographic information, these three documents also provide tantalizing clues about social class background, Sarah's geographical and social mobility through her teaching career and the fact that she had a daughter. If these were the only documents relating to Sarah Jane Bannister available, however, there would be a lot of missing information. Nowhere on these registration documents, for example, is there any reference to Sarah's own professional career.

Official probate records

Having accessed accurate biographical data from the registration documents, I was then able, with the full details of her death, to apply to the Probate Office and find out whether Sarah had made a will. Wills, like registration documents, are official, legal documents. In order to search the probate index, certain information is necessary: the full name of the deceased; the exact or approximate date of death and the last known address or area of residence. Sometimes wills are brief and contain minimal factual information, but they can also offer potentially rich insights into a person's life, family and friendship networks and financial status. Sarah's will helped to flesh out some of the bare bones of the factual registration data. Made on 6 September 1930, when Sarah was over 70 years old, the will reveals that she was at this stage a widow and living at 1 Hill Close, NW11, as indeed we know she was at the time of her death 12 years later. Her only daughter, Winifred Katharine May Bannister, and Miss Jane B. McCrea were appointed as executors. Sarah's daughter is listed as the main beneficiary of her estate, with 13 detailed provisions of personal gifts to individual family members and friends. The extraordinary detail of these provisions is illuminating and helps to build a picture of a woman with particular tastes in art and literature, and also demonstrates how much Sarah herself must have valued a number of gifts that had been presented to her from former students, both at Moorfields College and the Stepney Pupil Teacher Centre. These include, for example, for 'Mrs Agnes Kent the oak stool with Persian tile top given me by Moorfields College Students' and to Mrs John Seymour Lindsay, 'my plaque in beaten copper, giving the Moorfields College motto and the blue china bowl given me by Moorfields College students'. There is also a bequest to Mrs Stephen Graham for the 'framed picture of "The Angelus" given by Students of the Stepney Pupil Teacher Centre' and to Miss Emma F. Peart 'the plaque in beaten copper giving the motto of the Stepney Pupil Teacher Centre'. Other bequests include specific items of jewellery, one being her moonstone pendant with chain attached, which is such a prominent feature of both the official Hendon Borough Council photograph and portrait in oils of her that I found at the Barnet Local Studies Centre, as well as pictures and books. Some of the friends listed had clearly been professional colleagues of Sarah's, for example Miss E. Jeffries Davis and Miss Margaret S. Ryan who were bequeathed 'in grateful recognition of their devoted work for and with me at Moorfields Training College and of valued friendship in later years'. In addition to the factual information contained in Sarah's will, a 'reading between the lines', as described in McCulloch's work, is possible and does generate some deeper understanding of Sarah as a person, her friends, her professional context and her literary and cultural preferences.

The press

The press and its treatment of a range of social and political issues, as well as being a source of basic information, is very important for the documentary researcher.

An obituary of Sarah Jane Bannister which I located in the *Hendon Times and Guardian* both corroborates some of the detail of her personal and professional life accessed through other sources, but also fills in some of the missing gaps. Published on the 20 March 1942, and some 600 words long, this obituary summarizes Sarah's educational career and provides hitherto unknown information about her early professional life. For example, the obituary states that she undertook her initial teacher training at St Katherine's College, Tottenham, and was subsequently appointed as a resident lecturer on the college staff before her marriage to Henry Bannister two years later. There is also a reference to her appointment as an inspector of schools in Bradford before her appointment as head teacher of the Stepney Pupil Teacher Centre. This new information raised a number of further research questions for me. It is unclear whether Sarah was required to relocate to Bradford for this purpose, or whether she remained in London and travelled to Bradford on a regular basis. What is clear is that right from the start of her marriage, Sarah continued to actively develop her own career, combining marriage, motherhood and professional life. Sarah and Henry had one daughter – Winifred Katherine. Quite how Sarah found the management of this potentially conflicting lifestyle is unknown but it cannot have been an easy balancing act, particularly when social mores and expectations at that period of history were unsympathetic towards working wives and mothers.

Over half of the obituary catalogues Sarah's services to Hendon Council, which spanned over 20 years. In 1915 she retired from professional work and was invited by the Hendon Women Citizens' Council to offer herself for election to the then Hendon Urban District Council. She was duly elected and served without interruption until 1938, when she finally retired. When Hendon became a borough in 1932 Sarah was one of the first aldermen to be elected and the only woman to receive that distinction. She served on almost every statutory committee of the council, as well as on many subcommittees. The bulk of her work, however, lay with the Education Committee and she was the prime mover in the founding of the Hendon Free Library. At one time, she was the council's representative on the National Association of Education Committees and on the Assessment Committee for Central Middlesex. She was also council representative on the Garden Suburb Institute Council, on the governing body of the Henrietta Barnett School and the Hendon County School. To mark 20 years of service to the civic life of Hendon, Sarah was presented with a portrait of herself in oils at a special ceremony in the town hall in March 1939. This insight into her public role suggests a woman with a strong public service work ethic and a personal commitment to education.

Official government publications: the 1898 Departmental Committee on the Pupil Teacher System

It was through a detailed reading of an official government report, which documented the meetings and findings of a prestigious and influential Departmental Committee on the Pupil Teacher System which was appointed in January 1897 to investigate the working of the pupil-teacher system and to recommend any improvements that I became curious about Sarah Bannister. She was one of three women on a committee of 12, which was mainly represented by leading HMI, clergy and training college principals. She was actively committed to her position on the committee, which met twice weekly from January to June 1897 on Monday afternoons and Thursday mornings to hear evidence from witnesses. She only missed one of 30 such sessions and presumably had to attend many more committee meetings for the assessment of the overall findings and writing of the final report. As well as giving her own evidence as a witness, she pursued a clear agenda in questioning other witnesses, contributing to nearly every session. It is from her evidence and questioning that much of her vision for teacher training can be drawn. In essence the 1898 Departmental Committee was unable to condone the long-term future of pupil teaching and recommended that intending teachers should be relocated into the secondary sector where greater emphasis would be placed on their academic rather than professional preparation. The pupil-teacher centres were criticized for their professional and social narrowness and for subordinating educational aims to pressure of examinations. Part of its vision was for the perceived educational and cultural 'narrowness' of the elementary school sector to be bolstered and enhanced by the injection of intending teachers from more cultured and higher social class backgrounds. This vision resonated with Sarah's own outlook on the future of pupil teaching. She was not afraid of stating her position on the pupil-teacher system – a position which for its extremity was at odds with that of her colleagues as well as her employer. I know from other sources that so incensed were many of her fellow London centre principals at her evidence to the 1898 Committee, that they submitted an official complaint to the London School Board. Sarah was accused of exaggerating the extent to which overwork and overstrain among female pupil teachers was a problem as well as the extent to which probationers were appointed before they reached the age of 14 years. Faced with such evidence it is difficult to asses whether Sarah, for the overall sake of pupil teachers, exaggerated her dissatisfaction, or whether she presented a true picture. Whatever the answer, it can only be inferred that this difficult situation must have been awkward for Sarah's husband in his own position as headmaster of the Hackney Pupil Teacher Centre.

Finding meaning

For over 60 years, Sarah Jane Bannister occupied an important place in the educational world of elementary teacher training, school inspection and local government. When she retired from official working life as a local inspector of schools, she moved into Hendon's local politics where she continued to champion various educational causes. While she clearly achieved some local acclaim by the time of her retirement, the substance of her professional life and career had been lost to history. Individual women teachers as unique individuals with specific personal and domestic as well as professional circumstances remain fairly elusive, shadowy figures to the educational historian. Dina Copelman (1996: xvi), in her extensive work on London's women teachers, eloquently expresses this frustration: 'How intimately can we get to know the individual teacher? The sources are fickle, sometimes yielding sharply focused snapshots of life and a personality, other times hinting at deep mysteries but providing little detail, yet other times remaining obdurately silent'. It is likely that there were many other women teachers like Sarah, who led important and interesting professional lives but who have not as yet caught the attention or the imagination of researchers willing to pursue the faint, patchy or even empty traces they have left behind. The documentary record clearly offers a critical lens on the lives and work of women teachers who have been largely forgotten and overlooked in official educational histories. Yet by its very nature, this documentary record is only partial.

Box 12.3 Key points in documentary research

- Documentary research has been marginalized in education and social science research but clearly has an important role to play.
- Documentary research draws heavily on historical methodology – it is about the appropriate identification, selection and interpretation of different types of document.
- Documentary research has strengths and weaknesses: there is the question of survival and representativeness of documents; their bias; and the nature and means of interpretation of data.
- Documents have to be subjected to rigorous external and internal criticism and understood in their proper context.
- Documents can be classified and categorized in different ways.
- The distinction between primary and secondary data is important.
- Documents are social and cultural constructs.
- A documentary study needs to amass as wide a range of different types of document as possible.

Summary

In this chapter, the possibilities and parameters of documentary analysis for educational and social science research have been defined and explained. Currently, somewhat peripheral and marginalized in educational and social science research, documentary research has been reviewed as an important and worthwhile research tool. Its perceived problems to the researcher (bias, removal from the real research subject, partiality, reliability and interpretation) have been examined in the light of the various checks and measures applied to the documentary research process. These concern the different ways of identifying, classifying, compiling and interpreting evidence from documentary sources, drawn largely from historical methodology. A case study of a piece of documentary research has been used to illustrate both the rich potential of documentary research but also its frustrations and limitations. When assessing the contribution of documentary research to educational and social science research, it is helpful to remember that the problems faced by the documentary researcher are not a world away from the more generic problems associated with qualitative and interpretative approaches. Furthermore, whether it is used for reference or as a substantive resource, documentary research has the added attraction of being able to offer unique insights into historical problems and to tap into a different dimension of time.

References

Copelman, D. (2006) *London's Women Teachers: Gender, Class and Feminism 1870–1939*. London: Routledge.

McCulloch, G. (2004) *Documentary Research in Education, History and the Social Sciences*. London: RoutledgeFalmer.

Robinson, W. (2004) Entry for Sarah Bannister, *New Dictionary of National Biography*. Oxford: Oxford University Press.

Scott, J. (1990) *A Matter of Record: Documentary Sources in Social Research*. Cambridge: Polity Press.

Tosh, J. (2002) *The Pursuit of History: Aims, Methods and New Directions in the Study of Modern History*, revised 3rd edn. London: Longman.

The Application of Visual Methodology in the Exploration of the Visual Culture of Schools

Jon Prosser and Andrew Loxley

Introduction

The purpose of this chapter is to consider how a visual-based methodology can be applied in the context of educational research. Although the use of the visual is not new to the social sciences, it has been a relatively 'fringe' activity for many decades and has only in the past few years begun to be seen as less marginal and, quite literally, as a legitimate approach to research. Our intention is to discuss an array of visual methods applied to schooling and we will argue for a methodologically framed, visually orientated, mixed-methods approach to examining over-arching and substantive educational themes and research questions which are central to understanding the quotidian (as well the less mundane) nature of educational institutions and practices. However, like all other approaches to research, the visual has grown into a complex and multifaceted area, and our intention is to provide a 'flavour' of this approach. By the end of this chapter you should be able to:

- Describe a visual methodology.
- Explain why visual methods are useful.
- Explain how visual data can be interpreted.
- Discuss the ethical issues for visual researchers.

What is Visual Methodology?

Visual research is concerned with the production, organization and interpretation of imagery. Its subject draws on analytical perspectives including sociology, anthropology, media studies, psychology and cultural geography to study a wide range of topics ranging from community, power and gender studies, to spatial relationships and spectatorship. In educational research in particular, over the last three decades, visual studies have come to play a particularly meaningful role. However, the use of the visual in the social sciences has a long and complicated genealogy, and is as much bound up with the technology of constructing images as it is with changing methodological fashions and developments since the early nineteenth century (see e.g. Stasz 1979; Banks 1998; Harper 1998; Wagner 2006; Prosser and Loxley 2008). More specifically, many of the critiques of the use of imagery are as equally directed at the technology researchers use (cameras, processing techniques, modes of reproduction etc.), as with the more conventional issues around trustworthiness, credibility, sampling and analytical strategies.

On another level (and as with most research approaches), the visual research community was (and still is) fragmented into two broad camps: the 'critical' and the 'empirical'. The main difference is that the latter group work with visual data which they are predominately responsible for producing (see e.g. Harper 1987; Prosser and Schwartz 1998; Prosser 2006), whereas the former group of researchers tend to work with material which comes in a 'pre-digested' form such as advertisements, soap operas, film and so on. Researchers who work in the area of cultural studies (see e.g. Hall 1997; Tagg 1988; Wells 2003) would be typical of the second group. However, it can be argued that such lines of demarcation are rapidly becoming invalid and inappropriate in applied visual studies. There is a discernible shift in that the more versatile and able visual researchers are applying their skills across a wide range of research questions and situations which entails combining 'researcher created', 'participant generated', 'researcher found', and 'representational practices'. This continuum of theoretical approaches includes postmodernism, critical theory, cultural studies, semiotics, sociosemiotics and visual symbolism, used to interpret existing images, and visual ethnography and visual sociology to generate additional imagery.

What Counts as an Image?

Wagner (2006: 55) provides a useful insight into the question of 'what counts as an image' by providing two definitions:

> The term 'visible' refers to physical-optical attributes of phenomena or materials, regardless of how interesting or meaningful they are to researchers or research subjects. Something is 'visible' if it can or could be seen, whether or not anyone notices or cares about it. 'Visual', on the other hand, refers to an attribute, dimension or mode of sense of perception, not to objects per se.

However, Wagner's definitions are only of partial use to us, as the more problematic concerns for most researchers (both neophyte and experienced) are about what we can legitimately label 'visual' data. This needs to be addressed by asking three simple questions:

1 What is the relevance of visual data to the research question?
2 How are they to be constructed (i.e. the process and methods used to 'create' the data)?
3 What is it that you have or will have when you have constructed the data (i.e. the epistemological status of the data)?

For researchers, all three questions are interlinked in some form; the question(s) will suggest the methods and the methods in turn will shape the nature of the data in terms of what they may 'mean', which in turn might generate new questions (see Chapter 5 for a discussion on the interplay between research questions and methods). However, a further cognate concern 'sitting behind' the relationship between methods and questions relates to the theoretical orientation which profoundly shapes a researcher's 'conduct' in any study. The differences between academic disciplines, theoretical concepts, empirical versus critical, impact on epistemology and methodology and so on, all collude to generate further different reference points in what constitutes the visual and how it can be used. For example, a study of pupils' perception of playground space (i.e. an empirical sociological investigation) is very different from a study of the visual semiotics of pages of a science textbook (i.e. critical cultural studies). There is also the added complexity that alongside the 'bigger' conceptual markers of difference, visual researchers (and not too dissimilar to historians, ethnographers, psychologists etc.) have their own methodological 'rules, rituals and regulations' within which they work. Hence each discipline has its own notions about what constitutes legitimate research questions as well as appropriate forms of data construction, analysis and reporting strategies.

Disciplinary boundaries notwithstanding, a more concrete way of looking at what counts as an image is by loosely classifying visual research data into three broad types (shown in Table 13.1), which can be used individually or in combination within a study. In looking at these types in

Table 13.1 Types of images that can form the part of a study

Type of image	Definition	Example
Researcher found	Any image which has been found or 'discovered' which is considered to be relevant to the study. Typically little is known about the context of creation.	Images in an old school prospectus; children's work on classroom walls or in exercise books; playground graffiti.
Researcher created	Images which are constructed by a researcher specifically for a specific study.	Researcher-created video of complex interactions; drawings and diagrams in a field diary.
Participant generated	Images which are either created by research participants specifically for the study they are involved in, or an image which has been found or 'discovered' by participants which is considered to be relevant to the study.	Participants' own photographs which may be used for elicitation purposes; participant's diagrams or 'maps' showing, for example, ideas, concepts or social relationships.

more detail, from a methodological perspective we need to be mindful that, for example, researcher images (found, created or generated) have an ambiguous 'existence' and significance as data. In the case of images, a photograph, for example, is not only of something (i.e. possess content, such as a family portrait, a Dublin bus) and has an aesthetic form, but it is also an artefact in its own right which possesses a social biography – even objects have a history (see Edwards 2001). As such, the photograph as a found and created document is a three-dimensional object which contains 'within it' a two-dimensional representation of something and the medium, as much as the content, can become, as Marshall Mcluhan (1967) would argue, the message, or at least part of it.

Added to this, there is the space, place and context in which a photograph is viewed. An image framed on a wall, stuck on a fridge door or within a family album may give the photograph additional significance. Hence it is important to consider the materiality of the image, in that what *kind* of presentational media is used can exert an influence over our readings of the image. Photographs can come in different sizes, colours, texture, tonalities, slides, negatives, contact sheets and so on which are all factors that modulate our interaction with them as artefacts in our attempt to construct meaning from 'out' of them. A further point to note is that the image itself is also a construct, as well as a record of something (Leeuwen and Jewitt 2001). The photograph that we refer to as 'data' (1) is the outcome of sophisticated social and technological practices, for example, the relationship between the photographer and the persons being photographed, and to what extent has the lens distorted what is before the camera; (2) has been produced for other possibly unknown reasons (if found) and for specific reasons (if researcher created).

Why are Visual Methods Useful?

In the past, researchers have focused on words and numbers to make sense of society and have adopted methods to meet their needs. However, as an often used cliché runs, we live in a world replete in visual images – we plan, think and create in terms of imagery, therefore we need appropriate visual methods to aid our understanding of these phenomena. On a basic level, visual methods are useful because:

- they slow down observation and enhance the focus on looking
- they provide an important counterbalancing mechanism to numbers and words methods
- the visual in the form of objects, photographs or drawings, provides a versatile elicitation media that evokes ideas and memories in respondents
- found material potentially provide insights into the past and present culture of schooling
- they build bridges between researchers and researched and are less threatening than words/numbers-based methods and are thus empowering
- they can be used to capture ineffable and illusive concepts and enhance empathetic understanding (Webber 2008)

Exploring the Visual Cultures of Schooling: An Example of Using Visual Methods

One example of why a researcher would wish to employ visual methods would be for the study of the visual culture of schooling. The so-called 'visual but hidden curriculum' is important because it reflects implicit and elusive powerful forces that shape everyday activities in education (Prosser 2007). It can be argued that the visual can provide an intersection between what ethnographers would refer to as the 'non-material dimension of culture' (values, norms, rituals, roles, power etc.) and the material dimension (furniture, signs, clothing, photographs, tools etc.). In this sense, a material object such as a school uniform is imbibed with meaning and values, which we can explore in relation to a larger cultural network of schooling.

Arguably, the 'visual culture of schools' is as important as word- and number-based constructions of school culture in three critical ways. First, a visual-centric method gives primacy to what is visually perceived in schools rather than what is said, written, tabulated or statistically measured. The second element (i.e., 'culture') draws attention to taken-for-grantedness and the unquestioned and unwritten codes of habitual practice. The third element (i.e. 'schooling') is process-orientated and provides the context in which visual culture is situated and enacted. When combined, the three elements provide us with a working definition of the visual culture of schools which is:

> the ready-made standardised visual scheme handed down by previous generations of teachers and authorities as an unquestioned and unquestionable guide to all observable events, rituals, situations, objects, materials, spaces and behaviours which normally occur within everyday schooling. It is the trace and markings of the past, present and probably the future hidden curriculum.
>
> (Adapted from Schutz 1964)

It is important to recognize that the visual culture of a school is a combination of generic and unique elements. Generic visual culture describes observable, inscribed and encrypted similarities of schools in terms of visual norms, values and practices, which constitute taken-for-granted visual schooling. In other words, there are common features of schooling (pupils, teachers, curriculum, assessment, timetables, etc.) that we can recognize more or less regardless of the kind of institution (infant school, special school, boarding school etc.) we are in. However, because schools comprise individuals who can have the capacity to (re)interpret generic visual culture, school people create their own unique visual culture. To paraphrase Marx, people make their own schools, but not just as they please.

By way of an example of how to apply visual methods in a study around two dimensions of the visual culture of schools, in this section we will focus on non-teaching space and visual methods and, in the following section, consider the messy process of interpreting images by looking at the *teaching and learning space*. It is important to add that what we offer does not exhaust the constitutive possibilities of the visual culture of schooling, but is merely illustrative of the kind of contribution visual methods can make to our understanding of these phenomena.

Table 13.2 Using visual methods to explore the visual culture of schools

Focus	Method	Category	Rationale/example
Non-teaching space	Cultural inventory	Researcher created	The placement of objects in space is not arbitrary and communicates information about the use of a space and its significance to learners and teachers. Analysis of the organization and layout of objects emerges through understanding of cultural inventories. Applicable to a headteacher's office, school corridors and school entrances.
Non-teaching space	Close reading	Researcher created	Close or in-depth reading is critical looking. This entails researcher sociosemiotic interpretation of what is visible. We can ask analytic questions of playgrounds, for example: why are they a particular shape, what do the surface markings mean to pupils, who controls different territories and how is geopolitical space managed?
Non-teaching space	Graphical elicitation	Respondent generated	This is a pencil and paper exercise where, for example, pupils draw a map of a playground and mark how and what space they use. This means they set the agenda and work at their own speed rather than the researcher's.
Non-teaching space	Walk and talk	Respondent generated	Sometimes called a 'walkabout' this is a participatory technique that entails the researcher being guided around a space or territory by a student. Treats students as experts and agents in their own lives. Often sound- or video-recorded.
Teaching space	Draw and talk	Researcher created	A 'talk and draw' approach is useful for exploring pupil's perspectives (Clark and Moss 2001) and is useful not only for identifying pupils' own agenda and priorities but also their perspectives on power, control, and the visible hidden curriculum.
Teaching space	Video record	Researcher created	Video has long been used to record classroom interaction. Recent improvements in technology and software led to an upsurge of interest in video feedback. Videos facilitate transcription, coding and qualitative analysis.
Teaching space	Concept mapping	Respondent generated	Concept mapping or mind mapping is used to trace the way children build concepts and relationships. It is most commonly used for tracking the development of children's learning, as a diagnostic tool for evaluating progress (Buzan and Buzan, 1993). Concept mapping is also useful as an interview device with children because it allows them to set the agenda, to decide what is important.

Table 13.2 sets out a summary of these methods, how they might be used and for what particular purpose. As can be seen, there is a range of different methods which can be incorporated into a single design. From this we can literally and metaphorically construct a complex and rich picture of the visual culture of a school. In applying some of these methods to the study of pupils' non-learning space, we can begin to get a sense of how they may be usefully employed.

Playground space has an ambiguous status for pupils. On one level it is a place they are most likely to feel confident and empowered in. However, it is also one of the spaces where bullying takes place. Hence space and how it is used have meaning for children and, for researchers, space is a key sensitizing concept and not merely a three-dimensional backdrop to social action. It is the context for complex and often competing interactions (see Donoghue 2007 for more on this). The study of playgrounds can employ a combination of visual methods and theoretical orientations to elicit and interpret data. Methods include researcher-generated images; found images such as old school photographs and architectural drawings, video as a record of complex interaction and/or used for photo elicitation, participant-generated images such as children's drawings and photographs, researcher-generated maps and photographs and of course researchers' observations.

One theoretical approach is to document what children actually *do* (e.g. video, photographs, sketches) and use techniques of member checking and photo elicitation to check researchers' interpretations with children's meanings. An alternative approach is to invite the pupils themselves to take photographs (Schratz and Steiner-Loffler 1998), make paintings (Anning and Ring 2004; Gharahbeiglu 2007) or draw maps with coloured pencils (see Figure 13.1). These participant-constructed images tap into children's abilities and enthusiasms (Clark and Moss 2001).

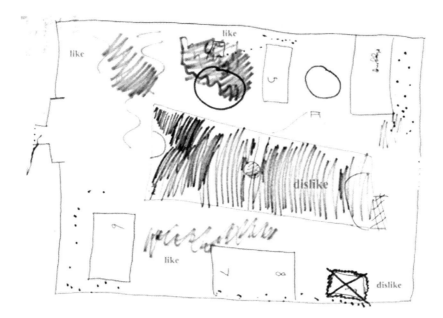

Figure 13.1 Mapping playground space – pupil likes and dislikes

The man in Figure 13.2 is Jon Prosser (acting as a researcher's assistant) standing in 'no-man's land' in an empty playground. The picture-taker is Steven, a 9 year-old boy, and I am being instructed by him to move to an exact location which marks the outer limits of his Year 5 soccer pitch and the start of the Year 6 soccer pitch. This is important to him since if his ball incurs too often on the Year 6 pitch it will be 'booted' over the wall. Steven was revealing the visible but

Figure 13.2 Limit of Year 5 soccer pitch and the start of the Year 6 soccer pitch

hidden territory of his playground. This 'walk and talk' method shifts data collection from research 'on' to research 'with' and 'by' children (see Chapter 9 on doing research *with* children). Such participatory methods are becoming central to contemporary visual research.

If playgrounds are not to be viewed as 'neutral backdrops', then an understanding of evolving meanings of them as contested space requires a combined visual and historical perspective to be embraced (Depaepe and Henkens 2000). Playground spaces are transient. Their significance for children's play is dependent on a combination of interactive factors, which change over time. The capacity to access differing sets of historical documents and readings of playground surfaces contribute to understanding why children choose to play the way they do in particular settings. The capacity to study, for example, original architectural plans, subsequent records kept by a school and markings on a playground surface are all insightful (Prosser and Loxley, 2002).

Figure 13.3 is a Victorian school built in 1872, typical of the national school design of this period. Armitage (2005: 541) described the impact of this design on playground shape as producing a number of 'nooks and crannies' that provide 'in effect small "rooms"', and this is exactly how children use them'. Visual researchers can use techniques such as 're-photography' to explore social change and the evolution of the buildings or a site.

Figure 13.4 is a girl's map of the playground marking the 'likes' (where she felt safe) and 'dislikes' (the boys' soccer pitch). By oscillating between researcher-found historical data, close readings of the playground surface, students' drawings of 'liked' and 'disliked' play space and a student questionnaire, an 'equality' issue emerged. The majority of girls in the school (94 per cent) were 'upset' or 'very upset' at being left with second-rate play space. It is widely recognized and accepted but unquestioned in school tradition that girls work around playground space dominated by boys' soccer pitches. As a result of the evolutionary 'improvement' in school buildings the girls had lost their 'nooks and crannies' space to straight lines and irregular paving stones and the boys had gained yet another soccer pitch. Three years after the study was undertaken the school moved to a new location and building and the gender

Figure 13.3 Victorian school

Figure 13.4 Mapping playground space – pupil likes and dislikes

inequity, in terms of amount and quality of play space, was redressed. Mixed-method approaches can be powerful initiators of educational change.

How Can Visual Data be Interpreted?

In this section, we will use the example of teaching and learning space as a way to engage in the analysis of images. It should be noted that a critical factor when planning to apply the visual is to consider what use the data will be put to. At one level, this refers to the analytical strategies adopted and on another to the representational function of the data at the reporting stage. Analysis should therefore not be seen as an afterthought when all the data have been gathered/ constructed, but iteratively tied into that very process (see Chapter 18 on the interplay between analysis and data collection). In short, a visual researcher needs to embed the analytical strategy he or she may use into the design. How the analysis is undertaken will partly be decided by the disciplinary framework we are working within, as that will shape the interpretative parameters of the study as a whole, as well as specific segments of data. However, there are a number of related techniques which can be applied, that while not entirely 'discipline free', can be deemed as useful to help organize the data collection and analysis.

The first example is the use of a cultural inventory, with an emphasis on the *systematic* mapping of content via a visual survey of primary school classrooms. The photographs of eight classrooms in the case study school from our study were taken using an agreed protocol as to how the images would be produced (e.g. angle at which they were taken, lens width setting, number of frames taken and so on) and what we would focus on: in this instance the walls, furniture and interior space of the classrooms. At this stage, there was no preconception as to the *detail* of what we wanted to document; only that we would visually map as completely as possible the classrooms to allow us to undertake a more fine-grained analysis. On completing this process the next step was to begin to analyse the images. Our initial question pivoted around 'What are the similarities and differences between the classrooms?' This in turn led us to construct two further, but much more focused questions:

1   What is the specific content of the classrooms?
2   How might we organize and classify our content given the remit of the study?

The images were initially 'handled' by Bryman's (2001) *ethnographic content analysis*. This technique is traditionally seen as a process for working with documents or images which allows researchers to enumerate the occurrence of 'things' (e.g. single words, phrases, names, images and so on) via the use of pre-specified categories. In other words, we can simply use the categories as a sorting device and count the number of times something 'falls into' that category. An ethnographic mode of content analysis, while still being concerned with enumeration, has a more reflexive twist to it as it is less concerned with procedural exactitude and focuses upon the way in which researchers interact with the material to not only construct the categories but also determine how different segments of data are selected for allocation.

Our attitude towards content analysis mirrored the mode of analysis that would not seem out of place in a grounded theory study (see Strauss and Corbin 1994), or any other form of study that would be recognized as coming from the qualitative research tradition (Dey 1994). The categories that were developed to help explore the data were a result of two forms of interaction: a joint initial viewing of some of the images by the researchers to assess their properties and drawing on our own theoretical and disciplinary frameworks to try and understand these properties. Table 13.3 was developed out of an emergent reading of the images, to enable us to be both systematic in terms of the enumeration of phenomena and yet sensitive to the nuances within each category.

However, one of the problems associated with a simplistic application of content analysis is that if the categories are too fine-grained to enable you to 'capture' the range of difference within an image, then it becomes very difficult to establish any patterns based on regularities or irregularities. Conversely, if the categories are too broad, any subtle play of difference is lost in the effort to work at what seems to be a more manageable level of generality. In an attempt to get around this problem and allow for a degree of interpretative latitude and the assignment of a

Table 13.3 Content analysis grid

Classroom: Teacher 6 – Year 6	
Image number: 10	
General description of image:	

Category	Count/comment

Directional signs and text
    Regulatory (must be obeyed)
    Information (for guidance)	

Interactive materials (tactile: picked up, touched, manipulated etc.)	
Political aesthetics and impression management	

Locational and spatial positioning
    2-D materials
    Artefacts	

Furniture
    Type
    Function
    Position	

Colouration (number of colours, types of colour) and medium used (ink, paint chalk)	

Origin of material
    Child originated
    Teacher originated
    Commercial origination	

Types of images
    Photographs
    Drawings
    Moving images	

Use of text (font size, font type, colour etc.)	
Mix of text and the visual	
Curricula materials (which area)	
Size of images	
Juxtaposition of images and text	
Permanent and transient displays	

segment of data to what we considered to be an appropriate category, we devised the grid shown in Table 13.3.

Figure 13.5 A primary school classroom (image 10)

The grid in Table 13.3 refers to the content in Figure 13.5 and begins to help us construct a systematic and thematic understanding of the properties of visual data. This grid is intended to be used with single images and/or a portfolio of images, though depending upon the richness of them it has the potential to become unmanageable, as well as difficult to interpret. As can be seen the number of categories and, where needed, subcategories, is quite large. But, as we argued above, this is both a function of what emerged from our initial viewing of the images – which can be seen as rich and varied – and our understanding about primary teaching and learning. Two other common approaches to interpreting visual data are visual semiotics and narrative analysis, which we discuss below.

Visual semiotics

The application of visual semiotics provides researchers with a powerful set of analytical tools with which to excavate or generate meaning out of complex systems of symbols or, to be more specific, signs. It needs to be added that visual semiotics is but one member of an extended family of approaches which share a common genealogy (explicitly or not) in the work of Sassure (1974), Peirce ([1940] 1965), Barthes (1957), Eco (1977), Goffman (1979) and Hodge and Kress (1988) to name but a few. As Rose (2001) notes, the use of visual semiotics has been particularly important for writers who take a critical stance towards social structures and issues. Culler (1976) argues that

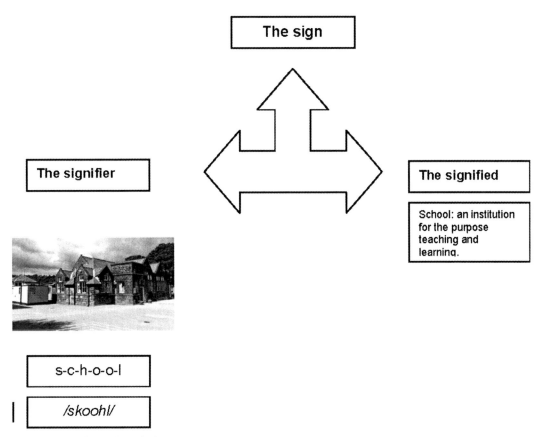

Figure 13.6 Signifier and signified

language is a system of signs which, as Hall (1997: 31) observes, can include 'sounds, images, written words, paintings, photographs [and] material objects'. Originating in the work of Ferdinand Saussure (1857–1913), who also gave us the term 'semiology', the sign is the basic unit of meaning, but contains within it two related elements known as: the signifier (word, image, sound) and the signified (the idea or concept associated with the above). These are combined to form the 'sign'. In the following example, when we see a picture of a school or see the word 'school' (the *signifier*) it should connect with the concept we carry around in our heads of a school (the *signified*) (see Figure 13.6). But as Hall (1997) argues, it is our cultural codes that give signs, as modes of representation, their relative stability.

Although we understand signs as being socially constituted and agreed upon (for the most part), the critical part of Saussure's scheme is that the relationship between the signifier and the signified is an arbitrary one. This is a powerful idea as it implies that there is no necessary connection between the label 'school' and the idea of a school. We could easy substitute the label *ecole* or *schule* or *szkolny* or *sukuru* and attach it to the generalized concept of 'school'. Thus, the supposed naturalness between a signifier and signified can be open to question. What also adds to the analytical prowess of the sign is the notion of difference. As such, what also gives a sign its meaning is not just the internal relationship between the signifier and signified, but its difference relative to other signs. Hence the meaning of 'school' is contingent upon what it is not (e.g. a shop, a shed, a monkey, a Dublin bus and so on).

In developing Saussure's basic framework beyond the purely linguistic and into the visual, the

American philosopher Charles Peirce (1839–1914) provided us with another set of tools by which we can begin to explore meaning derived from mainly non-textual signs. These, he divides up into (1) the iconographic, (2) the indexical and (3) the symbolic. The first thing to note is that they are not mutually exclusive and can, as we will briefly demonstrate, 'reside' in a single sign. But before that, it is useful to provide some definitional clarity of what these three functions refer to using Figure 13.7, usually found near or on public toilets, as an example.

Figure 13.7 Common image

Iconographical – the image, while not intending to be a realist depiction of an object/subject that for the sake of argument has corporeal existence, nonetheless functions as a mimetic approximation of the object/subject. In other words, it looks like what it is 'meant' to be but with large amounts of detail removed; or in most cases not even applied. The image relies on culturally dominant characteristics of what constitutes generalized (and socially shared) concepts of 'maleness' (trousers), 'femaleness' (dresses) and disabledness (a wheelchair) to convey and articulate its meaning. Also the inclusion of text ('toilets') reduces the polysemicity (many different interpretations) of the image and provides what Barthes calls a 'relay-function', simply a meaningful relationship between image and text.

Indexical – with this kind of sign, there is meant to be a relationship between what is depicted and its 'real-life' correlate, which in this case are usually public toilets. Non-textual road signs are good examples of combining the iconic with the indexical as they are intended to 'point' to something that is real.

Symbolic – the relationship between the symbol(s) and what it is intended to signify is arbitrary; this is different to the icon and the index, which are supposedly mimetic. There is no reason why these three images placed in relation to each other as a single sign should be associated with toilets or maleness, femaleness and disabledness; any image could function in the same way. At the symbolic level, they can operate in different modes (metaphorical, poetic, political, ideological) contingent upon the context in which they are positioned. They go beyond mere depiction and into a higher order of abstraction, whose meaning is not directly related to the image.

Like the indexical and the iconographic, the symbols are only meaningful via the cultural frameworks we bring to them. The meaning is not intrinsically embedded in the images but 'extracted' by us. We need to be able to piece together the various elements in order to make sense of the whole (the wheelchair, the 'people', the drawing style etc.).

The French critic and philosopher Roland Barthes (1915–80) extended both the work of Saussure and Peirce in a set of essays entitled *Mythologies* (1957) and *Camera Lucida* (1984) in a way which

Figure 13.8 Trinity College Dublin

has greatly added to our analytical sophistication. His focus was essentially on what is commonly referred to as popular culture (wrestling, red wine, soap powder etc.) and explored how 'representation is working at a broader cultural level' (Hall 1997) which Barthes refers to as 'myth'. But before unpacking that concept we need to define two underlying concepts of *denotation* and *connotation* used by Barthes to make sense of signs. Denotation refers to the literal description of an image. Figure 13.8 is a photograph of the front square of Trinity College Dublin (where Andrew Loxley works). What it denotes is a series of Georgian style buildings placed around a cobbled square. To the left and right of the building in the front are two large trees, three marquees (set up for the annual student ball) and a small number of people. Connotation is intended to function at a higher level and connects with more abstract and diffused ideas around ideology, values and culture. As Rose (2001) points out, connotation can operate in two (closely related) ways. Firstly *metonymic*, in which the sign, in this case Trinity College, is associated with something else, which is the idea of the university as a place of learning or research. Alternatively, it could be seen as metonym for elitism, social exclusion and a key institution of past British colonial rule. The second, *synecdochal*, is where the sign represents part of something or the whole represents a part. In the case of Trinity College it could be used to stand for Dublin city as a whole. Or the front square could stand for the whole university. In either case, the sign *in toto* or elements within (the marquees are put up at the time of the college ball and can be read as signs within a sign) provide for a much complex and multilayered reading. Though denotation is not that straightforward, as our so-called literal reading of an image, it draws on a host of cultural concepts, for example, on an understanding of architecture no matter how basic.

In specifically discussing photographs in *Camera Lucida*, Barthes argues that we can further make sense of them in two main ways. Firstly, by the use of what he classes as the *studium*, which is the orthodox culturally mediated interpretation of the image. The *punctum* in contrast works against this normative reading: it is a 'sting, speck, cut, little hole [...] [an] accident which pricks me' (Barthes 1984: 27). There is for Barthes a unique and idiosyncratic response to an image, or, more specifically, to a detail within it, which goes beyond the mundane, which we find jarring or unsettling or illuminative. In turn this alters and challenges our taken-for-granted understanding of the image as a whole. The last concept which Barthes (1972) developed was that of the *myth* which to a certain degree is a more elaborate form of connotation. This provides us with a different level of analytical sophistication, which is concerned with treating the image (signifier + signified = sign) as a signifier, which in turn has its own associated signified and forms its own sign. As a simplified example of myth at work, the picture of Trinity College contains a number of signifiers (elements) and signified (buildings, marquees, lawns, trees, a clock, a flag pole). This cluster of signs generates a literal meaning (denotation): a set of marquees in the grounds of a grand Georgian building being set up for a party. But as Barthes argues, this sign itself needs to be made intelligible – i.e. what does this mean within a larger cultural and ideological framework? This is where we enter into a second level of signification. We could, for example, read it as meaning that the students in this veritable old place of learning celebrate the end of each academic year with a ritual gathering involving music, dancing and drinking which reinforces the notion of belonging to an academic community. It is a sign about student life in a traditional university, a place where predominately young people from privileged backgrounds prepare for entry into adult life. In getting to this next level of meaning, Barthes argues that the first sign (the marquees set up for the ball) becomes the signifier for the signified we have just outlined (end of year 'jolly japes'), from which a new sign (or more accurately myth) is generated. For Barthes, this second-order semiological system (as he calls it) pre-exists that of our first sign. And it is our use of myth as a metalanguage that enables us to position the first sign in a wider cultural and ideological domain (see Table 13.4).

An interesting example of using semiotics to explore school cultures is Gewirtz *et al.*'s (1995) study of the marketization of secondary schooling in England and Wales. The study (among a range of issues related to markets and education), looked at the different strategies schools adopted to gain a positional advantage over other institutions. In other words, it explored the question 'What did the schools do to attract parents to consider sending their children there?'. As well as the more obvious factors such as the perceived or actual standards of education as indicated by examination results, Gewirtz *et al.* identified a whole ensemble of signs which they

Table 13.4

1 Signifer (things in the picture)	2 Signified (marquees, buildings etc.)		
3 Sign (ritual of end-of-year student celebration)		II SIGNIFIED (Student life as preparation for adulthood)	
I SIGNIFIER			
III SIGN (Unification of I & II)			

argued were an attempt to express 'messages about ethos, culture, values and priorities'. What is useful about their study is that they draw into their analysis both the material ('things' that are visible and/or have a physical existence) and the non-material (values, relationships etc.). Although they argue that historically schools have been concerned with the presentation of themselves both internally (to staff, students, parents) and externally (potential students, the local community etc.), the introduction of educational markets in the early 1990s and the imperative to 'attract' students made schools more conscious of this particular dimension of life in the 'marketplace'. To this end, they explored in their work the following dimensions:

- school practices and policies
- the language and format of school documentation and activities
- the age fabric and design of the school grounds and buildings, facilities and furnishings
- styles of management and headship
- school designations (church, county, single-sex, comprehensive, grammar)
- socioeconomic characteristics of catchments areas
- the size and nature of student composition (1995: 122)

The above list is extensive and is a mix of the material and non-material cultural forms. Although Gewirtz *et al.* do not specifically refer to Roland Barthes they nonetheless intimate that taken together and used in varying combinations the above list of 'things' attempts to construct a 'mythology of schooling'. However, in particular, they draw attention to the care taken by the schools in their study to produce prospectuses and host promotional events (open days and evenings) as significant carriers of meaning about what kind of 'image' they wished to present to the outside world. Prospectuses ceased to be amateur photocopied sheets and became glossy, professionally printed and designed booklets. They noted the careful use and positioning of logos, school images and typefaces to try and convey a specific kind of institution. They argue that this was not done out of any aesthetic concerns per se, but was what the schools saw as a necessary technique to attract students.

Narrative analysis

Whereas visual semiotics provides a very systematic model to analyse images, under the rubric of 'external' or 'internal' narratives there is a much looser strategy, partially related to the cultural inventory. Approaching visual research from the perspective of an anthropologist, Marcus Banks (2001) provides us with a simple but highly effective pair of tools with which to explore images and (potentially) artefacts. An internal narrative refers not only to the content or in Banks' terms, properties, of the image, but the relationship between the individual(s) and the phenomena within the image. This goes beyond merely producing a content analysis based on prespecified categories, and represents an attempt to tell the 'story' of the content in terms of *connotation* (the symbolic and metaphorical meaning of the image) and *denotation* (literally what is in it). However, our reading and/or construction of these narratives is multifaceted, which in turn is further exacerbated by the polysemic (capable of having many meanings) nature of the images. Each viewer will bring with them their own culturally mediated interpretation (e.g. age, gender, ethnicity, educational attainment etc.) which not only affects the way in which content is selected, but also the meaning ascribed to it. As a caveat against overly individualizing these 'viewings', we need to also be aware of the degree to which certain features of the image and interpretations contain shared meanings, that is 'things' which are ostensibly recognized by most people who view them (participants *and* researchers). But, equally, there are meanings that are not shared, and which only become partially accessible through some form of dialogue. An obvious example is the way our different disciplinary positions (as well as other social positions – gender, ethnicity, age etc.) influence how we interact with and hence create a narrative. In other words, we can envisage a sociological narrative, an anthropological narrative, a psychological narrative and so on that would tell slightly different stories of, for example, Figure 13.8.

An external narrative as defined by Banks refers to the world beyond the photograph or image. As we argued above, it is important to remember that an image is not only a portrayal of something, but an artefact in its own right. In other words, a photograph can be treated as a three-dimensional object which happens to be a two-dimensional representation of 'someone' or 'something'. The external narrative is a mixture of conjoined analytical layers:

1 *The context production:* this refers to the time, place and circumstances (posed, 'naturally occurring', spontaneous, structured etc.) of the image coming into being, including the technology used (still, video, digital, chemical, lenses, artificial and natural lighting etc.), and, importantly, the intention, as well as perhaps the meanings ascribed to the 'someone' or 'something' which is 'captured' in the photograph. Take for example the difference between a family photograph taken by a family member and a family portrait taken by a professional photographer. The former is rich with different emotional resonances; the relationships between the individuals are complex and dynamic, full of pre-and post-history (treating the image as a single and significant point in time and space). The latter is a financial transaction, but one which is nonetheless mediated around cultural assumptions concerning the composition of family portraits (e.g. parents at the front, seated, children at the back, standing, and so forth).

2 *The social relations of the context in which the image is viewed at any given time:* the circumstances under which the image is viewed or discussed, and with whom it is being discussed, will add another layer to the meaning of the image. For instance, the use of family photographs as a tool to guide students through the process of photo-elicitation will generate a different kind of discourse to viewing them with a group of friends at a social gathering. Again, when placed in an academic context, it is quite easy to see that different disciplines (and specialized subsections), at different historical, institutional and theoretical junctures, will interpret an image or portfolio of images differently.

3 *The image as a historical artefact:* if the photograph or image is treated as an artefact, it can be located within its own historical context and hence we can trace some sort of historical trajectory that it has undergone. Although this is probably more appropriate in the context of researcher-found images, it can also be applied to images that are researcher-generated in certain instances. For example, the different intergenerational ownership of family photographs can tell us about the patterns of ownership and how they came to be possessed.

How Might Visual Methods be Used in Research Design?

The above sections were intended to provide a reference point as to how visual researchers use visual data and make sense of visual methods. This section will briefly consider some of the broader issues to be addressed around the research design aspect of visual studies. Generally, the issues are not too divergent from other research approaches, but it is useful to be sensitive to our central argument about the use of the visual – that it should be enveloped within a coherent and well-defined research design. As with any other research approach or method, it should not be used in an ad hoc or random manner, but considered in relation to the purpose of the research as a whole. This is of course contingent upon what questions are being posed as well as the underlying disciplinary frameworks (history, sociology, cultural studies etc.). Although there is no isomorphic relationship between any given set of questions and research designs, some are more appropriate than others. Hence, you need to have a very good reason why you want to incorporate a visual dimension and know how it may help you 'answer' the questions posed. The dynamic forces that combine to influence topic-method relationships are ambiguous. The idea of research design makes explicit the need for a plan for conducting a study, and provides a framework for establishing the trustworthiness of data and the inferences drawn from them. In short, a research design offers a 'blueprint' for the conduct of research, incorporating the overall approach and rationale. Any design normally encompasses decisions about site and sample collection; the researcher's role; data collection methods; data management; analysis strategy; trustworthiness features; and the time management plan.

We would suggest that when planning to use the visual it should be done within a mixed-methods design (qualitative and quantitative research designs). This has the added advantage of providing for data and methods triangulation with the added dimension of a visual modality. Within this, we would also encourage researchers to use a mix of visual methods as well. This can help provide a more fine-grained visual sensitivity to the phenomena being explored.

One of the critical decisions to be made at the early stages of the design is what kind of role the researcher will play. Deciding on an appropriate role is only the beginning of 'getting in and staying in' the field. All qualitative researchers tackle the process of establishing rapport with respondents by considering the role they will play and establishing a trusting relationship. This is particularly important when incorporating a visual dimension. There are fairly obvious ethical and methodological issues at stake which can be related back to whether the data will be researcher-generated, participant-created or researcher-found – or a mix of the three. The incorporation of participant-created data in a design involves developing a different kind of relationship with the participants, as they take on a certain role of co-researchers (see Wang *et al.* 2000 for a detailed discussion of this). This will involve some kind of technical (e.g. how to use the cameras etc.) and methodological (e.g. ethics, sampling etc.) training in order to optimize data generation. Simply giving people cameras and a rough idea of what to photograph is somewhat remiss (Prosser and Loxley 2008).

The issue of sampling also needs to be considered both at the design stage and during the process of data construction. Again, most visual researchers will take an emergent attitude towards this activity, but there is an added layer of complexity, which is as much technical as it is methodological and relates back to the context of production. This probably has closer parallels to the traditional business of producing observational data. As we argued above, how an image is made is critical to how it is interpreted by both researcher and other viewers/readers and this involves an awareness of two main factors:

1   The *technical* at the point of constructing the image (moving or still), for example, shutter speeds, f-stops, ISO, lenses and angles, digital or chemical, megapixles, alignment of planets and so on.
2   The *compositional* – for example, what is 'in' and 'outside' the frame relationship with those people or objects in the image relationship with the research questions and design parameters (e.g. sampling, ethics) relationship with theoretical and conceptual frameworks.

Thus, the 'taking' of an image needs to be subjected to the same degree of reflection as any other method of data-gathering. Perhaps even more so given the ethical approbation that taking an image can generate if not handled sensitively by the researcher.

What are the Ethical Issues for Visual Researchers?

Partially due the relative newness of visually-orientated research, there is a limited agreement among ethics committees and visual researchers on the ethical guidelines and the subsequent practices (see Chapter 7 on research ethics). It is clear that funding bodies, universities, academic departments, regional and local authorities and researchers are only now beginning to consider establishing comprehensive and viable visual ethics policies. This is no easy task since image-based research comprises a range of visual media applied in a multitude of ways and does not form a homogeneous set of technologies, techniques or practices. We would argue that the visual ethics vacuum should be filled, as a matter of urgency, with situated exemplars of good practice.

Becoming knowledgeable in visual ethics is no easy matter since what constitutes good practice in different contexts and different sociopolitical environments is not clear. There are few significant ethical benchmarks or support mechanisms for visual researchers. Not all institutions and departments have ethical committees and those that do may be overly restrictive and focused on protecting the organization rather than respondents, and may only work within the prevailing methodological and epistemological orthodoxies. Codes of practice and guidelines applied by UK universities act as gatekeepers and offer a general ethical framework but are of limited use to visual researchers and may in practice work against them. There are two related reasons for this. The first is that university ethics committees vary in nature, their discretionary scope, their monitoring capacity, enthusiasm and their application of sanctions in cases of transgression. The second reason is that committees consist of members from epistemologically dissimilar academic disciplines who would scrutinize proposals differently and may look on minority (visual) methods judgementally. However, viewed positively, it could be said that institutional ethics committees will be knowledgeable on number- and word-based research.

However, more practically, when planning to use the visual, good starting points would be to consult the codes of practice published by professional associations – for example, the British Sociological Association provides a valuable resource acting as a foundation for ethical practice. The ESRC Ethical Framework document is another valuable source of guidance. The ESRC also offers an important insight into specific elements within ethics, for example, informed consentand general ethics training through the Researcher Development Initiative. Another avenue worth exploring is special interest groups with an interest in things visual: the British Sociological Association's Visual Sociology Study Group and the International Visual Sociology Association'sdiscussion group whose members regularly discuss visual ethics.

Box 13.1: Exercises

The following are simple tasks that you might want to try out with a partner.

Drawing a cultural inventory

For this task, you and your partner will need to construct separately, as a hand drawing, a cultural inventory of your non-professional identity. In other words, how you would represent yourself to others as an assemblage of artefacts, signs, symbols etc. This is as not as easy as it might seem as you need to think about where you would position these 'objects' in relation to each other, as well as yourself and other people in the drawing. Spend about 10 to 15 minutes on your drawing.

When you have both finished your separate drawings, one of you should act as the researcher (e.g. the interviewer) and your partner as the researched (e.g. the interviewee).

Photo-elicitation

You will again need a partner and two *found* photographs (i.e. not taken for the purposes of this exercise) each. The photographs can be of anything, but it is important that they have some kind of meaning for you (e.g. family photographs, you as a child, your favourite pet dog and so on). Take turns with your partner to explore:

1 *The internal narrative* – what is the 'story' in the picture (e.g. who is in it, what is their relationship, what is the location and so on).
2 *The external narrative* – when was the photograph taken, why was it taken, who took it, what is their relationship to the people or object in the photograph and so on.

Hopefully you will find that the relationship between the image(s), the viewing of the image(s) and the context of image production is a messy and interrelated process.

Photographing people

This is a very difficult task. You are both connected with the (fictitious for this exercise) 'Living Resemblances' research project and you've been asked to take photographs on the theme of 'likenesses between friends'. You can interpret 'likeness' in any way you wish (e.g. clothes, facial expressions, body language or hair). You can take a maximum of 20 photographs. As you photograph think about the sorts of issues which arise – for example, ethics or your particular interpretation of 'likeness'. Visual ethics is problematic – you will need to think about what you are going to tell the people you are photographing (e.g. 'we will destroy the images at the end of the day').

Summary

In this chapter we have merely scratched the surface of some of the concepts, techniques and issues involved in visual research. We would argue that the use of the visual in research can provide rich and multilayered insights into educational lifeworlds. However, it is not an easy route to take for either experienced or new researchers. This is further compounded by its alleged 'newness' as an approach, as well as the labyrinthine ethical issues that can be seen as a real impediment to applying visual methods.

In summarizing the main points covered in this chapter we would advise both new and established researchers to be mindful of the following areas when embarking on the visual path:

- *Be ethically sensitive:* be alert to your responsibilities as a researcher when engaging in research-created or participant-generated image work.
- *Know your technology:* similar to understanding the workings of your audio recording equipment, it is vital to have a sense of what your camera (moving or still) and image processing software can and cannot do. This is critical in terms of setting the parameters for the interpretation of the data generated.
- *Work within a mixed methods design:* this will add a richness and depth to your study as well as bolster trustworthiness and credibility. Also, try not to rely on one visual method, mix these up as well.
- *Make sure the research questions and visual methods are linked:* a poor fit between questions and methods (and ultimately data) will create problems when trying to draw adequate and meaningful conclusions or inferences.
- *Be sensitive to the context of production and analysis:* the relationship between how an image is made and how it is interpreted is an intimate one and can lead to all sorts of problems usually concerning inappropriate analysis if this is not treated as a first principle in visual work.
- *Think about the representation of images in research reports:* pay careful attention to what you will do and what can be done with images when presenting you research. The medium (print or screen) can affect how the image is 'read'. More specifically, what will the role of the image be? It may be useful to think of images as taking the form of visual 'quotes' in the same way we present a segment of an interview to indicate some conceptual point. There is also the relationship between text *and* images and their function to be considered. That is, how much 'anchor' work or explanatory work does the text engage in? How will what you write affect how people view the images you present? Do you wish to circumvent their own interpretation of the image by imposing meaning in it via the text or allow them to provide their own interpretation?

The above are by no means a complete list of 'caveats' but should, if applied carefully, guide you through the convoluted and unkempt maze that is visual research.

References

Anning, A. and Ring, K. (2004) *Making Sense of Children's Drawings*. Buckingham: Open University Press.

Armitage, M. (2005) 'The influence of school architecture and design on the outdoor play experience within the primary school', *Paedagogica Historica*, 41(4–5): 535–53.

Banks, M. (1998) Visual anthropology: image, object and interpretation, in J Prosser (ed.) *Image-based Research: A Sourcebook for Qualitative Researchers*. London: Falmer Press.

Banks, M. (2001) *Visual Methods in Social Research*. London: Sage.

Barthes, R. (1957) *Mythologies*. London: Cape.

Barthes, R. (1972) *Mythologies*. London: Cape.

Barthes, R. (1984) *Camera Lucida: Reflections on photography*. London: Fontana.

Bryman, A. (2001) *Social Research Methods*. Oxford: Oxford University Press.

Buzan, T. and Buzan, B. (1993) *The Mind Map Book*. London: BBC Books.

Clark, A. and Moss, P. (2001) *Listening to Young Children: The Mosaic Approach*. London: The National Children's Bureau and Joseph Rowntree Foundation.

Culler, J. (1976) 'Literary history, allegory, and semiology', *New Literary History*, 7(2): *Poetics: Some Methodological Problems*.

Depaepe, M. and Henkens, B. (2000) The challenge of the visual in the history of education, *Pedagogogica Historica, International Journal of the History of Education*.

Dey, I. (1994) Qualitative Data Analysis: A User-friendly Guide for Social Scientists. London: Routledge.

Donoghue, D. (2007) James always hangs out here: making space for place in studying masculinities at school, *Visual Studies*, 22(1): 62–73.

Eco, U. (1976) *A Theory of Semiotics*. Bloomington, IN: Indiana University Press.

Edwards, E. (2001) *Raw Histories: Photographs, Anthropology and Museums*. Oxford: Berg.

Gewirtz, S., Ball, S. and Bowe, R. (1995) *Markets, Choice and Equity in Education*. Maidenhead: Open University Press.

Gharahbeiglu, M. (2007) 'Children's interaction with urban play spaces',
Visual Studies, 22(1): 48–52.

Goffman, E. (1979) *Gender Advertisements*. London: Macmillan.

Hall, S. (ed.) (1997) *Representation: Cultural Representations and Signifying Practices*. London: Sage.

Harper, D. (1987) *Working Knowledge: Skill and Community in a Small Shop*. Chicago: University of Chicago Press.

Harper, D. (1998) 'An argument for visual sociology', in J. Prosser (ed.) *Image-Based Research: A Sourcebook for Qualitative Researchers*. Falmer Press.

Hodge, R. and Kress, G. (1988) *Social Semiotics*. London: Polity Press.

Leeuwen, T. and Jewitt, C. (eds) (2001) *Handbook of Visual Analysis*. London: Sage.

Mcluhan, M. (1967) *The Medium is the Message*. London: Penguin.

Peirce, C. S. ([1940] 1965) *Collected Papers*. Cambridge, MA: Belknap Press.

Prosser, J. (2006) 'The darker side of visual research', in D. Hamilton (ed.) *Visual Research Methods*. London: Sage.

Prosser, J. (2007) 'Visual methods and the visual culture of schools', *Visual Studies*, 22(1): 13–30.

Prosser, J. and Loxley, A. (2008) 'Enhancing the contribution of visual methods to inclusive education', *Journal of Research in Special Educational Needs*, 7(1): 55–68.

Prosser J. and Schwartz, D. (1998) 'Photographs within the sociological process' in J. Prosser (ed.) *Image- Based Research: A Sourcebook for Qualitative Researchers*. London: Falmer Press.

Rose, G. (2001) *Visual Methodologies: An Introduction to the Interpretation of Visual Materials*. London: Sage.

Sassure, F. (1974) *Course in General Linguistics*. London: Fontana.

Schratz, M. and Steiner-Loffler, U. (1998) 'Pupils using photographs in school self-evaluation', in J. Prosser (ed.) *Image Based Research: A Sourcebook for Qualitative Researchers*. London: Falmer Press .

Schutz, A. (1964) *Collected Papers*. The Hague: Martinus Nijhoff.

Stasz. C. (1979) 'The early history of visual sociology', in J. Wagner (ed.) *Images of Information: Still Photography in the Social Sciences*. Beverly Hills, CA: Sage.

Strauss A. and Corbin, J. (1994) *Basics of Qualitative Research: Techniques and Procedures for Developing Grounded Theory*. London: Sage.

Tagg, J. (1988) The Burden of Representation: Essays on Photographies and Histories. Basingstoke: Macmillan.

Wagner, J. (2006) 'Visible materials, visualised theory and images of social research', *Visual Studies*, 21(1): 55–69.

Wang, C., Cash, J. and Powers, L. (2000) 'Photovoice who knows the streets as well as the homeless? Promoting personal and community action through photovoice', *Health Promotion Practice* 1(1): 81–9.

Webber, S. (2008) Visual images in research, in J. G.Knowles and A. Cole (eds) *Handbook of the Arts in Qualitative Research*. London: Sage.

Wells, E. (2003) *The Photography Reader*. London: Routledge.

Interviewing as Educational Research Method(s) 14

Andrew J. Hobson and Andrew Townsend

Introduction

This chapter deals with a cluster of the most frequently used methods of generating data in educational (and social) research, namely research interviews. We say 'cluster' because the existence and use of a wide variety of different kinds of interview means that in some respects it is simplistic to speak of 'the interview' as a single method.

By the end of this chapter, you should be able to:

- explain the different ways in which interviews can be used in educational research
- explain the relative strengths and limitations of different kinds of research interviews
- understand the theoretical and practical issues relating to interviewing in educational research

We begin the chapter by explaining the nature and diversity of research interviews, and go on to discuss some of the advantages and disadvantages of different forms of one-to-one interview, before examining alternative approaches to conducting interviews with groups of participants. We conclude by highlighting a number of important, practical considerations associated with conducting research interviews.

Definitions and Typologies

Sharing Kvale's view that research interviews are 'construction sites for knowledge' (1996: 14), in which 'the outcome is a co-production of the interviewer and the [research] subject' (p. xvii), we recommend the following definition: 'An interview is literally an *inter view*, an inter-change of views between two persons conversing about a theme of mutual interest' (Kvale 1996: 14, emphasis added).

Data generated by interviews are normally recorded in the form of an interview *transcript*, a verbatim record of the spoken word translated into written form (see Chapter 18 for a detailed discussion of transcripts). Some researchers seek, in addition (or occasionally instead), to produce a record of the nonverbal communication involved in the interview.

While, as suggested in the definition provided above, research interviews are normally conducted on a one-to-one basis involving a single interviewer and a single interviewee, interviews may also be employed with more than one research participant at a time in a 'group interview' – that is, an exchange of views between an interviewer and several interviewees. Some writers use the term 'focus group' interchangeably with that of 'group interview' (Bryman 2004: 346) but, as we demonstrate below, focus groups are best regarded as either a specific form of group interviewing or a separate method altogether.

The vast majority of interviews (and focus groups) carried out in educational and social research are administered in person, and it is this kind of administration on which we focus in this chapter. Although many of the points made nonetheless also apply to interviews conducted by telephone and to interviews or focus groups conducted online, for a discussion of the relative merits and demerits of telephone interviewing and 'e-research' readers should consult sources such as Bryman (2004, Chapters 5 and 23 respectively).

Interview typologies

As Kvale suggests, '[t]he varieties of research interviews approach the spectrum of human conversations' (1996: 13) and a wide range of different typologies may be found in the literature. Here we confine our discussion to some of the more familiar typologies. We focus mainly on the much-used contrast between 'structured' and 'unstructured' interviews, but also distinguish between 'formal' and 'informal' interviews and 'respondent' and 'informant' interviews. These contrasts are presented in Figure 14.1, which groups the respective types with the general methodological approach with which they tend to be associated.

With structured interviews, it is said that the content and procedures are set out in advance, that the questions asked are predominantly 'closed' (whereby interviewees are offered two or more fixed response alternatives), and that the same questions are read out in the same order to all interviewees, with relatively little freedom of manoeuvre for interviewer and interviewee.[1] Conversely, unstructured interviews are said to resemble everyday conversations in so far as:

- they are more free-flowing
- they are *less likely* to have as many specific, predetermined questions
- they are *less likely* to require that questions are asked in a particular order
- the questions asked are *more likely* to be 'open-ended' than closed (see Box 14.1)

As Figure 14.1 suggests, structured interviews tend to be associated with 'quantitative' research or 'quantitative' strands of mixed-method studies, while unstructured interviews are associated with a 'qualitative' approach to research.[2]

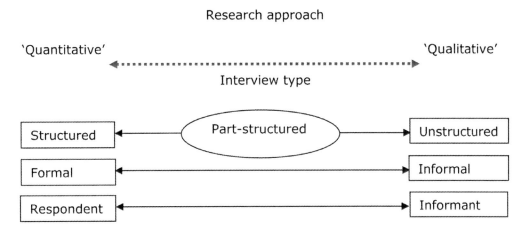

Figure 14.1 Commonly used research interview typologies

The distinction between structured and unstructured interviews is, however, somewhat simplistic for a number of reasons. First, the association between structured interviews and closed questions on the one hand and unstructured interviews and open-ended questions on the other is exaggerated. It is possible, for example, to develop an interview agenda that is highly structured in terms of having a series of set questions which should be asked of all interviewees in the same order, yet which comprises mostly open-ended questions. Secondly, it is not possible to have a completely structure-free interview, not only because the researcher must have some purpose or agenda (Jones 2004) but also because 'the agendas and assumptions of both interviewer and interviewee will inevitably impose frameworks for meaningful interaction' (Mason 2002: 231). Thirdly, an examination of interview protocols developed and used by educational and social researchers would reveal that a high proportion of them cannot unproblematically be classified as either 'structured' or 'unstructured', and the majority might best be described as 'semi-structured' or (as we prefer to call them) 'part-structured' interviews.

The structured-unstructured distinction might also be regarded as unsatisfactory in so far as it fails to address other important issues which ought to be considered by researchers deliberating the use of research interviews. One such issue relates to the degree of formality in the interaction between interviewer and interviewee. Some writers (e.g. Schmuck 2006) thus differentiate between 'formal' and 'informal' interviews. Again, however, the distinction is somewhat over-generalized and, in practice, it would be difficult to categorize most interviews as either completely formal or completely informal. A further problem is that some writers seem to conflate the two sets of distinctions referred to above and use the formal-informal and structured-unstructured distinctions synonymously. For example, Letherby (2003: 84) states that: 'The most formal type of interview is fully structured and the wording of questions and the order in which they are asked is the same from one interview to the next [...] The most informal interview is the unstructured in-depth interview'.[3]

The degree of formality and the degree of structure involved in a research interview are not the same thing, however. The former refers to the nature of the relationship and interaction between

---

Box 14.1 Degrees of structure via 'closed' and 'open-ended' questions

Suppose we want to know why student teachers choose to follow particular kinds of teacher training programme from a range of options (including a variety of university and employer administered courses). We might do it by asking student teachers an open-ended question, such as:

'Why did you choose to follow this particular training route and programme?'

Alternatively, we might choose to employ a more structured or 'closed' question, such as the following (versions of which might be employed in 'structured' interviews or in self-completion questionnaires):

'Can you tell me whether any of the following considerations influenced your choice of initial teacher training (ITT) route or programme?':

- *Did you think prospective employers may prefer applicants who had followed this route? (Yes or No)*
- *Was it important for you to train alongside people in your peer group or in a similar situation as yourself? (Yes or No)*
- *Was the availability of programmes in your local area a consideration? (Yes or No)*
- *Did the balance of in-school and out-of school training on this route appeal to you? (Yes or No)*
- *Did you think this kind of programme was the best option financially? (Yes or No)*

(Adapted from Malderez *et al.* 2007)

---

interviewer and interviewee, the latter to the extent to which interview questions are predetermined, 'open' or 'closed' and asked in the same order to all interviewees. While informal interviews tend to have less structure than formal ones, and vice versa, this need not necessarily be the case.

By way of introducing a different kind of interview typology, Powney and Watts (1987) argue that the key distinction between different kinds of interviewing relates not to the degree of structure but to the question of 'where lies the locus of control' (p. 17). These authors distinguish between *respondent interviews*, in which the interviewer assumes and remains in control throughout the whole process, and *informant interviews*, where the interviewee has much more control over the agenda and the direction of the conversation. Again, respondent interviews tend to be associated with a 'quantitative' approach to research and informant interviews with a more qualitative or interpretive approach. Yet while 'respondent' interviews are likely to be relatively structured (and formal) and 'informant' interviews to be less structured (and more informal), it is nevertheless possible to envisage not only unstructured 'respondent interviews' but also structured 'informant interviews', in which the interviewee provides the structure.

Although the distinction between 'structured' and 'unstructured' interviews represents something of an oversimplification and omits some important considerations associated with different varieties of interview, researchers who wish to employ research interviews nonetheless do have a meaningful choice to make regarding the extent to which they might structure: (1) their interview agenda in general and (2) specific questions which may form part of such an agenda. In addition, the perceived strengths and limitations associated with these *ideal types* provide a helpful framework against which to critique one's own interviewing practice. Later in the chapter we outline some of the main benefits and drawbacks associated with relatively structured and relatively unstructured interviews, and consider some of the attractions of hybrid part-structured interviews. First, though, we explore why researchers may wish to conduct interviews of any kind, and identify some of the common drawbacks and limitations associated with research interviews of all varieties.

Advantages and Disadvantages of Research Interviews

Strengths and limitations of interviews in general

Research interviews take advantage of the fact that humans can 'tell you things about themselves' (Robson 1993: 227). They are a versatile method of generating data which can be used in a variety of different kinds of study and can help researchers to address a wide range of goals and purposes. Van Manen (1990: 66) suggested, for example, that interviews could be employed in qualitative studies:

> [t]o study ways of doing and seeing things peculiar to certain cultures or cultural groups [. . .], to study the way individuals see themselves and others in certain situations [. . .]; to study the way people feel about certain issues [. . .] as a means for exploring and gathering experiential narrative material that may serve as a resource for developing a richer and deeper understanding of a human phenomenon, and [. . .] as a vehicle to develop a conversational relation with a partner (interviewee) about the meaning of an experience.

Research interviews have a number of advantages over other commonly used methods of data generation such as observation and questionnaire surveys. For example, interviews provide the opportunity to cover a broader range of issues than would be possible via observation. They also allow us to discover things that we would not find out through observation alone or would not find out if we did not ask (although some forms of 'observation' also provide opportunities to ask questions). For example, for a research study which sought to discover student teachers' preconceptions and concerns about initial teacher training (ITT) programmes (Hobson *et al.* 2006), observational methods would be inappropriate, since it is less likely to witness many participants speaking about this issue would be small. While a questionnaire survey employing 'closed' questions, conducted before or at the start of their training courses, might allow the researcher to address this research question, it would be difficult to anticipate the possible range of types of answer that research participants might give, suggesting that interviews which include at least some open-ended questions might be more appropriate. Other advantages of interviews over questionnaires are that the researcher is able to explain the meaning of any terms the participant may not understand, that the interviewer is able to *probe* participants' responses in order to gain more detailed data, and that they can seek clarification regarding the meaning of particular (e.g. ambiguous) answers (Leonard 2003). In addition, interviews tend to attract higher response rates:

It is a curious fact that people are, in general, far more willing to devote an hour and a half to an interview (even of no benefit to themselves) than to give fifteen minutes to the completion of a questionnaire. There are various reasons for this [. . .] but a fundamental one is simple: people like the attention, they like to be listened to, they like their opinions being considered [. . .] These are basic human needs, which we all share, and a great strength of the interview is that, in a small way, it fulfils them.

(Gillham 2000: 15)

It is important to recognize, however, that the research interview 'is not a neutral conversation allowing us to decide about the true nature of the social world [. . .] [but rather] is part of the social world studied' (Kvale 1996: 296). This feature of interviews as 'a site of knowledge production' has been utilized to support the respective arguments of both champions and critics of research interviews. Proponents of interviewing in educational and social research have thus argued that one of the main advantages is that it takes advantage of the human characteristics of the interviewer. As Kvale (1996: 125) put it, by virtue of being human:

[t]he interviewer has an empathetic access to the world of the interviewee; the interviewee's lived meanings may be [. . .] communicated not only by words, but by tone of voice, expressions, and gestures in the natural flow of a conversation. The research interviewer uses him- or herself as a research instrument, drawing upon an implicit bodily and emotional mode of knowing that allows a privileged access to the subject's lived world.

Critics, however, have argued that since the interviewer is a 'co-producer' of knowledge, interviews are an 'unreliable' method of data generation. That is, we cannot rely on findings that result from interview studies because the data would inevitably have been different had they been generated or 'produced' by a different interviewer. This critique tends to be associated with a traditional, positivist approach to research, which has become increasingly challenged in recent decades. Researchers who recognize the inevitability of researchers' influence on data generation and who argue that this can be an advantage, notably those who embrace a more qualitative approach to research, tend not to recognize the concept of reliability as a plausible goal of research or a meaningful criterion by which educational and social research should be evaluated (Jones 2004).

Nevertheless, since '[i]nterviewers and interviewees alike bring their own, often unconscious experiential and biographical baggage with them into the interview situation' (Cohen *et al.* 2000: 121), which means that the researcher influences both the interviewee and the data that are generated, it follows that questions may also be raised about the validity or credibility of the data. Most 'qualitative' researchers accept that this is the case, suggesting that it is an inevitable consequence of all methods of data generation, and that what is important is to embrace reflexivity, to be transparent about the 'baggage' that they may have brought to the research, and open about potential effects that this may have had on their research findings.

Other threats to the validity or trustworthiness of interview data can arise because some participants may not give accurate or truthful answers to questions posed, in some cases because of the issue of 'social desirability', which suggests that, in general, people like to present themselves in a favourable light. Moreover, the extent to which interviewees are likely to provide *accounts*

(Dingwall 1997) which accurately reflect what they really believe will be influenced by a number of factors relating to their relationships with or to the interviewer. These include: 'differences or similarities in class, ethnic origin, gender, age and status' (Robson 1993: 237); and the level of expertise of the interviewer, who may, for example, unwittingly influence the interviewee's responses by giving non-verbal cues, such as frowning. The effects on the validity or credibility of data of status or power differences between interviewer and interviewee may be particularly acute in relation to school teachers interviewing their own (or others') pupils/students.

It is also important to recognize that different interviewees may interpret (even the same) questions in different ways, that participants' intended meanings in their interview responses may be different from the meanings ascribed by the researcher, and that the influence of the interviewer on the 'data production' process may vary from one interview (and interviewee) to the next, since the *inter-views* produced on each occasion are part-shaped by each unique *inter-action*. These issues challenge the extent to which comparisons can *legitimately* be made between the responses of different participants or categories of participant.

Compared with some research methods, such as questionnaire surveys, interviews can be both *time-consuming* (especially where the decision is made to produce verbatim transcripts of all interviews prior to data analysis) and *costly* (especially where research participants live far apart and/or a long way away from the researcher, and where it is necessary to pay someone to undertake transcription). This can mean that sample sizes are relatively small and, assuming that your epistemological and ontological stance enables you to entertain such a notion, claims to generalizability tend to be much harder to sustain (see Chapter 4 for a discussion on generalizability, mainly in the context of quantitative research).

Having identified some of the advantages and limitations that are common to interviews in general, we now list some of the commonly stated advantages and disadvantages of undertaking relatively 'structured' and 'unstructured' interviews respectively. We should add, however, that many of these points are contestable, and that the extent to which each of the advantages and disadvantages listed may be realized in practice would depend on the specific context in which interviews were employed.

Advantages of 'structured' and disadvantages of less structured interviews

1 With structured interviews, it is relatively easy to ensure coverage of the researcher's agenda, since appropriate questions are put directly to participants. This is harder with 'unstructured' interviews, as the interviewee may not sufficiently address issues of interest to the researcher.

2 With structured interviews, the nature of the data generated is less likely to be influenced – and arguably, the validity of the data less likely to be threatened – by the personalities and moods of, and interpersonal dynamics between, the interviewer and interviewee.

3 Structured interviews are, therefore, said to be more reliable and more easily verifiable than 'unstructured' interviews.

4 Studies involving structured interviews may be more accurately replicated in the future, which facilitates comparisons over time.

5 The use of pre-coded, standardized questions makes it possible to analyse data relatively quickly and accurately using computer programmes such as SPSS (Statistical Package for Social Sciences).[4] The analysis of data generated from unstructured interviews tends to be more time-consuming.

6 With 'structured' interviews, the fact that different interviewees are asked the same questions and in the same order is said to facilitate more legitimate comparisons between different interviewees and categories of interviewees.

7 Structured interviews are sometimes regarded as less intrusive than 'unstructured' ones in which, occasionally to their subsequent regret, participants may reveal more information than they might have intended or expected to reveal (but see point 7 below).

Advantages of less structured and disadvantages of 'structured' interviews

1 In opposition to point 2 in the previous section, the data generated by structured interviews are largely shaped by the way in which the researcher defines and uses concepts, structures the interview schedule, and phrases and orders individual questions, all of which are dependent upon the researcher's values. For these reasons, it might be argued that data generated from structured interviews are likely to be *less* valid or credible than those generated from relatively unstructured interviews.

2 In addition since, in unstructured interviews, the data are less predefined by questions set, interviewees participating have a greater opportunity to speak, in their own words, about what is significant to them. The premature closure of questions in 'structured' interviews dictates that interviewees may only be able to give an approximation to their true feeling or conception.

3 Relatively unstructured interviews and open-ended questions can produce valuable 'answers' to questions the researcher may not have thought to ask or include in a 'structured' interview schedule.

4 Relatively unstructured (and informal/'informant') interviews provide a greater opportunity to develop a rapport with and gain the trust of the interviewee, which may have the effect of the participant being more likely to provide honest and accurate information or (again) more valid or credible data. Oakley (2004: 263) thus argues that:

> [I]n most cases, the goal of finding out about people through interviewing is best achieved when the relationship of interviewer and interviewee is non-hierarchical and when the interviewer is prepared to invest his or her own personal identity in the relationship.

5 The greater degree of flexibility associated with 'unstructured' interviews allows interviewers to clarify and probe interviewees' answers and follow up leads, which facilitates the generation of a richer dataset than is possible from more structured interviews.

6 In response to points 4 and 6 in the previous section, it may be argued that data generated from participants in structured interviews are not as comparable as is often claimed because different interviewees may not understand the same questions in the same ways, or in the ways intended by the researcher(s).

7 Further to point 7 in the previous section, since in 'unstructured' interviews research participants are free to choose which issues to speak about, such interviews may be regarded as *less* intrusive than structured ones, in which some of the specific questions asked may make some participants feel uncomfortable.

Part-structured interviews

Conscious of the relative advantages and disadvantages of extreme ('structured' and 'unstructured') forms of interviewing, some (probably most) researchers who employ interview methods choose to conduct 'part-structured' (or 'semistructured') interviews. The part-structured interview tends to include a number of specific questions, and often includes both 'closed' and 'open-ended' questions, while the interviewer and interviewee are relatively free to depart from the predetermined list or ordering of questions where they feel it is appropriate.

One of the main benefits of part-structured interviews is that they can help to ensure coverage of the researcher's agenda while also providing opportunities for interviewees to talk about what is significant to them, in their own words. Related to this, researchers employing part-structured interviews can achieve both breadth and depth in their datasets – though perhaps not as much breadth *or* depth as might be achieved through the use of more, or less, structured interviews respectively.

Tomlinson (1989) developed a particular and flexible version of a part-structured interview, which he termed *hierarchical focusing*, with the aim of helping researchers to 'have it both ways' and achieve two goals which are aspired to by most interviewer-researchers yet sometimes regarded as incompatible, namely:

- ensuring coverage of the interviewer's agenda
- minimizing the interviewer's influence on interviewees' responses

In order to conduct a 'hierarchically focused' interview, it is necessary to construct an interview agenda which starts with the most general question, which theoretically allows the interviewee to speak about all of the things in which you are potentially interested. The agenda will also include more specific questions and prompts, to be used only if they are needed – that is, if the interviewee does not spontaneously address those issues. The basic aim is for the interviewer to 'elicit as spontaneous a coverage of as much of the interview agenda as possible' (Tomlinson 1989: 169), and this is achieved by:

- encouraging interviewees, in a non-directive manner, to elaborate and expand upon the views they are expressing, using both verbal and non-verbal strategies (e.g. deliberate silences, modest encouragement such as 'I see, do go on', and more explicit requests like 'Would you like to take that a bit further?')
- prompting interviewees to discuss those aspects of the agenda which they do not spontaneously address, but as far as possible by using only terminology which has already been introduced by the interviewee and not by introducing one's own terms

An example of a hierarchically-structured interview agenda is provided in Figure 14.2.

Group Interviews and Focus Groups

An alternative to conducting one-to-one interviews is to interview groups of participants simultaneously. In addition to generating data through interaction between researcher and

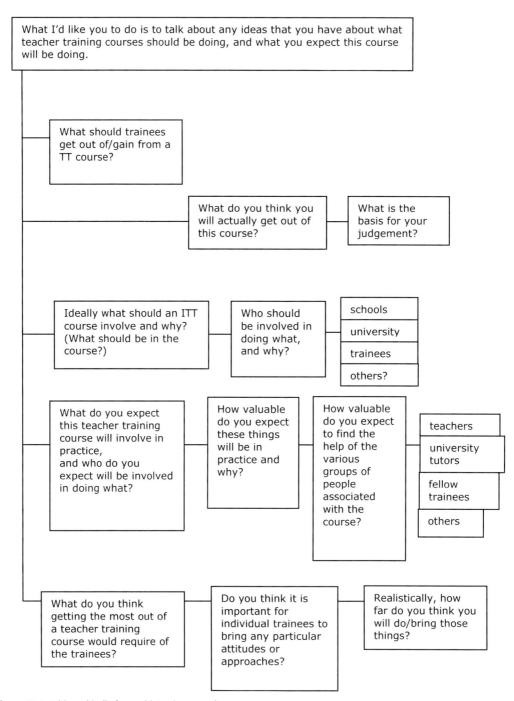

Figure 14.2 A hierarchically-focused interview agenda

participant, interviewing groups involves the added dynamic of data production via interaction between participants, which can come in a number of (direct and indirect) guises, including:

- a participant directly associating or disassociating with other participants' comments when answering a question set by the researcher
- a participant extending, elaborating upon or illustrating other participants' comments when answering a question directed to them by the researcher
- a participant doing these things, and others, by engaging in sustained dialogue with other participants, rather than directly with the researcher

Two main approaches to conducting interviews with groups of participants may be distinguished: the group interview and the focus group, a method which has its origins in market research (Gray 2004). We highlight the main differences between the two approaches around three dimensions (see Figure 14.3).

Dimension 1: the role of the researcher

In both one-to-one and group interviews the extent to which the interviewer leads the conversation will vary according to the degree of structure in the interview agenda and the extent to which the researcher seeks to conduct a 'respondent' or 'informant' interview. Nevertheless, it is generally the case that the researcher plays a more prominent role in leading a group interview discussion than would be the case in a focus group. In a focus group, the role of the researcher is to *facilitate* discussion which is led by participants, albeit around a focus identified by the researcher. This is recognized in the use of the term *moderator* to describe the role of the researcher (Krueger and Casey 2000; Stewart *et al.* 2006).

Dimension 2: the nature of data

A second area of difference between group interviews and focus groups lies in what constitutes data in each case. As we have suggested, researchers employing one-to-one interviews are normally concerned with the content of speech (mostly that of the interviewee-participants), and this is the same for group interviews. Researchers employing focus groups, however, may be at least as concerned with the pattern of interactions between participants as they are with the content of speech (Morgan 1988; O'Sullivan 2003).

Dimension 3: the breadth of focus

Thirdly, one of the key differences between group interviews and focus groups is that, as their name suggests, focus groups tend to have a narrower and more specific 'focus' on a particular topic or question, which participants are encouraged to debate or explore, in detail, among themselves. Group interviews (in common with most one-to-one interviews) tend to cover a broader range of issues.

Through the discussion presented above we are not suggesting that focus groups and group interviews exist as polarized extremes of methodological approaches. Indeed, any particular case of interviewing groups of people may fall at any point along the three continua whose main points of contrast we have identified above, such that in some cases it is difficult to decide whether the approach to data generation which a researcher is employing is best described as a group interview or a focus group.

Conducting interviews with groups of participants brings a number of advantages. For example, it can save the researcher both time and the financial costs associated with travelling to research sites (Bryman 2004). There are also potential benefits associated with the 'participant-to-participant' dynamic. One of these is that the influence of the researcher on data production is minimized. Another is that participants may be stimulated into thinking more deeply about the matter in hand. In focus groups in particular, participants often probe each other's reasons for holding certain views in ways that one might be reluctant to do as an interviewer, which can help the researcher to develop a fuller understanding of *why* people feel or behave the way they do. It might also be argued that group discussion better reflects the processes through which meaning is constructed in everyday life and may thus be said to be more naturalistic, which, in turn, might produce more legitimate claims to the validity or credibility of data.

The group dimension can also bring limitations, however. For example, since the responses of individual participants may be influenced and potentially shaped by the presence and perspectives of other participants as well as by the researcher, group interviews may be regarded

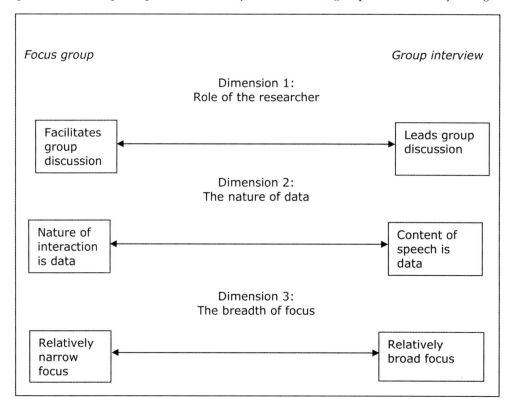

Figure 14.3 Dimensions of interviewing groups of participants

as posing greater threats to the validity or credibility of the data. In addition, and on a more pragmatic level, group discussions are generally more difficult for the researcher to manage than one-to-one interviews. Moreover, the recording of interviews where a large number of people are talking (sometimes simultaneously) poses a major challenge for transcription and data analysis where it is considered important to attribute particular comments to individuals.[5]

Summary

Interviews are a widely used and popular means of generating data in educational and social research and, as discussed, there exists a broad diversity of interview methods that can be used by the researcher. Our underlying preference is for approaches to interviewing which maximize the scope for participants to explore their perceptions and beliefs, and in their own terms. Nevertheless, we recognize the potential value of interview techniques ranging from highly structured researcher-led one-to-one interviews on the one hand, to relatively unstructured participant-led focus groups on the other, and we feel that the selection of the interview technique should be guided primarily by the notion of *fitness for purpose* to the research study in question.

In this chapter, which provides an introduction to the use of interviews in educational research, we have explored:

- the main features of research interviews
- distinctions between different forms and styles of interviewing, including variations relating to the degree of structure and formality of interviews
- a range of advantages and disadvantages associated with interviews in general and with different approaches to conducting interviews
- the nature of and distinctions between different forms of group interviews, including focus groups

Interested readers may wish to explore the interviewing literature in more depth and, to that end, we have provided a list of additional reading below. For those planning to use interviews in their educational research studies, we highlight, in Box 14.2, a number of practical considerations which might aid your planning or provide a useful checklist. We should add that, on the one hand, some of the points that we make also relate to other forms of research while, on the other hand, they should not be taken to comprise an exhaustive account of all the issues that you will need to address in conducting an interview. For example, we only briefly touch on a small number of ethical issues which researchers need to address regardless of the particular methods of data generation they employ (see Chapter 7 for a detailed discussion of research ethics), and we leave to others (e.g. Miles and Huberman 1994) the discussion of alternative ways of analysing the different kinds of data that interview studies can produce. In addition, the considerations that we highlight are not equally relevant to all forms of interviewing. For example, the use of probes is more suitable for relatively unstructured and part-structured interviews than for focus groups, where the researcher acts as moderator, or for highly structured interviews, where attempts are made to consistently apply the questions to all participants.

Box 14.2 Some practical considerations in conducting interviews

Stage 1: initial preparation/planning

Decide what type or style of interview (if any) is most appropriate for addressing the research questions or aims of your study and for facilitating the kind of data analysis that you plan to conduct. You thus need to:

- consider your proposed methods of data analysis in advance.
- consider how your data will be recorded and stored to facilitate analysis.
- seek appropriate permissions from research participants if audio or video recordings are needed.
- consider how long the interview would ideally last, and what the maximum duration of any single interview is likely to be.
- consider the most appropriate, convenient and safe meeting time and place for both interviewees and yourself.

Stage 2: developing the interview agenda

- Decide how you wish to begin the interview and what introductory points you wish to make (e.g. you may wish to reassure participants about confidentiality and anonymity).
- Develop questions and prompts which you feel will allow you to generate the data that you require (and consult 'experts' and previous studies to help you do so).
- Attempt to ensure that your questions are not ambiguous or 'leading' (unless this is deliberate).
- Try to order the questions appropriately so that the interview 'flows'.
- Decide which questions or prompts are relatively low priority and might be omitted in the event that you are in danger of running out of time during an interview.
- Undertake a 'pilot study' or trial of the interview. This will allow you to judge (for example) whether the planned duration of the interviews is realistic and whether the questions developed are appropriate.
- Revise your interview agenda according to the lessons learned from your pilot.

Stage 3: during the interview

- Be polite and attempt to develop a rapport with the interviewee.
- Avoid passing judgement on the interviewees' comments (be aware of your body language, including frowning, as well as what you say).
- Do not put words into the interviewees' mouths.
- Probe interviewees' responses (asking them to clarify, explain, expand or illustrate) as (and if) appropriate.
- If interviewees 'wander' away from the question or the focus of the interview, attempt to bring them back on task in a sensitive manner.
- Keep your eye on the clock to try to ensure that you get through all of your key questions and do not exceed the agreed duration of the interview.
- Towards the end of the interview, ensure that you give the interviewee the opportunity to make any additional comments.
- Thank the interviewee for their participation and clarify the arrangements for any subsequent contact (e.g. you might send interviewees a copy of the transcript for their information, verification or 'validation').

Stage 4: after the interview

- Thank the participants in writing if possible (this is not only polite but might also encourage future participation).
- If producing interview transcripts, use participants' words throughout, not your interpretation of what they said (this will come later, at the data analysis stage).
- Ensure that you keep any promises made to participants (e.g. will you provide them with an account of the findings of your study or some other means of acknowledging their participation?).

Finally, at all stages throughout the interview/research process

- Develop contingency plans (attempt to anticipate what might go wrong and how you might deal with it if it does).

Notes

1 The structured interview schedule thus resembles a questionnaire (see Chapter 15), the main difference being that, with the former, the questions are read out and the answers recorded by an interviewer, while with the latter, research participants read the questions and record their responses themselves.

2 We use the terms 'quantitative' and 'qualitative' with caution. Hammersley (1996), among others, has argued that contrasts between quantitative and qualitative methods are simplistic and exaggerated (see Chapter 2 for a discussion on paradigmatic divisions).

3 The term 'in-depth' interview is sometimes used to refer to interviews which are relatively unstructured and/or informal, and which are associated with qualitative studies or qualitative strands of mixed-method studies.

4 This assumes that the achieved interview sample is sufficiently large and possesses other suitable characteristics to facilitate different methods of quantitative analysis (see Chapters 16–23).

5 This is not intended to be an exhaustive account of the pros and cons of group interviews and focus groups. For a fuller treatment see, for example, Krueger and Casey (2000), Gibbs (1997) and Morgan (1988).

References

Bryman, A. (2004) *Social Research Methods*, 2nd edn. Oxford: Oxford University Press.

Cohen, L., Manion, L. and Morrison, K. (2000) *Research Methods in Education*, 5th edn. London: RoutledgeFalmer.

Dingwall, R. (1997) 'Accounts, interviews and observations', in G. Miller and R. Dingwall (eds) *Context and Method in Qualitative Research*. London: Sage.

Gillham, B. (2000) *The Research Interview*. London: Continuum.

Gibbs, A. (1997) 'Focus groups', *Social Research Update*, 19.

Gray, D. (2004) *Doing Research in the Real World*. London: Sage.

Hammersley, M. (1996) 'The relationship between qualitative and quantitative research: paradigm loyalty versus methodological eclecticism', in J. T. E. Richardson (ed.) *Handbook of Qualitative Research Methods for Psychology and the Social Sciences*. Leicester: British Psychological Society.

Hobson, A. J. (2001) 'Postgraduate history specialists' perspectives on their initial teacher preparation: preconceptions, experiences and evaluations', unpublished PhD thesis, University of Leeds School of Education.

Hobson, A. J., Malderez, A., Tracey, L. and Pell, G. (2006) 'Pathways and stepping stones: student teachers' preconceptions and concerns about initial teacher preparation in England', *Scottish Educational Review*, 37 (supplement): 59–78.

Jones, S. (2004) 'Depth interviewing;, in C. Seale (ed.) *Social Research Methods: A Reader*. London: Routledge.

Krueger, R. A. and Casey, M. A. (2000) *Focus Groups: A Practical Guide for Applied Research*. Thousand Oaks, CA: Sage.

Kvale, S. (1996) *InterViews: An Introduction to Qualitative Research Interviewing*. Thousand Oaks, CA: Sage.

Leonard, M. (2003) 'Interviews', in R. L. Miller and J. D. Brewer (eds) *The A–Z of Social Research*. Thousand Oaks, CA: Sage.

Malderez, A., Hobson, A. J., Tracey, L. and Pell, G. (2007) 'Choosing initial teacher preparation (ITP) in England: why student teachers undertake ITP and why they choose particular ITP pathways', paper presented at the annual meeting of the American Educational Research Association (AERA), Chicago, 9–13 April.

Mason, J. (2002) *Qualitative Researching*. London: Sage.

Miles, M. B. and Huberman, A. M. (1994) *Qualitative Data Analysis: An Expanded Sourcebook*. Thousand Oaks, CA: Sage.

Morgan, D. L. (1988) *Focus Groups as Qualitative Research*. Newbury Park, CA: Sage.

O'Sullivan, R. (2003) 'Focus groups', in R. L. Miller and J. D. Brewer (eds) *The A–Z of Social Research*. Thousand Oaks, CA: Sage.

Oakley, A. (2004) 'Interviewing women: a contradiction in terms', in C. Seale (ed.) *Social Research Methods: A Reader*. London: Routledge.

Powney, J. and Watts, M. (1987) *Interviewing in Educational Research*. London: Routledge.

Schmuck, R. A. (2006) *Practical Action Research for Change*. Thousand Oaks, CA: Corwin Press.

Stewart, D. W., Shamdasani, P. N. and Rook, D.W. (2006) *Focus Groups, Theory and Practice*. London: Sage.

Tomlinson, P. D. (1989) 'Having it both ways: hierarchical focusing as research interview method', *British Educational Research Journal*, 15(2): 155–76.

Van Manen, M. (1990) *Researching Lived Experience: Human Science for an Action Sensitive Pedagogy*. Albany, NY: State University of New York Press.

Experimental and Quasi-experimental Designs in Educational Research

Dimitra Hartas

Introduction

Group comparisons for the purpose of testing the effects of a treatment on an outcome constitute an important strand in quantitative research, and have been traditionally situated within experimental research. Experimental research has been described as the 'gold standard of research designs' (Gorard 2001: 133). It has been typically carried out in laboratory settings to remove or decontextualize the object of investigation from its context for the purpose of controlling for extraneous factors, to maximize the validity of the research (Gorard and Taylor 2004). In this chapter, we discuss experimental, including randomized, trials and design experiments, and quasi-experimental designs, focusing on issues of feasibility, appropriateness and fitness for purpose. Non-experimental designs – i.e., survey and correlational research – are discussed in Chapters 16 and 23, respectively (see Figure 15.1).

By the end of this chapter, you should be able to:

- identify the distinctive characteristics of experimental research – i.e. randomized trial and design experiments, and quasi-experimental research
- describe the theoretical and methodological assumptions that underlie each quantitative research design
- critically engage with the advantages and disadvantages of each design type

Experimental Designs in Education

Over the last decade, in education, the use of experimental designs has gained ground, stimulated mainly by the US National Research Council's drive towards a scientific approach to educational research. Shavelson and Towne argue for methods that link directly to the research problem and facilitate the development of a 'logical chain of reasoning based on the interplay among

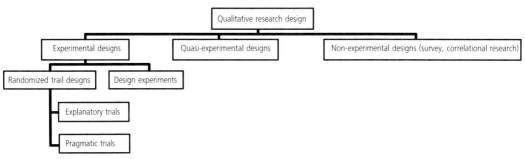

Figure 15.1 Types of quantitative research design in education

investigative techniques, data and hypotheses to reach justifiable conclusions' (2002: 63). As such, they consider experimental designs to be 'ideal for establishing whether one or more factors caused change in an outcome because of their strong ability to enable fair comparisons' (p. 110). Considering experimental designs to be the only scientific approach to educational research, however, has been criticized widely (see Chapter 1 for debates in educational research). Berliner argues that to view 'randomized experiments as the only scientific approach to gaining knowledge [...] suggests a myopic view of science in general and a misunderstanding of educational research in particular' (2002: 18).

Traditionally, experimental designs originate within the positivist and postpositivist world-views where objectivity, causality, generalization and theory-driven hypotheses are key principles (see Box 15.1). Experimental designs are pre and post-test or pre- and post-treatment designs because intervention, or the systematic manipulation of certain factors, constitutes the main component of an experiment. The pre-test/post-test design is considered to be robust in that both groups of participants are pre-tested on the outcome variable and post-tested after an intervention has taken place in the experimental group (Cresswell 2005). In experimental designs, to delineate the effects (systematic variation) of one factor on another, we need to exercise control in terms of setting the parameters of the context of the experiment (e.g. laboratory) and, most crucially, defining the factors/variables to be included in the design to avoid interference or unsystematic variation from extraneous factors. In addition, a control group – i.e. a group that does not receive treatment – is required for comparison purposes. The use of a group that does not receive treatment has raised concerns in that, in education, not receiving treatment at all is unrealistic and potentially unethical. In the following sections, we elaborate on the principles (e.g. control, causality), that frame experimental designs.

Box 15.1 Principles of experimental designs

- Formulation of theory-based, a priori hypotheses.
- Control through randomization (i.e. random selection and assignment of persons to groups, in order to increase generalizability and minimize the impact of confounding variables on outcome).
- Emphasis on intervention/treatment (or pre- and post-treatment designs).
- Use of a control group (one that does not receive treatment at all, 'placebo' only).
- Exploration of causal relationships between independent variables and outcome.

Control

In experimental designs, controlling for unsystematic variation due to extraneous factors is achieved through randomization. Randomization (random assignment of persons to treatment and control groups) refers to the process whereby the effects of extraneous factors on outcome measures are distributed evenly across groups. For example, participants' characteristics such as intelligence or prior learning experience are distributed evenly across groups, rather than being concentrated in one group. In so doing, these factors exert a random rather than a systematic effect on the outcome measures (see Chapter 4 for a discussion on randomization).

Another way to control for the effects of extraneous variables is to keep a factor constant (e.g. Year 3 pupils in a particular school). The decision about which factor is kept constant depends on the scope of the study. Finally, we may control for the effects of extraneous variables statistically, by incorporating them into the research design and controlling for their effects through the application of statistical procedures – namely, stratification, partial correlation and analysis of covariance (ANCOVA) (Punch 2005). The decision as to which factors to study and which to control for is an important one, and should be based on the aims of the study and the research questions. Limiting the effects of confounding variables (variables that cannot be controlled for) maximizes the internal validity (see Chapter 4 for a discussion on validity) and sets the stage to explore causal relationships within the context of experimental designs.

Box 15.2 How to control for extraneous factors

- Ensure random assignment of persons to groups.
- Keep an extraneous factor constant (depending on the purpose of the research).
- Incorporate extraneous factors in the study (if their effects are judged to be important).
- Control for extraneous variables through statistical procedures, namely partial correlation and analysis of covariance (ANCOVA).

Causality

The concept of causality is elusive. A view of causation, due mostly to the work of Curt John Ducasse (1881–1969), states that what makes a sequence of events causal is the local link (an intrinsic feature of the particular sequence) between the cause and the effect. In a sense, causality, and thus causal explanations, is singular: a matter of *this* causing *that*. We know that correlation does not imply causation; however, what does causation mean? To draw causal relationships between two factors requires us to understand the dynamic and hierarchical structures of the factors involved, and to delineate their relationship by taking into account time order (preceding/antecedent factors), and the possibility of the existence of confounding variables or counter-hypotheses. In experimental designs, it is important to rule out possible counter-hypotheses. This is not straightforward, in that we do not know all the confounding factors from the outset.

If two factors, A and B, are in a causal relationship, for example, *A causes B* means:

- A and B must be related
- A must precede B, in that the cause must precede the effect
- other plausible hypotheses must be rejected (Punch 2005)

In education, it is debatable whether a single factor causes an outcome, in that many factors are likely to operate simultaneously, producing different results depending on the context within which they operate (see Box 15.3). For example, the influence of ethnicity on academic achievement differs depending on the socioeconomic and cultural context of a school or the level of parental involvement in their children's education. Moreover, it may be the case that a single factor produces different results (e.g. differentiation of the curriculum may support learning but also stigmatize pupils with special educational needs) or an outcome may be produced by multiple factors (e.g. you can raise academic performance by changing many factors, such as pupil motivation, ethos of the school or parental participation). Thus, the factors and their causal relationships need to be examined within their local contexts to capture their complexity, understand their dynamic and hierarchical structures and capture their transformations as they occur.

Box 15.3 An example of the elusiveness of causality

Increasingly, research shows a relationship between behavioural/emotional difficulties and language difficulties in children and young people (e.g. Donahue *et al.* 1999). In these studies, the relationship between language and social/behavioural difficulties is approached as a 'correlational' and not a 'causal' one. Establishing causality is difficult in that the order of influence is less clear. Specifically, it is difficult to determine whether language or emotional/behavioural difficulties occur first. Do we rely on the chronological order of the manifestation of the difficulty per se, or the time of a formal diagnosis, or the condition that had the most pronounced impact? Also, previous research suggests that there is a multitude of variables, such as family social circumstances, gender and age that also influence the relationship between behaviour, social and language development.

The use of a control group and pre-test measures improve an experimental design. Pre-test and post-test differences denote changes in the outcome, which are crucial in establishing causality. The existence of a control group and pre-test measures are not enough however to eliminate bias from confounding variables impacting on the treatment and outcome. To ensure that initial differences due to extraneous factors are small, a large sample size and random assignment are important. Otherwise, post-intervention group differences that are caused by pre-intervention differences between the groups may be mistakenly understood as being caused by the intervention. Consequently, the internal validity of the study is compromised in that we may mistakenly think that the intervention has (or has not) had an effect on the outcome.

This problem can be resolved by carrying out randomized experiments, in which units, (e.g. participants or classrooms) are randomly allocated to treatment and control groups (see Box 15.4). Random assignment does not result in the means of the variable of interest in both groups being identical; the means will vary probabilistically, and the degree of variation is determined by the sample size (Cook and Sinha 2006). In other words, the experimental and control groups are probabilistically equivalent. With randomized designs, the observed differences are due to treatment and not to differences in the composition of the groups or the characteristics/attributes of the participants.

Box 15.4 Three important features of experimental designs

- Random assignment to groups.
- Pre-test measures.
- Control group.

Randomized trial designs

Randomized trials are considered to be more rigorous than any other quantitative method (e.g. Torgerson and Torgerson 2001). There are two types of randomized trial design, namely, *explanatory* and *pragmatic* trials. Explanatory trials, through randomization, achieve homogeneous groups with minimum variation so we can ascribe any differences found in the post-test measures to the intervention. However, explanatory trials present practical and educational limitations, in that although the variation is kept to the minimum, the control group does not receive any intervention, and the results are less likely to be generalizable. For example, we want to establish whether an intervention works for pupils across ages, ethnicity groupings and gender and, most importantly, whether it can transfer into real-life classrooms. Explanatory trials are not deemed appropriate for this type of evaluation, whereas pragmatic trials are because they counterbalance the artificiality of the explanatory trials by creating as realistic a real-life situation as possible. In pragmatic trials, instead of giving placebo to the control group we offer them another, equally meaningful, educational intervention (see Box 15.5). However, because the groups in pragmatic trials tend to be less homogeneous, we need large effect sizes (see Chapter 19 for a discussion on effect size) to detect variation due to intervention (Cresswell 2005). With less homogeneous groups, the existence of extraneous factors is a concern and, by increasing the sample size, the confounding factors are likely to cancel each other out.

One type of randomized trial is *factorial designs*, with which we examine the simultaneous effects (independent and interactive) of more than one independent variable, each examined at two or more levels/conditions on an outcome (Creswell 2005). In factorial designs, at least one of the independent variables is manipulated experimentally, and the research participants are randomly assigned to groups (i.e. cells, which are combinations of independent variables). Suppose the independent variables are gender and ethnicity; the cells created are White female, White male, Chinese female etc. The research participants receive a combination of independent variables that corresponds to the cell to which they have been assigned (e.g. White female). With a factorial analysis, we estimate the effects of each independent variable separately (main effects) and the interaction between the independent variables (interaction effects). There are as many main effects as there are independent variables (see Chapter 22 on factorial analysis).

Box 15.5 An example of a randomized trial

In educational research, a relatively small number of studies have employed randomized trial designs. The Tennessee study, conducted in the USA, is discussed here to illustrate the structure and assumptions that underlie randomized trial designs (Finn and Achilles 1990, 1999). The aim of the Tennessee study was to investigate the impact of class size on achievement, by employing an experimental design (random assignment, control group), aiming to draw a causal relationship between class size and academic achievement. Within the 79 schools across the state, 11,600 students were randomly assigned to three groups: a regular class (26 students); a class with an aide (20 students); and a reduced class size (13–17 students). Through random assignment, confounding factors such as SES, prior learning experiences or ability were equally distributed in all three groups, cancelling each other out.

The findings from this study suggest that students in small class sizes outperformed their peers in the other two groups; minority students were benefited most; and the effects on academic achievement persisted when students returned to their regular class. Overall, the findings showed that reducing class size had a positive effect on students' performance. However, we need to understand the causal mechanisms that underlie the relationship between class size and academic performance in terms of the interaction between factors and the context within which they operate. For example, is it the case that, in small classes, student-teacher interactions are more sustained and of a better quality? Are students in small classes likely to exhibit less off-task behaviour? Is there less distraction in the classroom, likely to encourage better student and teacher engagement? Does the quality of teaching improve in a small class due to the fact that a teacher does not have to put so much effort into behaviour management?

Establishing a causal relationship between class size and academic performance, as in the class size study, is a good starting point. However, what we need is to understand the mechanisms that underlie causality so that we can implement meaningful and sustained educational interventions, especially considering the elusive nature of causality. A thorough knowledge of the intervention context in terms of resources, staffing and school ethos, and the particulars of context-actors' interaction plays a major part in delineating the mechanisms that underlie causality. Randomized control trials are rarely used in educational research although they have been used in medical research extensively. The ethical and practical issues regarding the implementation and applicability of experimental designs, including randomized trial designs, limit their use. Highly controlled environments in experimental designs are seen as being artificial, and controlling for the factors involved is likely to make the results less generalizable and applicable in educational settings. A limited generalizability is a problem in that causal interpretations of an educational phenomenon may fit a particular context but not another (see Chapter 4 for a discussion on generalizability). With this in mind, questions about causal inferences and the effectiveness of an intervention should be followed by questions of 'under what circumstances' and 'by whom and for whom' an intervention is effective.

Experimental designs have received extensive criticism on theoretical/philosophical and practical grounds (Cook and Sinha 2006). Some of the philosophical arguments focus on the notion of causality, stating that simple causal relationships between A and B do not represent real-life educational situations and contexts. The meaningfulness of drawing cause and effect relationships between two factors is debateable, especially in education, where many factors influence the phenomenon under consideration. Moreover, educational theories are not fixed and observations are theory-laden. The practical arguments against randomized experiments focus on the ethical and political issues, undesirable trade-offs and their limited relevance to school settings. Design experiments and quasi-experimental designs have emerged as a response to these concerns, to encourage collaboration between researchers and practitioners to ensure that causal explanations relate to real-life events.

Design experiments in education

Design experiments are a new and still evolving genre of educational research, which combines the rigour of experimental designs with considerations of local contexts and the particularities of teaching and learning in classrooms and schools. The use of design experiments signifies a departure from traditional experimental and quasi-experimental designs. Although the term 'design experiment' is fairly new, the processes involved such as building, testing, evaluating and calibrating interventions have been used for the last three decades, mainly within North American educational research (e.g. Schoenfeld 1979, 1985; Cobb and Steffe 1983; Cobb 2000). Design experiments counteract the limitations of traditional experimental designs such as artificiality and lack of opportunity to calibrate an intervention and retest it in a real-life context. Within design experiments, theory is used to develop an intervention or an 'educational artefact' that is tested, calibrated and redesigned until a version is developed that can be used in classrooms to facilitate teaching and learning (Gorard with Taylor 2004). Design experiments involve cycles of generating, testing and redefining hypotheses and interventions with the aim of calibrate them to meet teaching and learning demands (Steffe and Thompson 2000).

Brown describes design experiments as 'an attempt to engineer innovative educational environments' (1992: 141) and, based on prior research and theory, 'trace the evolution of learning in complex, messy classrooms and schools, test and build theories of teaching and learning and produce instructional tools that survive the challenge of everyday practice' (Shavelson *et al.* 2003: 25). In other words, design experiments take place within real-life contexts with the intent to produce educational artefacts or instructional tools to support teaching and learning. With design experiments, although the factors incorporated in a design cannot be controlled entirely, their influence can be traced through a systematic analysis of quantitative and narrative data compiled over an extensive period of time.

Design experiments are described as being 'iterative, process focused, interventionist, collaborative, multileveled, utility oriented and theory driven'. They are:

- *iterative* in that they involve cycles of developing, testing and calibrating theories, activities and educational artefacts
- *process-focused* because they intend to trace pupils' learning by understanding successive patterns in reasoning and thinking, and the impact of instructional artefacts on reasoning and thinking
- *interventionist* because they test theories and try out instructional artefacts by designing and modifying real-world classroom settings
- *collaborative* in that they involve researchers and practitioners, working together in testing strategies and instructional tools
- *multilevelled* because they test multiple variables simultaneously, incorporating factors that have been found to affect teaching and learning at school and community levels

- *utility oriented* because they aim to develop instructional tools to support learning
- theory driven in that they test theory through cycles of design-analysis-redesign of instructional activities and artefacts (Shavelson *et al.* 2003: 26)

Box 15.6 What makes a good design experiment?

The Design-Based Research Collaborative (2003: 5) refers to the following characteristics to describe a good design experiment.

- The central goals of designing learning environments and developing theories or 'prototheories' are intertwined.
- Development and research take place through continuous cycles of design, enactment, analysis and redesign.
- Research on designs must lead to sharable theories that help communicate relevant implications to practitioners.
- Research must account for how design functions in authentic settings.
- The development of such accounts relies on methods that can document and connect processes of enactment to outcome of interest.

The phases of design experiments

Being longitudinal, design studies allow researchers to engage with the many phases of a research study, from the initial exploration to establishing causal relationships and retesting/redesigning learning environments. The exploratory phase, or what Shavelson *et al.* (2003) call 'What is happening?', seeks to establish the nature of an inquiry and formulate initial hypotheses based on existing theory. During this phase, a variety of methods are used such as survey research, ethnography and case studies to identify the nature of the phenomenon and bring together insiders' and outsiders' perspectives on the issues under investigation. With the use of both qualitative and quantitative approaches, an overview of the key issues is gained and detailed narratives are formed and communicated to the practitioners, upon which suggestions about redesigning the learning environment are based.

The second phase refers to the 'Is there a systematic effect?' aspect of the research which aims at establishing cause and effect relationships. This phase involves processes similar to those in randomized trials. Based on the outcomes from the exploratory phase, hypotheses are formulated and a small randomized trial is delivered in classrooms to test the effects of the factors involved. A design study is interventionist in nature and, at the second phase, the outcomes of an intervention (e.g. instructional tools and activities) are tested to determine the magnitude and direction of their effects.

The third phase, or the 'Why or how it is happening?' phase, seeks to establish the mechanisms that underlie causal relationships. During the previous two phases, systematic effects between factors are established, moving the research into the next stage of delineating the causal mechanisms. This is the most challenging phase of a design experiment in that, being multilevelled, there are many factors that should be examined simultaneously, and thus tracing cause-and-effect relationships in a multivariate context can be tricky. Moreover, the nature of the intervention itself may change over the lifetime of the research project as well as the requirements of the participants and the setting.

Box 15.7 Phases of a design experiment

1 'What is happening?' phase (establishes the nature of an inquiry where initial hypotheses based on existing theory are formed.
2 'Is there a systematic effect?' phase (aims at establishing cause and effect relationships).
3 'Why or how it is happening?' phase (seeks to establish the mechanisms that underlie causal relationships) (Shavelson *et al.*, 2003).

The Medical Research Council (2000) developed a model for complex interventions based on the principles that underlie design experiments with the intent to use it in educational studies. The model relies on prior theory and knowledge and modifies them, illustrating the steps of identifying what works and why, with the researcher working together with the teaching staff to develop and deliver educational interventions in the classroom context. According to this model, the phases of a design experiment are explicated further (see Box 15.8).

Box 15.8 A model for design experiments

Preliminary phase: using prior theory
At this phase, current theory is used to enable the formulation of hypotheses and to delineate all the factors that have been found to relate to the topic under consideration.

Phase I: modelling
Modelling would allow the researcher to identify paths of influence and make predictions about future outcomes. Specifically, it identifies the factors and their underlying relationships as well as the direction of their influence on outcome variables.

Phase II: exploratory trial
During this phase, the model developed during Phase I is tested, and an appropriate alternative model for comparison is also developed for the following randomized control trial (experimental design).

Phase III: definitive randomized control trial
The model developed is compared with an alternative one using a protocol that is theoretically defensible, and applying the principles of randomized control trials (eg, randomization) properly.

Phase IV: long-term impact
At this phase, it is important to determine whether the trial can be replicated in different settings over time. Moreover, the efficacy of educational tools is judged, finalizing all the required calibrations required to ensure that they can be used for teaching and learning.

Although design experiments share many similarities with traditional experimental designs, they present several differences. Collins (1999: 290–3) has identified six fundamental ones:

1   *Laboratory vs. messy situations.* Design experiments are set in the messy situations that characterize real-life learning to avoid the distortions of laboratory experiments.
2   *A single dependent variable vs. multiple dependent variables.* In design experiments, there are many dependent variables that matter: variables can be studied by observation, interviews and surveys, outcome variables can be studied by giving pre- and post-tests or evaluating products and performances, and system variables can be studied by follow-up observations, surveys, interviews and longitudinal studies.
3   *Controlling variables vs. describing a situation.* In design experiments the goal is to identify all the variables, or characteristics of the situation, that affect any dependent variables of interest. Not only is the goal to characterize what affects any dependent variable, but also to identify the nature and extent of the effect.
4   *Fixed procedures vs. flexible design revision.*
5   *Testing a hypothesis vs. developing a profile.*
6   *Experimenter vs. co-participant design and analysis*

Box 15.9 An example of a design experiment (discussed in Schoenfeld 2006)

Schoenfeld conducted a series of laboratory studies on students' problem-solving strategies during maths, focusing on the processes involved in employing problem-solving and learning how to make a selection of strategies. Then he taught a course in mathematical problem-solving, based on the outcomes of the experiment. However, he soon realized that the interaction and conversations in the classroom were different from the structured activities that took place in the laboratory. In the classroom, with regard to strategy selection, students would often select inappropriate strategies towards problem-solving, which raised the need to investigate monitoring and self-regulation, both relevant to metacognition. This led Schoenfeld to refine theory and practice by examining students' decision-making about strategy selection, as well as metacognitive strategies. The idea that metacognition plays an important role in deciding which strategy to select during problem-solving was taken back to the laboratory to create tools and techniques to be used and tested in the classroom to refine them. Refinement of the theory also took place by exploring students' work on problems and realizing the importance of belief systems in problem-solving. In Schoenfeld's study, theory, research procedures and instructional tools were co-developed during interactions between classroom and laboratory, offering opportunities for ideas to be developed, tested and refined.

The advantages of design experiments

Design experiments are considered to be useful in exploring the 'learning ecology – a complex, interacting system involving multiple elements of different types and levels – by designing its elements and by anticipating how these elements function together to support learning' (Cobb *et al.* 2003: 9). They have the potential to tackle the complexity inherent in classroom environments, take on board the discourses and narrative accounts of students and practitioners and generate theory. Design studies have an 'intermediate theoretical scope', in that they occupy a middle ground, focusing on a specific local system (e.g. a classroom), and a broader theoretical scope in terms of producing new theory through cycles of testing and redesigning (Cobb *et al.* 2003: 11). They are characterized by a 'highly interventionist methodology' which sets the stage for developing and testing theories, and they have 'pragmatic roots' in that they are concerned with specific learning experiences and not just 'what works' (Cobb *et al.* 2003: 9–10). Finally, design experiments share many features with participatory action research (see Chapter 8) in terms of engaging in cycles of evaluation and redesign to ascertain not only 'what works' but also 'how, when and why it works, and by a specification of what it is' (Cobb *et al.* 2003: 13).

Another important feature of design experiments is the development and testing of educational artefacts (e.g. a particular way to use ICT during maths) based on established causal relationships (e.g. causal relationship between ICT use and maths performance). Artefacts are tested and calibrated in real-world classrooms by taking into account the context-specific mechanisms of causality and theory revision. Finally, design experiments are considered to be robust because they employ mixed methods that counteract the polarization between quantitative and qualitative research methodologies (see Box 15.10).

Box 15.10 Advantages of design experiments

- They combine the rigour of experimental designs with local contexts.
- They mix both qualitative and quantitative methodologies.
- They seek to establish causal relationships in a real-life context.
- They offer cycles of generating, testing and redefining hypotheses.
- They examine multiple factors simultaneously.
- They develop and calibrate educational tools or artefacts.
- They focus on what it is, what works, how, when and why it works.

The limitations of design experiments

Design experiments aim at delineating 'what works' through engineering the learning environment. The critics of design experiments contest the idea of educational engineering with regard to teaching and learning, advocating naturalistic investigations (e.g. Berliner 2002). The view that education is a design science, in the same way that engineering or artificial intelligence is, has been challenged, raising issues connected to the epistemology and nature of education as a discipline. Design experiments have also been criticized for their over-reliance on the assumption that the phenomenon under consideration has been theorized sufficiently to formulate a priori hypotheses (e.g. National Research Council 2002).

The conceptual and methodological basis of causality in design experiments has also been contested, for the same reasons that causality in traditional experimental designs has been critiqued. A number of concerns with causal inferences and the mechanisms that underpin causality have been raised. First, interventions are social entities themselves that change during the experiment and thus establishing causal effects is not a clear-cut process when the phenomenon under investigation is shifting. Against this view, we need to question whether it was the original intervention or a different version of the original that has had a causal effect on an outcome. Secondly, once an educational artefact is constructed, there is bound to be variability in its implementation across different classroom contexts, stressing the need to account for this variation in the design. Thirdly, outcome measures may not fully represent the domain we want to study. For example, academic achievement may be defined along a single dimension (e.g. reading skills), which does not fully capture its entirety. Outcome measures, such as intelligence or self-esteem, are multidimensional, and this makes it difficult to draw precise causal pathways between them and an intervention (Shavelson and Towne 2002) (see Box 15.11).

Box 15.11 Limitations of design experiments

- Engineering the learning environment (education is not a design science).
- A priori hypotheses are based on the assumption that the field of inquiry is adequately theorized.
- Interventions are social phenomena that change over the course of a study, especially in longitudinal studies.
- Variability in the application of educational artefacts exists across classrooms.
- The outcome may not represent the domain we want to study in its entirety.

The criticisms with regard to the appropriateness of experimental designs in education typically revolve around ethics, artificiality of context and reductionism in terms of reducing complex, multilevelled educational phenomena to causal relationships between single factors. Although these criticisms are serious, we need to place them in the context of the purpose of research. Experimental designs are most suitable for research with sharply focused questions about causation where randomization is feasible. However, for studies that, for ethical or practical reasons, the use of a control group and randomization are not feasible, quasi-experimental designs present a viable option (see Table 15.1).

Quasi-experimental Designs

Quasi-experimental designs are like randomized designs in terms of purpose and structure; however, they do not involve random allocation and assignment of persons to groups. Lack of randomization means that other procedures, such as group matching, should be in place to control for the unsystematic effects of extraneous variables. For example, to evaluate a classroom-based intervention, while keeping classrooms intact, the schools and pupils who receive an intervention are matched with schools that do not receive the same intervention. For the groups to be equivalent, the two schools or groups of pupils need to be matched along variables that have been found to affect the outcome. A caveat of this approach is that no matter how well the groups are matched, there are always factors that may have escaped matching, ultimately affecting the results. Overall, the control over extraneous factors within quasi-experimental designs tends to be limited.

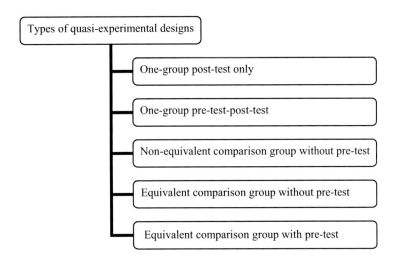

Figure 15.2 Types of quasi-experimental design

Types of quasi-experimental design

Shadish and Luellen (2006) discuss the following types of quasi-experimental design (see Figure 15.2) based on the existence of pre-test measures and a comparison group.

One-group post-test only design

This design involves one group of respondents only, and obtains measurements/observations from this group at the end of the intervention. This design is considered to be weak. Due to the lack of pre-test measures, we do not know whether any changes have occurred as a result of the treatment. Because of the lack of a comparison group, we cannot ascertain what the outcomes would have been for a similar group of people if they had not received any treatment. Even in the case that change has occurred, we are not in a position to know whether the group changes more than it would have changed without intervention.

Suppose we introduce a new reading scheme for the entire school term. At the end of the term, we get measures of pupils' reading comprehension through a reading comprehension test. With this design, we cannot ascertain whether any changes have occurred since the new reading scheme was introduced (because of the lack of pre-test or baseline measures), and what the outcome would have been for a similar group of pupils had they not received any treatment.

One-group pre-test, post-test design

This is a slightly better design in that by having pre-test measures we can ascertain whether there are any changes from before to after intervention. However, because we do not have a comparison group, we cannot say whether the same changes would have been observed in a similar group if it had not received any treatment. Moreover, without a comparison group, we cannot tease out changes due to intervention from changes that would have happened anyway due to maturation (developmental changes over time).

Going back to the previous example, with an one-group pre-test, post-test design we obtain measures of reading comprehension before and after we introduce the new reading scheme. With this design, we can observe whether any changes have occurred; however, we cannot say that the changes observed (if there are any) are due to introducing a new reading scheme. Because of the lack of a comparison group, we cannot tell what the outcome would have been if a similar group of pupils had not received the new reading scheme.

Non-equivalent comparison group design without pre-test

With this type of design, a comparison group is used. However, the comparison and experimental groups are not equivalent because of the nonrandom assignment of persons to groups. Thus, the participants' characteristics that may interfere with the outcome have not been distributed equally between the groups (selection bias). This poses a threat to the internal validity (see Chapter 4). Even if there are differences in the outcome measures between the two groups, because the groups are composed of respondents with different characteristics we cannot attribute the differences to intervention. It is likely that the groups would have had different outcomes even in the absence of a treatment because they bring different characteristics and predispositions.

In our example, a non-equivalent comparison group design means that, although we have an experimental and a comparison group of pupils, the groups are not equivalent because of the lack of a random assignment of pupils to groups (in order to distribute their characteristics evenly). As in the first design type, the lack of pre-test measures from both groups does not allow us to say whether there are any differences attributed to reading intervention. Any observed differences between the two groups cannot be attributed to the reading scheme because extraneous factors (e.g. testing – students becoming better at tests due to practice or perform worse due to the boredom of taking the test many times) or language skills may explain their differences in their reading performance. Due to the lack of matching or other ways of establishing group equivalence, we cannot control for selection bias.

Equivalent comparison group design without pre-test

This is a better design because having experimental and comparison groups that are equivalent (via matching) means that the participants' characteristics are likely to be distributed evenly. Thus, any observed differences between the groups may be attributed to the intervention (because extraneous factors are controlled for). However, due to the lack of pre-test measures, we cannot ascertain the exact magnitude of the differences, and the extent to which these differences are due to intervention, given that the groups would have had different outcomes even in the absence of an intervention.

We should also question the equivalency of groups with this design because in order to achieve a good matching between groups, a series of pre-test measures are required to ensure similar starting points. The results can be strengthened if we provide evidence that the groups were very similar to begin with, especially along the factors that have been found to influence the outcome. In our example, some of the factors that are thought to influence reading comprehension are verbal ability, prior reading exposure, gender or home literacy environment. Having taken pre-test measures we will be able to see whether the groups are equivalent along these factors.

Equivalent comparison group design with pre-test

This is the best design type of all discussed here. The pre-test measures allow us to determine whether there are changes before and after the intervention as well as the magnitude of these changes. Equivalent experimental and comparison groups allow us to control for extraneous factors, and deduce that the observed differences are due to the intervention. As discussed before, the equivalence of groups is not easy to attain, and the extent to which the groups are equivalent always generates heated debates when quasi-experimental designs are used in education.

Box 15.12 An example of quasi-experimental design

A study by Hobbs employed a quasi-experimental design to investigate students' ability to critically analyse advertising as part of their English language arts class. The research question was 'whether instruction in media literacy affects students' ability to critically analyse advertising' (Hobbs 2004: 5). In terms of defining the key terms, the notion of 'critical analysis of an advertisement' refers to an analysis of the purpose, target audience, point of view and the persuasive techniques used.

There were two groups formed, the experimental and the comparison group. The experimental group consisted of 293 students in seven classrooms who were taught how to analyse advertisements in terms of purpose, audience, point of view and persuasive techniques used. This teaching was provided as part of the classroom instruction. A comparison group, which did not receive the instruction as part of their course, was matched with the experimental group along important demographic factors. The instructional activities (intervention) included writing to describe target audience, appeal of emotional language, a visit to an advertising agency and interviewing staff members. All seven teachers involved in this study shared resources and materials; however, they developed the content/activities of the interaction along the priorities of the setting (and the activities took place in a different sequential order in all seven classrooms).

In terms of group matching, the experimental and comparison groups were matched along the dimension of instructional quality. However, instructional quality is multidimensional and not easy to define, making it difficult to reach consensus on its components. Moreover, although the two groups were matched along demographic characteristics and school size, there are probably other important factors that were not accounted for, such as language and communication skills, which were likely to interfere and alter the outcome.

The advantages and limitations of quasi-experimental designs

An important advantage of quasi-experimental designs is that we compare naturally occurring groups (e.g. intact classrooms, schools). Because of this, the groups represent real-world classrooms better, maximizing the external validity or generalizability of the findings. For example, we can compare two classrooms in the same or different schools, with one classroom being the 'experimental' and the other the 'comparison' group.

In quasi-experimental designs, the possibility of a selection bias is high because persons are not randomly assigned to groups, compromising the internal validity of a study. A selection bias and the limited control over extraneous factors limit the scope of quasi-experimental designs, raising concerns about internal validity. For example, a pilot study on evaluating the National Literacy Strategy (NLS) in the UK employed a quasi-experimental design, and concluded that there were no differences in the results between schools that had introduced NLS and those who had not (Smith and Hardman 2000). However, can we be certain that there are no differences knowing that the schools were not selected randomly? Not having a control group or appropriately matched groups, we are not in a position to control other factors that are likely to interfere and alter the results.

Moreover, experimental groups tend to include participants or units of analysis that are selected for a purpose. For example, schools in disadvantaged areas or schools that volunteer may function as the experimental group and thus the members in the group are likely to have characteristics that set them apart from the control group in a systematic way. A common practice is to pilot new educational initiatives among 'volunteer' schools. However, volunteer staff are likely to display characteristics and behaviours such as initiative, willingness to try new methods of teaching and learning, and self-efficacy, that introduce bias in the study (see Table 15.1).

Quasi-experimental designs, no matter how well they are planned and executed, are no substitute for experimental designs. However, despite their limitations, they can provide useful information, especially in the field of education where randomized trial designs are not always feasible, due to ethical or practical reasons.

Table 15.1 Advantages and disadvantages of experimental and quasi-experimental designs

Type of design	Advantages	Disadvantages
Experimental designs Randomized trial designs	• Control (through randomization) • Exploration of causal relationships • Good internal validity • Use of control group	• Reduced generalizability/ applicability (external validity) • Artificial, lab-like setting • Ethical concerns
Design studies	• Produce artefacts or instructional tools • Experiment in real-life contexts • Mixed-method designs • Generate theory • Longitudinal and multivariate analyses • Cycles of design-analyses-redesign • Causality • Interprofessional collaboration • Good internal and external validity	• Educational engineering • Against the nature of education as discipline (not a design science) • Changing nature of intervention • Over-reliance on prior theory • Lack of naturalistic interventions • Intervention outcomes vary across contexts
Quasi-experimental designs	• Matching groups • Using intact classrooms • Comparison of naturally occurring events • Good external validity • Good applicability	• Limited control of confounding variables • Internal validity can be compromised • Possibility of selection bias • The notion of equivalence of groups is questionable

Summary

In this chapter, two major types of quantitative research design, namely experimental and quasi-experimental, were discussed. Each design type has advantages and disadvantages, and the decisions on their use ultimately depend on the purpose of the research. Achieving internal validity and generalizability/applicability will always be a balancing act, requiring researchers to make judgements about control, artificial vs. naturalistic contexts, causal relationships and the nature of an intervention. Increasingly, the shift towards evidence-based practice places demands on policy-makers and practitioners to employ experimental designs to delineate causal relationships and identify what works. As educational researchers, we should be aware of the strengths and limitations of experimental designs, and balance the need for randomization and causal inferences with the pedagogical nature of an intervention and the particularities of its context.

References

Berliner, D. C. (2002) 'Comment: educational research: the hardest science of all', *Educational Researcher*, 31(8): 18–20.

Brown, A. L. (1992) 'Design experiments: theoretical and methodological challenges in creating complex interventions in classroom settings', *The Journal of the Learning Sciences*, 2: 141–78.

Cobb, P. (2000) 'Conducting teaching experiments in collaboration with teachers', in A. E. Kelly and R. A. Lesh (eds) *Handbook of Research Design in Mathematics and Science Education*. Mahwah, NJ: Lawrence Erlbaum Associates.

Cobb, P. and Steffe, L. P. (1983) 'The constructivist researcher as teacher and model builder', *Journal for Research in Mathematics Education*, 14: 83–94.

Cobb, P., Confrey, J., diSessa, A., Lehrer, R. and Schauble, L. (2003) 'Design experiments in educational research', *Educational Researcher*, 32(1): 9–13.

Cook, T. D. and Sinha, V. (2006) 'Randomised experiments in educational research', in J. L. Green, G. Camilli, G. and P. B. Elmore (eds.), *Handbook of Complementary Methods in Education Research*. Mahwah, NJ: American Educational Research Association/Lawrence Erlbaum Associates.

Cresswell, J. W. (2005) *Educational Research*. Upper Saddle River, NJ: Pearson.

Design-Based Research Collaborative (2003) 'Design-based research: An emerging paradigm for educational inquiry', *Educational Researcher*, 32(1): 5–8.

Donahue, M., Hartas, D. and Cole, D. (1999) 'Research on interactions among oral language and emotional/behavioural disorders', in D. Rogers-Adkinson and P. Griffiths (eds) *Communication Disorders and Children with Psychiatric and Behavioural Disorders*. San Diego, CA: Singular Publishing Group.

Finn, J. and Achilles, C. (1990) 'Answers and questions about class size: a statewide experiment', *American Educational Research Journal*, 27(3): 557–77.

Finn, J. and Achilles, C. (1999) 'Tennessee's class size study: findings, implications, misconceptions', *Educational Evaluation and Policy Analysis*, 21(2): 97–109.

Gorard, S. (2001) *Quantitative Methods in Educational Research: The Role of Numbers Made Easy*. London: Continuum.

Gorard, S. with Taylor, C. (2004) Combining Methods in Educational and Social Research. Maidenhead: Open University Press.

Hobbs, R. (2004) 'Analysing advertising in the English language arts classroom: a quasi-experimental study', *Studies in Media and Information Literacy Education*, 4(2).

Medical Research Council (2000) *Good Research Practice*. London: Medical Research Council.

National Research Council (2002) *Scientific Research in Education*. Washington, DC: National Academy Press.

Punch, K. (2005) *Introduction to Social Research: Quantitative and Qualitative Approaches*. London: Sage.

Schoenfeld, A. H. (1979) 'Can heuristics be taught? The element of a theory, and a report on the teaching of general mathematical problem solving skills', in J. Lochhead and J. Clement (eds) *Cognitive Process Instruction*. Philadelphia, PA: Franklin Institute Press.

Schoenfeld, A. H. (1985) *Mathematical Problem Solving*. Orlando, FL: Academic.

Schoenfeld, A. H. (2006) 'Design experiments', in J. L. Green, G. Camilli and P. B. Elmore (eds) *Handbook of Complementary Methods in Education Research*. Mahwah, NJ: American Educational Research Association, Lawrence Erlbaum Associates.

Shadish, W. and Luellen, J. (2006) 'Quasi-experimental designs', in J. L. Green, G. Camilli and P. B. Elmore (eds) *Handbook of Complementary Methods in Education Research*. Mahwah, NJ: American Educational Research Association, Lawrence Erlbaum Associates.

Shavelson, R. J. and Towne, L. (2002) *Scientific Research in Education: Committee on Scientific Principles for Education Research*. Washington, DC: National Academies Press.

Shalveson, R. J., Phillips, D. C., Towne, L. and Feuer, M. J. (2003) On the science of education design studies, *Educational Researcher*, 32(1): 25–8.

Smith, F. and Hardman, F. (2000) 'Evaluating the effectiveness of the National Literacy Strategy: identifying indicators of success', *Educational Studies*, 26(3): 365–78.

Steffe, P. and Thompson, P. (2000) 'Teaching experiment methodology: underlying principles and essential elements', in A. E. Kelly and R. Lesh (eds) *Handbook of Research Design in Mathematics and Science Education*. Mahwah, NJ: Lawrence Erlbaum Associates.

Torgerson, C. and Torgerson, D. (2001) 'The need for randomised controlled trials in educational research', *British Journal of Educational Studies*, 49(3): 316–28.

Survey Research in Education 16
Dimitra Hartas

Chapter Outline

Introduction

Survey research is a non-experimental type of research, within which data are collected via self-reports, questionnaires or interviews. What makes it different from an experimental type of research is the lack of randomization (random selection and/or random assignment) and an experimental manipulation to explain cause-and-effect relationships. Notions of control, prediction and causality cannot be applied in survey research, in that we examine naturally occurring events, such as teacher attitudes towards inclusion or practitioners' views about curriculum differentiation, and provide descriptions of the characteristics (e.g. attitudes, beliefs, opinion, behaviour) of a population.

Historically, surveys were used to collect data on epidemics during the 1600s and also census and population surveys in the 1700s and 1800s (Converse 1987). Charles Booth's study on the social conditions in London in the 1800s is considered to be the first large-scale survey in social research, albeit limited in its scientific merit (Hutchinson and Lovell 2004). In 1934, in the USA, surveys received a widespread acceptance as a result of George Gallup's accurate prediction of Roosevelt's presidency based on the opinion of a relatively small portion of the population (Rea and Parker 1997). In the UK, large national surveys include the British Cohort Studies, the Millennium Cohort Study, British Social Attitudes (BSA) and the Young People's Social Attitudes (YPSA). Some of the main themes explored in these surveys include people's views of and attitudes towards friendships and social networks, civic participation and decision-making, family issues, education, social prejudice and trust.

By the end of this chapter, you should be able to:

- understand the scope of survey research
- appreciate the strengths and limitations of on-site and online survey research

- consider the phases in carrying out survey research
- explain the processes involved in questionnaire construction

Survey Research in Education

Research studies in education have used survey and correlational research designs extensively, because they offer flexibility and adaptability. They are especially useful when studying educational issues and events that are fluid and cannot be manipulated experimentally, due to practical and ethical reasons, involving multiple contexts and diverse participants. Surveys have been a widespread method for collecting data in higher education, with a staggering 82 per cent of the 209 studies reviewed using survey data (Hutchinson 2004).

The purpose of conducting surveys is to obtain people's views and attitudes about social situations by gathering descriptive, behavioural and attitudinal data (Rea and Parker 1997). There is a misconception about survey research as being simplistic, bias-ridden, easy to conduct and limited in its utility and applicability. These views have been stimulated by a plethora of poorly constructed and delivered surveys over the years. However, good surveys are capable of producing valid and meaningful results regarding educational issues, requiring an initial planning and consideration of the main principles that underlie research in education in general and survey item construction in particular.

Bateson (1984) discusses three conditions that are necessary to conduct survey research, namely, respondents' understanding, ability and willingness. It is common sense that respondents who misunderstand the survey items or cannot recall information will not offer meaningful and accurate answers. Most crucially, even if the respondents are capable of understanding the items, they may not be committed to the research, resulting in answering the questions carelessly and offering socially desirable answers or consistently neutral answers. Other factors such as cultural differences, respondents' language skills, translation of the responses and vested interests in completing a survey also influence the response rate and, subsequently, the validity of the results.

The assumptions of survey research

Survey research relies on a general assumption that the respondents' views and opinions agree with their actions. However, there are fundamental differences between expressing a view and acting upon it. Although respondents may answer truthfully, they may not be aware of the possibility of a dissonance between their beliefs and behaviour. Respondents may translate opinion into action indirectly, through the mechanisms of suppression and inaction, displacement into other arenas and rationalization (Hutchinson 2004). Moreover, respondents may not be willing to disclose their views about certain sensitive or controversial matters, or they may lack the informational resources (e.g. knowledge, language skills) and the opportunities or self-efficacy to act. Potential gaps between respondents' attitudes and behaviour are likely to affect the validity of a survey.

Another assumption that underlies survey research is that the sample constitutes a homogeneous group with comparable cases, where all respondents interpret the survey items in similar ways. This is an oversimplification of the complexity inherent in interpretation, assumptions and prior knowledge and the experience that people bring into a situation. Social reality is 'multi-nested' and cannot be reduced to a single nesting of people within regions (Oslen and Morgan 2005). Finally, the extent to which survey responses reflect the 'truth' as an objective entity, a normative understanding of events and relationships, or as an entity embedded in meanings constructed within a community of practice is debatable.

Types of Survey

The common methods for data collection in survey research include face-to face interviews, telephone surveys, post surveys and online surveys to mention but a few. For a detailed discussion on interview methods see Chapter 14. In this chapter, we discuss the types and the construction of questionnaires used in much survey research. In terms of design, there are two main types of survey research: *cross-sectional* and *longitudinal*. With a cross-sectional design, we collect data at one point in time, whereas a longitudinal design allows us to collect data and investigate a phenomenon over time (Cresswell 2005). Which type we use depends on the purpose of the research. With longitudinal designs, we map change or trends in a specific population or subpopulation over time, whereas with cross-sectional designs, we collect data to describe attitudes and needs at a point in time. Finally, with regard to the mode of administering a survey and collecting the responses, there are two types of survey: *on-site* (e.g. mail and telephone surveys) and *online* (eg, web-based surveys).

Telephone surveys

There are many advantages to telephone surveys in terms of time, money, resources and flexibility regarding data collection. Telephone surveys enable us to have a conversation with the respondents, which facilitates the process of building rapport and offers opportunities for stating the aims of a study and clarifying issues related to research ethics. Although not as personal as face-to-face interviews, telephone surveys offer a space for conversation. As with every method of data collection, telephone surveys present limitations, one of which is being able to access participants who may not have a phone. Although households without a telephone represent a small percentage of the population, the capacity to access all respondents in a sample brings important considerations with regard to ethics and social justice, especially when dealing with marginalized groups who may not have other opportunities to voice issues that matter to them. Other practical issues that emanate from doing a telephone survey involve interruptions of people's busy lives, which makes it less likely that they will commit their time and offer good quality information. We can get around this problem by sending a letter in advance to set up a convenient time for the telephone survey to take place.

Mail surveys

A major advantage of this type of survey is that it can reach a large number of respondents in geographically dispersed areas with the minimum cost to a researcher. Although cost-effective, mail surveys do not offer direct contact with the respondents, which may contribute to a reduced commitment to complete the survey, and thus low response rates. As discussed elsewhere in this volume, the problem with low responses is response bias in the results, which can limit the quality of the data. Mail surveys can work well if they are constructed according to the rules described in this chapter (e.g. clear, well-worded items, short, easy to complete), and if, through a cover letter and other means, we are able to motivate the respondents to offer their views.

Online surveys

Increasingly, online surveys are gaining ground in the education research community. In an era of globalization, the need to internationalize research findings is pressing. Conducting international research requires methods of data collection that allow access to a geographically dispersed population at a reasonable cost to the researcher. Online surveys have the potential to reach a large number of respondents from different countries and special groups such as individuals with a disability, or marginalized groups (e.g. excluded pupils). Online surveys can supply data faster than other survey methods, guaranteeing informed consent, confidentiality and anonymity (Nesbary 2000).

Although there are many advantages in using online surveys, certain issues such as sampling, identity of respondents, relevance of items and response bias need to be considered. As with on-site surveys (e.g. telephone and mail surveys), online surveys have been criticized for including nonprobabilistic samples, such as convenience samples (e.g. volunteers). Using nonprobabilistic samples does not mean that the respondents do not represent the population, they may or may not, but we have no way of knowing. A question that arises is whether the respondents vary in a systematic way. Volunteers, for example, tend to have certain characteristics (e.g. motivation, interest) which may differentiate them from the rest of the population, introducing a systematic variation, which is likely to bias the findings.

Furthermore, with online surveys, the respondents' identity and frame of reference cannot be ascertained, raising concerns about the relevance of the respondents' characteristics and attributes to the survey and overall research purpose. Problems such as identity fraud (e.g. multiple submissions of a questionnaire by a single respondent) can potentially reduce the validity of the results. The decision to use on-site or online surveys should be based on the purpose and goals of the research and a careful balancing of the advantages and disadvantages of each method.

Phases of Survey Research

Initial planning

As with other types of educational research, the planning stage is crucial. The research questions should be clarified and mapped onto the main aims of the study. Lack of a matching between the research questions and the intended population are major pitfalls in survey research. To avoid this, a thorough review of the literature is needed to enable us identify the main issues and set the theoretical and methodological framework for survey research. A theoretical appreciation of the field of study is crucial to enable the transformation of theoretical constructs to questionnaire items and, ultimately, to variables. Clarity about the respondents' frame of reference is crucial to enable us construct survey items that can be easily understood by them. As Jaeger comments 'you don't want every respondent to give you the same answer, but you do want every respondent to hear or read the same question' (1997: 461). To this end, it is importance to define the constructs and delineate their dimensions, such as self-esteem, to ensure consistency and conceptual coherence across items and the variables that emerge from them.

At the initial planning stage, the type of survey research needs to be addressed. Determining the characteristics of the population and sample is part of conceptualizing the research questions and research design. Identification of the population and decisions regarding sampling should take place from the outset to ensure the feasibility of the study. Important considerations about who the respondents are, how they will be selected, how many are needed and what the manner of survey administration will be (on-site or online) take place at this stage. From the target population, we select a number of respondents through probabilistic sampling (e.g. random or stratified random), if we can access large groups as in national surveys, or, most commonly, non-probabilistic sampling (e.g. convenience and purposive sampling) (see Chapter 4 for sampling techniques). The decisions about these matters should mirror the general aims and the research questions identified at the planning stage.

The number of respondents required mainly depends on the type of the statistical analyses of the quantitative data (certain statistical analyses require a minimum sample size) and the scope of the survey research. It is quite common for survey response rates to be around 20–30 per cent, which means sending out five times as many questionnaires as we want returning. For example, if we want to obtain 60 responses we need to send out 300 questionnaires (see Chapter 4 for information on sample size).

Survey item construction

Questionnaires are the most widely used method for data-gathering in survey research. In this chapter, the development of survey items focuses on questionnaire construction. Self-administered questionnaires require clarity in the use of language and structure, in terms of:

- deciding the type and format of the survey items
- developing the content of the survey items in a way that is consistent with research purpose and questions (content/construct validity)
- organizing/sequencing the survey items

Question type and format

Broadly, there are four types of question that are included in a questionnaire: knowledge,

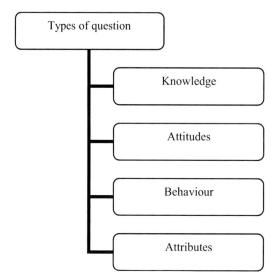

Figure 16.1 Types of question

attitudes, behaviour and attributes. Knowledge questions refer to what people know, their awareness about an issue (e.g. 'Are you aware of the Disability and Discrimination Act?'). Attitudes questions refer to people's opinions, beliefs and ideals about the issues under investigation (e.g. 'What are your views about young people's decision-making regarding educational matters?'). Behaviour questions address what people actually do, their observable actions (e.g. 'Have you participated in a charity event over the last year?'). Finally, attributes questions refer to what people are and what they have in terms of specific characteristics such as demographic information, gender, age or professional status.

'Format' refers to the way questions are presented. There are two broad types, open-ended and close-ended questions. With open-ended questions, the answer is not constrained by a fixed set of possible responses; instead, we invite the respondents to provide an answer without offering options or predefined categories from which to choose. Open-ended questions invite a completely unstructured response in terms of a narrative account or in the form of word association, sentence/story completion and a thematic appreciation test. For example, a completely unstructured question might be 'What makes a good teacher?', where the responded is expected to offer a narrative account of what makes a good teacher. The same question may be answered through words being presented with the respondent mentioning the first word that comes to mind (word association). Or, the respondent may be asked to complete an incomplete sentence (e.g. 'The most important consideration in my decision to become a teacher is . . .') or complete an incomplete story. Finally, with the use of a thematic appreciation test, respondents explain a picture or tell a story about what they think is happening in the picture.

On the other hand, with close-ended questions, respondents choose an answer from the response categories we have provided. Types of close-ended question typically used in questionnaires are:

- dichotomous questions
- multiple-choice questions
- rank-order questions
- matrix questions
- contingency questions
- scaled questions

With dichotomous questions, the respondent answers with a 'yes' or a 'no', ticking one of two mutually exclusive categories. For example:

What is your gender?
- *Male*
- *Female*

With multiple-choice questions, respondents have several options from which to choose. For example:

In your view, what is disability? (circle as many choices as appropriate)
- *the outcome of posing barriers in the physical environment (e.g., lack of lifts and ramps, narrow pavements)*
- *the outcome of societal barriers (e.g. prejudice, discrimination, stigma)*
- *the outcome of having limited access to good quality education and employment opportunities*
- *the outcome of having a medical and/or a mental health condition*
- *the outcome of a culture that places a great emphasis on the 'perfect body'*
- *the implications of socioeconomic disadvantage (e.g. homelessness, poverty, poor education)*
- *other factors/situations (please write in the space below)*

With rank-order questions, a respondent is asked to rank the responses that are already provided in terms of to sorting them in the order of 'most to least serious' or 'most to least important'. For example:

Please, rank the implications of disability on individuals (1 = 'least important' to 5 = 'most important')
- *social isolation and loneliness*
- *limited access to the physical environment*
- *limited participation in cultural life (e.g., going to cinema, clubs, concerts)*
- *limited participation in political life (e.g. voting, organizing charity events)*
- *self-doubt and low self-esteem*
- *negative self-image*
- *parents having feelings of loss and grief*
- *limited employment opportunities (e.g. restricted promotion, lower than standard salary)*
- *poverty*
- *other (please explain)*

With matrix questions, we can ask several questions that have the same set of answer categories by forming a matrix of items and answers. For example:

From your experience, as a person with disability or a care/guardian of a person with disability, to what extent (please tick the box)

	A great deal	Somewhat	Slightly	Not at all	Do not know
Is the physical environment disabling?					
Are societal attitudes disabling?					
Are medical or a mental health conditions disabling?					
Is popular culture disabling?					
Are socioeconomic disadvantages disabling?					

With contingency questions, a question is answered only if the respondent gives a particular response to a previous question (filter question). This avoids asking respondents questions that do not apply to them. For example:

Do you use the internet for homework support?
[Before asking this question we may ask 'Do you use the internet?' If Yes, then ask 'Do you use the internet for homework support?']

With scaled questions, the responses are graded on a continuum. For example:

Rate the effectiveness of a specific teaching strategy on a scale from 1 to 10 (1 being the least effective and 10 being the most effective).

Another type of scale is the Likert scale, which, typically, offers five responses, including a 'neutral' or 'don't know' response. For example:

To what extend do you feel that students benefit from PE lessons?
(Respond by circling the number that represents your view)
1 = A great extent, 2 = Somewhat, 3 = Slightly, 4 = Not at all, 5 = Do not know

1   2   3   4   5

There are certain considerations to bear in mind when constructing Likert-scale measures. These are:

- the items in the questionnaire must be statements and not questions
- the items must all relate to the same object
- the items that make up the scale should be interrelated, which is to ensure the internal consistency (reliability) of the scale (Bryman 2004).

There are advantages and disadvantages with both open-ended and close-ended questions, and the choice of a format depends on the research aims. For exploratory research, open-ended questions can be useful to allow important issues to emerge in order to identify the parameters of an inquiry. In contrast, once the field of research has been established and we want to collect data on specific issues, close-ended questions are likely to offer a sharper focus.

The content of survey items

The content of the questions should be developed in a way as to reflect/capture the research questions and aims. The writing style should be conversational, yet concise, free of jargon and accurate. The language used in target vocabulary, sentence structure and grammar should be at the respondents' level. We need to consider the respondents' ability, interests and motivation, and their frame of reference. Specifically, the respondents' background and how it may affect their interpretation of the questions, and whether they have enough information or expertise to answer the questions accurately. We should always ask whether an item is really necessary in that questionnaires containing many questions tend to attract a low response rate. Most crucially, we need to ensure that the questions are relevant and embedded in the research context. Some examples of common problems with item construction in survey research are presented in Table 16.1.

In the current climate of internationalization of educational research, the translation of questionnaires to different languages raises concerns about the content and meaning of the questions. The translation of survey items can be challenging, considering that linguistic expression is laden with cultural meanings and interpretations. With this in mind, we should consider three dimensions of survey translation, namely, the semantic equivalence, conceptual equivalence and normative equivalence of items.

A semantic equivalence is sought through the translation/back translation method, having independent translators translate from one language to another, and then back again, to check whether the original and retranslated items remain the same. A conceptual equivalence may be sought by statistical methods such as factor analysis (see Chapter 24), demonstrating that items in one language version have the same factor structure (load similarly on underlying factors) as in another language version. However, Behling and Law (2000) recommend caution in the use of statistical tests, urging that theory should be used instead to validate each language version independently. A normative equivalence requires such strategies as developing close relations with the respondents, using trusted agents for interviewing, providing assurance of anonymity or confidentiality, and pilot testing extensively (Garson 2006).

The layout of survey items

The organization of questionnaire items is important to ensure clarity and cohesiveness. A brief introductory statement is useful; this can be included in the questionnaire itself (in case introductory letters go adrift). In the introduction, we state briefly the importance of the participants and the value of their responses, the purpose of the research and the ethical considerations in terms of anonymity and confidentiality. Contact and return information, including return date, should be stated in the covering letter. To establish credibility, we need to state our professional affiliation and the research funding body (if there is one). It is good practice to offer the respondents the opportunity to contact us if they wish to be informed about the research findings. Box 16.1 presents a brief description of the components of a covering letter (or an introductory statement).

Table 16.1 Common problems with item construction in questionnaires

Example of a poorly constructed question	Problem (content, format, type)	Example of an improved question
Do you agree with the behaviour policies in today's *failing* schools?	False premises	Do you agree with the behaviour policies in the current climate of school performance?
Do you *disagree* that teachers should *not* offer pastoral support to students?	Use double negative	Do you agree that teachers should offer pastoral support to students?
Do you agree that the early years curriculum is play-orientated *and* stresses parental involvement?	Double-barreled question	i) Do you agree that the early years curriculum is play-orientated? ii) Do you agree that the early years curriculum stresses parental involvement?
Assuming that pupils are retained, do you agree that some students' self-esteem may suffer?	Hypothetical question	How, and to what extent, has disability changed your *worldview*?
How, and to what extent, has disability changed your views about friendships?	Vagueness	
Do you *agree* that *disrespectful* students should be excluded from schools?	Emotional language, prestige bias and leading question	
Do pupils with autism have difficulties with the *pragmatic aspect* of language?	Use of jargon or technical language	Do pupils with autism have difficulties with using language socially?
What is your age range? • 0–18 • 18–25 • 26–35 • 35 +	Response overlap (not mutually exclusive categories)	What is your age range? • 0–18 • 19–25 • 26–35 • 36 +
To what extent have people's views about '*normality*' changed over the years?	Ambiguity and confusion about the meanings of 'normality'	To what extent have people's views about able-bodied and disabled individuals changed over the years?
What is the nature of your disability? Physical impairment Hearing impairment Visual impairment Emotional/social difficulties Mental health difficulties Learning Difficulties	Categories are not inclusive (respondents cannot find themselves in any of the given categories)	What is the nature of your disability? Physical impairment Hearing impairment Visual impairment Emotional/social difficulties Mental health difficulties Learning Difficulties Other (please specify)
To what extent do you use the internet for long-distance learning (e-learning)	Not all respondents can answer the question – filter is needed	Do you use the internet? • Yes • No If Yes, to what extent do you use it for long-distance learning (e-learning)?
To what extend do you feel that students benefit from PE lessons? • Very important • Important • Little importance	Mismatch between the question and the responses	To what extent do you feel that students benefit from PE lessons? • To a great extent • Somewhat • Slightly • Not at all

In terms of sequencing, the questionnaire items should be ordered to flow logically from general to specific themes, from factual and behavioural to attitudinal and opinion questions, and from the least sensitive to the most sensitive questions. It is advisable to address important questions early rather than late in a questionnaire and avoid controversial questions, especially at the start of the questionnaire. It is also good practice to place open-ended questions that require narrative responses at the end of the questionnaire, and ensure that previous questions will not bias later questions. The organization can be improved by clustering items into 'natural' groupings that share conceptual similarities. Finally, in terms of style, avoid cluttering the form with unnecessary headings and designs; the title and date, and the numbering of individual questions offer sufficient information to aid data entry and analysis.

Box 16.1 Cover letter

Whether you use a separate cover letter or an introductory statement written on the questionnaire itself, it should include the following components:

- *Purpose:* it is crucial you describe the purpose of the survey research with clarity, and in a way that takes into account the respondents' frame of reference. In so doing, you place respondents in the context of the study, to maximize the relevance of their responses.
- *Ethical considerations:* it is important to assure respondents about maintaining the anonymity of their responses. You may state that the information provided will not be shared with others (confidentiality) or will be shared in a way that does not identify the respondent (anonymity). This is an important consideration, in that depending on the research purpose, you need to decide whether you can report certain findings that may identify the respondents. If the respondents are to remain anonymous then the survey items should be written in such a way that respondents cannot be identified from the responses they offer. Finally, the covering letter should stress the voluntary nature of respondents' involvement.
- *Contact information:* accurate contact information should be provided as well as the researchers' professional affiliation, to offer credibility to the study.
- *Return date:* the return date should be stated in **bold letters** and addressed and stamped envelopes should be provided for mail surveys.

Piloting a questionnaire

Piloting is an important phase of questionnaire construction to identify problems and refine the items. Important aspects to be checked during the pilot phase are content, flow and naturalness of the sections; the order of the questions; respondents' misunderstandings, typically expressed by skipping an item or consistently offering an inappropriate response; timing; respondent interest and attention; and respondents' well-being (sensitive nature of items). It is advisable to ask the pilot participants to write down any comments they have regarding the nature, appropriateness and sequencing of survey items.

Survey item analysis

A survey item analysis refers to a questionnaire analysis. The quantitative data from a questionnaire can be analysed by employing a wide range of statistical procedures, from descriptive statistics to correlational and multiple regression analyses. With survey research, we examine relationships between variables, instead of comparing groups, as is the case with experimental and quasi-experimental designs. Estimating variance within the context of survey research can be achieved through certain statistical procedures: namely, correlation and regression (see Chapter 23). This variance refers to the difference observed/measured in the outcome variable that is 'explained' or 'accounted for' (and not caused) by some other variables selected, based on previous theory.

In this chapter we will not go into detail with regard to the type of analysis that can be conducted on survey data. However, we need to employ certain analyses to establish the construct validity and reliability as internal consistency of the questionnaire (see Chapter 4 for more details on reliability and validity). Statistically, by calculating the Cronbach's alpha reliability coefficient we can ascertain whether a group of items measure the same underlying construct (the closer the coefficient is to 1 the higher the reliability is).

Another statistical technique for testing whether a set of items measures the same construct is *exploratory factor analysis* (see Chapter 24). With a factor analysis, we can determine all the factors/constructs that underpin a set of survey items. However, it is important to note that the conceptual work of developing survey items from theoretical constructs is very important and needs to take place *before* doing a confirmatory factor analysis, which means that the theoretical model and the subsequent constructs are specified a priori rather than relying on a computer to cluster items together and identify the underlying factors. This is to ensure that item construction has a strong theoretical basis. If we can justify that certain items can be clustered together, then we can use a confirmatory factor analysis to test whether the suggested construct actually fits the theoretical model within which we work.

Summary

Survey research is not new; it has been used for a couple of centuries to explore of educational and social phenomena. It is multi-purpose, flexible, adaptable and applicable. It is typically employed to describe the attitudes and trends in the public's views about important issues such as disability rights or youth participation in civic society. Survey research is also used to map the needs of certain groups, delineate opinions about educational policy matters and evaluate the implementation and effectiveness of educational programmes or artefacts in schools. Questionnaires are a useful tool for data collection in survey research in that they are versatile in obtaining descriptions of the respondents' characteristics and views. A major criticism of survey research is its reliance on self-report measures, and subsequently, on the integrity, interest and motivation of the respondents to provide accurate accounts. As with all research methods, there are advantages and limitations, and our decision to choose a survey research design should be driven by the aims and scope of our research.

Box 16.2 Checklist: survey research

Here is a summary of the main points to consider as you go through the phases of survey research.

1 Define your research aims and questions and offer a rationale for using a survey research design.
2 Decide/explain the type of the survey (e.g. cross-sectional or longitudinal) to match the research aims/questions.
3 Identify the population and specify the sampling procedures (e.g. random or non-probabilistic sampling).
4 Clarify the sampling technique, decide on the sample size and explain the basis on which you chose the sample from the target population.
5 Identify the administration procedures, including collection of the responses (e.g. mail surveys, email/web questionnaires, telephone surveys or face-to-face interviews).
6 Construct the items of a questionnaire (and try to avoid the pitfalls described in Table 16.1).
7 Consider issues regarding construct validity and reliability.
8 Run a pilot test to refine/calibrate the survey items.
9 Employ data analyses that map onto the research purpose and aims.
10 Present the results in a sound and ethically acceptable manner.

References

Bateson, N. (1984) *Data Construction in Social Surveys*. Winchester, MA: Allen and Unwin.

Behling, O. and Law, K. S. (2000) *Translating Questionnaires and other Research Instruments*. Thousand Oaks, CA: Sage.

Bryman, A. (2004) *Social Research Methods*, 2nd edn. Oxford: Oxford University Press.

Converse, J. M. (1987) *Survey* Research in the United States: Roots and Emergence, 1890–1960. Berkeley, CA: University of California Press.

Cresswell, J. W. (2005) *Educational Research*. Upper Saddle River, NJ: Pearson.

Denscombe, M. (2003) *The Good Research Guide*. Maidenhead: Open University Press.

Garson, G. D. (2006). *Quantitative Research in Public Administration, Section Reliability Analysis*, http://www2.chass.ncsu.edu/garson/pa765/reliab.htm, acessed 7 February 2006.

Hutchinson, S. (2004) Survey research, in K. B. deMarrais and S. D. Lapan (eds) *Foundations for Research: Methods of Inquiry in Education and the Social Sciences*. Mahwah, NJ: Lawrence Erlbaum Associates.

Hutchinson, S. and Lovell, C. (2004) 'A review of methodological characteristics of research published in key journals in higher education: implications for graduate research training', *Research in Higher Education*, 45(4): 383–403.

Jaeger, R.M. (1997) Survey methods in education, in M. R. Jaeger (ed.) *Contemporary Methods for Research in Education*. Washington, DC: American Educational Research Association.

Nesbary, D. (2000) *Survey Research and the World Wide Web*. Upper Saddle River, NJ: Allyn & Bacon.

Oslen, W. and Morgan, J. (2005) 'A critical epistemology of analytical statistics: addressing the sceptical realist', *Journal for the Theory of Social Behaviour*, 35(3): 255–84.

Rea, L. M. and Parker, R. A. (1997) *Designing and Conducting Research Surveys*. San Francisco: Jossey Bass.

17

Evaluation Research in Education

Dimitra Hartas

Introduction

Evaluation research has developed over the years as an interdisciplinary field. In the last two decades, evaluation studies of educational programmes and policy initiatives have become widespread (Lapan 2004). Broadly, evaluation is defined as 'any effort to increase human effectiveness through systematic data-based inquiry' (Patton 1990: 11).

In education, evaluation refers to a process whereby we appraise the worth of an educational activity in a systematic manner, by delineating its goals and objectives and setting criteria and standards against which we assess its merit.

This chapter discusses evaluation research and the challenges it poses and offers examples to illustrate the evaluation of an educational programme and a policy initiative in terms of their aims, implementation and operation, their impact on users and their effectiveness and merit in achieving standards. Participants' views and cultures, mixed methodologies and the dilemmas of a democratic evaluation are discussed in the context of two evaluation studies to illustrate the processes involved in evaluation research in education.

By the end of this chapter, you should be able to:

- explain the different models of evaluation, participatory evaluationin particular, and the dilemmas that evaluators are likely to encounter
- outline the structure of evaluation research in education in terms of its purpose and dimensions – i.e. implementation, context and the human factor
- delineate the cycles of evaluation research, namely, setting the criteria and evaluation questions, deciding upon the methodology, delineating outcomes and reflecting on standards
- describe mixed-method designs
- understand participatory evaluation, power structures and the diversity in participants' views and intentions

Evaluation Research

Although evaluation studies in education share many elements with educational and social research in general (e.g. mixed methodologies), evaluation research is considered to be distinct from academic research. Evaluation research has a pragmatic focus in terms of solving practical problems, with the outcomes being utilized by the sponsors, primary users, evaluators and the public at large (Rossi and Freeman 1993; Kelly 2007). Scriven separates evaluation from social science in that it 'identifies relevant values or standards that apply [...] performs empirical investigation using techniques from the social sciences and then integrates conclusions with the standards into an overall evaluation. Social science research, by contrast, does not aim for or achieve evaluative conclusions' (2003: 1).

This view of evaluation research raises questions about the role and nature of evaluation in education. Are evaluation and research in education distinct entities? Does research in education aim for evaluative conclusions? As the landscape of educational research is shifting, the distinction between academic and applied research becomes less clear. This has implications with regard to user-stakeholder relationships, methodology, the role of the context and participants, ethical standards and applicability of research. To understand the nature and role of evaluation studies, three perspectives have been offered, namely, *technocratic*, *political* and *cultural* (House 1979; Stufflebeam *et al.* 2000). A technocratic perspective views evaluation programme as a means to achieving a desirable end, and change as a linear and rational progress. It accepts that intervention and the subsequent educational/social changes lead to positive outcomes and, ultimately, enhance people's lives.

Within a technocratic viewpoint, the evaluation of an educational programme is instrumental, mainly focusing on articulating changes in classroom practice. This view is simplistic because it places much emphasis on output in comparison with the input and understands added value in measurable terms. It hardly questions 'Whose added value?', 'For whom are the changes desirable?' or 'How are the primary users to benefit from it?', and it does not consider unexpected outcomes and reflexivity in terms of critiquing the political structures and ethics that surround evaluation. The technocratic view has been sustained by a managerialist culture in education, and by notions of performativity (see Ball 1999), and has stimulated debates about the outcome-orientated nature of such programmes (Stufflebeam *et al.* 2000), and 'the belief that welfare can be improved through planned change' (Kushner and Adelman 2006: 714).

Evaluation is a complex process that involves people's experiences, decision-making and judgements within diverse political and cultural contexts (Stake 1967). From a political perspective, educational programmes are viewed as sites for political action, which involve consensus but also dissent, conflict and compromise. From a cultural perspective, an educational programme should fit into people's lives and account for their experiences and local knowledge by engaging with pluralism, difference and diversity (Kushner and Adelman 2006). A cultural/political view of a programme evaluation raises questions about democracy and decision-making over social change, whether change is desirable and who decides about its desirability. An evaluation of such programmes is expected to take on board the contested nature of change and its implications for people's lives.

Evaluation should be 'responsive', stressing its participatory and dialogic nature where the views and experiences of the primary users play an important role in evaluating a programme and its outcomes (Stake 1967). Involving users and stakeholders in evaluation enables a dynamic adaptation to organizational changes (Cousins and Earl 1992). A distinction is drawn between a participatory and a stakeholder-orientated evaluation, with the former involving primary users in all evaluation cycles – i.e. from formulating the questions to the data collection and the dissemination of the findings, and advocating joint responsibility and mutual accountability – whereas the latter prioritizes the stakeholders' agenda with a minimum input from the end-user. A participatory evaluation relies on an ongoing dialogue and responsiveness between stakeholders and users, and encourages the formation of communities of practice, with organizational learning becoming an integral part of the evaluation. The political and cultural perspective has construed evaluation as a site where democracy is practised by accounting for difference, equality, advocacy and human rights, and from where 'the evaluator emerges as a practitioner of democracy' (Kushner and Adelman, 2006: 718).

The dilemmas of evaluation research

Over the last two decades, many competing views of evaluation have been offered, culminating in postmodern views of evaluation as a site for scepticism and dissent (see Stronach 1997). Postmodern views of evaluation refute assumptions about causal predictions, determinism and truth-seeking as an objective endeavour, offering a relativistic view of different actor's contributions and stories. The adoption of a relativistic framework in evaluation research is however considered to be less conducive to stimulating action in the public domain. We need, instead, to 'reconcile iconoclastic assumptions' that underpin evaluation research (Kushner and Adelman 2006: 719), and to engage with the dilemmas towards difference, social change and social inequality to ensure that the rights of users, evaluators and stakeholders are not competing against each other. It is also important to ensure that change benefits the primary users' lives and that advocacy permeates all the cycles of an evaluation, especially when encountering difference and the notion of a social contract – i.e. citizens' rights and corresponding responsibilities. Goodhart (2004) refers to these dilemmas as 'progressive dilemmas' in that they emerge from discourses and practices on diversity and social justice.

A 'dilemmatic' approach towards evaluation research is likely to encourage an open discussion about the political values and conflicts and the social/cultural context of an evaluation to move Stake's 'responsive evaluation' to a more egalitarian field. An important function of democracy is to support citizens to become involved in policy decision-making, policy implementation and policy evaluation (MacDonald and Norris, 1981). A participatory evaluation has the potential to enable citizens, be they stakeholders, primary users or evaluators, to engage with policy implementation and evaluation. Dealing with the dilemmas of ethics and democratic participation, as well as balancing personal and professional interests and rights and obligations, is an inherent part of an evaluation. Evaluation research should challenge assumptions of the norm as being given (and its implications regarding the desirability of action and social change); neutrality as the absence of other perspectives (by considering the multiple perspectives that individuals bring into an evaluation); and the status quo as being natural and unchanged (by questioning the changes that a programme intends to make in some aspects of the status quo and not in others). Finally, it should challenge the assumption that any change is good for the end-users.

A participatory evaluation engages with these assumptions and the dilemmas that emanate from them, and considers the resource implications that underpin programmes or initiatives, which are typically funded by the tax payers' money and are expected to be responsive to the needs of the public at large. Most importantly, what makes an evaluation democratic is its critical stance towards outcomes and the capacity to distinguish solutions that may mask or sidetrack the real issues from knowledge and insight that propel social action with a genuine transformative potential.

Evaluation Studies in Education: A Conceptual Framework

Nevo's evaluation framework was adapted to consider the purpose and dimensions of evaluation in education and delineate its cycles (1989). This framework does not claim to provide a blueprint on how to design and conduct evaluation studies in education, nor does it suggest that the described phases occur in a linear fashion; the process is, rather, iterative. This framework is to guide the steps that we are likely to take to establish the *purpose/aims* (i.e. accountability, development /refinement, knowledge generation) and delineate the *dimensions* (i.e. implementation, context and human factors) of an evaluation. It also describes the *evaluation cycles*, including setting the evaluation criteria and questions; justifying the methodology used; developing an interpretative framework to articulate impact/outcomes; and, finally, discussing standards (see Figure 17.1).

Aims of evaluation research in education

The aims of evaluation research are diverse, including appraising educational programmes, interventions or policy initiatives, increasing effectiveness in managing people and resources, stimulating changes in organizational cultures, developing community-based initiatives and meeting the needs of primary users (Kelly 2007).

Broadly, evaluation research in education has three main aims. The first is to evaluate the mechanisms and processes of a programme or activity over time to ensure accountability through the provision of evidence about the benefits of the object of evaluation. The second aim is, through the cycles of evaluation, to inform the development of a programme in terms of calibrating ideas about design and implementation. The third aim is to generate knowledge and articulate insights gained from the evaluation to support further knowledge generation.

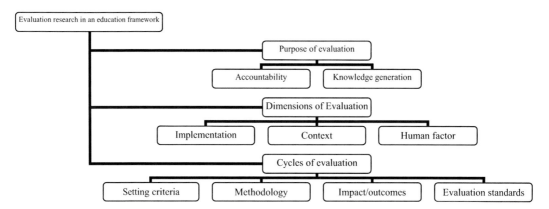

Figure 17.1 Evaluation research in education

Theoretically, a broad distinction is made between the aims of a formative and a summative evaluation or, as Nevo (1983) describes it, proactive and retroactive evaluation. A proactive evaluation is to facilitate decision-making and influence the development of programmes, policy initiatives or artefacts. A retroactive evaluation aims at providing feedback for accountability purposes, selection and further development of a programme. These aims mirror a formative and summative evaluation, with the former capturing the ongoing, fluid nature of a programme, and the latter accumulating the evidence regarding its worth. Nevo (1989) adds the sociopolitical aims of an evaluation in terms of motivating its primary users, promoting public relations and raising awareness about issues deemed to be important by the stakeholders.

At a practical level, the aims of an evaluation are to ascertain whether a programme meets the needs of its users, contributes insights about its future management, satisfies accountability demands and makes judgements about whether it should continue, expand or be curtailed (Freeman *et al.* 2003). Educational programmes do not necessarily have to meet all these aims, in that some programmes and initiatives may emphasize knowledge generation rather than accountability. Moreover, these aims are not mutually exclusive, in that understanding how something works and altering its workings to achieve maximum impact can stimulate change. The purpose of evaluation studies should be delineated from the outset by asking questions that involve exploration, explanation and transformation, such as 'who wants to know what' which will help you to plan the 'how' and understand the 'why' or the mechanisms that underpin a programme in order to alter its functioning.

An important principle of evaluation is not to assume that the programme's aims and objectives are coherent and agreed upon by all involved. Kushner and Adelman (2006) differentiate between coherence and consistency, pointing out that the confusion between the two is common. It is often assumed that the views of all participants have to be coherent for a programme to achieve consistency. A programme can be consistent in its functioning and phases of implementation, however the individuals involved may bring diverse perspectives, aims and aspirations that do not necessarily form a cohesive whole. Programmes, from their initial conception and development to evaluation, involve people (e.g. clients/users, sponsors, government, competitors, managers) with multiple interests and intents, who are equally likely to reach consensus or offer competing views.

In evaluation research, notions of voice and participation should prioritize inquiry, especially as we tackle complex issues such as effectiveness, impact, transformation and change in people's lives (Kelly 2007). Evaluation research should aim at developing models to explain how educational programmes or policy initiatives work, the changes that are required to maximize their impact, and whether they function according to egalitarian principles. Most crucially, an evaluation should ask questions about the desirability of change and the extent to which changes occur as a result of democratic processes that take on board the 'iconoclastic assumptions' that underpin evaluation.

Dimensions of evaluation in education

There are three important dimensions in any evaluation, namely implementation, context and the human factor.

Implementation

Implementation refers to decisions regarding the resources required to carry out the evaluation, timelines, the structure of the activities, the logistics of user involvement, as well as issues of efficiency and cost-effectiveness. A successful implementation of an evaluation relies on understanding the components of a programme or policy initiative, and the intentions of the participants and those involved in setting up the activities, including equality of opportunity and negotiation of access with gatekeepers.

Context

The dynamics of the physical, social/cultural and political context of an evaluation have the potential to influence its outcomes. Programmes have their own culture in terms of rules and patterns of interaction, hierarchy, tensions between personal and professional goals/aspirations and vested interests (Kushner and Adelman 2006). As an important part of an evaluation, we need to delineate the physical, social and cultural dimensions of its context, and identify its facilitative and hindering features in relation to the aims of the evaluation. The following questions are important in delineating the context of an evaluation in education:

- What is the policy/legislative context of the intervention?
- How do the primary users interact with each other socially and politically?
- Do the primary users and stakeholders form a cohesive group?
- Has the physical and social context changed to accommodate a programme?
- Has the programme changed to fit into the context and people's lives?

Human factor

Kushner and Adelman (2006) observed that people fit into programmes but programmes also fit into their lives. A programme evaluation should start from this premise and examine the human factor in terms of people's views about a programme and how well the programme fits with their lives. 'Human factor' refers to the roles, responsibilities, actions and degrees of involvement of primary users, stakeholders and evaluators, and the extent to which their voices are genuinely heard. In evaluation studies, several terms have been used to describe individuals and groups that have a stake in appraising the worth of a programme or policy, including 'stakeholders', 'primary users' or what Cronbach (1980) calls a 'policy-shaping community'.

The human factor is an important element in an evaluation in that the characteristics, attitudes, motivation and changes of behaviour of the stakeholders, evaluators, decision-makers and primary users (i.e. individuals for whom the intervention is designed) influence the nature and outcomes of the evaluation. Understanding the social dynamics enables us to delineate the required changes and, most crucially, the mechanisms that underlie these changes in terms of who decides upon the nature and ethics of public action towards social transformation. The interaction between stakeholders, users/benefactors and evaluators is an interaction between scientific and political communities (Wingens 1990). Much current evaluation of social and educational programmes tends to be unidimensional in that it often focuses on how well people fit into a programme and not the other way around.

As evaluators, we need to identify the benefactors or primary users and stakeholders of an evaluation, and through partnerships, encourage them to offer their views to delineate the nature and outcomes of an intervention. A partnership can achieve multiple outcomes. First, it clarifies the requirements of an organization, its individual users and funding bodies, enabling evaluators to ask the right questions. Secondly, it builds bridges with the participants to increase their commitment to the project. Thirdly, it maximizes the impact of an evaluation in that users who feel part of a project are more likely to take on board the recommendations and insights generated. Finally, partnerships encourage a participatory evaluation, which changes the centre of control and the nature of power relationships between the users/benefactors and stakeholders. A participatory evaluation is likely to make relationships more transparent and the structure of evaluation conducive for the participants to exercise agency. Given the increasingly political nature of evaluation in education, questions of credibility, bias/vested interests should be discussed in a context of partnership and participation (Garaway 2004).

Garaway defends participatory evaluation along the lines of 'utilisation, empowerment, creation of an interactive organisational learning environment and establishing partners' (2004: 265). These principles set the framework for participants' roles and responsibilities, maximizing their personal/professional investment. As Whyte (1991: 21) comments, 'science is not achieved by distancing oneself from the world; as generations of scientists know, the greatest conceptual and methodological challenge comes from engagement with the world'. Perhaps the same view can be applied to evaluation research.

The cycles of evaluation research in education

Evaluation criteria and questions

The evaluation criteria define what constitutes evidence in evaluation research. Different types of information that can function as evidence include descriptive information, information that is responsive to concerns raised by the primary users/stakeholders, information about relevant issues, information about values and information about standards (Cuba and Lincoln 1981).

Setting the criteria for judging the worth of an educational programme or policy is not easy. Broadly, the criteria should map onto the goals/objectives of an evaluation, based on the needs of its primary users and stakeholders, and the culture and economic parameters of an organization. The evaluator is expected to justify the choice of criteria to ensure that they account for the local context, values and diverse needs of the participants.

Setting the criteria against which we measure the impact of a programme is an important step towards the formulation of evaluation questions. Evaluation questions typically cover the nature and structure of a programme, the similarities and differences between the programme being evaluated and other similar programmes, the needs of the primary users and stakeholders and their views about impact and effectiveness (see Box 17.1).

Box 17.1 Evaluation questions

- What are the components of this educational programme?
- What is the nature of the intervention?
- What is its policy/legislative context?
- Does the programme or policy initiative occupy a unique territory, a niche?
- What are the differences and similarities with other programmes/policies?
- What are the users' views about effectiveness and impact (need to distinguish between impact and effectiveness)?
- How is effectiveness defined in the context of this evaluation?
- What are the outcomes at an individual and collective level (organizational institutional, policy, practice)?
- What are the benefits of the programme, and who benefits, directly or indirectly?
- Has the programme shown any potential for positive social change?

Methodology (mixed approaches)

Evaluation research involves mixed methods for data collection and analysis, typically using both qualitative and quantitative methods of inquiry. The data collection techniques that are typically used in evaluation studies in education include questionnaires, observations, interviews, focus groups, document analysis and standardized tests. In many evaluation studies, sampling is purposive in that the evaluator engages in a 'deliberate selection of information-rich sources' (Lapan 2004: 242). In some cases, such as the evaluation of national educational programmes with large groups, random sampling is used to allow evaluators to make generalizations from the sample to the population.

Evaluation research requires methodologies that bring together complementing strengths and compensate for weaknesses and limitations inherent in methodological approaches. With quantitative research, we can get the 'big picture' by using large, possibly representative samples, delineate the relationships between factors and engage in group comparisons to test whether the differences/relationships we observe in the samples can also be observed in the population at large. With qualitative research, we gain rich interpretations and understandings of the context that surround an event, and are able to trace change and elaborate on the relationship between the researcher and the researched.

The use of mixed methods encourages multiplism, triangulation and complementarity. Multiplism refers to the process of employing multiple methods when there is doubt about the adequacy of each method if used independently (Cook 1985). Multiplism is achieved by positing questions in different ways; it is a form of triangulation applied to both questions and methods, and aims at enhancing the validity of an evaluation. Triangulation involves the use of multiple methods (e.g. interviews and observations) and data sources (e.g. teachers, administrators, government officials) to investigate the same programme or policy. Through triangulation, we generate overlapping data, offer multiple perspectives and enhance the internal validity of a study. Greene and McClintock (1985) advise that the employment of different methods should take place simultaneously to avoid bias inherent in each method when applied independently. Complementarity is achieved through the application of different methods to address different aspects of an evaluation. It differs from triangulation because it involves different methods to explore different aspects of a research question, whereas with triangulation, more than one method is applied to corroborate results on the same aspect of an evaluation.

The use of mixed-method designs has raised debates about mixing methods that are underpinned by different, and sometimes clashing, theoretical frameworks. In the context of evaluation research, Rossman and Wilson (1985) place the incompatibility thesis on a continuum with researchers being described as purists, situationists and pragmatists. The purists (e.g. Smith and Heshusius 1986) argue that different paradigms encompass incompatible assumptions that cannot be brought together in a research design. On the other hand, pragmatists (e.g. Greene and Caracelli 2003) argue that paradigmatic positions are logically independent and can be brought together to fit into the research questions and support the integrity of an evaluation. Paradigmatic purity is not a prerequisite to the completion of a research project, pointing to a pragmatic approach to inquiry (Miles and Huberman 1994). Most crucially, the research questions, and not the methods used or the paradigmatic positions that underpin the methods, should drive research, including evaluation research.

Situationists accept the principles that underlie paradigms and wish to retain a paradigmatic integrity; however, they understand that approaching evaluation research from multiple perspectives is likely to enhance the meaningfulness of interpretation and explanation. Mixed-method designs serve three functions, namely, corroboration (establishing convergence), elaboration (offering rich interpretations) and initiations (bringing fresh perspectives to illuminate the issues under consideration) (Rossman and Wilson 1985). With mixed-method designs we can describe and explore data, generate theories inductively and test hypotheses to gain a holistic understanding of social complexity. At the same time, we strive for embeddedness and sensitivity of the contexts and actors' voices. The emphasis on rich explanation and interpretation regarding educational phenomena challenges the use of purely experimental methods and encourages case studies and ethnography to offer a qualitative view of the political and cultural contexts that surround evaluation studies (Parlett and Hamilton 1972).

Two commonly used mixed-method designs are explanatory and exploratory (Punch 2009). An explanatory design consists of two phases: the first phase is quantitative and the second phase is qualitative. Through the quantitative phase, we explore the wider field for the purpose of locating a sub-area for an in-depth qualitative investigation. For example, with a survey, we collect data on teachers' attitudes towards inclusion on a large scale. At the second phase, we may interview a group of teachers who have been identified during the first phase to present a particular interest to the study (e.g. teachers in schools with large numbers of pupils from minority linguistic and ethnic backgrounds). In so doing, we are in a better position to explain/interpret the quantitative data we collected at the first phase.

With an exploratory design, the qualitative data is collected during the first phase and the quantitative data during the second phase. The rationale is that we need to explore the field first before we formulate and test hypotheses and collect quantitative data. This design is useful when we investigate a new area or an original idea which is under-researched and thus need to do some groundwork before undertaking further research. For example, we may want to do an initial exploration of parents' views about childcare for their disabled children for the purpose of identifying the key issues/factors (e.g. affordability, access, flexibility) that affect their choice of childcare provision. The idea is that once we identify the key factors we are in a better position to construct a survey that captures relevant and timely issues regarding childcare provision, as identified by parents, and send it to a large sample to collect quantitative data. Both exploratory and explanatory designs are illustrated in Study 1 and Study 2 discussed later in this chapter.

Outcome/impact

Delineating the outcomes of an intervention on its users is an important dimension of an evaluation (see Box 17.2). Indeed, the quality of an evaluation should be judged by 'its intended use by the intended users' (Patton 1988: 14). In evaluation studies, the terms 'impact' and 'outcome' are used synonymously. However, they are distinct in that impact refers to the long-term effect of a programme achieved through a conceptual and pragmatic shift in its users, whereas outcome refers to an immediate, direct result of an activity.

The use of an interpretive framework is necessary to analyse and interpret the findings of an evaluation, and delineate its impact. An interpretive framework should map into the evaluation questions, criteria of merit and the standards of the evaluation processes itself (Fourier 1995). To delineate the outcomes/impact of an evaluation, we should consider multiple facets such as resources, activities, participation, reactions to learning and action to achieving a long-term impact. This offers a useful framework to distinguish outcomes from impact, or immediate gains,

---

Box 17.2 Impact/outcome at an individual and collective level

- What do people (e.g. students, teachers, administrators, policy-makers, stakeholders) do differently as a result of this programme or policy initiative?
- To what extent has the programme changed their views, attitudes and behaviour?
- Are the recipients of the services satisfied with the programme?
- What are the benefits and their recommendations for further improvement?
- Are the resources invested worth the outcome (cost-effectiveness)?
- What are the strengths and weaknesses of the programme?
- Are there any unintended outcomes (positive or negative) for the users and their communities?
- What is the long-term impact?
- What type of social action did the programme stimulate?

(e.g. access to resources), materials from long-lasting gains (e.g. primary users becoming agents of change) (see Box 17.3).

In evaluation studies, outcome and impact should be articulated and presented in a way that offers a concise description and explanation to encourage different audiences to respond effectively. For example, the results from evaluating an educational programme should be presented to parents in an accessible format, and in the form of an executive summary to policy-makers to ensure that evidence is communicated with clarity. Summaries, including executive summaries, should contain concise statements regarding the goals/evaluation questions, findings and recommendations of the evaluation. The format and length of the final report are usually negotiated with the funding bodies to abide by their dissemination guidelines and organizational requirements.

Evaluation standards

The joint Committee on Standards for Evaluation (1981) developed four sets of standards to underlie an evaluation. These are: utility standards to meet the practical needs of the primary users; feasibility standards to ensure that the evaluation is realistic; propriety standards to ensure the evaluation abides by ethical and legal standards; and accuracy standards to ensure that the collection and analysis of data are technically and theoretically accurate (Nevo 1989: 124).

Evaluation research has been criticized as being atheoretical and value-free (Kelly 2007). This argument is somewhat simplistic, in that all research has a theoretical framework which informs decisions about research design and the interpretation of the results. It is true that reports of evaluation tend to allocate a small space for theoretical discussions because the focus of an evaluation is on presenting evidence about effectiveness and articulating the implications for policy and practice. However, this does not mean that the conceptualization of all facets of an evaluation cannot draw on theory.

Evaluation is a political activity with a public audience. Findings from an evaluation are likely to contribute to ethically and politically contested situations, especially when they contradict

Box 17.3 Becoming an agent of change

An exploration of identified issues/problem solving:
- To what extent has the intervention enabled you as a primary user/stakeholder to identify problems and find solutions?
- To what extent did you identify and address particular issues, challenges or ideas?

Application of divergent thinking and new ideas:
- To what extent has the project enabled you to think creatively and in different ways?
- Did you ask questions and challenge assumptions through the project?
- Were you able to share new ideas with colleagues and the community?

Engagement in co-learning:
- To what extent have you been able to learn alongside colleagues?
- Were you all equal partners in learning?
- Has there been a conceptual shift in ideas, self-awareness and perspectives, as well as a policy and practical shift?

Becoming engaged:
- To what extent have you been motivated/empowered to become an agent of change?
- Has this affected your long-term attitudes towards learning?

Risk-taking:
- To what extent did this project encourage you to take risks and experiment with new ideas and practices?
- Do you feel that you have been challenged enough?

Development of critical reflexivity:
- Are you more likely now to persist and refine your work?
- Have you developed towards being a reflective practitioner?

sensitive issues. Ethical and political questions are raised regarding the role and degree of involvement of evaluators in situations where evidence contradicts the stakeholders' views, and the extent to which the findings should be defended in these circumstances. Moreover, articulating the ethics and politics embedded in evaluation research on the effectiveness and cost-effectiveness of a programme requires open dialogue and partnership. This is particularly pertinent considering the increasing politicization of educational research. Regardless of its political and ideological context, evaluation research should be done in a rigorous manner, with opportunities for peer review and sharing of the findings with a community of practice (see Box 17.4 for an overview).

Examples of Evaluation Studies in Education

To illustrate the nature and cycles of evaluation research in education, two studies on a programme and a policy initiative are presented here. These studies vary in terms of their outcomes and impact (individual vs. collectiv-organizational), and the object of the evaluation,

Box 17.4 Evaluation research in education

Aims of evaluation in education:

- Accountability (increasing effectiveness in managing people/resources).
- Appraisal of educational programmes/policy initiatives.
- Changes in organizational cultures.
- Facilitating further refinement of a programme.
- Knowledge generation to stimulate public action.

Dimensions of evaluation in education:

- Implementation (e.g. initial decisions about resources, timeline, activities, efficiency, cost-effectiveness).
- Context (e.g. dynamics of the physical, social, political and legislative context).
- Human factor (e.g. roles, responsibilities, action and degrees of involvement of primary users, stakeholders and evaluators, as well as their reaction, motivation, learning, change of behaviour; who benefits and who decides on the desirability of change).

The cycles of evaluation in education:

- Set the criteria (e.g. what constitutes evidence) and formulate the evaluation question (e.g. main question and sub-questions) which, in turn may refine the initial criteria.
- Present and justify the methodology (e.g. mixed-method design).
  - i) Consider issues regarding procedures for data collection (e.g. feasibility, appropriateness given the context, and validity).
  - ii) Employ multiple methods of data collection (e.g. document analysis, case studies, surveys, peer reviews and unobtrusive measures such as keeping a journal).
  - iii) Draw a reasonable timeline (e.g. pre- and post- intervention phases; timespan for data collection, periodic follow up, longitudinal evaluation).
- Delineate the impact/outcomes of the evaluation at an individual and collective level through the development of an interpretive framework (e.g. differentiate between outcomes and impact, dissemination of findings to communities of practice).
- Set the standards of evaluation.
  - i) Utility standards.
  - ii) Feasibility standards.
  - iii) Propriety standards.
  - iv) Ethical and legal standards.
  - v) Accuracy standards.

namely an educational programme and a government policy. The evaluation of an education programme focuses on a teacher continuing development programme, PGCE Plus, and its context of delivery, evaluating its effectiveness at an individual teacher level. The evaluation of the policy initiative focuses on electronic registration, and the structures and factors that shaped its functioning at an organizational and policy level.

Study 1: evaluation of PGCE Plus

In 2004 and 2005, two two-week PGCE Plus courses, in mathematics and science respectively, were offered by the National Academy for Gifted and Talented Youth (NAGTY), and participants were recruited nationally. The PGCE Plus courses ran in conjunction with NAGTY's summer schools for students aged 11–16 years. An evaluation was conducted to investigate the effectiveness of PGCE Plus on newly qualified teachers' (NQTs) professional development (see Arweck *et al.* 2005, 2006).

Aims

PGCE Plus was intended to extend initial teacher training by focusing on gifted and talented (G&T) education and creating a supportive structure for NQTs to engage in professional learning. The purpose of this evaluation was to delineate the outcomes of PGCE Plus at an individual teacher level. Specifically, the goals were threefold: to satisfy accountability, refine the programme and possibly extend it to other subjects and generate knowledge about pedagogies for all, and the nature of teachers' continuing professional development.

Dimensions

Implementation
Implementation refers to the structure and the logistics of an evaluation. The PGCE Plus evaluation took place during the two-week course period, with a follow-up component after teachers had completed their first year at a school. The timeline of data collection was flexible to accommodate the primary users' schedule. In terms of cost-effectiveness, cohorts from 2004 and 2005 and their tutors were asked to offer their views.

Context
Regarding the physical context, PGCE Plus was a residential course delivered at a university setting. This offered primary users the opportunity to create a social space where they exchanged ideas about their work and built professional networks. The main structural components of PGCE Plus included the design and implementation of a two-week course in the summer following the PGCE, the provision of a masters-level accreditation, termly meetings once the NQTs were in schools, and the establishment of an online community. Its functional components covered theory, policy and practice regarding G&T pedagogy, remedial support to ameliorate gaps in PGCE training and capacity-building towards responsive teaching for all children. The PGCE Plus course comprised pre-course reading, a combination of course elements (self-study, teaching episodes/peer teaching, taught sessions), observations of NAGTY students and a masterclass (open to all summer school students). The course provided the theoretical and policy background regarding G&T provision in the first week and focused specifically on mathematics and science in the second week.

The policy context of PGCE Plus was the Excellence in Cities framework, with a focus on supporting teachers to teach G&T pupils. The evaluation explored the physical, social and legislative context and its potential to shape the primary users' perceptions about the effectiveness of the programme. Delineating the context was crucial in that PGCE Plus occupied a unique territory, resembling initial teacher training without the 'real' teaching dimension, and an INSET model without a mentoring component.

Human factor

An important part of every evaluation is to clarify the roles, responsibilities and input of the individuals involved, namely, primary users/benefactors, stakeholders and evaluators. In this evaluation, the primary users were NQTs and their tutors, and the stakeholders were the funding agency and NAGTY. The stakeholders were encouraged to become involved in the evaluation in terms of offering their accounts and disseminating the evaluation findings.

In examining the human factor, the evaluation focused on participants' views about their capacity-building and potential for agency at the end of the PGCE Plus course. The capability approach (Sen 2006) was taken to examine PGCE Plus users' perceptions of the capacity of the programme to support them to convert resources, knowledge and professional skills into changed practices in schools. As Sen observes, factors such as the interaction between individual teachers and the social/ideological/political milieu of their schools can influence the translation of professional knowledge and skills into valued functionings to benefit children academically and socially.

Cycles

Evaluation criteria and questions

The criteria should map onto the goal of the evaluation, namely, to prepare NQTs to teach G&T pupils. With this in mind, the criteria referred to the knowledge, professional skills and competence that teachers needed to become effective in teaching G&T pupils. Specifically:

- develop knowledge regarding the social, emotional and learning needs of G&T pupils, beyond the PGCE level
- understand the legislative framework of G&T education
- apply differentiation in class to respond to pupils' diverse needs
- incorporate materials and resources in their teaching
- become more confident and motivated to teach G&T pupils
- engage critically with notions of giftedness and the pedagogies for difference

With the above criteria in mind, the evaluation questions included:

- What are the functional and structural components of PGCE Plus?
- What is the nature of the programme as a model of professional development?
- Does PGCE Plus occupy a unique territory or is it similar to other teacher development programmes?
- What are the stakeholders' and users' views about its outcomes/impact at an individual teacher level?
- What are their views/predictions regarding its long-term impact?

Methodology

The evaluation took a mixed-method approach including interviews and questionnaires as well as observations and documentary analyses. Two sets of semistructured interviews were carried out with participants from the 2005 PGCE Plus courses, both mathematics and science, and tutors at each university. All seven tutors present at the time of the field visits were interviewed, as were the two respective subject coordinators of the summer school strands. The total number of interviews conducted in 2005 was 35. Also, three questionnaires were distributed to the PGCE Plus participants. The first comprised a follow-up questionnaire for the 2004 cohort, sent at the end of the summer term 2005. The second was sent to the 2005 PGCE Plus participants *before* their respective courses and the third was sent to them *after* they had completed the course. A total of 53 questionnaires were returned. Aspects of this design are explanatory because some of the questionnaires were sent before the qualitative data collection took place. With the interviews and observations, we were able to collect rich and contextualized information about key issues identified from the questionnaires.

Interpretive framework

PGCE plus teachers' personal and professional development was analysed by adapting Harland and Kinder's (1997) typology to explore material/resources and provisionary outcomes; professional knowledge and skills; new awareness, social/affective outcomes; and critical reflexivity. Specifically, the evaluation examined teachers' receptiveness to new ideas and teaching practices, and their capability to experiment with new materials and resources and use knowledge to achieve outcomes. Moreover, their capability for critical reflexivity was also examined in terms of being able to re-examine and revise professional practices in the light of new knowledge, and professional dialogue and collaboration with their colleagues.

Outcomes

The perceived outcomes from the PGCE Plus evaluation at an individual teacher level were:

- Material/resources: teachers were proactive to locate and use materials and resources to differentiate in the classroom.
- Knowledge and professional skills: teachers' knowledge expanded by acquiring cognitive knowledge – i.e. an understanding about G&Tstudents' learning and social and emotional needs, and the legislative framework of G&Teducation in the UK; applied knowledge – i.e. teaching styles and differentiation, with regard to the practical usefulness of the course in their classroom teaching; integrated knowledge constructed through teachers' collaborative inquiry and professional dialogue; and dynamic knowledge, in terms of knowledge and insight that stimulate changes in teaching and learning.
- Awareness: teachers' increased awareness of the shifts in the concept of giftedness.
- Affective outcomes: teachers' attitudes, motivation and self-confidence are important for changing classroom practice, and can be supported through the creation of a social space and a community of practice.
- Critical reflexivity: a crucial component of teacher professional development, this requires a critical space for debating ideas about teaching to engage in critical scrutiny and develop a sense of ownership, professional control and self-regulation.

Impact

The majority of participants described the benefits of PGCE Plus in terms of acquiring and applying new teaching techniques, such as differentiation, curriculum content and resources/materials with regard to G&T provision. Moreover, a smaller number of participants perceived the wider benefits of

PGCE Plus in terms of being exposed to models of professional development and interprofessional dialogue, and an active involvement in developing, refining and reviewing teaching practices.

Teachers articulating of patterns of professional learning and changes at a personal and professional level is an important indicator of impact and the first step towards delineating learners' experiences (Burchell *et al.* 2002). The shifts in teachers' awareness of G&T, the refinement of their professional skills and knowledge and critical reflexivity suggested that teachers' learning and professional development had been internalized (Kirkwood and Christie 2006). In this regard, PGCE Plus was a successful programme in encouraging teachers to develop as professional learners and learning professionals, with the potential for action at a classroom level. However, it would be worth exploring to what extent PGCE Plus laid the foundation for sustaining communities of practice, and whether the participants developed the capacity to reshape practices of pedagogy and engage the wider community in their schools.

Standards of evaluation

The standards set for the PGCE Plus evaluation involved:

- utility standards in terms of meeting the needs of the NQTs and their tutors during the evaluation (e.g. negotiating appropriate time for data collection)
- feasibility standards in terms of ensuring that the evaluation could realistically be carried out given the timeline, context and structure of PGCE Plus
- propriety standards in terms of abiding by ethical standards (e.g. informed consent and confidentiality, encouraging multiple voices to be heard) and legal structures (e.g. the legality of dealing with funding bodies)
- accuracy standards in terms of ensuring that the methodological (e.g. mixed methods) and theoretical frameworks (e.g. previous studies on continuing professional development for teachers) were well argued and reasoned.

Study 2: evaluation of electronic registration (policy initiative)

Aims

This was an evaluation of electronic registration systems in secondary schools in England (Lindsay *et al.* 2005). The aim of the evaluation was to investigate school staff's type of engagement with e-registration to monitor pupil attendance, and the system's capacity to work in synergy with other school attendance initiatives. It also addressed whether the use of a monitoring technology has the potential to prevent school absenteeism and support the inclusion of disaffected pupils, especially when e-registration operates in synergy with other attendance policies and is supported by staff.

Dimensions

Implementation

The evaluation was conducted with 538 secondary schools in England over a three-year period. These schools were identified by the then Department for Education and Employment as having the highest levels of unauthorized absence, with the majority of them operating with an OMR system.

Context

Regarding the policy context, the implementation of electronic systems was part of the Capital Modernization Programme, a government initiative to reduce non-attendance by one third by 2002. The evaluation took place at selected schools in different geographical areas in England, mainly located in areas of socioeconomic disadvantage. To delineate the evaluation context, Berman's (1978) stages in policy implementation were adapted:

- Policy decision (to promote school attendance in secondary schools) →
- Government programme (Capital Modernization Programme) →
- Local adoption (to be adopted in selected local secondary schools) →
- Local practice (to be implemented in conjunction with other local systems) →
- Policy outcomes (impact of e- egistration on reducing school absence)

The multiplicity of the factors that underpin non-attendance require interagency and interprofessional collaboration to tackle absence, as well as a whole-school and community approach with electronic attendance monitoring being an integral component. The causes for non-attendance include disaffection and conscious decisions not to attend, or mental health problems, which adversely impact upon young people's ability to attend school. This evaluation focused mainly on the local adoption and practice (or attempts towards putting electronic registration into practice). The evaluators and the primary users did not offer an input regarding the other phases, (i.e. policy decisions about school attendance, government's conception of the Capital Modernization Programme, and how its implementation actually impacted on policy and the young people's lives and communities).

Human factor

A wide range of school staff were involved in this evaluation including members from the senior management team, teachers tutors, administration officers and education welfare officers. Also, consultations took place with officials from the then Department for Education and Skills. The participants offered different perspectives on the use and effectiveness of e-registration. Within-school variations in opinions can be explained by considering the range of functions of e-registration, and the roles and the responsibilities of the staff involved. For tutors, e-registration facilitated access to diverse information (including attendance), albeit in a time-consuming manner, whereas for the senior management team the focus was on gathering statistics and producing attendance reports efficiently. For the Department for Education and Skills officials, e-registration was a policy initiative towards reducing absence.

Cycles

Evaluation criteria and questions

As in the PGCE Plus evaluation, the criteria should map onto the goals of the e-registration evaluation, namely, staff confidence and attitudes towards e-registration, as well as staff views regarding effectiveness, school infrastructure, technical support and training.

The evaluation questions were:

- What is the capacity of e-registration to work in synergy with other school initiatives/systems?
- Does e-registration have the capacity to reinforce, facilitate and generate changes with regard to absenteeism?
- What are the school staff views and attitudes towards the use of e-registration?
- Do school staff consider e-registration to be easy to use and effective in reducing absenteeism?

Methodology

This evaluation used a mixed-methods design to capture the complexity and interactions between the factors associated with the use of e-registration. Qualitative case studies were used and interviews were carried out to address issues related to the introduction, implementation and operation of e-registration. Also, questionnaires sent to non-case study participating schools were employed to capture staff views about e-registration in operation and its function within the wider context of school policies and initiatives. Finally, school-level authorized and unauthorized absence rates were examined. In part, this evaluation employed an exploratory design. With the case studies, we identified key issues with the implementation and operation of e-registration (a fairly new and under-researched initiative) and, based on the information collected during the exploratory phase, constructed the surveys sent to non-case study schools.

Interpretive framework

To develop an interpretive framework, an eclectic approach was taken by adapting and synthesizing models of teacher engagement with ICT and its policy context developed by Cuban (1993), Schnitz and Azbell (1990) and Clariana (1992). This framework was used to analyse and discuss issues related to e-registration implementation in secondary schools by investigating staff's type of engagement with e-registration and the system's capacity to work in synergy with other attendance initiatives. In so doing, a continuum of three phases of e-registration use and capacity-building, namely *practitioner*, *integrator* and *extender*, was developed. The type of staff engagement with e-registration systems (i.e. novice, preservationist, sceptical and cautious optimist) was analysed within the practitioner phase. The capacity of e-registration to work in synergy with other initiatives as a reinforcement tool and facilitator, capable of generating changes and extending practice, was investigated within the integrator and extender phases.

Outcomes/impact

In the ICT literature, it is widely accepted that what makes technology in schools work is the extent to which its users perceive it to be facilitative, relevant to teaching and professional development, and capable of being implemented in a socially and pedagogically constructive way (Mumtaz 2000). The findings from this evaluation suggested that, for e-registration to be a catalyst for change and an integral component for tackling school absence, the triadic interactions between e-registration users, the capabilities of the system and the school policy context should be considered. The transition from the practitioner to the integrator and extender phases relied on the capacity of e-registration to operate in synergy with other attendance systems as a reinforcement and facilitator of their practices.

Standards of evaluation

As in the PGCE Plus evaluation, the same framework of standards (i.e., utility, propriety, feasibility and accuracy of evaluation) applies here. An important question raised in this evaluation was whether the use of monitoring technology has the potential to prevent absenteeism and support the inclusion of disaffected pupils. This has ethical implications with regard to children's rights, citizenship and pastoral care, especially considering the debates that surround the use of monitoring technology and its pedagogic significance.

Summary

Evaluation research in education is widespread, carried out in a variety of contexts across the public and private sector. Policy initiatives and programmes rely on evaluation research mainly for public accountability purposes, raising questions of effectiveness and accomplishment. The rise of an audit culture relies on evaluation research to provide evidence about what works and most importantly how and under what circumstances to shape educational policy and practice. In this context, rigorous evaluation research is needed to allow evaluators to defend their findings to stakeholders and others who have vested interests in the evaluation. However, evaluation in education should not be instrumental only, but also a type of research that is embedded in complex social, organizational and political contexts with utility, relevance and participation being important aspects.

References

Arweck, E., Cullen, M. A., Cullen, S. and Lindsay, G. (2005) *Evaluation of the PGCE Plus 2005. Interim Report 1.* Warwick: Centre for Educational Development, Appraisal and Research (CEDAR).

Arweck, E., Cullen, S., Hartas, D. and Lindsay, G. (2006) *Evaluation of the PGCE Plus 2006. Interim Report 2.* Warwick: Centre for Educational Development, Appraisal and Research (CEDAR).

Ball, S. (1999) 'Performativity and fragmentation in "postmodern schooling"', in J. Carter (ed.) *Postmodernity and the Fragmentation of Welfare*. London: Routledge.

Berman, P. (1978) 'The study of macro and micro-implementation', *Public Policy*, 26: 157–84.

Burchell, H., Dyson, J. and Rees, M. (2002) 'Making a difference: a study of the impact of continuing professional development on professional practice', *Journal of In-Service Education*, 28(2): 219–29.

Clariana, R. (1992) 'Integrated learning systems and standardized test improvement'. Invited presentation at WICAT Users Conference, Sandy, Utah.

Committee on Standards for Evaluation (1981) *Joint Committee on Standards for Educational Evaluation. Standards for Evaluations of Educational Programmes, Projects and Materials*. New York: McGraw-Hill.

Cook, T. D. (1985) 'Post-positivist critical multiplism', in R. L. Shotland and M. M. Mark (eds) *Social Science and Social Policy*. Beverly Hills, CA: Sage.

Cousins, J. and Earl, L. (1992) 'The case for participatory evaluation', *Educational Evaluation and Policy Analysis*, 14(4): 397–418.

Cronbach, L. J. (1980) *Toward Reform of Program Evaluation: Aims, Methods, and Institutional Arrangements*. San Francisco: Jossey-Bass.

Cuba, E. G., and Lincoln, Y. S. (1981) *Effective Evaluation*. San Francisco: Jossey-Bass.

Cuban, L. (1993) 'Computers meet classrooms: classrooms win', *Teachers College Record*, 95: 185–210.

Fourier, D. M. (1995) 'Establishing evaluative conclusions: a distinction between general and working logic', *New Directions for Evaluation*, 68.

Freeman, H., Rossi, P. and Lipsey, (2003) *Evaluation: a Systematic Approach*, 7th edn. Newbury Park, CA: Sage.

Garaway, G. (2004) Participatory evaluation, in K. deMarrais and S. D. Lapan (eds) *Foundations for Research: Methods of Inquiry in Education and the Social Sciences* Mahwah, NJ: Lawrence Erlbaum.

Goodhart, D. (2004) 'Too diverse?' *Prospect*, February, www.prospectmagazine.

Greene, J., and McClintock, S. (1985) 'Triangulation in evaluation', *Evaluation Review*, 9(5): 523–45.

Greene, J. C., and Caracelli, V. J. (2003) 'Making paradigmatic sense of mixed method practice', in A. Tashakkori and C. Teddlie (eds) *Handbook of Mixed Methods in Social and Behavioural Research*. Thousand Oaks, CA: Sage.

Harland, J. and Kinder, K. (1997) 'Teachers' continuing professional development: framing a model of outcomes', *British Journal of In-service Education*, 23(1): 71–84.

House, E. R. (1979) 'Technology vs craft: a ten years perspective on innovation', *Journal of Curriculum Studies*, 11: 1–15.

Kelly, M. (2007) 'Qualitative evaluation research', in C. Seale, G. Gobo, J. Gubrium and D. Silverman (eds) *Qualitative Research Practice*. London: Sage.

Kirkwood, M. and Christie, D. (2006) 'The role of teacher research in continuing professional development', *British Journal of Educational Studies*, 54(4): 429–48.

Kushner, S. and Adelman, C. (2006) 'Program evaluation: a democratic practice', in J. Green, G. Camilli and P. Elmore (eds) *Handbook of Complementary Methods in Education Research*. Mahwah, NJ: American Educational Research Association/Lawrence Erlbaum Associates.

Lapan, R. T. (2004) *Career Development across the K-16 years: Bridging the Present to Satisfying and Successful Futures*. Alexandria, VA: American Counseling Association.

Lindsay, G., Muijs, D., Hartas, D. and Band, S. (2005) *Evaluation of Capital Modernisation Funding for Electronic Registration in Selected Secondary Schools* (research report RR759). London: Department for Education and Skills.

MacDonald, B. and Norris, N. (1981) 'Twin political horizons in evaluation fieldwork', in T. S. Popkiewicz and B. R. Tabachnik (eds) *The Study of Schooling: Field Based Methodologies in Educational Research and Evaluation*. New York: Praeger.

Miles, E. G., and Huberman, A. M. (1994) *Qualitative Data Analysis: An Expanded Sourcebook*. London: Sage.

Mumtaz, S. (2000) 'Factors affecting teachers' use of information and communications technology: a review of the literature', *Journal of Information Technology for Teacher Education*, 9(3): 319–42.

Nevo, D. (1989) 'The conceptualization of educational evaluation: an analytical review of the literature', *Review of Educational Research*, 53(1): 117–28.

Nevo, D. (1983) 'The conceptualization of educational evaluation: a review of the literature', *Review of Educational Research*, 53(1): 117–28.

Parlett, M. and Hamilton, D. (1972) *Evaluation as Illumination: A New Approach to the Study of Innovatory Programs* (occasional paper No 9). Edinburgh: University of Edinburgh Centre for Research in the Educational Sciences.

Patton, M. Q. (1988) Paradigms and pragmatism, D. M. Fettermann (ed.) *Qualitative Approaches to Evaluation in Education: The Silent Scientific Revolution*. Santa Barbara, CA: Praeger.

Patton, M. Q. (1990) *Qualitative Evaluation and Research Methods*, 2nd edn. Newbury Park, CA: Sage.

Punch, K. (2009) *Introduction to Research Methods in Education*. London: Sage.

Rossi, P. and Freeman, H. (1993) *Evaluation: A Systematic Approach*. 5th edn. Newbury Park, CA: Sage.

Rossman, G. and Wilson, B. (1985) 'Numbers and words combining quantitative and qualitative methods in a single large-scale evaluation study', *Evaluation Review*, 9(5): 627–43.

Sen, A. (2006) *Identity and Violence: The Illusion of Destiny*. London: Penguin.

Schnitz, J. and Azbell, J. (1990) 'Training for third-generation management systems effecting integrator implementation models', *Proceedings of the Eighth Annual Conference on Interactive Instructional Technology*.

Scriven, M. (2003) 'Evaluation in the new millennium: the transdisciplinary vision', in S. I. Donaldson and M. Scriven (eds) *Evaluating Social Programs and Problems*. London: Erlbaum.

Smith, J. and Heshusius, L. (1986) 'Closing down the conversation: the end of the quantitative-qualitative debate among educational inquirers', *Educational Researcher*, 15(1): 4–12.

Stake, R. E. (1967) 'The countenance of educational evaluation', *Teachers College Record*, 68: 523–40.

Stronach, I. (1997) 'Evaluation with the lights out: deconstructing illuminative evaluation and new paradigm research', in L. Mabry (ed.) *Evaluation and the Postmodern Dilemma*. Greenwich: CT: JAI.

Stufflebeam, D. L., Madaus, G. and Kellaghan, T. (2000) *Evaluation Models: Viewpoints on Educational and Human Services Evaluation*. Boston, MA: Kluwer.

Whyte, W. F. (1991) *Social Theory for Action: How Individuals and Organizations Learn to Change*. London: Sage.

Wingens, M. (1990) 'Toward a general utilisation theory: a systems theory reformulation of the two-community metaphor', *Knowledge*, 27–42.

Part IV
Making Sense of Research in Education – Analysing our Data

Qualitative Research Analysis in Education

Will Gibson

18

Introduction

In Chapter 3, I was concerned with thinking about how researchers can usefully conceptualize and orientate to a qualitative research analysis. I now turn my attention to some of the practices of data work, focusing particularly on transcription, the use of software and the application of modes of qualitative analysis. As a forerunner to this, I will briefly discuss the distinctive aspects of qualitative data analysis in education.

By the end of this chapter, you should be able to:

- understand various approaches to transcription
- consider the use of computer software in qualitative analysis
- describe critically the different modes of qualitative analysis

Qualitative Analysis in Education

In many respects, the matter of qualitative analysis in the field of education is no different to any other field or discipline, such as healthcare, human geography, social psychology, sociology or anthropology. As outlined in Chapter 3, the principles of treating data analysis as an iterative feature of the research process rather than as a 'stage', and of building the design of one's research around the generation of relevant data, are applicable in whichever field one operates. Much of what I have to say in this chapter also pertains to qualitative research *in general* and not to distinctive fields of its application, such as education.

That said, there are nonetheless aspects of work in education that can present particular challenges. Education is a multidisciplinary field, in which many disciplines converge, such as sociology, history, psychology, economics, mathematics, computer science, social anthropology, philosophy, art, music, drama and languages, each bringing distinctive conventions of work and theoretical ideas and commitments. The field of education, or perhaps more precisely, education studies, is enriched by this eclectic range. However, from the point of view of analysis, this multidisciplinarity (and often *interdisciplinarity*) can mean that researchers work in teams where the analytic framework of a given study is a matter of negotiation. As I noted in Chapter 3, for researchers new to the field, such as postgraduate researchers, one of the challenges can be in defining one's theoretical focus in the context of a very wide range of disciplinary affiliations. Importantly, while the alignment to a particular discipline can make life easier, it is by no means a necessary step. Effective analysis involves the specification and use of concepts that are far more focused than a general discipline.

Another common characteristic in educational research is that there is a strong link between professional work and research practice. In sociology, for example, while there are some connections with other professions, such as social work, researchers tend to be academics or professional researchers. In education, by contrast, researchers are very often, first and foremost, members of the communities being researched (like teachers, policy advisers, students and so on). The strong link between profession and research in education means that analysis is often more connected to professional expertise than in other areas, where researchers may not have the skills necessary to interrogate very specialized complex institutional knowledge. There are advantages and disadvantages to this situation. The familiarity with settings means that researchers come with what Harold Garfinkel (1967) has termed 'unique adequacy' – the distinctive sets of knowledge and know-how through which they see and understand those settings from the 'insider's' point of view. On the other hand, this familiarity can mean that features of the setting that an outsider may pick up on become hard to bring into focus. One of the challenges for researchers operating in their own areas is in trying to make the commonplace look *strange* such that they can begin to ask questions of its composition and character.

With these thoughts in mind, I now turn to look at some of the practices of qualitative data work more generally. The remainder of this chapter is divided into three key sections: transcription, technology and analysis, and modes of analysis. In the first section, I discuss three different approaches to transcription and outline the importance of conceptualizing and approaching transcription as a form of analysis rather than as simply a matter of data representation. In the second section, I look at some of the ways in which comparatively recent technological advances have influenced the process of qualitative analysis, focusing on the role of particular analytic software, recording technology, collaborative analysis and multimedia analysis. In the final section, I outline a common (although not universal, and certainly not *theorized*) way of approaching the organization of qualitative data. I describe this approach as a set of procedures to data work, and make a distinction between these and the conceptual work involved in data analysis.

Transcription

Transcription is often thought of as a process that is undertaken *prior* to conducting analysis. However, it is actually a fundamental aspect of the analysis process itself in which researchers give sense to and interrogate their data. Transcription is not a 'neutral' process of representing what someone said in an interview or observation setting; it is, more accurately, a matter of selectively deciding on which aspects of a given dataset are relevant. All transcription involves *re-presenting* some feature of the data in a way that enables the researcher to do some analytic work with it. When analysing an interview, researchers need to present verbal conversation in a written form, using conventions of writing and speech representation as shorthand for the very detailed features of spoken language. In observational transcripts, researchers use symbols, codes, drawings and pictures as means of *re-presenting* some analytically relevant features of the interaction. A key aspect of producing a transcription, then, involves trying to figure out what information is relevant. I outline three approaches to transcription: indexical, focused and detailed. These three approaches represent a sliding scale in the representation of detail in data; they are not defined, distinct or codified methodologies for data work.

Indexical transcription

As the name implies, indexical transcription involves creating an *index* of the points at which key occurrences happened within data. In an interview, for example, a researcher may wish to mark the points at which a question was asked by the interviewee, or at which particular interesting answers were provided. Typically, researchers will write the times of the events down the side of the page and then annotate the events next to them. In this way, researchers are able to easily identify relevant aspects of the data. Making decisions about 'what counts as relevant or interesting' in relation to one's data involves making analytic judgements about that data and deciding that one particular event is more important than another. In this respect, indexical transcription involves generating a very focused selection of interesting and relevant features of data.

Indexical transcriptions serve as a guide to data and may be used as a way of simply mapping the data out before more detailed analysis begins. It can be useful to produce a timeline of an interview before using any of the other approaches as it enables researchers to check that the data contained in the interview are relevant, and to choose particular aspects of the data to transcribe. Compared to the 'focused' and 'unfocused' approaches outlined below, indexical transcriptions are relatively quick to produce.

Unfocused transcription

The term 'unfocused' refers to the process of simply trying to represent what was said or *meant* in a particular event or interview setting, without paying attention to the details of *how* that meaning was created. James Paul Gee (1999) has referred to this mode of transcription as 'broad' transcription. In this approach, researchers try to write down the meaning that they heard within a given set of utterances, rather than write down or represent the *exact* ways in which those utterances were produced. Researchers who use unfocused transcription do not typically have an interest in systematically representing the way that features such as overlap or hesitation feature in the talk, although they may draw attention to some of these aspects at points in the data where they feel it is particularly relevant.

The extract in Box 18.1 is a brief example of this mode of transcribing and comes from a recording of two friends talking in a kitchen. In the extract, the transcription is organized through chronological turns in the speech, with the speaker being identified by an initial. Typical punctuation marks such as question marks, commas, full stops and apostrophes are used to give sense to the talk. The question marks at the end of the first three lines, for example, indicate that the words immediately preceding them are phrased as a question. The full stop after 'Not sure' in the second line implies that this was phrased as an answer to M's preceding question and not, for example, as connected to uncertainty about whether or not Sarah was going.

Box 18.1: Extract of an unfocused transcription of two friends talking

M: Are you coming over later?
S: Not sure. Is Sarah going?
M: Sarah, No, I haven't spoken to her. Shall I call her?
S: I'll call her. I have to speak to her anyway.

It is advisable for researchers to ask other members of the research team, colleagues or friends to check their transcript against the data in order to make sure that the researcher's re-presentation is appropriate to the data. It is common for researchers to work largely from the transcripts once they have been produced, but there is a real benefit in re-listening to interviews throughout the research as new hearings can often result in new interpretations of the significance of particular utterances.

Unfocused transcription is quite time-consuming; it can take around four hours to transcribe one hour of talk, depending on one's typing speed and the speed and clarity of the recorded speech. It can be useful to use some form of transcription machine, which allows the listener to control the tape player or digital recording through pedals and to type continuously. This makes the transcription process a little faster and easier to manage.

Focused transcription

Focused transcription is used where researchers are interested in recording some of the ways in which a given set of discourse was produced. In this approach, researchers try to represent not what was meant by what was said, but *how* it was said. Researchers have developed elaborate systems of representation that help to display the particular verbal mechanisms by which people give meaning to speech. Richard Dressler and Roger Kreuz (2000) have provided a list of some of the most commonly used symbols, some of which are shown in Box 18.2.

Box 18.2 The Dressler and Kruez transcription system

?	=	Rising intonation at end of sentence
.	=	Falling intonation at end of sentence
/ \	=	Rising and falling intonation within text
,	=	Continuing intonation (like in a list)
CAPS	=	Stress or emphasis in the text
(0.5)	=	Pause in tenths of a second
. . .	=	Short untimed pause
< >	=	Talk spoken slowly
> <	=	Talk spoken rapidly
:	=	Lengthened syllable
-	=	Word cutoff (abrupt self-termination)
=	=	Latched talk (no gap between two speakers)
[ ]	=	Overlap speech
{ }	=	'Backchannel' talk (someone who is not being transcribed)
○ ○	=	Spoken softly
ITALICS	=	Spoken loudly
H	=	Audible breath
.h	=	Inward breath
h	=	Outward breath
(( ))	=	Paralinguistic behaviour
( )	=	Unclear or unintelligible speech

When using focused forms of transcription, researchers do not attempt to represent *every* nuance and feature of speech, but simply try to identify and draw attention to those features that are relevant to their research. Indeed, transcription systems that use too many of these representation resources are very difficult to interpret. Focused transcription is extremely time-consuming, and it can take as long as one hour of work to transcribe one *minute* of talk. Typically, with this transcription type, researchers do not therefore transcribe very large sections of talk, but select through careful listening and re-listening the areas of a given dataset that they want to focus upon. Because these transcriptions are so focused, researchers may need to produce more than one transcription for a given section of talk in order to draw attention to different features of the data. These forms of transcription are particularly common in types of discourse analysis.

Technology and Analysis

Like all areas of social life and work practice, the analysis of qualitative data has been dramatically altered through developments in digital technology, web communications and ubiquitous computing. Researchers have a range of software, recording tools and modes of distributed collaboration that are fundamentally changing the nature of qualitative analysis work. In this section, I look at some of these basic features in relation to the process of analysis in qualitative research.

CAQDAS

The term CAQDAS stands for 'computer-assisted qualitative data analysis' software, and refers to a range of commercial products that have been developed to help researchers manage their data. Such technologies are, in essence, databases that allow researchers to index and retrieve their data according to user-defined criteria and categories. There is, however, a distinction between these basic 'code and retrieve' functions and more elaborate 'theory-building' functions, where the technologies are said to facilitate the development of theory within research.

Code and retrieve software enables researchers to create codes for particular aspects of their data and to *retrieve* the data that they have coded. To take an example, a researcher may have a large number of transcripts of interviews, and code that data according to a number of emergent and/or predefined categories. The software allows the researcher to retrieve and to view together all of the instances of a given code. This facilitates the creation of comparative coding – i.e. the creation, application and evaluation of code categories by applying codes and comparing the instances of data to which those codes have been assigned. Most CAQDAS software packages enable researchers to undertake this form of analysis.

Some software packages are designed to aid slightly more elaborate data management processes. Theory-building packages contain a range of features that enable researchers to develop theory from their data. Such programmes offer tools for interrogating both data and emergent coding structures in more detailed ways than simpler code and retrieve tools. Software packages such as Atlas.ti and NVivo, to take two of the market-leading packages, allow researchers to look at the ways in which the codes they have developed relate to each other (e.g. the frequencies of codes, and the specified relationships and hierarchies between codes).

There are important caveats to bear in mind when using CAQDAS. The first quite obvious but nonetheless instructive point to remember is that software programmes do not analyse data: researchers do. The software is simply a tool to help researchers to organize their data work in effective ways. Secondly, not all technologies are relevant to all analytic frameworks. Researchers conducting conversation analysis are unlikely to find the theory development tools found in software such as NVivo particularly relevant to their aims. It is not the case, then, that CAQDAS is necessarily appropriate to a researcher's work. Working out whether or not such tools may be useful is one aspect of designing an analytic strategy for dealing with data and is, as with every part of analysis, a contextual matter. Where they are relevant to a researcher's project, these programmes can be very useful for helping researchers to organize and interrogate their data.

Recording technologies, digital data and analysis

For many years, researchers relied on cassette-based recording devices to capture their data (such as interviews, audio-fieldnotes or video observations). However, many researchers now prefer to use digital recording devices that can connect to a computer to transfer the data across for storage, transcription and analysis. Many CAQDAS programmes are compatible with audio-video materials, and can be used to analyse and organize these media-rich data forms. By using these technologies, researchers can analyse their data directly, instead of relying solely on transcriptions of that data. This is not to suggest that transcriptions are therefore unnecessary: as I previously discussed, transcriptions are an important aspect of working through data.

However, the integration of transcriptions together with data can be a very profitable approach. Orientating to the original data forms enables researchers to check their transcriptions and to analyse their original data in new ways. Similarly, rather than relying on re-descriptions, researchers can shuttle between analytic descriptions (transcriptions) and data, as a means of shifting their analytic focus, moving from a focused iteration of their data to the data itself, and back. This frees researchers from the confines of one particular interpretation of their data and allows them to keep the data as an analytic resource. Multimedia compliant forms of CAQDAS are particularly useful tools for aiding this process.

The use of digital data does not stop at with the analysis of data. Online publication formats, such as electronic journals, are increasingly encouraging researchers to use electronic data forms. The use of electronic data has some distinct advantages for researchers: transcribed exemplars of data take up significant word space and restrict the number of examples that researchers can use, whereas, through hyperlinks, researchers can connect their data to their analysis and include multiple examples, without adding to their word count. Furthermore, such data are more 'alive' than transcriptions, and create more of a sense of the social setting being investigated. These matters also have important implications for some of the persistent methodological debates in qualitative research. A common criticism towards some forms of qualitative research has been the suggestion that analysis can be invisible and therefore difficult to validate. When researchers publish their work, it is common for them to include only a few selective examples of their data. By using hyperlinks in online publication formats, it is possible to produce better access to their analysis.

However, there are serious ethical dilemmas surrounding such usage. Research participants are much more identifiable through digital recordings than they are through anonymized transcripts. As a result, it can be more difficult to hold to the very common promise of anonymity that researchers give to their research participants (Akeroyd 1998; Parry and Mauthner 2004). Perhaps because of this, in spite of the increasing number of exclusively online publication formats, very few researchers have taken up the challenge of integrating data into their writing in this way. However, the technology does bring important opportunities for contemporary qualitative researchers that enable them to overcome important methodological critiques.

CAQDAS packages often include features that help researchers to coordinate their analytic work by enabling them to:

- work on the same project at the same time and to see each other's analysis
- filter the analysis that is displayed in the package (e.g. to see just the analysis conducted by a particular person, or just the analysis conducted on a particular day)
- keep all the features of analysis (analytic notes, fieldnotes, transcripts, and coding) in the same 'place'

CAQDAS is not the only tool at researchers' disposal however. Social networking software, such as wikis and blogs provide potentially very useful ways of coordinating one's analysis across a team of researchers. To take an example, a wiki is a series of web pages that can be created and linked together without the need for specialist web design or editing skills. Researchers can use wikis as a useful way of coordinating their work. Even an individual researcher not working in collaborative spaces can use wikis as a means of centralizing his or her writing and analysis. Researchers may use individual web pages to present alternative analyses of a given data section; they may link sections of data from different pages to each other, and add comments and ideas for conceptual development. These sorts of relatively new collaborative online working tools provide new opportunities for organizing and managing data work.

Modes of Analysis

Collaborative analysis

While it is not always possible, collaborative analysis can be useful for researchers as it gives them a means of ensuring both internal and external reliability (see Box 18.3). The 'internal reliability' of a coding scheme is ensured when more than one researcher agrees on the coding that has been generated. External reliability is ensured by researchers from beyond the particular research team reaching the same or very similar coding structure (see Chapter 4 for a discussion on inter-coder reliability). At a simpler level, collaborative work can also be more productive, as researchers can share out what is often a considerable amount of work. Further, offering more than one perspective on data can sometimes create a richer analytic process.

Box 18.3: Internal/external reliability

The internal reliability of analysis is achieved when members of the same research team agree on the analysis that is conducted. External reliability involves members of the research community who do not participate in the project reaching similar analyses. However, not all qualitative researchers agree that either of these types of reliability are actually required for an analysis to be robust. Some researchers suggest that the notion of 'reliability' as a check for consistency between researchers can be inappropriate in qualitative research, where the individuality of a researcher's biography and analytic angle is seen as important for how an analytic 'story' is told. In such instances notions such as 'transparency' are often used, where the aim is to show *how* the analysis was reached rather than achieving agreement on the analysis (Guba and Lincoln 1982).

Thematic analysis

I use the phrase 'thematic analysis' to describe a very common set of procedures used for organizing and working through data. Thematic analysis is not a unified entity, but describes quite a general interest in the exploration of themes. Most CAQDAS software is designed to facilitate this form of data work. Two examples of specific approaches that can be described as instances of thematic analysis are Glaser and Strauss's (1967) formulation of grounded theory and Miles and Huberman's (1994) 'cross case' analysis. Thematic analysis is based around the creation of *themes* that are described in terms of categories. The category or *code* is a concept that describes some recurring feature of the data. Importantly, this type of work should be thought of as *procedural*, and as concerning the ways that data can be managed. It does not relate in any way to the conceptual issues underlying the research problems being pursued and worked through in this type of data analysis. While the types of strategies outlined below may offer ways of *working with data*, they should not be thought of as *constituting* data analysis or as representing a universal approach. I have chosen to focus on this type of data work as it is very common in educational contexts.

Below are several important principles within thematic analysis.

- *Create clear and distinct code definitions* – all codes need to be clearly defined and operationally distinct from each other. However, it is not uncommon for the definition of codes to evolve through the analysis, as researchers often find a section of data that broadly fits a code definition but which contains some new property that requires the definition to be broadened. When definitions do change, researchers need to check that this change does not alter the relevance of previously included data to the code.
- *Keep a code log books* – it is important to keep a list of the codes that are generated – the date of their creation, their definition and, where relevant, who created them. It can also be insightful to note the participants or data sections to which the codes have been applied. Such information is important for keeping track of analysis, ensuring that repetition does not occur, keeping codes distinct and working out how and why codes were developed in the first instance.
- *Don't create too many codes* – this rather imprecise instruction is based on the idea that using a lot of codes can get very confusing. I have tended to work on the basis that more than around 30 codes is probably too many; however, this is a very arbitrary formulation. The point is that researchers need to be able to remember their codes and distinctive features, and to be able to use them consistently.
- *Make sure that there is a purpose to the code* – code categories should only be created when there is a clear purpose to them. It can be tempting to create codes whenever a theme is detected, but themes are only necessary where they are analytically relevant. Of course, because analysis is iterative, it may be the case that codes seem relevant but become superfluous. Coding is very much an experimental and iterative process, so such occurrences are inevitable to a certain extent.

One way to think about codes and to give them a little more analytic depth is in terms of properties. A property is simply a characteristic that can vary along a sliding scale. For example, a researcher examining the uses of drugs by university students may create a code for 'drug use' that has a sliding scale for the types of drugs that are used, based, perhaps, on some legal classification scheme. Sometimes the specification of a scale might be made in the first instance, while on other occasions it might be derived from the data. Not all codes will be classifiable in this way of course; indeed, much of the data created in qualitative research cannot be described in terms of scales.

Groupings

A significant aspect of thematic analysis involves developing relationships between codes: defining the ways in which different codes relate to one another. There are two key aspects to this: groupings and relations. Groupings are collectivities of codes that have some property or other in common. Relations are specifications of the connection between two or more codes.

One way of thinking about groupings is in terms of code families (which is simply another term for a collection of codes). An example of a code family is provided in Box 18.4, and comes from my study about the processes of jazz improvisation. The two code families, namely, 'instrument specific contingencies' and 'collaborative performance practices', represent two different sets of contingencies within which musicians operate. The first set relates to the specific instrument played by an individual musician and the second to the contingencies of the group. Within the individual contingencies, the instrument itself provides a context for thinking about the music – a conceptual framework for thinking about how musical sounds are organized. Musicians also have personal and individualized stylistic preferences and improvisation practices. These practices are worked out in the context of a group set of interests, in which musicians work out how to collaboratively orientate to certain contingencies such as the expectations of an audience or the particular challenges of improvising in the specific harmonic context of a given song. It is well beyond the scope of this discussion to go into the details of this analysis (see Gibson 2006 for further discussion of these ideas). The point to make here is that the two collections are sets of codes that are grouped according to particular similarities as defined by the grouping.

Box 18.4 Two code families in a study of jazz improvisation

Individual 'instrument specific' contingencies	Collaborative performance practices
Volume	Turn-taking
Timbre	Specific performance roles
Speed	Collaborative aesthetics
Register	Audience aesthetics
Tone	Harmonic/melodic/rhythmic context
Conceptual framework	Genre
Personal stylistic preferences	

Researchers may also create groupings within code groupings, *or sub-families*. These are sets of codes that belong to the same family, but which also have some other property that makes them similar. In the example given in Box 18.4, the codes 'Turn-taking' and 'specific performance roles' could be placed in a sub-family called 'general performance conventions' – these would still be a part of the family 'collaborative performance practices' but would be a specific aspect of the concept collated in the wider family. Through families and sub-families, researchers can create relational groupings of codes to describe their data.

Relations

The specification of relations involves giving some meaningful connection between codes other than that they are simply related. Box 18.5 outlines some of the possible relations that may be used to connect codes to each other. These are just examples however: as a relation is simply the delineation of a type of connection, any relational word could, in principle, be of value in creating this conceptual linking.

Box 18.5 A list of possible relations between codes

Causes	Reinforces
Contradicts	Is a property of
Results from	Is the opposite of
Influences	Is an aspect of
Implies	

To give an example, in a study of professional education and practice in pharmacy I conducted some years ago, a code for 'satisfaction' was thought to be related in some way to the achievement of good parity between the educational experience of those practitioners and the roles that they had in their professional context. Specifically, it was supposed that pharmacists who had a varied role and used a significant amount of their advanced pharmacy training were more satisfied than those who did not use their training skills and had a more limited set of roles and responsibilities. This supposition formed a loose hypothesis that was formulated in terms of code relations:

'Varied role' + 'Use of educational experience' = job satisfaction

The creation of relationships may also be used to connect to other objects of analysis, such as interviewees, or particular parts of the data. With this in mind, researchers may wish to demonstrate that a code is 'derived from', 'relates strongly to' or is 'demonstrated by' a particular interviewee. They may similarly wish to note that a particular code family 'results in', 'results from' or 'contradicts' a particular code. Equally, different families/sub-families or the codes within a given family may be given a more detailed analysis through the creation of particular relations. Working through categories in this way results in the generation of a conceptual framework that operates as a sort of 'meta-description' of the data themselves.

The relevance of thematic analysis

This discussion shows that approaches to thematic work such as this simply comprise strategies for working through data but do not provide any theoretical resource for thinking about that data. The methods do not offer ways of thinking about what should count as a code or concept, but merely give some basic ways of thinking about how these might be worked through once they are created. As such, these sorts of techniques should not be thought of as constituting analysis, but merely as some of the ways that researchers *might* think about some aspects of their data work. This heavily equivocal statement draws attention to the great difficulty of offering techniques to data work that are generally applicable and relevant to all researchers in education. The point of including the brief discussion of these particular techniques to data organization is simply because of their remarkable popularity.

Summary

Technology is a very useful aid in qualitative analysis. When deciding on which CAQDAS package to use, researchers need to think about the mode of analysis to be used and the ways that the distinctive packages on offer may aid their use of that approach.

Transcription is not a means of preparing for analysis but is a fundamental feature of data work. By working with various transcription methods and approaches, researchers can create interesting juxtapositions of data re-presentations as a means of focusing and refocusing on different features of their data

Qualitative research is characterized by a wide variety of analytic modes and approaches. Not all of those modes are relevant to all research projects. Researchers need to think through the alignment of their research problem, their research design, their methods of data collection, their transcription modes and their analytic mode in order to make sure that they have a coherent and consistent analytic strategy.

To speak of qualitative analysis in a generalized way (as I have been doing here) is to remove the very thing that gives analysis its sense, namely, *data*. That said, for analysis to proceed smoothly, it is important to understand both the process of analysis and some of the key practices that constitute much data work, and it is these that have formed my topic of discussion.

It is extremely common for researchers undertaking qualitative analysis, particularly when they are doing so for the first time, to have some trepidation about the process. In large part, this uneasiness is due to the unknown character of the journey through the data. Very often, when researchers ask for advice on 'doing data analysis' what they really want is some map through this terrain, but precisely because it is an exploratory and iterative process, no particularly clear map is available. To reverse the analogy, qualitative analysis is an exploratory activity, and one of the *outcomes* is a map of the process. What researchers can use to guide them, though, is some of the accumulated practices, tools and experiences that other researchers have developed and put to use in their own explorations. I hope that some of the reflections I have provided here may offer researchers some ways of thinking about their own contexts of work, and assist them in working out their own orientation to the complex literary terrain of qualitative research.

References

Akeroyd, A. (1998) 'Personal information and qualitative research data: some practical and ethical problems arising from data protection legislation', in R. M. Lee (ed.) *Using Computers in Qualitative Research*. London: Sage.

Dressler, R. and Kreuz, R. (2000) 'Transcribing oral discourse: a survey and a model system', *Discourse Processes*, 29: 25–36.

Garfinkel, H. (1967) *Studies in Ethnomethodology*. Englewood Cliffs, NJ: Prentice Hall.

Gee, J. P. (1999) *An Introduction to Discourse Analysis: Theory and Method*. London: Routledge.

Gibson, W. (2006) 'Material culture and embodied action: sociological notes on the examination of musical instruments in jazz improvisation', *The Sociological Review*, 54: 171–87.

Glaser, B. and Strauss, A. (1967) *The Discovery of Grounded Theory: Strategies for Qualitative Research.* New York: Aldine de Gruyter.

Guba, E. and Lincoln, Y. (1982) 'Epistemological and methodological bases of naturalistic inquiry', *Educational Communication and Technology Journal,* 30: 233–52.

Miles, M. and Huberman, A. (1994) *Qualitative Data Analysis.* Thousand Oaks, CA: Sage.

Parry, O. and Mauthner, N. (2004) 'Whose data are they anyway? practical, ethical and legal issues in archiving qualitative research data', *Sociology,* 38: 139–51.

19 Key Concepts and Assumptions in Quantitative Data Analysis

Dimitra Hartas

Introduction

Doing quantitative research brings many challenges, and employing appropriate statistical techniques is one of them. The choice of statistical procedures for quantitative data analysis is an important aspect of the research design, and requires an understanding of the key concepts and assumptions that underpin quantitative research. The technical requirements of statistical analyses can be met fairly easily. What is important however is to employ quantitative analyses in ways that are consistent with the research aims and questions, and clarify the nature of the data and the variables and the sources of variation in a study. These preliminary steps are crucial to enable us to formulate hypotheses, test the assumptions that underpin quantitative analyses and develop a rationale with regard to the statistical procedures we plan to employ to analyse our data. The aim of this chapter is to introduce you to the key concepts and assumptions in quantitative research design and analysis.

By the end of this chapter, you should be able to:

- understand key concepts in quantitative research – i.e., variables and variation; levels of measurement; confidence intervals; effect size and statistical power
- understand hypothesis testing and the critiques associated with the notion of significance
- differentiate between parametric and nonparametric data and statistics
- consider the assumptions that underpin quantitative data analyses

The Variables in a Study

Educational researchers collect qualitative or quantitative information about participants' characteristics, attributes, behaviour and actions. These entities, which can take on different values, are called *variables*. For example, age is a variable because it can take on different values for different people or for the same person at different points in time. Variables emerge from constructs via the process of *operationalization*. It is important to be aware of the differences between *constructs* and *variables*. A construct is an abstract entity – for example, intelligence or self-esteem – whereas a variable is a specific entity, such as reading comprehension, which takes on different values. A construct is multidimensional and cannot be measured or observed directly. In a research study, constructs need to be operationalized (defined as measurable and observable entities) in order for the variables to emerge from them. For example, the construct 'ability' may be defined as comprising verbal and nonverbal reasoning or problem-solving skills, depending on the theoretical orientation of a study. As such, the variables that emerge from 'ability' are verbal reasoning and nonverbal reasoning skills, which are measurable entities.

Three main types of variable can be identified in a research study, namely *independent* variables, *dependent* variables and *extraneous* or *confounding* variables (Cresswell 2005). The independent variables influence/affect the outcome, which is the dependent variable. The distinction between independent and dependent variables is particularly relevant when we investigate cause-effect relationships, in that the independent variable is the cause and the dependent variable is the effect. For example, suppose we study the effects of a new educational programme on reading achievement: the programme is the independent variable and measures of achievement constitute the dependent variable (outcome).

An independent variable can be a treatment or a measured variable. A treatment is an independent variable, which is manipulated as part of an intervention (e.g. a new educational programme). The measured variables are included in a research design to control for their effects (e.g. gender). The extraneous variables are those that are likely to influence the outcome of a study in a non-systematic way. We control for their unsystematic effects by including them in a research design. For example, in a study that explores the effects of a literacy programme on vocabulary skills, we should account for factors such as language skills or literary home environment (or any other factor/characteristic) that have been found to impact on children's vocabulary in order to minimize unsystematic variation (see Chapter 15 for a discussion on controlling for the effects of extraneous variables). The extraneous variables whose effect is accounted for are called *control* or *mediating* variables and those whose effect cannot be controlled are the *confounding* variables (see Figure 19.1). We should aim to minimize the effects of the confounding variables because they pose threats to internal validity (we have no way of knowing whether an outcome is due to the treatment or to a confounding variable). A good theoretical grounding and a careful consideration of the research design (e.g. a close fit between the research questions and the methods) may tackle the confounding variables in a study.

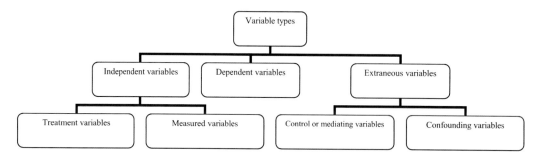

Figure 19.1 Types of variable

Systematic and unsystematic variation

Typically, two types of variation in the outcome variable are observed, namely *systematic* and *unsystematic*. A systematic variation is due to the experimental manipulation or treatment, whereas an unsystematic variation is due to the effects of extraneous factors (e.g. natural differences in a person's ability or prior learning experience) on an outcome. To reduce unsystematic variation, we can control for the effects of these factors through randomization, as in experimental designs, or group matching, as in quasi-experimental designs, or through a statistical manipulation (e.g. covariance).

By controlling for extraneous factors, we are in a better position to assert that the differences found between groups are due to the treatment or experimental manipulation (systematic variation) and not due to some uncontrolled, random factors (unsystematic variation). It is important to note that we can never control for all the factors that are likely to interfere with a study, especially when examining social phenomena in their context. As we discussed in the chapter on experimental designs, there are advantages and disadvantages attached to an experimental control. Controlling for extraneous factors through an experimental manipulation in a lab-like setting can increase the internal validity of a study. However, the outcome may not be relevant and applicable to a real-life setting (e.g. classrooms). The balance between systematic and unsystematic variation in a study is, essentially, a trade-off between the internal and external validity. In highly controlled settings, we can minimize the unsystematic variation and increase the internal validity; however, the results of the study may not be generalizable into other settings, reducing the external validity.

The Levels of Measurement

The data are collected in various forms, including self-reports, standardized scores, observation fieldnotes or interview accounts. A *measurement* is the process of recording numerical information on a characteristic. Scales of measurement or levels of measurement refer to the ways the responses, and subsequently the variables, are measured. Variables differ in how well they can be measured, or how much measurable information their measurement scale can provide. A key determinant of the amount of information provided by a variable is its type of measurement scale.

For example, opinion ratings are less specific than test scores, in that the former involves the rating of an opinion by assigning it to ordered categories, whereas the latter involves precise numerical values on a scale.

Determining the level of measurement has many implications. First, it influences decisions on the type of statistical analysis that is appropriate for the values assigned to the variables. Secondly, it influences the way in which the results are interpreted: with variables such as gender we address categories, whereas with variables that are based on scores we refer to precise numerical values. There are four levels of measurement, namely nominal, ordinal, interval or ratio, and variables can be classified as such (see Figure 19.2).

Nominal scales

The values of the variables measured at a nominal level (e.g. gender) are categories assigned with arbitrary values, for example, female = 1 and male = 2. The values 1 and 2 describe the variable and have no other meaning and no logical order. The properties of a nominal scale are: mutually exclusive categories; and categories have no logical order. The variables measured at the nominal level are categorical because they involve categories chosen by a respondent to provide information about characteristics.

Ordinal scales

With ordinal scales, the characteristics are ordered or ranked in terms of importance or the extent of occurrence, allowing responses to be placed on a continuum. For example, 'To what extent something happens', with the response categories being 'To a great extent, Somewhat, Slightly, Not at all'. Ordinal scales offer a logical order to the classification. The properties of ordinal scales are: mutually exclusive categories, categories have a logical order in that they are scaled according to the amount they possess.

In survey research, a Likert scale is a common technique used to measure the participants' responses to attitudinal items in a questionnaire. The Likert scale is a multiple indicator of a set of attitudes relating to a specific area (Bryman 2004) and measures the extent to which something happens or the intensity of feelings or attitudes towards something, generating ordinal data.

Interval scales

Interval scales function as a ruler with equal intervals. The points of the scale are continuous, and the distance between them is assumed to be equal. The properties of interval scales are: mutually exclusive, can be ordered logically and the distance between any two points is equal.

Ratio scales

Ratio scales have equal distances between the units and a point 0, which refers to an absence of a characteristic. An example of a ratio scale is scores in a reading test where 0 means no correct answers, and the difference between the 20 and 25 is the same as the difference between 30 and

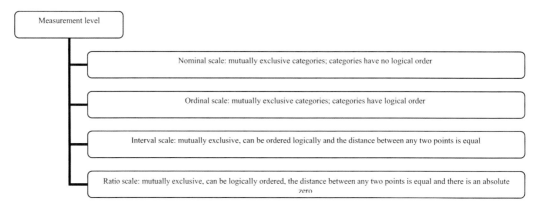

Figure 19.2 Levels of measurement and their properties

35. The properties of a ratio scale are: mutually exclusive, can be logically ordered, the distance between any two points is equal and there is an absolute zero.

The measurement levels are hierarchical: as we move from the nominal to ratio levels of measurement, the procedures employed for statistical analyses become less restrictive. With nominal and ordinal variables, we are constrained in the statistical analyses we employ, which are mainly nonparametric (see Chapters 21, 22, 23). Some statisticians argue that nominal and ordinal variables are not 'real' variables. However, in education and social sciences, they have an important function, given that much data are collected within the context of survey research.

What is a Hypothesis?

A hypothesis is an educated guess, a prediction we make about the outcome of an intervention or a relationship among factors that characterize social events and situations. The phrase 'educated guess' may be misleading because it conveys the notion of guessing. In quantitative research, we develop hypotheses based on theories and previous research findings (via deductive reasoning; see Chapter 1), and collect evidence to either verify or reject the hypotheses formed. In experimental and quasi-experimental designs in particular, a hypothesis links together the dependent and independent variables (Cross and Belli 2004).

Hypotheses are specific statements and thus the wording used should be precise and well defined (operationalized). A well-formed hypothesis is a concise statement that encapsulates information about the variables and their interplay, comparison of groups or relationships between variables and information about the participants and possibly the context of the research. It is important to note that a well-formed hypothesis is derived from a well-formed question and clear research goals.

An example of a hypothesis is:

Pupils whose mother has a higher education qualification complete more homework than those whose mother does not.

This hypothesis offers information about the independent variable (mother's higher education qualification), the dependent variable (amount of homework completion) and participants (pupils). Cresswell (2005) offers some useful guidelines with regard to stating a hypothesis. These are: the independent variables should be stated before the dependent variables; the groups (if the study involves group comparisons) should be stated explicitly; and the relationships among variables should be delineated. Finally, the overall hypothesis should be stated as a prediction or conjecture.

There are two types of hypothesis, the null hypothesis (H0) and the alternative hypothesis (H1). The null hypothesis predicts that there is not any relationship between the independent and dependent variables. Going back to the previous example, the alternative hypothesis is:

H1: Pupils whose mother has a higher education qualification complete more homework than those whose mother has not.

And the null hypothesis is:

H0: Pupils whose mother has a higher education qualification do not complete more homework than those whose mother has not.

Another way of stating the null hypothesis is:

H0: There is no relationship between mother's higher education qualifications and pupils' homework completion.

Or

H0: There is no difference in homework completion between pupils whose mother has higher education qualifications and those whose mother has not.

We can specify the direction of a prediction and formulate directional or one-tailed and nondirectional or two-tailed hypotheses. The terms 'one-tailed' and 'two-tailed' refer to the tails of the frequency distribution of the outcome scores (for details on frequency distribution see Chapter 21). With 'one-tailed' hypotheses, we predict the direction of an outcome (e.g. changes in the relationship between the variables or in the scores between groups). For example, the hypothesis *H1: Pupils whose mother has a higher education qualification complete more homework than those whose mother has not* is 'one-tailed' in that the prediction has one direction, i.e. pupils complete *more* homework.

To make it a 'two-tailed' hypothesis, we should state as H1: 'There is a difference in the amount of homework completion between pupils whose mother has higher education qualifications and those whose mother has not'. In this case, we do not specify the direction of the prediction; with an open-ended statement such as 'there is a difference in … ' the direction can be positive or negative (e.g. pupils complete more or less homework). Conceptually, the difference between one-tailed and two-tailed hypotheses is that, with the latter, we explore both directions that a relationship between variables can take, being less deterministic about the outcome. One-tailed hypotheses have been criticized for introducing bias in a research by taking a specific direction. The decisions over one- or two-tailed hypotheses should be grounded on previous research to offer a sound justification as to why we decide to explore a specific direction in a relationship.

Hypothesis-testing

With statistical analyses, we test whether there are any differences between the sample values on the variables we examine and the true values of the population at large. In other words, we test whether the sample mean (statistic) is a good estimate of the population mean (parameter). The term 'statistics' refers to measures such as mean and standard deviation, of a characteristic in a sample, whereas the corresponding characteristics in a population are called 'parameters'.

Through hypothesis-testing we produce probabilistic answers as to whether a hypothesis is confirmed or rejected when comparing groups or examining the magnitude of association between variables (Levin and Robinson 1999) (see Box 19.1). Hypothesis-testing has meaning for inferential statistics only. Statistical inference is the process whereby we make inductive statements about the population parameters based on the sample statistics. If the sample mean is a good estimate, then we are confident to generalize the findings from the sample to the population from which it was drawn.

To make inferences about a population based on the relationships we observe in a sample underpins the capacity to make generalizations, a desirable feature of quantitative research. With quantitative research, we can never be absolutely sure that the findings will be generalizable to the population from which the sample was drawn. There is always a possibility that a sampling error has occurred. In statistics, the term 'error' is used a great deal. Error indicates the extent to which the properties of a sample deviate from the corresponding values in the population (Kinnear and Gray 2006).

Box 19.1 Hypothesis-testing: an analogy

In many countries, the criminal justice system operates on the assumption that the defendant is innocent until proven guilty beyond a reasonable doubt. In hypothesis-testing, this assumption is called the null hypothesis (H0 = the defendant is not guilty). As in a court system, we assume that the null hypothesis is true until we gather evidence to either reject or accept it. As Johnson and Christensen (2004) put it, during hypothesis testing, we bring the null hypothesis to 'trial', and through the use of inferential statistics we determine the probability of the evidence under the assumption that the null hypothesis is true. If the null hypothesis is rejected, then we accept the alternative hypothesis (H1 = the defendant is guilty).

Probability level

In order to decide whether we accept or reject the null hypothesis, we need to set a level of acceptance/rejection, called *significance* or *probability level*. A statistical significance is the probability that the observed relationships between variables or the differences between group means in a sample have occurred by chance alone. In other words, a significance level refers to the level of risk we accept that the differences found are due to chance alone (Cresswell 2005). If the relationships observed in the sample are due to chance alone and, assuming that the sample is representative of the population, we infer that no such relationships or differences exist in the population.

By convention, the borderline or critical value for the significance level is set at .05 (meaning that 5 out of 100 times we do an experiment the results are due to chance alone) which involves a 5 per cent probability error. We are more confident about the results when the level is set at .01 (1 out of 100 times the results are due to chance alone). Results that are significant at the $p < .01$ level are commonly considered to be statistically significant, and those at $p < .005$ or $p < .001$ levels are often considered to be highly significant. The correspondence between the notion of chance and the probability level is expressed as: 0 per cent chance translates to $p = 0$; 5 per cent chance is $p = 0.05$; 25 per cent chance is $p = 0.25$ (Connolly 2007). It is important to note that those classifications represent nothing else but arbitrary conventions based on general research experience.

When setting the probability level, we need to consider the sample size, in that it is more likely to find statistically significant results with large sample sizes. When the sample size is large it is almost likely that the null hypothesis is rejected (Kinnear and Gray 2006), suggesting that the results are statistically significant. However, this does not always mean that the magnitude of the association between variables is of practical importance.

Type I and Type II errors

During hypothesis-testing, there are two possible errors that can be committed, namely Type I and Type II errors (see Box 19.2). A Type I error occurs when we think that there is a relationship or an effect but in fact there is not. In this case, we wrongly reject the null hypothesis and accept the alternative hypothesis (false positive). A Type II error occurs when we think that there is not a relationship or a difference/effect between groups where, in fact, there is. In this case, we wrongly accept the null hypothesis (false negative). A Type I error is worse than Type II error in that, in the former case, we indicate that there is a significant difference between the groups or a relationship between variables, whereas in reality there is not. This can be potentially misleading, especially when the results obtained from a sample are generalized to the population. With a Type II error, the opportunity to identify differences in the sample and generalize the findings to the population is missed. The level of statistical significance refers to the risk that we might commit a Type I or Type II error and, subsequently, the risk of making inferences about the population based on the sample.

Box 19.2 Type I and Type II errors

	Null Hypothesis is true	Null Hypothesis is false
Fail to reject null hypothesis	Correct decision	Type II error (false negative)
Reject null hypothesis	Type I error (false positive)	Correct decision

With this in mind, a probability level of p<.05 translates into 5 chances in 100 that we might be committing a Type I error, that is, to falsely conclude that we have confirmed the hypothesis we set out to investigate. In other words, 5 chances in 100 means that if we draw 100 samples from a population, there is a probability that in as much as 5 of them we confirm a relationship that cannot be found in the population. However, the relationship between variables in the remaining 95 samples is likely to be found in the population from which the samples were drawn. If we want to be more confident that we are not committing a Type I error, we set the significance level at p<0.01. This again translates into 1 chance in 100 that a relationship between variables exists by chance alone. Compared to p<0.05, the significance level p<0.01 is considered to be more rigorous in that the chance to get statistically significant results by chance alone is 1 out of 100 rather than 5 out of 100.

It is important to note that statistical significance does not always mean 'practical importance'. Levin (2006) raises a number of concerns regarding hypothesis-testing or significance testing, summarizing the arguments offered by the 'antisignificants' and the 'significants'. The 'antisignificants' attest that statistical significance does not necessarily mean that the findings are of any substantive importance. There is a great deal of criticism levelled against a significance testing, encapsulated in the following statements.

- To obtain information about whether something differs from a specified value is not always very useful, unless we can estimate the magnitude of the difference and judge its educational importance (Thompson 1996).
- There are concerns about producing statistically significant results when large sample sizes are involved (Tukey 1991). Conversely, in some studies with small samples, statistically significant results may not be shown.
- The term 'significant' in a hypothesis testing can be misleading in that it suggests that the results are important, when what it means is that the hypothesis was rejected at a set level (see Thompson 1996).
- There is a bias among researchers towards research where the hypothesis has been rejected, compared to research studies where the null hypothesis has not been rejected (Levin 2006: 531, paraphrased).

The 'significants', on the other hand, view hypothesis-testing as a useful device to distinguish research outcomes that are due to chance from those that are not, and delineate the direction of an outcome or a relationship. Levin and Robinson (1999: 147) argue that statistical hypothesis-testing can offer probabilistic answers to research areas such as:

- the average performance of SAT-takers is better or worse this year compared to national norms
- a company has exhibited discrimination practices in recruitment (based on the known ethnic representation in the community and the pool of qualified applicants)
- an experimental outcome differs from what was predicted (based on an accepted theoretical or mathematical model)

A statistical significance shows the probability that the differences or relationships found in the sample are not properties of the sample alone but also exist in the population. For this to be the case, sampling and the power of statistical tests need to be considered carefully. While it is useful to engage with hypothesis-testing, we always have to exercise caution with the interpretation of the findings, even when we are confident that the results are statistically significant. Being able to show statistically significant findings is not an end in itself. The most important aspect is to understand the nature and the theoretical and practical significance of the findings. In so doing, calculating the confidence interval, the effect size and statistical power is useful to develop an estimate of the magnitude or size of statistically significant differences. Another way of ascertaining the practical importance of hypothesis-testing is through replication. Replicating a study by testing the same hypothesis with different samples (independent replications) allows us to investigate whether the outcomes of the research hold weight.

The Confidence Interval

A confidence interval is a range of numbers within which the population mean is likely to fall. Although hypothesis-testing and statistical significance are important concepts to consider, they may be misleading when interpreting the results. For example, a 95 per cent confidence interval suggests that you are '95 per cent confident' that the data collected from the sample will include the population parameter. A 95 per cent confidence interval means that a range of values centred on the sample mean will include the population mean in 95 per cent of samples. To put it simply, if we derive 100 samples from the same population, in 95 of them the sample mean also includes the population mean, thus stating that we are 95 per cent confident that the population mean lies within the range (Kinnear and Gray 2006).

The Effect Size

The effect size refers to the size of the difference between groups, or the magnitude of the relationship between variables. The effect size is the ratio of the explained variance (systematic variance) and the total variance (both systematic and unsystematic variance) in a variable. We need to determine the magnitude of a difference or a relationship in practical terms, in order to ascertain its practical importance. Calculating the effect size helps us to identify the strength of the conclusions drawn in a study (Creswell 2005). Suppose we find that the differences between boys' and girls' maths scores are statistically significant. However, we should also ask whether the differences make sense from a practical point of view. To figure this out we need to calculate the effect size of the difference. The effect size is calculated differently in different statistical analyses, and its value typically ranges between 0 and 1, with .5 (one-half of a standard deviation) or above being considered strong (Cohen's d effect size range, between 0 and 1+). Several factors influence the effect size. These include:

- the sample size
- the violation (or not) of the assumptions that underpin statistical analyses (e.g. homogeneity of variance)
- the critical value we set for statistical significance (a level)
- the statistical power of a test

The extent to which the effect size is noteworthy depends on the nature and implications of a study. The interpretations of an effect size should account for the findings from previous studies in order to investigate the consistency across effect sizes. This is particularly important for policy decision-making that is based on quantitative research findings. Although a large effect size is useful, a small effect size can also be noteworthy when we investigate certain research topics. For example, small effect sizes may be important when exploring factors that have a policy/practical significance (e.g. a measure of quality of life) or factors that do not respond to intervention, or small effects that over time can bring a cumulative effect (Thompson 2006).

When estimating the effect size, we should avoid the rigidity of a classification based on small-, medium- and large-size effects. There are other factors that we should consider, such as the research context, to understand why an effect size is similar or different to other effect sizes, and what this means in practical terms. Even small sample sizes can be important if:

- the outcome is of importance, such as a class size or the impact of the Literacy Hour on academic achievement
- the outcome is particularly resistant to intervention (e.g. changing people's addictive habits)
- small effects, generated over time, accumulate into larger effects
- the outcome has multiple causes and thus some of the interventions are likely to have a limited impact if they target a causal factor that is not very prominent (Thompson 2006: 595, slightly paraphrased).

The Statistical Power of a Test

A statistical test refers to the procedures employed to test a hypothesis. The power of a statistical test is the probability that it will detect a relationship or a trend in a sample, assuming that a relationship actually exists in the population (Connolly 2007). This means that a test with low statistical power may not be able to show a relationship in a sample, despite the fact that the same relationship may exist in the population. Small statistical power is linked with a higher probability to commit a Type II error, which is to fail to detect a genuine effect.

Statistical power is affected by its type (parametric, nonparametric), the design (different or same participants observed under two conditions), sample sizes and the reliability of a measurement. The statistical power of a test should be determined prior to deciding on the statistical techniques for data analysis. Cohen (1988) recommends a statistical power of .8, which translates into an 80 per cent chance to detect a genuine effect). As seen in Box 19.3, when calculating the statistical power of a test, we need to account for many factors. For example, to achieve a statistical power of .8 to detect a genuine effect at a p<.05 level, we need 783 participants in order to achieve a weak effect size of r=.1; 85 participants to achieve a medium effect size of r= .3; and 28 participants for a strong effect size of r=.5 (Cohen 1992 cited in Field 2005: 34). It is important to stress the need for a balance between a sample size, the statistical power of a test and the effect size to reduce the probability of committing Type I or Type II errors.

Box 19.3 Factors affecting statistical power

- Sample size.
- Type of test (parametric or nonparametric).
- Research design (between-subject or within-subject design).
- Probability level p (the critical value set for statistical significance).
- Effect size or the magnitude of a relationship we try to detect.

Parametric and Nonparametric Data

The nature of a data – i.e. parametric and nonparametric – influences the type of statistical analyses we employ. Because statistical analyses use mathematical models, parametric data are fit for a wide range of analyses, whereas nonparametric data are thought to be unfit. In education, however, nonparametric data (e.g. attitude scores, categories such as ethnicity, gender, SES) offer useful information to address questions of educational and pedagogic significance.

As discussed before, the levels of measurement influence the decision about the type of statistical techniques employed in a research design. For example, if the variables in a study are nominal, they yield nonparametric data, which require nonparametric tests. The decisions about the type of variables, and the subsequent statistical analyses, should be made early in a study to consider the data collection and analyses procedures, such as questionnaires, interview schedules or tests. In addition to the type of variables, decisions should be made about the sample size, effect size and statistical power.

A quick way of categorizing variables is by asking the following questions:

- Can the categories be rank ordered? If no, then the variables are nominal/categorical; if yes, they are ordinal.
- Are the distances between the categories equal? If no, they are ordinal; if yes, they are interval/ratio (Bryman, 2004: 226).

Parametric data abide by the following assumptions:

- data are from normally distributed populations
- data are measured at interval level
- variance in different groups of people is roughly equal
- scores are independent (obtained from different people) (Field 2005: 287)

The first two assumptions – i.e. a normal distribution and level of measurement – refer to the nature of parametric data. The last two describe the comparison groups in terms of being homogeneous (have equal variance) and involving different people (independent scores). The statistical procedures such as an independent t-test, analysis of variance or factorial analysis, employ parametric data that rely on these assumptions (i.e. normality, interval data, homogeneity of variance and independence of scores). It is important to ensure that the nature of our data and the constitution of the groups are such that they meet these assumptions prior to running the above statistical analysis. In the following sections, we discuss the processes whereby we check these assumptions.

Normal distribution

Parametric tests assume that the data are derived from a normally distributed population, whereas nonparametric tests do not make assumptions about the population distribution. There are two ways to check the assumption of normality in a dataset. First, simply, by examining the histogram produced during descriptive analyses we check whether the outcome scores form a normal distribution. Secondly, to be confident about the normality assumption, we can also run a statistical test called Kolmogorov-Smirnov test.

Histogram

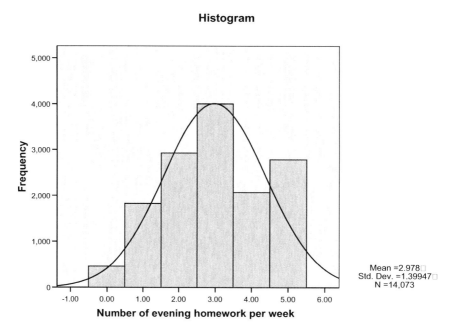

Figure 19.3 SPSS output

In the following example, we illustrate both ways of checking the assumption of normality by examining a variable from the LSYPE dataset – i.e. 'the number of homework evenings per week completed by pupils'. First we create a histogram of the number of the homework evenings per week. By looking at it, we can see that the scores form a near normal distribution (see Figure 19.3).

However, examining the histogram and the superimposed normal curve to determine whether the scores form a normal distribution is not an accurate method. Hence, we run the Kolmogorov-Smirnov test to test the null hypothesis H0 = 'there is no deviation from the normal distribution' or, in other words, H0 = 'there is no difference between this distribution and a normal distribution'. If the null hypothesis is correct, there is no difference between our distribution and a normal distribution and, essentially, the distribution of our data forms a normal distribution. If the null hypothesis is rejected, the distribution for this variable deviates from a normal distribution, and this violates the assumption of normality.

In SPSS this test is accessed through the 'Explore' command:

1 Go to **Analyze**
2 In the drop-down menu choose **Descriptive statistics**
3 Choose **Explore**, then click **Plots** and choose **Normality plots with tests** (see Figures 19.4, 19.5)

An example of testing for a normal distribution

Suppose we want to check whether the Key Stage 3 average scores (from LSYPE data) form a normal distribution. Looking at the histogram (Figure 19.6), we see that the KS3 scores form a distribution that is not bell shaped.

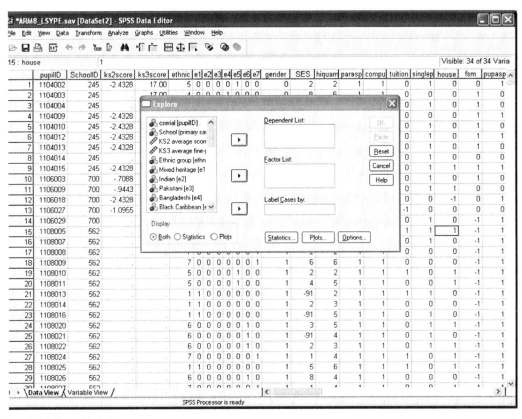

Figure 19.4 Normality test

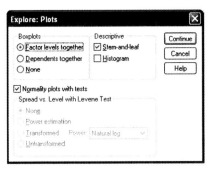

Figure 19.5 Explore plots

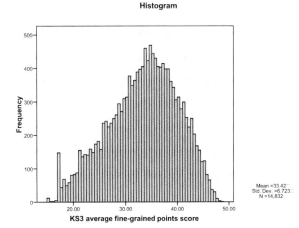

Histogram

Figure 19.6 Histogram

With the Kolmogorov-Smirnov test, the results came out statistically significant (p<.000, see Figure 19.7), meaning that the distribution is not normal, and hence the assumption of normality is violated.

The normal Q Q Plot offers a visual representation of the values we would have obtained if the

Tests of Normality

	Kolmogorov-Smirnov[a]		
	Statistic	df	Sig.
KS3 average fine-grained points score	.036	14832	.000

a. Lilliefors Significance Correction

Figure 19.7 SPSS output

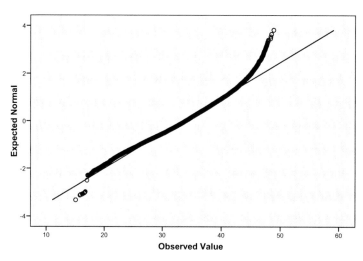

Figure 19.8 SPSS output

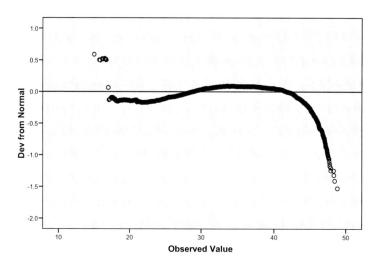

Figure 19.9 SPSS Output 19-5

distribution were normal (expected values). These values are compared to the actual/observed values in the dataset. If the data are normally distributed, the observed values (dots) follow very closely the straight line that represents the observed values. In this case, the dots form a non-straight, S-shaped line, and this is different from that in a normal distribution (see Figures 19.7 and 19.9). When the dots form an S shape the distribution is skewed, whereas when the dots consistently gather below or above the line, the distribution is kurtic (Field 2005).

The goodness of fit test (Kolmogorov-Smirnov test) compares the cumulative probabilities of the values in a dataset with the cumulative probabilities of the same values in a theoretical distribution. The goodness of fit indicates how well data are fitted by the theoretical distribution. If the discrepancy between the data distribution and a theoretical distribution is big, the data are not a good fit. When the assumption of normality is violated, we employ nonparametric tests (e.g. contingency analysis).

Data at an interval level

The data collected on the outcome variable should be at an interval level. Other terms used to describe such variables are *scale* or *continuous*, meaning that the distance between the points on a scale is equal across all points. An example of a continuous variable is reading skills as measured by a reading test. Assuming that the scores range between 0 and 50, the difference in the reading skills represented by moving from score 7 to 8 is the same as that occurring when moving from score 16 to 17.

Homogeneity of variance

The assumption of the homogeneity of variance attests that the data have been derived from normal distributions with an equal variance (Kinnear and Gray 2006). As we discuss in Chapter 23, a t-test or analysis of variance are considered to be rigorous statistical techniques and thus violation of the assumption of homogeneity of variance is acceptable as long as certain conditions are met. These are: (1) the samples are not small; (2) samples do not contain outliers (atypical scores); and (3) the group/cell sizes are nearly equal.

The Levene test is used to test the hypothesis that the variance across groups is equal. Hence, the null hypothesis is H0 = 'there is no difference in the variance between groups', whereas the alternative hypothesis is H1= 'there is difference in the variance between the groups'. Confirming the null hypothesis means that the variance is the same across the groups. In other words, the Levine test has to be non-significant to confirm that the variance is equal across groups.

If the null hypothesis is rejected, then the alternative hypothesis – i.e., 'there is difference in the variance between groups' – is accepted. In this case, the homogeneity assumption is violated. As mentioned, when a group variance is not equal, it is important to ensure that cell sizes are equal or near equal. With near-equal group sizes, violating the equal variance assumption does not affect the validity of the results. However, with unequal group sizes, violating the assumption of the homogeneity of variance increases the probability of making a Type I error. That is, to wrongly reject the null hypothesis and find statistically significant differences between groups whereas, in reality, there are none. To counteract the risk of committing a Type I error, we set a higher probability level for rejecting the null hypothesis (use conservative post hoc tests such as Bonferroni during ANOVA, see Chapter 22). Moreover, statistically, we may counteract unequal variance by 'correcting' the F value (the ratio of systematic variance to unsystematic variances) by selecting the option 'Welch F' during an ANOVA.

There are two ways to run the Levene test, as a part of the ANOVA analysis or separately. It is better to run it before we run the main ANOVA to check the assumption of homogeneity of variance. If the assumption is not met, we should select the option 'Welch F' when running an ANOVA (these procedures are detailed in Chapter 22).

To run a Levene test with SPSS:

1   Go to **Analyze**
2   Choose **Descriptive statistics**
3   Click **Explore**, then choose **Plots**
4   Click **Spread vs. level with Levene test** (see Figures 19.10, 19.11)
5   Then **OK**

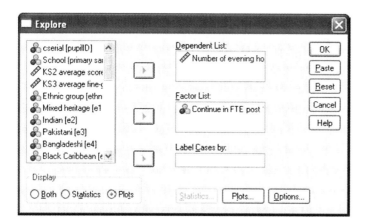

Figure 19.10: Levene Test

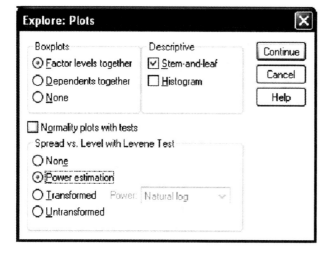

Figure 19.11: Normality plots

Independence of data

The groups are independent when the data are collected from different participants, or as Field puts it 'the behaviour of one participant does not influence the behaviour of another' (2005: 64). Between-subject designs involve different participants, whereas within-subject designs (e.g. repeated measures) involve the same participants at different points in time. In Chapter 22, we discuss independent t-tests and between-group ANOVAs, where different participants comprise the groups.

Summary

In this chapter, key concepts and assumptions pertaining to quantitative research were introduced to set the stage for analysing quantitative data. Identifying the variables, testing the hypotheses and delineating the nature of the data are crucial steps in quantitative data analysis that should be clarified prior to making decisions on statistical procedures for data analysis. It is important to stress that, in quantitative data analyses, the decision to reject or confirm the null hypothesis is based on probability *not* proof. Confirming the alternative hypothesis does not mean that it is proven; rather, it is tentatively confirmed until more evidence is gathered to either confirm or reject it. Moreover, when an alternative hypothesis is confirmed, statistical significance does not always mean practical importance. To add some weight to statistically significant results, we also estimate the confidence interval and the magnitude of a relationship or an impact (effect size). Finally, we challenged the notion of significance testing by considering alternative ways of looking at the nature and magnitude of relationships between variables.

References

Bryman, A. (2004) *Social Research Methods*, 2nd edn. Oxford: Oxford University Press.

Cohen, J. (1988) *Statistical Power Analysis for the Behavioural Sciences*, 2nd edn. New York: Academic Press.

Cohen, J. (1992) 'A power primer', *Psychological Bulletin*, 112(1): 155–9.

Connolly, P. (2007) *Quantitative Data Analysis in Education: A Critical Introduction Using SPSS*. London: Routledge.

Cresswell, J. W. (2005) *Research Methods in Education*, 6th edn. London: Routledge.

Cross, H. and Belli, G. (2004) 'Using multiple methodologies: the case of retention in Chicago', in K. B. DeMarrais and S. D. Lapan (eds) *Foundations for Research: Methods of Inquiry in Education and the Social Sciences*. Mahwah, NJ: Laurence Erlbaum.

Field, A. (2005) *Discovering Statistics Using SPSS*, 2nd edn. London: Sage.

Johnson R. B. and Christensen, L. B. (2004) *Educational Research: Qualitative, Quantitative and Mixed Research Approaches*. Boston, MA: Allyn & Bacon.

Kinnear, P. and Gray, C. (2006) *SPSS14 Made Simple*. Hove: Psychology Press.

Levin, J. R. (2006) 'Probability and hypothesis testing', in J. Green, G. Camilli, and P. Elmore (eds) *Complementary Methods in Education Research*. Mahwah, NJ: Lawrence Erlbaum.

Levin, J .R., and Robinson, D. H. (1999) 'Further reflections on hypothesis testing and editorial policy for primary research journals', *Educational Psychology Review*, 11: 143–55.

Thompson, B. (1996) 'AERA editorial policies regarding statistical significance testing: three suggested reforms', *Educational Researcher*, 25(2): 26–30.

Thompson, B. (2006) 'Research synthesis: effect sizes', in J. Green, G. Camilli, and P. B. Elmore (eds) *Complementary Methods in Education Research*. Mahwah, NJ: Lawrence Erlbaum.

Tukey, J. W. (1991) 'The philosophy of multiple comparisons', *Statistical Science*, 6: 100–116.

Preparing and Inputting Data in SPSS15
Dimitra Hartas

20

Introduction

This chapter offers a description of the SPSS (Statistical Package for the Social Sciences) environment. The statistical analyses discussed in this book were done via the use of the SPSS software for Windows. The aim of this chapter is to offer sufficient information on the practicalities of using SPSS software to get started by describing several windows in SPSS and the processes involved in creating variables, inputting data and navigating through the different functions necessary for running statistical analyses. The version of SPSS primarily used for this book is 15, which is very similar to a more recent version (SPSS16).

By the end of this chapter, you should be able to:

- use SPSS15 to input and analyse data.
- engage with different functions such as creating variables, inputting and storing data, and retrieving and transforming data

Getting Started

Once you open SPSS you are faced with the **SPSS data editor** which combines two windows, the **Data view** and the **Variable view** (see Figures 20.1, 20.2). You can move between these two views by clicking the tab at the bottom of the screen. In the **Data view** mode, which is in the form of a spreadsheet grid, you can see all the data on the screen and the statistical functions. In this mode, variables are referred to as var00001 before names are given to them. In **Variable view**, you input and edit the data, and can go back during the analysis to remind yourself of the coding of the data

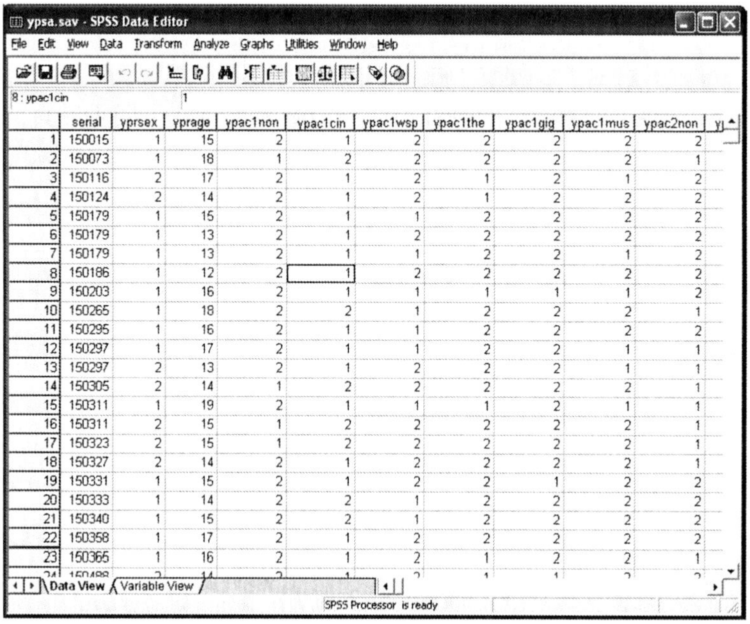

	serial	yprsex	yprage	ypac1non	ypac1cin	ypac1wsp	ypac1the	ypac1gig	ypac1mus	ypac2non
1	150015	1	15	2	1	2	2	2	2	2
2	150073	1	18	1	2	2	2	2	2	1
3	150116	2	17	2	1	2	1	2	1	2
4	150124	2	14	2	1	2	1	2	2	2
5	150179	1	15	2	1	1	2	2	2	2
6	150179	1	13	2	1	2	2	2	2	2
7	150179	1	13	2	1	1	2	2	1	2
8	150186	1	12	2	1	2	2	2	2	2
9	150203	1	16	2	1	1	1	1	1	2
10	150265	1	18	2	2	1	2	2	2	1
11	150295	1	16	2	1	1	2	2	2	2
12	150297	1	17	2	1	1	2	2	1	1
13	150297	2	13	2	1	2	2	2	1	1
14	150305	2	14	1	2	2	2	2	2	1
15	150311	1	19	2	1	1	1	2	1	1
16	150311	2	15	1	2	2	2	2	2	1
17	150323	2	15	1	2	2	2	2	2	1
18	150327	2	14	2	1	2	2	2	2	1
19	150331	1	15	2	1	2	2	1	2	2
20	150333	1	14	2	2	1	2	2	2	2
21	150340	1	15	2	2	1	2	2	2	2
22	150358	1	17	2	1	2	2	2	2	2
23	150365	1	16	2	1	2	1	2	2	1

Figure 20.1 Data view

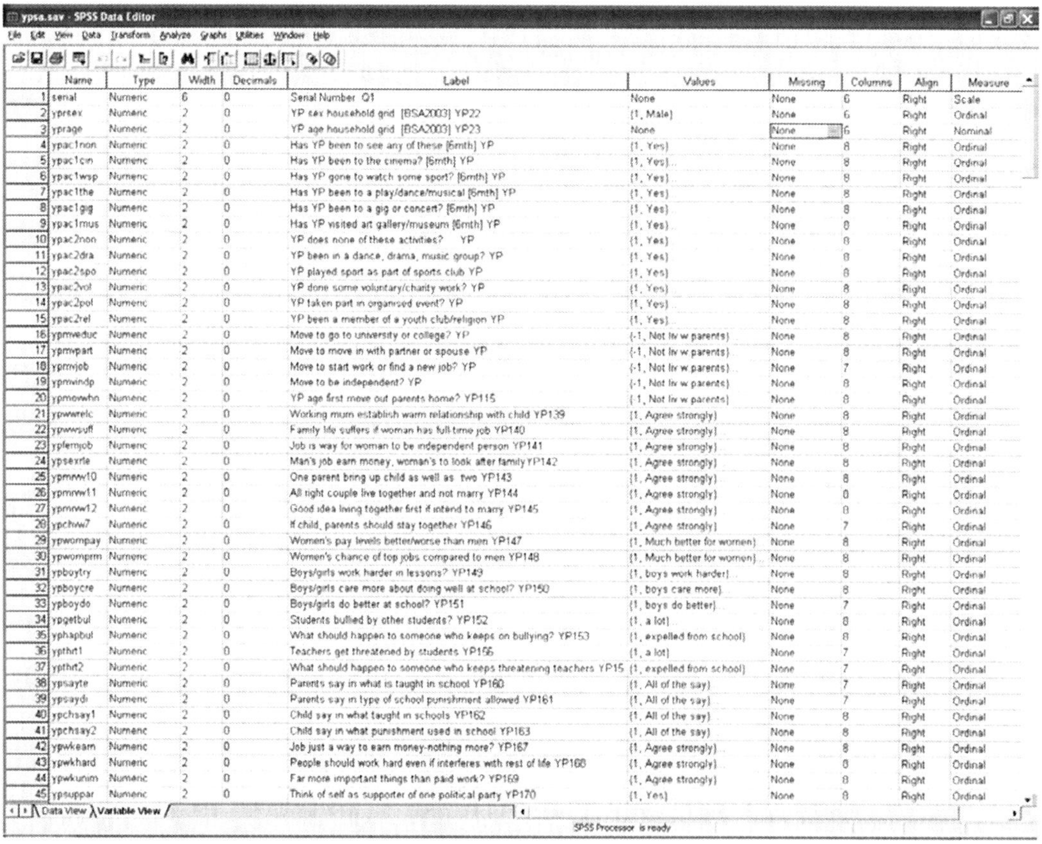

	Name	Type	Width	Decimals	Label	Values	Missing	Columns	Align	Measure
1	serial	Numeric	6	0	Serial Number Q1	None	None	6	Right	Scale
2	yprsex	Numeric	2	0	YP sex household grid [BSA2003] YP22	{1, Male}	None	6	Right	Ordinal
3	yprage	Numeric	2	0	YP age household grid [BSA2003] YP23	None	None	6	Right	Nominal
4	ypac1non	Numeric	2	0	Has YP been to see any of these [6mth] YP	{1, Yes}	None	8	Right	Ordinal
5	ypac1cin	Numeric	2	0	Has YP been to the cinema? [6mth] YP	{1, Yes}...	None	8	Right	Ordinal
6	ypac1wsp	Numeric	2	0	Has YP gone to watch some sport? [6mth] YP	{1, Yes}	None	8	Right	Ordinal
7	ypac1the	Numeric	2	0	Has YP been to a play/dance/musical [6mth] YP	{1, Yes}	None	8	Right	Ordinal
8	ypac1gig	Numeric	2	0	Has YP been to a gig or concert? [6mth] YP	{1, Yes}	None	8	Right	Ordinal
9	ypac1mus	Numeric	2	0	Has YP visited art gallery/museum [6mth] YP	{1, Yes}	None	8	Right	Ordinal
10	ypac2non	Numeric	2	0	YP does none of these activities? YP	{1, Yes}	None	8	Right	Ordinal
11	ypac2dra	Numeric	2	0	YP been in a dance, drama, music group? YP	{1, Yes}	None	8	Right	Ordinal
12	ypac2spo	Numeric	2	0	YP played sport as part of sports club YP	{1, Yes}	None	8	Right	Ordinal
13	ypac2vol	Numeric	2	0	YP done some voluntary/charity work? YP	{1, Yes}	None	8	Right	Ordinal
14	ypac2pol	Numeric	2	0	YP taken part in organised event? YP	{1, Yes}	None	8	Right	Ordinal
15	ypac2rel	Numeric	2	0	YP been a member of a youth club/religion YP	{1, Yes}	None	8	Right	Ordinal
16	ypmveduc	Numeric	2	0	Move to go to university or college? YP	{-1, Not liv w parents}	None	8	Right	Ordinal
17	ypmvpart	Numeric	2	0	Move to move in with partner or spouse YP	{-1, Not liv w parents}	None	8	Right	Ordinal
18	ypmvjob	Numeric	2	0	Move to start work or find a new job? YP	{-1, Not liv w parents}	None	7	Right	Ordinal
19	ypmvindp	Numeric	2	0	Move to be independent? YP	{-1, Not liv w parents}	None	8	Right	Ordinal
20	ypmovwhn	Numeric	2	0	YP age first move out parents home? YP115	{-1, Not liv w parents}	None	8	Right	Ordinal
21	ypwwrelc	Numeric	2	0	Working mum establish warm relationship with child YP139	{1, Agree strongly}	None	8	Right	Ordinal
22	ypwwsuff	Numeric	2	0	Family life suffers if woman has full-time job YP140	{1, Agree strongly}	None	8	Right	Ordinal
23	ypfemjob	Numeric	2	0	Job is way for woman to be independent person YP141	{1, Agree strongly}	None	8	Right	Ordinal
24	ypsexrle	Numeric	2	0	Man's job earn money, woman's to look after family YP142	{1, Agree strongly}	None	8	Right	Ordinal
25	ypmrrw10	Numeric	2	0	One parent bring up child as well as two YP143	{1, Agree strongly}	None	8	Right	Ordinal
26	ypmrrw11	Numeric	2	0	All right couple live together and not marry YP144	{1, Agree strongly}	None	8	Right	Ordinal
27	ypmrrw12	Numeric	2	0	Good idea living together first if intend to marry YP145	{1, Agree strongly}	None	8	Right	Ordinal
28	ypchw7	Numeric	2	0	If child, parents should stay together YP146	{1, Agree strongly}	None	7	Right	Ordinal
29	ypwompay	Numeric	2	0	Women's pay levels better/worse than men YP147	{1, Much better for women}	None	8	Right	Ordinal
30	ypwomprm	Numeric	2	0	Women's chance of top jobs compared to men YP148	{1, Much better for women}...	None	8	Right	Ordinal
31	ypboytry	Numeric	2	0	Boys/girls work harder in lessons? YP149	{1, boys work harder}	None	8	Right	Ordinal
32	ypboycre	Numeric	2	0	Boys/girls care more about doing well at school? YP150	{1, boys care more}	None	8	Right	Ordinal
33	ypboydo	Numeric	2	0	Boys/girls do better at school? YP151	{1, boys do better}	None	7	Right	Ordinal
34	ypgetbul	Numeric	2	0	Students bullied by other students? YP152	{1, a lot}	None	8	Right	Ordinal
35	yphapbul	Numeric	2	0	What should happen to someone who keeps on bullying? YP153	{1, expelled from school}	None	8	Right	Ordinal
36	ypthrt1	Numeric	2	0	Teachers get threatened by students YP156	{1, a lot}	None	7	Right	Ordinal
37	ypthrt2	Numeric	2	0	What should happen to someone who keeps threatening teachers YP15	{1, expelled from school}	None	7	Right	Ordinal
38	ypsayte	Numeric	2	0	Parents say in what is taught in school YP160	{1, All of the say}	None	7	Right	Ordinal
39	ypsaydi	Numeric	2	0	Parents say in type of school punishment allowed YP161	{1, All of the say}	None	7	Right	Ordinal
40	ypchsay1	Numeric	2	0	Child say in what taught in schools YP162	{1, All of the say}	None	8	Right	Ordinal
41	ypchsay2	Numeric	2	0	Child say in what punishment used in school YP163	{1, All of the say}	None	8	Right	Ordinal
42	ypwkearn	Numeric	2	0	Job just a way to earn money-nothing more? YP167	{1, Agree strongly}	None	8	Right	Ordinal
43	ypwkhard	Numeric	2	0	People should work hard even if interferes with rest of life YP168	{1, Agree strongly}	None	8	Right	Ordinal
44	ypwkunim	Numeric	2	0	Far more important things than paid work? YP169	{1, Agree strongly}	None	8	Right	Ordinal
45	ypsuppar	Numeric	2	0	Think of self as supporter of one political party YP170	{1, Yes}	None	8	Right	Ordinal

Figure 20.2 Variable view

and the labels you have given to the variables. The variables and the information on each variable are entered in the columns, and the cases, which can be people or other units of analysis such as schools, are entered in the rows.

Variable View: Creating Variables

Variable view is the environment where the variables are created. Here you can see a series of columns called 'Name', 'Type', 'Width', 'Decimals' etc. Their function is as follows.

Name: the name (label) of the variable appears here. To give a variable a name, go to the **Variable view** mode and click the current generic variable name (e.g. var00001), and type the name you want to give to the variable. The name cannot be more than eight characters and you cannot use spaces. In addition to the variable name that appears in the column, you can give a label, a descriptor of the variable, that will show in the SPSS output (after you run an analysis). For example, in the YPSA dataset (see web companion for this volume), the variable gender is entered as yprsex, and its label is YP sex household grid.

Label: the description of the variables. To insert the variable label, go to **Variable view** and click the cell in the **Label** column that corresponds to the variable you want to label, and type the label (e.g. YP sex household grid).

Values: the values given to the variables. After you have entered the label, the next step is to enter the value labels for the variable. A value is attached to a code used when entering the data. For example, for the categorical variable 'Gender', the values are M (male) = 0 and F (female) = 1. For an ordinal variable measured on a five-point Likert scale, the values may be entered as: Strongly disagree = 1, Disagree = 2, Undecided = 3, Agree = 4 and Strongly agree = 5. To enter a value, go to the **Values** column and click the right side of the cell (a small box with three dots …) that corresponds to the variable for which you want to enter a value. Then, a **Value labels** dialog box appears (see Figures 20.4, 20.5, 20.6), which allows you to enter the value and the value label (for this example, 1=low, 2=medium, 3=high). Then click **Add** and **OK** to finish.

Type: the type of the variable. By default, all the variables appear as numeric, that is, a variable with all the values being expressed in numbers. Variables that are not numeric, such as the name of a geographical region, are entered as 'string' variables. To change this, click on the … area within the cell in the **Type** column and the **Variable type** dialog box pops up. Select **String** and enter the number of characters.

Width: the width controls the maximum number of characters or digits that can be entered when working with a string or a numeric variable. The default setting for width is eight characters or digits but you can change it by choosing **Edit**, then **Options**, click **Data** and change the width setting.

Decimals: the number of decimal places displayed for each variable. Clearly, this is relevant for the numeric variables, thus for a string variable the value 0 is entered in the **Decimals** column.

Missing: the value for missing data. For example, you have missing data when a response was not offered in a questionnaire item or the responses are of the nature of 'Not applicable' or 'Do not

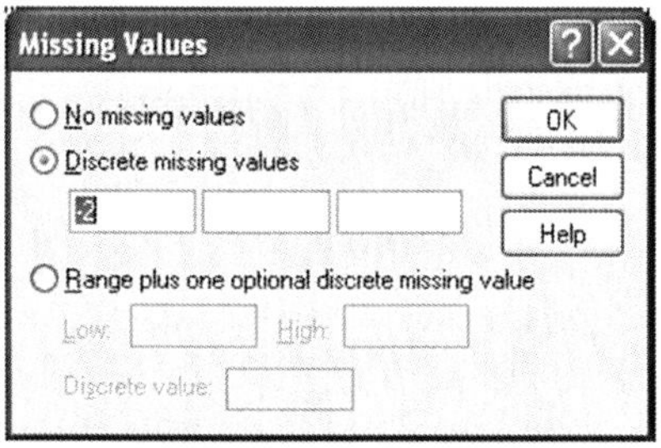

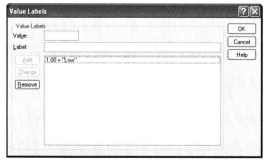

Figure 20.3 Missing values

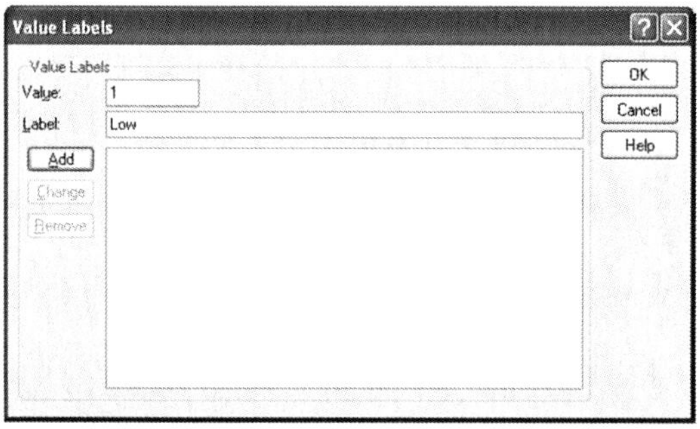

Figure 20.4 Value labels (a)

Figure 20.5 Value labels (b)

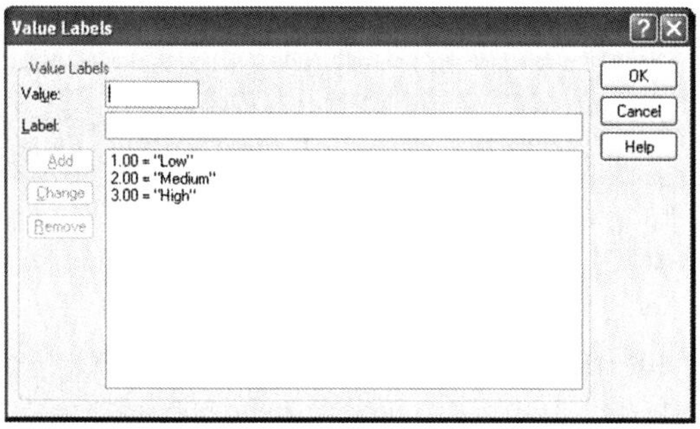

Figure 20.6 Value labels (c)

know'. If you have a missing value, you can leave the cell empty, in which case the SPSS automatically enters a dot to indicate that nothing has been entered. The problem with this is that it is not clear whether there was nothing entered because of a missing value or a mistake in entering the data. It is a better practice to assign a value to indicate the missing one, and use the same value consistently for all the variables. It is important to choose a code that does not correspond to any other data value. You can code responses such as 'Not applicable' or 'Do not know' as well as truly missing values. For example, for a scale with values ranging between 1 and 10 you cannot choose any value between 1 and 10 as a missing value. To assign the missing values for the variables that entail incomplete or missing responses, you click the cell under the **Missing** column (three dots at the right side of the cell) and a **Missing values** dialog box appears where you enter the missing value under **Discrete missing values** and then click on **OK** to finish (see Figure 20.3).

Columns: the actual widths for all the variables entered. To make the columns wider for a variable in a **Data view**, click the appropriate cell in **Columns** and adjust the setting.

Align: this refers to changing the column format. Data are aligned right, left or centre. The default setting is right.

Measure: the level of measurement for every variable entered. The default measure is scale (interval/ratio) because quantitative variables – i.e., weight, height, age – are measured in units on a scale, whereas the categorical variables are entered as nominal and rating scales as ordinal.

Inputting Data

After you finish inputting the labels and values for the variables, the next step is to enter the data. Each row includes data for one case/respondent, whereas each column represents a variable. In **Data view**, click on a cell and enter the data. Once data are entered, you can block or highlight a whole block of cells or entire rows and copy/paste them. To highlight a whole column or row, click the grey box containing the row number or the heading of the column. To highlight a block of cells within a row or column, click the first cell and drag the mouse pointer to the end of the block. To copy the numbers of one column into another, highlight them and choose **Edit** and click **Copy**, then once in the chosen column click **Edit** and then **Paste**.

Saving data

SPPS15 gives you the option to save the data:

1 In the **Data editor**
2 Click on **File**
3 Click **Save as**... give it a name and
4 Click **OK**

This procedure saves the data and any work done on the data. If you do not want to save the data as an SPSS file, but let's say as a Microsoft Excel file, then choose **Save as type** and a list with all possible formats will appear.

Retrieving data

To retrieve saved data or output:

1 In the **Data editor**
2 Click **File**
3 **Open** ... The **Open file** dialog box appears. You need to go to the location you have saved the data or output and then
4 Click **Open**

Saving and printing SPSS output

You can save the output as a separate file, following the same procedures as those applied when saving data. You can also print the output by clicking the **Print** button. You may also copy parts or the entire output and paste it into a Word document, by highlighting and using the copy and paste function.

Menus on SPSS15

In the toolbar, there are a number of menus available, including **File**, **Data**, **Transform** and **Analyse**. A brief description of each one follows.

File: as in any other Windows programme, **File** contains several functions such as **Save**, **Print** etc. You can open files (data or outputs) that have been previously saved.

Edit: contains edit functions for the data editor. A useful function here is 'cut and paste' to move blocks of data around.

View: presents the systems specification (e.g. whether you want grid lines or not).

Data: there are functions here that allow you to make changes to the data editor. You can **Insert a column** between two existing columns (insert a variable); **Insert a row** between two existing rows (insert a case); **Split file** (split a file by grouping variables) and **Select cases** to run analyses on selected cases.

Transform: this is a useful function for manipulating the variables. The **Recode** and **Compute** functions are important in that they allow you to change the values of certain variables, and create a new variable by combining two existing ones.

Analyse: this menu includes all the statistical techniques for analysing data. The techniques that are discussed in this book are as follows.

1. Descriptive statistics: this menu is used for running **Frequencies** and general data exploration (e.g. central tendency measures: mean, mode and median). Within this menu, there is also a function called **Crosstabs** that allows you to do crosstabulation (contingency tables) of two variables (see Chapter 21).

2. Compare means: within this menu, you can find the function for **Independent t-test** and **One-way analysis of variance** (ANOVA) (see Chapter 22), as well as other functions that are not covered in this book.

3. General linear model: this menu is to run n-way ANOVAs (e.g. factorial analysis; see Chapter 22).

4. Correlate: this menu is to run bivariate correlations, such as Spearman's rho and Pearson's R (see Chapter 23).

5. Regression: there are many regression techniques included here. The one discussed in this book is multiple linear regression (see Chapter 23).

6. Nonparametric tests: includes nonparametric tests such as Mann Whitney U and Kruskal Wallis tests (see Chapter 22).

There are other functions such as **Loglinear data, Reduction, Scale** etc. that go beyond the scope of this book. For our purposes, the two most important menus in SPSS are **Transform** and **Analyse**.

Graphs: offers the facility for graphs, such as histograms, pie charts, bar charts or scatterplots.

Window: enables you to switch from window to window (e.g. **Data** to **Output**).

Help: offers on-line support.

Transforming Variables

Within the **Transform** menu, **Recode** and **Select** are two functions often used to manipulate variables and prepare them for subsequent statistical analyses.

Recode

The **Recode** function is used to transform a variable before you analyse it. This function is typically used during regression analysis, which requires us to recode nominal variables to create dummy variables whose categories are coded 0 and 1 (see Chapter 23). The number of dummy variables we create for each nominal variable is equal to the number of categories minus one (reference category). For example, if we have a nominal variable with three categories, a, b and c, through **Recode**, we take one of the categories as a reference category to which the others are compared. Suppose b is the reference category, a is then compared with b and c is compared with b (there are two comparisons for three categories). Suppose we have a nominal variable with two categories such as gender (male, female). In this case, recoding can be done easily by coding one category 1 and the other 0 (there is no need to create a dummy variable for gender in a regression analysis). An important consideration in **Recode** is to decide on the category used as a reference category or baseline. We may choose a reference category that represents the majority or a control group. Having chosen the reference category, the next step is to code it as 0 for all the variables that will be created, and code 1 the category against which you want to compare the reference category.

To illustrate this, I recoded the variable 'year young people left school', from the YPSA data, which has three categories originally coded as $16 = 1$, $17–19 = 2$ and 19-plus $= 3$. This variable was recoded into two new dummy variables, and I chose as a reference category the one coded as 16 (reflecting the majority of young people). To create the first dummy variable, the reference category (young people who left school at 16) is coded as 0 and the other young people who left school $17–19$ as 1 (and the 19-plus $= 0$). In the second dummy variable, the reference category is $16 = 0$ and the other category 19-plus $= 1$ (and the $17–19 = 0$).

To run **Recode** with the SPSS 15:

1 From the toolbar, choose **Transform**
2 From the drop-down menu choose **Recode**
3 A new menu appears and offers two choices: **Into same variable** and **Into different variable**. If you choose **Into different variable**, a new variable is created and the original variable stays the same. For this example, I chose **Into different variable** (see Figure 20.7)
5 The **Recode into different variable** dialog box appears. Select the variable you want to recode and click the arrow
6 The variable enters a box and is followed by the arrow
7 Give the new variable a name by typing the new name under **Name** (let's call the new variable 'sixteen') then click **Change**. The arrow now points to the new variable 'sixteen'
8 Next, give the new variable a label, add it to the **Label** box
9 Click **Old** and **New Values** tab and a dialogue box appears
10 Enter the old variable's code in the **Old Value** box. In this example, to create the first dummy variable, the old value for the reference category is 1, and turns into a 0, the $17–19$ turns into 1 and the 19-plus turns into 0, and they are all entered in the **New nalue** box
11 Then click **Add**, and then **Continue**
12 Finally, click **OK** (see Figures 20.7 and 20.8)

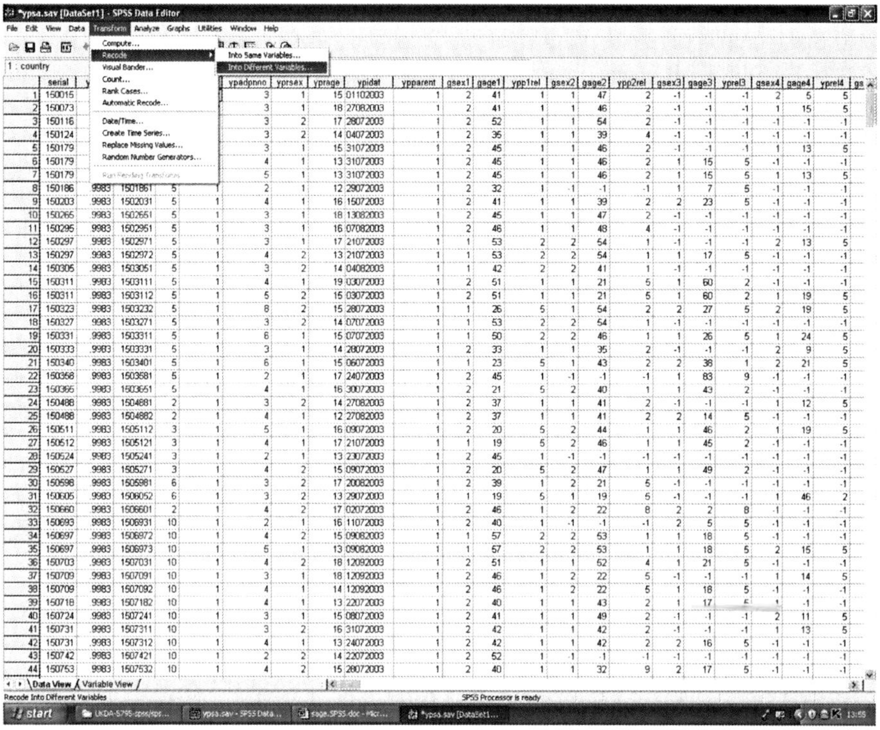

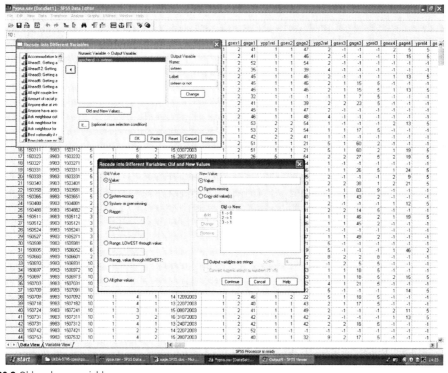

Figure 20.7 Recode

Figure 20.8 Old and new variables

The new variable appears at the last column of the grid in the **Data view** and also at the end of the list of variables at the **Variable view**. To find out more about the new variable, we may run frequencies with pie charts to give a visual representation of the variables. We follow the same procedures to create the second dummy variable.

Select cases

For some analyses, we may decide to focus on specific variables and exclude others temporarily. In other words, we may want to block some variables from entering into the analysis. Suppose we want to run an analysis selecting boys or girls only. To select cases:

1 From the tool bar click **Data**
2 A drop-down menu appears, click **Select cases**
3 The **Select cases** dialog box appears (see Figure 20.9)

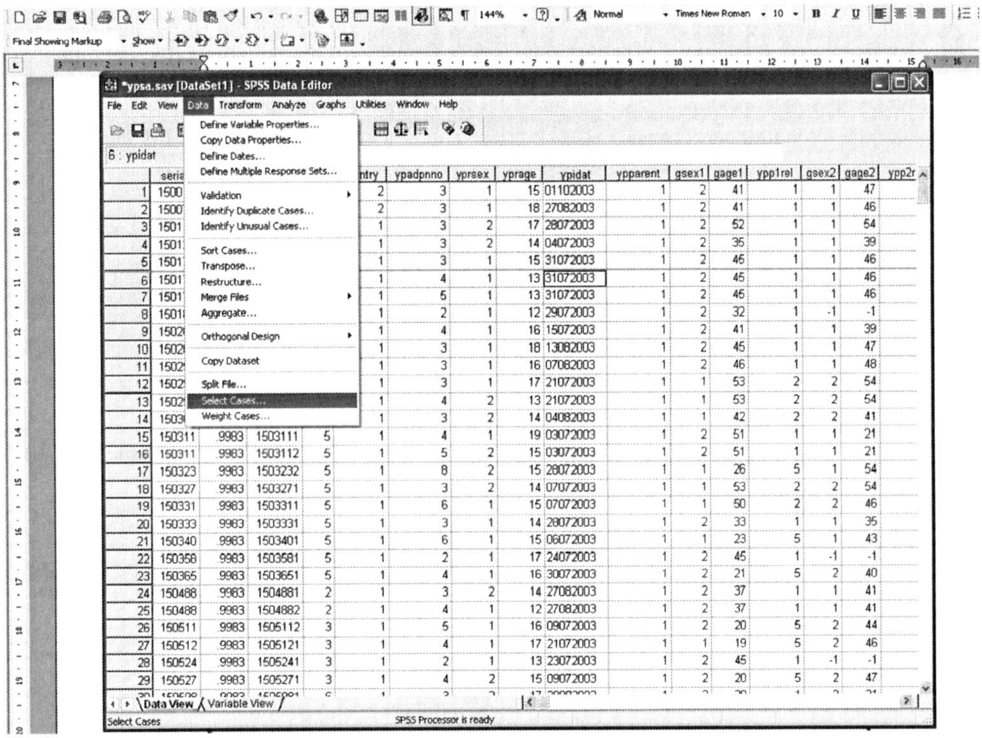

Figure 20.9 Select cases

4 Options are offered for selection (the default is **All cases** – all respondents are included in the sample) and you may select **If condition is satisfied** (click on the radio button **If** which lights up)
5 **Select cases: If** pops up, enter the variable from the list in the box, in our example the variable is ypsex
6 Specify the condition for variable ypsex by clicking on the panel with arithmetic symbols
7 for this example, the cases selected are males only, expressed as ypsex = 1, click **Continue** (see Figure 20.10)
8 Click **OK**

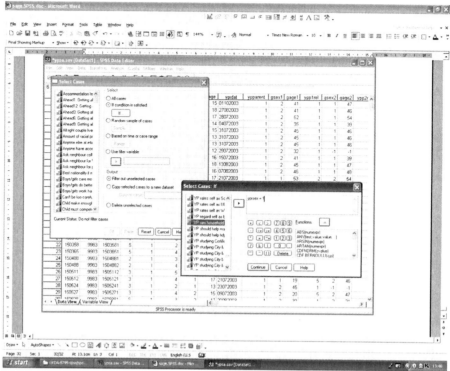

Figure 20.10 Select cases

	serial	ypwt	ypsmo	gor2	country	ypadpnno	yprsex	yprage	ypidat	ypparent	gsex1	gage1	ypp1rel	gsex2	gage2	ypp2r
1	150015	.9983	1500151	12	2	3	1	15	01102003	1	2	41	1	1	47	
2	150073	.9983	1500731	12	2	3	1	18	27082003	1	2	41	1	1	46	
3	150116	.9983	1501161	7	1	3	2	17	28072003	1	2	52	1	1	54	
4	150124	.9983	1501241	7	1	3	2	14	04072003	1	2	35	1	1	39	
5	150179	.9983	1501791	5	1	3	1	15	31072003	1	2	45	1	1	46	
6	150179	.9983	1501792	5	1	4	1	13	31072003	1	2	45	1	1	46	
7	150179	.9983	1501793	5	1	5	1	13	31072003	1	2	45	1	1	46	
8	150186	.9983	1501861	5	1	2	1	12	29072003	1	2	32	1	-1	-1	
9	150203	.9983	1502031	5	1	4	1	16	15072003	1	2	41	1	1	39	
10	150265	.9983	1502651	5	1	3	1	18	13082003	1	2	45	1	1	47	
11	150295	.9983	1502951	5	1	3	1	16	07082003	1	2	46	1	1	48	
12	150297	.9983	1502971	5	1	3	1	17	21072003	1	1	53	2	2	54	
13	150297	.9983	1502972	5	1	4	2	13	21072003	1	1	53	2	2	54	
14	150305	.9983	1503051	5	1	3	2	14	04082003	1	1	42	2	2	41	
15	150311	.9983	1503111	5	1	4	1	19	03072003	1	2	51	1	1	21	
16	150311	.9983	1503112	5	1	5	2	15	03072003	1	2	51	1	1	21	
17	150323	.9983	1503232	5	1	8	2	15	28072003	1	1	26	5	1	54	
18	150327	.9983	1503271	5	1	3	2	14	07072003	1	1	53	2	2	54	
19	150331	.9983	1503311	5	1	6	1	15	07072003	1	1	50	2	2	46	
20	150333	.9983	1503331	5	1	3	1	14	28072003	1	2	33	1	1	35	
21	150340	.9983	1503401	5	1	6	1	15	06072003	1	1	23	5	1	43	
22	150358	.9983	1503581	5	1	2	1	17	24072003	1	2	45	1	-1	-1	
23	150365	.9983	1503651	5	1	4	1	16	30072003	1	2	21	5	2	40	
24	150488	.9983	1504881	2	1	3	2	14	27082003	1	2	37	1	1	41	
25	150488	.9983	1504882	2	1	4	1	12	27082003	1	2	37	1	1	41	
26	150511	.9983	1505112	3	1	5	1	16	09072003	1	2	20	5	2	44	
27	150512	.9983	1505121	3	1	4	1	17	21072003	1	1	19	5	2	46	
28	150524	.9983	1505241	3	1	2	1	13	23072003	1	2	45	1	-1	-1	
29	150527	.9983	1505271	3	1	4	2	15	09072003	1	2	20	5	2	47	

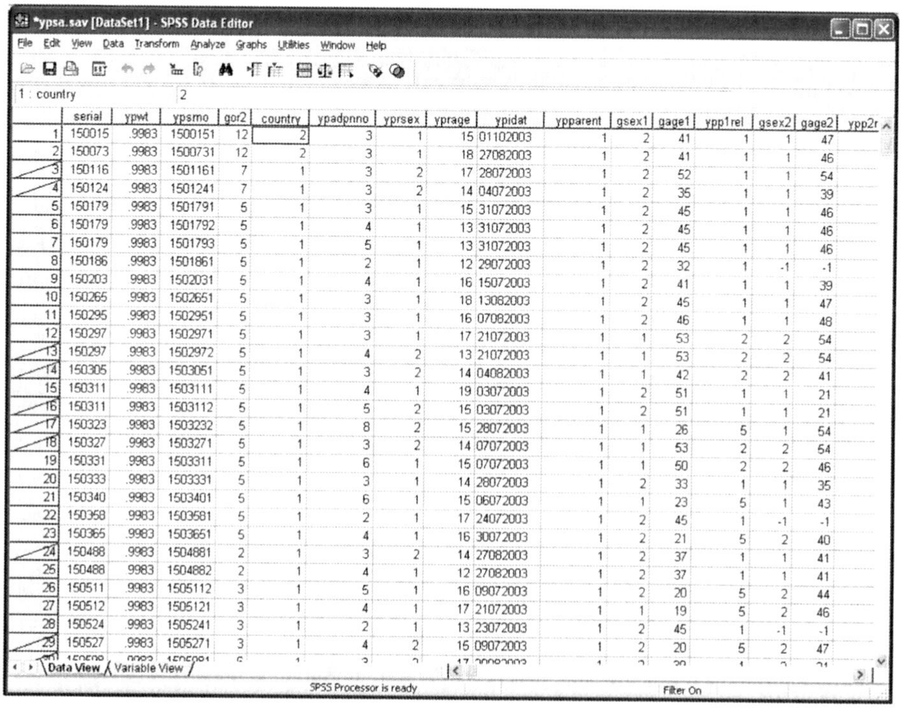

Figure 20.11 View of selected cases

In **Data View**, a number of cases are marked with an oblique bar, which means that they are not selected for all subsequent analyses. Now, we are ready to run an analysis with the selected cases only (e.g. selecting boys only) (see Figure 20-11). In order to go back to the original set of data, in the **Select cases** dialog box, click the radio button **All cases**, then click **OK**.

Summary

This chapter has offered a basic introduction to the SPSS environment. Its main aim was to assist you in the process of coding, creating and manipulating variables, and inputting and analysing data. A description of an array of functions has been offered to get you started. It is important to familiarize yourself with the main menus and functions of the SPSS environment before you venture into statistical analyses. Most crucially, you should prepare the variables and transform them (if required) before any analyses you plan to undertake. To this end, I presented two commonly used functions – i.e., **Recode** and **Select**. In the next chapter, initial explorations of quantitative data are discussed.

Box 20.1 Checklist: getting started with SPSS

- Code the variables that you plan to analyse and keep the coding consistent (e.g. male = 1, female = 2).
- Create variables by entering their names and their values (including missing values).
- Input the data in SPSS by entering the scores/codes.
- Edit and save the information entered.
- Manipulate the variables that require changes via **Recode** or **Select** functions.
- Consider the type of variables/levels of measurement (e.g. nominal or ordinal) (see Chapter 19).
- Clarify the relationships you want to explore and map them onto the hypotheses formed.

21 Exploring Quantitative Data

Dimitra Hartas

Introduction

In this chapter, explorations of quantitative data via univariate, bivariate and multivariate analyses are introduced, and will be discussed in detail in the next three chapters. As an initial exploration of a quantitative data, we start with descriptive statistics to obtain an overview of our data, via a univariate analysis – i.e. frequencies – and a bivariate analysis – i.e. contingency tables. With descriptive statistics we obtain a summary of the data by calculating the central tendency (i.e. mean, mode and median) and dispersion measures; however, we cannot make inferences and predictions about the population at large. This can be done by employing inferential statistics, which allow us to draw inferences about the population characteristics based on our knowledge of the sample (assuming the sample is representative of the population from which it was drawn; see Chapter 4).

The bivariate and multivariate analyses presented in this volume involve both parametric and nonparametric data. As discussed in Chapter 19, parametric data meet certain assumptions (i.e. normality, independence of scores, equality of variance and data at an interval level), and thus they are fit for inferential statistical analyses. The contingency analysis presented here is carried out with nonparametric data. Group comparisons to explore the impact of independent variable(s) on an outcome via a t-test, an analysis of variance (ANOVA) or a factorial analysis are typically done with parametric data (see Chapter 22). However, we can still compare groups with nonparametric data by employing certain tests such as the Kruskall Wallis test (see Chapter 22). A bivariate correlation and a multiple linear regression, which explore the strength of relationships or association between variables (see Chapter 23), and a factor analysis as a data reduction technique (see Chapter 24) can be carried out with parametric or nonparametric data.

By the end of this chapter, you should be able to:

- apply descriptive statistics to describe quantitative data
- consider variable characteristics such as central tendency, dispersion and frequency distribution
- understand the differences between descriptive and inferential statistics
- describe a contingency analysis

Descriptive Statistics

A data description is an essential part of a quantitative analysis, and is achieved though descriptive statistics. For example, we may want to calculate the percentage or frequency of participants' responses on a particular item in a questionnaire. Or, simply, we may want to gain an overall picture of our data to check for inaccuracies (e.g. mistakes) with data entry or data coding. There are three major characteristics of a single variable to describe:

- central tendency
- dispersion
- frequency distribution

Central tendency measures

There are three central tendency measures, namely mean, median and mode.

The *mean* is a hypothetical value that can be calculated to summarize the data. The mean does not have to be observed in the data, and makes sense for interval and ratio variables only (scale or continuous variables), although it is not uncommon to calculate the mean for ordinal variables.

The *mode* is the most frequently occurring score and has meaning for nominal, ordinal and interval/ratio variables.

The *median* is the middle category in a distribution, which is located by ordering the scores from high to low (50 per cent of the scores fall above and 50 per cent fall below the median), and has a meaning for ordinal and interval/ratio variables. Compared to the mean, the median summarizes the data more accurately because the mean can be affected by outliers or extreme scores. For example, if we take a range of salaries from low to high and then calculate the mean, its value will not summarize the data accurately because some salaries are very low and others are very high, introducing extreme values.

Dispersion

Dispersion refers to the spread of the values around the central tendency. There are two common measures of dispersion, namely *range* and *variance* (Standard Deviation SD). The range is simply the highest minus the lowest value in a distribution of values from an interval/ratio variable. For example, in a distribution with a high value of 36 and a low of 15, the range is 36 – 15 = 21.

A variance is a measure of the spread, the average error between the mean and the observed scores. Variance indicates how far or close the observed scores are from the mean. A large variance indicates that the observed scores are far from the mean, suggesting that the mean does not represent the data well. A small variance indicates that the mean represents the data well, because the scores are clustered around it.

A standard deviation is the square root of variance and, compared to the range, it is a more accurate and detailed estimate of dispersion because extreme scores can greatly exaggerate the range. A standard deviation is the average amount of variation around the mean, and assuming that the distribution of scores is normal (bell-shaped distribution), the following conclusions can be reached:

- approximately 68 per cent of the scores in the sample fall within 1 SD of the mean
- approximately 95 per cent of the scores in the sample fall within 2 SD of the mean
- approximately 99 per cent of the scores in the sample fall within 3 SD of the mean

Univariate analysis: frequency distribution

A univariate analysis involves the analysis of one variable. A common way to describe a single variable is with a frequency distribution, which is the summary of the frequency of individual values or ranges of values for a given variable. The simplest distribution lists every value of a variable and the number of persons who had each value. For instance, a typical way to describe the distribution of pupils is by school year, by listing the number or percentage of pupils at each of the six school years. We can have a sampling distribution, which is a frequency distribution of all the means of the samples that are drawn from a population (the average of the sample means gives us the population mean).

Frequency distributions are depicted as a table or a histogram. A histogram is a graph that shows the plotting values of observations on the horizontal axis with a bar showing how many times each value occurred in the dataset. It is important to note that a histogram is appropriate for data measured at an interval/ratio level. The SPSS offers the facility to superimpose a normal distribution on a histogram to show how well the scores form a normal distribution (see Figure 21.1).

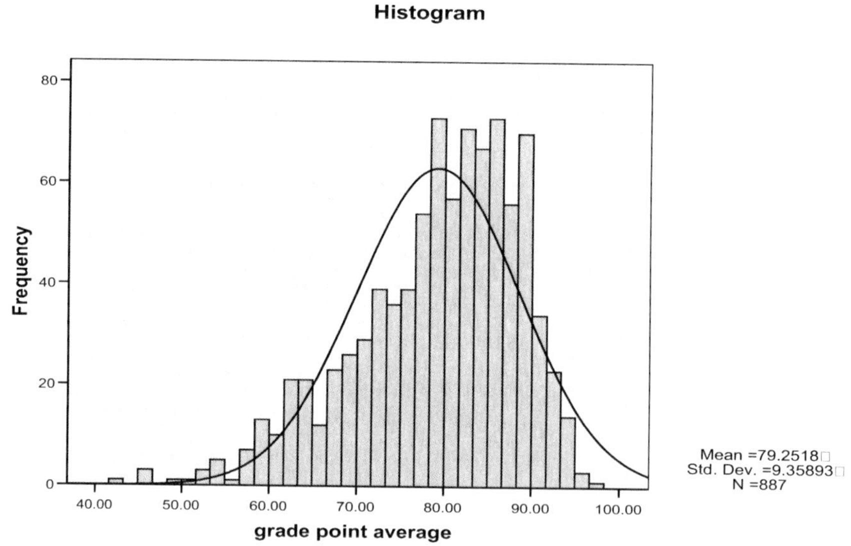

Histogram

Mean =79.2518
Std. Dev. =9.35893
N =887

Figure 21.1 SPSS output 1

For nominal and ordinal variables, the most commonly used graphs are pie charts and bar charts.

Types of frequency distribution

There are different types of a frequency distribution. The most commonly known is the normal distribution, a bell-shaped curve, which shows the majority of the scores being clustered around the centre of the distribution. In normal distributions, the mean represents the scores well because the majority of the scores cluster around the mean and thus measures of dispersion (i.e. variance and standard deviation) are small. In a normal distribution, as we move further away from the centre, the bars of the histogram become smaller and that indicates that the frequency of the scores decreases (see Section C in Figure 21.2).

A distribution can deviate from normal in terms of a lack of symmetry (skewness) and the extent to which it is pointy or flat (kurtosis). Skewed distributions are not symmetrical in that the majority of the scores cluster at one side with the frequency of scores tailing off the other side of the distribution. A skewed distribution can be either positively or negatively skewed (see Figure 21.2). In a positively skewed distribution, the majority of the scores are clustered towards the lower end of the scale and the tail extends towards the higher scores (hence positively skewed; see Section B in Figure 21.2). In a negatively skewed distribution, the majority of scores cluster towards the higher end of the scale, with the tail moving towards the lower scores (hence negatively skewed; see Section A in Figure 21.2).

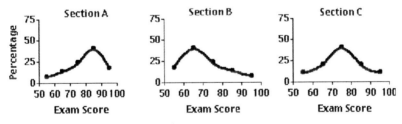

Figure 21.2 Skewness (adapted from Lowry 2008)

Distributions also vary according to how pointy or flat they are (kurtosis). Kurtosis refers to the extent to which the scores gather at the tails of the distribution. A distribution where many scores gather at the tails is called *platykurtic*, and its shape is wide or flat (see Section D in Figure 21.3). A distribution where a few scores gather at the tails is called *leptokurtic*, and its shape is thin (see Section E in Figure 21.3). A *mesokurtic* distribution is a halfway between a platykurtic and a leptokurtic distribution (see Section F in Figure 21.3).

In a normal (symmetrical) distribution, the central tendency measures are equal (mean = mode = median). In skewed distributions, the mean, median and mode are distinct from each other: the mean is located towards the tail of the skew, the mode towards the peak, away from the tail and the median between the mean and the mode (Lowry 2008). In a positively skewed distribution, the mean is towards the positive scores, whereas in a negatively skewed distribution, the mean is

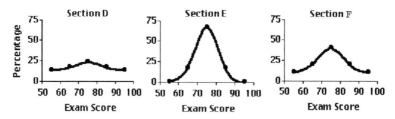

Figure 21.3 Kurtosis (adapted from Lowry 2008)

towards the negative scores. In both types, the mode is located at the peak of the distribution (see Figure 21.4).

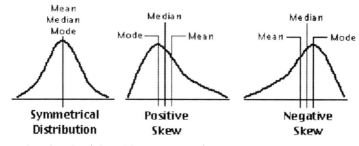

Figure 21.4 Mean, mode and median (adapted from Lowry 2008)

How to run frequencies with SPSS

Calculating the frequency is an important part of descriptive statistics. A frequency refers to the number/percentage of occurrences of an event, or responses to a specific category of a variable, for example, the number of responses to the question 'How often does a young person see friends?'. A frequency analysis involves the examination of one variable at a time across cases. To run **Frequencies**, on the SPSS tool bar:

1 Go to **Analyze**
2 A pop-up list appears, click on **Descriptive statistics**
3 Click **Frequencies** (see Figure 21.5)
4 The **Frequencies** dialogue box appears, enter the variable(s) from the list that we want to analyse (see Figure 21.6)
5 Click the **Charts** tab to produce a chart: a **pie chart/bar chart** for nominal and ordinal variables (see Figure 21.7), or a **histogram** for interval/ratio variables. In this example, the variable is interval/ratio and thus we choose **Histograms** with **Normal curve** (see Figure 21.8)
6 Click on **Statistics** and a dialog box appears
7 Click on **Central tendency** measures (**Mean, Median, Mode**) and **Dispersion** measures (**Std Deviation**) (see Figure 21.9), then **Continue**.
8 Finally, click **OK**

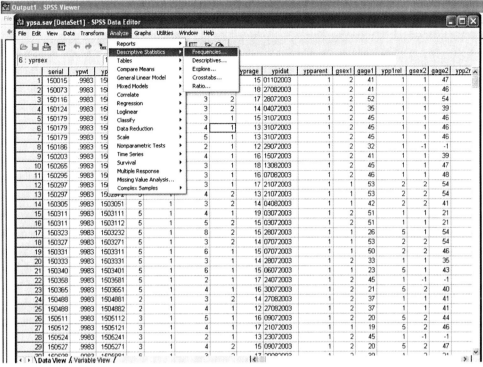

Figure 21.5 Frequencies

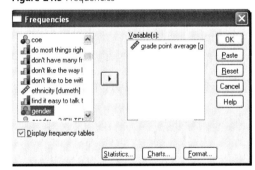

Figure 21.6 Frequency box

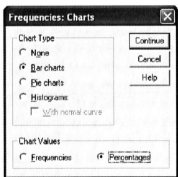

Figure 21.7 Bar/pie charts

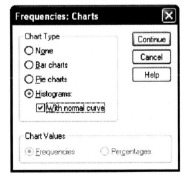

Figure 21.8 Histogram

Figure 21.9 Statistics box

Examples of frequency analyses

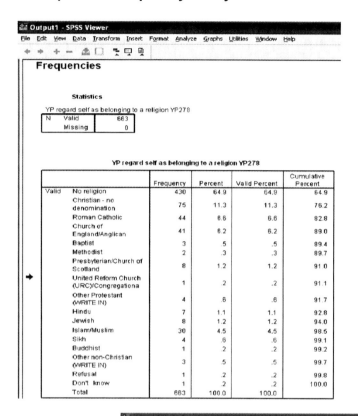

First, let's run frequencies on the variable 'young person regards self as belonging to a religion' from the YPSA database, choosing a pie chart as this variable is ordinal. The SPSS output provides information about the number of responses and their percentages. As Figure 21.10 shows, 64.9 per cent of young people stated that they do not belong to any religion. The remaining percentage is distributed to various religions as depicted in the pie chart (see Figure 21.11).

Frequencies

Statistics

YP regard self as belonging to a religion YP278

N	Valid	663
	Missing	0

YP regard self as belonging to a religion YP278

		Frequency	Percent	Valid Percent	Cumulative Percent
Valid	No religion	430	64.9	64.9	64.9
	Christian - no denomination	75	11.3	11.3	76.2
	Roman Catholic	44	6.6	6.6	82.8
	Church of England/Anglican	41	6.2	6.2	89.0
	Baptist	3	.5	.5	89.4
	Methodist	2	.3	.3	89.7
	Presbyterian/Church of Scotland	8	1.2	1.2	91.0
	United Reform Church (URC)/Congregationa	1	.2	.2	91.1
	Other Protestant (WRITE IN)	4	.6	.6	91.7
	Hindu	7	1.1	1.1	92.8
	Jewish	8	1.2	1.2	94.0
	Islam/Muslim	30	4.5	4.5	98.5
	Sikh	4	.6	.6	99.1
	Buddhist	1	.2	.2	99.2
	Other non-Christian (WRITE IN)	3	.5	.5	99.7
	Refusal	1	.2	.2	99.8
	Don't know	1	.2	.2	100.0
	Total	663	100.0	100.0	

Figure 21.10 SPSS output 2

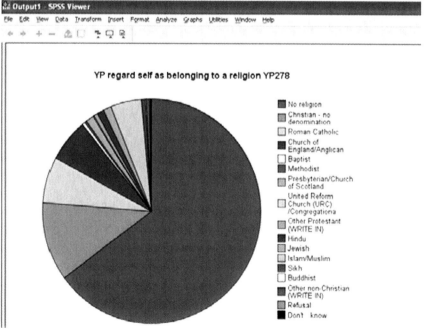

Figure 21.11
SPSS output 3

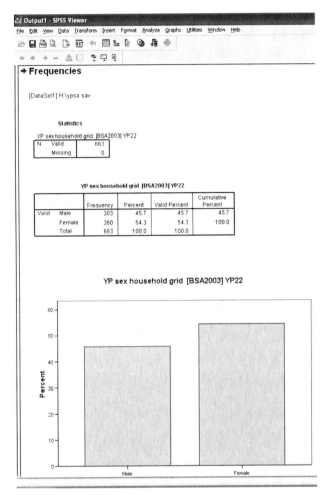

Figure 21.12 SPSS output 4

In the next example of a frequency analysis we enter a nominal variable (i.e., gender) to calculate the percentages of boys and girls who comprise the sample (see Figure 21.12; the bar chart displays the percentages).

In the third example we have a variable (i.e. grade point average) measured at an interval/ratio level. Figure 21.13 presents the central tendency measures. In this example, because the variable is interval, all three central tendency measures are appropriate.

N	Valid	887
	Missing	2
Mean		79.2518
Median		80.8100
Mode		90.00
Std. Deviation		9.35893

Figure 21.13 SPSS output 5

The frequency distribution is slightly negatively skewed because the tail extends towards the low scores (see Figure 21.1). The mean (M = 79.25) is located towards the tail of the skew, the mode = 90 towards the peak and the median = 80.8 is between the mean and the mode.

In the next section, we discuss a bivariate statistical analysis known as contingency analysis.

Bivariate Analyses

A bivariate analysis involves two variables at a time to explore the association/relationship between two variables or the effects of one variable on another. There is an array of statistical techniques used for this purpose (see Table 21.1), depending on the type of the variables (level of measurement, parametric/nonparametric data) in the research design. For example, to explore the relationship between two nominal (categorical) variables, or one nominal and one ordinal, we employ a statistical technique called contingency analysis (chi-square test). With ordinal variables, we can run a correlation and calculate Spearman's rho coefficient, which is a measure of the magnitude of their association (see Chapter 23).

A contingency analysis

While a frequency analysis shows the number of cases in each level of a categorical variable, it does not provide any information about the relationship between nominal or ordinal variables. For example, a frequency analysis can provide the number of men and women in each ethnic group category separately, whereas with a contingency table we present the intersection (crosstabulation) of gender and ethnicity (the number of men and women in each of the ethnic groups). A crosstabulation of gender and ethnicity however does not tell us whether there is a significant relationship between them. To find this out, we run a chi-square test.

A chi-square test for independence examines whether a statistically significant relationship between two categorical or one categorical and one ordinal or two ordinal variables (nonparametric data) exists. With a chi-square test, the null hypothesis is that the row and column variables are independent, in the sense of not relating to each other. The difference between the observed and expected values forms the basis of the chi-square statistic, which evaluates the likelihood that the differences between the observed and expected values would not occur by chance alone. With a chi-square test, we explore the differences between the frequencies across categories, rather than the differences between group means (as in the case of a t-test or ANOVA), to examine whether the observed pattern is statistically different from that expected by chance.

The assumptions that underlie a chi-square test are:

- variables are nonparametric (nominal or ordinal)
- no cell should have an expected value of less than 1
- No more than 20 per cent of cells should have expected values less than 5

To run a contingency analysis with SPSS:

1 Click on **Analyze**
2 A pop-up list appears, click on **Descriptive statistics**
3 A new pop-up list appears, choose **Crosstabs** (see Figure 21.14)

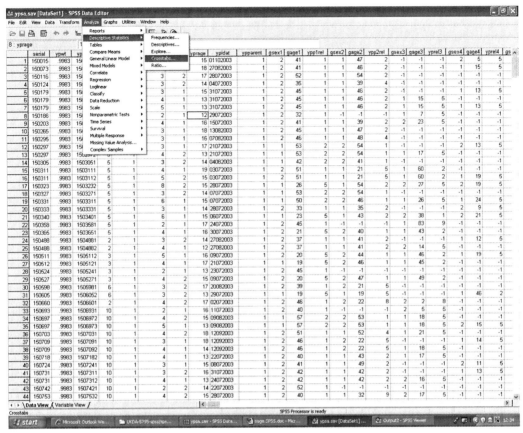

Figure 21.14 Crosstabs

4   Click on **Crosstabs**

5   A new dialogue box appears (see Figure 21.15) to enter the variables in the left-hand side for analysis. It does not matter which variable goes to the **Row(s)** box and which one goes to the **Column(s)** box

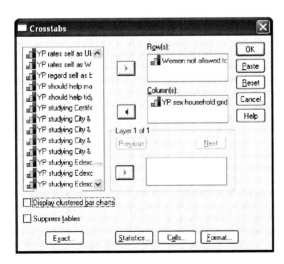

Figure 21.15 Crosstabs box

6   Click on the first variable and then click the arrow to transfer it in the **Row(s)** box,
7   Click on the second variable and then click the arrow to transfer it in the **Column(s)** box
8   Click on the **Cells** tab, click on **Expected** and **Observed counts** (and percentages, if required), then click **Continue** (see Figure 21.16)
9   Click on **Statistics** tab, and click on **Chi-square**, then click **Continue** (see Figure 21.17)
10 Click **OK**

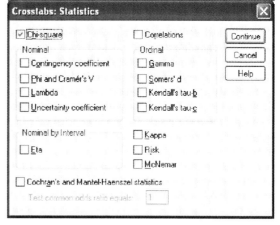

Figure 21.16 Crosstabs, cell display   **Figure 21.17** Crosstabs, statistics

To estimate the effect size (the strength of a relationship; see Chapter 19 for a discussion on effect sizes), we click **Phi** (for 2×2) and **Cramer's V** (for more than 4 cells). The effect size can be estimated manually by taking the square root of the chi-square value divided by the overall sample size (if the Phi value is negative we ignore the sign in that we are interested in its value, which ranges between 0 and 1). As discussed in Chapter 19, an effect size with a value greater than .5 is considered to be strong.

An example of a contingency analysis

Suppose we want to find out the percentage of boys and girls who think 'true/false' about the statement 'women are not allowed to sit in the House of Lords' (YPSA dataset). The null hypothesis is that there are no differences between boys and girls with regard to their responses on the statement. We also want to explore whether any observed differences in this sample between boys' and girls' views on this statement can be found in the population from which they were drawn. This requires us to use a statistical test to calculate the significance level (via the probability value, p).

As shown in the crosstabulation table (Figure 21.18), both the expected and observed frequency counts have been calculated for each variable. With a chi-square test, we test the differences between the expected (the number of occurrences in the population) and the observed (the number of occurrences in the sample) counts, and its value is interpreted in relation to the level of significance.

Looking at Figure 21.18, the '**Chi-Square Tests**' table, the value of Pearson's chi-square = 16.48, df = 2 and p<.000. This suggests that the results are statistically significant and, thus, the null

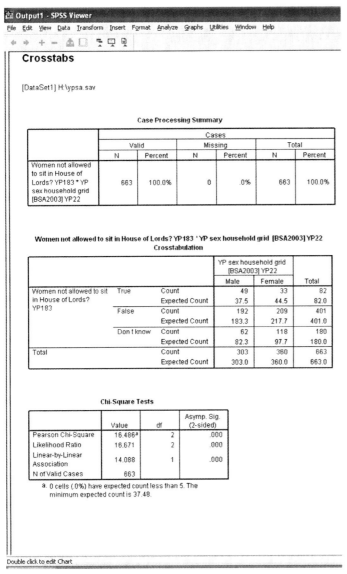

Figure 21.18 SPSS output 6

hypothesis H0 = there are no differences between boys and girls on their responses regarding 'women are not allowed to sit in the House of Lords' is rejected. Thus, boys' and girls' responses to this statement differ. Specifically, compared to girls, more boys thought that this statement was true. The effect size is .15 (weak/ modest), suggesting that although the results are statistically significant, we need to be careful with the conclusions we draw.

Multivariate Analyses

A multivariate analysis involves the analysis of more than two variables. Examples of multivariate analyses in this volume are a factorial analysis (Chapter 22), a multiple linear regression (Chapter 23) and a factor analysis (Chapter 24). (Note that a factorial analysis is different from a factor analysis: the former explores the impact of two independent variables on a dependent variable, whereas the latter is used for data reduction purposes.) In the following chapters, bivariate (e.g. t-test) and multivariate (e.g. factorial analysis) analyses will be presented with examples to illustrate them. At the empirical stage of a quantitative research, there are many issues to be considered in terms of the nature of sampling, the type of variables and the nature of data they yield, the assumptions that underpin the use of statistical tests and the employment of descriptive and inferential statistics. In Box 21.1, a number of questions are offered to guide us through the empirical stage.

Table 21.1 A guide for selecting statistical tests

Type of variable (Independent/ dependent)	Type of data collected	Assumptions/ conditions to be met	Number of comparisons	Appropriate statistical test
Nominal/nominal	Non-parametric	• No cell should have an expected value of less than 1 • No more than 20 per cent of cells should have expected values less than 5	Two or more categories in each nominal variable	Chi-Square Test (Chapter 21)
Nominal/ordinal	Non-parametric		Comparison of two categories of the nominal variable (eg, gender: male and female)	Mann Whitney U Test (Chapter 22)
Nominal (two or more categories)/ ordinal	Non-parametric		Comparison of more than two categories of the nominal variable	Kruskal- Wallis Test (Chapter 22)
Nominal/interval (scale)	Parametric	• Homogeneity of variance • Independence of groups • Scale variable is normally distributed	Comparison of two categories of the nominal variable (eg, gender: male and female)	Independent Samples T-Test (Chapter 22)
Nominal/interval (scale)	Parametric	• Scale variable is normally distributed • Homogeneity of variance (roughly equal spread) • Independence of groups	Comparison of more than two categories of the nominal variable	One-way ANOVA (Chapter 22)
Nominal/interval (scale)	Parametric	• Scale variable is normally distributed • Homogeneity of variance (roughly equal spread) • Independence of groups	Comparison of two or more categories of the nominal variable. Also, the number of the nominal variables is 2 or more.	Multivariate Analysis (General Linear Modeling) eg, Factorial Analysis (Chapter 22)
Interval/interval	Parametric		Measure of association	Pearson product- moment correlation (Chapter 23)
Ordinal/ordinal	Non-parametric		Measure of association	Spearman rho correlation (see Chapter 23)
Ordinal or categorical/ interval (scale)	Parametric	• Low correlation between predictor variables • The outcome variable is continuous (scale)	Measure of association and prediction – data reduction	Multiple Linear Regression (Chapter 23) – Factor Analysis (Chapter 24)

Box 21.1 Checklist: Decisions at the empirical stage

- Are you aware of the types of variable (i.e. nominal, ordinal, interval/ratio) you have included in the research design?
- Are you familiar with the fundamental differences between descriptive and inferential statistics, and the assumptions that underpin the latter?
- Can you differentiate between parametric and nonparametric data?
- Have you decided what statistical technique(s) you will employ for data analysis?
- Have you considered the sample size before the data collection?
- What are the conceptual (the purpose/aims of the study) and technical (e.g. sample size, type of variables) considerations that underpin the choice of your statistical technique? Have you matched the type of variables with the appropriate choice of statistical techniques (see Table 21.1)?
- Have you considered the sampling procedure? If the sample is nonprobabilistic (i.e., not randomly selected), are you aware of the limitations in making generalizations?
- Have you considered what the probability level would be for your statistical analyses?

Summary

In this chapter initial explorations of quantitative data were presented. Descriptive statistics were used to gain an overview of the data through the calculation of the central tendency measures (i.e. mean, mode and median) and dispersion (i.e. variance and standard deviation). The distinction between descriptive and inferential statistics was discussed, and three types of analysis were introduced, namely univariate, bivariate and multivariate. A univariate analysis (i.e. frequencies) and a bivariate analysis (i.e. contingency analysis) were presented to summarize data and explore the differences between the observed and expected frequencies and determine whether they were statistically significant. In the next chapter, bivariate analyses for parametric or nonparametric data (i.e. independent t-test and ANOVA, Mann Whitney U test and Kruskal-Wallis test) will be presented.

References

Lowry, R. (2008) Frequency distributions, http://faculty.vassar.edu/lowry/ch2pt1.html.

22 Between-group Differences: Comparing Two or More Means

Dimitra Hartas

Introduction

In educational research, between-group comparisons have been traditionally located within the context of experimental and quasi-experimental designs, where the experimental group receives some form of treatment, through an experimental manipulation of variables, and the other group (i.e. control or comparison group) receives a placebo. Ultimately, with experimental designs, we examine whether any differences in the outcome are attributable to treatment. A comparison of two or more groups involves a comparison of two or more mean values to determine whether, on average, the groups score differently. Group comparisons are different from exploring relationships between two or more variables (as in the case of bivariate correlation and multiple regression, discussed in Chapter 23).

The statistical procedures employed for between-group designs are the independent t-test, analysis of variance (ANOVA) and general linear modelling (e.g. factorial analysis). In the previous chapter, the assumptions that underpin parametric statistics – i.e. normally distributed data, equality of variance, independence of scores and variables measured at an interval level – were discussed. The statistical techniques discussed here rely on these assumptions. Although the independent t-test and ANOVA are considered to be robust tests capable of withstanding violations of the above assumptions, we need to be aware of these violations and interpret the results accordingly.

By the end of this chapter, you should be able to:

- understand the theoretical and technical assumptions that underpin the use of independent t-tests, one-way ANOVA and factorial analysis
- carry out t-tests and n-way ANOVAs and read and present the SPSS output with accuracy
- interpret and write up the results from t-tests and ANOVAs
- use nonparametric statistical techniques as alternatives to an independent t-test and an ANOVA

In this chapter, the statistical techniques employed to compare two or more groups are presented with examples to illustrate the 'how to do' aspect of statistical analyses. When we compare groups, essentially, we compare the mean values and variance of the dependent variable (outcome) for different treatments or conditions of a treatment. Depending on the research design and the sampling procedures, we may have the same or different participants in the groups. The research designs in which different groups of people are exposed to different experimental treatments are called 'between-group' or 'independent' designs. In repeated-measures designs, the same group of people is exposed to different treatments at different points in time (Field 2005). Put differently, in between-subject designs, the participants are tested under one condition only, whereas in within-subject or repeated designs the same participants are tested under all conditions of an intervention. In this chapter we focus on between-group designs.

Independent-samples T-test

A t-test is a useful statistical technique for comparing the mean values of two sets of scores. This comparison provides us with a statistic to evaluate whether the numerical difference between two means is statistically significant. In other words, we compare the mean values of two groups on a measured variable that we would have obtained by chance to those obtained at the end of an experimental (or quasi-experimental) manipulation. Large differences in the mean values that are beyond what is expected to occur by chance indicate genuine differences in the outcome scores.

The type of t-test I present in this chapter is an independent-samples t-test employed to compare two independent groups.

To run an independent-samples t-test using SPSS15:

1. Click on **Analyze**
2. A drop-down list menu appears, then click on **Compare means**
3. Choose **Independent-samples t-test** (see Figure 22.1)
4. A dialogue box pops up, presenting us with a space to insert the **Test variable** and the **Grouping variable**. The **Test variable** is the dependent variable or outcome, and the **Grouping variable** is the independent variable. With the t-test we can analyse one independent variable with two levels only, for example gender, which has two levels – i.e. male and female. In other words, with a t-test, we can compare two groups only
5. From the list of variables in the left-hand side of the dialogue box, choose the independent and dependent variables and click the arrow to transfer them into the appropriate boxes
6. After having entered the grouping variable (independent variable), a bracket containing question marks appears. This is because we are required to specify the levels of the variable, or the coding of the groups

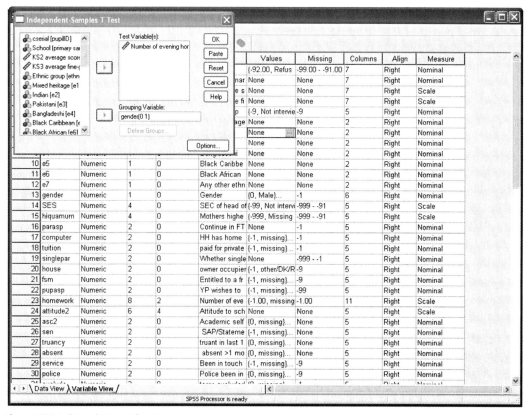

Figure 22.1 Independent-samples t-test

    'we compare. To do so, click the **Define groups** tab (it lights up once the grouping variable is entered in the box) and a new dialogue box appears

7   Enter the codes of the grouping variable in the **Group 1** and **Group 2** boxes, then click **Continue**

8   Back on the **Independent-samples t-test**, click **Options** to run **Descriptive statistics**

9   Finally, click **OK**

Examples of independent-samples t-tests

Based on a LSYPE dataset (see volume website), suppose we want to investigate whether there is a difference in the amount of homework completed by boys and girls. The null hypothesis is H0 = 'There is no difference between boys and girls with regard to the amount of homework completed'. The alternative hypothesis is H1 = 'There is a difference between boys and girls with regard to the amount of homework completed'. This is a two-tailed hypothesis in that, by referring to 'difference' we do not specify a direction, leaving it open to two possibilities (more or less homework). Once we run the independent t-test, the first output table, labelled **Group statistics**, displays descriptive statistics – i.e., mean, standard deviation (SD) for each group, as well as group sizes (see Figure 22.2).

    The second output table, labelled **Independent-samples test**, contains the statistics that are critical to testing the above hypothesis and the assumption of homogeneity of variance (e.g.

Group Statistics

	Gender	N	Mean	Std. Deviation	Std. Error Mean
Number of evening homework per week	Male	6997	2.8314	1.39984	.01673
	female	7076	3.1231	1.38400	.01645

Figure 22.2 SPSS output 1

Independent Samples Test

		Levene's Test for Equality of Variances		t-test for Equality of Means						95% Confidence Interval of the Difference	
		F	Sig.	t	df	Sig. (2-tailed)	Mean Difference	Std. Error Difference		Lower	Upper
Number of evening homework per week	Equal variances assumed	2.248	.134	-12.432	14071	.000	-.29174	.02347		-.33773	-.24574
	Equal variances not assumed			-12.431	14063.812	.000	-.29174	.02347		-.33774	-.24574

Figure 22.3 SPSS output 2

Levene's test) (see Figure 22.3). We also test for the normality assumption (Kormologov-Smirnov test as demonstrated in the previous chapter). If violated, we should consider employing the nonparametric equivalent of the independent t-test (i.e. Mann-Whitney u-test).

In Figure 22.3, the Levene's test (F = 2.248, p<.134) is not significant, meaning that there is no difference in the variance between the two groups (e.g., boys and girls). In other words, the variance in the two groups is homogeneous, and thus we can assume equal variances. The t statistic is –12.432 and is statistically significant (p<.000), pointing to differences between boys and girls with regard to homework completion. The next question is: who completed more homework? To answer this, we look at the mean values in the group statistics table (see Figure 22.2), with girls (M = 3.12) displaying a higher mean value than the boys (M = 2.83). Thus, we can say that, on average, girls do more homework compared with boys in this dataset (we may generalize this finding to the population from which the sample was drawn only if the sample was randomly selected – see Chapter 4). For the independent t-test, the degrees of freedom (df) are calculated by adding the sample sizes of the groups and then subtracting the number of samples (df = N1 + N2 – 2). In this example, the df = 6997 + 7076 – 2 = 14071 (the SPSS calculates the df).

In the independent-samples t-test, the effect size (r) is calculated as r = the square root of t squared divided by t squared + df (t is the t-test statistic and df the degrees of freedom). The effect size index takes values between 0 and 1, interpreted as: 0–0.1 is a weak effect; 0.1–0.3 is a modest effect, 0.3–0.5 is a moderate effect and anything greater than 0.5 represents a strong effect. These cut-off points are somewhat arbitrary and should be used to guide our judgement as researchers. In this example, r = $\sqrt{(-12.43)} \times (-12.43) / (-12.43) \times (-12.43) + 14071 = 0.1$. This is considered to be a weak effect size, and thus we need to interpret the t-test results with caution.

When testing the null hypothesis, we test for either a two-tailed or one-tailed hypothesis (see Chapter 19). The SPSS produces results for a two-tailed hypothesis only. If we want to test an one-tailed hypothesis (because we have a rationale as to why we want to test a directional hypothesis), then we need to divide the two-tailed significance value by two in order to calculate the one-tailed probability value. We can do this with a t-test but not with an ANOVA (see next section). As Field (2005) discusses, an ANOVA is a non-specific test in that it tells us whether there is a difference between more than two means. Thus, we cannot divide the significance value we get from the ANOVA table by 2 to test for a one-tailed hypothesis.

Let's present another example of an independent t-test that involves unequal variance between groups. Suppose we want to examine homework completion across two groups of pupils – i.e. those who are entitled to a free school meal and those who are not (eligibility to free school meals is seen as a measure of social class).

Group Statistics

	Entitled to a free school meal	N	Mean	Std. Deviation	Std. Error Mean
Number of evening homework per week	No	10787	2.9649	1.37106	.01320
	Yes	2562	2.7338	1.39817	.02762

Figure 22.4 SPSS output 3

		Levene's Test for Equality of Variances		t-test for Equality of Means					95% Confidence Interval of the Difference	
		F	Sig.	t	df	Sig. (2-tailed)	Mean Difference	Std. Error Difference	Lower	Upper
Number of evening homework per week	Equal variances assumed	13.517	.000	7.639	13347	.000	.23106	.03025	.17177	.29035
	Equal variances not assumed			7.547	3817.112	.000	.23106	.03062	.17104	.29109

Figure 22.5 SPSS output: 4

In this example, the Levene test is significant (F = 13.51; p<.000) which means that the variance between the two groups is not equal (see Figure 22.5). This means that the assumption of the homogeneity of variance was violated, and so we need to be cautious about interpreting the results. In Figure 22.5, the t statistic t = 7.639 is statistically significant (p<.000), indicating that there is a difference in the amount of homework between pupils who are eligible for a free school meal (M = 2.73) and those who are not (M = 2.96), with the latter group doing more homework (means are presented in Figure 22.4). Although a t-test is rigorous, we need to consider the large sample size in this dataset, the unequal group sizes and the fact that the difference in the mean values is relatively small. Based on this analysis, we may extrapolate (with caution!) that there is a relationship between homework completion and social class (defined as eligibility to free school meals).

Analysis of Variance (ANOVA)

Anaysis of variance (ANOVA) is a statistical analysis that is, conceptually, very similar to an independent-samples t-test. An ANOVA is employed to compare more than two sets of scores, whereas with a t-test we can compare two groups only at a time. Thus, the advantage of an ANOVA over a t-test is that we can perform post-hoc testing to delineate the comparison pairs and ascertain which ones are statistically significant. (The results from a one-way ANOVA are exactly the same with those obtained from an independent t-test when the independent variable has two levels only.)

Suppose that we want to compare three ethnic groups (e.g. black, white, Indian) on measures of academic achievement. Typically, there are three pair-wise comparisons to be performed: black–white, black–Indian, white–Indian. One may suggest that we can perform these pair-wise comparisons by employing three t-tests. In so doing, however, we maximize the probability of making a Type I error by rejecting the null hypothesis wrongly and stating that there is a statistically significant difference between the groups where in fact there is not (see Chapter 19 on Type I and II errors). To demonstrate the increase in the probability of making a Type I error, suppose that when we run one t-test, the probability of making a Type I error is 5 per cent ($p<.05$). If we run three separate t-tests, then the probability becomes $.5 \times .5 \times .5 = .143$. The new p value indicates the probability that the differences observed between the groups is due to chance is 14.3 per cent, which is not acceptable because the cut-off point is less than 5 per cent or, put simply, $p<.05$.

To avoid this problem, an ANOVA offers the choice of several post-hoc tests, with some being more conservative than others. The notion of a conservative vs. a liberal test is linked with the probability of making Type I errors. With a conservative test, the probability of making a Type I error is small. At the same time, the statistical power of the test is small in terms of being able to detect a genuine effect. As discussed in Chapter 19, there is a fine balance between a good statistical power to allow for real differences to emerge and the probability of making a Type I error.

With such a choice of post-hoc tests, an important question is how to decide which post-hoc test to choose. Bonferroni and Tukey post-hoc tests are considered to be conservative tests in that they show significance only when there are large differences between the group means. The advantage of this is that they reduce the possibility of making a Type I error. The downside is that the possibility of making a Type II error increases because a conservative test may not detect statistically significant comparisons in data. The Scheffe test is also conservative and is preferred for complex group comparisons, whereas the Newman-Keuls is a liberal test. Field (2005) points out that Bonferroni is a good post-hoc choice for a small number of comparisons, whereas Tukey is good for a large number of comparisons.

With an ANOVA, we calculate the F statistic, which is the ratio of between-group variance and within-group variance (it compares the between-group and within-group mean squares). The between-group variance refers to systematic variation, which is due to the 'treatment' or other factors that have been included in the study, whose impact on the outcome variable has been examined. The within-group variance refers to the statistical error that arises from unsystematic variation, for example, variation due to chance or confounding factors (e.g. individual characteristics) whose effect was not controlled for. As discussed in earlier chapters, an important advantage of experimental designs is that through randomization, unsystematic variation is controlled and thus minimized, ensuring that the only source of variance is the between-group variance.

When testing for genuine effects, we expect the between-group variance to be much larger than the within-group variance. A statistically significant F value reflects an outcome that is due to treatment/intervention, which is much higher than an outcome obtained by chance. The F value also reflects the sample size of the groups, the variance in the outcome scores and the differences in the mean values. The F value is more likely to be statistically significant when the difference in mean values is large, the sample size is large and the variance is low – i.e. outcome scores cluster around the mean of the frequency distribution (see Chapter 21).

As discussed in Chapter 23, ANOVA and regression share many characteristics, mainly because both explore relationships between independent variables, or 'predictor variables' as they are called in regression, and an outcome variable. An important difference between ANOVA and regression lies in the epistemological framework of quantitative research within which they operate. ANOVA originates within the experimental and quasi-experimental tradition and involves group comparisons. Regression, on the other hand, originates in nonexperimental research. Regression analyses are considered to be more flexible than ANOVAs because they include all variable types, whereas in an ANOVA the outcome variable should be measured at an interval level.

To run an one-way ANOVA using SPSS15:

1 Go to **Analyze**
2 A drop-down list menu appears, click **Compare means**
3 Choose **One-way ANOVA** (see Figure 22.6)
4 A dialogue box appears, enter the dependent variable in the **Dependent list** and the independent variable in the **Factor** (see Figure 22.7)
5 Then click the **Post hoc** tab to specify the pair-wise comparisons (if the grouping variable has two levels then there is only one comparison to be made. In this case, the results from the One-way ANOVA are the same with those produced via a t-test analysis. However, one-way ANOVA allows you to compare more than one pair of groups and thus the post- hoc function is important
6 Once you click **Post hoc** a new dialogue box appears: **Post hoc multiple comparisons**
7 Choose a post-hoc test, in this example, **Tukey** and click **Continue**
8 Back to the ANOVA dialogue box: click the **Options** tab, and then click **Homogeneity of variance** and**Means plot**, and click **Continue** (see Figure 22.8)
9 Finally, click **OK**

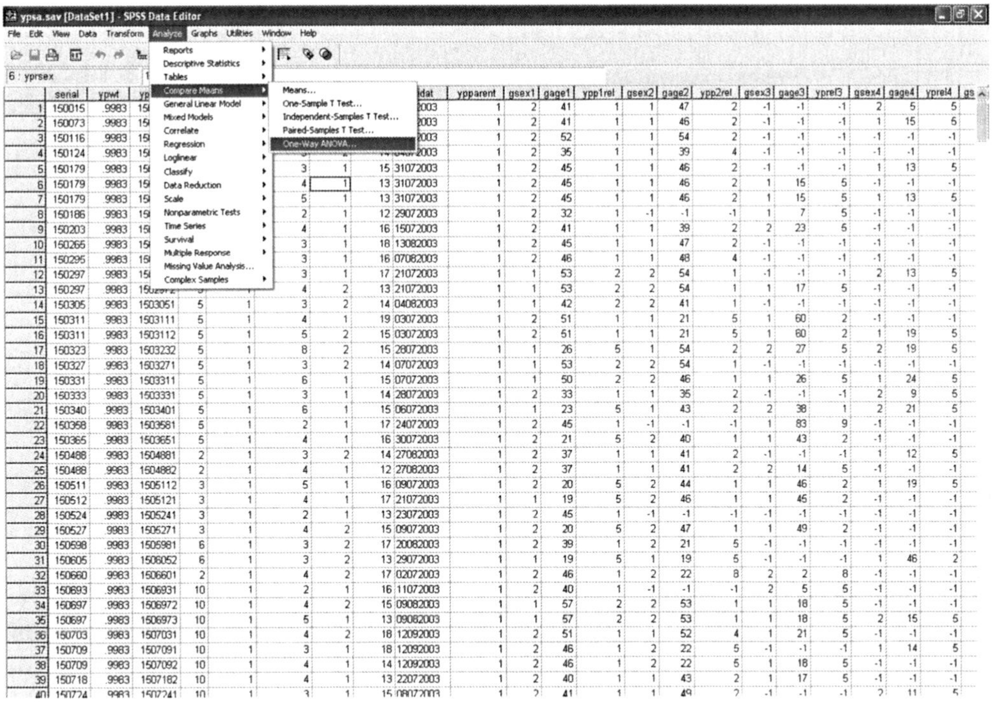

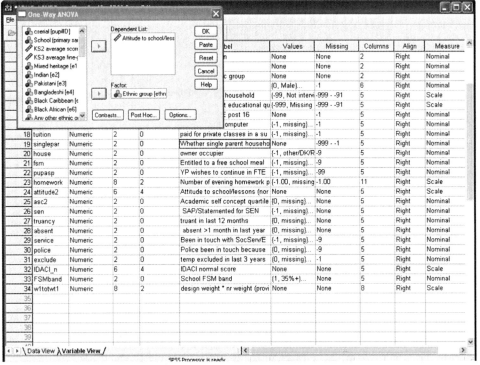

Figure 22.6 One-way ANOVA

Figure 22.7 One-way ANOVA (dialogue box)

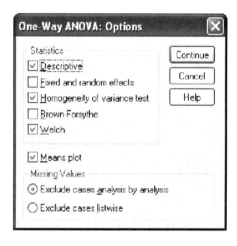

Figure 22.8 One-way ANOVA (options)

Examples of one-way ANOVA

Using a subset of the LSYPE data, let's explore the relationship between pupil academic self-concept and the number of homework evenings per week. Looking at Figure 22.9, we see information about descriptive statistics,= – i.e. mean and SD, for each condition/level of the independent variable (i.e. very high, high, low, very low).

Descriptives

Number of evening homework per week

	N	Mean	Std. Deviation	Std. Error	95% Confidence Interval for Mean		Minimum	Maximum
					Lower Bound	Upper Bound		
missing	944	2.6314	1.48649	.04838	2.5364	2.7263	.00	5.00
very high	2999	3.3815	1.34129	.02449	3.3334	3.4295	.00	5.00
high	4776	3.0976	1.33817	.01936	3.0596	3.1355	.00	5.00
low	4097	2.7942	1.38187	.02159	2.7519	2.8366	.00	5.00
very low	1257	2.4208	1.41432	.03989	2.3426	2.4991	.00	5.00
Total	14073	2.9780	1.39947	.01180	2.9549	3.0012	.00	5.00

Figure 22.9 SPSS output 5

First, we test for the assumption of equality of variance with the Levene test (as we did with the independent-samples t-test). In this example, the Levene statistic of 15.40 is statistically significant, p<.000 (see Figure 22.10),which means that there is a difference in the variance between the two groups. Thus, the assumption of homogeneity of variance is violated. However, we can correct this by choosing the Welch F (see Figure 22.8).

Test of Homogeneity of Variances

Number of evening homework per week

Levene Statistic	df1	df2	Sig.
15.409	4	14068	.000

Figure 22.10 SPSS output 6

Looking at the ANOVA table (see Figure 22.11) and the 'Robust Tests of Equality of Means' table (see Figure 22.12) we get the F and the Welch F values, respectively. Both the F = 159.88 (p<.000) and the Welch F = 152.95 (p<.000) came out to be statistically significant. We report the Welch F value, which is the corrected F value. In one-way ANOVA, the degrees of freedom (df) of the between-groups mean square is the number of treatment groups minus one (df = k–1). In this example, df = 5 – 1 = 4 (the number of treatment groups is five including the 'missing' condition).

ANOVA

Number of evening homework per week

	Sum of Squares	df	Mean Square	F	Sig.
Between Groups	1198.444	4	299.611	159.888	.000
Within Groups	26361.771	14068	1.874		
Total	27560.215	14072			

Figure 22.11 SPSS output 7

Robust Tests of Equality of Means

Number of evening homework per week

	Statistic^a	df1	df2	Sig.
Brown-Forsythe	152.953	4	7174.328	.000

a. Asymptotically F distributed.

Figure 22.12 SPSS output 8

Post-hoc testing

The 'Multiple Comparisons' table (see Figure 22.13) offers information on the pair-wise comparisons. Because the overall F came out statistically significant, it does not necessarily mean that all pair-wise comparisons are statistically significant. Post-hoc testing distinguishes pair-wise comparisons that are statistically significant from those that are not. In this example, the 'very high' group vs. the 'high' group (p<.000); 'very high' vs. 'low' (p<.000); and 'very high' vs. 'very low' (p<.000) comparisons are all statistically significant. (When reporting the results, we may also include the means from Figure 22.9].

Means plots

The plot of means offers a visual representation of the differences between the mean values (see Figure 22.14). Statistically significant results are not sufficient to claim that a factor has a substantial effect on the outcome variable. The effect size offers an important index with regard to the strength of the effect of the independent variable(s) on the dependent one. For ANOVA the effect size is calculated by the *eta squared*. Manually, the eta squared is calculated by dividing the 'within group sum of squares' with the 'total sum of squares' and then taking the square root of the ratio (SPSS calculates this). The values for the within-group sum of squares and the total sum of squares can be found in Figure 22.11.

Multiple Comparisons

Dependent Variable: Number of evening homework per week

Scheffe

(I) Academic self concept quartiles	(J) Academic self concept quartiles	Mean Difference (I-J)	Std. Error	Sig.	95% Confidence Interval	
					Lower Bound	Upper Bound
missing	very high	-.75010*	.05109	.000	-.9075	-.5927
	high	-.46622*	.04876	.000	-.6164	-.3160
	low	-.16288*	.04942	.028	-.3151	-.0106
	very low	.21051*	.05896	.013	.0289	.3921
very high	missing	.75010*	.05109	.000	.5927	.9075
	high	.28389*	.03189	.000	.1856	.3821
	low	.58722*	.03290	.000	.4859	.6886
	very low	.96062*	.04600	.000	.8189	1.1023
high	missing	.46622*	.04876	.000	.3160	.6164
	very high	-.28389*	.03189	.000	-.3821	-.1856
	low	.30333*	.02915	.000	.2135	.3931
	very low	.67673*	.04339	.000	.5430	.8104
low	missing	.16288*	.04942	.028	.0106	.3151
	very high	-.58722*	.03290	.000	-.6886	-.4859
	high	-.30333*	.02915	.000	-.3931	-.2135
	very low	.37340*	.04414	.000	.2374	.5094
very low	missing	-.21051*	.05896	.013	-.3921	-.0289
	very high	-.96062*	.04600	.000	-1.1023	-.8189
	high	-.67673*	.04339	.000	-.8104	-.5430
	low	-.37340*	.04414	.000	-.5094	-.2374

*. The mean difference is significant at the .05 level.

Figure 22.13 SPSS output 9

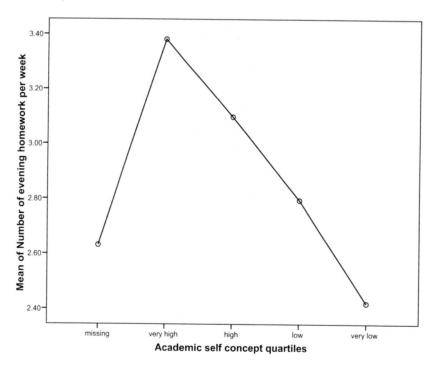

Figure 22.14 SPSS output 10

General Linear Modelling (GLM)

An analysis of variance is used in many situations to determine whether there are differences between groups in one or more outcome variables. In the previous section, a one-way ANOVA was discussed as a statistical technique for multiple pair-wise comparisons involving one independent variable only. In education and social sciences, we are interested in investigating the effects of more than one independent variable (and their interactions) simultaneously. In so doing, we employ a series of statistical techniques that are clustered under *general linear modelling*. There are three main types of the general linear model, namely univariate, multivariate and repeated measures (see Box 22.1). The univariate general linear model involves a single outcome (dependent variable), and can have several independent variables (e.g. fixed between-subjects factors, random between-subjects factors or covariates). The multivariate general linear model involves more than one dependent/outcome variable, and can have more than one independent variable. In the repeated measures general linear model, the dependent variable is measured at different points in time (repeated measures over time). The procedures used for conducting these three types of analysis of variance are found under the **General linear modelling** menu item in the **Analyse** menu of the SPSS.

In summary, these types of ANOVA differ along (1) the number of independent variables, (2) the number of dependent variables and (3) whether the same or different participants take part (within vs. between subjects).

In this section, I present the univariate type of a general linear model with different participants (independent factorial analysis). The univariate general linear model is used to compare differences between group means and estimate the effect of covariates on a single outcome. For example, we may want to examine children's academic performance in reading as a function of several factors, such as household income, ability and language skills, all of which have been shown to affect reading. To do this, we would want to demonstrate that the average

---

Box 22.1 Statistical techniques under GLM

- One-way independent ANOVA: involves one independent variable that is measured using different participants (independent scores).
- N-way independent ANOVA: involves more than one independent variable measured by using different participants (between groups). Another term used for this is independent factorial analysis.
- Repeated measures n-way ANOVA: involves more than one independent variable measured by using the same participants (within groups). Another term used for this design is related factorial design.
- Multivariate ANOVA (MANOVA): involves more than one dependent variable (outcome), and may have one or more independent variables.
- Mixed ANOVA: combines both between- and within-group designs. In other words, it combines both independent and repeated measures ANOVAs. For example, a mixed design may involve two independent variables: one measured by using different participants (between groups) and the other by using the same participants at different points in time (within groups).

reading scores are significantly different between, for example, children who come from low-/high-income households or children with high and low language skills, and also explore the interaction of the two factors (e.g. children with low language skills in high-income households). With a one-way ANOVA, we could have examined one factor (independent variable) only. However, we know from the literature that multiple factors affect children's reading and, thus, it is important to incorporate some of these factors into the research design to either examine their effects or statistically control for their influence on reading.

The independent variables exert two types of effects on outcome, namely, main effects and interaction effects. Main is the effect that each independent variable separately has on the outcome variable. An interaction effect exists when differences in one factor depend on the level of another factor. An interaction effect is not the combined effect of two or more independent variables. Rather, interaction means that the effect of an independent variable on the outcome is affected by another independent variable. For example, suppose that we want to examine the effects of gender and ethnicity on reading comprehension. Main effects are the effects that gender and ethnicity separately have on reading comprehension, whereas an interaction effect refers to the influence that both gender and ethnicity exert on reading comprehension. A significant interaction would mean that boys/girls from certain ethnic groups perform better/worse in reading comprehension. Had we had looked at the main effects only, we would not have been able to say that, within the same ethnic group (or across different ethnic groups), differences in measures of reading comprehension depend on the young person's gender. Put differently, we would not have been able to examine whether the differences between boys and girls in reading comprehension are affected by their ethnicity.

There are three ways to determine whether there is an interaction effect. First, looking at the SPSS output, the ANOVA statistical table reports on all main and interaction effects. Secondly, an interaction effect is evident in the discussion of the results. When we discuss the effects one factor has on outcome and mention the conditions of the other factor, essentially, what we say is that these effects have been mediated by the conditions of another factor. Thirdly, we can always spot an interaction in the graphs of group means – whenever the lines are not parallel, there is an interaction effect (see Figure 22.29).

To interpret a two-way ANOVA, looking at the test of interaction effects is the logical first step. The results of this test influence the interpretation of the main effects. For example, if the interaction is statistically significant, less attention is generally paid to the interpretation of the main effects. As Pedhazur and Pedhazur-Schmelkin note, the 'motivation for studying interactions is to ascertain whether the effects of a given factor vary depending on the levels of the other factor with which they are combined' (1991: 514). Having found that the interaction is statistically significant, it makes little sense to focus on the main effects. However, a statistically significant interaction does not mean that no attention at all should be paid to the main effects. A large main effect, relative to the interaction effect, indicates that we should consider both the main effect and the interaction when we interpret the results (Keppel 1999). On the other hand, if the interaction is not statistically significant, or if it is statistically significant but trivial (according to the effect size), our attention should focus on the main effects (see Box 22.2).

> ### Box 22.2 An example of factorial design in educational research
>
> In a study by Bornholt *et al.* (1994), adolescents' perception of their own achievement in English and maths was examined in the context of school year and gender. A two-way ANOVA was used to examine the effects of gender and school year (independent factors) on students' perception of their own achievement, as well as on measures of actual achievement obtained through reading and maths tests. Significant differences were found in both English and maths as a function of school year (Year 7 and Year 10), in that there was a significant increase in academic performance moving from Year 7 to Year 10. However, no significant differences in academic performance were found as a function of gender. This study was based on a quasi-experimental design where intact classrooms/year groups were used to form the comparison groups, rather than forming an experimental and control group via random allocation of students to groups. (See Chapter 15 for examples of experimental and quasi-experimental studies, which typically employ n-way ANOVA as a statistical technique.)

Advantages of independent factorial designs

Pedhazur (1982: 135) discussed four major advantages of factorial designs.

- Factorial designs make it possible to determine interaction effects. An independent variable can explain a relatively small proportion of variance in a dependent variable, whereas its interaction with other independent variables may explain a relatively large proportion of variance. The effects of, let's say, two independent variables in isolation (e.g. running two separate one-way ANOVAs) cannot reveal the interaction between them.
- Factorial designs allow the researcher to incorporate extraneous factors in the design, in the form of covariates, to maximize experimental control. Moreover, because two or more factors are tested simultaneously, the possibility of committing a Type I error is reduced.
- Factorial designs are efficient. One can test the separate and combined effects of several variables using the same number of subjects one would have used for separate experiments.
- In factorial designs, the effect of a treatment can be studied across different conditions of other treatments. Consequently, generalizations from factorial experiments are broader than are generalizations from single-variable experiments.

To run a two-way independent ANOVA using SPSS15:

1 Go to **Analyze**
2 Choose **General linear model** from the drop-down menu
3 Then click **Univariate** (see Figure 22.16)
4 The **Univariate** dialogue box appears
5 Several little boxes appear to enter the variables you want to analyse in the **Dependent variable** box, and the independent variables in the **Fixed factor(s)** box (see Figure 22.17)

In Figure 22.17, we also see a **Random factor(s)** box. Random factors refer to conditions or levels that are a random selection from a group of possible conditions, a selection of specific characteristics from a pool of characteristics. Suppose that the conditions of the factor 'decoding skills' are made up of a collection of characteristics such as phonemic analysis, alliteration or sound blending, characteristics that, as research has shown, relate to decoding words. In this

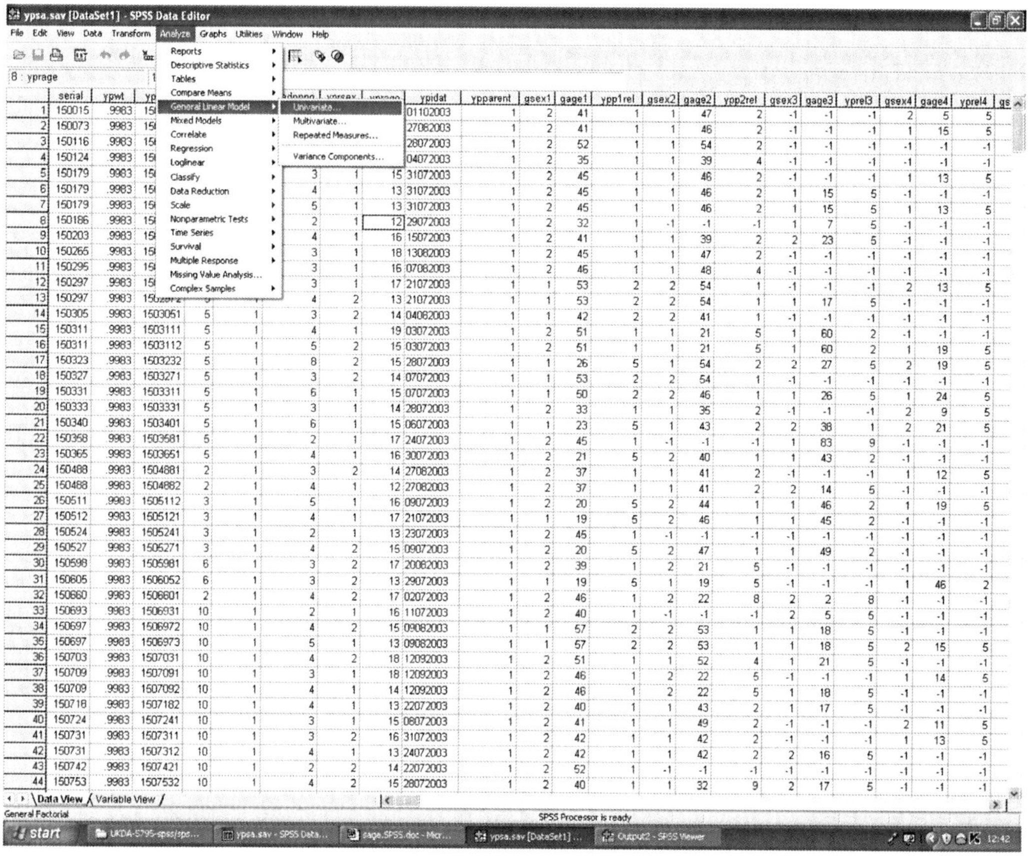

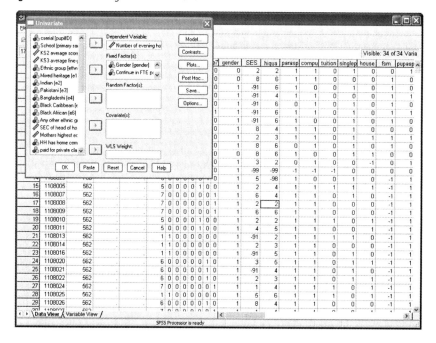

Figure 22.16 Univariate general linear model

Figure 22.17
Unvariate dialogue box

example, decoding skills is a random factor because we can select a number of characteristics (e.g. alliteration) from a pool of equally relevant characteristics. In contrast, fixed factors are made up by conditions that are fixed – for example, gender – with two fixed conditions (male, female).

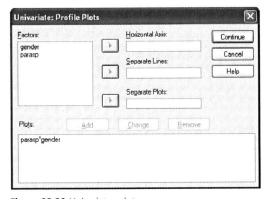

Figure 22.18 Post-hoc comparisons

6 Click **Post hoc** and a new dialogue box, Univariate: post hoc multiple comparisons for observed means appears (see Figure 22.18)

If the main effects of a variable/factor with more than two levels are statistically significant, post- hoc comparisons are required to delineate all the pair-wise comparisons and ascertain which ones are statistically significant.

7 We choose the independent variables (from the **Factors** box) that require a post- hoc testing. These are variables that have more than two levels; in this example, ethnicity has more than two levels, white, Indian, African etc.

8 Then click the arrow to transfer them to the box called **Post hoc tests for:** we specify the type of post-hoc test (e.g. Scheffe), then click **Continue** (see Figure 22.18)

9 Back to the **Univariate** dialogue box – click **Plot** to get the plot of group means (this is useful to look at the interaction or lack of it between the independent variables). You enter one variable in the × **axis** and the other in the **Y axis**, then click **Add** and then **Continue** (see Figures 22.19)

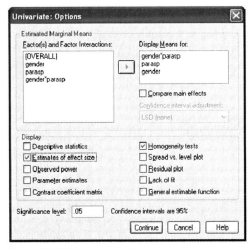

Figure 22.20 Univariate: plots

Figure 22.20 Univariate: option

10 Back to the **Univariate** dialogue box, click **Options** to click **Homogeneity tests**, **Descriptive statistics** and **Estimates of effect size,** then click **Continue** (see Figure 22.20)

In Figure 22.20, we click **Estimates of effect size** to calculate the effect size. The effect size for ANOVA is the eta squared and is a standardized measure of the strength of a relationship. In a factorial analysis, the effect sizes are computed for the main effects and the interaction effects. Also, in Figure 22.20, we click **Homogeneity tests** to test the assumption of homogeneity of variance (Levene test).

11 Back at the **Univariate** dialogue box, click **OK** to run the analysis

As with a one-way ANOVA, in an independent factorial design we need to consider the assumptions of normality, homogeneity of variance, independence of scores and outcome variables measured at an interval/ratio level. In factorial analyses with two or more independent variables each having two or more levels, we check for multivariate normality, expressed in the scores of the dependent variable having a normal distribution for each value category of the independent variables.

An example of an independent factorial analysis

With the LSYPE dataset, suppose we want to examine the effects of truancy and entitlement to free meals at school (a measure of socioeconomic status) on the number of homework evenings per week. The null hypothesis is H0 = 'there are not any differences in the number of homework evenings as a function of truancy and entitlement to free meals at school'. Looking at Figure 22.21, we see the independent factors, their conditions and the coding given to each. There is also information about the number of cases per condition (N).

Between-Subjects Factors

		Value Label	N
Entitled to a free school meal	-1	missing	723
	0	no	10787
	1	yes	2562
truant in last 12 months	0	missing	875
	1	yes	1733
	2	no	11464

Figure 22.21 SPSS output 12

In Figure 22.22, the first table is the Levene test (F = 9.67, p<.000; statistically significant), indicating that the groups do not have equal variance. Thus, the assumption of the homogeneity of variance is *not* met. As discussed before, ANOVAs are rigorous designs that can withstand violations regarding homogeneity of variance. However, it is important to ensure that the cell sizes are not very unequal. If we look at the 'Between-Subjects Factors' table (Figure 22.22), the number of cases (cell sizes) varies across conditions, pointing to unequal cell sizes. In this case, to minimize the possibility of committing a Type I error, we need to choose a conservative post-hoc test (e.g. Bonferroni).

Levene's Test of Equality of Error Variances^a

Dependent Variable: Number of evening homework per week

F	df1	df2	Sig.
9.672	8	14063	.000

Tests the null hypothesis that the error variance of the dependent variable is equal across groups.

a. Design: Intercept+fsm+truancy+fsm * truancy

Figure 22.22 SPSS output 13

Next, we look at 'Test of Between-Subjects Effects' table (Figure 22.23), which offers information on both main and interaction effects. In a factorial analysis, we examine the interaction effects as a first step (Figure 22.23). The F value is a ratio calculated by dividing the mean squares for the effect by the mean square for the residuals. In this example, the interaction is expressed in terms of fsm*truancy, which is statistically significant, $F = 3.13$, $df = 2 \times 2 = 4$, $p < .014$, with the effect size (partial eta squared) = .001. As with the one-way ANOVA, we report the results by stating the F value, the degrees of freedom from which it was calculated, and the p level. The terms 'corrected model' and 'intercept' refer to the regression method that was used to run the ANOVA. We do not refer to these terms when interpreting the output.

In a two-way ANOVA, the degrees of freedom (df) for each factor are the number of the conditions that make up this factor minus 1. In our example, the factor 'truancy' has three conditions (yes, no, missing); thus the $df = 3 - 1 = 2$. Likewise, the factor 'fsm' has three conditions (yes, no, missing) and $df = 2$. The df for the interaction is the product of the df of the factors involved; for the interaction fsm*truancy, the $df = 2 \times 2 = 4$.

We need now to estimate the effect size. In this example, the eta squared is .001, and is very weak. With such a small effect size, we need to be careful how we interpret the interaction effects, and also to examine the main effects, which came out statistically significant for both factors – i.e., fsm and truancy.

Tests of Between-Subjects Effects

Dependent Variable: Number of evening homework per week

Source	Type III Sum of Squares	df	Mean Square	F	Sig.	Partial Eta Squared
Corrected Model	1723.066ᵃ	8	215.383	117.250	.000	.063
Intercept	14154.510	1	14154.510	7705.431	.000	.354
fsm	181.682	2	90.841	49.452	.000	.007
truancy	294.606	2	147.303	80.189	.000	.011
fsm * truancy	23.046	4	5.761	3.136	.014	.001
Error	25833.061	14063	1.837			
Total	152345.000	14072				
Corrected Total	27556.127	14071				

a. R Squared = .063 (Adjusted R Squared = .062)

Figure 22.23 SPSS output 14

Figures 22.24 and 22.25 offer information on descriptive statistics (mean, standard error) for each factor separately and their interaction. Because both factors (i.e. truant and fsm) have more

1. Entitled to a free school meal

Dependent Variable: Number of evening homework per week

Entitled to a free school meal	Mean	Std. Error	95% Confidence Interval	
			Lower Bound	Upper Bound
missing	3.541	.090	3.363	3.718
no	2.700	.023	2.654	2.746
yes	2.570	.037	2.498	2.642

Figure 22.24 SPSS output 15

2. truant in last 12 months

Dependent Variable: Number of evening homework per week

truant in last 12 months	Mean	Std. Error	95% Confidence Interval	
			Lower Bound	Upper Bound
missing	2.774	.077	2.624	2.925
yes	2.667	.061	2.548	2.787
no	3.369	.022	3.327	3.411

Figure 22.25 SPSS output 16

than two conditions, multiple pair-wise comparisons are required (e.g. Scheffe). Figure 22.26 offers information on multiple comparisons with regard to the factor 'fsm'. Likewise, Figure 22.27 presents three group comparisons for the factor 'truant' – i.e. 'missing' vs. 'yes', 'missing' vs. 'no' and 'yes' vs. 'no'. All the pair-wise comparisons are statistically significant, pointing to differences in the number of evening homeworks per week between truant and non-truant children and those

Multiple Comparisons

Dependent Variable: Number of evening homework per week
Scheffe

(I) Entitled to a free school meal	(J) Entitled to a free school meal	Mean Difference (I-J)	Std. Error	Sig.	95% Confidence Interval	
					Lower Bound	Upper Bound
missing	no	1.0725*	.05207	.000	.9450	1.1999
	yes	1.3035*	.05708	.000	1.1638	1.4433
no	missing	-1.0725*	.05207	.000	-1.1999	-.9450
	yes	.2311*	.02979	.000	.1581	.3040
yes	missing	-1.3035*	.05708	.000	-1.4433	-1.1638
	no	-.2311*	.02979	.000	-.3040	-.1581

Based on observed means.
*. The mean difference is significant at the .05 level.

Figure 22.26 SPSS output 17

Multiple Comparisons

Dependent Variable: Number of evening homework per week
Scheffe

(I) truant in last 12 months	(J) truant in last 12 months	Mean Difference (I-J)	Std. Error	Sig.	95% Confidence Interval	
					Lower Bound	Upper Bound
missing	yes	.2407*	.05621	.000	.1031	.3783
	no	-.4498*	.04754	.000	-.5661	-.3334
yes	missing	-.2407*	.05621	.000	-.3783	-.1031
	no	-.6904*	.03493	.000	-.7759	-.6049
no	missing	.4498*	.04754	.000	.3334	.5661
	yes	.6904*	.03493	.000	.6049	.7759

Based on observed means.
*. The mean difference is significant at the .05 level.

Figure 22.27 SPSS output 18

who did not respond to this item (missing). Thus, the number of evening homeworks per week differs between children who are entitled to free school meal and those who are not, as well as between those who are truant and those who are not. (In some analyses, the category 'missing' is not included. It depends on whether 'missing' is considered to be a valuable category to examine.)

In many cases, when the interaction effects are statistically significant, we do not present the main effects (and their pair-wise comparisons). However, in this example, we present both main and interaction effects because the effect size for the interaction effects is weak.

Interaction

The hypothesis explored in this example is whether there are any statistically significant differences in the number of evenings a week a pupil completes homework as a function of truancy and eligibility for free school meals. The results suggest (see Figure 22.28) that there are, and that the effects of one factor (truancy) depend on (or are mediated by) the condition of the other factor (fsm). In other words, the interaction between 'truant' and 'fsm' is statistically significant. Pupils who were not entitled to free school meals and had been truant in the last 12 months did a smaller number of homework evenings (M = 2.38) than those who had not been truant (M = 3.06). Among pupils who were entitled to free school meals, those who had been truant presented a smaller number of homework evenings (M = 2.31) than those who had not (M = 2.86). These results suggest that being truant has a negative effect on the numbers of homework evenings a young person puts in, and this effect is evident for both pupils who are entitled to free school meals and those who are not. We need to exercise caution with these results in the light of (1) the weak effect sizes; (2) the fact that the assumption of homogeneity of variance was not met; and (3) the unequal cell sizes, all conditions that maximize the likelihood of committing a Type I error. In this example, it is worth examining both the interaction and the main effects.

An easy way to look at these interactions is with the 'profile plot' (see Figure 22.29) which is the interaction graph. Typically, non-parallel lines indicate significant interactions; however, the

3. Entitled to a free school meal * truant in last 12 months

Dependent Variable: Number of evening homework per week

Entitled to a free school meal	truant in last 12 months	Mean	Std. Error	95% Confidence Interval	
				Lower Bound	Upper Bound
missing	missing	3.140	.207	2.734	3.545
	yes	3.303	.167	2.976	3.630
	no	4.179	.055	4.072	4.286
no	missing	2.653	.056	2.543	2.764
	yes	2.383	.039	2.307	2.460
	no	3.063	.014	3.035	3.091
yes	missing	2.529	.085	2.363	2.696
	yes	2.315	.063	2.191	2.439
	no	2.865	.032	2.804	2.927

Figure 22.28 SPSS output 19

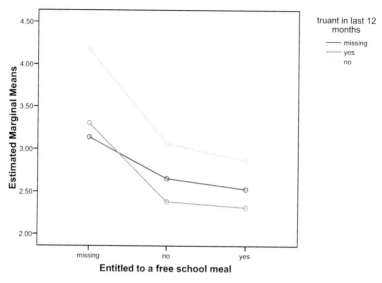

Figure 22.29 SPSS output 20

existence of non-parallel lines does not automatically mean that the interaction is significant. For an interaction to be significant, the lines have to cross over to a significant degree (Field 2005).

Nonparametric Tests

As discussed before, when the assumption of normality is violated, the data do not form a normal distribution, requiring us to employ nonparametric tests for data analysis (see Box 22.3).

Box 22.3 What if?

- What if the homogeneity assumption is violated?
  In ANOVA, a violation of the homogeneity of variance (Levene test turning out to be significant) points out that the variance between groups is not equal. Unequal variance and cell sizes that are also unequal can have serious consequences in terms of increasing the risk of committing a Type I error. A way of going around this is by using the Welch F that is available in SPSS. The Welch F has been found to be robust when the homogeneity of variance assumption is violated (Field 2005).
- What if the data collected on the outcome variable are not normally distributed?
  If the assumption of normality is violated (the Kolmogorov-Smirnov test turns out to be statistically significant) then this translates to nonparametric data. There are nonparametric tests that function as counterparts to the independent t-test and one-way ANOVA, namely Mann-Whitney u and Kruskal-Wallis tests, respectively.

Mann-Whitney u-test

The Mann-Whitney u-test is an alternative to the independent-samples t-test. To explore the effects of a nominal variable (independent variable) on the outcome (ordinal variable), both producing nonparametric data, the appropriate statistical test is the Mann-Whitney u-test.

To run a Mann-Whitney u-test using SPSS15:

1 Go to **Analyze**
2 Non-parametric tests, then click **2 Independent samples**

The **2 Independent samples** test window pops up, then, in a very similar manner to the independent t-test, you enter the outcome variable in the **Test variable list**, and the independent nominal variable in the **Grouping variable** (see Figure 22.30)

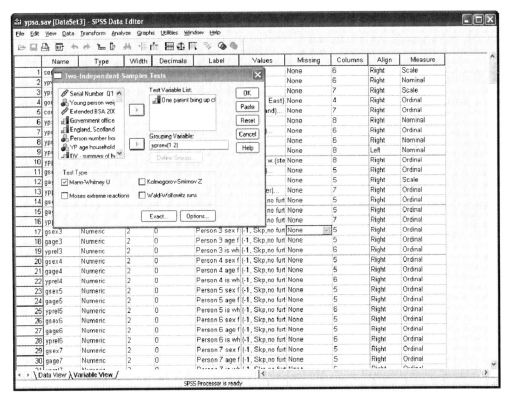

Figure 22.30 Mann Whitney u-test

1 Then click **Define groups** and enter the codes for the conditions of the nominal variable
2 Click **Continue**
3 Click **Mann-Whitney u**
4 Click **OK**

An example of a Mann-Whitney u-test

Suppose we want to examine boys' and girls' views on the statement 'one parent can bring up a child as well as two' from the YPSA data. Because the outcome variable is measured at an ordinal level, the data are nonparametric and violate the assumption of normality. In this case, we employ a nonparametric test.

In Figure 22.32, the 'mean rank' is an important indicator of the nature of the differences between the groups with regard to the ordinal variable. Depending on how the ordinal variable is ordered (in this example, the small numbers indicate agreement), the lower the mean rank the higher the agreement is. The group with the highest score will have the highest rank.

	YP sex household grid [BSA2003] YP22	N	Mean Rank	Sum of Ranks
One parent bring up child as well as two YP143	Male	303	363.25	110064.50
	Female	360	305.70	110051.50
	Total	663		

Figure 22.31 SPSS output 21

From the Figure 22.32, three important pieces of information are offered: The Mann-Whitney u, the 'Z score' and the 'Asymp. Sig.' or the significance level. In this example, there is a statistically significant difference between boys and girls in their views about the adequacy of one parent to bring up a child as well as two.

We need to calculate the effect size (r), which can be easily done by dividing the Z score with the square root of the total sample size ($r = Z/\sqrt{N}$). In this example, the effect size is: $r = -4.249/\sqrt{663} = 0.16$, and this is a weak effect size.

	One parent bring up child as well as two YP143
Mann-Whitney U	45071.500
Wilcoxon W	110051.500
Z	-4.249
Asymp. Sig. (2-tailed)	.000

Figure 22.32 SPSS output 22

Kruskal Wallis test

The Kruskal Wallis test is a nonparametric test, alternative to one-way ANOVA, used for ordinal outcome variables.

To run the est with SPSS15:

1 Go to **Analyze**
2 Click **Nonparameric tests**
3 Choose **K independent samples**

The **Tests for several independent samples** dialogue box appears (see Figure 22.33). Enter the outcome variable in the **Test variable list** and the independent (nominal) variable in the **Grouping variable**.

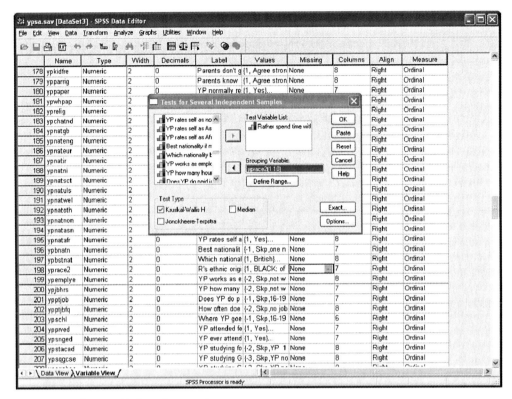

Figure 22.33 Tests for several independent samples

1 Click **Define range,** and enter the range (codes) for categories of the grouping variable, then click
   Continue
2 Select **Kruskal Wallis H**
3 Click **OK**

An example of Kruskal Wallis test

Suppose that we want to explore ethnic group differences in young people's preferences with regard to social interactions with friends and family members. Using a subset of the YPSA data, we run a Kruskal Wallis test given that the outcome variable is ordinal (social preferences are measured on an ordinal scale). The independent variable is ethnicity with

	R's ethnic origin (self-ascribed) YP307	N	Mean Rank
Rather spend time with friend then family YP269	BLACK: of African origin	6	332.58
	BLACK: of Caribbean origin	5	335.00
	BLACK: of other origin (WRITE IN)	2	277.25
	ASIAN: of Indian origin	9	292.28
	ASIAN: of Pakistani origin	20	384.75
	ASIAN: of other origin (WRITE IN)	6	395.00
	WHITE: of any European origin	583	319.42
	WHITE: of other origin (WRITE IN)	10	261.80
	Total	641	

Figure 22.34 SPSS output 23

	Rather spend time with friend then family YP269
Chi-Square	5.328
df	7
Asymp. Sig.	.620

Figure 22.35 SPSS output 24

eight levels (see vol-ume companion website for a description of variables).

Figure 22.34 and 22.35 show ranks and test statistics. In the ranks table, the information on mean rank is valuable. In the test statistic table (Figure 22.35), three pieces of information are important: the chi-square value (the Kruskal Wallis H statistic is called chi square), the statistic's degrees of freedom (df) and the Asymp.Sig. (significance level). In our example, the Asymp.Sig. is not statistically significant and thus there are no differences found between ethnic groups with regard to social interaction preferences.

A major limitation of the Kruskal Wallis H test is that it does not offer the facility for post-hoc testing (test the statistical significance for pair-wise comparisons). In this example, the Kruskal Wallis test indicates that there are no statistically significant differences across all ethnic groups with regard to young people's social preferences and thus there is no need to run any post-hoc tests. If the Kruskal Wallis had come out significant, we would have needed to find out where the significance lies, and delineate the pair-wise comparisons that are significant.

One way of finding out which pair-wise comparisons are significant is to run three separate Kruskal Wallis H tests. (A similar issue was raised with the independent-samples t-test, which also does not have a facility for post-hoc comparisons. A solution to this problem was to run a one-way ANOVA.) As with the t-test, the problem of running multiple Kruskal Wallis tests is that we increase the probability of committing a Type I error. To explain this differently, if we are to run three tests, and if we accept 5 per cent level (p<.05) as the critical value of significance for each test, then for all three tests the critical level would work out as $.05 \times .05 \times .05 = 0.143$. This means that there is a 14.3 per cent probability that between-group differences are due to chance, which is way beyond the cut-off point, 5 per cent.

We can get around this problem is by using the Bonferroni correction, which translates into dividing the critical level of significance (P<.05) by the number of pair-wise comparisons that we plan to do, and use this as the new critical level for each test. It is important to exercise judgement as to how many comparisons are important in order to avoid doing too many. The more tests we run, the smaller the critical level for significance becomes. Also, the statistical power of the test is reduced, making it a more conservative test and thus risking a Type II error.

As these examples illustrate, the choice of statistical technique is underpinned by a number of theoretical as well as technical considerations. Considerations such as sampling, sample size, nature and type of variables and statistical assumptions, to mention but a few, should be dealt with from the start of a research project, because they influence the research design and the decisions regarding data analyses. Making decisions about sample size, the number and type of variables, the strength of the effects of the independent variables on outcomes, the strength of tests to detect significant differences between groups and what a statistical significance actually means is a balancing act, which should be guided by the research aims and design.

Summary

In this chapter, an independent t-test and ANOVAs for comparing groups were examined, and examples were offered to illustrate their use. A comparison of two or more groups translates into a comparison of two or more mean values to determine whether, on average, the groups scored differently with regard to an outcome. These statistical techniques rely on a set of assumptions such as normality and equality of variance. Violation of these assumptions (normality) requires us to employ alternative statistical tests – i.e., nonparametric tests – to compare groups on variables that produce nonparametric data. The statistical techniques presented here originate in experimental research, and thus they are not typically employed with nonexperimental research. In the next chapter, Steve Strand presents statistical techniques, such as correlation and regression, which are more flexible than ANOVAs, and are suitable for the statistical analysis of all types of data that educational researchers are likely to encounter.

References

Bornholt, L. J., Goodnow, J. J. and Cooney, G. H. (1994) 'Influences of gender stereotypes on adolescents' perceptions of their own achievement', *American Educational Research Journal*, 31(30): 675–92.

Field, A. (2005) *Discovering Statistics Using SPSS*, 2nd edn. London: Sage.

Keppel, G. (1999) *Design and Analysis: A Researcher's Handbook*, 3rd edn. Prentice-Hall, Englewood Cliffs, NJ: Prentice Hall.

Pedhazur, J. and Pedhazur-Schmelkin, E. (1991) *Measurement, Design, and Analysis: An Integrated Approach*. Mahwah, NJ: Lawrence Erlbaum.

23 Correlation and Regression

Steve Strand

Introduction

This chapter is divided into three parts. Th first part introduces the idea of association between variables, and particularly the correlation coefficient as a means of summarizing the strength of the relationship. The second part explores regression as a means of assessing the predictive relationship between a continuous variable and an educational outcome, and the final part extends this analysis to multiple regression, where we are concerned to understand the relationship between multiple predictor variables and an educational outcome.

By the end of this chapter, you should be able to:

- graph and explore associations in data (scatterplots etc.)
- understand the conceptual basis of statistical summaries of association (such as variance, covariance, and the Pearson r)
- appreciate the strength of multiple regression as a technique for untangling cause and effect relationships
- calculate and interpret correctly correlations, simple regressions and multiple regressions by using SPSS15
- understand how multiple regression can be used to answer substantive questions about educational attainment, using the Longitudinal Study of Young People in England (LSYPE)
- have the confidence to use these techniques in your own research

Association and Correlation

What are correlation and regression good for? Here are a number of research questions to consider:

- Are some schools more effective than others?

- Is a pupil underachieving in their school work?
- What factors influence the likelihood of attaining a university degree?
- Does changing school (pupil mobility) impact on pupils' educational progress?

To answer all of these questions we need a measure of the association between variables. For several of these questions we want to go further, evaluating the extent to which we can predict an outcome while also controlling (statistically) for other related variables. This chapter will show you how you can go about answering such research questions.

Measuring association

We looked in Chapter 21 at how to measure an association between nominal variables using Crosstabulation. The general principle is that the proportion of observations in each category of the variable differs from what would be expected by chance if there were no association in the population as a whole.

For example, say we take 100 pupils (50 boys and 50 girls) and ask them whether they intend to leave full-time education after the age of 16. Table 23.1 shows the results for this hypothetical study. We can see that 15 out of 50 boys (30 per cent) indicated they intended to leave education, compared to only 5 of the 50 girls (10 per cent). We can compare the cell counts to what would be expected if there was no association between gender and intention to leave education at 16 (this would use the overall level for the whole sample, i.e. 10 boys and 10 girls would be expected to leave education). The significance of the association can be tested using the *chi-square test* (see Chapter 21).

Table 23.1 Example of a crosstabulation of nominal variables

Group	Leave education at age 16	Stay in education after age 16	Marginal total
Boys	15	35	50
Girls	5	45	50
Marginal total	20	80	100

		Q6 I am good with numbers				
		1 Strongly agree	2 Agree	3 Neither agree nor disagree	4 Disagree	5 Strongly disagree
Q2 I enjoy statistics	1 Strongly agree	1				
	2 Agree	1	4	1	1	
	3 Neither agree nor disagree	2	2		1	
	4 Disagree			2	1	1
	5 Strongly disagree				1	2

Figure 23.1 SPSS output 1: example of an crosstabulation of ordinal variables

We can extend this to ordinal variables. For example, consider the association between two attitude questions, 'I am good with numbers' and 'I enjoy statistics', each rated on a five-point scale. This is reproduced in Figure 23.1. We can see that responses to the two items are strongly associated. The respondents who strongly agree/agree with 'I enjoy statistics' are more likely to also strongly agree/agree with 'I am good with numbers'. Those that strongly disagree/disagree that they enjoy statistics are more likely to also strongly disagree/disagree that they are good with numbers. This association could be tested with chi-square, although more appropriately with *Spearman's rho* to evaluate the association between the ranks (see web companion for more examples of Spearman's rho correlation between two ordinal variables).

But what about when our outcome is a continuous or scale variable? For example, scores on standardized attainment tests typically range from 60 through to 141. Clearly, the table would be very wide if we were to plot all possible values of a continuous variable such as a standardized attainment test score. The answer is to graph the relationship.

Scatterplots

The scatterplots in Figure 23.2 show how different patterns of data produce different degrees of association between two measures or variables. Several points are evident from the scatterplots.

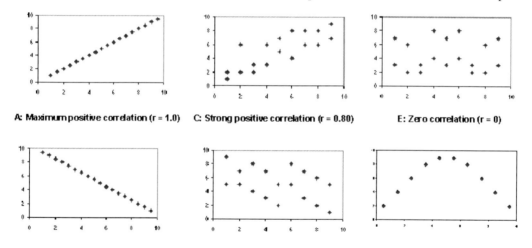

A: Maximum positive correlation (r = 1.0)   C: Strong positive correlation (r = 0.80)   E: Zero correlation (r = 0)

B: Maximum negative correlation (r = −1.0) D: Moderate negative correlation (r = -0.43)   F: Strong relation but correlation (r = 0)

Note: Adapted from StatTrek at http://stattrek.com/AP-Statistics-1/Correlation.aspx?Tutorial=AP

Figure 23.2 Examples of different relationships illustrated through scatterplots

These are:

- When the slope of the line in the plot is positive, the correlation is positive (graph C); and when the slope is negative the correlation is negative (graph D).
- The strongest correlations (r = 1.0 and r = −1.0) occur when all data points fall *exactly* in a straight line (graphs A and B).
- The correlation becomes weaker as the data points become more scattered. If the data points fall in a random pattern, the correlation is equal to 0 (graph E).

We should remember that the Pearson product-moment correlation coefficient (r) measures linear relationships only. Therefore, a correlation of 0 does not mean zero relationship between two variables; rather, it means zero *linear* relationship. For example, let's look at the last scatterplot graph, F. Here there is zero linear relationship but a strong curvilinear relationship. This is a rather extreme example, but is sometimes noted in research on arousal and performance. For example, small to moderate amounts of alcohol may improve performance on a task, but beyond a certain threshold increased alcohol actually reduces performance.

How to create a scatterplot in SPSS

I will demonstrate the process using data drawn from an example dataset. The data were collected during the LSYPE. A sample of 15,570 young people and their parents were interviewed in their homes when the pupil was aged 14. A wide range of demographic data were collected, as well as details of pupils' attitudes and opinions about school, teachers and lessons. The dataset is described in detail in the web companion of this volume.

Here I ask a specific question: 'What is the relationship between end of Key Stage 2 (KS2) test score at age 11 and end of Key Stage 3 (KS3) test score at age 14?' Follow the steps below to create the scatterplot using SPSS15.

1 From the menu select **Graphs** > **Legacy dialogues** > **Scatter/dot**. Your screen should look like that in Figure 23.3
2 Click on **ks2score** from the variable list and copy (▶) to × **axis**
3 Click on **ks3score** from the variable list and copy (▶) to Y **axis**
4 Click **OK**

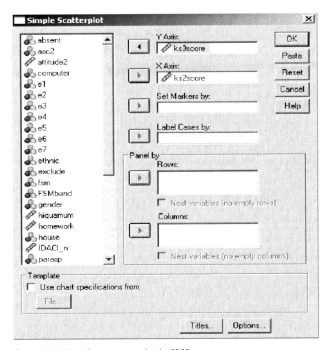

Figure 23.3 Creating a scatterplot in SPSS

The results are shown in Figure 23.4. This shows a positive association since the higher the KS2 score the higher the KS3 score.

Correlation coefficients

Graphical plotting of your data is essential to understanding what your data are telling you. Never rush to the statistics, get to know your data first (see Chapter 21 for details on describing your data via descriptive statistics). You should always examine a scatterplot of your data. However, it is useful to have a numeric measure of how strong the relationship is. The Pearson r correlation coefficient is a way of describing the strength of this association in a simple numerical form.

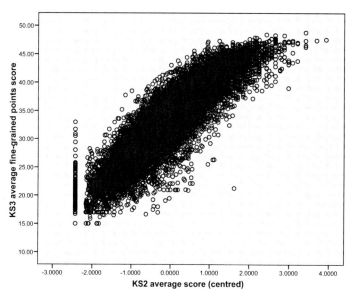

Figure 23.4 Scatterplot of KS2 score against KS3 score

How is Pearson's r calculated?

I am not going to blind you with formulae, but it is helpful to have some grasp of how the statistics work. The basic principle is to measure how strongly the two variables relate to each other – that is, the extent to which they *covary*. We can calculate the *covariance* by multiplying for each observation how far it is above (or below) the mean for × and by how far it is above (or below) the mean for Y. If an observation is above the mean on × and also above the mean on Y, the product will be positive (top right quadrant). Also if the observation is both below the mean on × and below the mean on Y the product will be positive (bottom left quadrant). However if the observation is below the mean on × but above the mean on Y (top left quadrant), or above the mean on × but below the mean on Y (bottom right quadrant), the product will be negative. These scores for all observations are summed to get a total and this is divided by the product of the standard deviations of both variables to scale it. This gives us the Pearson correlation coefficient.

The correlation coefficient tells us four key things about the association between the variables:

1 *Direction*. A positive correlation means that if one variable gets bigger, the other variable tends to get bigger. A negative correlation means that if one variable gets bigger, the other variable tends to get smaller (e.g. greater test anxiety may be related to poorer examination performance).

2 *Strength*. The weakest linear relationship is indicated by a correlation coefficient equal to 0. The strongest linear relationship is indicated by a correlation coefficient of –1 or 1. The strength of the relationship is indicated by the magnitude of the value regardless of sign, so a correlation of –0.6 is equally strong as a correlation of +0.6, it is just that the direction of the relationship differs.

3 *Statistical significance*. We also want to know if the relationship is statistically significant. Is the relationship likely to exist in the sample if it does not exist in the population? This is included in the SPSS output.

4 *How well the correlation describes the data.* This is best expressed by considering how much of the variance in the outcome can be explained by the predictor. This is described as the proportion of variance explained (R^2), sometimes also called the coefficient of determination. Conveniently the R^2 can also be found just by squaring the Pearson correlation coefficient. The usefulness of R^2 is that it provides us with a good gauge of the substantive size of the relationship. Thus, I can say that a correlation of 0.6 explains 36 per cent of the variance in my outcome variable. If you want to understand exactly how this is calculated, the process is explained in the web companion of this volume.

Calculating Pearson's r in SPSS

1 From the menu select **Analyze > Correlate > Bivariate**. A window should open as shown in Figure 23.5

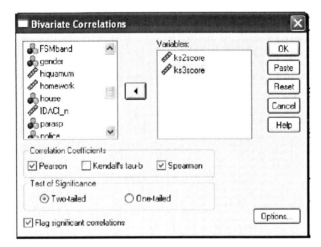

Figure 23.5 Calculating Pearson's r in SPSS

2 Click on **KS2score** and **KS3score** and copy (▶) to **Variables** list
3 Put a tick in the **Pearson** box, and click **OK**

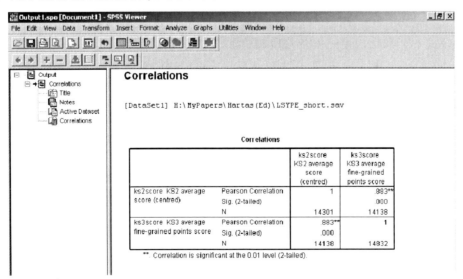

Figure 23.6 Pearson's r

Figure 23.6 tells us that:

- there is a positive association between KS2 score and KS3 score
- the correlation coefficient is 0.88, which is very high
- the coefficient is highly statistically significant (p < .01). It is therefore very likely that this correlation exists not just in our sample but in the population as a whole
- KS2 score can account for 77 per cent of the variance in KS3 score. This is substantial, but reminds us that 23 per cent of the variance is not accounted for.

Correlation for ordinal variables

What if you have a continuous outcome variable but your predictor variable is not continuous – say it is an ordinal variable? An example from our dataset would be the socioeconomic classification (SEC) of the pupil's home. SEC was classified on the occupation of the head of the household into one of eight groups running from 1 (higher managerial and professional occupations) through to 8 (long-term unemployed).

First, as always, you should graph your data to get a visual impression of the relationship. We are interested in whether there is an association between SEC and KS3 attainment (the null hypothesis is H0 = there is no relationship between SEC and KS3 attainment). Here a scatterplot is not very revealing, partly because of the limited range of possible values for SEC but also due to the large number of cases in the file (over 15,000). As an alternative we can plot a bar chart of the mean KS3 score for each social group.

1 Select Analyze > Legacy dialogues > bar
2 Click **Define**. The window shown in Figure 23.7 should open

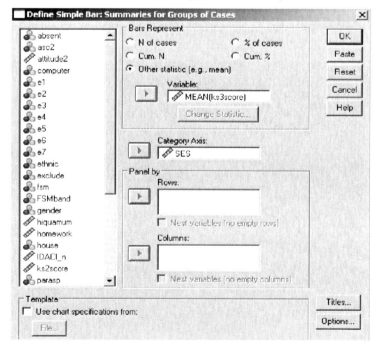

Figure 23.7 Creating a bar chart in SPSS

3 Click on **SES** from the variable list and copy (▶) to **Category axis**

4 Click on **ks3score** from the variable list and copy (▶) variable

5 Click on the **Options** at the bottom right of Figure 23.8

6 A new window will open. Place a tick in the **Display error bars** check box, and then click **Continue** followed by **OK**

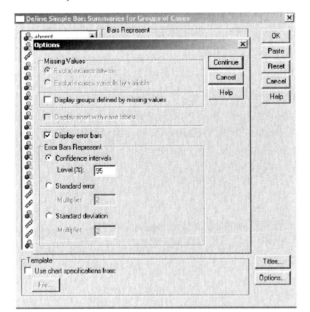

Figure 23.8 The options window for bar charts

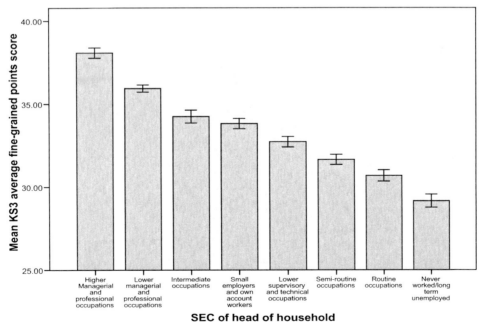

Figure 23.9 SPSS output 4: mean KS3 score by socioeconomic classification of the home

The results are shown in Figure 23.9. I have rescaled the Y axis to start at 25 to show the differences in mean score more clearly. It is clear that there is a strong negative association between the SEC of the family and the pupils' KS3 score. The error bars are important because they say something about the significance of the differences in mean scores between SEC groups. The error bars represent the range in which we are 95 per cent confident the 'true' mean score will lie, after allowing for score variability and sample size (see Chapter 4 for a discussion on sample size). That is, if we were to repeat the LSYPE study 100 times, drawing a different sample of pupils on each occasion, 95 times out of 100 we would expect the mean scores to fall within the range defined by the error bars. If these error bars do not overlap for two groups then there is a significant difference in the mean score for those groups.

As SEC is an ordinal variable, we use the Spearman rho rank order correlation. To do this we follow the same instructions as we did to calculate the Pearson's correlation, but this time place a tick in the radio button for **Spearman**. The results are shown in Figure 23.10. This output is

			ks3score KS3 average fine-grained points score	SES SEC of head of household
Spearman's rho	Ks3score KS3 average fine-grained points score	Correlation coefficient	1.000	-.390(**)
		Sig. (2-tailed)	.	.000
		N	14832	12100
	SES SEC of head of household	Correlation coefficient	-.390(**)	1.000
		Sig. (2-tailed)	.000	.
		N	12100	12829

Figure 23.10 SPSS output 5: Spearman's rho correlation

interpreted in the same way as the Pearson's r. From Figure 23.9, we answer the following questions:

- What is the direction of the relationship between SEC and KS3 score?
- What is the strength of the relationship (the correlation coefficient)? Is this a strong or weak relationship?
- What is the p value for the test of statistical significance of the relationship? Is this statistically significant?
- What proportion of variance in KS3 score can be explained by SEC?

Correlation and causation

It is important not to confuse correlation with causation. We can only say that our two variables are related, not that one has necessarily caused the other. Consider the following example.

When looking at national test results, pupils who joined their school part-way through a key stage tend to have lower end of key stage attainment that those who attended the school for the whole of the key stage. For example, in a recent study in a local authority (Strand and Demie 2007) 42 per cent of the pupils who were in the same school for the whole of the secondary phase achieved 5 or more A*–C grades at GCSE, while only 18 per cent of those pupils who joined their secondary schools during Year 11 achieved similar grades.

Can we conclude from this example that there is a causal relationship between pupil mobility and lower attainment? The answer is not necessarily. There may be reverse causation at work. For example, it may be that pupils with low attainment and behaviour problems are excluded from school, so the low attainment is actually a cause of the mobility. Or, it might be that the relationship between mobility and attainment arises because both are related to a third variable(s), such as socioeconomic disadvantage. Pupils from more disadvantaged circumstances may be more likely to be both mobile (e.g. refugees or asylum seekers) and have low attainment (see Chapter 15 for a discussion on the nature of causality).

In the final part of this chapter, I will look at a multiple linear regression, which allows us to explore the simultaneous effect of several predictor variables on an outcome and lets us tease out some of the above questions.

Box 23.1 Quick revision exercise

A national consumer magazine reported the following correlations.
- The correlation between car weight and car reliability is –0.30.
- The correlation between car weight and annual maintenance cost is 0.20.

Which of the following statements are true?

I   Heavier cars tend to be less reliable.
II   Heavier cars tend to cost more to maintain.
III. Car weight is related more strongly to reliability than it is to maintenance cost.

(A) I only
(B) II only
(C) III only
(D) I and II only
(E) I, II and III

Adapted from StatTrek at http://stattrek.com/AP-Statistics-1/Correlation.aspx?Tutorial=AP

Simple Linear Regression

Regression and correlation are actually fundamentally the same statistical procedure. The difference is essentially in *purpose*. In correlation we are generally looking at the strength of the relationship between × and Y, whereas in regression we are specifically concerned with how well we can *predict* Y from X.

Examples of the use of regression in education research include defining and identifying underachievement or specific learning difficulties, for example by determining whether a pupil's reading attainment is at the level that would be predicted from an IQ test. Another example is the use of entrance tests: in the USA, the Scholastic Aptitude Test (SAT) is used to predict whether a candidate is likely to achieve success at college. Screening tests, used to identify young children who are 'at risk' of later educational failure for the purpose of informing early intervention and additional support also use regression analyses.

Calculating the regression line

In regression, it is conventional to define × as the predictor or independent variable and Y as the outcome or dependent variable. We are concerned to determine how well × can predict Y. Let's look at an example.

1 Figure 23.11 (a) plots five observations (XY pairs). We can summarize the linear relationship between × and Y by drawing the best-fitting straight line through the points. This is called the *regression line.*

2 Figure 23.11 (b) shows the regression line. It is the line that minimizes the square of the differences between the actual Y value and the predicted Y value, hence the term 'ordinary least squares' (OLS) regression. You don't have to worry about how you calculate the line, as the SPSS software will do this for you.

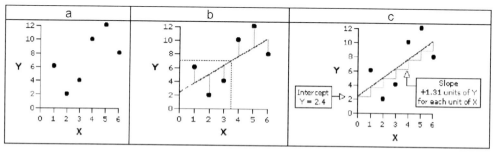

Figure 23.11 The process of calculating a regression line

3 The line has the formula Y = a + bx, where:
   a = the intercept (the point where it crosses the Y axis)
   b = the slope (the unit increase in Y for each unit increase in X).
   Figure 23.11 (c) shows for this example that the intercept (where the line crosses the Y axis) is 2.4. The slope is 1.31, for every unit increase in × the value of Y increase by 1.31.

4 The regression line represents the predicted value of Y. We can generate a predicted value of Y for any given value of X, even if we don't have a specific data point which covers this value. From the regression equation Y = a + bx we can calculate that for an × score of 3.5 the predicted value of Y is 7, since 2.4 + (1.31*3.5) = 7. This is the same as reading off the Y value on the regression line that corresponds to an × of 3.5, as shown by the dotted lines in Figure 23.11 (b).

5 However, the model (that is the regression line) is not perfect. The vertical distance from the data points to the regression line (see Figure 23.11 (b)) is called the *residual,* and represents the errors of prediction. We can take the average of these errors to get the standard error of measurement (SEM), an indication of the average amount that the regression equation over- or under-predicts. The higher the correlation the lower the SEM is, and the more accurate the predictions are likely to be.

Using SPSS to complete simple linear regression

First, I shall run a simple regression of KS2 score (independent variable) as a predictor of KS3 score (dependent variable).

1 From the menu select **Analyze > Regression > Linear**. The window shown in Figure 2.12 should appear
2 Click on **KS3score** from the variable list and copy (▶) to **Dependent**

3 Click on **KS2score** from the variable list and copy (▶) to **Independent(s)**

4 Click **OK**

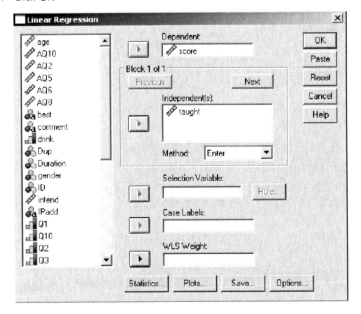

Figure 23.12 Completing a linear regression in SPSS

The results will appear in the output window. First, let's look at the **Model summary** as shown in Figure 23.13.

Model summary

Model	R	R square	Adjusted R square	Std. error of the estimate
1	.883(a)	.780	.780	3.07563

a Predictors: (constant), ks2score KS2 average score (centred)

Figure 23.13 SPSS output 26

This output presents some key results. The 'R' value tells us that the correlation between the predictor(s) and the outcome is .883, an extremely high correlation. 'R square' indicates the proportion of variance in Y accounted for by the statistical model. KS2 score can explain 78 per ent of the variance in KS3 score. Because we have a single predictor, we obtained the same values as those we got from the Pearson's r correlation coefficient earlier. Regression will really come into its own when we have multiple predictors.

Figure 23.13 also reports the SEM, which is 3.1. This is the average value of all the residuals (the differences between the predicted and actual values of KS3 score). We can use the SEM to calculate a band around any predicted value of Y within which we believe the 'true' value of Y lies. Add the SEM to the predicted value to get the top of the band, and subtract the SEM from the predicted value to get the bottom of the band: +/-1 SEM is the range within which we are 67 per cent confident that the 'true' score is likely to fall, i.e. for two out of three cases.

The ANOVA table (see Figure 23.14) tells us whether our model explains a statistically significant proportion of the variance in KS3 score. Not surprisingly, given the strength of the correlation, our model is extremely statistically significant (p<.000).

ANOVA(b)

Model		Sum of Squares	df	Mean Square	F	Sig.
1	Regression	475099.516	1	475099.516	50224.726	.000(a)
	Residual	133719.131	14136	9.459		
	Total	608818.647	14137			

a Predictors: (Constant), ks2score KS2 average score (centred)
b Dependent variable: ks3score KS3 average fine-grained points score

Figure 23.14 SPSS output 7

The coefficient table (see Figure 23.15) gives us the values for the regression line as we described in 23.11 (c). The intercept is indicated by the constant, and its value is 33.6. The slope is indicated by (B) and is 5.83, which indicates that for every unit increase in KS2 score, KS3 score increases by 5.83 points. The KS2 score used here has been standardized to have a mean of 0 and standard deviation (SD) of 1. Thus at age 11 the average pupil had a KS2 score of 0, while an above average pupil had a KS2 score of 1. The difference in the KS3 score of these two pupils is 5.83 points. So returning to our example the predicted value for a KS2 score of 1 is 33.6 + (1*5.8) = 39.4. The 67 per cent confidence band around this prediction is 39.4 +/- 3.1 which gives the range 36.3–42.5. There is the option to save the predicted values and the residuals back to the SPSS data file if we want.

Coefficients(a)

Model		Unstandardized coefficients		Standardized coefficients		
		B	Std. Error	Beta	t	Sig.
1	(Constant)	33.602	.026		1298.982	.000
	ks2score KS2 average score (centred)	5.828	.026	.883	224.109	.000

a Dependent Variable: ks3score KS3 average fine-grained points score

Figure 23.15 SPSS output 8

What do 5.83 points mean? Is it a 'big' or 'small' in educational terms? National Curriculum levels are assumed to represent two years of achievement. There are six points within a level, so each point represents one term of achievement. A difference of 5.83 points therefore places pupils almost six terms (or two years) ahead, and is extremely substantial!

This analysis has several practical uses. For example, by comparing the actual KS3 score achieved by a pupil against the KS3 score that was predicted from their KS2 score (i.e. by looking at the residual) we get an indication of whether a pupil has achieved more (or less) than would be expected given their prior score, i.e., made more (or less) than expected progress. This can be used diagnostically with individual pupils. We can also look at the average residual for different groups of pupils and ask the following questions: 'Do boys and girls make the same amount of progress?' 'Have pupils who missed a lot of lessons made less than expected progress?'

Multiple Regression

Regression models are implicitly causal models where the predictor variables are assumed to have a cause-effect connection with the outcome variable. In a simple linear regression, we are concerned with how well a single variable can predict an educational outcome. In a multiple linear regression, we can look at the simultaneous influence of a wide range of predictor variables on an educational outcome. This is an extremely powerful technique for untangling the complex and interrelated relationships between variables, as is typical in education.

Consider the example of understanding educational attainment. It is well known that there is a strong and positive correlation between social class and educational attainment. There is also evidence that pupils from some (though not all) minority ethnic groups do not achieve as well in the English education system as the majority white British group. However, there is also a strong relationship between ethnic group and social class, with many minority ethnic groups experiencing higher socioeconomic disadvantage than white British pupils. It is therefore not possible to say whether the lower attainment of some minority ethnic groups reflects something particular about belonging to that ethnic group or reflects the fact that some groups are particularly socially and economically disadvantaged.

A multiple regression offers a way to address these issues. If we put all the variables we have into one analysis, we can assess the impact of one factor when the effect of another is simultaneously taken into account. This is important because in real life, variables are often interrelated in complex ways. Thus, in our example, a multiple regression analysis allows us to assess the association between ethnicity and attainment *after the variance in attainment associated with SEC is taken into account*. A wide range of further variables (e.g. family composition, maternal educational qualifications, attitude to school, parental aspirations etc.) can also be included to build up highly detailed and complex models.

Here I use a multiple regression to answer the following questions:

- What factors are associated with educational attainment as measured by national tests at age 14?
- Do minority ethnic pupils differ from their ehite British peers in their educational attainment?
- Can we explain differences in the attainment of different minority ethnic groups using a wide range of pupil, family, school and neighbourhood factors?

This example is drawn from a 'real-life' dataset, i.e., LSYPE, described in this book's website resource. This will give you an idea of why a multiple regression is a useful technique, and how it can be used to answer real-life research and policy-relevant questions.

Completing a multiple regression analysis in SPSS

I start from the simple linear model I described in the second section of this chapter, modelling the relationship between KS2 score and KS3 score, which we shall describe as model 1. I now wish to add two further variables to the regression model (see Box 23.2).

Box 23.2 Selecting independent variables

It is important to have a strong rationale for the independent variables you include in your models. This might come from previous research or from observation or informed hypotheses. There is a method of entering your variables called *stepwise* entry. This allows you to include *all* your independent variables as potential predictors and to select all those with a significant independent association with the outcome. I have not described the stepwise method here because it can lead to a sloppy 'scattergun' approach.[1] This may result in some associations that are statistically significant within your particular dataset but have no strong basis for generalization to other datasets. It is important to have a theoretically guided approach to selecting relevant independent variables.

Model 2: Adding ordinal predictor variables

The two variables we are interested in are the socioeconomic classification (SEC) of the home and mother's highest educational qualifications (Hiquamum). These are ordinal variables, but regression is a very robust procedure and in practice ordinal variables can be used, although there should be at least five levels within the variable and a spread of cases across the levels, and of course a linear relationship with the outcome. These conditions are satisfied for both SEC as we saw earlier, and are also satisfied for Hiquamum.

1 From the menu select **Analyze > Regression > Linear**. The window shown in Figure 23.16 should appear
2 Click on **KS3score** from the variable list and copy (▶) to **Dependent**
3 Click on **KS2score** from the variable list and copy (▶) to **Independent(s)**
4 Also add **SES** and **Hiquamum** to the **Independent(s)** list, and click **OK**

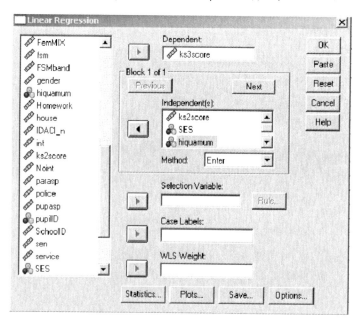

Figure 23.16 Multiple regression

In the **Model summary, R** now indicates the multiple correlation, that is the overall correlation of our combined predictor variables with KS3 score. We see that the correlation has increased slightly to .889, explaining around an additional 1 per cent of the KS3 variance (increasing from 78 to 79 per cent).

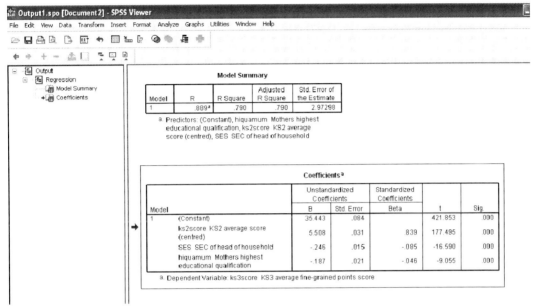

Figure 23.17 SPSS output 9

The 'Coefficients' table now includes two additional predictor variables. Remember that the regression weight (B) is the change in KS3 score for a one-unit change in the predictor variable. The SES variable ranged from 1 (higher managerial and professional) to 8 (long-term unemployed), so the difference between the lowest and highest social class is 8* – .246 = 2.0 points. Mother's highest educational qualification ranges from 1 (degree or equivalent) to 6 (no educational qualifications), so the difference between a pupil with a mother educated to degree level and a pupil with a mother with no educational qualifications is 6* – .187 = 1.1 points.

What are the relative strengths of KS2 score, SES and mother's educational qualifications in predicting KS3 score? We cannot tell this directly from the B weights since these are not expressed on a common scale. A one-unit increase in KS2 score does not mean the same thing as a one-unit increase in SES. In contrast, the *beta weights* are a standardised form of B,[2] which range between 0 and 1 and give a common metric which can be compared across all predictor variables. The effects of SES and mother's qualifications are small relative to KS2 score, as can be seen by the small betas relative to the beta for KS2 score.

However both SES, and mother's educational qualifications are highly statistically significant. This is shown by the p value in the last column where both are significant at p<.000. They are also substantial in real-world terms, as even a 1.0 point difference is equivalent to a whole term of progress in National Curriculum levels.

Model 3: adding nominal predictor variables

The outcome variable in a multiple regression *must* be a continuous variable. However, we are not limited to only continuous variables as predictors in the regression. In this example, I add three nominal variables to the model as follows.

Entitlement to a *free school meal (FSM)* is a dichotomous variable, taking the value 0 if the pupil is not entitled to an FSM and 1 if the pupil is entitled to an FSM. Thus a one unit change in the variable represents the contrast between not entitled to FSM (value 0) and entitled to FSM (value 1). The B coefficient for FSM coefficient will therefore indicate how the attainment of pupils entitled to FSM contrasts with the reference group of those not entitled to FSM.

Gender is also a dichotomous variable taking the value 0 for boys and 1 for girls. Because girls are scored 1, the coefficient for gender will indicate how much better (or worse) girls score relative to boys (the reference category).

Ethnic group presents a different challenge. The variable ethnic is coded 0 to 8. However we cannot treat this as an ordinal variable as we did with SEC. We cannot say that black Caribbean (value 5) is 'more' of something that white British (value 0). What we want to do is compare each ethnic group against a reference category. The most sensible reference category is white British, since this is the largest group constituting 82 per cent of all pupils, so we want to contrast each minority ethnic group against white British. We do this by creating seven separate variables, one for each minority ethnic group, called dummy variables, by applying a procedure called *recode* (see Chapter 20 for how to recode a variable). Thus, we create a new variable (e1) which takes the value 1 if a pupil is of mixed heritage and 0 otherwise, a second variable (e2), which takes the value of 1 if the pupil is Indian and 0 otherwise, and so on.

The appropriate syntax is given in Figure 23.18.

```
RECODE Ethnic (1=1)(else=0) into e1.
RECODE Ethnic (2=1)(else=0) into e2.
RECODE Ethnic (3=1)(else=0) into e3.
RECODE Ethnic (4=1)(else=0) into e4.
RECODE Ethnic (5=1)(else=0) into e5.
RECODE Ethnic (6=1)(else=0) into e6.
RECODE Ethnic (7=1)(else=0) into e7.
VAR LABELS
  e1  "Mixed heritage"
  e2  "Indian"
  e3  "Pakistani"
  e4  "Bangladeshi"
  e5  "Black Caribbean"
  e6  "Black African"
  e7  "Any other ethnic group".
```

Figure 23.18 Coding

I have created these seven variables and stored them in the file. The B coefficients for these seven new variables are interpreted in exactly the same way as described for FSM and gender, that is, they tell us how much better (or worse) a particular ethnic group has performed relative to the reference group (white British).

The next step is to add these new variables (FSM, gender, e1, e2, e3, e4, e5, e6 and e7) to the regression and run the analysis. The results are presented in Figure 23.19.

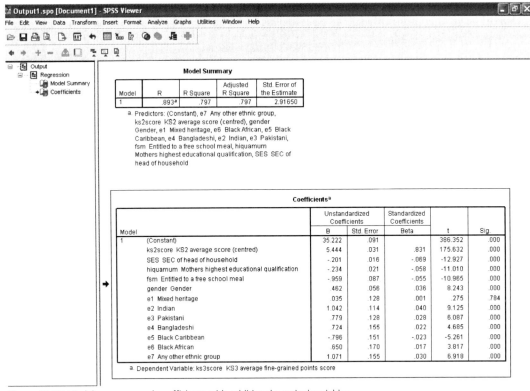

Figure 23.19 Model summary and coefficients with additional nominal variables

The model summary shows that there has been a very modest increase in the R from .883 to .893, and in the R^2 from 79.0 to 79.7 per cent. The SEM has decreased slightly (from 2.97 to 2.92) reflecting the improved fit of the model.

The B for entitlement to an FSM is quite large (–0.96) indicating that pupils entitled to an FSM have a KS3 score one point lower than those not entitled to an FSM, even after controlling for all the other variables in the model. This is highly statistically significant (p<.000). Put another way, pupils entitled to an FSM make around one term less progress than those not entitled.

The B for gender is 0.46 points, and indicates that girls on average achieve a KS3 score half a point higher than boys, again after controlling for all the other variables in the model. This is highly statistically significant (p<.000). Put another way, girls make around half a term more progress than boys.

Finally, in relation to ethnic group, the contrasts with white British are statistically significant for all ethnic groups except the mixed heritage group. Indian pupils do better than white British pupils, making 1.0 point (one term) more progress. However the next largest difference, and the only negative effect, is for black Caribbean pupils. The B for black Caribbean is –0.80, indicating black Caribbean pupils achieve a KS3 score 0.80 points below their white British peers even after controlling for (or net of) prior attainment, SEC, maternal education, entitlement to FSM and gender; 0.80 may be a small number in absolute terms, but it indicates three-quarters of a term less progress than expected.

Checking the assumptions of multiple regression analysis

Linear regression is appropriate when the following conditions are satisfied.

First, the outcome variable must be *continuous*. Simply, don't do a linear regression unless this is the case! (For dichotomous outcome variables there is an analysis that can be used called *binary logistic regression*, or *multinomial regression* if there are more than two levels in your nominal outcome. For ordinal outcome variables, there is an analysis called *ordinal regression*. However, these analyses go beyond the scope of this chapter.)

Second, there must be a *linear relationship* between the predictor(s) and the outcome. Inspect your scatterplot to check this assumption. You can also check whether the relationship is linear or not by looking at the residuals, as described later.

Third, the correlation may be low, and the model weak, if there is *restriction in range* in either $\times$ or Y. The example below shows the correlation between mean cognitive abilities test (CAT) score at age 11 and GCSE score at age 16 separately for (a) a random sample of 1,000 pupils, and (b) a selection from the sample of just those pupils with above average CAT scores (scores>100).

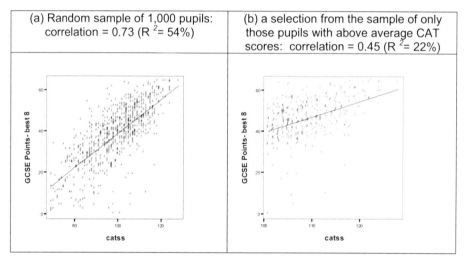

Figure 23.20 SPSS output 1: example of the effect of restriction of range on the correlation coefficient

The restriction in range in the latter case severely limits the size of the correlation, which drops from 0.73 for the random sample to just 0.45 for the restricted sample, explaining only 22 per cent rather than 54 per cent of the variance in GCSE score. This was a frequent source of misunderstanding in grammar schools whose teaching staff wondered why the reasoning tests they used for selection did not appear to be a strong predictor of GCSE outcomes. The moral of the story is your sample must be representative of the full range of potential values on any variables relevant to your research question.

Fourth, the presence of *outliers* can substantially reduce the correlation. Again inspect your scatterplot to identify any potential outliers. You can also set a flag in the SPSS regression procedure to identify significant outliers and print the cases by requesting **Casewise diagnostics** from the **Linear regression: statistics** window (see Figure 23.21).

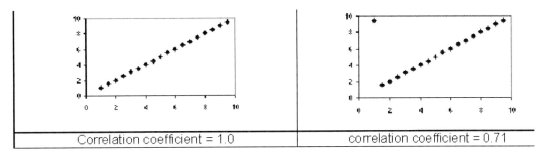

| Correlation coefficient = 1.0 | correlation coefficient = 0.71 |

Figure 23.21 SPSS output 12: example of the impact of an outlier on the correlation coefficient

Often outliers are data entry errors and can be corrected or deleted. There will always be some outliers, but if there are more than 10 per cent of cases that are more than 2 SD from the predicted value this indicates that a model does not fit the data very well and may suggest a nonlinear relationship. It is worth noting that outliers make interesting case studies. For example, it may be valuable to make case studies of both very successful and very unsuccessful schools and contrast the cases.

Fifth, **influential cases** are a special subset of outliers that greatly affect the slope of the regression line (see Figure 23.22). The charts compare regression statistics for a dataset with and without an influential point. The chart on the right has a single influential point, located at the high end of the x axis (where $x = 24$). As a result of that single influential point, the slope of the regression line decreases dramatically, from –2.5 to –1.6. Note that this influential point, unlike the outliers discussed above, did not reduce the R^2. In fact, the R^2 was bigger when the influential point was present. The solution again is to check your scatterplot to identify potential cases. Such cases can often be data entry errors and can be eliminated.

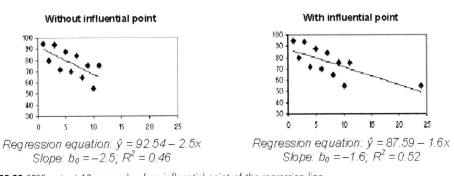

Figure 23.22 SPSS output 13: example of an influential point of the regression line

Sixth, we need to *analyse the residuals* to ensure there are no systematic biases in our model. Two important checks are (a) that the residuals (errors) in our model are normally distributed, and (b) that the residuals (errors) do not vary systematically with the predicted values. These checks are given in more detail below.

Running Residual plots with SPSS

1 Click the **Plots** button at the foot of the **Linear regression** window, as shown in Figure 23.23

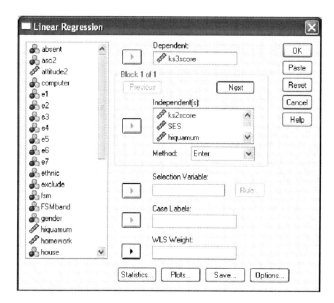

Figure 23.23 Requesting residual plots

2 This will open the **Plots** window shown in Figure 23.24. First, place a tick in the histogram checkbox. Secondly, drag **ZPRED** to the × axis and **ZRESID** to the Y axis

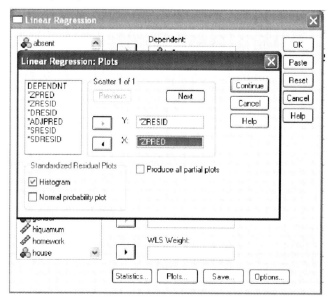

Figure 23.24 Linear regression plots window

3 Click **Continue** to return to the regression window and then **OK** to run the analysis

Figure 23.25 shows the outputs from the residual plots. The histogram shows the residuals are normally distributed. Many are around zero (as we would expect with a good model) with a few being towards the extremes.

The scatterplot shows no consistent relationship between the residuals (ZRESID) and the predicted values (ZPRED). There is a tendency for relatively few large positive residuals at very

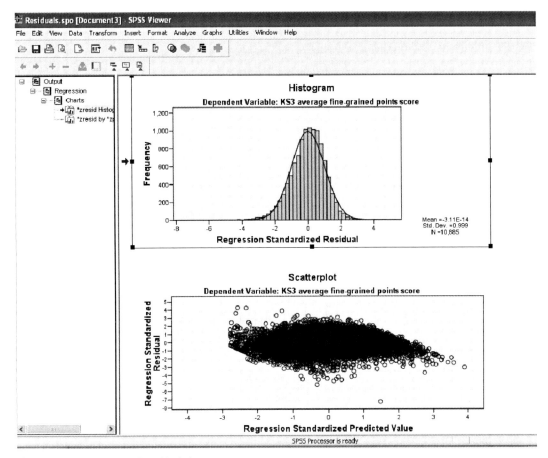

Figure 23.25 SPSS output 14: residual plots

higher predicted values (more than 2 SD), indicating a possible ceiling effect. However, generally both positive and negative residuals are reasonably distributed across the predicted values.

Multicollinearity

Seventh, and finally, *multicollinearity*. Problems can also arise when the predictor variables are very strongly correlated with each other. If they are, it is difficult to isolate the individual contribution of each predictor variable and this can cause problems in estimating the relationship between the predictors and the outcome. A rough rule of thumb would be the presence of correlation of 0.8 or 0.9 or above between predictors. Luckily, SPSS produces various multicollinearity diagnostics to ease this process.

To obtain collinearity diagnostics, first click the **Statistic** button at the bottom of the **Linear regression** window, as shown in Figure 23.26. This opens the **Linear regression: statistics** window where you should place a tick in the collinearity diagnostics box as shown in Figure 23.27. Click **Continue** and then **OK**.

SPSS will add two statistics (tolerance and VIF) to your coefficients output. If the VIF for any

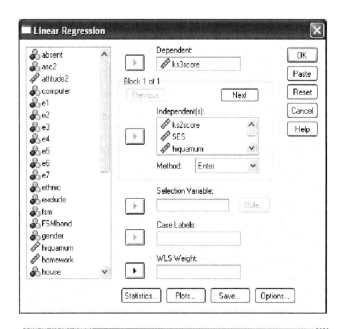

Figure 23.26 Requesting statistics

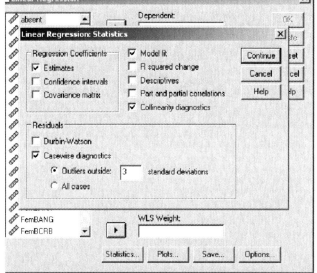

Figure 23.27 Requesting collinearity diagnostics

variable is greater than 10, then this would be a good reason to worry. The tolerance is just the reciprocal of VIF (1/VIF). If the tolerance for any variable is below 0.1 then this is similarly a cause for concern. We can see that on this basis there is no need to worry about excessive multicollinearity in the model (see Figure 23.28).

Summary

In this chapter, I introduced the idea of association between variables, and particularly the correlation coefficient as a means of summarizing the strength of a relationship. Regression

Coefficients[a]

Model		Unstandardized Coefficients		Standardized Coefficients	t	Sig.	Collinearity Statistics	
		B	Std. Error	Beta			Tolerance	VIF
1	(Constant)	35.222	.091		386.352	.000		
	ks2score KS2 average score (centred)	5.444	.031	.831	175.632	.000	.834	1.200
	SES SEC of head of household	-.201	.016	-.069	-12.927	.000	.650	1.539
	hiquamum Mothers highest educational qualification	-.234	.021	-.058	-11.010	.000	.670	1.493
	fsm Entitled to a free school meal	-.959	.087	-.055	-10.965	.000	.748	1.338
	gender Gender	.462	.056	.036	8.243	.000	.997	1.004
	e1 Mixed heritage	.035	.128	.001	.275	.784	.972	1.028
	e2 Indian	1.042	.114	.040	9.125	.000	.954	1.048
	e3 Pakistani	.779	.128	.028	6.087	.000	.905	1.105
	e4 Bangladeshi	.724	.155	.022	4.685	.000	.883	1.132
	e5 Black Caribbean	-.796	.151	-.023	-5.261	.000	.968	1.033
	e6 Black African	.650	.170	.017	3.817	.000	.969	1.032
	e7 Any other ethnic group	1.071	.155	.030	6.918	.000	.973	1.028

a. Dependent Variable: ks3score KS3 average fine-grained points score

Figure 23.28 SPSS output 15: collinearity diagnostics

analyses – i.e. simple linear and multiple linear regression, as a means of assessing the predictive relationship between one or more predictor variables and an educational outcome, were presented and illustrated with examples using the LSYPE data. The multiple regression analysis described here is a simplified version of the LSYPE research, which incorporates many more variables and a more complex procedure including adjustments for clustering and design and nonresponse weights. Nevertheless, the results presented in this chapter demonstrate the ways in which regression can be used and the type of educational research questions that can be addressed. The full report on LSYPE data analyses can be accessed from the Department for Children, Schools and Families (DCSF) research report website – see Strand 2007).

Notes

[1] There are specific circumstances when stepwise methods may be of use, for example if you want to demonstrate how much more of the variance in your outcome variable is explained by each additional independent variable.

[2] To get the betas all variables are divided by their SD so the beta tells us the number of SDs the outcome would change for a one SD change in any predictor (see Field 2005: 193–4).

References

Field, A. (2005) *Discovering Statistics Using SPSS*, 2nd edn. London: Sage.

Strand, S. (2007) *Minority Ethnic Pupils in the Longitudinal Study of Young People in England. DCSF Research Report RR-002*. London: Department for Children, Schools and Families.

Strand, S. and Demie, F. (2006) 'Pupil mobility, attainment and progress in primary school', *British Educational Research Journal*, 32(4): 551–68.

Strand, S. and Demie, F. (2007) 'Pupil mobility, attainment and progress at secondary school', *Educational Studies*, 33(3): 313–31.

Appendix: the Coefficient of Determination

This is best expressed by considering how much of the variance in the outcome can be explained by the predictor. This is described as the proportion of variance explained (R^2), sometimes also called the *coefficient of determination*. To find these we calculate two measures of variance and compare them.

a *Variance from the mean (SSM):* this is an index of the total variability in our dependent variable. We calculate the difference between each Y value and the mean of Y. Sometimes these differences will be positive and sometimes the differences will be negative. If we just took the average of these values they would cancel each other out, so we square the differences to make all the values positive. Thus a difference score of –2 and a difference score of +2 have the same absolute difference from the mean (remember 2*2 = 4 and –2*–2 = 4). The figure on the left below shows the mean value for our attitude to statistics score. You can think of this as the best predictor of Y if there was zero correlation between the variables.

b *Variance from the regression (SSR):* however, some of the variance in Y is explained by X. We calculate the deviation scores in the same way as described above, but this time take the differences between the Y observation and the line that best describes the linear relationship between X and Y. If there is any correlation between X and Y, the sum of these differences will be smaller than the total variance.

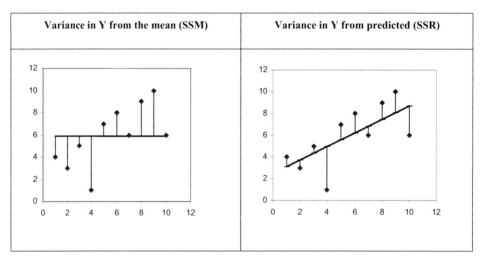

Variance in Y from the mean (SSM)	Variance in Y from predicted (SSR)

The ratio of the two reveals how much we have improved the explanation of Y relative to just using the mean.

$$R^2 = 1 - \frac{(SSR)}{(SSM)}$$

The usefulness of R^2 is that it provides us with a good gauge of the substantive size of the relationship. Thus I can say that a correlation of 0.6 explains 36 per cent of the variance in my outcome variable.

Table 23.2 Relationship between correlation coefficient and percentage of variance in the outcome explained

Correlation coefficient	Variance explained (%)
0	0
.10	1
.20	4
.30	9
.40	16
.50	25
.60	36
.70	49
.80	64
.90	81
1	100

24 Exploratory Factor Analysis

Dimitra Hartas

Introduction

Often, educational research involves investigations of people's attitudes, feelings or beliefs that cannot directly be measured. We refer to these as latent variables and try to measure them by identifying aspects or dimensions which, thematically, underpin them. For example, let's say we want to measure children's sociability. We look at the relevant research literature to identify the conceptual dimensions or constructs used to describe sociability. Some studies have defined sociability along the lines of peer interactions, pro-social behaviour (empathy) or emotional control. So, one way of measuring sociability is by obtaining measures on these separate yet interrelated constructs and their underlying dimensions. Based on previous research, the construct of pro-social behaviour consists of dimensions such as capacity to show empathy to others' distress, helping behaviours or social problem-solving skills. An important question here is whether, and if so how, we know that these dimensions actually underpin a single construct. To ensure that a set of variables/dimensions reflects the same construct, we need to identify the common patterns in data. To this end, we employ a statistical technique called *factor analysis*.

There are two types of factor analysis, exploratory and confirmatory. An exploratory factor analysis (EFA) seeks to uncover the underlying patterns of a relatively large set of variables. With an EFA, we do not bring a priori assumptions or views about possible interrelations among the variables under consideration into the research. Rather, we attempt to identify patterns in a dataset and cluster variables that appear to be related thematically to offer a simpler data structure, without assuming that each factor is associated with a specific subset of variables. A confirmatory factor analysis (CFA), on the other hand, aims at testing predetermined clusters of variables, whose interrelations rely on a strong theoretical grounding. This chapter examines EFA, including principal component analysis, and offers examples to illustrate the theoretical considerations and statistical processes involved.

By the end of this chapter, you should be able to:

- consider the appropriateness of employing an EFA
- understand the theoretical and statistical processes involved in EFA
- understand the methodological issues that surround factor extraction and rotation
- interpret the results obtained from an EFA

Why do an Exploratory Factor Analysis (EFA)?

There are three, interrelated purposes for doing an EFA. First, EFA is used to unearth the theoretical underpinnings of a construct (e.g. what are the dimensions/aspects of sociability in children?). Secondly, for the purpose of designing a questionnaire, it is important to demonstrate that its items actually reflect the construct(s) we want to investigate to ensure construct validity (see Chapter 4 for details on validity). An example of this is the Strengths and Difficulties Questionnaire (SDQ) (Goodman 1997) in which its constituent items (e.g. 'Restless, overactive, cannot sit still', 'Tends to play alone', 'Considerate of others' feelings') are loaded onto a number of factors (e.g. hyperactivity, peer relations, pro-social behaviour) (see exercise in the web companion). The third purpose of doing an EFA is to reduce a large dataset by selecting a subset of variables based on which original variables have the highest correlations with the principal component factors, and identifying clusters of variables that load onto factors (see example in this chapter).

A factor analysis is commonly used in quantitative research in education, especially in the context of survey research where questionnaire construction and survey data analysis are central. Typically, a factor analysis is used to reduce a large number of interrelated variables into a smaller set of factors without compromising their explanatory capacity. It is a useful technique to produce factors that do not correlate (or correlate very slightly) with each other in order to avoid problems of multicollinearity (strong correlations between factors, see Chapter 23) and sphericity (perfect correlations between factors). As a statistical technique, a factor analysis is part of the general linear model family of procedures (see Chapter 22), and is underpinned by the same assumptions, namely, linear relationships, interval or near-interval data, lack of high correlations and normality (data that is normally distributed). The last assumption is important if we want to generalize the results beyond the sample.

The phases of an EFA

EFA is a 'complex statistical procedure with few absolute guidelines and many options' (Costello and Osborne 2005: 1). To untangle the processes involved, EFA is presented in three phases.

1 *Preliminary phase:* for diagnostic purposes, we check the initial correlations among the variables via a matrix of correlation coefficients (R-matrix), which is generated for all possible correlations between variables.

2 *Extraction phase:* factors are extracted by identifying the common components in a set of variables. The most commonly used method for factor extraction is principal factor analysis.

3 *Rotation phase:* rotation of the extracted factors occurs to regularize the structure of the factors by maximizing the loadings of the variables onto some of the factors and reducing the loadings onto others.

Preliminary phase

The first step in factor analysis is to check the magnitude of interrelations among the selected variables. To this end, we run a series of correlations between the variables we want to reduce. If the variables indeed measure the same conceptual entity or construct, we would expect them to correlate with each other to a degree (with a coefficient, r, of around .3). However, if the variables are found to correlate with each other highly (r>.8) or not to correlate at all (r = 0), then it is useful at this stage to exclude them from the analysis. The problem with variables correlating highly with each other is that they tend to measure the same thing. If this is the case, we cannot determine their unique contribution to a factor. At the same time, we would expect a fair amount of correlation among variables that reflect similar constructs because, if there are no interrelations, there is no point in trying to identify common patterns and generate clusters among the variables.

For diagnostic purposes, the SPSS produces the R-matrix table (see Figure 24.8), which shows the Pearson product-moment correlation coefficient (r) between all pair of variables and the significance level (p) of these coefficients. With the matrix we can check correlation coefficients and make decisions about the variables we keep and those we exclude from subsequent factor analysis. Specifically, we exclude variables that are highly correlated (r>.8) as well as those that do not correlate with any other variables (r<.2).

Extraction phase

At the extraction phase, the loading of variables onto factors takes place for the factors to emerge. During a factor extraction, the shared variance of a variable (variance that is in common with another variable) is partitioned from its unique variance and error variance in order to reveal the underlying factor structure (Costello and Osborne 2005). Many methods of factor extraction, namely, principal component, generalized least squares, principal axis factoring etc. are available in the SPSS, with principal component analysis being the default option. There is a lack of consensus among researchers as to which extraction method should be used. This is due to a limited theoretical and statistical understanding of the relative advantages and limitations of these methods. Principal component analysis is a preferred method for extracting factors, and is used to establish the linear components that exist within data and the ways in which variables contribute to each component. The choice of extraction method has important implications because over- or under-extraction affect the validity of the results. To simplify matters, in this chapter we employ a principle component analysis (a thorough discussion on the similarities and differences between principal component analysis and factor analysis is presented in Field 2009).

In theory, via an EFA, we can extract as many factors as the original variables. Being a data-reduction technique though, not all the factors are retained. A key issue is to determine the importance of the generated factors (which factors do we keep and which ones are statistically significant?). To determine the substantive importance of a factor, we need to know the *eigenvalue* associated with each factor. An eigenvalue refers to the amount of variation in a variable that is explained by a given factor. A large eigenvalue indicates a meaningful factor. However, this raises the question of how we know whether an eingenvalue is sufficiently large to represent a substantive factor.

Kaiser (1960) argues that eigenvalues greater than 1 represent a good amount of variation, whereas Jolliffe (1986) states that eigenvalues greater than .7 are sufficiently large to retain factors. Cattell (1966) recommends a graph of each eigenvalue (Y axis) against the factor (X axis) it represents to create a *scree plot*. A scree plot is an uncomplicated way of deciding on the number of the generated factors. Cattell recommends the point of inflection in the curve (where the curve flattens out) to be the cut-off point. The number of data points (above the inflection point but not including it) indicates the number of factors to retain.

Looking at a scree plot in Figure 24.1, the relative importance of each factor becomes apparent: a fairly small number of factors have high eigenvalues, whereas many factors have small eigenvalues, shown by a sharp descent in the curve followed by a tailing off. The first factor extracted has the largest eigenvalue, the second factor the next largest eigenvalue and so on. With a large sample (more than 200 cases), the scree plot is thought to provide a reliable technique for selecting factors (Field 2009). By default, the SPSS accepts Kaiser's criterion (eigenvalues greater than 1) for factor retention.

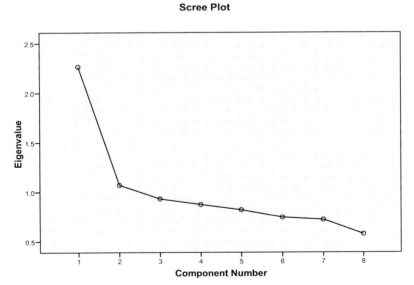

Figure 24.1 SPSS Output 1

Rotation phase

The purpose of rotation is to simplify the factor structure and unearth a pattern of loadings of variables onto the generated factors that is clear and meaningful to interpret. The pattern of loading changes after rotation because the majority of the variables are loaded onto a small number of factors. This is to create a good approximation to the correlations between the original variables, whose coefficients are shown in the R-matrix (see Figure 24.8). Rotation also changes the eigenvalues so the variance accounted for by each factor becomes more evenly distributed among the rotated factors. In so doing, we reduce data without losing substantive information. The communalities (common variance) do not change during rotation because they relate to the generated factors, which remain the same.

There are two methods of rotation, namely orthogonal and oblique. An orthogonal rotation produces factors that are uncorrelated, whereas an oblique rotation allows the factors to correlate (Costello and Osborne 2005). Commonly available methods of orthogonal rotation in the SPSS are varimax, quantimax and equamax. For an oblique rotation the methods are direct oblimin and promax (see Figure 24.5). The SPSS default values for oblimin is delta = 0 and for promax is kappa = 4. Changing the default values for delta or kappa changes the magnitude of correlations among the factors. We are advised to keep the default values to ensure that correlations are very small (Costello and Osborn 2005; Field 2009).

To generate factors that are independent, an orthogonal rotation is the preferred method especially if we want to enter the factors into subsequent regression models where intercorrelations among variables have to be low (see Chapter 23). However, in education and social sciences, variables are expected to correlate with each other given that human behaviour, attitudes or beliefs do not present themselves in mutually exclusive forms. With this in mind, with an orthogonal rotation, we may lose important information, if indeed the factors are correlated with each other. If the factors are truly uncorrelated then orthogonal rotation produces similar results as those by oblique rotation.

Sample size

The sample size does affect correlation coefficients and thus the more cases we have the better it is for a factor analysis. Tabachnick and Fidell (2007) recommend that we need at least 300 cases to run a factor analysis. A common rule for sample adequacy is to have around 10 cases per variable. The adequacy of a sample size is also determined by the nature of the data, in terms of how high the communalities are and how many variables load onto a small number of factors. In a typical dataset, the communality ranges between .4 and .7 (Field 2009); however, for low communalities, a large sample is required. Field recommends that for communalities above .6, relatively small samples consisting of around 100 cases are adequate. With regard to the number of variables, Guadagnoli and Velicer (1988) suggest that factors with four or more variables and with loadings greater than .6 are strong regardless of the sample size. However, for large sample sizes (200 cases or more), correlations between factors and variables greater than .35 are considered to be reliable. As presented in the following sections, the calculation of KMO Bartlett's test for sphericity (see Figure 24.3) checks for the adequacy of a sample.

The sample size also determines the significance of a factor. For a sample of 50 cases, a loading (correlation coefficient between variable and factor) of .722 is considered significant; for 100 cases the loading should be greater than .512, for 200 it should be greater than 0.364, for 300 it should be greater than .298, for 600 it should be greater than .21 and for 1,000 it should be greater than .162 (Field 2009). This means that in large samples even small loadings can be considered significant. However, as Field argues, the value of a loading is not a good indicator of the substantive importance of a variable to a factor. He suggests calculating the square value of a loading of a factor in order to estimate the amount of variance that is accounted for by a variable. In such case, it is recommended that an absolute value greater than .4 is acceptable because it explains 16 per cent of the variance in the variable (Stevens 2002, cited in Field 2009).

Example: Young people's attitudes and feelings towards school

To illustrate an EFA, we utilized a data subset from the Millennium Cohort Study (the third survey – MCS3 – 'Older Sibling Questionnaire' with 10,876 participants). MCS3 is a national longitudinal birth cohort study, which offers large-scale information about the 'New Century's Children' and their families in the four countries of the UK (England, Wales, Scotland and Northern Ireland). Some of the items of the Older Sibling Questionnaire refer to young people's views/attitudes towards school, learning and teachers. An EFA was employed to identify the underlying patterns in the following subset of variables:

Q1 *leave school at 16 or go on to sixth-form or college*
Q2 *how important are good marks in school work, exams or tests*
Q3 *like most of the teachers*
Q4 *think teachers are always getting at you*
Q5 *care what teachers think about you*
Q6 *OK to break a bad school rule*
Q7 *agree or disagree that teachers like ordering pupils around to show who is in charge*
Q8 *in last 12 months, ever skipped or bunked off school*

Running an EFA

1 Click **Analyze**, then
2 **Data Reduction**, then
3 **Factor**

A **Factor analysis** dialogue box pops up

4 Select the variables you want to enter in the factor analytic model and click the arrow to insert them into the **Variables** area (see Figure 24.2)

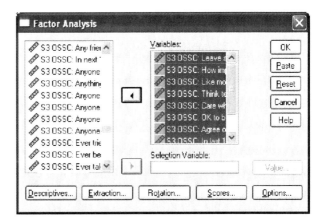

Figure 24.2 Factor Analysis

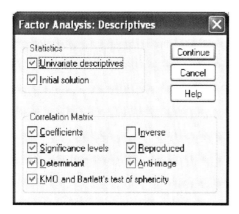

Figure 24.3 Descriptives

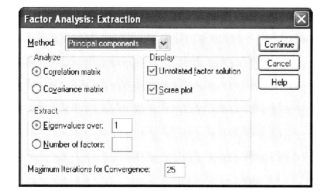

Figure 24.4 Extraction

5   Click **Descriptives** and the **Factor analysis descriptives** dialogue box pops up (see Figure 24.3)

6   Next, click **Statistics**, and then the **Univariate descriptives** option to provide information on mean and standard deviation (SD), and then click **Initial solution** (Figure 24.3). Within the **Correlation matrix** options, click **Coefficients** (to produce the R-matrix), then **Significance levels** (to check the significance value for each correlation), **Determinant** (to test for multicollinearity or singularity) and **KMO and Bartlett's test of sphericity** (to check for correlations between variables and adequacy of sample). The KMO test has to be greater than .5. If it is less the sample is not adequate and thus we need to collect more data or reduce the number of variables in the factor analytic model (see Figure 24.3).

7   Click **Continue**

8   Back to the **Factor analysis** dialogue box (see Figure 24.2) click **Extraction** to access the **Factor analysis: extraction** dialogue box (see Figure 24.4)

9   There are several factor extraction methods and, for this example, we chose **Principal component analysis**

10 In the **Analyze** section in Figure 24.4, there are two options, **Correlation matrix** and **Covariance matrix**; the former is a standardized version of the covariance matrix. Click **Correlation matrix** for a standardized version because you are likely to have variables measured at different scales

11 The **Display** section in Figure 24.4 offers two options: **Unrotated factor solution** and **Scree plot**. As discussed before, the scree plot is a useful way to decide how many factors will be retained. The **Unrotated factor solution** helps you to check how improved the factor structure is after rotation. If you find that the rotated solution is not much better than the unrotated one, you need to think about the appropriateness of the rotation method, as well as the nature of data

12 The **Extract** section in Figure 24.4 presents options with regard to deciding how many factors to retain. The SPSS default option sets eigenvalue greater than 1 (applying Kaiser's criterion), and thus every factor with this value is retained. You can change the eigenvalue to .7 (applying Jolliffe's criterion), which means that factors with a value greater than .7 are retained. However, for large samples such as the MCS3, you should set the eigenvalue over 1

13 **Maximum iterations for convergence** in Figure 24.4 refers to how many times SPSS searches for an optimal solution (it is set by default to 25 times). For a large dataset, you may want to increase the number of iterations to ensure an optimal solution

14 Click **Continue**

15 Going back to the **Factor analysis** dialog box (see Figure 24.2), click **Rotation** (Figure 24.5). Rotation improves the process of loading variables to the extracted factors to enable you see how each variable relates to a factor

16 From the **Factor analysis: rotation** dialogue box (see Figure 24.5) choose the rotation method. **Varimax, Quartimax and Equamax** are orthogonal rotation methods, with **Varimax** being the most commonly used. The **Direct oblimin** and **Promax** are oblique rotation methods. The choice of rotation method is based on whether or not you have a theoretical justification that the extracted factors are correlated. If you think they are, choose an oblique rotation (e.g. **Direct oblimin**); if they are not related, choose an orthogonal

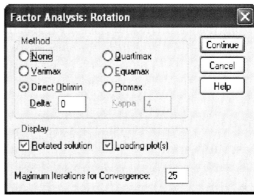

Figure 24.5 Rotation

rotation (e.g. **Varimax**). In our example, we chose an oblique rotation because variables such as, 'How important are good marks in school work, exams or tests'; 'Like most of the teachers'; 'Think teachers are always getting at you' relate to each other. Because in an oblique rotation the factors are allowed to correlate, the degree of correlation needs to be determined, and this is done via the **Delta** or **Kappa** value. The SPSS default delta value is 0, which means that the factors are not allowed to correlate. It is a good idea to leave it 0 in that by changing it we allow for correlations to take place

17 The **Display** section (see Figure 24.5) offers **Rotated solution** and **Loading plots**. The **Rotated solution** is important for factor analysis and **Loading plots** offers a graph of each variable plotted against the factors (three factors maximum)

18 Again, the **Maximum iterations for convergence** is set at 25 times (default value)

19 Click **Continue**

20 Back to the main menu (Figure 24.2) click Scores and the **Factor analysis: factor scores** dialogue box pops up (see Figure 24.6) to save the factor scores generated for every individual case in the data editor. SPSS will create a new column for each factor extracted and place it at the end in the data editor

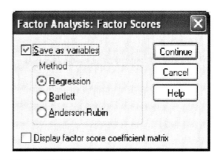

Figure 24.6 Factor Scores

21 There are three options offered for obtaining the scores, **Regression, Bartlett** and **Anderson-Rubin** (see Figure 24.6). To ensure that the factor scores are not correlated, choose **Anderson-Rubin**, but if correlations are acceptable, choose **Regression**. In our example, we chose **Regression** because the

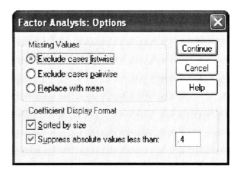

Figure 24.7 Options

factors are likely to correlate with each other (and this is the reason we chose an oblique rotation in the previous sections)

22 From the main menu (Figure 24.2), click **Options** and the **Factor analysis: options** dialogue box pops up (see Figure 24.7). From the **Missing values** section, click **Exclude cases listwise** to account for missing data. By excluding cases listwise we exclude any case with missing data on any variable

23 From the **Coefficient display format**, choose **Sorted by size** to sort variables by their factor loadings (all variables that load highly into a factor are clustered together). The other option is **Suppress absolute values less than** a value that we specify (default value is .1). In our example, we specified a value less than .4, and thus we would expect to see loadings of variables onto factors greater than .4 (see Figure 24.7)

Interpreting the results from an EFA

A correlation matrix or R-matrix offers diagnostic information. The first half of this output presents the correlation coefficients between variables (Q1 to Q8 as in the Example), and the remaining half the significance level (p). At the bottom of Figure 24.8, the **Determinant** value is

		Q1	Q2	Q3	Q4	Q5	Q6	Q7	Q8
Correlation	Q1	1.000	.208	-.175	.109	-.185	.086	.148	.142
	Q2	.208	1.000	-.207	.090	-.247	.140	.096	.148
	Q3	-.175	-.207	1.000	-.350	.351	-.165	-.263	-.186
	Q4	.109	.090	-.350	1.000	-.170	.167	.270	.092
	Q5	-.185	-.247	.351	-.170	1.000	-.201	-.165	-.188
	Q6	.086	.140	-.165	.167	-.201	1.000	.101	.123
	Q7	.148	.096	-.263	.270	-.165	.101	1.000	.133
	Q8	.142	.148	-.186	.092	-.188	.123	.133	1.000
Sig. (1-tailed)	Q1		.000	.000	.000	.000	.000	.000	.000
	Q2	.000		.000	.000	.000	.000	.000	.000
	Q3	.000	.000		.000	.000	.000	.000	.000
	Q4	.000	.000	.000		.000	.000	.000	.000
	Q5	.000	.000	.000	.000		.000	.000	.000
	Q6	.000	.000	.000	.000	.000		.000	.000
	Q7	.000	.000	.000	.000	.000	.000		.000
	Q8	.000	.000	.000	.000	.000	.000	.000	

a Determinant = .499

Figure 24.8: SPSS Output 1

stated. In our example, the value is .449, which is greater than .00001, indicating that multicollinearity is not a problem for these variables.

The KMO and Bartlett's test of sphericity offers information about multiple and individual variables. In this example, the Kaiser-Mayer-Olkin Measure of Sampling Adequacy is .754. A value greater than .5 is recommended, with values between .5 and .7 being medium, between .7 and .8 good and values greater than .9 being very good. In our example, the KMO value for all variables is .754, suggesting that the sample is adequate and that a factor analysis is appropriate for this data.

Kaiser-Meyer-Olkin Measure of Sampling Adequacy.		.754
Bartlett's Test of Sphericity	Approx. Chi-Square	1028.534
	Df	28
	Sig.	.000

Figure 24.9: SPSS Output 2

For individual variables, the KMO can be obtained from the anti-image correlation (see Figure 24.10). An anti-image correlation is a standardized version of the anti-image covariance. To examine the anti-image correlation, we look at the diagonal values of coefficients (highlighted in **bold**), which should be greater than .5. In this case, they are greater than .5 (values are around .7 as highlighted in **bold** in Figure 24.10). The variables with a diagonal coefficient less than .5 should be excluded from the factor analysis. In such a case, we need to re-run the analysis to produce an anti-image correlation because the KMO is affected by the removal of variables. The other (non-diagonal) coefficients in Figure 24.10 are partial correlations and their values should be small.

		Q1	Q2	Q3	Q4	Q5	Q6	Q7	Q8
Anti-image Correlation	Q1	**.788(a)**	-.147	.059	-.025	.085	-.014	-.082	-.076
	Q2	-.147	**.764(a)**	.094	.008	.150	-.072	-.007	-.072
	Q3	.059	.094	**.727(a)**	.262	-.244	.041	.137	.086
	Q4	-.025	.008	.262	**.708(a)**	.021	-.103	-.186	.002
	Q5	.085	.150	-.244	.021	**.753(a)**	.122	.046	.092
	Q6	-.014	-.072	.041	-.103	.122	**.799(a)**	-.020	-.064
	Q7	-.082	-.007	.137	-.186	.046	-.020	**.773(a)**	-.065
	Q8	-.076	-.072	.086	.002	.092	-.064	-.065	**.813(a)**

a Measures of Sampling Adequacy(MSA)
SPSS Output 24-4: Anti-image Matrices

Figure 24.10: SPSS Output 3

The **Total Variance Explained** (Figure 24.11) shows the variance explained *before extraction, after extraction and after rotation*. The part titled **Initial eigenvalues** shows the proportion of variance explained by each component (factor) before extraction. There are as many components as the variables entered for factor analysis. Before and after factor extraction, the components 1 and 2 explain a large amount of variance (cumulative 41.69 per cent of the total variance; see **Initial eigenvalues** columns in Figure 24.11). Before extraction, the other components (i.e., 3, 4, 5, 5, 7 and 8) explain a smaller variance. After extraction (see **Extraction Sums of Squared Loadings** columns in Figure 24.11), there are only two components left, and the others are discarded. This is because we specified that variables with eigenvalues greater than 1 should be retained (Kaiser's criterion). Because a rotation optimizes the structure of the factors, after rotation (see last column **Rotation Sums of Squared Loadings(a)** in Figure 24.11), the relative importance of the two factors is equalized (component 1 = 1.894 and component 2 = 1.801).

Component	Initial Eigenvalues			Extraction Sums of Squared Loadings			Rotation Sums of Squared Loadings(a)
	Total	% of Variance	Cumulative %	Total	% of Variance	Cumulative %	Total
1	2.266	28.322	28.322	2.266	28.322	28.322	1.894
2	1.070	13.371	41.693	1.070	13.371	41.693	1.801
3	.932	11.644	53.337				
4	.874	10.927	64.264				
5	.820	10.246	74.510				
6	.744	9.299	83.808				
7	.720	8.998	92.807				
8	.575	7.193	100.000				

Extraction Method: Principal Component Analysis

Figure 24.11: SPSS Output 4

The Communalities (see Figure 24.12) shows the proportion of common variance (communality) in a variable that is shared with other variables, before and after factor extraction. Before factor extraction, it is assumed that all variance is common and thus the value of 1 for all variables (first column of Figure 24.12). After factor extraction, we have a realistic view of the shared variance. In question 2 ('How important are good marks in school work, exams or tests) of our example, 50 per cent of variance is common, whereas for question 1 (Leave school at 16 or go to sixth-form or college) shares 33.1 per cent of variance (see 0.500 and .331, respectively, in second column of Figure 24.12).

	Initial	Extraction
Q1	1.000	.331
Q2	1.000	.500
Q3	1.000	.528
Q4	1.000	.621
Q5	1.000	.434
Q6	1.000	.188
Q7	1.000	.458
Q8	1.000	.275

Extraction Method: Principal Component Analysis

Figure 24.12: SPSS Output 5

	Component	
	1	2
Q1	-.696	
Q2	-.629	
Q3	.513	-.441
Q4	.454	
Q5	.439	
Q6	.431	
Q7	.548	-.566
Q8	.488	.512

Extraction Method: Principal Component Analysis.
a 2 components extracted

Figure 24.13: SPSS Output 6

The component matrix (see Figure 24.13) shows the loading of each variable onto the components (factors). In this example, the majority of the variables load onto the first factor (see Component 1 column in Figure 24.13). This is expected given that the first factor accounts for a large amount of variance. The component matrix output shows loading greater than .4 because we set it for any loadings below .4 to be suppressed (see Figure 24.7). Tabachinick and Fidell (2007) cite .32 as a good value for minimum loading of a variable/item onto a factor, which suggests 10 per cent of shared variance.

After factor rotation, SPSS produces two tables – i.e., 'Pattern Matrix' and 'Structure Matrix' (see Figures 24.14 and 24.15, respectively). The 'Structure Matrix' presents the correlation coefficients and the 'Pattern Matrix' shows the regression coefficients between factors and variables. With an orthogonal rotation, it is assumed that the factors are unrelated to each other and the factor loading is the correlation coefficient which has the same value as the regression coefficient. With an oblique rotation, it is assumed that the factors are not independent

	Component	
	1	2
Q1	.739	
Q2	.587	
Q3	-.573	
Q4	.523	
Q5		
Q6		-.813
Q7		-.684
Q8		.589

Extraction Method: Principal Component Analysis.
Rotation Method: Oblimin with Kaiser Normalization.
a Rotation converged in 7 iterations

Figure 24.14: SPSS Output 7

and thus the correlation coefficient is not the same as the regression coefficient. In our example, the factors were not assumed to be independent and thus the correlation and regression coefficient values are not the same. We use the 'Pattern Matrix' to obtain the regression coefficients, whereas the 'Structure Matrix' is used for double checking the loadings after rotation.

Under component 1 (see Figure 24.14), the four variables have regression coefficients that range between .5 and .7. Under component 2, there are three variables whose regression coefficients range between .5 and 8. Conceptually, the first factor reflects pupil attitudes towards school, and the second factor reflects beliefs/feelings about teachers. A factor with fewer than three variables is consid-

	Component	
	1	2
Q1	.691	
Q2	-.632	
Q3	.574	
Q4	.525	
Q5		
Q6		-.781
Q7		-.676
Q8	-.461	.675

Extraction Method: Principal Component Analysis.
Rotation Method: Oblimin with Kaiser Normalization

Figure 24.15: SPSS Output 8

ered to be weak, whereas five or more variables make a solid factor (Costello and Osborne 2005). In this example the second factor is weak because it consists of three variables.

Once we have identified the factors, it is important to check how well they explain the observed data. Factors are derived entities and, as such, we want to check the extent to which they approximate the original variables in our dataset. A factor model is a reduced version of the original data. With this in mind, it is important to examine whether there is a close fit between the factors and the original variables they represent. The 'Reproduced Correlations' (see Figure 24.16) displays the correlations between variables/items

		Q1	Q2	Q3	Q4	Q5	Q6	Q7	Q8
Reproduced Correlation	Q1	**.331(b)**	.403	-.241	.049	-.355	.213	.077	.301
	Q2	.403	**.500(b)**	-.232	-.022	-.408	.236	.025	.361
	Q3	-.241	-.232	**.528(b)**	-.500	.396	-.289	-.450	-.245
	Q4	.049	-.022	-.500	**.621(b)**	-.233	.207	.531	.078
	Q5	-.355	-.408	.396	-.233	**.434(b)**	-.281	-.236	-.333
	Q6	.213	.236	-.289	.207	-.281	**.188(b)**	.199	.204
	Q7	.077	.025	-.450	.531	-.236	.199	**.458(b)**	.099
	Q8	.301	.361	-.245	.078	-.333	.204	.099	**.275(b)**
Residual(a)	Q1		-.195	.067	.060	.170	-.127	.071	-.159
	Q2	-.195		.025	.112	.160	-.096	.071	-.213
	Q3	.067	.025		.150	-.045	.124	.187	.059
	Q4	.060	.112	.150		.063	-.041	-.261	.013
	Q5	.170	.160	-.045	.063		.080	.071	.145
	Q6	-.127	-.096	.124	-.041	.080		-.098	-.081
	Q7	.071	.071	.187	-.261	.071	-.098		.034
	Q8	-.159	-.213	.059	.013	.145	-.081	.034	

Extraction Method: Principal Component Analysis.
a Residuals are computed between observed and reproduced correlations. There are 23 (82.0%) nonredundant residuals with absolute values greater than 0.05.
b Reproduced communalities

Figure 24.16: SPSS Output 9

based on the factor model, not the original data. We would expect to see differences in the communalities before and after factor extraction. The coefficients in 'Reproduced Correlations' (after extraction) differ from those displayed in the R-matrix (before extraction) because the latter are based on the original data. As in R-matrix, we look at the diagonal coefficients (highlighted in **bold**).

Comparing the R-matrix and 'Reproduced Correlations' we see that the coefficients between variables are not the same. Small differences between the observed and reproduced coefficients mean that the factor model is a good fit to the data, whereas large differences indicate a poor fit. SPSS calculates these differences, which are shown in the 'Residual' table (bottom half of Figure 24.16). The cut-off value is 0.05 to ensure that the gap between the factors and original data is not large. In this example, however, a large number (82 per cent) of residuals are greater than 0.05, and this raises concerns with regard to the fitness of this factor analytic model. Field (2009) recommends that 50 per cent (or fewer) of the correlations should present values less than 0.05 to ensure a good fit.

Factor Correlation

As mentioned earlier, the reason for employing a principal component analysis is to form factors that are not related to each other, so they can be used for subsequent analyses (e.g. regression). We can now check the correlation between the two generated factors through the 'Component Correlation Matrix' (see Figure 24.17). There is a weak correlation between components 1 and 2, and this is good because we want to ensure that the factors are correlated slightly but not highly to avoid problems with multicollinearity. Although the correlation is weak, it does confirm the decision that an oblique rather than an orthogonal rotation was appropriate with the data in our example. This makes sense when considering that the two factors refer to young people's attitudes towards school and beliefs about/feelings for teachers.

Componen t	1	2
1	1.000	-.302
2	-.302	1.000

Extraction Method: Principal Component Analysis.
Rotation Method: Oblimin with Kaiser Normalization.

Figure 24.17: SPSS Output 10

Factor Score

When reducing variables, the factor score gives us the individual score for a set of measures, and subsequent statistical analyses (e.g. t-test or multiple regression) are carried on the factor score rather than the original data. For each individual case, the factor score combines the scores of a subset of measures that underpin the factor (Field 2009). The scores for the new factors are placed in columns at the end of the SPSS data editor.

Summary

An EFA aims at reducing a large number of interrelated variables into a smaller set of factors without missing important explanatory information. There are three steps to a factor analysis, namely screening of variables/items, factor extraction and factor rotation. Initially, we screen our variables by exploring the interrelations among them and calculating their coefficients. We expect to find a degree of correlation in that the reason for selecting these variables in the first place is that they appear to display a common pattern. At the same time, we hope that their correlations are not strong because this would compromise their unique contribution to the generated factors. The next step is to extract the factors. In our example, through principal component analysis, two factors emerged, and we calculated the common variance (communality) and the loading (coefficients) of each variable to these factors. We also discussed the appropriateness of orthogonal and oblique rotation methods, and chose an oblique rotation for our analysis to create a simpler factor structure. Finally, we estimated the extent to which the generated factors approximate the original variables to ensure a good fit. This is important because factors, as derived entities, are useful only when they offer a meaningful representation of the original data.

References

Cattell, R. B. (1966) 'The scree test for the number of factors', *Multivariate Behavioral Research*, 1: 245–76.

Costello, A. B. and Osborne, J. (2005) 'Best practices in exploratory factor analysis: four recommendations for getting the most from your analysis', *Practical Assessment Research & Evaluation*, 10(7), available online at http://pareonline.net/getvn.asp.

Field, A. (2009) *Discovering Statistics Using SPSS*, 3rd edn. London: Sage.

Goodman, R. (1997) The Strengths and Difficulties Questionnaire: a research note, *Journal of Child Psychology and Psychiatry*, 38: 581–6.

Guadagnoli, E. and Velicer, W. (1988) 'Relation of sample size to the stability of component patterns', *Psychological Bulletin*, 103: 265–75.

Jolliffe, I. T. (1986) *Principal Component Analysis*. New York: Springer-Verlag.

Kaiser, H. F. (1960) 'The application of electronic computers to factor analysis', *Educational and Psychological Measurement*, 20: 141–51.

Tabachnick, B. and Fidell, L. S. (2007) *Using Multivariate Statistics*, 5th edn. Boston, MA: Allyn & Bacon.

Part V
Presentation of Educational Research

Writing up and Presenting Research 25
Alan Pritchard

Chapter Outline

Introduction

The end product of virtually all research will be a written report of one kind or another. In the case of research which has been undertaken in the course of working towards the award of a higher degree this will be in the form of a detailed dissertation. If the dissertation is to be acceptable it must have many positive features, the most important of which could be considered to be clarity. The content, analysis, discussion and conclusions must be sound, and the presentation should be good, but all of this will be for nothing if what you have written is not easy to read and straightforward to understand. Clarity at every stage of the process of reporting is vital. Imprecise or difficult to follow writing will not be well received no matter what the importance of the findings of the research; similarly, muddled oral presentations will be poorly received and will not serve the researcher/presenter well.

In your academic work you will have read many research reports and articles, and it is quite possible that either consciously, or more likely unconsciously, you will have taken in many of the stylistic and other features of what you have read. It is likely that you may have come across examples of writing which lack clarity. In working towards becoming an academic writer, it is very helpful and important to be aware of the conventions and structure of the writing of others who are better established.

Some of the important considerations when writing for publication or for the award of a higher degree are: *style*, *format*, *audience*, *purpose*, the dangers of *plagiarism* and the importance of *referencing*. In some cases the nature of these considerations will be dictated by the context of your work – degree regulations, departmental guidelines or the protocols of the journal that you have targeted to publish your work. Notwithstanding any external constraints, there are personal considerations to be taken into account when undertaking the presentation of research. We will return to the considerations above later. Firstly, we will look at the nature and structure of a typical dissertation which would be the result of research and inquiry in the field of educational studies.

By the end of this chapter you should be able to:

- describe the structure of a standard dissertation
- understand the importance of considering style, format and audience when writing a dissertation
- understand the dangers of either intentional or unintentional plagiarism
- understand the crucial importance of referencing
- consider use of language for academic purposes, and recognize common errors

The Dissertation

The end product of your work will most likely be a dissertation, but equally it could be a different type of research report. To explore the nature of the dissertation we will consider it with reference to other types of written report.

Where research reports and dissertations tend to differ is in their length and complexity. As dissertations are produced as part of an academic exercise leading to an award, there is a need to explain, qualify and justify aspects of the study which is being reported in more detail than would be required for some reports – for example, the methodology section of the dissertation will need to be given greater prominence than it would in some other contexts.

Before looking at a standard dissertation structure, we will look at the features which dissertations and other research reports have in common.

Common features of research reports and dissertations

Formally presented research must have certain key features in order to ensure clarity, credibility and accessibility. Edwards and Talbot (1994: 141) suggest the following:

- *readability*: so that it can be clearly and quickly understood
- *clear organization:* so that the reader is easily led through the text
- *a logical reference system:* so that the reader can quickly follow up any references
- *information presented in a logical order:* so that the reader does not at any point have to guess, for example, how the data were analysed or the conclusion was reached
- *substantiation:* so that each claim can be seen to be based on evidence

It is not uncommon for reports to emerge from the completion of a dissertation. This is a very useful tool for disseminating the outcomes of research, for presentation to peers, to colleagues in the organization where the research took place, or as a part of the preparation process for possible publication or conference presentation.

In producing a dissertation, presentation is important, and we will return to this later, but it is not as important as:

- content
- clarity
- accuracy

- order of argument
- the validity of the conclusions drawn

It is important to remember that not all reports and dissertations take the same form, and it is difficult to cover all possibilities and requirements in any sort of general guidance material, especially in a short chapter of this nature. You should therefore use your discretion in following this guide and, if you have any doubts, seek advice from your supervisor. *Always* check through any guidelines you have been given.

The structure of a dissertation

The bare framework for a research dissertation is relatively simple to follow and looks like this:

- literature review
- methodology
- findings/results
- discussion

With this sparse outline we should also include an abstract, an introduction, a statement of the purpose of the research (usually posed as a research question), references, perhaps a bibliography and possibly one or more appendices. There is scope for other short additions by way of acknowledgements perhaps, or other brief explanatory notes. In the light of this we can develop a more detailed structure for a dissertation, as follows:

- introduction
- literature review
- research design
- results
- discussion
- conclusion
- references
- appendices

Introduction

The introduction to your work will be the first part that the reader engages with and, as such, it should quickly and directly set the context. It need not be a long section, but it does have a specific job to do. As the name suggests the introduction will introduce a number of points which will be developed later. Your introduction should include the following:

- background to the area being studied and any contextual points
- rationale for the study, including the reasons why you are undertaking the work
- significance of the work in the wider context of its setting
- theoretical or conceptual framework within which your work is situated
- definitions of concepts and terms
- hypothesis, if appropriate, which will be challenged by your work
- aims of the study
- research question, if appropriate

In conjunction with the literature review, the introduction will inform the development of the work that you are presenting, in particular, the aims, objectives, the hypothesis (if there is one) and the methodology that will be described in detail later.

Literature review

Your literature review will be the end product of an extensive search of the existing published work in the field and of your analysis of and thoughts about what you have found. In Chapter 6 you were given a detailed consideration of the place and importance of the literature review. The chapter emphasized the benefits of the literature review to your work from a conceptual/ theoretical and methodological perspective. Here we will focus more on the mechanical and stylistic aspects of formatting and presenting the review.

In the context of a dissertation submitted for an award the purpose of the literature review is to present a critical synthesis of as much of the available published work on the topic of your research as possible. The reason for doing this is to illustrate that you have a full understanding of the work carried out by others in the area, and to put your particular research into a wide context.

It is important that you include the work and opinions of the major researchers and writers in the field. To this end you must ensure that you have made a wide-ranging search, following up leads from as many sources as is practical, and that the content of what you report is accurate and fully referenced.

The literature review is a place where your own ideas and opinions might be included, but they must be justified by the facts, which should also be presented. Judgement about the value, or otherwise, of your review will be based on on the depth and breadth of what you have included, the accuracy of your reporting and on the fairness of any criticism that you put forward.

At the level of higher degree work, it is critical for you to consult and refer to the original sources of the material that you include. It is generally considered to be poor academic work if you rely on the reporting and analyses of others. Occasionally this is not possible, but 'second-hand' references should be avoided. One of the reasons for this is that you cannot guarantee the accuracy of the work where you find the reference, or even the fairness with which it has been treated.

A common format for the process of constructing a literature review is as follows:

- a search for and review of existing literature relating to the area of investigation
- a critical analysis of previous relevant research
- an analysis of the concepts involved illustrating a theoretical understanding
- a comparison and analysis of previous work in the area
- a discussion of the significance of previous findings
- the identification of areas or research gaps for future study

Research design

This section of your dissertation will set out the reasoning behind the particular approach that you have taken to your research. It will explain your thinking about research design, and also explain the precise approach, or methodology, that you will use. There is a need here to refer to recognized research methodologies, and to fully justify the choices that you have made during the planning process leading to the work that you will be reporting on.

The design of your research and the methodology that you eventually employ form the theoretical basis for your research. By having a clear description of the ways in which you will work you allow yourself to work within set theoretical and methodological boundaries and to refer to broadly agreed assumptions concerning the approaches that you will take.

Results

It is important that in this section you do *nothing more* than present your results. It is *not* the place for any consideration of the implications of your work or for consideration of the work of others. The results section is not the place for comment or discussion either.

In some cases, particularly in the case of quantitative studies, the results should be presented as tables, graphs and figures. They should always be referred to and described in the text. It is possible that without an explanation some of your results will not be meaningful to others. You will, naturally, feel close to your data, having collected them and worked closely with them, and understand what you are presenting. However, this will not necessarily be the case for others. What you present must be clear and unambiguous and this will not be possible unless you clearly describe and explain the presentation of your results.

Also, for the sake of clarity and ease of reading, you should be sure to label and number your charts and tables in a consistent and understandable way. This will be particularly helpful when referring to particular points in later sections.

Extensive sets of raw data should not appear in the main results section of your work but should be moved to appendices. However, where appropriate, simplified mean datasets can be shown in the results section. Do not display the same datasets as a table and a figure, as this is likely to lead to confusion. Statistical analyses should also be placed in an appendix.

You should be wary of describing your results as *significant* unless you have performed statistical tests upon them (see Chapters 21, 22 and 23 for information on various statistical analyses). The word *significant* has a formal and technical meaning concerning the statistical likelihood of any particular event, and is often used informally in a way that can be misleading, or just plain wrong. Beware of this and of the use of other words which may have technical meanings alongside more informal and everyday meanings.

When setting out your results section the use of subheadings which relate to specific research objectives or to specific items from the methods section may well be useful. This technique for breaking up text with useful and meaningful subheadings is a good way of allowing easy access to your work for the reader and you should consider its use throughout.

Discussion

The discussion section of a dissertation is the crucially important step that must be taken from the presentation of results to a critical engagement with them. There has been a good deal written about all aspects of the process of research, but as far as the final written product is concerned, more has been written about the discussion of results than about any other part of the process. The discussion section can be one of the most difficult to write. It involves more than reporting; it involves a high level of critical thinking, and this needs to be translated into text in a way that meets the requirements of the project as a whole. The research question must be to the fore, and all of the results reported earlier must be considered.

Probably the most important pitfall to avoid in a discussion section is simply restating the results. *Discussion* implies a good deal more than any sort of restating what has gone before. The results should be referred to, but it is your job to add a good deal more to them in terms of analysis and development of ideas and argument.

Boote and Beile (2005) tell us that we have to synthesize results in a way that permits a new perspective to be developed and this requires us to be involved in making links, comparisons and contrasts, and to juxtapose the results with the findings of others. Hart (1999) encourages us to provide a new perspective of the situation under investigation by considering the results in the context of the literature, by referring back to both the literature review and the detailed results. It is also possible that you may need to consider methodological matters as well, and discuss the suitability of what you have done in relation to what you have discovered.

You should provide an analysis and discussion of the findings and their implications for professional practice, research and education, or whichever combination of these is appropriate in the context of your work. You should consider the overall strengths, weaknesses and limitations of the study which will lead you to include recommendations, both for practice and for further research.

One further possible pitfall is including speculation, which goes beyond the evidence which arises from the research undertaken. The discussion must be based fully on the results, their significance and their relationship to previous work. A survey reported by Onwuegbuzie and Daniel (2005) on the most commonly criticized aspects of discussion in research writing submitted for publication found that:

- the discussion was too brief
- there was repetition of material from the results section
- there were too many cases of over-generalization (going beyond the data)

With these three points in mind and with a focus on a thorough critical treatment of the results, the likelihood is that you will write a good discussion section.

Conclusion

The importance of a well thought-out and comprehensive conclusion must not be under-estimated. Tutors and examiners are likely to pay detailed attention to this section. It is crucial that you remember that your conclusion is the conclusion to your dissertation, based upon the evidence that you have presented and analysed, and not any conclusions concerning the subject in general. It must be a conclusion and not a further discussion. A common mistake at this stage is to treat the conclusion as a place for further discussion. Instead, it should be the place where the conclusions drawn from the evidence that you have collected, analysed and discussed are made and presented.

The conclusion to your dissertation should start with an overall summary of your work and go on to include: detail of the implications of any limitations which you have identified; the identification of implications and recommendations for theory, policy or practice, with an outline of how these can be put in place; and an outline of any recommendations for future research. If you include recommendations in your conclusion they should not just be listed but should be explained with reference to the information you have presented. A simple list of recommendations is not enough.

It is sometimes suggested that the conclusion and introduction should be written at the same time once the bulk of the work has been completed. This may or may not be good advice, but what is certain is that the conclusion should have direct and obvious links to your initial aims and research questions, which were set out in the introductory sections. Whatever you have set out in the introduction as the focus of your investigation should form the framework for your conclusion. If you draw conclusions about issues which you have not mentioned earlier then there is something wrong. Similarly, if you raise issues in the introduction which are not addressed in your conclusion there is something wrong. It is sound advice, as you write the conclusion, to consider each point in turn that you have raised in your introduction, even to the point where you have a checklist in front of you as you work.

References

Referencing has a far greater importance in academic writing than new researchers usually recognize. Certainly, at an undergraduate level, you will have been required to provide adequate referencing, but it is unlikely that a piece of work would fail for the want of proper referencing alone. However it is not a rare occurrence for a thesis to be declined as a result of inaccurate or incomplete references.

There will be detailed guidelines provided by, or at the very least, made available by, your department or institution. Only the foolish will fail to pay attention to these and other requirements. It is usually best to write out your references in full, in the approved format, as you go along. If you decide to write first and reference later it is almost a given that you will not be able to trace certain sources, or that you will make a mistake of one kind or another.

It is possible that you will be expected to provide a bibliography in addition to a list of references. The difference between the two is straightforward, but does sometimes cause confusion. The reference list contains the full details of anything referred to directly in your work, whether it is a cited quotation or a reference made in your own words; a bibliography contains the detail of *other* sources which you have consulted but *not* referred to, even tangentially, in what you have written.

The Harvard system for referencing is probably the most usual system that you will be required to use, but there are others and you must be clear about the required format and stick to it scrupulously. Detail of the Harvard system of referencing, and any of the other systems, is readily available in a number of different places including many internet sites. The best source of information, though, will come from the institution where you are based.

Appendices

The purpose of an appendix is to provide the reader of your work with extra detail which may be required without causing any sort of written congestion in the main text. An appendix should be clear and contain items which cannot be easily fitted into the text. Examples include copies of questionnaires, copies of letters requesting permission to access participants, interview schedules, samples of responses from participants or lengthy quotations from relevant published work. An appendix could contain detailed numerical data.

Appendices are not usually counted as a part of the word limit but they should not be a place to deposit material you are not sure what to do with. The content of an appendix must have a purpose, and it should also be referred to at the appropriate point in the main text. You should consider using the rule that if the material in question is not essential to an understanding of the text, then it should be placed in an appendix.

Word lengths and relative section sizes

There are no hard and fast rules about the relative lengths of the different sections of a dissertation, but Table 25.1 gives an indication of what might be acceptable.

Table 25.1 Word lengths

Section	% of whole	Approximate word count for a 15,000 word dissertation
Abstract	2.5	250–350 words
Literature review	30 (5 for introduction)	4,500 words (700–750 words for introduction)
Methodology	17.5	2,500 words
Findings	30	4,500 words
Discussion	20	3,000 words

Common mistakes in academic writing

There is a real danger in academic writing of trying too hard to give an erudite tone to your work. By doing this you are likely to do the exact opposite. That is, you give the impression of stupidity. Academic writing does not need to be made up of long words served up in long and complicated sentences. Academic writing has to be *clear* and *precise*. The importance of clarity was mentioned at the beginning of the chapter. One certain way to remove clarity from your work is to use words which seem to be appropriate, when a simpler word will do the job, and to string together excessively long and complex sentences. You should aim to be sure that your reader (supervisor, examiner, peer) does not have to re-read any sentence or paragraph in an attempt to understand it.

Look at the following examples of long and cumbersome sentences.

1 Overlong sentence

In response to an increasingly complex and diverse society and a rapidly changing, technology-based national economy, in a similar worldwide context, schools are being asked to educate across a wider range of subjects than ever before, the most diverse body in history to higher academic standards than ever before and the strain is beginning to show on both the teaching workforce, which is apparently suffering from extremely low morale currently, and more importantly, perhaps, on the general health and well-being of the students in our schools, which is something that we must seek to rectify as a matter of urgency.

2 Too long and far too verbose

English Robins (Erithacus rubecula), under typical meteorological and nutrient availability conditions, are a solitary, non-migratory subspecies; however when prevailing underlying contextual situations extend to extreme conditions with respect to climate and nutrition, this isolatory tendency may be seen to be reversed.

3 Imprecise language

Quite a few people think that the National Front are racists.

4 Several inaccuracies with grammar and punctuation

Thousand's of deaths were reported on the first day of the battle which was more than everyone could of imagined. The government, were shocked, and announced that they would never sanction nothing like that again.

You might like to consider the examples above and think about how they could be written in a more acceptable and clearer way.

Table 25.2 shows some of the common mistakes that appear in work submitted for assessment, even at higher-degree level. They really should be avoided. In almost all cases, the solution to the problem is careful proof-reading; in many cases reading out loud is a better way to proof-read as it invokes the use of an additional sense.

You will see from the list of possible solutions to the problems that there is no real substitute for very careful proof-reading and checking by both you and by others. Often a reciprocal arrangement for proof-reading can be very worthwhile.

Some of the 'rules' in the Table 25.2 could be considered archaic. Whether we consider them archaic or not, the situation is that they do still apply in formal written English, and you will be expected to abide by them. There are, naturally, some who disagree with some of these rules, or see times when exceptions can be made. In general you should try to keep to the customary formalities of written English, even in times when our language is clearly changing, as all living languages do.

A brief word about the reliability of the spell-checking features of word processors is perhaps appropriate here. Spell-checkers will pick out an enormous number of errors, but not if the word which you have written by mistake actually exists. For example, pretty:petty; high:sigh; also a spell-checker will not differentiate between such words as: practice (noun) and practise (verb). If there is ever any doubt about a spelling then an up-to-date dictionary should be on hand and should be consulted.

If you are unsure about any writing conventions there are many sources of reference. A good first port of call might be a web-based resource at www.mantex.co.uk where you will find

Table 25.2 Problems and possible solutions

Problem	Possible solution
Missing out a word: 'the work was carried in complete silence'	Careful proof-reading by you, or by a friend
Incorrect use of adjectives and adverbs: You should 'be carefully to use them correct'	Careful proof-reading by you, or by a friend
Sentence fragments presented as full sentences: 'About Key Stage 3 testing and other exams.'	Careful proof-reading by you, or by a friend
The use of double negatives: 'They soon discovered that the place where they visited did not have none of the Roman artefacts they wanted'	Careful proof-reading by you, or by a friend. When proof-reading try rewording the negative as a positive statement
Pronouns not agreeing: 'Each teacher had their own classroom to organize'	Careful proof-reading by you, or by a friend
Incorrect use of commas: 'The reasons, being economic circumstances.	Careful proof-reading by you, or by a friend. Pause for each comma to check for sense
Incorrect use of apostrophes: 'Parent's were consulted and kept informed throughout'	Careful proof-reading by you, or by a friend
Splitting infinitives: 'To finally arrive at the conclusions below'	Careful proof-reading by you, or by a friend
Incorrect capitalization: 'The use of the Internet in modern classrooms'	Careful proof-reading by you, or by a friend
Verbs not agreeing with their subject: 'The senior management team advise heads of department at appropriate times through the year'	Careful proof-reading by you, or by a friend
Change in point of view of the writer: 'As a writer you must not shift his point of view'	Careful proof-reading by you, or by a friend
Incorrect use of irregular verbs: 'Newer teaching methods gradually creeped into use'	Careful proof-reading by you, or by a friend
Use of clichés. To give just a few examples of the many possibilities: 'in the same boat'; 'all walks of life'; 'calm before the storm'; 'from time immemorial'; 'nipped in the bud'	Careful proof-reading by you, or by a friend

excellent freely downloadable help, as well as options to buy a range of printed guides. Another good starting point might be the support site of your own university, for example the Learner Development Unit site at www.ssdd.uce.ac.uk/learner, a site belonging to the University of Central England (now Birmingham City University) which offers a good range of support for academic writing and related topics. There are other book-based sources of support listed at the end of the chapter.

Obviously in a chapter of this nature there is not scope for providing either numerous examples of lapses in writing style, or the amount of advice which would be suitable elsewhere. Other, more detailed sources of reference are available from the sources listed at the end of the chapter.

Problems of plagiarism

Plagiarism is always a violation of intellectual and academic honesty. It exists in many forms, but it all has the same concept at its heart, namely representing somebody else's words or ideas as your own. There are many different sources for advice and definitions concerning plagiarism. At its simplest, plagiarism is copying the work of others. More technically, the *Oxford English Dictionary* gives the following definition: 'The action or practice of taking someone else's work, idea, etc., and passing it off as one's own; literary theft'. Each institution will have a strict policy with regard to plagiarism and this will include a working definition that you must be fully aware of.

Plagiarism can be intentional or accidental. If it is accidental then it could be described as plagiarism through stupidity, because whether intentional or not the consequences remain the same. In some cases the consequence can be de-registration, meaning that you are required to leave the institution. 'It doesn't matter if you intend to plagiarise or not. In the eyes of the law, most publishers and academic institutions, any form of plagiarism is an offence that demands punitive action. Ignorance is never an excuse" (Turn it In 2008).

'Accidental' plagiarism includes:

- misunderstanding referencing and citation
- relying too heavily on original source material
- following practices encouraged or accepted in previous educational experience or culture
- not fully understanding when group work ceases and individual work begins
- compensating for poor English language skills
- poor note-taking practice
- laziness

'Intentional' plagiarism includes:

- leaving the work to the last minute and choosing an easy solution
- needing desperately to succeed
- having problems with workload management
- deciding consciously that copying is easier than producing original work
- sensing that it will not be detected and that it will not matter anyway
- laziness

To avoid any suspicion of plagiarism in your work you must avoid:

- cutting and pasting from electronic journals, websites or other sources to create a piece of work for submission
- passing off someone else's work as your own
- recycling essays from previous assessment situations (known as 'self-plagiarism')
- using a professional source of academic writing or anyone else to produce work for you (e.g. websites which will produce written work for a price, known as 'cheat sites')
- submitting a piece of work based on someone else's ideas without fully referencing them in accordance with the institution's requirements

To sum up, plagiarism can be passages copied word for word without acknowledgment, but paraphrasing authors' ideas or quoting even limited portions of their texts without proper citation is also an act of plagiarism. Even putting someone else's ideas into your own words without acknowledgment is a form of plagiarism, albeit less serious than wholesale copying. In any of its forms, plagiarism cannot be tolerated in the academic, or for that matter any other, domain. When detected, which is inevitable with modern software systems linked with your tutors' expert knowledge, plagiarism is likely to constitute grounds for at least a fail. In more extreme cases, stronger sanctions are imposed. Plagiarism is wrong, likely to get you into trouble of one sort or another, and can be detected surprisingly easily.

Oral Presentations

Giving presentations has become a common feature of undergraduate programmes and is increasingly used as a means of developing wider understanding of specific topics in postgraduate teaching situations. The ability to communicate in a range of different ways, including oral presentations, is considered to be an essential graduate skill (see AGCAS 1999 or Pritchard 2008 for a fuller discussion of graduate skills). For many graduate students, giving presentations will not be considered particularly troublesome, but for others it will present seemingly insurmountable difficulties. In the academic domain there is an increasing emphasis on disseminating the findings of research in this way. This takes place in such diverse locations as a small internal seminar or at the podium of prestigious international conferences.

If a presentation is to be deemed successful it needs to pass on information in an effective, understandable way. In order to ensure this there are certain points which need to be considered.

The importance of thorough preparation

When producing any final product for presentation, or for assessment, the importance of attention to detail cannot be overemphasized. For a successful presentation you must prepare thoroughly. Jotting down a few notes and expecting to 'wing' your way through may work for some, but as a rule this is not a sound approach to a quality presentation. For some, thorough preparation means writing a detailed script to be followed to the letter, and this may well be your preferred approach, however, reciting, or reading from your prepared script, does not usually make for an interesting and engaging audience experience.

The best preparation tends to involve preparing a full and detailed set of notes with which you can then become thoroughly familiar and use as a basis for what you are going to say, and as the basic content of any visual aids or handouts that you produce.

In terms of notes, it is usually a good practice to have a set to refer to. The question of how detailed they are is really a personal choice. Some will prefer small cards with a headline point and a series of subpoints, others a fuller set with specific titles and points emboldened or highlighted in a bright colour. In most cases the notes should be your guidance and *not* your script, but there may be some quotes or particularly important points that you might want to read word for word.

The use of electronic and other visual aids

Sometimes, especially in situations where your presentation is being assessed, you will be given detailed guidance about how much time you have, whether you should provide handouts or if you should use a chart, poster or an electronic system such as PowerPoint. (This is also the case at most academic conferences.) In other situations, you may have to decide for yourself. There is a danger of overdoing the electronic presentation approach and invoking a condition referred to as 'death by PowerPoint'. This involves having too many slides packed with too much information and including too many gimmicks and animations.

The following points can be considered as simple rules of thumb for the use of electronic presentations:

- in a presentation lasting between 10 and 15 minutes you should aim to have no more than ten slides
- eight slides for ten minutes is probably about right
- each slide should have no more than six lines of text
- avoid too many effects and animations, they can be distracting (some consider that any effects apart from simple slide-to-slide transitions are unnecessary)
- the text must be easily read by everyone in the room, simply copying standard-size text into PowerPoint is unacceptable

Obviously these rules are notional, and should not be seen as 'hard and fast', except the last one.

A mistake which is often made by those new to presenting is to write too much on a slide and then read out what the slide has on it. Coupled with also providing a handout with exactly the same information, this tends to lead to a certain disengagement by the audience. One good way to approach this is to put up to five or six main points on a slide and then to provide a measure of detail for each in what you say. The use of diagrams, charts or graphs is something which can help with the audience's understanding, but only if they are simple and explained adequately.

Handouts can be used to provide a record of your presentation and also more detail for some of the points that you will not have time to expand upon, including further reading or references. Good handouts often have space for personal notes to be added during your talk.

Keeping calm and appearing confident

It is very easy to give advice about staying calm and relaxed, but for some presenters this is very difficult. In some cases the anxiety engendered by the prospect of addressing a group verges on the debilitating. Simple techniques for relaxing, such as slow and measured breathing, or at a slightly higher level, following the instructions from a relaxation tape or CD at intervals prior to the presentation, can often alleviate some of your symptoms. If relaxing thoughts and keeping the whole exercise in perspective do not work for you, you could consider one of the herbal remedies which claim to soothe, or you could consult a professional. Orthodox medicine can offer some help, and so can alternative practitioners, such as hypnotists.

In order to appear confident, despite your inner feelings, you need to be sure to stand up straight and give an impression of efficiency. You need to smile, but not excessively, and give eye contact to members of the audience. If you are able to do these things, and to breathe slowly and deeply, your detailed preparation will come into play and your presentation should go well. Some novice presenters like to practise in advance of giving their presentation in earnest. This is not at all a bad idea. You can do this alone, you can record and listen to your performance, or you can ask a trusted friend to listen and give feedback. As in many cases, practice does lead to improvement, and the more presentations you deliver, the easier it is likely to become.

Often in presentations it is usual to allow time for questions and comments. This can be an unsettling time, thinking that you will perhaps be criticized, or that you will be unable to answer points raised. First of all you need to pay careful attention to the questioner and then respond in both a personal and general way. If you do not know something it is, naturally, best to say just that. Sometimes a point that has been raised can be turned back to either the questioner, or to the audience in general, for comments or possible answers/solutions. A detailed and thorough preparation is a way of safeguarding against being caught out.

Learning more

The section of this chapter devoted to the topic of giving a presentation can only provide space for an overview. If you feel you would like to learn more, try *Lend Me Your Ears*, by Max Atkinson (2004), a former political spech-writer and now a consultant and trainer in making speeches and presentations, which has an amazing array of information and good advice. On a less grand scale, *Studying and Learning at University* (Pritchard 2007) devotes a chapter to the topic.

Summary

This chapter has set out the essential elements of the presentation of research in the form of an extended dissertation. Consideration was made of structure, style, the importance of accurate referencing and the dangers of plagiarism. Emphasis was laid upon the importance of clarity at every stage and how 'good' research can be spoiled by careless and imprecise reporting. A short section also considered oral presentations.

References

AGCAS (1999) The Association of Graduate Careers Advisory Services, www.agcas.org.uk, accessed 22 February 2008.

Atkinson, M. (2004) *Lend Me Your Ears: All You Need to Know About Making Speeches and Presentations*. London: Vermilion.

Boote, D. and Beile, P. (2005) 'Scholars before researchers: on the centrality of the dissertation literature review in research preparation', *Educational Researcher*, 34(6): 3–15.

Edwards, A. and Talbot, R. (1994) *The Hard Pressed Researcher*. London: Longman.

Hart, C. (1999) Doing a Literature Review: Releasing the Social Science Research Imagination. London: Sage.

Onwuegbuzie, A. and Daniel, L. (2005) Evidence-based guidelines for publishing articles in *Research in the Schools* and beyond, *Research In The Schools*, 12(2): 1–11.

Pritchard, A. (2008) *Studying and Learning at University.* London: Sage.

Turn it In (2008) *Research Resources: Plagiarism FAQs,* http://turnitin.com/research_site/ e_faqs.html, accessed 20 February 2008.

Epilogue
Dimitra Hartas

In this volume on research in education, we discussed a range of strategies of inquiry and techniques for addressing research questions and making sense of data. We engaged with the criticisms of educational research and its diverse epistemologies and discussed the politicization of research and its implications for research users. Throughout the book we elaborated on the 'how' of conducting research in education and, most importantly, on the need to balance research as an inquiry and as a technical enterprise, a method or a means to an end. For new researchers, there is a strong temptation to let the methods drive the inquiry while limited consideration is given to the thought processes involved in setting the parameters of the field of investigation and the research design. This is compounded by the fact that, despite the proliferation of paradigms, little attention has been paid to exploring alternative epistemologies and complementary methods to address complex issues in education and their implication for policy and practice at a local level.

To strike a balance between inquiry and methodology during research training, learners should be encouraged to develop a view of educational inquiry that:

- situates the research processes and outcomes within social/political and educational contexts that address issues of social justice and equality, with an emphasis on the common good of the communities from which the participants come
- attempts to understand the gap between the participants' experiences and the institutional contexts, (e.g. schools, universities) within which they operate, and view learning from the point of view of learners by including them in all phases of research
- expands current notions of research rigour located within experimental designs to qualitative and mixed-method studies
- engages with the ethics that emanate from intruding into people's lives
- bridges qualitative and quantitative approaches
- accounts for the institutional structures that surround research

Over the years, many contradictory views have been raised about the ways in which educational research and educational policy and practice interact and inform each other, and this book has not attempted to reconcile these contradictions. We acknowledge that the nature of research is inherently contradictory, as reflected in the diversity of paradigms and philosophical positions on the nature of knowledge and its influence on social reality. The politicization of research in education, as seen in the 'what works' movement, has undermined the view that problem-solving and research should be framed as inquiry and take into account its social, moral and cultural context. The way we conceptualize and conduct research has implications for social action and democracy. As Biesta argues, the extent to which an institution, private or public, 'actively supports and encourages researchers to go beyond simplistic questions about "what works," may well be an indication of the degree to which a society can be called democratic' (2007: 12). Debates about the nature of an inquiry, its social/political context and the epistemology that underpins not only what works, but also what should work, its desirability and who decides about it, are much needed to inform research in education.

Educational research should address not only the effectiveness of strategies, interventions or instructional artefacts but also the quality of the means (e.g. the quality of an instructional approach). To improve the relationship between educational research and professional practice we need to develop models of inquiry that address teaching and learning in relation to their political and social context, and ensure that action-orientated knowledge and innovative practices are possible as long as inquiry is open to peer review within communities of practice. Research in education plays a crucial role in making sense of the rapidly changing social and technological reality, where simplistic views about what it is and whether it works are not adequate to capture the multifaceted nature of teaching and learning and the role of education in a world that is 'out of joint' and which 'must be constantly set right anew' (Arendt 1993).

Educational research can (and should) inform educational practice without being confined to offering technical solutions to technical problems. Through inquiry, educational researchers and practitioners contribute to knowledge generation and knowledge transfer, being 'socially accountable and reflexive' (Code 1991). They can tell good and persuasive stories that are rigorous and relevant to their lived experience (Hodkinson 2004). Moreover, for research to develop a transformative capacity and stimulate desirable changes, it needs to engage with the polyphony of its contexts, and acknowledge the pluralism in the voice of teachers and learners, and the positionality and ethics of researchers. It needs, above all, a political as well as a cultural presence to widen its scope and 're-image' teaching and learning and their implications for active citizenship and democracy.

References

Arendt, H. (1993) *Between Past and Future: Eight Exercises in Political Thought*. New York: Penguin.

Biesta, G. (2007) 'Why "what works" won't work: evidence-based practice and the democratic deficit in educational research', *Educational Theory*, 57(1): 1–22.

Code, L. (1991) *Epistemic Responsibility*. Oxford: Oxford University Press.

Hodkinson, P. (2004) 'Research as a form of work: expertise, community and methodological objectivity', *British Educational Research Journal*, 30(1): 9–26.

Glossary

a priori theory	the use of concepts and ideas that are specified and defined prior to the generation and interrogation of data.
action research	an approach to achieving change in which the social actions of individuals are examined and developed (often in collaboration) through a cyclically reflective, research-informed process.
adjusted R squared	a measure of variance in the outcome (how much variance is accounted for) considering that the model had been derived from the population from which the sample was drawn.
agency	the idea that people's actions can make a difference. Agency is normally set against the structural constraints in people's lives.
alternative hypothesis	a statement that the population parameter has some value other than the value stated by the null hypothesis.
analysis of covariance (ANCOVA)	a statistical method that can be used to statistically equate groups that differ on a pretest or some other variable; a statistical method that is used to examine the relationship between one categorical independent variable and one quantitative dependent variable controlling for one or more extraneous variables.
analysis of variance (ANOVA)	a statistical technique that compares group means to test if they differ.
anonymity	the process of concealing the identity of a research participant.
audience	when we look at an image we form an audience and determine its meaning. Different audiences viewing the same image at a different time or place may arrive at a different meaning.
authenticity (in the context of documentary research)	testing a document to verify the authorship, place and date of writing.
baseline	the behaviour of participants prior to the administration of a treatment condition.

between-subject designs	designs where each group of participants is tested once and under only one condition. Another term used to describe this type of design is 'independent samples'.
biased sample	a sample that is systematically different from the population in a direction/ characteristic that is not of interest to the study.
bivariate analysis	an examination of the relationship between two variables.
bivariate correlation	a correlation between two variables.
Bonferroni correction	a correction that is applied to a level to minimize the probability of making a Type I error when multiple significance tests are carried out (post-hoc comparisons).
CAQDAS (computer assisted qualitative data analysis software)	software packages that are designed to aid the process of analysis.
case study	an in-depth study of a single phenomenon, for example, a school, a professional body, or a year group of pupils in a particular school.
categorical variables	variables that consist of categories such as gender (male, female).
category analyses	systems for analysing classroom interaction which approach the phenomena to be analysed with predetermined categories into which an interactive behaviour is assumed to fit.
causal description	a description of the consequences of manipulating independent variables.
causality	the process of establishing a causal link between two variables.
cell	a combination of two or more independent variables in a factorial design.
central tendency	measures of mean, mode and median in a distribution.
chi-square distribution	a probability distribution used to test hypotheses about categorical data.
chi-square test	a test of the independence of two categorical variables; a test run during a contingency analysis.
citizenship	status bestowed on members of a community or nation on the basis of ownership of economic, political and social rights.
classical positivism	a view that reality is experienced and observed and that knowledge is objective, derived from directly observed events.

classroom interaction	all the ways in which participants in classrooms interact with one another, including oral interaction, non-verbal interaction and shared activity.
closed question	a fixed-choice question with predetermined answers (e.g. respondents choose an answer from the response categories provided).
coding scheme	a theoretical framework that incorporates the codes emerging from the analysis of qualitative data or a priori codes based on previous theory.
coefficient alpha	a formula that provides an estimate of the reliability of a homogeneous test or an estimate of the reliability of each dimension in a multidimensional test.
communality	the total proportion of the shared variance in a variable that can be accounted for by the extracted factor.
comparative case study	a multi-case approach, which allows the researcher to compare and contrast a number of equivalent cases.
confidence interval	a range of numbers inferred from a sample that has a certain probability or chance of including the population parameter.
confidentiality	the process of keeping information provided by the research participants confidential.
confirmatory factor analysis	a statistical procedure that aims at testing a predetermined cluster of variables whose interrelations rely on a strong theoretical grounding.
confounding factor	a type of extraneous variable (nuisance variable) that may interfere with the treatment and exert unwanted effects on the outcome; a confounding variable varies systematically with the independent variable and influences the dependent variable.
contingency table	a cross-tabulation or cross-classification of two categorical variables.
control group	a group that does not receive experimental treatment.
convenience sample	a sample selected because it is available to the researcher.
correlation	an analysis of the magnitude and direction of the relationship between two variables.
correlation coefficient	a standardized measure of the linear association between two variables, expressed on a scale from 0 to 1 (indicating a perfect positive relationship) or –1 (indicating a perfect negative relationship); it is called **Pearson's product moment r** when the variables concerned are interval/ratio, and **Spearman's rho** when the variables are ordinal.
coverage	how well a literature review covers studies in the field of specialization.

critical	can have a variety of meanings including the ways in which action research is intended to interrogate social conditions and accepted actions. Another use of the term is associated with critical theorists and refers to the challenge that action researchers make to existing social inequalities.
critical realism	a view that social reality consists of multiple layers and that knowledge relates to the time and place of an inquiry.
critical theory	a descriptive and philosophical framework for social inquiry aimed at emancipation. Critical theorists argue that to understand social reality is to approach participants as agents and makers of their own histories.
cultures of communication	the communicative structures that children use to express and represent their views in different contexts of their everyday lives.
currency/ implications	how influential the reviewed studies are in shaping theory, policy and practice.
data editor	the main window in SPSS which presents the functions to enter data and run statistical analyses.
data view	he view of the contents (i.e. raw data – numbers) of the data editor in SPSS.
deductive reasoning	the process whereby we deduce a hypothesis from theory to be subjected to empirical scrutiny (usually associated with quantitative research).
degrees of freedom	a statistic that is expressed as the number of observations minus the number of the parameters estimated.
dependent variable	a variable (outcome) that is presumed to be influenced by one or more independent variables.
descriptive statistics	statistics that focus on describing, summarizing or explaining data.
designing research	the process of theorizing and conceptualizing a theme or topic.
dispersion	a measure of the spread of data from the mean.
distribution	a table where the values that a variable can take are paired with a frequency or probability.
documentary analysis	a method of research that involves the analysis of primary documentary data, such as official policy material and records of events and actions.
dummy variable	a way of recoding a nominal variable with more three or more values so that each value is contrasted with a baseline or reference value. Each dummy variable is dichotomous and takes the value of either 0 or 1.
ecological validity	refers to the applicability and meaningfulness of findings across different

settings (beyond the immediate setting of research).

educational research a multidisciplinary field and a cognate discipline of the social sciences.

effect size a standardized measure of the strength of an effect. It normally takes values between 0 and 1 (Cohen's d takes values between 0 and 1+). Examples of effect sizes are: Cohen's d, eta squared and Pearson's correlation coefficient r.

eigenvalue the total variance accounted for by a factor.

emancipatory research emancipatory research seeks to address people's historical and political contexts, and help them to achieve emancipation; research that 'gives' voice to vulnerable and marginalized individuals.

empirical theory theorizing that involves generating ideas, concepts and categories through the data that can be combined and interrogated to create theory.

empiricism a doctrine which frames knowledge as experience or, put differently, experience is seen as the only source of knowledge.

epistemic fallacy the tangling of ontology (what it is) with epistemology (what it is to be known).

epistemology the philosophy of the nature of knowledge.

eta squared an effect size index used in ANOVA.

evaluation determines the worth, merit or quality of a programme/initiative or policy.

experimental design causal study with random allocation of persons to groups (experimental and control groups).

exploratory factor analysis a statistical procedure that seeks to uncover the underlying patterns in a relatively large set of variables.

external validity refers to the generalizability of findings to the population from which the sample was drawn.

extraneous variable a variable other than the independent variable that might influence the dependent variable; a variable that may compete with the independent variable in explaining the outcome; any variable other than the independent variable that might influence the dependent variable.

F value or ratio the ratio of systematic/unsystematic variation. It tests the overall fit of a model in regression analysis, and the overall group differences in ANOVA.

factor (as in factorial analysis)	an independent variable (a treatment or condition).
Factor (in factor analysis)	a derived entity, a statistically generated component in a dataset.
factor rotation	the process whereby a factor structure is simplified.
factorial analysis	an analysis that involves two or more independent variables or factors.
focus group	a means of data generation whereby a group of participants is involved in discussion, moderated by the researcher, of a single issue or a topic with a relatively narrow focus.
formative evaluation	ongoing evaluation that aims at offering feedback to a programme or activity as it occurs.
general linear modelling	see **factorial analysis**.
generalizability	the applicability and meaningfulness of findings to the population from which the sample was drawn.
generativity	the process of generating new knowledge based on prior scholarship.
genre	images (still or moving) associated or recognized as belonging to an accepted class are said to be representative of a 'genre'. Situation comedies or action-hero cartoons, for example, form particular genres.
getting started	defining the issue, topic or problem of research; asking questions.
grounded analysis	attempt to interpret classroom interaction which does not use predetermined categories but derives the analysis from the data itself.
group interview	interview conducted with more than one research participant simultaneously, where the participants respond to a series of questions posed by the interviewer.
histogram	a frequency distribution for interval/ratio variables.
homogeneity of variance	an assumption that the variance of a variable is equal across groups.
hypothesis	an informed speculation, an educated guess about the possible relationship between two or more variables.
icon	a sign that communicates its meaning by resembling the object it refers to.
impact	a long-lasting effect of the independent variable(s) on an outcome.

independent-samples t-test	a test that uses the t-statistic to explore whether two group means differ significantly. The groups are independent, i.e., between groups.
independent variable	a variable that influences outcome (also called a predictor variable).
inductive reasoning	a process whereby we draw generalizable inferences from the data to build a theory (theory is the outcome of research; theory is data-driven).
inferential statistics	statistical techniques that allow for making inferences from the sample to the population from which it was drawn.
informed consent	a consent that participants give in order to participate in research after they have been informed about the purpose of the research and the stages and modes of data collection.
rater) reliability	item. This is required for content analysis to ensure consistency in the coding of the emerging themes in qualitative data.
interaction effect	the effect of an independent variable on an outcome that is mediated by another variable; or when the effect of one independent variable depends on the level of another independent variable.
inter-coder (inter-interval data	the degree of consistency/agreement between two coders coding the same data measured on a scale where the intervals between any two points are equal.
interview agenda	sometimes called an interview schedule or protocol, a written guide for the researcher which normally includes a number of questions and/or prompts, to assist them to conduct an interview.
Kolmogorov-Smirnov test	a test used to check the assumption of normality or whether the distribution of scores is different from a normal distribution. A statistically significant result suggests that the distribution of scores is different (or deviate) from the normal distribution.
Kruskal Wallis test	the nonparametric equivalent for a one-way independent ANOVA (for data that is not parametric).
kurtosis	the extent to which the scores are clustered in the two tails of a frequency distribution. A platykurtic distribution is quite flat because the scores gather at the tails, whereas in the leptokurtic distribution the scores cluster around the mean.
latent variable	a variable that cannot be measured directly. A construct such as self-esteem represents a latent variable that needs to be 'deconstructed' into other variables that relate to it conceptually in order to measure it.

Levene test	a test conducted to check whether variance is homogeneous between groups.
Likert scale	a format develop by Rensis Likert to evaluate responses to attitude questions. The responses typically include degrees of agreement on a series of statements.
linear model	a model based on a line.
loading	a correlation between a variable and a factor (the greater the loadings of variables onto a factor the more important the factor is).
logical positivism	a view that logic is crucial in understanding cause-and-effect relationships.
main effect	he effect of each independent variable on the dependent variable.
Mann-Whitney u-test	the nonparametric equivalent of the independent-samples t-test.
materiality	the physical composition of an object. This is important since it indicates something other than what it is made of. Words written in sand may denote impermanence while words in marble suggest permanence.
mean	the arithmetic average.
measurement	a process whereby we assign symbols or numbers to something by following a specific set of rules.
median	the middle score of ordered scores. If the number of observations is even then the median is the average of the two scores that fall either side of the middle value.
method	a strategy for data collection and analysis.
methodological appraisal	appraisal of the main methodologies and research techniques used in the studies reviewed, focusing on their advantages and limitations.
methodology	the study of research methods.
mode	the most frequently occurring score in a data.
multicollinearity	the outcome of two or more predictor variables being closely related (or highly correlated).
multivariate analysis	an analysis of more than two variables at a time.
narrative structure	how a story is communicated or 'unfolds' (e.g. linear, chronological, fragmented and so on). May refer to a set of documentary photographs, a film or comic strips.
negatively skewed	a distribution that is skewed to the left (tail towards the negative scores).

nominal scale   a scale of measurement that uses symbols, such as words or numbers, to label, classify or identify people or objects.

nonparametric data   data that do not form a normal distribution.

nonparametric tests   tests that do not rely on the assumptions that underpin parametric data, mainly the assumption of normality.

normal distribution   a bell-shaped (symmetrical) distribution in which skewness and kurtosis are zero.

objectivity   the notion that knowledge is independent of the knower.

oblique rotation   a type of rotation that allows the generated factors to correlate.

official documents   formal, mostly published, documents produced by governments which are in the public domain.

online/onsite surveys   different modes of administering surveys.

ontology   the science of 'what it is'.

open-ended questions   respondents are invited to offer an answer without being provided with response categories.

operationalization   the process of defining a construct along the operations involved in measuring it.

orthogonal rotation   a type of rotation that creates independent factors.

outcome   immediate results of an intervention.

outlier   a number that is very atypical of the other numbers in a distribution; an extreme value (high or low) in a distribution of values. With outliers, the median and not the mean provides a meaningful measure.

paradigm   a worldview, a perspective which influences what should be studied, how research is conducted and the ways the results are interpreted.

paradigm wars   a clash of different worldviews about the nature of knowledge and how to conduct research.

paradigmatic transition   the process whereby one worldview is replaced by another.

parameter   a numerical characteristic of a population.

parametric data   data that form a normal distribution.

participation	the ability to contribute and become actively involved in decision-making processes.
photo-elicitation	the use of a photograph as a stimulant in an interview situation. Akin to object, drawing or painting elicitation.
political representation	a political system or a set of political arrangements that emphasize the role of a small group of people to represent the interests of a larger group of people.
politicization of research	the selective use of research for political purposes, mainly as a tool to justify political agendas.
polysemic	a sign is said to be polysemic when it has more than one meaning. Images are ambiguous and have many possible meanings.
positively skewed	a distribution that is skewed to the right (tail towards positive scores).
positivism/ post-hoc comparisons	doctrines that consider knowledge to be objective, value-free, based on required when a variable has more than two levels to detect statistically significant pair-wise comparisons.
postmodernism	a perspective that does not privilege a single authority, accepting that knowledge is polyphonic and contested.
postpositivism	cause and effect and law-like relationships.
poststructuralism	a worldview that it is impossible to step out of discourse to understand social reality objectively. To poststructuralists, language is not neutral and discourse is perpetually contested.
power (statistical power)	the likelihood of rejecting the null hypothesis when it is false (or the capacity of a test to detect genuine effects).
pragmatism	a worldview that stresses the role of knowledge to support social action. It offers a practical and utilitarian view of knowledge.
predictor variable	a variable that is used to predict the outcome variable.
primary documents	those created closest to the origin of the information or idea under study. This definition is not straightforward and depends on how the document is used and its context.
principal component analysis	a method for extracting factors.
principle ethics	an approach that attempts to identify universal principles.
private documents	personal documents with closed or restricted access, such as diaries or letters.

probability   a measure of likelihood that varies between 0 and 1.

probabilistic sample a sample that has been formed by using a random method.

probes   questions used by a researcher to further examine issues raised by participants during an interview.

prompts   comments made by the researcher to help encourage participants to talk about issues of interest to the researcher.

qualitative variable a variable that is expressed in kind and not in values, such as gender, ethnicity; it is comprised of categories.

quality/authority   the quality of the reviewed sources and materials (primary sources in peer-reviewed journals).

quantitative   a variable such as weight or height whose attributes are expressed in degrees
variable   – i.e. having more or less of a given property. A variable that is comprised of values.

randomization   a process of assigning participants into groups randomly.

range   the difference between the highest and lowest numbers.

ranking   the ordering of responses into ascending or descending order.

rate   the percentage of people with a specific characteristic in a group.

rating scale   a continuum of response choices.

ratio scale   a scale of measurement that has a true zero point as well as the characteristics of the nominal (labelling), ordinal (rank ordering) and interval (equal distance) scales.

reflexivity   an approach in which the methods of study are 'bent back'. In action research this often means using an approach which intentionally examines the preconceptions, beliefs and attitudes of the action researcher themselves.

regression   a statistical model in which one variable or outcome is predicted from a linear combination of one or more predictor variables. Each predictor has a regression coefficient b associated with it, which indicates the change in the outcome variable associated with a one-unit change in the independent variable.

relevance   refers to how well the research questions have been formulated, and how clear the aims and the objectives of the research are.

reliability   a criterion for the consistency and replicability of the measures in a study.
research   a systematic inquiry made public.

research as dialogue research as a dialogical practice where both the researcher and the informant are seen as active in the production and interpretation of data.

research design the specific design for undertaking research (e.g. ethnography, case studies, surveys or action research) and a more general process of designing projects by creating strategies for generating appropriate data. Not all research regards itself as adopting a specific design, but all research must involve a *process* of design.

research interview a discussion between at least two individuals (normally a researcher and research participants) from which data are generated.

residual the difference between the original and reproduced correlation coefficients (or coefficients between the original variables/items and the emerging factors).

response bias a bias due to a small response rate. Refers to bias that emerges from the characteristics/attributes of the respondents who decide to return a survey, as opposed to those who do not.

response rate the percentage of the completed surveys received.

sampling the process of drawing a sample from a pragmatic population.

sampling error the difference between a sample statistic and a population parameter.

scatterplot a bivariate distribution; an elliptical cluster of points which indicates a linear association between two variables.

scientism the reduction of science to a method (one method to be used for all purposes), regardless of whether the method is quantitative or qualitative.

scree plot a graph of factors and their eigenvalues, used for determining the number of the extracted factors.

secondary documents documents in the form of a synthesis or interpretation of primary sources, thus further removed from the original source.

semi-official documents documents produced by corporations and associations, largely concerned with day-to-day workings and business.

semiotics the study of the social production of meanings through signs.

semi-structured research research that involves a flexible approach to finding out about prespecified interests, but with the aim of having an openness to new and interesting issues.

skewness	a measure of how symmetrical a frequency distribution is. Positively skewed is a distribution where the scores are clustered at the lower end of the distribution and the tail points toward the positive scores. Negatively skewed is a distribution where the scores cluster at the higher end of the distribution and the tail points towards the negative scores.
social constructivism	a worldview that approaches knowledge as being socially and culturally constructed and grounded in human experience. Within this paradigm, learning is relational, and individual experiences are mediated by historical, cultural and social circumstances.
sociogeographical variable	a variable drawn on by social scientists to differentiate a sample according to location, social class and ethnicity.
sphericity	refers to perfect correlations between factors.
standard deviation (SD)	an estimate of the average variability of scores; the square root of the variance.
standard error	the standard deviation of sample means (in a sampling distribution) that indicates variability in the means of different samples.
standard error of difference	an estimate of the difference between sample means. The standard deviation of the sampling distribution (i.e. distribution of all sample means) is the standard error of difference.
statistic	a numerical characteristic of a sample.
stratified sample	a sample formation by dividing the population into mutually exclusive groups and selecting a random sample from each group.
structuralism	a worldview that individuals are not simply constrained by linguistic, cultural or social structures; they also play an active role in producing these structures.
structured research	involves prespecifying one's analytic interests, and creating tools (such as observation schedules or interview schedules) to find out about those interests.
suitability	how well the reviewed studies suit the topic and aims of the research.
summative evaluation	the feedback given at the end of an evaluation with regard its merit.
survey research	a non-experimental type of research.
systematic variation	a variation that is due to the treatment effect, or the factors we are interested in examining.

thematic analysis	a general term that describes approaches to coding and thematically-orientating to data.
transcript	a verbatim record of an interview discussion.
transcription	the process of *re-presenting* data into a form that brings to light certain analytically relevant features of that data.
transformative research	emancipatory research that asks questions about the lives of people who have been marginalized or discriminated against; seeks to address social justice.
two-tailed test	a test of a two-tailed hypothesis (non-directional hypothesis).
Type I error	the outcome of rejecting a true null hypothesis (to believe that there is a genuine effect in the population when there is not).
Type II error	the outcome of failing to reject a false null hypothesis (to believe that there is not a genuine effect in the population when there is).
univariate analysis	an analysis of one variable at a time.
unstructured research	involves very little specification of interests and is used to find out as much as possible about a given topic, practice, set of people etc. Unstructured approaches are often used as a precursor to more structured forms.
unsystematic variation	variation that is not due to treatment or manipulation effects but to other factors such as the characteristics of participants or context.
unwitting evidence	information gathered from a document that is interpreted and understood in a way that was not originally intended by the author.
validity	a criterion for the integrity of a study in terms of accuracy of inferences and the trustworthiness of results; the accuracy of the inferences, interpretations or actions made on the basis of test scores.
vantage point	the view or perspective of the world taken by members of a researched community.
variable	a condition or characteristic that can take on different values or categories.
variable view	a view of the content (i.e. the properties of the variables) of the data editor in SPSS.
variance	a measure of variation within a distribution, determined by averaging the squared deviations from the mean of a distribution.
variation	the dispersion of data points around the mean of a distribution.

virtue ethics   code of ethics that is intended to be *aspirational*, encouraging a professional to seek the highest level of practice.

Welch's F test   an alternative test selected during an ANOVA in circumstances when the assumption of the homogeneity of variance has been violated.

within-subject design a design in which a group of participants or units are tested more than once in two or more conditions.

witting evidence   information gathered from a document that the author intended to be understood – usually factual.

Index